MU

a personal memoir of life with American Sufi Samuel L. Lewis

Murshid wearing his dervish robe at the wedding of Jehanara and Hassan Herz, 1968.

Mansur Johnson

MURSHID

a personal memoir of life
with American Sufi
Samuel L. Lewis

PeaceWorks Publications,
Seattle, Washington, USA

Published by PeaceWorks Publications. PeaceWorks Publications is a trademark of the International
Network for the Dances of Universal Peace, PO Box 55994, Seattle, WA 98155-0994, USA
PeaceworksPubs@dancesofuniversalpeace.org

Printed in the United States by Thompson-Shore, Inc., Dempster, Michigan.

Cover and book design by Hauke Sturm, Berlin, Germany.

Cover photo: Murshid at Mt. Shasta, California, 1969. Back cover photo: Mansur and Murshid, 1967
(photographer unknown). All photos by Mansur Johnson © 2006 by Mansur Johnson, except two
photos of the author by Dennis Stock in Chapter 17, the group photo including the author on page 335
and the back cover photo—both by unknown photographers—and the shot of Murshid on page 459
by Sylvaine Vaucher of Geneva, Switzerland.
ISBN 0-915424-16-9 paperback
ISBN 0-915424-17-7 hardback

Library of Congress Cataloging-in-Publication Data:

Johnson, Mansur, 1941-
   Murshid : a personal memoir of life with American Sufi Samuel L. Lewis / Mansur Johnson.
      p. cm.
   Includes bibliographical references and index.
   ISBN 0-915424-16-9 (pbk. : alk. paper) -- ISBN 0-915424-17-7 (hardcover : alk. paper)
   1. Lewis, Samuel L., 1896-1971. 2. Johnson, Mansur, 1941- 3.
Sufis--United
States--Biography. I. Title.
   BP80.L49J64 2006
   297.4092--dc22
   [B]
            2006024330

Content

Foreword

Dear Reader:

Prepare for a unique adventure of spiritual discovery and transformation. Comparing favorably to Irina Tweedie's *Daughter of Fire*,
her autobiographical account of her Sufi discipleship with an Indian
teacher, *Murshid* describes an even more unique relationship, that of
an American student of the American Sufi-Buddhist teacher Samuel L.
Lewis.

In his massive study of Western teachers in Eastern traditions (*The
Book of Enlightened Masters: Western Teachers in Eastern Traditions*, 1997),
Dr. Andrew Rawlinson cites Samuel L. Lewis as "one of the first exponents
of experiential comparative religion." Lewis studied both Buddhist and
Sufi paths with Eastern teachers for his entire adult life, and before his
death was initiated as a Sufi sheikh by Indian and Pakistani Sufis and as a
zen-shi by Japanese and Korean Zen Buddhists. In addition to carrying on
a lineage of Chishti Sufism, Lewis is known for his creation of the Dances
of Universal Peace movement, which has branches around the world. An
introductory sketch of Lewis' unusual life and work by another of his close
students, Wali Ali Meyer, follows this foreword and prepares the reader for
the heart of *Murshid*.

Mansur Johnson's tale of his discipleship with Samuel Lewis is as
honest, refreshing and unselfconscious as was the life of his teacher. This
is not an account of any idealized, new age spirituality, but a warts-and-all
story of what real discipleship with a real Sufi, operating in a completely
Western context is like. Rather than being largely about cultural differences
(as are other stories of Western students studying with Eastern teachers),
Johnson's *Murshid* includes all of the stress, expectation, love, hope,
betrayal, disappointment and humor that fill everyday human life. The
plot here does not thicken around how to manage the food in India or
Japan, but on how to manage the break-up of a relationship in the midst of
intense experiences of awakening.

For those who already know and love the work of Murshid Samuel Lewis,
Murshid offers the reader completely new insights about what life with
him was really like. The only previous biographical accounts (published
in *In the Garden*, 1972) focused on disconnected anecdotes of memorable
moments with Murshid. My own compilation of Samuel Lewis's letters

and diaries (*Sufi Vision and Initiation*, 1986), focused on his life through his own words. Johnson's book not only shows us what was behind the anecdotes, but also provides a full context for the voluminous writing of Samuel Lewis' last years, years that saw him at the center of a spiritual awakening that included colleagues and correspondents like Pir Vilayat Inayat Khan, Yogi Bhajan, Swami Satchidananda, Mother Krishnabai, Huston Smith and many more notables of the late 1960s and early 1970s. In addition, far from being only interested in overtly spiritual matters, Lewis was deeply interested in cultural transformation, as witnessed by his ongoing correspondence with journalists, scientists, ecologists, the General Semantics association, early spiritual communes and various universities. Solely as a document of what has been called the birth of America's New Religious Movements, *Murshid* is invaluable. In this regard, to help the reader to keep track of the almost bewildering array of correspondents that Murshid engages, a list of "dramatis personae" is included as an appendix to this book.

When I read the semi-final draft of this book two years ago, I knew that it needed to be published in as full a form as possible. For this reason, I donated my time as editor of the project. At some point, a more highly edited version may be produced. Certainly there is a much larger audience for current popular spiritual books that tend to promise facile, how-to solutions to complex human and societal problems. The spiritual life, as presented in *Murshid,* cannot be reduced to either ten easy steps ("everything I ever needed to know...") or to a series of glorified incidents. As Samuel Lewis once said, "If you understand me but don't understand yourselves, you've failed. If you don't understand me, but understand yourselves better, you've passed."

For now, reader, you have before you a wild, bucking-bronco of a spiritual ride. Hold on!

Neil Douglas-Klotz
Edinburgh, Scotland
May, 2006

Introduction

Murshid Samuel L. Lewis
(Sufi Ahmed Murad Chisti)

by Murshid Wali Ali Meyer

Samuel Leonard Lewis was born on October 18, 1896, to Jacob Lewis, a vice-president of the Levi Strauss Company, and the former Harriet Rothschild, of the international banking family. He once said, "My parents never forgave me for being conceived out of wedlock." He was an unusual child, a child prodigy; his mother often claimed to have had a dream of the Prophet Samuel before the child's birth and therefore gave him that name. But these unusual qualities did not endear him to his family. His father never could accept the otherworldly tendencies of his oldest son. He was angered time and again that Samuel was not interested in business, competition and material success. In all matters his younger brother Elliott was preferred; even when he lied and stole this was at least showing interest in money.

This introverted and deeply studious young man, with his memories of previous lives and his mystical inclinations, graduated from San Francisco's top high school, Lowell, with the highest grades in its history to that point. But his well-to-do family refused to send him to college. This family rejection and conflict was one of the crosses he had to bear until the end of his life. He achieved reconciliation with his parents and with his brother shortly before their respective deaths, and the small trust fund which his father then left him allowed him to take up college at a late date in his life (the 1940s). He continued to take college courses until his death in 1971; his passion for knowledge was inexhaustible.

He told his students on several occasions that it was his own family rejection which made him naturally sympathetic to the young people who came to him with similar problems in the last few years of his life. It was one of the ways God prepared him to be of help to others, he later came to believe. Through rejection after rejection in life he developed great patience and perseverance, until at the end of his life the flow of time and evolution began to catch up with him, especially in the persons of the youth of the late sixties. He repeated again and again the phrase of Christ: "The stone which is rejected is become the cornerstone." He said that this was the *koan* for his life. While he had "intimations of immortality" from early childhood and reported reading about psychic research at age 13, his mystical training was set into motion a few years later.

In 1915, at the age of 18, he goes to the Palace of Education at the World's Fair which was held in San Francisco. There he becomes acquainted with Theosophy, which teaches "All religions are right. They differ on the outside when taken exoterically, they agree on the inside if taken esoterically. All religions are from God. There are seven planes of existence, the lower ones experienced in life after life, the higher ones only by sages and the illumined." He knows in the depth of his being that this is true. He believes he has found the Way. He continues to read all the world's scriptures voraciously. He is still living at home, something of a recluse. But the teachings of the Theosophists prove to be only intellectual and he renews his search. In November 1919, he sees a display of books while walking on Sutter Street. He is unaware of how but soon he is upstairs facing a little dark-haired lady. She is Jewish. "You can explain the Kabbala?" he asks. "Yes, and all religions." "What is Sufism?" "Sufism is the essence of all religions. It has been brought to the West by Hazrat Inayat Khan." The woman is Murshida Rabia A. Martin, then Inayat Khan's senior disciple, and his first appointed Murshida. Shortly after this, Samuel formally begins his study of Zen, meeting the Zen teacher Reverend M.T. Kirby, a disciple of the Rinzai Abbot Soyen Shaku. His study of religion has now taken a much deeper turn.

In June of 1923, he has a vision of the arrival of Hazrat Inayat Khan and his mystical mergence with him. The next day at noon, the summer solstice, he is summoned to meet the Pir-o-Murshid. Samuel walks into the room only to see a tremendous light. "Come, don't be afraid," says the Murshid. He takes initiation. He is loyal to his teacher through thick and thin for the rest of his life: "Inayat Khan was the first person to ever touch my heart." Thereafter, he introduces Rinzai Zen master Nyogen Senzaki and Hazrat Inayat Khan, who "entered samadhi together." Samuel begins to write poetry and numerous essays on religious themes. His being is beginning to ferment. His behavior patterns become stranger and even more difficult for his family to understand; his health begins to deteriorate. In 1925, he is on the verge of a nervous breakdown. By his own report he goes into the wilderness to die. This is on land in Fairfax, California, owned by Murshida Martin, dedicated to the Sufi work and called *Kaaba Allah*. He is to make a *khilvat* or spiritual retreat. In the midst of it, the legendary

Khwaja Khizr appears and offers him the gift of music or poetry. He chooses poetry. Khizr appears again the next night. And then all the Prophets of God appear in vision; Elijah presents him with a robe, and Mohammed appears to him as the Seal of the Prophets. For the next 45 years until his death he never questions the validity of these experiences. He remains silent about them until Hazrat Inayat Khan's return to America in 1926, when he seeks an interview and tells the Sufi master of his experiences. Inayat Khan summons him back for five more interviews and gives him tremendous responsibilities for the Sufi work. He makes him "Protector of the Message." During the course of these interviews, Inayat Khan yells at him that he has not as many trustworthy disciples as he has fingers on one hand. This yell literally knocks him over, and he later says that it was at this moment that he received the full transmission of *baraka* (love-blessing-magnetism) from his teacher. It was to be, he later declares, the strength for his whole life.

Hazrat Inayat Khan reads Samuel's early efforts at spiritual commentary, and tells him that he is to be a leader in the Brotherhood work, particularly in efforts to build a bridge of communication between the mystics and the intellectuals. Inayat Khan has Samuel and Paul Reps take a special pledge to protect and be loyal to Rabia Martin, not to let her defend herself in public or take up money matters. On these latter points he fails. Hazrat Inayat Khan dies the following year, and the Sufi Movement which he established becomes divided by politics. Murshida Martin uses Samuel as her foil for making her claim to succession, having him write numerous letters to Sufi Movement headquarters in Europe. Even on her deathbed many years later, though he pleads with her, she refuses to release him from his pledge.

In 1930, three years after his passing, Hazrat Inayat Khan appears to Samuel in vision and exerts pressure upon his crown center. From then on Samuel receives communications from Inayat. He writes lesson paper after paper for the Sufi *mureeds*. He writes numerous commentaries on the esoteric teachings of the Pir-o-Murshid. These commentaries he continues to write until his death, often rewriting them three or four times.

The 1930s and 1940s are a fertile period for his writing, particularly the prophetic types of materials which are all that survived a fire at *Kaaba Allah* in 1949. He begins to live at *Kaaba Allah*, and stays there throughout most of the depression years. He has no salary; his work is as a gardener and groundskeeper. He lives off the land. Murshida Martin appoints him as her *khalif* (representative) and he bears much of the responsibility for running the Sufi Khankah. But as the years go on, they have increasingly more differences. He is being taken through inner initiations all the time and his outer behavior patterns reflect this inner intoxication. There is no one around to be his teacher. He takes the spiritual name *Murad*, meaning one who receives by Grace.

During the 1930s, Samuel also spends time in Los Angeles with Luther Whiteman, collaborating on the book *Glory Roads*, a classic study of Utopian movements in the state of California, and conducting what they call "propaganda analysis." He is becoming more involved with social issues. He lives for a time at the bohemian community called the Dunes in Oceano. He is still a celibate, not by choice but by fate; he rarely even touches a woman and never men. The outbreak of World War II finds him working as a historical consultant and secretary for Army Intelligence (G2). His immediate superior Colonel Edward Landsdale tells him to burn all his diaries of this period. "This was easy because nobody believed me anyway," he says later. He was fighting the war in the inner planes, and his diaries were a chronicle of this. After the war years, Murshida Martin appoints Ivy Duce as her successor, someone nobody in the Sufi Order knew, bypassing Samuel who had been her chief representative for years. Ivy Duce decides to turn everything over to Meher Baba. Samuel tries to accept this out of loyalty; he goes to South Carolina where he lives as a beachcomber. Finally after two years he is given a vision of the grand mosque of the heavens where Jesus sweeps the floors, Mohammed takes up the shoes, and this lady goes around demanding and demanding from others. He is allowed to leave. He collects one box of his multitudinous writings and leaves *Kaaba Allah*. It burns down the next day. He is wrongfully accused of burning it down and finds himself disgraced, penniless, broken. The sacred writings of Hazrat Inayat Khan are withheld from him.

Around this time he gets a vision from Jesus Christ of how to bring peace in Palestine. He goes to school, takes odd jobs, has some very small allowance from his family, does many spiritual practices, writes copiously, works with orphaned children, takes up horseback riding, folk dancing, ornamental horticulture, and works with road crews planting shrubs and flowers. In 1956, Samuel makes his first trip to Asia and is accepted everywhere. He is recognized by spiritual teachers of all schools. He takes up many world projects. In 1961, he makes his second trip abroad. He studies and teaches Sufism in the East. Among many other recognitions, he is made a Murshid in the Chishti Order of Sufis, the parent school of Hazrat Inayat Khan. He works actively distributing different kinds of seeds around the world and working on solutions to world food problems. In 1963, he returns to the United States.

In 1966, he begins to attract a few young disciples. The following year he lands flat on his back in the hospital where God comes to him and appoints him "Spiritual Leader of the Hippies." It's something he never expected, but shortly after this time the young people begin to flock to his door. He finds the family he never had. At the end of his life he is hugging and kissing men and women all the time. He originates the Dances of Universal Peace and dedicates them to the Temple of Understanding which is committed, as was Inayat Khan, to providing a house of prayer for all peoples.

These dances, which take sacred phrases from all the world's religions, have since spread worldwide. He originates the work of the Sufi Choir and institutes spiritual instruction through music. He credits his "fairy godmother" Ruth St. Denis with his ability to draw Dance forms out of the cosmos and for his inspiration to teach through the Walk.

In 1968, he joins forces with Pir Vilayat Khan, the eldest son of his first teacher, and there follows a great flowering of the Sufi work in the United States. Murshid Sufi Ahmed Murad Chishti, as Samuel is now known, appoints his own spiritual successor, Moineddin Jablonski, from among his disciples, as well as several *sheikhs* and *khalifs*.

In December 1970, a fall down the stairs of his San Francisco home gives him a brain concussion; after two and a half weeks in the hospital he dies on January 15, 1971. His work is continued by his energetic and devoted disciples. "For years," Samuel said about himself, "I followed a Gandhian attitude, always yielding, and got nothing for it. When once I was able to be firm and take the path of the master, everything came my way." The events of the last years of Samuel's life were so full they deserve a chronicle all their own. This brief biographical sketch focuses on less known periods of his early life. At the end, all the seeds of his earlier efforts and experiences came to fruition. Finally, he received the Divine instruction: "Harvest what you can, and leave the rest to Me."

Chapter 1

Introduction to
Murshid

What was foreseen when Mansur wrote to Murshid at Lama has now fully manifested in all aspects. Mansur is meeting some of the really great persons of the world, and they like him. This completes his initiation, the price was paid, and now the 'prize' is bestowed. (Murshid's letter from Geneva, Switzerland, to Wali Ali and the Garden of Inayat, April 1, 1970)

This book concerns events that took place in the late 1960s. Since finishing the first draft in 1981, I was not able to work on the manuscript again until 1995. Reading one or two pages during those intervening years was so deep for me, so filled me with emotion, taking me into memories of the unwritten, I had to close the book.

I don't know if anybody else has any interest in the subject of Murshid, but like St. John said about his beloved Jesus: "If I were to use all the water in the oceans for ink, I could not exhaust what there is to say about Jesus." The meaning, I think, is that the heart is an ocean, and love has no boundaries, no shoreline.

I am weeping now as I write this, my back up against a Ponderosa pine 8,600 feet above sea level in the Sangre de Cristo Mountains—just below Murshid's *maqbara* (grave), up at 9,000 feet. I just drummed for dancing led by a committee of dance leaders at the Lama Foundation in New Mexico on Visitor's Day. It's been twenty-six years since I first brought a few of Murshid's dances to this mountain—1969 was the year Murshid's dervish dance cycle was presented here. Today, the canon of dances has expanded, and they are spreading throughout the world as "Dances of Universal Peace."

Not having led or drummed for dances for fifteen years, I am unaccustomed to standing in the center of the circle and receiving the projections of the dancers. I feel sick after the dance. A cup of coffee aggravates my already emotionally charged stomach. This isn't relieved by sleeping, eating, or defecating. It takes the weeping, and the weeping takes me into the love, which is Murshid.

Murshid said that people either develop love on their own, or they are forced into this realization through the trials and tribulations of life. I am one of the latter. The suffering I experienced when my wife left me—because she thought I didn't love her—went a long way toward opening my heart.

But I think my deepest experience of love came at the Temple of Understanding, a meeting of representatives of all the world's religions, in Geneva, Switzerland, which I attended with Murshid in 1970.

I had been watching Swami Ranganathananda Maharaj of the Vedanta Order for days. The swamis of the Vedanta Order are celibate, but before we came to Geneva Murshid repeatedly described Swami Ranganathananda to classes as a "manly man," as if we thought someone celibate was effeminate. I found when watching him that he would disappear in light. Whenever he was speaking, my eyes were constantly focused on him—until he vanished in light.

One day, Murshid and I were eating lunch in the bottom floor restaurant of the Hotel Internationale. Swami Ranganathananda came by and chatted with Murshid for a while. Then, perhaps to underscore a point he was making, Swami slapped me on the back and rested his hand on my left shoulder. My right hand darted to his hand on my shoulder and made gentle contact to acknowledge its presence. I did it without thinking. I was very shy, and quickly withdrew my hand.

Swami Ranganathananda Maharaj at the Temple of Understanding conference in Geneva, 1970.

Nothing more of importance transpired until Murshid and I were back up in our room. I was in the bathtub when tears started to come.

"What's the matter?" Murshid asked.

"The love," I sobbed. "The love," is all I was able to say as my body convulsed with weeping.

After six days in Geneva in April of 1970, Murshid and I spent ten days in London and nine days in Boston. We returned to our homes in San Francisco and Marin County, California, on April 25th. Summer came, and

I drove Murshid, my son Nathan, Saul, Selima, and her two kids—Kevin and Shirin—in my green and white 1966 Volkswagen bus to the Lama Foundation for the month of June. I took dictation from Murshid every day. Every night Murshid presented talks, spiritual practices, and dances to the Lama community.

While we were returning to California, a curious thing happened. I was driving along Interstate 40, somewhere between Albuquerque and Flagstaff, when Murshid became angry with me over nothing. Out of the blue, he became quarrelsome. With hindsight, I knew where this impulse

came from. It was the spirit of guidance urging Murshid to do something, without him necessarily knowing the reason. A servant of God—anyone attuned to their inner guidance—follows through when they receive such a message.

Confronted with Murshid's anger, I responded first on the inner plane. It brought up the recurring issue of my life since I began functioning as Murshid's secretary: the issue of not taking care of myself. True, I did what I had to do to survive. I pulled weeds for Manpower, Inc., dug ditches for the local lumber yard, and assembled hospital beds in Greenbrae, California. I collected government subsidies for Families with Dependent Children. The type of job didn't matter—serving Murshid was the most important thing.

Still, there was always a sort of tension: I had a family to support, I had no regular job, and I was arriving home from Lama $800 in debt. Murshid's anger made me resolve to distance myself from him and focus on myself for a change. And so it was after we arrived home. I obtained more film work with Amertat (Fred Cohn), who was still working on *Sunseed*, his film about Murshid and other spiritual teachers. I left the service of Murshid to Wali Ali in the city and Moineddin in Novato. I thought little about the incident that produced this change.

Less than six months later, on December 28, 1970, Murshid fell down the stairs in his house and hit his head. I remembered an impression I had in London when we were fulfilling one of Murshid's dreams, to visit Kew Gardens. Murshid and I had just gotten out of a cab at the Royal Botanical Gardens, and Murshid started to bolt across the street. I caught his arm before he walked in front of a bus. My thought was: *Murshid is not going to die a natural death. He's going to have an accident.*

I visited Murshid in the Chinatown hospital in San Francisco on Sunday the 10th of January, 1971. He'd been in a coma since the accident. His expression was as one sleeping. I took him some smoked kippers. He liked kippers. The nurse took the dried, unappetizing-looking fish from me with an indulgent smile, and promised to serve them to him next mealtime.

Although Murshid lay in a coma, I spoke to him as if he were fully conscious. There was no response, yet I felt a tremendous power, like the charged atmosphere at a holy place. He had a gold light around his head. I had taken his hand while communing with him like this. When I got up to go, Murshid raised goose bumps on my body by scratching the palm of my hand with his middle finger. With that gesture I knew he heard me and was acknowledging my presence. When I got outside I circumambulated the building while chanting a sacred phrase.

On another visit to the hospital with a group of *mureeds* (disciples), it hit me: I understood why Murshid picked a fight with me on the way back from Lama. He drove me away to mitigate the pain of separation, the devastation and loss his death would produce! How did he know this was going to happen to him? He probably didn't, but was just following his guidance, as usual. Still, I credited him with loving me so much that he pushed me away to save me the excruciating pain I would have felt if I'd still been so close.

During this group visit, I went into ecstasy. My mood was totally contrary to that of the rest of the *mureeds*. For them, the real possibility that their beloved Murshid might perish soon was slowly and painfully sinking in. No one was happy. Certainly, no one was ecstatic—except me. Being with so many disciples at a hospital near Chinatown, I was inspired to dash out and bring back a potpourri of Chinese dinners for fifteen or twenty people. No one was hungry. Very few ate. Tribal people call this sort of contrariness—i.e., ecstasy when others are sad—*heyoka*. I found the term in Archie Fire Lame Deer's book *Gift of Power*. Some Sufis might call it *madzub*. It became my hallmark, as I began to spread Murshid's teachings beyond the San Francisco Bay Area.

In 1972 I asked Pir Vilayat Khan, the head of the Sufi Order where I might start a Sufi center. He offered me Los Angeles or Boston. L.A., with its smog, I considered uninhabitable. I landed briefly in Roxbury, a suburb of Boston and then after a year bought a house near the Atlantic coast in Hull, Massachusetts. There, The Einstein Academy, a school of Sufi studies, which was founded in Roxbury, found a home. I spent the seventies giving Sufi seminars throughout the U.S. and Canada, presenting to others what Murshid had given me. I was still living in Hull in 1981, when I completed the first draft of *Murshid*. By 1991 I had matured enough not to be shamed by the character who had written the journal it was based on.

The truth is sometimes embarrassing. Most everything I have written is autobiographical. I'm not a journalist. I have difficulty writing about people and things. Rather, I write about how I feel, and how I interact with people and things. I am an introvert-intuitive type. This presented a problem when Murshid asked me to write his biography. "You'll have to help me," was my first reaction. Then Murshid died before he ever spoke to me about his life before I met him. Fortunately, Murshid's autobiography is in his letters. Merge those letters with my confessional journal and you have the basis for this memoir.

"Pupil and teacher are one," Murshid taught. Between 1967 and 1970 our lives had merged. Murshid was one with me and all his *mureeds*. During this period I kept an "esoteric journal"—which Murshid asked me to do—wherein he figured prominently. What little is known about Murshid's early life has been presented as an editor's note in Neil Douglas-Klotz's *Sufi Vision and Initiation*, pages 5-8. In the appendix to that book are nine pages (pp. 351–360) entitled "Dates from the Life of Samuel L. Lewis," beginning "1896. Born on October 18, at 2:20 A.M. in San Francisco," and ending, "January 15, 1971, dies at age 75 [*sic*]. Buried at Lama Foundation near Taos, New Mexico."

Before plunging into this book, the reader may want to know more about the author. I would not add these details except my editor tells me a context for this "unfamiliar world" you are about to enter would be useful. My bio begins: Otis B. Johnson was born in Bloomington, Illinois on November 18, 1941. My father, Otis B. Johnson, died two months before I was born. His father, Otis B. Johnson, was the first Secretary of the Federal Trade Commission under United States President Franklin D. Roosevelt. Upon the death of his son, my father, he prematurely retired to Florida. His wife, Mabel McDermott Johnson, was a Washington, D.C. socialite. My mother, Betty Klemm Johnson, and I lived with her parents, Carl and Francis Metz Klemm in Bloomington. Klemm's Department Store was a four-story building on the town square. My grandmother's family business, the Metz Brewery, operated in Omaha, Nebraska, finally closed in 1980. We went to the Presbyterian Church every Sunday. I studied the Bible in order to join the church. Betty married Stan Holzhauer when I was twelve and gave birth to a son, Gregory Lynn Holzhauer, when I left for college in 1959. I got a B.A. from Miami University in Oxford, Ohio in 1962 and an M.A. from the University of Illinois in 1963. For both degrees, English was my major. After receiving my master's degree, I went to Mexico for a year to write a novel.

In 1965 I married Carolyn Buckmaster whom I met while accumulating 60 hours towards a Ph.D. in English at the University of Iowa. Mostly, I was enrolled to stay out of the war in Vietnam. After my wife had a baby in 1966, I dropped out and taught English at Northern Michigan University for one year. I named the boy Nathan B. Johnson.

With two college degrees, a wife and family, I felt old at 26. The questions that consumed me at this time were simple: What to do? How to live? I had taken LSD once in Mexico and experienced the oneness of life. This was a religious experience for me. My friends and I craved that experience and experimented with other psychedelic drugs.

Among those friends from Iowa City were Carl and Pat Jablonski, who moved to San Francisco. They shared the ambience of the hippie explosion with us in Michigan. I especially remember a recording of the Human Be-In in Golden Gate Park with music and speakers like Allen Ginsberg and Timothy Leary. Then, when they met Murshid, Carl told me Murshid's message was, "Joy without Drugs," and it struck a chord.

"Sufism is based on experience," Murshid said. Very well: drug-induced mysticism was our experience. We yearned for more, and we needed guidance. We thought Murshid could take us where we wanted to go the fastest. I resigned my position in Michigan. So there we were in 1967: one month after Murshid moved to 410 Precita in San Francisco, my wife and I celebrated Independence Day, July 4th, in his living room with the Jablonskis. To Murshid, we were "young people." Murshid was then 71 years old. The Vietnam War and the hippie phenomenon associated with the Haight-Ashbury district in San Francisco were nothing to me after this meeting with Murshid. His two bedroom townhouse above a one car garage facing Precita Park in the Mission district became my school. And little by little, the living room above the garage filled up with students. Murshid was retired and lived on a small inheritance, so he was free to attend to those he was attracting.

Two months later I was keeping an "esoteric journal." I never asked Murshid what an esoteric journal was or should contain. All kinds of things went in the journal: from dreams and experiences I considered noteworthy to travels, books, personalities, and teachings I met on the path.

In short, what impressed or moved me went in, and everything was related to Murshid. He impressed me. I kept coming back. He was my teacher, the father I never had, my friend, my mentor, my self.

My story during this time is Murshid's story. His story is my story. That's why this book is called *Murshid* with the subtitle, *a personal memoir of life with American Sufi Samuel L. Lewis*. The youthful protagonist called Mansur in this tale is no longer with us. Neither is the old man named Samuel. But once upon a time they came together as one and something was created. Only the fragrance remains. Only the love can give a clue. Lovers everywhere know what I am talking about.

May this book awaken you and inspire you to continue to strive for more life, more love, more joy, and more peace.

I salute all the beings, seen and unseen, who guide us and protect us.

Thank you all for your life.

Murshid teaching in his living room with
his back up against a bookcase; he faces the
windows seen in the photo on page 299.

Chapter 2

First
Experience

There is a teaching of Pir-O-Murshid [Inayat Khan] that in the Zaval [the end] part of life we get the results of what was done earlier... Sunday week we had open house here with a Pakistani catered dinner and about fifty people came and those who have known me a long time said it was the best affair I had ever put on... The prayer that one might have a dozen male disciples seems to have come true and now there are also some women...

One has broken with Vilayat [son of Inayat Khan]. And he will have to pay on the Day of Judgment. Instead of a Sufi seeing from the point of view of another as well as of himself, he has refused even unconditional surrender!... His refusal to release his father's papers under any circumstance will be held against him on the Day of Judgment. (Murshid's diary letter to Sharab and Paul, September 1967)

September 6, 1967, Wednesday

A reading of Papa Ramdas's *God Experience* this week awakens a sense of the human ideal (*fana-fi-rassul*), a longing for realization, and an awareness of my sense of mission. There is a strong pulsation in my head when I retain breath or mentally repeat the sacred phrase *OM SRI RAM JAI RAM JAI JAI RAM* (i.e. the name of God in the form of Ram; the whole mantra is sometimes just called *Ramnam, Ram* meaning God, *nam* meaning name). Papa Ramdas gave the mantra to Murshid at Anandashram in Kanhangad during Murshid's first visit to India in 1956.

In a dream this afternoon, I am aware of heartbeats in my head, a rocket launch of energy out my crown center while I back my car out of a one-way street that I had entered mistakenly (me in daily life going the right way backwards) with Jemila (my real-life wife Carolyn's spiritual name she received from Murshid) in the passenger's seat. I have the sensation of ego loss, which I interpret while dreaming as God's grace.

While going to sleep tonight, I am so attuned to the pulse in my head that I can't stop my ears from flapping. No, you wouldn't see them flapping. Understand, the consciousness of the blood pulsing in my ears makes me say it like this. I mean the blood pulsed so strongly that I felt as though my ears were flapping. The reality of these experiences alters my perception of why I think I am with Sam (Murshid). In the beginning, I was curious to learn esoteric practices for the sake of learning what is hidden.

And now, after reading Ramdas, I want to go to India, renounce the world, and chant *Ramnam* all the time. *God Experience* speaks of renunciation. Ramdas leaves his job and family *before* beginning his quest for God. He suggests that this renunciation is a strong reason for his success.

I'm reminded of my lifelong Don Juan tendencies toward life (romantic in the literary sense of Lord Byron's Don Juan, rather than in the spirit of Carlos Castaneda's sorcerer). Don Juan's were the clothes I came dressed in. Ramdas's story offered a type of advanced accomplishment. I realize that this path with Sam is the beginning of the beginning.

September 10, 1967, Sunday

Sam mentions that he will be going to "hippieland" (San Francisco's Haight-Ashbury district) on Tuesday nights. He is going to give the hippies the same practices he gives us, as presented in Paul Reps's *Zen Flesh, Zen Bones*. A fee will be charged, but Sam is going to take a secretary who will get in free. Although Sam has said so publicly in this impersonal way, I've already volunteered to help him and I know I am that secretary.

September 13, 1967, Wednesday

I dream that as Jemila (my feminine self) and I are coming up to a dock (safety from emotional turmoil) in a boat, my son Nathan (my child part within) drowns (goes under emotionally) as a result of my negligence.

September 14, 1967, Thursday

I have certain visual experiences while chanting *Allaho Akbar* (God is Great) and *La Ilaha El Il Allah* (There is no God but God), and concentrating on Sam. During each of these three different activities, something happens visually. I'm not prepared to say what exactly happened at this point. My normal way of seeing is altered. After the meeting is over I say, "Sam, while doing *Allaho Akbar*, I lost my body." Sam replies, "Good for you, good for you." My breathing during the chanting is not deep breathing, but rather a kind of hyperventilation. It makes me very short of breath. Once, it causes me to stop chanting and take a deep breath.

Sam says that Saturday he will go to his friend Katherine's dress shop and get Pat (Carl's wife) and Jemila each a sari. Then at a later date, we will all walk chanting down Haight Street. "This," Sam says, "will be good business for Katherine."

Murshid says there are three heavens to be attained: first, that of your heart's desire; second, the *sifat* (qualities) of God; third, manhood. I duly record these concepts, but of the three I really only have a clue about the qualities. Why? Because Murshid gives us the experience of these qualities.

Utilizing the mantric value of the original language, Murshid has presented in Arabic qualities like *jemal* (beauty) and *jelal* (strength). We have repeated these phrases while walking and used *mudras* (gestures) to suggest the meaning. As for "heart's desire," I am not in touch with my heart. And manhood? I think I am too young to understand this now.

Murshid means spiritual guide. At some point before this journal begins, Sam said, "Call me Murshid." I'm still not comfortable calling him this, so for a while I go back and forth between Sam and Murshid, but to avoid confusion here, from now on it will be Murshid.

September 15, 1967, Friday

Tonight at Murshid's I silently wish for a lesson on the Upanishads. Murshid goes to the bookcase and pulls out a book. He tells us the Upanishads are difficult to understand without having had the experiences these scriptures describe. "It is difficult to know," Murshid says, "what the 'bees' and other symbols mean without the experience."

September 17, 1967, Sunday

Eugene Wagner, a lay Buddhist priest friend of Murshid's and spiritual advisor to the Maharani of Sikkim, comes to Murshid's. He says to Carl and myself, "I'm very much impressed with you two. You are very close." Close to what? I wonder. Whatever, I'm flattered.

September 18, 1967, Monday

Last night I got just a flash of the same visual blurring that happened while chanting *Allaho Akbar* last Thursday. Today Clark, one of Murshid's earlier disciples, comes over to Murshid's and is talking about "the white light." I remember the blurring and make a connection. I get that the blurring is *the light*. In fact, I think this light phenomenon is what I experienced at Murshid's the first time I concentrated on his Buddha statue, two months ago. I ask Murshid what to do about the opaqueness I perceive impinging on my vision, when everything is lighted with a dull orange-yellow, gray luminosity. "Ignore it," Murshid says.

September 22, 1967, Friday

I flash tonight while reading the man who was Murshid's murshid, Inayat Khan. In *Aqibat, Life after Death*, Khan writes,

> Sometimes there are visions of the murshids, the higher beings; these come to the initiate. They come to guide and to help in all difficulties. Someone who is quite absorbed in the thought of a prophet or murshid may be so lost in him, that if he calls upon him in any difficulty, the one upon whom he calls will always come and help him. (*The Sufi Message of Hazrat Inayat Khan*, vol.5, p.70)

I flash because sometime before I read this, Hazrat Inayat Khan appeared to me. He looked in vision as he looks in his picture on the flyleaf of the book. While reading the next page, I recall having a thought that I want to tell Murshid but can't remember it. Something tells me: Just keep reading. The next paragraph begins, "Animals..." and I remember the thought concerns our Labrador, Bigger. I visualize Bigger as a sort of Cerberus, guarding a gate in some future life. In my vision, Bigger lets me pass because of kindness given to him in this life. This whole stream of activity, which feels so holy, creates the same feeling I used to have when I was high. Those were the times when poetry flowed in rivers of lyrics. There was nothing that was not seed or flower of poetry.

September 23, 1967, Saturday

Murshid announces in class he will publish the different kinds of walks in a book. Since we have been doing walks with qualities, it takes awhile before I realize I'm being set up. It's a joke. First, Murshid continues, he will teach the walks to his Comparative Religion class. I think "That's us!", and I am so happy to be in this exclusive group. He goes on, "There will be the Hindu walk, which will consist of sitting on your haunches and talking about walking. There is the Pakistani walk, which takes place in a hammock. Finally, the Jewish walk involves vigorously waving the hands," says Murshid. Murshid says he will desecrate religion and then teach Zen, which has to be desecrated to be taught. He will paint a picture of Lord Buddha or Bodhidharma—the one who brought Buddhism to China from India—on a football, and kick it hard.

The small group that meets at Murshid's is going to Fairfax tomorrow to visit the Sufi rock, an outcropping Hazrat Inayat Khan identified as sacred and named *Pir Dahan* (the voice of the Prophet). Murshid wrote that Nyogen Senzaki, one of his Zen teachers, "went to the rock and immediately went into *samadhi* (a state of oneness). He reported it had the highest vibration of any place he had known in America." The outcropping is located next to the lot where Murshid's old home *Kaaba Allah* (God's place of pilgrimage) used to be. The house burned in 1949, destroying most of Murshid's writings and library. Murshid invites people to be aware of what they feel when we go to the rock. I feel nothing.

After making the trip to Fairfax, Jemila and I bring Murshid back to Bolinas. Murshid will stay overnight Sunday at Pat and Carl's. Monday, I will take Murshid back to San Francisco.

September 24, 1967, Sunday

Murshid says Pat had "a true vision" when she heard a ram's horn at *Pir Dahan*. Murshid used to blow on a conch shell there and the sound is in the space, he says. I heard nothing. In the course of doing research for a trip to Peru, I found a report of a place called Ichu where local people hear a bell. It is interesting to read an archaeologist's explanation that the sound may exist as a "folk belief":

Ichu is believed by some of the local people to be the dwelling place of a supernatural bell which tolls on certain days in the religious calendar. This is a widespread Andean belief, but in the case of Ichu, a real bell may have rung in the Colonial period and the memory may persist in this folk belief. (*Huanuco Pampa*, p.143)

Jemila and I join Murshid for dinner at Pat and Carl's in Bolinas. Jemila says to Murshid, "When you're around, our husbands don't know what they're doing. Otis cleaned the house today before you came." Murshid answers, "How do you know he didn't know what he was doing?"

September 25, 1967, Monday

Driving through Lagunitas, I try to make a joke by pointing out the sign reading, "No braziers allowed in the woods." "Does that mean no women can go in the woods?" I ask. My attempt to link "braziers" and "brassières" falls flat. Continuing along these lines, I ask about a kissing game Murshid had mentioned Sunday in Fairfax. He had organized it at a children's party he directed years ago in the park near the rock. I must have been leering slightly. In the car going back to San Francisco, Murshid responds finally to the above (I believe) saying, "Personally, I don't like obscenity." Our earlier exchange about brassieres and my insinuation about children's kissing games come back to haunt me.

On the road, I ask Murshid if he was a translator in a past life. I want to verify Clark's report that according to Dr. Neville Warwick, a local Buddhist, Murshid was Marpa the Translator in a past life. Marpa was the teacher of Milarepa (1038-1122), the great Tibetan yogi. Murshid says he doesn't know. He doesn't pay too much attention to his past lives, he says, unless they help him know himself, or help him with his creative work. The only time I asked, "What past lives do you remember?" was the same day I asked to be a disciple. That was way before I started keeping this journal. Murshid answered then that it wasn't a disciple's business to know about the teacher. Correspondingly, he noted, the teacher's only job is to help the student know himself. But Murshid added, "I died in all my past lives either by drowning or by having my head cut off." Murshid also said he had frequently been a social rebel or a court jester type. So at the same time Murshid gently told me not to ask, he answered me. I felt both chastened and satisfied.

In San Francisco, Murshid gives me a carbon copy of his poem, *The Rejected Avatar*. In the car driving in, he says, "You're going to go high (when you read the poem)." Murshid says that even if I don't go to the Orient, I will be protected. I don't know where the bit about going "to the Orient" came from but I am happy I will be protected. Murshid says Carl or I will be guardian of his poetry. Murshid says he will need a ride to San Rafael sometime to see his lawyer about forming a corporation. I don't know what he is talking about.

One thing Murshid does today to gratify my ego is to talk candidly around me. When his old friend Bill Hathaway comes, they talk openly about their families. Several times, Murshid puts me "on oath." It gratifies my ego that he takes me into his confidence. The first occasion concerns Robert (Phra Sumangalo) Clifton, who said, "Samuel, we ain't got it." I understand that "it" meant spiritual realization. Murshid says he answered Phra Sumangalo, "Well, we got it." It is this supreme confidence and suggestion of his ability that keeps me coming back for more. The second time Murshid puts me on oath is when he tells me Clark believes that homosexuality is wrong. I didn't know or care if Clark was homosexual——and still don't.

Murshid tells me which people seem to him to be candidates for initiation. I learn what, according to Murshid, a teacher does when a pupil has enlightenment. The teacher goes off into the woods. Murshid tells me about the time his Muslim friend in Lahore, Pakistan, had an experience of Christ. "Irony was," Murshid says, "that I had a Mohammed experience."

When I ask how long it would take me to know as much as he, Murshid says, "It doesn't matter. It could be years. It could be tomorrow. There is the quantitative thing, and the other which depends on the grace of God. The thing between us," Murshid continues, "is like a fire engine which has a steering wheel in front and one in back, and both of us steer. Do you understand?"

The stories continue. There was the time Murshid arrived early for a bus to the airport, and there was an early bus. So he got to the airport early, and it turned out that the plane was early, too. In my mind, this episode is incredibly uncanny.

Murshid met a certain woman in the company of a Zen master at the airport. Murshid learned that she used to be Nyogen Senzaki's secretary. He said to her, "I'm going to whisper something in your ear, and you are going to have enlightenment." He tells us, "It never happened before, it may never happen again. But she did (get enlightened)." Later I ask, "What were the words you whispered?" "It doesn't matter," Murshid says. "I could give you a Zen answer." He pauses. "The best restaurants serve outhouse dung." But since he isn't being a Zen master at this moment, Murshid goes on without missing a beat and says some words explaining why the words don't matter.

September 26, 1967, Tuesday

The faucet at home takes all day to fix. This is significant. I feel remiss. There's no time to do any typing for Murshid. To impress my consciousness with spiritual teachings, Murshid assigns me to copy some. The very first is a short essay on "The Intoxication of Life," from the works of Sufi Inayat Khan.

September 27, 1967, Wednesday

I type a little and smoke grass, so I don't get Murshid's poem *Shiva, Shiva* read. I feel guilty.

September 28, 1967, Thursday

A lot comes out at Murshid's today. He repeats the story I heard him tell before about Lottie Von Stahl:

> There was once a remarkable clairvoyant who came to San Francisco to explain auras, their light and color, and the significance thereof. A number of socially prominent people came, all expecting to be told they had brilliant auras. And not a single one had a brilliant color. When they remonstrated, the clairvoyant said, "Not only do I see what I see, but I shall be telling what you have been doing. You do not hide from me, you do not hide from God; you merely hide from those who have the incapacity to see." It was very fortunate she did not tell about those who had the brilliant colors or the yellow or golden light (he is referring covertly to himself.) The audience would not have understood it. This audience is the type that has been running from one teacher to another incessantly and is never satisfied. They seek miracles, not awakening.

Then, Murshid tells an oft repeated reincarnation story: There was an ongoing argument about the existence or nonexistence of reincarnation taking place at the house of astrologer Gavin Arthur (the grandson of United States President Chester Arthur). Murshid busts up the meeting (his phrase) when he says, "What am I to say? I remember all my past lives."

Later on, Murshid asks me for some literary and mystical criticism of his poetry. I don't remember it clearly enough to comment. I say I'll have to read it again. I think the poem he is asking me about is *Shiva, Shiva*, but it isn't. He is asking about his autobiographical poem, *The Rejected Avatar*. I read that one three days ago. Why is the word "rejected" in the title? I wonder. Why would anyone reject an avatar? Now Murshid wants to know how *The Rejected Avatar* stacks up against contemporary verse. He names people and poems I've never read. How does it compare to Marianne Moore's work? I've never heard of her. I'm proud to have a Master's degree in English, and feel ashamed for not knowing who Marianne Moore is.

Murshid says people reveal themselves when they feel ashamed, and leaves the room.

Murshid returns, talking about integrity, intuition, and humor. He says his words have solid intellect behind them; that they aren't all Irish stubbornness. Murshid stresses that one must be honest with oneself. "Well, was it [the poem] interesting?" Murshid asks finally. "Yes," I can answer honestly.

September 29, 1967, Friday

I am lying in a hammock watching my breath. I do a breathing practice involving rhythmically inhaling, holding, and exhaling. Then I practice thinking, "There is no mind" while exhaling; "but heart" while inhaling. I fall into a kind of dream trance. I think I'm holding a manuscript, which I begin to read. I've dreamed this before. Mentally, I repeat the lines consciously to myself. But when I open my eyes from the waking dream, I see there is no manuscript and I can't remember the lines. This really upsets me. I want to know the words from the dream manuscript, but they're gone.

Many details included in last week's journal entries come back tonight while I spend all night typing a manuscript by Seo San, an ancient Korean Zen patriarch, called *Text for Zen Buddhism,* which was translated by Murshid's Korean Zen master, Dr. Kyung-Bo Seo. The date of this text, "the only textbook of Zen used by Korean Buddhists" according to Dr. Kyung-Bo Seo in the Introduction, is 1564. Seo is the one who gave Murshid the title *Zen-Shi* (Zen Master).

I don't know that Murshid will later send this manuscript to publisher Charles Tuttle, or that he has written to Master Seo and said, "I have found enough book materials for [a book we might call] *The Roshis Speak.*" Murshid told Seo he had found notes written by Shaku Soyen "entirely different from his *Sermons of a Buddhist Abbot,*" as well as "another manuscript of a friend of Shaku Soyen translated into English by the late Nyogen Senzaki," plus "the lectures of Master Tai Hsu"—all this "apart from my own autobiographical notes which will be revised and put into book forms."

September 30, 1967, Saturday

Carl and I proofread the *Text for Zen Buddhism.* Then Murshid leads a group of us on a walk, where we concentrate on our breath while walking. We walk thinking "Toward the One" breathing in, and "Toward the One" breathing out. This is basic training to teach awareness of the breath. We use the phrases *Ya Hayy* (O Life) and *Ya Haqq* (O Truth). We think or chant one of the phrases when we step on our right foot and the other phrase when we step on our left foot. They are energizing. More advanced work while walking involves concentration on different physical centers. The *hara* center in the solar plexus, the heart center, and the third eye— all are used. It is uncanny sometimes the way my attention shifts from one concentration to another a block or so before Murshid suggests that the group change its concentration. Whether the ground is level or hilly influences how we concentrate.

October 1, 1967, Sunday
The chants are especially good at Murshid's tonight. Murshid says, "I think some of you are beginning to get something out of this." Murshid gives a concentration on the *sushumna* (the center of the spinal column), and I feel a sense of spiral, like a sea shell. Later I think of the book about the *kundalini* (energy) by Woodruff called *Coiled Serpent Power,* and note the verbal similarities between "spiral" and "coiled", but that is all—no revelations.

October 5, 1967, Thursday
The view from Bolinas Lagoon to Stinson Beach and beyond is very similar to a Technicolor vision I had three years ago in Mexico. I knew the vision represented San Francisco, but I had never been to this place. Some people have forevisions of their teacher. This was a forevision of where I was going to get the teachings.

While I'm enjoying an idyllic morning in Bolinas, Murshid is writing U.S. Senator John Sherman Cooper, "We have failed to see that we can not win the hearts of Asians by ignoring their humanity and their culture... [There is] no excuse for our refusals to have candid cultural exchange with these people [Arabs] and our selection of Englishmen as chief mentors in Islamics." June, 1967, had seen the Six Day War in Israel, and now the Viet Nam war is going on. Murshid informs Senator Cooper, "Next week I begin my own lectures in the religions of the world, based on deep studies..." (see October 25, 1967) Just two sentences later, he shifts back: "It is a tragedy that to us Europeans are human beings, Asians are thought-forms. There will be no peace in Viet Nam until we change this attitude."

Some of us go early to Murshid's, where he dictates to me four numbers— each a page long—of "Self-Protection" *Githekas* (Sufi study papers). Ten numbers comprises a complete series of Sufi study papers. When I ask him why he stops dictating, Murshid says his intuition told him to stop. "Intuition is always right," he says. Murshid says that he doesn't—I forget his exact words—check me out from a distance. The reason, he explains, is because I might be experiencing psychic phenomena and he doesn't want to interfere.

October 15, 1967, Sunday

A new girl named Marcia tells Murshid, "You're more like what I've been looking for than anything I've found so far." And Murshid says, "I may be more than that."

October 16, 1967, Monday

When I told Murshid that we had some super hash from Morocco, he said, "Don't smoke dope." But when asked later, he says he doesn't care one way or the other if people smoke. It has been two weeks since I smoked cigarettes, grass, or hash. I've been aware of the somatic and soporific effects of pot for some time. I'd smoke, eat a lot, and then have to sleep. By quitting tobacco and marijuana, I hope to open myself to the finer vibrations. I am also becoming very conscious of the effect that food has on the body, and sometimes I resent those somatic and soporific effects, too. I am realizing the significance of the biblical fast, as well as of Mohammed's sayings on "Abstinence" that Murshid introduced. Some of these are:

1. Remember the Lord in retirement from the people and make prayer thy sleep, and hunger thy food...

3. Illumine your hearts by hunger, and strive to conquer your self by hunger and thirst; continue to knock at the gates of Paradise by hunger...

7. Keep fast and eat also, stay awake at night and sleep also... and nobody hath kept fast who fasted always; the fast of three days in every month is equal to constant fasting; then keep three days' fast in every month. (*The Sayings of Mohammed*, London, 1941)

"The world of heart." "She has a good heart." "Cold-hearted." None of these phrases meant anything to me before Murshid. Now I am learning that heart is higher than mind. Mind, that thing everybody goes to college to exercise; college, where people are taught to think. Ha. Our so-called "education" is lamentable.

October 17, 1967, Tuesday

I dream Murshid and disciple Ginger are at my house. Ginger is making spaghetti. I climb down out of my attic, asking, "Are we going to eat soon? Or shall I climb up and do some more typing?" All the time I'm thinking I don't want to eat spaghetti, because it makes me heavy and tired and then I have to sleep. The dream continues: Picking up on my thought, Murshid immediately takes everyone out to dinner. The two images are: Ginger tasting spaghetti sauce off the spoon, and a long line of us going to cars to drive to the restaurant.

Murshid wore a suit and a tie for his lecture, based on the works of 19th century Biblical scholar Fabre D'Olivet, at the Church of Man. This is a place where a long-time associate of Murshid's teaches youngsters like ourselves to make a reality of Christ. During Murshid's talk at the church founded by Father Earl Blighton, I ask Murshid what "Thou shalt not kill" means. Murshid answers by speaking about "unity" as Hindus do when they say: *"Tat Twam Asi"* (Thou art that). All is One. I took LSD, so I know exactly what Murshid is talking about, because when I saw the energy in everything the oneness was my realization. Inevitably, when *Tat Twam Asi* is mentioned, Murshid will tell this story.

I got into India quickly last time by shouting *TAM TVAT ASI* to all the customs and immigration officials; last in line I was the first through. This effort is something prepared for for years. But I warn you there is a vast difference between words used by dialecticians and orators from the same words used by a realized mystic. (Murshid's letter to Julie Medlock, Auroville, India, May 8, 1968)

Still on the topic of "Thou shalt not kill," I ask about the morality of swatting flies. Murshid talks about the evolution of life from the mineral, vegetable, and animal kingdoms to the human. The death of insects, Murshid implies, promotes their evolution. He quotes Rumi:

Man slept in the mineral kingdom
Dreamt in the vegetable kingdom
Woke in the animal kingdom
And realized himself as man.

Murshid's view is that a creature on the lower plane shouldn't annoy human beings. People may kill flies if they do it without malice, is Murshid's teaching.

October 26, 1967, Thursday

Murshid doesn't have a car. I begin to drive him places. When I pick him up at his Comparative Religion class today, I tell him I feel the need for more discipline. This is a direct result of reading Philip Kapleau's *The Three Pillars of Zen*. Murshid recommended the book especially because it emphasizes spiritual experience, rather than concepts about spiritual experience. (I later reviewed this book in our publication *The San Francisco Oracle*.) Murshid gives me a *tashbih* (prayer beads) and these practices: Morning: Twenty purification breaths and prayer; then *ziker*, (remembrance) 101 times. Evening: w*azifas*, (qualities of God) 101 times each; then heart concentration.

November 1, 1967, Wednesday

During the question period after Murshid's lecture at Father Blighton's, I ask, "Can a fully enlightened man see in the dark?" Murshid counters, "What kind of dark?" "In a mine." Murshid says, "Yes, he can see."

November 5, 1967, Sunday

A number of years ago Murshid joined a group of Chinese Buddhists who "do not believe in God."

During a lecture at the Holy Order of MANS ...

But they do believe in humanity, kindness, generosity, consideration, and all those assumed virtues of metaphysical and religious people. They were using exactly the methods that Hazrat Inayat Khan taught Sam [accept donations of any size]. They started with a debt of $10,000 and an empty lot. They now have a beautiful $400,000 structure. (Murshid's letter to Vera Van Voris, September 17, 1968)

I take Murshid to this same, $400,000 United Buddhist Church in Chinatown. Murshid was involved in building this church—I'm not sure how—when he wanted to learn about Chinese philosophy. Murshid implies that the Chinese were secretive and not especially open to sharing their philosophy with Westerners.

Lacking that well known virtue *humility*, I worked as a flunky for 11 years at the Buddha Universal Church on Washington Street. I was a nobody, but I wanted to learn about Chinese psychology. Someone had said, "If you want to learn Confucianism, live with the Chinese." (Murshid's letter to Art Hoppe, January 27, 1970)

When I take Murshid to the church, they're having an anniversary party to commemorate the day construction was completed—a birthday party of sorts. The service is so Christianized it feels like the Presbyterian Church I grew up in. I am puzzled as to why it is even called "Buddhist." I note in church literature an emphasis on their adherence to scripture. Wise guy that I am, I ask Dr. Fung, the church's director, if the scriptures sanction building a church. "No," he says, "but we needed a place to meet." My disgust for organized religion is showing. The service was like any Christian, nonexperiential church, but Fung's words are beautiful in their simplicity. I miss the beauty, and label this church an example of those who talk and don't seek the reality: the experience upon which religion is based—what Murshid teaches.

At his meeting tonight, Murshid answers my question about one of the centering exercises in Paul Reps's book *Zen Flesh, Zen Bones*. The exercises are Lord Shiva's 112 answers, in the form of practices, to Devi's questions: "What is this life beyond form pervading forms?" and "How may we

... Murshid was so animated, he was difficult to photograph.

enter it fully, above space and time, names and descriptions?" Some practices important to me appear later in the book. Murshid says even though "Murshid's son" (Vilayat, son of Inayat Khan) won't give him his father's teachings, he "has been told" (by what I take to be inner guidance) that he has enough teachings to get me to God-realization. Murshid has enough teachings to get me to God-realization! I am excited twice; Murshid has the tools, and he thinks I have the capability. Recording this, I feel exalted. The spiritual path is too much. I feel unworthy. If I'm going to become wise, I need to learn more. I admire Murshid's spontaneity in action and in answering. I have to be impeccable, really honest with myself.

November 8, 1967, Wednesday

At the Holy Order of MANS tonight, Murshid introduces me as his secretary. Being a famous man's secretary, I realize, is my heart's desire, and being Murshid's secretary is the fulfillment of my heart's desire. My heart starts pounding while at Father Blighton's moments before Murshid says that in the *Bhagavad Gita* Kurukshetra, the battlefield, represents the human heart. The battle that takes place in that book represents the battle of the seeker with himself. The main difference between spiritual and worldly battles is that the spiritual battle is inward. The supreme victory to be won is over oneself, rather than, for example, in succeeding at business.

November 9, 1967, Thursday

At the Sufi Night gathering tonight, Murshid waits until I come in from doing the dishes and sit down before he announces, "I am about to realize a goal that I have been waiting forty years to accomplish." What? "I now have the most complete esoteric teaching that the world has ever known..." –that's impressive– "for those who ask for it." After the meeting I ask, "When is the proper time to ask for what you mentioned?" "What?" Murshid says. "The esoteric teaching," say I. "You remember, don't you, that I said, 'I am *about* to realize a goal?'" Murshid says. Then he gives me a piercing look and disappears behind his bedroom door. He reappears a few beats later. "It's going on all the time," he says, smiling. I feel stupid for asking, but don't care. If I hadn't responded, I would have condemned myself as well. Murshid asks me to come early next Thursday, so that we can make an esoteric notebook listing people's names and spiritual practices.

I used to get into my third eye by inhaling. Tonight, driving in to the meeting, I get into my third eye by exhaling. At the meeting, when I concentrate on Murshid speaking, I lose consciousness of my body to some extent. Invariably, my joined hands lose feeling. I understand what Murshid says about being restricted by his disciples. He says he can soar only as high as they are able to go. Why? Because he must be *with* them. Where they are, he must be. Murshid says a *Gatha* (Sufi study paper) class will be starting up in Bolinas. He predicts that realizations are inevitable for some of us at certain tombs in Pakistan, but does not mention his own powerful experiences in Lahore, Pakistan, at the tomb of al-Hujwiri (Data Gang Baksh). Of this, he wrote, "On every occasion when visiting the shrine, the Saint appeared." Something just as amazing happened in Japan. In Murshid's words:

Once the commentator had been taken to the Royal Cemetery in Japan. He was told that no non-Asian had ever been brought there, and only one Asian, and that Asian was not very respectful. They went to the tomb of the former Emperor and made obeisance. Then all the Japanese disappeared.

The commentator was a disciple in Sufism. He had been trained by both Hazrat Inayat Khan and Ruth St. Denis to employ insight to read from the ethers, so to speak. To many the term "ether" or "akasha" is transcendental, but non-conscious. But to the mystics they are very conscious. And as is taught in *Cosmic Language*, one learns to read effectively from the "space" and all "vibrations".

So being alone, the commentator stood before the shrine of the Empress, bowed, meditated; walked forward until some 30 paces from the tomb, bowed, meditated, bowed again; and walked backward facing the tomb until at the original place, bowed again, meditated, and gave a final bow and waited.

Then the three Japanese came forward from their hiding places and told him they had been watching him, and he had done what was absolutely correct. So he was taken in turn to the Stupa for Lord Buddha on the mountain; to an esoteric Shingi-Shingon temple; to the top of the mountain where some pictures were taken; and later was a guest of honor at the Imperial Gardens in Tokyo, an honor never before bestowed on a simple person, or on non-Asians excepting of the highest grades.

Actually, the same thing had happened before, when Murshid met Roshi Sogen Asahina at the Engaku-ji in Kamakura, a most famous Zen temple. The two just glanced at each other and became one—or nothing, or transcendent. I don't know what to call it.

This has happened many times to and with mystics, but is seldom an experience of metaphysical book-writers who may become famous and wealthy, but who do not bestow understanding on themselves or on the human race. (Murshid's *Commentary on Superstitions, Customs & Belief*)

I'm beginning to realize the reality of telepathy, or mind attunement. Football scores on TV are an example. The scores were being given several weeks ago. "Purdue beats Minnesota, Illinois defeated...," and I thought,

Ohio State. The sportscaster said, "Ohio State." Telepathy is faster than the TV transmission from New York to California. When I report such phenomena to Murshid, he's nonchalant—like yesterday, when I told him how my heart pounded before he gave his interpretation that the heart is the battleground the *Bhagavad Gita* calls Kurukshetra. "Yes", Murshid said, his voice falling with solemnity—not rising with excitement. When I compare my expectations of how I think Murshid is going to respond with his actual response, I always learn something. Like this time, when I got: *What you just experienced is no big deal, or nothing to get excited about.*

November 12, 1967, Sunday

Murshid reads from "Perversion" in Hazrat Inayat Khan's *Rasa Shastra*, and I have to choke off the tears when he talks about neglect. The passage says, "There is a tendency in every child that needs guidance, the neglect of which is a most fertile soil for perversion." I feel that I have lacked guidance my whole life. I relate another passage Murshid reads to my relationship with Jemila: "But the average child will suffer in other ways; for instance, it may with the years develop a distaste for marriage or a coldness that affects relationship in marriage." My life without a father—my life without guidance—all flashes back, and I feel so sorry for myself.

Later, my recollection of a wonderful dream gets my mind off the self pity, and I ask Murshid, "What does it mean when you wake up from a dream in which you feel good about the fact that the grass gets green by itself?" "It means you're getting close to home, and when you reach your home, you don't have to pay rent," Murshid says joyfully.

Murshid speaks again of the initiations next Thursday. I am to get a book to record the name, address, occupation, and aim in life of all Murshid's disciples—what he calls his pupils. Murshid will require a fee or personal service from all new initiates. The principle involved in asking for a payment of some kind is sacrifice.

November 13, 1967, Monday

Today, feeling pitiful while sawing logs for our fireplace, I think of calling Murshid and asking about self pity. I want to ask for a practice to do while sawing logs. My feeling of self pity leads to the thought: *nobody loves me.* I enter the back door to find Jemila. She is full of love. The question I thought to ask Murshid—what to do about lack of love—is answered. But my problem is *not to be solved by another individual loving me.*

November 14, 1967, Tuesday

When typing *Education* by Hazrat Inayat Khan, I am particularly struck by a part about how children should not be sent off to "cry for a time." If that happens, they may become impressed with being neglected.

Subsequently, they may be displeased and disappointed with everything in life. This fits me perfectly. I feel the emotion start to constrict my neck. The passages from *Rasa Shastra* at Murshid's the other night brought up self pity and produced the same emotion. I don't feel comfortable letting it out. I wonder what to do. I keep reading.

Then in Rumi's *Discourses*, I read that at the beginning of the spiritual path there may be epiphanies of weeping. Weeping helps clear out the sorrow and make way for the joy. Glad to learn that my emotion is not abnormal, I don't attempt to hold back the tears. Now I am really cooking. My psyche produces a dream—recorded in the middle of the night—that takes material from the three main periods of my life. In the first sequence I am rooming with an elderly couple (I grew up in my grandparents' home). There is much tension, and I leave when they discover that I left the water (emotional energy) running—this was the final blame.

Next I have a row with my stepfather (who came into my life at age 12). He isn't satisfied with a job I'm doing for him. My stepfather chases me out of the house, throwing beer cans at me, and then offers me a drink. Bewildered and angry, I take the can and pour the beer on the ground. The stepfather laughs as I fail his test of tolerance and equanimity.

In the final sequence, Murshid's disciples have just gotten back from a bus trip. Everyone has been blessed. During some blessings I'm a little surprised to find that I can see the sex organs of those on whose stomachs Murshid was laying hands in blessing. All of us were warned: One needs a special body for spiritual development. Murshid's head looks hideous, no eyes or nose, a clenched neck with the skin missing, and no mouth—only a membrane connected with metal. Where Murshid's neck tendons should be, there's a long relaxed spring on each side. I ask Murshid, "What do we have in place of springs?" Murshid reaches inside my neck to my chest, and I start squirming. He begins pounding with a steel hammer in my stomach area. I squirm more and finally shout repeatedly, "I'll resist, I'll resist..." But Murshid keeps pounding and smoke rises. There is no pain, but great commotion. Finally, I realize Murshid is going after my pain and suffering. I stop shouting and bring to bear a great quantity of heat in the area he's working in, to aid his hammering. Out of my solar plexus, Murshid and I produce—deliver, really—a small, clear glass ashtray with oh-so-small hammer marks on it. We laugh hysterically. Near the end of the laughing, I think Murshid and I will hug, but instead he retires to the kitchen.

November 15, 1967, Wednesday

"You are progressing well," Murshid says when I tell him I had ecstasies of weeping sparked by self pity last night and Sunday. Murshid advises,

"Be strong. Imagine you are a fish in an ocean, or a drop of blood in your bloodstream. You are full of sin, and you go to the lungs, get purified, and you come back. "I have two jobs for you tomorrow," Murshid continues. "One is to initiate the esoteric notebook for disciples. The other is to start an esoteric journal." Proud of having anticipated his assignment, I smile, "It's already in progress."

Another realization comes during the winding ride home from San Francisco to Bolinas, somewhere between Muir Woods State Park and Stinson Beach. It is that I can't—or don't—love Jemila. My first thought is to take another wife along with her. Then the absurd logic of this catches up with me. The problem isn't Jemila. The problem is that I can't or don't love. Gaining more wives will not cure the problem. I need to fix myself.

Chapter 3

Masts and Madzubs (God-Intoxicated Beings)

As one was visiting the tomb of Amir Khusrau at the Nizam-ed-din Auliya in New Delhi in company with Pir-O-Murshid Hassan Sani Nizami, the poet [Khusrau] appeared—open daylight mushahida [contemplation]—put a robe around one and said: "I appoint you successor to Mohammed Iqbal in the school of Jelal-ed-din Rumi." When I reached Pakistan that same robe was ready and is now with me. And as to cosmic poetry, it is already written and someday, inshallah [God willing] shall be published. (Murshid's letter to Reza Arasteh, author of Rumi the Persian, February 13, 1968)

November 16, 1967, Thursday

Murshid initiates eight people in a ceremony so powerful that my heart starts palpitating inexplicably several times. Each initiate's name and occupation are noted and, after each person has an interview with Murshid, I record the practices he gives them. Then, the new initiates are provided with written instructions for the purification breaths and copies of the Sufi prayers given by Hazrat Inayat Khan. This, essentially, is my esoteric secretarial work. I mass produce the instructions and prayers on my typewriter, using several sheets of carbon paper.

November 22, 1967, Wednesday

One topic in Murshid's lecture at Father Blighton's Holy Order of MANS church is about monkey people and cat people. Murshid explains that monkey people are dependent—they give Christ their burdens—and cat people are independent. I have been a monkey person vis-à-vis Murshid, and I assume he is talking to me. I think he wants me to be independent. Then I realize: I *ought* to be independent.

I tell Murshid that Jemila probably isn't going to be selected for the lead role that she has auditioned for in John Korty's movie *Riverrun*; however, my chances of being employed by the film company are good. They need my Volkswagen bus to haul the crew from Stinson Beach to Marshall, California, location of the farmhouse being used as a movie set. Up there, I may function as a driver, film loader, grip, and electrician.

< Murshid in the front seat of my VW van before our visit to San Francisco's DeYoung Museum, 1967.

November 23, 1967, Thursday, Thanksgiving

Afternoon dream: At sea (enormous emotional potential). In a stuffed chair (my position in life). Murshid. Waves (changes) coming. All flee. Nathan (my son). I ask, "Is Nathan (the masculine child part within myself) the son of Nyogen Senzaki (the source of spiritual energy and truth)?" "Yes," Murshid responds.

November 25, 1967, Saturday

Since I told Murshid I might get a job with Korty Films, he has been saying how much he needs a typist. I actually give notice today, and Murshid immediately announces an opening. It is impossible for me to ignore the conflict between my outside job and Murshid's need for help. I feel slightly stressed.

Murshid in Precita Park, 1967.

November 30, 1967, Thursday

Murshid tests my ability to take dictation. It works out fine and at the meeting tonight, he reiterates his need for a typist. Tonight is Sufi Night. A thematic rhythm is developing: Thursday, Sufi material is presented. Why is that? Murshid says Sufis traditionally meet on Thursday. The planet Venus is associated with Thursday. Venus is associated with love. Sufism might be considered the religion of love; hence, Thursday. For the rest, no reason that I know: Saturday is devoted to the Walks Class, and Sunday is *Dharma* (the teachings of Buddha) Night, where Zen Buddhist and Ramdas or Vedantic material is offered.

At the meeting, Murshid interprets a picture he bought from Cleary's Oriental Art store, near Katherine's dress shop. The sacred Islamic reproduction pictures a veiled Prophet Mohammed riding a winged steed in the sky. It represents the *miraj* (the ascension) of Mohammed on the creature named *Buraq* (a symbol for the breath). Maybe it's my Scorpio nature that wants to understand what is behind appearances, but I experience interpretations such as this, which illuminate sacred art, as a sort of enlightenment. I feel included in a secret that hitherto was inaccessible and inscrutable: the meaning of a man riding a flying horse in the sky.

After the meeting tonight, my cousin Bill Wachob, who is enrolled in a graduate program at Stanford, calls and leaves a message that Professor H.

Bruce Franklin is lecturing on *The Confidence Man* by Herman Melville at 1:15 P.M. tomorrow. I decide to go, but can't reach Bill for more information. I want to ask Franklin for a job. I know I've just given notice to Murshid so I can take a movie job, if offered, but, since I need work, I haven't completely let go of teaching college again.

Books from Murshid's collection that I've borrowed and read since July include: Rumi's *Discourses*, Ramdas's *God-Consciousness*, Dwight Goddard's *The Buddhist Bible*, Redhouse's *Legends of the Sufis*, and two volumes of *The Sufi Message of Hazrat Inayat Khan*. Volume 2 contains four books (*The Mysticism of Sound; Music; The Power of the Word; Cosmic Language*), and volume 5 has six (*A Sufi Message of Spiritual Liberty; Aqibat, Life after Death; The Phenomenon of the Soul; Love, Human and Divine; Pearls from the Ocean Unseen; Metaphysics*).

December 1, 1967, Friday

I want to type for Murshid, but we need $200 a month to live on. He has given me $150 over the last two months. I committed to help when Murshid asked for help. I never asked him for money, even though his willingness to pay was in the original job offer. Nor did I discuss money with him; the subject is too delicate for me. Murshid said he was willing to pay somebody to do this work, so I volunteered with the expectation I would be paid.

Today after morning prayers, John Korty's secretary calls to see if I am available to start work on their film tomorrow. I have to pick up some props in San Rafael, California, and drive them to Marshall. My prayer for guidance is more than answered, with what I need most: a paying job.

December 16, 1967, Saturday

The Walks Class meets in San Francisco's Golden Gate Park at the de Young Museum, where we wander among the museum's permanent colonial American art collection. The six photos I took today show Murshid, clean shaven and smiling, sitting in the passenger seat of my van. There's a shot of Murshid and nine of us outside the museum, three shots

Moineddin, Marcia, Murshid, Jehanara

of paintings, and one of Murshid, Carl, Jehanara (Ginger's new spiritual name) and a new disciple, Marcia Pavolic, looking at a painting.

December 18, 1967, Monday

I dream I am initiated again. The ceremony is mysterious, the figures unclear.

December 19, 1967, Tuesday

My practices and concentration used to be upset by worry about money and the fact that I wasn't working. Now that I'm working, I catch myself lamenting the necessity of having a job. Then I remember what Murshid said when I suggested that having a job was just not fulfilling. "Why can't a job fulfill you?" he asked.

December 21, 1967, Thursday

I tell Murshid about the dream where I am initiated. He initiates me for the second time, to the second grade. This gives me the idea that dreams reveal inner processes to Murshid, who makes them come true. As far as the difference between the first and second grade initiation, I haven't a clue.

December 23, 1967, Saturday

There is a Christmas party at the Garden of Allah, Stan Quance and Katherine Erickson's (Amin and Amina's) place. It is located on a hillside in Corte Madera, just north of the Golden Gate Bridge, with a view of San Francisco Bay. Murshid and I drive to San Rafael and pick up Margaret Albanese, a poet friend of Murshid's from the days before we arrived. Murshid invited her to the Christmas party because Margaret is a poet, and Murshid is going to read a portion of his cosmic poem "What Christ? What Peace?" When Murshid and I are getting out of the car to get Margaret, he crosses the street in an abstracted way, seemingly unaware of the earth plane. It is obvious to me that in this condition, he could get hit by a car.

Except when he "checked me out," Murshid was too busy working in the garden ...

I have a foreshadowing of Murshid's death in an accident. This freaks me out. It feels disrespectful to describe Murshid as "unaware." Judgment aside, I realize that one can be so fully concentrated on the mind world, so fully absorbed in thought, that one is unaware of traffic in the street.

At the Garden of Allah, I shoot a roll of black and white film. The first ten shots show Murshid working outside in a long sleeved plaid shirt, thinning the thick vegetation surrounding the house. Disciple David Hoffmaster is seen in a couple of shots working with him. I catch Amin coming out of his house and a female arriving, carrying something for the potluck. The next eleven shots are taken inside the house.

Murshid now wears a lighter colored, short-sleeved shirt and eats with chopsticks out of a bowl. He's sitting on the floor with his legs crossed and his back up against the wall. Now he's talking, without food in his hand. In one picture there's my wife, Jemila, listening seriously; Murshid with a big smile in another. Carl scored a comfortable easy chair, where we see him listening intently. My one and a half year old son, Nathan, joins Jemila in the next two shots. When I change angles, you can see Murshid sitting to the left of Jemila.

My picture of Murshid balancing a broom on his finger precedes the final two shots, which show eight people listening to his talk. Murshid's "impish" behavior with the broom blends with this talk, because both reflect the same ecstatic mood. "One is somewhat of an imp," Murshid says in the Reza Arasteh letter of February 13, from which this chapter's epigraph is excerpted. He continues,

In a revisit to the tomb of another Shams-i-Tabriz at Multan in Pakistan, one was with Americans whom one dearly loves to shock, especially when they reject one's credentials. There was a Saint there. [The saint said,] "Why are you here?" "I came to teach you," [Murshid replied]. "What?" "*ISHK* [love], *ILM* [knowledge], *SHAHUD* [bearing witness that God alone exists]." "All right, teach..." I have the pictures of this Saint and myself... It is this *ISHK* which the American young need and it is

... to "pose" for a picture at Amin's, 1967.

going to work... Anyhow for one who has had the strangest experiences with *Masts* [God-conscious beings] and *Madzubs*...these young people are very easy.

Dennis McGinley (left) and Moineddin (right) watching Murshid balance a broom on his finger during the party at Amin's, 1967.

Murshid's bizarre broom dance leads to a discussion of *madzubs*. Murshid tells us he is the only American that *madzubs* actually seek out. Murshid defined *madzub* when he wrote his commentary on Inayat Khan's book *The Inner Life*:

> *Madzub* literally means 'possessed'. Such a one is possessed by the divine spirit. Sometimes the word is applied in another sense to those who have advanced through many stages and states and become conscious of God alone. But this is not an abstraction; it is a completion and fulfillment. There is a story of Mohammed and his close associates. Abu Bakr could see the whole universe, God and creation together, while Ali was conscious only of Allah. So Abu Bakr has remained the perfect *Saluk* or sober type, and Ali the perfect *Madzub* or ecstatic type. But both should be regarded as perfect.

Inayat Khan, Murshid reveals, sought out *madzubs*, and they always fled from him. It was the opposite for Murshid. In Pakistan there was a *madzub*, normally high and incommunicado, who sobered up when Murshid came. Again, from the same commentary:

> There is a great *Madzub* at Salarwala in Pakistan, in the Lyallpur District, so great that he is often known as MADZUB SAHIB, and mostly he never says anything, or gives out strength noises (corresponding to the unintelligible Zen 'Kwatz'), but he has confirmed the teaching of the Message by Murshid and its spread in the West

and given all blessings and magnetism, and out of that has come the power and wisdom which makes this an accomplishment.

When Murshid gets on the subject of *madzubs*, the progression of details is the same, whether it's in the talk tonight, in his commentary, or in the Arasteh letter. Murshid goes from *madzubs* to blessing to what the external confirmation by the saint al-Alawi has meant to him.

After that, wherever the commentator went the *Madzubs* greeted him, and spoke to him, and blessed him, and he brought to America the *BARAKA* [blessing]. It was not accepted, but once when a great Sufi Saint, Abu Salem al-Alawi came from North Africa, he saw this Blessing and what it meant, and this has given the strength and wisdom to help bring the Message to the people of the West on all levels.

Murshid writes more about the acknowledgement of his *baraka* by al-Alawi at a meeting in his letter to Arasteh.

One of my colleagues hosted Sidi al-Alawi some time back. This colleague [Rev. Neville Warwick, a local Buddhist] announced himself as a Mevlevi [a Turkish Sufi] disciple. The audience [comprised of old people] asked the Saint to establish a *khankah* (a Sufi community house) here. 'No, it is not necessary.' 'Why not?' 'You have somebody in this audience who has the *baraka*.' I am thankful to say nobody accepted this but the crypto-Mevlevi. So I do not have the older, metaphysical people but the young, the alive, the God-seekers and more and more every week. This Mevlevi is also a Buddhist Master!

In conclusion tonight, Murshid blesses everybody with a breath-kiss on the forehead and an embrace. I am the first one to receive his blessing and can still feel the breath.

December 24, 1967, Sunday

I have been experiencing "the creeping of an ant" for some time, and it isn't until I read ahead in Reps that I realize it is an opportunity to do a practice.

Stop the doors of senses when feeling the creeping of an ant. *Then*. ("Lord Shiva's 42nd Practice," *Zen Flesh, Zen Bones*, p.200)

January 13, 1968, Saturday

Murshid's goddaughter, Saadia-Khawar Khan, wrote Murshid from her home in Pakistan. Today he answers her at length: four single-spaced pages. The headlines, in bold type, range from FINANCES ("Last year the income doubled but the expenses more than doubled") to DISCIPLES ("One had hoped to have a dozen men disciples, one has more") to TAWAJJEH (sharing magnetism through the glance) ("The *Tawajjeh* of Hazrat Inayat Khan is the source of the strength, vitality, energy and all else") to DR. SEYYED HOSSEIN NASR ("the world leader in the intellectualization if not popularization of Sufi teachings"). "The only way to complete this [letter]," Murshid writes, "is to send some notes on *TASSAWUF* [Sufism] from Hazrat Inayat Khan's *ryazat* [spiritual practices]." Earlier, referring to these practices, Murshid says, "It is obvious in going over these papers if one should publish them, one would be accused of having fabricated them. But if you saw them, you, Saadia-Khawar, would know they are true and in perfect harmony with the age-old teachings known as *tassawuf* and with the spiritual and mystical teachings of all times."

January 14, 1968, Sunday

Murshid gives me the name *Mansur*, which means "victorious." I feel no wiser or more knowledgeable about myself now than I did years ago. Back then I told girlfriends I couldn't make promises. I didn't know who would keep them.

January 17, 1968, Wednesday

Ernie, a follower of Father Blighton's, notices Murshid's low shoulder and suggests he visit a chiropractor. (Murshid exhibits what I later call "shield shoulder." Shield shoulder is when the left shoulder is higher than the right, as if the person is holding up a shield to ward off the blows of the world. Murshid never visits a chiropractor, but starts manifesting "sword shoulder" as success emboldens his attacks on his enemies of the past. Sword shoulder is when the right shoulder is higher.) I smoke some marijuana and tobacco now and, as usual when I smoke grass, I forget to say my prayers. Not good.

January 19, 1968, Friday

Murshid repeatedly talks about the realization he attained at Anandashram, Ramdas's place in India. His story is that after spending three days there, he approached Ramdas and said, "Papa, it's time to go." "Why is it time to go?" Ramdas asked. "For three days I feel that I am Papa," Murshid answered. Murshid had achieved the unity that Indian philosophy describes in three words: *Tat Twam Asi*. Thou art That. After finishing Ramdas's *In the Vision of God* on the beach along Tomales Bay, I remember Murshid's story about the time Ramdas came to San Francisco.

The wise regard their opponents in debate as also God's children. Once when Swami Ramdas came to San Francisco, many wanted to dispute with him on the platform. And some assumed they were on his side, but when he was away they did not accept him, only when he was there. But there was one man who said he would be glad to dispute with the Swami, and he prepared all kinds of questions and dualistic arguments. It was only five minutes when the Swami not only answered all questions, but considered the disputant as one who favored him by asking challenging questions and also tried to please his inward being with the answers. True the disputant did not gain, but the whole audience was attracted by the Swami, who had the God-realization and saw God in everything and everybody. (Murshid's *Commentary on The Inner Life*, p.26)

January 21, 1968, Sunday

"They substitute devotion for morality. Religious people are all like that," Murshid says, after we have waited hours for Dr. Thien Thich An, the Vietnamese Zen Master, to come to dinner and class. It's 8 P.M. and Murshid's dinner is cold when Dr. An finally calls from somewhere on Lake Street and says, "I will eat here." Murshid phones Rev. Eugene Wagner, who has an apartment on Ninth Avenue near An's location, and asks him to walk over and confirm that Dr. An is really where he says he is. Then Murshid and I pick An up and chauffeur him to Murshid's. When the Vietnamese Buddhist speaks at the meeting, the atmosphere is like the experience of reading a Zen manuscript. Questions seem silly. The sense of the "one thing" is so strong. I choose this term because it appears in one of my typing projects for Murshid, Seo-san's *Text for Zen Buddhism*:

> There is one thing, which is originally bright and divine, which neither appeared nor disappeared, and of which one can get neither its name nor shape.
>
> Note: What is the one thing? An old saying goes: Even before the old Buddha was born, it was infinitely bright all round. Even Sakyamuni cannot know its meaning, much less Mahakasyapa can transmit its mysteries. This is the reason why the one thing is not born or dead, cannot be named nor its form described. The Sixth Patriarch once asked, "I have one thing which has no name or form. Do you know what it is?" Then Master Shen-Hui (Shin Hoi) answered at once, "It is the origin of all Buddhas and my Buddhistic mind." With this answer he became his disciple. And when Master Juai-Jang (Hoi Yang) came from Sung San to see the Sixth Patriarch, the former was asked by the latter, "What kind of thing came to see me?" He was dumbfounded, but realized after only eight years and answered, "Even though it be only the one thing, it is not that." With this answer he became his eldest [most accomplished] disciple.

During Dr. An's question period, I have a big laugh with him when I ask, "What is evil?" "When you have an idea that you cannot tell someone," An replies. Since I had long forgotten my idea that Dr. An was an inconsiderate ass for not being on time to dinner, I am unembarrassed by his answer. "Do you understand?" An says. "No, what did you say?" "When you have an idea that you cannot tell someone. Do you understand?" he repeats. "No. What did you say? I'm sorry." "When you have an idea you cannot tell someone," he says, for the third time.

Once, twice; not until he says it for the third time do I hear his answer. If Dr. An is commenting on my forgotten attitude about him, my deafness unwittingly turns the joke back on him—by his own definition, he becomes evil for having an idea he can't tell someone.

At the end of the evening, Dr. Thien Thich An forcefully asks Murshid to give him an expensive set of Buddhist scriptures sitting in Murshid's bookcase. It feels to me like he is testing Murshid. His challenge seems infused with a sneering, gleeful attitude that says, "You won't pass this test." Murshid acquiesces to An's demand, and the Zen master leaves with at least four heavy volumes of Buddhist scriptures.

January 24, 1968, Wednesday

Last night in dream, Ramdas (the master teacher within me) has a bad back (shows I'm not channeling spiritual power well). Murshid prescribes a walk on the back to cure it. As he is bouncing on Ramdas's back, I see Ramdas's head is off the floor; indeed, his body is horizontal, a few inches off the ground, as if he were doing a push-up with his fingertips. I also dream of burying a body alive (stuffing a part of my self) in a casket in some slimy mud.

January 26, 1968, Friday

In his January 13 letter to Saadia, Murshid alluded to his old friend Shamcher (Bryn Beorse). He wrote, "[Murshid's] 'Six Interviews with Hazrat Inayat Khan' were rejected excepting by one *mureed* of this great Pir-O-Murshid." Shamcher is the one *mureed*, and Murshid's letters to him are as if to his nearest, dearest friend: open, frank, and so he sometimes calls them "diary entries." Murshid writes Shamcher today,

When the Vietnamese Master was here Samuel could not get into his own living room... Last night there was an even larger gathering, quite different people—mureeds, candidates, and young who want to be candidates... Many have given up LSD and grass and those who find the spiritual practices far more excellent than any chemical or vegetable are bringing their friends and acquaintances... On Wednesday and Sunday nights we have the Love-breath, the Joy-breath and the Peace-breath from Lord Buddha, and on Mondays, Saturdays and Thursday nights, we have the corresponding practices from Hazrat Inayat Khan.

January 28, 1968, Sunday

Jemila's friend Barbara comes to visit; I am so low. My condition is almost paralyzed, as if I were on psilocybin, when massive paranoia sets in. On the drug, I was afraid to go downstairs and meet people. Today, social situations are intolerable, awkward. I can't figure out what I'm doing here.

February 5, 1968, Monday

This last week, I felt regressed to the point where I was disconnected from everything: my family—wife and son—could come or go. I was not related. I feel that this is a certain kind of madness, but won't think about it. In contrast, Murshid wrote Shamcher on January 26th about his disciples' "rapid inner development." Not mine. "This is especially true," Murshid said, "of the man who has the Sufi Symbol in his forehead"—namely, Carl.

On February 2nd, Murshid wrote Anandashram, addressing no one in particular, his usual form of address being "Dear Ram." "The other night Sam showed his disciples the Peace and two had *samadhic* [experience of oneness] experiences. Two others have had these last week. And we have stories of mergence in Jesus Christ, Sri Ramakrishna and Papa Ram Das."

I think I understood some time ago the meaning of the phrase from the Sufi Invocation, "united with all the illuminated souls." I puzzled: How am I united with all the illuminated souls? I got: We are united (in breath) when I am conscious of my breath.

February 8, 1968, Thursday

Before mounting the stairs at Murshid's, I am thinking about calling Korty Films (where I have been working on John Korty's film *Riverrun* but am still able to come to Murshid's meetings). I mistakenly brought a lens of theirs worth $5,000 with me to San Francisco. As soon as Murshid sees Jemila, he asks her, "Where is your lord?" Korty Films had called, looking for their lens.

It is as if Murshid's whole discourse tonight is for me. I tell Jemila before going that I'm bored with Murshid. I'll go to the meeting tonight, I tell her, but I have no expectation. The first thing Murshid says, in parody of the Ten Commandments: "Thou shalt not be bored." Next, Murshid speaks of seclusion: how his retreat in 1925 was pivotal in his life. Here, he refers to himself in the third person. "He was put on a special diet by Murshida Rabia Martin, [Hazrat Inayat Khan's representative in San Francisco], one based on teachings and directives of Hazrat Inayat Khan. This was the basic *khilvat*, or seclusion diet, very much akin to that used by Sufis in seclusion all over the world." Moving on, Murshid says one of the secrets of his vitality is always studying. Then he goes to look for a book. I think: *Are we going to hear Inayat Khan on* The Metaphysics of Sound? Murshid asks, "Did someone borrow *The Metaphysics of Sound?*"

Murshid tells how debates in India are contests in search of areas of agreement between the contestants. The disputants seek common ground, rather than emphasizing differences. He mentions the first paper I copied, "The Intoxication of Life." (see September 26, 1967) He says he knows we have experienced intoxication in various ways and hopes to teach us sobriety. Murshid reads in the *Gayan* by Hazrat Inayat Khan that the study of life for a mystic is full of endless delight. To the seer, Inayat Khan wrote, every leaf of the tree is expressive.

For not the first time, I keep my shoes in Murshid's bedroom, so the meeting room isn't so cluttered. Again, just like last Thursday, when I go to get them, I get his *darshan* (a teaching through the eyes) and tonight respond by kissing his neck. Much later, I get the benefit of reading what this *darshan* is meant to be.

Darshan has been translated as meaning 'view', 'outlook', 'idea' (the word 'idea' itself seems to be etymologically connected with the use of the eye)—in fact, *darshan* has been used to mean everything from simple glance to total philosophy. At the same time, the term *darshan* has been applied in a particular sense to a person using his eyes for purposes of communication and magnetism and blessing to one or more people, either in a matter-of-fact way or in ceremony. In the highest instances, the glance has been used by teachers to help elevate pupils and audiences. (Murshid's *Commentary on Nakshibandi* [Symbology] *Gatha*)

I borrow Hakuin Zenji's *The Embossed Tea Kettle* tonight. Murshid gives me a playful warning. "Read it and see," he says. An evening I began wading in *ennui* ends on a different note. Ah, how the ability of a master to change atmospheres is revealed to me. Once again, I have given up smoking and—for the first time, meat—because the word 'Sufi' means purity. Murshid has said, "If meat is eaten, certain centers can't open."

February 10, 1968, Saturday

I remember tonight the increasingly familiar state of looking inward and discerning my feeling. Related to this is acting when an impulse is discerned. I remember these states when I encounter the 64th practice from *Zen Flesh, Zen Bones*. It is a strange exercise for one so long paralyzed.

Just as you have the impulse to do something, *stop*. (p.203)

February 11, 1968, Sunday

I get a chance to practice some of Murshid's teachings. Jemila and I accept an invitation to visit my Aunt Jeanne in Santa Rosa, California. Jeanne isn't home when we arrive, so we are welcomed at the Schwartzes', Aunt Jeanne's friendly neighbors, who have received Christ as their Savior and have been blessed with the baptism of the Holy Spirit. One of the Schwartzes ask me, "Why is your hair so long? Do you like being different?" I say, "I don't think I'm that different." "Why do you try to be different?" they persist.

I key on the "why" in their question and offer that it was my psychedelic drug experience that taught me the silliness of "why" questions. (Actually, it was Murshid who taught me that.) Things just are, I tell them. This is a big mistake, because then the Schwartzes ask probing questions about my drug experiences.

Answering them, I become very agitated (I don't understand I am reflecting *their* inner state). I can't control my agitation by saying a *wazifa* under my breath or with *fikar* (mentally repeating a sacred phrase). Holding my breath works a little, while the *wazifa* and *fikar* don't work at all. Thinking *toward the one* when I breathe in, and *united with all the illuminated souls* when I breathe out completes the summary of all the methods I utilize, mostly to no avail. (Later I learn to stay with the rhythmic breath for best results.) After it is all over, Jemila and I kiss and embrace the Schwartzes, all of us together in a mass hug, with them praying fervently in my ear.

Tonight, Murshid speaks to me of giving me, Stan, and the disciples in Novato more esoteric practices. When I embrace him ardently, Murshid says I am just like a Pakistani general he knows. Then he takes me into the kitchen and gives me my Valentine's Day present, a lemon coffee cake. I kiss his forehead, and he goes away giggling. I am still tickled, but have no idea how moved Murshid is by the love of his disciples. One didn't know at the time Murshid wrote Saadia January 13th about "the unusual love between nearly all of them for their Murshid and for each other. This," he noted, "was unexpected."

When I come to class after finishing the dishes, Murshid holds off starting until I sit down. He says he has to wait for me, not I for him, to start class. Murshid calls me his "favorite." I infer from this that he is there for me. Murshid pledges to give us the complete teachings. This will require, he says, that he write many commentaries, all necessitating careful meditation.

February 13, 1968, Tuesday

Murshid writes to Arasteh Reza today. As the earlier ecstatic excerpts demonstrate, Murshid's *hal* (inspired state) of the weekend continues. He no longer feels constrained from speaking. In the beginning of his letter, Murshid illuminates his experience as a mystic in the first half of the twentieth century.

There is nothing more horrifying to metaphysical egocentrics than [to] have mystics come out openly on the same basis as scientists do and relate their experiences. Legends...have arisen, that if man knows he keeps silent. And this has led to a wholesale acceptance of all sorts of persons who are welcomed socially and sometimes also intellectually, and if a man shows any sign to the contrary, he is ipso facto [by this fact itself] excluded. If we did that in the sciences, we should be in the Dark Ages. There is no reason or justice before Allah that silence must be kept to please other than Allah. And when Allah speaks if man obeys he is immediately accused. And until recently barred absolutely, but no longer, *alhamdu lillah* [praise to God]. This is a New Age...

February 19, 1968, Monday

I dream today that I am with Murshid and some other people. I pick up Murshid's thought about doing something with a water sprinkler. Impetuously, I pick up the sprinkler and deposit water in front of each person. When I'm done, Murshid takes my right hand firmly in his left, and I sprinkle water over each of their heads. Next I present someone with three cubes of incense. After I tell Murshid the dream tonight, he says, "Yes, that's right." And he tells me about his plans for a class for those of us who will be teachers: Carl, Stanley, Sheila, maybe Fatima (Pat's new spiritual name). Although I am not mentioned, I assume I am in this elite group.

Murshid reads about celibacy from the book *Rasa Shastra* by Hazrat Inayat Khan. This is a timely presentation, because I have just explained to Jemila my reasons for continence. I told her that my lack of interest in sex at this time was a natural consequence of my breath practices. It is that I am constantly focused on my breath, seeking to learn by practicing the art of watching my breath.

February 21-26, 1968, Wednesday through Monday

Murshid talks like a Zen master, a Buddha *Hridaya*. Buddha means illuminated mind; *Hridaya* means heart. I ask Murshid what would help me to keep track of my breath all the time. He says, "Toward the One," which is what I have been thinking on each inhalation and exhalation all day. As I gaze at a stick of incense, all becomes white except the burning tip. This is the third day I've been practicing "Toward the One." I find my mind returning to the phrase after a conversation, for example, when I just find the phrase hanging around. In dream, Murshid gives me some *gathas* (Sufi study papers).

February 23, 1968, Friday

"The family estate matter has come up" for Murshid. He writes his attorney, Theodore C. Lachelt, "All I want is the money, not ego-satisfaction." When the Wells Fargo Bank report shows a substantial increase in the estate's capital, Murshid tells Lachelt, "I feel that this should be divided in part between Elliott [his brother] and myself."

February 28, 1968, Wednesday

The class tonight is replete with reincarnation stories. Murshid tells stories from the Tibetan tradition of Marpa and Milarepa, where reincarnation is an integral part of the teaching. Murshid speaks of his experience, detailed in the epigraph to this chapter, of receiving a robe that had been bestowed on him in a vision at the *dargah* (tomb) of the poet Amir Khusrau. He tells of a visit to the Royal Asiatic Society in London, where he asked if they had ever heard of Prince Dara Shikoh, a descendant of Akbar, the first emperor of India. They hadn't, and they apologized. Murshid feels he is a reincarnation of Prince Dara Shikoh. All this lore is exciting, uplifting. The mood is one of exhilarating freedom. I am embarrassed when Murshid interrupts his talk about love to tell Ray, sitting next to me, "Look at the love in the fellow next to you."

Most all of the time, I continue my "Toward the One" practice. I am breathing "Toward the One" in, and I am breathing "Toward the One" out. After the talk, Eugene Wagner, spiritual advisor to the Maharani of Sikkim arrives and we embrace. I hug and kiss Murshid, and Murshid begins telling no one in particular how last night he went somewhere and kissed the girls. A man asks Murshid if he only kisses girls. "Definitely not," Murshid says, and kisses me on the forehead to demonstrate.

March 1, 1968, Friday

I dreamed last night about fishing (the need for spiritual food). This makes me remember a dream of several nights ago, in which I had a feeling about humanity's similarity to sheep (giving all responsibility for self to others). In an early morning dream, I am followed by a great number of people going to see Murshid. His secretary sees me. Then Murshid comes out of the office, invites me in, and we embrace.

March 3, 1968, Sunday

The lack of attention I am paying to Jemila prompts her to call home today and ask for money to leave me, to fly home.

March 4, 1968, Monday

In class last night, Murshid taught the five levels of love: animal, human, jinn, angelic, and divine. I use this to explain myself to Jemila. I tell her that I think she is at the human level, and I am elsewhere—"angelic" is the level I have in mind. (see August 7, 1969 for more about angels) This, I suggest, is why I can't reach her, why we aren't connecting. I've been thinking lately about how Lord Buddha left his wife. I open Martin Lings' book *A Muslim Saint of the 20th Century* to a paragraph that tells how al-Alawi lost his wife because he stayed up all night studying with his sheikh. I reverberate with his meaning.

March 7, 1968, Thursday

Today I take Jemila and Nathan to the airport. She's going home to Waterloo, Iowa. She's leaving me, she said, because I don't love her. First I give myself a headache choking back the tears. Then I end up sobbing with a headache. It's all so dreamlike: home without Jemila and Nathan. I miss them. I begged her not to go. She hopes I'll see how much she means to me and ask them to come back. I didn't want them to leave in the first place, but I couldn't do the things necessary to keep them here.

Murshid asks us at the meeting tonight to keep a record of our impressions, desires, and wishes. I'm not sure what he means by "impression." Webster's dictionary defines impression as "an imprint; a communicating of a mold, trait, or character by an external force or influence." There is more in Murshid's commentaries.

The holding of impression is called creating *samskaras* in the Hindu teachings... All holdings of impressions or *samskaras* produce further *skandhas* [attributes of personality], as they are called in Sanskrit. Man, to be free, must become free both from the web of the *skandhas* and from his own adding to them. This is done by the various means of practicing the presence of God. (Murshid's *Commentary on Everyday Life*, p.51)

Meditation is theoretically practiced so that one can select his own impressions. Breathing practices and esoteric exercises are given so that one can reject those *samskaras* which do not serve a purpose. (Murshid's *Commentary on Insight*, p.58)

The more one listens, so to speak, to impression and inner responses, the more one will find that truth in them which can lead to a greater comprehension of the Divine Wisdom both in the seen and unseen. (Murshid's *Commentary on Superstitions, Customs & Beliefs*, p.62)

March 16, 1968, Saturday

So many things have happened lately. I know the sense of doing everything by feeling, which Murshid demonstrates—going from intuition to intuition, accomplishing tasks. I am beginning to function like this, to feel like Murshid. Today I am applying a "hint" that Murshid gave in class last Thursday. The hint is to be relaxed when you are tense, and tense when relaxed. When I apply this while concentrating on a white wall on the movie set near Tomales, I see green. Concentrating on the Sufi symbol (a winged heart containing a five-pointed star sitting on a cresent moon), I get an after-image with my eyes open. Another hint from Murshid is to look for more and more refinement in breath.

Today Rick, the producer of *Riverrun*, the feature film I'm working on about a couple that leaves Berkeley for life in the country, has me go to Marshall on an errand. He reaches me by telephone and asks me to bring some cotton rags up to the set. Before leaving, I have a feeling I should call to see if there is anything else they need. Lazy and unresponsive, I don't call. There is something else they need. Failure to follow my intuition costs me an extra trip into Tomales—an errand I might have avoided. Of course, there is no blame from the boss, but it shows me that hiring responsive adepts might promote efficiency. I'm learning by having these experiences.

March 17, 1968, Sunday

Murshid gives yet another hint: The breath and the heart are together. Then he demonstrates. His demonstration involves having Duncan, the yoga instructor, sit in front of Murshid and look at him. "Watch my breath," Murshid instructs. I perceive this as a demonstration of refinement of breath. I miss whatever there is about heart.

Tonight Murshid instructs me on my seclusion (Murshid's word), or retreat, as we would say today. Jemila's leaving motivates me to seclude myself. I'll continue until Murshid stops me, or Jemila returns. Murshid's instructions are simple: No meat, the same light meal each day, study *Koran* and—not compulsory—read Nicholson's *Idea of Personality in Sufism*, Affifi's *Mystical Philosophy of Ibnul Arabi*, Paul Brunton's *The Secret Path*, and more of Rumi's *Tales from the Masnavi*. I am able to borrow all these from Murshid's bookshelf.

Krishna   Rama   Jesus

– and Buddha.
One afternoon at Sheila's Murshid invited me to photograph him as he
became Krishna, Rama, Jesus and Buddha, 1967.

Chapter 4

Khilvat (Seclusion)

Remember the name of your Lord morning and evening; in the night time worship Him: praise Him all night long.

Happy shall be the man who purifies himself, who remembers the name of the Lord, and prays to Him.

I have vowed a fast to the Merciful and will not speak with any man today. (Koran, Sura: Man, p.18; Sura: The Most High, p.32; Sura: Mary, p.33)

March 20, 1968, Wednesday

I am secluded to meet God. I am fasting to experience purity. I took coffee this morning, water during the day, and another coffee now at 8 P.M. Perhaps it is a coincidence that my seclusion begins today; Murshid began his on March 10, 1925. One of the lessons Murshid gave in class last Thursday was to become a living example of virtue. The word "virtue" comes from a Latin root meaning "strength," Murshid says. When you are virtuous, you are strong. During chanting, I see my face from inside—lips moving, eyes closed. Ibnul Arabi says, "He who sees God in himself with God's sight is a Gnostic." My fulcrum of perception is changing.

March 21, 1968, Thursday

On this day in 1925, Murshid wrote that with "all health and vigor" restored, he "prepared an initiatory ceremony for noon, March 21, the equinoctial hour." He describes in a paper the exaltation that followed:

One prepared a ceremony with concentration, and in turn Shiva, Buddha, Zoroaster, Moses and Jesus appeared. Then Mohammed appeared, but double (on the left and right) and on horseback. All the others came singly. Then the six Messengers of God, so to speak, formed a circle and danced and became one and, as they danced, the Prophet Elijah appeared and bestowed a Robe. This is the Robe, not a Lloyd Douglas fiction. The same Robe was bestowed in vision by Khwaja Moinuddin Chisti at Ajmer, India, in 1956 and by Amir Khusrau at Nizamuddin Auliya in New Delhi in 1962. And when Ahmed Murad, as he was then called, returned to Pakistan after that, he was given this Robe, actually. He has it in his possession now. It is functional. It has been recognized by Sufis who are Sufis. (Murshid, *Sufi Vision and Initiation*. San Francisco, 1986, p.30)

I slept from 10 last night until 7:30 this morning and, upon rising, feel very weak. Decide to break the fast with a bowl of Familia this morning. If stronger, I can stay up longer praising God. Fasting but eating, the parameters of this retreat are loose. My second meal, at 10 A.M., consists of an egg salad sandwich, sunflower and pumpkin seeds, figs, nuts, raisins, milk, and coffee. Shouldn't have fasted. This overeating is required to compensate for the emptiness. Finish the *Koran* to page 136 by 11:15 and practice the last two pages of "centering" practices in *Zen Flesh, Zen Bones.* At 11:30 A.M. I eat peanut butter. At 11:35 A.M. I eat more seeds, raisins, figs, and almonds, and drink a cup of coffee. I read till twelve thirty and do more centering practices. Work in the yard until four thirty and eat an orange. I talk (secluded but talking, the parameters are loose) to the vegetable man who shouts from his truck, "Do you want any vegetables?" and to Art, my neighbor. To say "neighbor" suggests that we live in a subdivision. In fact, our cabin and Art Carpenter's circular home, behind his wood shop, are the only structures along Bolinas Lagoon for more than a mile. The lagoon fills and empties in tune with the rhythms of the tides of the Pacific Ocean. Long necked storks and long legged herons can usually be seen. After a dinner of curried fried rice with mushrooms, onions, and Canton asparagus, plus tea, I say the Sufi prayers.

Recite your prayers at sunset, at nightfall, and at dawn: the dawn prayer has its witnesses. Pray during the night as well, an additional duty for the fulfillment of which your Lord may exalt you to an honorable station. (*Koran*, Sura: The Night Journey, p.233)

Doing Centering Practice number 39—"With utmost devotion center on the two junctions of breath and know the *knower*"—leads to one of my deepest meditations. My heartbeat vanishes, and the breath moves so lightly it seems to stop. One of the hard words in this practice is the word "center." I have a tendency to think: *up down* or *up around, down around.*

For the next month, more or less, time is marked in my esoteric journal by selections copied from the *Koran*. With a few exceptions, I'm mostly unaware of what day it is. I am no longer fasting, but I continue to study. There is no indication whether the movie *Riverrun,* which employed me, offers any post-production employment. I go to classes, say my prayers, and do my practices. The following paragraphs show some of what comes to me as I follow Murshid's injunction to "study the *Koran.*"

Suddenly out in the front yard today, I think of our Mill Valley landlord, and Mill Valley Greyhound calls. More and more lately, I *feel* when a telephone call is coming.

Then We said to the angels: "Prostrate yourselves before Adam." They all prostrated themselves except Satan, who refused. "Why did you not prostrate yourself?" Allah asked. "I am nobler than Adam," he replied. "You created me of fire and him of clay." He said: "Begone from Paradise! This is no place for your contemptuous pride. Away with you! Henceforth you shall be humble." (*Koran*, Sura: The Heights, pp.239-40)

As part of evening prayers, I concentrate on a burning stick of incense and see an oval of gold light at my feet as I sit.

Most excellent are the names of Allah. Call on Him by His names and keep away from those that pervert them. (*Koran*, Sura: The Heights, p.254)

Oh boy. I feel more involved in this study since I bought four books at Fields Book Store today: Nicholson's *Studies in Islamic Mysticism*, Saadi's *Bustam*, al-Ghazzali's *Niche of Light*, and Burckhardt's *Introduction to Sufi Doctrine*.

Believers, do not enter the houses of the Prophet for a meal without waiting for the proper time unless you are given leave. [I did this once to Murshid—without "leave." Oh boy.] But if you are invited, enter; and when you have eaten, disperse. Do not engage in familiar talk, for this would annoy the Prophet, and he would be ashamed to bid you go; but of the truth Allah is not ashamed." (*Koran*, Sura: The Confederate Tribes, p.286)

What my work should be has crystallized itself to me as—broadly speaking—Sufi studies, gardening, and work for Murshid.

Some say: "It is but a medley of dreams." Others: "He has invented it himself." And yet others: "He is a poet: let him show us some sign, as did the apostles in days gone by." Yet though We showed them signs, the nations whom We destroyed never believed in them. Will *they* believe in them? The apostles We sent before you were no more than men whom We inspired. Let them ask the followers of the Scriptures, if they do not know this. The bodies We gave them could not dispense with food, nor were they immortal. (*Koran*, Sura: The Prophets, p.288)

March 31, 1968, Sunday

I remember Murshid telling us at a meeting how he became a *wali*, which means one versed in all religions. He started by asking rhetorically, "You want to know how to become a *wali*? Well..." And Murshid placed himself in the company of three holy men somewhere in the orient. "One of them asked me, 'Are you a *wali*?' 'No.' The questioner asked the second man while pointing at me, 'Is he a *wali*?' The man shook his head yes. He asked the third man and got the same affirmative answer. He turned to me and said, 'You are a *wali*.'"

April 6, 1968, Saturday

After Walks Class, Murshid gives specific guidelines for a Sufi *khankah* where we'd all live together. It should be a large house with many bedrooms, a large central room for meetings, and a special room for smoking, as there should be no smoke in the meeting room. The obvious reason for that is that we'd be doing breath exercises there. One of the bedrooms would be designated as a guest room. Silence would be maintained one night a week, and for an hour at night after the meetings. A person would be assigned to answer the phone during silent hours. Murshid says he will contribute $200 per month to our rent. Those of us who are to live in the *khankah* are Moineddin (Carl's new spiritual name), Fatima, Jehanara, Hassan (Jehanara's husband Sigmund Hertz's new spiritual name), and myself. Jemila's not back yet. There would be specific people responsible for each of the twenty-one hypothetical weekly meals. Two motor cars would have to be available. We could consider building on to an existing structure to make it fit our needs. Murshid will not be on the committee to choose a site; he will only approve the one chosen.

Believers, when you rise to pray, wash your faces and your hands as far as the elbow, and wipe your heads and your feet to the ankle. (*Koran*, Sura: The Table, p.375)

My study of the *Koran* has intensified a sense of making vows and establishing goals, and this has spurred action and accomplishment. To ritualize this new realization, I determine to finish typing *Drawing in the Furtherance of Education* a week from Thursday. This is a book on the education of children, by Mme. L. Artus-Perrelet. Murshid wants it copied. When Murshid repeats the Bible verse, "The son of man cometh in the hour [when] ye think least," I hear "when" for the first time. This, even though Murshid didn't say it when he read the verse. Plus, I get a new meaning. It's not when you least expect him he comes, but when you are *not thinking*, he comes.

April 8, 1968, Monday

To give the reader a sense of what Murshid was up to at this time, I look back at his correspondence. Murshid does not mention Shamcher by name in a letter he wrote without my help, but alludes to him in a letter today to both U.S. Senators from California, George Murphy and Thomas Kuchel.

Almost immediately after hearing from Senator Percy I was summoned by a friend [Shamcher] in Seattle, Washington. He is on excellent terms with one of President Johnson's closest advisers [Arthur Schlesinger, Jr.] and the adviser has consulted my friend about sending Americans to Asia who will be able to cement better relations because of their empathy and knowledge of Asian culture.

Commenting on former Ambassador John Kenneth Galbraith's article in *The Saturday Evening Post* magazine, Murshid writes that the article "is along the same general lines of *The Ugly American* and *Sarkhan* from which we have apparently learned little."

Some of the contentions in this work are, most unfortunately true. We are verbalizing democracy but have the most autocratic and dictatorial Foreign Office in existence. But this is the first time when an insider has so advised.

April 13, 1968, Saturday

Murshid reminds me I'll be with him next Thursday during interviews with new initiates. The Sufi prayer *Khatum* (literally, "closing") includes the line, "Open our hearts that we may hear Thy voice which constantly cometh from within." I hear that voice! All night long whenever I listen! And not for the first time tonight. I first heard it while doing the walk of the saint Mian Mir. Tonight I associate it with the voice in the line from *Khatum*. When I plug my ears, I hear two sounds: the blood rushing in my veins and the white sound. This discovery brings me to the verge of ecstasy.

Bathe in the center of sound, as in the continuous sound of a waterfall. Or, by putting fingers in ears, hear *the sound of sounds*. (*Zen Flesh, Zen Bones*, p.196)

April 16, 1968, Tuesday

Sometimes things take a while to sink in. In his talk at our house—even though Jemila's gone I have to refer to it like this—last Saturday, Murshid said, "We are free at every moment." And when I finally caught a vision today of the freedom he was talking about, it prompted weeping. During my second meditation tonight, I get a strong impression of Eugene Wagner—tonight is his class—and recall one of my first impressions of Murshid: his big nose. The significance of my observation came to me later, and was published in a book.

I have written to the magazine *Sufi Speaks* an unpublished letter, in which I relate my first meeting with Murshid. I thought he had a big nose, I wrote. Fatima and Moineddin wrote me about him. They told me that he taught walking and breathing, and that they believed he could take them the fastest to where they wanted to go. Shortly after I arrived in San Francisco, he taught me to walk up the steepest hills without any fatigue. I noticed his nose because he is a master of breath. (*In the Garden*, p.22)

April 17, 1968, Wednesday

Murshid writes to the Secretary General of the Sufi Movement in Geneva, Switzerland, whom I later learn did not accept Murshid's *Six Interviews with Inayat Khan*. (The non-acceptance of these interviews is a recurring theme. The failure of others to acknowledge Inayat Khan's recognition of him was the issue.) He quotes from one of their publications, *A Sufi Message of Spiritual Liberty*: "'When I [Inayat Khan] arrived in San Francisco, I found much to interest me there, and my desire *for the revelation of truth had its outlet*.' Did it? [Murshid asks] I wonder. Before God, I wonder. What outlet?" Murshid tells this organization, which was founded by Inayat Khan, "I have signed papers of affiliation [with you] and nothing has ever been received." He concludes, "One regrets that after all the efforts of

Hazrat Inayat Khan, his relatives have taken the lead, not in spreading his Message, but in abrogating it." (The subject of Murshid's connection to the European Sufis is taken up later. See November 10, 1969)

April 18, 1968, Thursday

Tonight I help Murshid dress; act as recording secretary during interviews; and receive a *fikar* (thinking the name of God) practice to be done during evening prayers.

April 20, 1968, Saturday

It's too much, the synchronicity of it all! The other night, I picked up Martin Lings's book *A Sufi Saint of the 20th Century* about Shaikh al-Alawi. A mention of the *Koran* in chapter 2 reminded me of my Koranic studies, which had been delayed. Tonight, after reciting some *wazifas*, I open Lings's book again and find Shaikh al-Alawi talking about the way his teacher used *dhikr* (a different spelling of *ziker*).

> As to his way of guiding his disciples, stage by stage, it varied. He would talk to some about the form in which Adam was created and to others about the cardinal virtues and to others about the Divine Actions, each instruction being especially suited to the disciple in question. But the course which he most often followed, and which I also followed after him, was to enjoin upon the disciple the invocation of the single Name [Allah] with distinct visualization of its letters until they were written in his imagination. Then he would tell him to spread them out and enlarge them until they filled the entire horizon. The *dhikr* would continue in this form until the letters became like light. (p.54)

One result of al-Alawi's success with *dhikr* was that he "understood things in advance before the Shaikh who was teaching us had finished expounding them." (p.58) I feel supported in my desire to serve Murshid when I read, "I was so taken up...with the service of the Shaikh and with furthering the increase of our order, that I neglected the demands of my own livelihood." (p. 60) He did it; so can I. I identify still more with al-Alawi when he reports that he "never crossed him [his teacher] even about the smallest point" in fifteen years of discipleship. I, too, feel that impeccable. Elsewhere, Lings emphasizes this impeccability when he writes, "No Sufi would consider himself qualified to practice methodically an invocation unless he had been formally initiated into it." (p.73)

April 22, 1968, Monday

The Temple of Understanding is planning a fall conference in Calcutta, and a few days ago Murshid received a positive letter from them. He answers,

> To me in an ego sense it is very ingratiating that a person accepts the objective experiences and objective reports from let us say, an unknown. This is the curse of

our land: that ideas, suggestions, etc. *must* come from prominent people and at the same time we verbally insist on democracy and then go out and fight for it. This has produced dismay in so many lands, among so many people.

April 23, 1968, Tuesday

You can't help but compare your own progress to the precocity of your teacher, and Murshid's early life amazes me. Moineddin reads me an autobiographical paper of Murshid's that might have been titled "Intimations of a Child Prodigy." Murshid was talking when he was one year old, and learned the alphabet immediately after his mother repeated it for him when he was three. He read the Old Testament of the Bible when he was six years old and his concept of God was "a white sky."

April 25, 1968, Thursday

8 A.M. In dream, Murshid appears to be in a hurry. He beckons with his hand. Glad to follow him, I grasp his finger in my hand. Once I let my hand open to see if Murshid wants to remove it. He doesn't. Murshid and I go to a place where I have to try on a robe. Next, Murshid leads me to a long Japanese type table, low to the ground. There is room for both of us to sit next to each other on top of it. Then all the disciples come and sit on the floor near this table. Murshid and I get off the table and sit with them on the ground.

April 27, 1968, Saturday

In a class at our house tonight Murshid works with the glance (*tawajjeh*). His glance of loving-kindness makes me smile constantly. Then, when I concentrate, Murshid's facial features are obliterated—all but his form goes. Could this be the *samadhic* experience Murshid wrote about others having? Later I think so, but don't know it at the time. Murshid talks very frankly of his work with people. He is taking us into his confidence. He mentions the work to come, saying he doesn't know whether we see it. I do—and feel I must devote myself full time to helping. This reawakens my recurring conflict between service to Murshid and earning a living. Expressing this conflict to myself starts a stream of consciousness that ends with me recalling how Murshid serves other people.He told us that yesterday he was bored with books and TV. Then two people who had problems walked in and stayed two hours. "That's how it was all day," Murshid says.

April 28, 1968, Sunday

Implying that there is a great deal in his silence, Murshid says, "My words are merely the interferences of what I'm giving." All day long I keep feeling Murshid attuning himself to me. He calls me an "astute student." This in reference to my telling everybody at the evening meeting what his concentration was when he walked up the hill during the Saturday class and how he was breathing.

May 2, 1968, Thursday

When the Ramdas book near Murshid drops, a girl sitting on the floor holds it out to him and says, "Would you like me to hold it?" The mixed message is her gesture to return the book and her words offering to keep it. If I were Murshid, I probably would have grabbed the book. Murshid stops as he is reaching toward it, and only then proceeds to take it from her. In that instant the meaning of self-control is revealed to me.

Just as you have the impulse to do something, *stop*. (*Zen Flesh, Zen Bones*, p. 203)

Some activities that keep me busy this evening at Murshid's are washing the toilet, making notes during the interviews Murshid conducts with *mureeds*, and finding copies of the Sufi prayers for folks who don't know them by heart. I am Murshid's dresser, a privilege he grants me. The heightened vibrational charge of his bedroom amplifies the intimacy of being there, helping him into his robe. It is an honor that I view as being just part of life. The *Bhagavad Gita* teaching of equal-mindedness in pleasure or pain has me striving to accept honor or dishonor without being inflated or deflated. During interviews, starting tonight, Murshid has me hand out the *Candidate's Gathekas* I typed to people interested in initiation.

May 8, 1968, Wednesday

In December, 1961, Murshid and Julie Medlock, whom I never met because she lives in India, went to hear an American choir sing Christmas carols in Lahore, Pakistan. Julie (the expatriot, ex-wife of a Hearst Newspapers editor) recently sent him a brochure on the place where she lives, the Sri Aurobindo's Auroville ashram in Pondicherry. This may have been their first communication since that Christmas concert. In Murshid's letter to the Temple of Understanding (April 22, 1968), he called Julie "perhaps the worst treated of all the 'Sarkhanians' to adopt a term from the book of the late Professor [Eugene] Burdick," who wrote *The Ugly American*. Today Murshid wrote Julie.

A year ago Sam Lewis was flat on his back in a hospital. He had just won in litigation, went out celebrating, had an attack of ptomaine, and bingo. There he had a kind of mystical experience which happens only to mystics and never to bright Englishmen and scholars who write books on experiences they have never had. And it was to the effect that he was to become the "Guru" of the Hippies.

Then Murshid relates something from the more distant past.

Several years ago, I said to Miss Ruth St. Denis: "Mother, I am going to revolutionize the world." "How are you going to do it?" "By teaching children how to walk." Ruth taught me how to draw dances from the *Akasha* [space] and later I told her of having performed a "Dance of Universal Peace" at Fathepur Sikri [in India]. It was the same dance that she and Ted Shawn had performed in the same place 30 years before. It is based on the rituals of the four major religions. And I am now training a few young people in it, showing them what our "superior more equal people" a priori [without examination] reject, God bless them.

While Murshid writes Julie, Murshid's friend Gavin Arthur reads my astrological chart. The reading is taped, and later I listen and take notes on the salient points on the tape. It is the most thorough analysis anyone has ever done of my personality. People ask me: Do you believe in astrology? My answer is: It's not a question of belief. Astrology provides an accurate psychological profile.

May 11, 1968, Saturday

Murshid takes me to an afternoon lecture by Gina Cerminara, author of *Many Mansions*, a book about reincarnation. She is sponsored by the Edgar Cayce Foundation, now known as the Association for Research and Enlightenment (A.R.E.). Cayce, called the "sleeping prophet" because he would give readings while apparently asleep, brought healing to many by using his psychic knowledge of their past lives. Murshid dozes off during the lecture. I let him sleep. In a future letter (May 26, 1968) to his godson Norman McGee in New York, Murshid refers to a prior affair sponsored by A.R.E.

A very characteristic "only in America" affair took place here recently. Elsie Secrist and Hugh Lynn Cayce of the Association for Research and Enlightenment were here. They talk and say that jogging cures many ills; that prayer is man talking to God, and meditation is God talking to man. The audience is delighted: Jogging can cure many ills and meditation is God talking to man! But did any of the dear-old-ladies jog! Did they permit God to talk to them! Words! Words! Words!

Then we go to Fields Book Store to check Paul Reps's announcement that he will speak Saturday in Sausalito. Murshid tells of Reps's failure to stay in Los Angeles after Inayat Khan appointed him guardian of the city, which reminds me to be true to my word. Sufis are not allowed to be hypocrites, Murshid teaches. I must say what I mean, and do what I say.

At dinner at the Gibson House in Bolinas, Murshid relates some out-of-body experiences he had during World War II. When word came to him that Hitler was going to utilize psychics, Murshid asked God what to do. "Go upstairs" was his guidance. Murshid speaks of the inner work he did with the Jewish victims of the German concentration camps at Dachau and elsewhere. In matters of spiritual hierarchy, Murshid says, you are not permitted to know who your fellow workers are—only your superior, who in this case was Abdul Qadir Jilani (1077-1166). This story illuminates my

understanding of how the spiritual hierarchy functions with saints long
dead in today's world.

May 12, 1968, Sunday

Murshid gives me a practice to do together with Jemila—concentrating
on a heart. I guess she's back; the esoteric journal is not a diary per se. I
had been doing the heart concentration from the beginning. The fact that
my journal does not record Jemila's return shows my bias toward inner life
activity and my tendency to avoid detailing the melodramas of everyday life.

PBS is running a TV series on Krishnamurti, whom C.W. Leadbeater
and Annie Besant of the Theosophical Society hailed as the next World
Teacher or messiah when he was 13. Krishnamurti is Murshid's age, 72.
Murshid often wisecracks about Krishnamurti, characterizing his teachings
as, "Do what I say, not what I do." The TV series is still in production and
is edited by disciple Fred Cohn, who will later employ me to work as his
assistant. Before I was privy to Murshid's opinion, Krishnamurti struck me
as an Alan Watts type intellectual. I had first hand experience with Watts
in 1966, the year before I met Murshid. Attracted by his Zen books and
sincerely searching for wisdom and guidance, I traveled from the Upper
Peninsula of Michigan to a seminar Watts gave in Chicago. I walked out
before it was over, disappointed that I wasn't getting the reality I later found
with Murshid.

May 13, 1968, Monday

Shamcher thinks Murshid is giving money away. It has Murshid "roaring
all over the place. I am not giving money away. There are disciples, growing
in number and prowess. Two are establishing a print shop. They want to
do just what you say without it costing this person a cent." Thus, Murshid
answers Shamcher. "Last night," Murshid writes to Shamcher, "a very
wealthy man was here, some of whose followers are disciples and some
applicants." He's referring to Don McCoy, founder of Olompali ranch, the
hippie commune where Sheila lives. Sheila is one of the would be teachers
Murshid mentioned above. (see February 19, 1968) "We are teaching
mystical and occult sciences here as fast as possible—the way of the Eye,
the way of Breath, the Way of Heart," Murshid tells Shamcher. He doesn't
credit Paul Brunton, who originated this method. Comparing himself and
Reps, Murshid writes, "Reps is a master of non-words. Sam uses words or
non-words, either, neither, or both, according to the impressions on the
audience."

May 18, 1968, Saturday

It was last July or August when I asked Murshid, "What about this yoga
breathing that I've heard about? Yogis do something with the breath, in

one or the other nostril. Is it a trick like I think sitting on a bed of nails is a trick, or what?" Today Murshid has me sit at his typewriter, and dictates the following *Ryazat for Mansur*, which explains the relation between the so-called Sun, Moon, Mars, and Venus energies and the breath.

In Sufism the breath in the right nostril is called *Jelal*, and in the left nostril it is called *Jemal*. But in Hinduism the breath in the right nostril is called solar, and the breath in the left nostril is called lunar. As interpreted in Sufic mysticism there is some difference: the Sun breath is in the right nostril, but the inhalation is stronger than the exhalation; the lunar (or Moon) is in the left nostril where the exhalation is stronger than the inhalation. Thus the Sufic Jelal breath is different from the Sun breath in that inhalation and exhalation may be equal; and the Jemal breath is also different from the moon breath in that the inhalation and exhalation may be equal. The Mars breath is also in the right nostril. Its exhalation is different from that of the Jelal breath for it is stronger than the inhalation. Thus in the right nostril strong inhalation signifies the Sun, and strong exhalation signifies Mars. Or we can symbolize the Sun by light, Jelal by heat, and Mars by lightning or electricity. Similarly, a strong inhalation in the left nostril followed by a weak exhalation is characterized by the Venus breath. It differs from the Jemal breath in that its inhalation is stronger than its exhalation. Thus if Jemal is equated to water (not exactly so), Venus would represent steam or rising water, and the moon would represent rain, streams and falling water.

Paul Reps speaks tonight on a Sausalito houseboat. His new book is *Ask a Potato*. Although named "Saladin" by Hazrat Inayat Khan, Reps dropped that, and now just goes by Reps. I meet and embrace him before the meeting. After the talk, Reps says, "It was the most wonderful night of my life." He'll eat dinner tomorrow at Murshid's, then give a talk at the Holy Order of MANS. May 23rd Murshid will write Reps back home in Hawaii "an evaluation report... You will not be surprised that your two chief critics were the oldest men there; at the same time they were each far more opposed to each other."

People from 28 to 35 in general liked you, but were slightly ashamed of the dualistic picture which came during the proceedings. Those under 28 loved you, and in general the love and devotion increased as one went down the age scale. The youngest ones were enraptured and nothing one can say can add to that. One's only comment is that it fits in with the general picture I have of the psychic evolution going on. If there is any suggestion from me—and do not take it too seriously—it would be to revive some of your earlier works. [Murshid was reviving *Zen Flesh, Zen Bones* in the sense that he was giving us practices from it.] I leave that to you.

May 26, 1968, Sunday

Murshid specifies in his letter today to godson Norman McGee why the older people disapproved of Reps.

To the old this man is impossible: he is not a bright-eyed Englishman, he is not a graduate of any German or other famous foreign university; he studied Oriental philosophies under Orientals, some here and some in Asia, and being *one of us* he *cawn't* [*sic*] possibly have anything to offer.

In this letter, Murshid tells how he got together with Paul Brunton. He begins by listing Brunton's methods.

Actually, there are the ways of the Heart, the Breath and the Eye. When Paul Brunton was here the old ladies arranged he speak only to the rich and movie actors. He had the impertinence to apply telepathy without asking any of our metaphysical "experts" and summoned six men, all unknown socially, taught them by silence and results followed. As this could not possibly be, skip it. But as the Asian-Asians accept it and Sam and the young find he does not always brag or lie, they are learning, and they are learning more than empty words.

June 2, 1968, Sunday

Aunt Jeanne comes down with the Schwartzes, the people who talk in tongues and have religious ecstasies, whom we met in Santa Rosa (February 11, 1968). I offer Aunt Jeanne Gina Cerminara's book *Many Mansions* to soothe her sister, my Aunt Patty, who is fighting cancer. My thinking is that knowledge of reincarnation might console someone dying. The Schwartzes' reaction: There is no reincarnation. I compare my ability to follow my breath this time with the upset I experienced last time. I notice some improvement. The greatest difficulty, again, is the agitation and excitement I create by expressing unacceptable positions.

June 16, 1968, Sunday

Murshid asks everyone to breathe in and out a question. I ask: *Who am I?* (a question Ramana Maharshi used to give to his disciples). Moments later, gesturing with one arm, Murshid says, "Seize the first impression. Did you get any answers?" My answer is: I am Murshid's gesturing arm.

Later, Murshid begins describing a banquet in his honor, scheduled by his Sufi brothers in Pakistan after he announced his intention to leave. Just when Murshid gets to the part about the invitation, he points to me and says, "You've seen it!" Maybe I was visualizing it as he spoke, maybe I had seen it the last time he told the story. My reaction is to ask myself: *Have I?* I don't remember. My mind is a total blank.

June 17, 1968, Monday

Opening the scrapbook Murshid told Moineddin to give me, I turn directly to a letter to Fred and Corinne Reinhold about the banquet in Pakistan Murshid described last night. This is not déjà-vu, a word that occurs to me while I search for the right one, but it is synchronicity.

June 18, 1968, Tuesday

When a spiritual teacher demonstrates sympathy for the pupil, it makes an impression that recurs in the memory and warms the heart. Today I remember when I gave Murshid the report on my visit to the numerologist and Murshid said, "You haven't had it so easy since I've known you." The quality of sympathy was similar when I told Murshid I couldn't drive everyone in to the Wednesday meeting because I had invited some people to dinner. Then, he said, "You've made enough sacrifices."

June 19, 1968, Wednesday

Before I take Murshid to Sheila's this afternoon, he writes University of Pittsburgh philosophy professor Dr. Oliver Reiser—a friend acquainted with Julie Medlock.

I was living with Gavin Arthur and there was a man who came every day and argued with Gavin; it did not matter what Gavin said. Then Gavin went away and the man, who was a sailor, did the same with me. Finally, exasperated, I turned and said: "When did your wife leave you?" "That was hitting below the belt." "No, that was the only fair question I have ever asked you. You pounce on a stranger for the troubles close to you." After that we became friends and there is no doubt that if I hit Don [Hayakawa] below the belt he might become far more compassionate about the short-comings of others.

Lloyd Morain, Don Hayakawa, and Russ Joyner of the International Society of General Semantics were all sent carbon copies of this letter.

This person (the author) sits next to Murshid tonight on Sheila's couch at her house in Mill Valley. I choose this way of speaking about myself because Murshid does it from time to time. Before the meeting Murshid has me photograph him in his teaching robe: sitting on the couch meditating like Lord Buddha, and standing, assimilated in Lord Krishna. Murshid goes high this evening, and so do we all, I assume.

Sheila McKendrick

Days earlier (May 2), I saw control in Murshid's gesture when he didn't immediately take the book that girl offered, and I called it "self-control." Let's be clear—this kind of self-control is breath control. As to my own practice tonight, I maintained remembrance (practicing *fikar* of the *ziker*) well.

Murshid wants me to remain at the house Sunday while he, Hassan, and Moineddin pick up Vilayat Khan, the son and successor of Hazrat Inayat Khan, at San Francisco airport.

Pir Vilayat Khan at meditation retreat, Olompali ranch, 1968.

Chapter 5

Vilayat

There was a most beautiful meeting here Sunday. After waiting for over forty years, there is total peace and harmony with Pir Vilayat I. Khan... A number of wonderful things came out at the Pir's meeting. We did no advertising, but invited a few older spiritual friends. The whole house was packed and the impressions were most favorable.

We are going to put into operation as soon as God wills all the things the Pir spoke about... None of this intellectual nonsense one gets from university professors, but real Yogic and mystical practices, especially in the vast domain of the Breath. Then the spiritual dancing, which has already been started. All those things he spoke about will be done and the things he did not mention will not be done, exactly as if it had been the Voice of God (or Nada Brahma) or what you will; to me it was just that. He is representing the Message of God as his father did and not himself and not in any limited sense, "Sufism."

Besides, the New Civilization is arising here, multitudes of reincarnated Indians who are so easy to awaken, rather than to teach. It is necessary now to double the disciples from 30 to 60 and help fulfill whatever seems to have been in the Pir's mind and heart.... When the Pir started, we gave a Sufi prayer and when he concluded the Ramnam and no intellectual or dualistic comments. There was so much love and enthusiasm aroused. It was most wonderful... (Murshid's letter to W.D. Begg, Topdara, Ajmer, India, June 26, 1968)

June 23, 1968, Sunday

Tonight Vilayat Khan comes to the Mentorgarten, Murshid's home at 410 Precita in San Francisco. My duties around the house consist in answering the phone and showing seats to honored guests. I also sit in during interviews that Vilayat has with various people. It seems to me a momentous event when I overhear Vilayat and Dr. Neville Warwick planning a conference of the world's religions for January, 1969. It is a very concentrated evening for me, and the house has a new sound when the people go.

This occasion may prove to be pivotal in Murshid's continued creation of spiritual dances. Vilayat mentions something about "the whirling of the spheres" [the planets] in his general remarks, and Murshid takes the ball and continues to run with it. On January 30, 1970, Murshid will write to a group in Australia,

A Sufi teacher passing this way told about 'the whirling of the spheres' practiced by the Mevlevi Dervishes. Two years later, he saw us demonstrate these whirls, not only the whirls of the seven planets, but also actively that of Uranus and potentially of Neptune. We are demonstrating this publicly and privately.

Murshid meets with Vilayat, with only myself present. He tells how Mrs. Ivy Duce (the successor of Murshida Rabia Martin) demanded that he give her all the more advanced spiritual papers—the *githas* (for grades 4-6) and the *sangathas* and *sangithas* (for grades 7-12). Mrs. Duce used the papers for the benefit of Meher Baba in an organization she founded called Sufism Reoriented; Murshid never saw them again. Vilayat says he will get these papers for Murshid. Murshid stresses in his interview that he will not extend his teaching range beyond San Francisco and its immediate environs, because he does not want to repeat "the mistakes of the past." I don't have a clue what "mistakes" he is talking about.

Vilayat, pursuing his agenda to strengthen his own organization, asks if he can list the Mentorgarten as a center of the Sufi Order. As Murshid well knows, the Sufi Movement founded by Hazrat Inayat Khan and headquartered in Geneva, Switzerland, is under the control of other members of Inayat Khan's family—not of Vilayat, the eldest son. Inayat Khan invested Vilayat with spiritual responsibility for the Sufi Movement at age 10, then died less than a year later, on February 5, 1926. Following his death, a committee appointed Inayat's brother Maheboob Khan to caretake the organization until Vilayat grew up. When Vilayat was ready to function, however, control of the Sufi Movement wasn't relinquished to him. So he started the Sufi Order as a basket in which to gather those flowers (followers) who recognized his authority.

The first person Murshid allows to see Vilayat is Sheila. Murshid is grooming Sheila to go to India, and she has opened her house in Mill Valley on Wednesday nights for Murshid to hold meetings. In her interview with Vilayat, Sheila does most of the talking. She talks about Don McCoy's Olompali ranch in Novato, where the Grateful Dead play, people swim nude, several of Murshid's disciples live, and Murshid and I visit from time to time.

Vilayat's next interview is with Gavin Arthur, who says he and "Bryn Beorse [whom readers know as Shamcher] from Seattle" are friends. Vilayat says Shamcher is the person who recommended that he see Murshid. Gavin tells Vilayat about "the Dunes," located somewhere between San Francisco and Los Angeles. I get the impression that the bohemians of Gavin's generation lived and made their art at this place. [The Dunes in earlier days was a place for beachcombing artists. They are known today as the Guadalupe-Nipomo Dunes and stretch 18 miles from Point Sol in the south to Pismo State Beach in the north.] Gavin invites Vilayat to a regular

Friday night gathering at his apartment, saying, "I will of course be at your complete disposal"—so aristocratic and debonair. Gavin and Vilayat exchange addresses, as Sheila and Vilayat did earlier.

The next interview is with Nancy Fish, a working actress who identifies herself as Murshid's "goddaughter in the U.S."—an oblique reference to Saadia Khawar Khan from Pakistan. Nancy tells Vilayat that she feels his heart quality and that she sees light on his forehead. Vilayat says he uses his third eye, not for seeing, but for radiating light. Nancy admires Vilayat's robe. Vilayat shows Nancy the rare, yellow, sapphire heart-with-wings necklace under his robe, which Hazrat Inayat Khan himself wore. I feel like a voyeur witnessing a seduction scene. Nancy says all the women must fall in love with him. Vilayat responds by speaking about impersonal love. The scene winds down.

Next, here comes Dr. Neville Warwick, with a lot of energy. Warwick's father was in the initiate class of the well known Orientalist Alexandria David-Neel. He tells Vilayat, "My father knew your father."

Warwick, the sometime Mevlevi Sufi (see December 23, 1967), tells how Sheikh Sidi Abusalem al-Alawi—the one who recognized Murshid's *baraka*—predicted that Vilayat would come to San Francisco. Warwick promotes San Francisco as a location for a conference of religions. This city has the potential to explode spiritually, says Warwick. He identifies a local cleric, Bishop Pike, as a tremendous vortex of power who could help make the conference a reality. Vilayat is acquainted with Bishop Pike; he says they talked prior to an appearance on the same TV talk show.

Showing sympathy for Vilayat's work to organize the Sufi Order, Dr. Warwick says spiritual movements are reborn every thirty to forty years. "I can cognize in here the problem of getting a spiritual movement reborn," Warwick says, pointing to his heart, "because I've done it." Warwick says he was warned that if he accepted the leadership of an organization, he would lose his spiritual powers. So he gave someone else the leadership, and he claimed for himself the nonassuming title of "Chief Mountaineer." Similarly, Warwick suggests, Vilayat was protected by those who usurped his father's Sufi Movement.

June 25, 1968, Tuesday

Reading Thoreau, writing in *Walden* about the bubbles in the ice of the pond and the leaves on the snow, has made me more observant. Today I see the strangler shoots from the cucumber in our garden and witness the work of a gopher re-covering the tunnel that I uncovered.

In an effort to get the attention of his adversaries whom Murshid calls "enemies" at the International Society of General Semantics, Lloyd Morain and Don Hayakawa, Murshid writes a letter to the poets Lawrence

Ferlinghetti and Allen Ginsburg at Ferlinghetti's City Lights book store on Columbus Avenue in San Francisco, and sends copies to Morain and Hayakawa. [I'm giving this story to you in dribbles, dear reader. At this point, I don't have any context to share with you. See August 17, 1968 for background.]

You will find here a carbon of a paper on "The Hippie Problem" which I am submitting to the International Society for General Semantics. I am hoping they will give it consideration but unfortunate past experiences find one facing those who believe that some people are more equal than others.

Murshid continues with a brief history.

Early in life I committed a sin for which there has been no forgiveness. I studied in turn various branches of Mathematics with the late Prof. Cassius Keyser of Columbia, friend and mentor of the then living Count Alfred Korzbyski [author of *Manhood of Humanity* and *Science and Sanity*].

Murshid mastered both books and saw "cures for many ills, but not having a prerequisited university degree, every effort to use the matrices and principles of *Science and Sanity* was brushed aside."

June 26, 1968, Wednesday

Before the evening meeting at Sheila's in Mill Valley, Murshid reflects on Vilayat's visit in his letter to W.D. Begg (see epigraph to this chapter), apologizing for his delayed answer, which he ascribes to "the pressure of events."

Murshid also writes Don Hayakawa, "I beg you to reconsider your stand." He mentions an attack on him by Hayakawa associate John Keel, while Murshid was defending Hayakawa: "And there Sam Lewis was left far afield trying to defend Prof. Hayakawa amid a lot of foes and John Keel joins in the attack." A carbon copy of the Hayakawa letter goes to Russell Joyner, the office manager of the International Society of General Semantics.

Murshid's exaltation over Vilayat's visit seems to empower him in his dealings with these old enemies; indeed, Murshid links the two. He writes to Joyner,

In my private life I have just been successful in a forty-two year effort, to try and prove that I had certain interviews with a certain person [Inayat Khan] on some very important matters concerning bringing East and West together, not the symbolic "East" and "West" of some narrow agreement between Alan Watts and Don Hayakawa *called* "vivid awareness of the world" but some actualities including geographical and demographic "time" and "space."

At Sheila's, Murshid calls editing the *ryazat* my life work. Murshid implies that Hazrat Inayat Khan was a reincarnation of Jesus when he answers a question about Inayat Khan's age by saying, "It says in the

Hadith [a collection of eyewitness reports of Prophet Mohammed's actions in everyday life] that Christ will come to Earth again, beget children, and die at age 45. This is not important." Hazrat Inayat Khan died when he was 45. In other words, to Murshid, it was no big deal if Inayat Khan was Christ. What is important for Murshid is what each did to make the world a better place.

June 27, 1968, Thursday

I have a joyous day with Murshid in Bolinas, even though we miss each other when Murshid walks to our house early in the morning from Moineddin's, which is down the road toward Bolinas about a mile. I'd gone walking the other way. Later, we all pick berries at the patch behind the Armstrongs' up on the mesa in Bolinas. Afterward, we play bridge at the Jablonskis' (Moineddin and Fatima's) rented place on a corner, a few blocks from central Bolinas. While we are there, Murshid refers to his own voice as "the voice of life itself."

At 3 P.M. I drive Murshid in to San Francisco. He talks of visiting his attorney next week or the following week. I don't know enough about his personal life to ask whether this concerns his father's estate or something else. Murshid listed visiting his attorney, among the things he was to do while I was driving him into the City last year. Also on the list at the time was a writing work on the subject of walking (*Walk Papers 1-10*) which he subsequently dictated to me, and which has been completed.

Murshid says he would not accept disciples who are inclined to go on arbitrary fasts or who have inflexible ideas about diet—a comment motivated, in my opinion, by encounters with rigid pupils. Murshid mentions that he had a dream of a barren tree stump. This seems to indicate the death of someone who is an obstacle to our work, he says. Murshid reaffirms that my task is to edit *ryazat*, Moineddin's is to write commentaries, and Amin's is to organize the spiritual papers from Europe. Murshid solicits my thoughts about the way Vilayat dealt with people. I don't get that he is asking for my perception of Vilayat during the interviews I witnessed. I can't answer at first. I have no thoughts. Then I censor a critical thought that he was overly scholarly. I finally say I don't know, but that I was very high being in Vilayat's presence.

It is possible to be more specific now. I felt Vilayat's pain, his childlike spirit, the gentleness without weakness. He was so kind as to verbalize what he thought was on Nancy's mind when she didn't speak. O the spiritual exchange! I couldn't help but embrace him after we escorted someone he interviewed to the door, overcome as I was with the sweetness.

My experience with my proximity to Vilayat, I confess to Murshid, made me wonder whether I was feeling Vilayat's atmosphere or self-generated excitement from being in the presence of celebrity. It's not movie star celebrity, but Vilayat's position as "successor" in a spiritual chain going back to Prophet Mohammed (570-632) that impresses me. *Vilayat is Hazrat Inayat Khan's son and successor.* I really caught a heavy glance from Murshid when I said I'd done Vilayat's astrological chart.

After I leave Murshid in San Francisco, he reads the newspaper. Items on desalinization and cotton insects inspire him to write U.S. Senator Thomas H. Kuchel. Murshid complains about having received no response to his queries about desalting progress in the Middle East: "I have written previously on this subject but to date have heard nothing either from the Department of Interior or your office." On cotton pests, Murshid tells Kuchel the press is "far behind actualities. I was not in Cairo one week in 1960 before I was informed about this hazard to Agriculture." Murshid calls for "some of us to sit down with each other before demanding Arabs and Israelis do that." He sends copies of this letter to the University of California's Entymology Department, American Friends of the Middle East, and the *San Francisco Chronicle.*

Back in Bolinas, I make peanut butter with Spanish peanuts after dinner and take some of our morning blackberry harvest to Hussain (Dennis McGinley). I met Hussain in Marquette, Michigan, when I taught English at Northern Michigan University. He was the night clerk at the only hotel in town. We might never have met were it not for Huston Smith, M.I.T. professor of religion and author of *The Religions of Man.*

Before Huston Smith was invited to give a lecture at Northern Michigan University, he lectured at the University of Iowa. I was studying there, and those of us who were experimenting with drugs were particularly interested in his *Psychedelic Review* article on the use of psychedelics to produce religious experience. We felt that Huston Smith was a kindred soul. When the head of the Humanities Department at Northern Michigan learned I was familiar with Smith and his work, he appointed me to be his host. Jemila (then Carolyn) and I picked the professor up at the airport, took him out to dinner, and delivered him to Hussain's hotel.

Years later, when Jemila asked Huston Smith if he remembered us, he said, "You know, I give maybe 200 lectures a year, but I'll never forget meeting you two in Marquette, Michigan. It was as if we'd known each other for many lifetimes. I'll never forget that meeting."

After dropping the berries at Hussain's, I return a borrowed guitar to Moineddin, along with Murshid's gift of coffee and a message that Fridays would be fine for *Gatha* readings at their house. Murshid rejected Tuesdays, because there were too many good TV programs he wanted to watch.

On the inner plane, I am concentrating on the Sufi symbol (a heart with wings, with a star and crescent moon in the heart), newly painted by Jemila. With open eyes, I see the complementary color (green) of the red heart. When I go to bed, I see light out of the corner of my eyes. My body is more responsive to vibrations produced by chanting. My breath is more refined. Moon and Venus breaths in *ryazat* (see May 18, 1968) are more delicate. The Venus breath, especially, promotes a wave of love for Murshid.

June 28, 1968, Friday

We sold our furniture when we left Marquette, Michigan. I made $7,500 for nine months' work as a professor at Northern Michigan University. The family was not destitute; nevertheless, I was not working and I heard I might qualify for Aid to Dependent Children: I go to the Welfare Office. To qualify for a stipend, you must show up. From now on, I will keep my appointments with them, just as I would show up for work on time.

Murshid and I visit Akbar, one of the three people Murshid has designated *khalif* (literally, representative; the tenth grade in the Sufi Order). Akbar, a Chinese-American who rarely comes to meetings, reads a paper by Vilayat and empathizes, feeling as though he'd written it himself. Akbar reports to Murshid his experiences of light and his desire for full enlightenment. He shows us some beautiful *T'ai Chi* moves. Contrasting Akbar's experiences with my own, I feel like an absolute novice, but my longing for union with the Divine increases.

Murshid takes me to dinner at the Taj. Then there is the Sufi dancing. At the class, Murshid announces Vilayat is coming back July 6th. He has a letter for Sheila from Vilayat. Shirin, one of Murshid's disciples who lives at Olompali ranch, has a problem with Sheila. It is partially discussed in front of the group. Although my narrative doesn't dramatize this incident, I write at the end of the day: *It was a very exhausting day.*

June 29, 1968, Saturday

Today I feel very low, tired, sad, and separated from the Divine. My mother gets bummed during a telephone call when she learns her son's family is collecting welfare. She says, "I have never felt so bad."

June 30, 1968, Sunday

Before coming to Murshid's tonight, I followed these impulses: to make coffee, to water the bean sprout garden, to pet the kittens, to go to the john, and to bring Hazrat Inayat Khan's *The Mysticism of Sound* upstairs for reading. Why am I following my impulses? Because Inayat Khan identifies impulses as being divine.

To a mystic, impulse has divine significance. In every impulse a mystic sees the divine direction... One may ask, Why is not every impulse divine for everybody, since every impulse has its origin within? It is because not everybody knows it to be so. The divine part of the impulse is in realizing it is divine. The moment we are conscious of the divine origin of the impulse, from that moment it is divine. Although all through life it has come from within, it is the fact of knowing this which makes it divine. (*The Sufi Message of Hazrat Inayat Khan*, vol. 10, p.20)

Murshid is sympathetic when I tell him how bad I felt yesterday. He says yesterday was bad for him, too. He misplaced his watch, and both his typewriter and refrigerator broke. But he heard from Sheila, who told him that there is another millionaire on our side. If so, I will be hired full or half time! Later tonight Murshid repeats, "You'll be on the payroll." Naturally, word of a paying job piques my curiosity, like a rumor from a reliable source.

Murshid is talking today about human consideration, fellowship, love, and consideration for others. These things, he says, are *not* developed when people get high doing Krishna dances. God is not found in the exotic, he stresses, but in human kindness and consideration for others.

This reminds me of Papa Ramdas, who considers everything as divine. One of his books is called *World Is God*. His awareness is what I've tuned into again. I practice being open and listening. Balancing my breath (1, 2, 3, 4 in and 1, 2, 3, 4 out) and swinging a question—for example, "What shall I do now?"—on the breath; then taking the first impulse as the divine guidance. When I live a day like that—and so far it's been only parts of a day—it is wonderful.

I sometimes ask myself, "Why do I have the honor of helping Murshid dress?" I understand that it is him grooming me for something. I feel it is an undeserved honor. Now he's saying I'm going to be on the payroll! I cannot begin to let pride or ego question these things. Toward the One.

At Murshid's tonight, he repeats the story of Saladin Reps when Reps was guardian of Los Angeles. Inayat Khan told Reps the city would be protected as long as Reps stayed there. Reps lived on a hill above much of the city. One day a heavy rain produced a flash flood. Reps sat in meditation, eyes open, and when the water was fifty yards from his house, it split apart. The torrent divided and dissipated. The city was saved.

I ask Murshid if I can do the practice of seeing God in everything, in accordance with Ramdas's unchanging point of view. Permission is granted.

At the meeting I experience an impulse to collect all of Hazrat Inayat Khan's books, after Murshid reveals that Shirin, one of his most beautiful disciples who lives at Olompali ranch and wants to build a kiln, owns all the books of Jung and Gurdjieff (Greco-Armenian mystic and philosopher,

1872?-1949). Taking off on that thought, Murshid adds, "The Gurdjieffians have promoted confusion with their complexity. They're never wrong, but they're so complex."

I have to remember to take my tape recorder into the City on Tuesday for Murshid's lecture on Noah's ark at the Holy Order of MANS. The topic is meaningful: Their church is to be dedicated as a refuge, and the word "ark" means *refuge* in Hebrew, while "Noah" means *repose*.

I am busier than ever at Murshid's, taking names of new people. There were twenty-three tonight who were not disciples.

Following impulses and *keeping my word* are up for me now. When Jehanara asks me if our blender will chop soy beans, I say I'll ask Jemila what the instruction book says. Before I go ahead, the guidance comes: Don't give the job to someone else; look yourself. I do and call Jehanara back. I have to fight an innate laziness and deal individually with each situation. Consciousness. That's what being conscious is.

The coming week is packed full. Tuesday, I'll go very early to San Francisco from Bolinas to help Murshid. Wednesday, there is the program in Mill Valley at Sheila's. Before the program, Murshid, Moineddin, and Fatima are going to Louise Snyfeld, a famed 84 year old numerologist who lives down the Peninsula. She has done number charts for movie stars like Robert Taylor. Louise was responsible for putting the "B." in Cecil B. DeMille's name. She gives people what they need to overcome their numerological "karmic lessons" by changing the spellings, adding letters, or renaming the person.

For example, the number seven (knowledge) is my karmic lesson. It's not in my name, so my new middle name from Louise will be "Graydon," which includes two sevens, a "g" and a "y." (You get numbers for the letters in the alphabet by giving "a" one, and continuing one through nine, over and over.) I use it for a while—weirding out, I'm sure, old friends back East when I sign letters and include an explanation of my second new name. This doesn't last long. Knowledge gained by studying with Murshid, I decide, takes care of having no seven.

After the program at Sheila's Wednesday, Murshid will spend Thursday in Bolinas. Saturday and Sunday, Vilayat Khan is returning for a meditation retreat at the ranch, and Jemila and I will camp there overnight. Murshid has called off his meetings in San Francisco next Thursday and Sunday because of it.

Two people have told Murshid that Vilayat is trying to steal his disciples. Murshid doesn't care. "My rent is paid; I'll go to Ajmer or Anandashram if it happens. I'm just keeping my heart open," Murshid says.

July 1, 1968, Monday

Murshid writes a letter to Mr. and Mrs. Russell Smith, Sr., old friends of his and functionaries of the Asia Foundation, telling them to expect a large meeting at "the San Francisco Theological Seminary not far from you." Murshid mentions possibly seeing them at the Ross Art and Garden Center, which is not likely, but which shows them that "Sam" still remembers them in connection with that place they both shared in a past time I know nothing about. Murshid's inspiration to write the Smiths is mainly goddaughter Saadia's recent fashion show, which happened when, Murshid explains, Saadia "stopped off here for a few hours en route to Los Angeles from Cornell University." He continued, "She is enrolled at this institution working for her PhD in clothing, fabrics and home economics."

Practicing what he preaches about cultural exchange, Murshid tells the Smiths (remember, they're with the Asia Foundation) that he has spoken "both to the Pakistani Consulate and Asia Foundation (South Asia Desk) about the possibility of a small fashion show or exhibition later on. The women in both places became immediately interested."

I watch Murshid plant seeds like this and note his Bhagavad Gitan nonattachment as to whether his labors bear fruit.

July 3, 1968, Wednesday

"God told me not to go to the ranch for the meditation part of Vilayat's program," Murshid says. He will check his guidance later to see about coming for the Universal Worship service late Sunday. "There are several messages for you to deliver to Vilayat," Murshid tells me. One is that Murshid wants Moineddin, Amin, and myself to have interviews. I ask Murshid what I am supposed to say to Vilayat. He says, "Say that you are being trained as Esoteric Secretary."

I am to give Vilayat a carbon copy of the papers I copied yesterday on *wazifa*, as an example of the teachings in Murshid's possession. The papers were originally dictated by Hazrat Inayat Khan to Rabia Martin, and Murshid is using them as a silent statement of his bona fides.

Murshid's use of the *wazifas* is a potential point of conflict with Vilayat. In his interview with Murshid, Vilayat said he freely gave everything to audiences except *wazifa*. To receive *wazifa* instruction from him, Vilayat requires initiation. Murshid responded that he gave *wazifas* to audiences, but didn't tell them what they were. We would repeat *Bismillah er-rahman, er-rahim* (in the Name of Allah, the Merciful and the Compassionate) at public meetings. Murshid sometimes translates *Er-rahman* and *Er-rahim*, mercy and compassion, as "the compassionator and the compassionated." These are attributes, *wazifas*, qualities of God. Our class walks while chanting these and other phrases with *mudras*. Vilayat eventually imitated Murshid's public use of *wazifa* to present the divine qualities.

Murshid gives Akbar a practice for his hearing; he *saw* Akbar had difficulty in this area. Murshid also saw that Clark has an obstruction in his nose. When the septum blocks one nostril, Murshid invariably advises in favor of corrective surgery; without it, the natural breath is obstructed, and the individual lacks balance. *Correct the breath and many symptoms vanish,* is Murshid's maxim.

I go to the Brotherhood House of the Holy Order of MANS with Murshid for his Noah's ark lecture and the dedication of the room as a refuge. Underscoring his depth of feeling, Murshid uses the term "Before God," spoken with a lot of energy, to preface answers to several questions. I have the tape. [This is fortunate, because Murshid never lectured again on the mystical interpretations of the Old Testament. Wali Ali took the tapes of Murshid's lectures on the Old Testament from me after his death. Copies were made and sold to disciples. Without these tapes, perhaps the inspiration for *Desert Wisdom* by Neil Douglas-Klotz would be incomplete, and Murshid's mastery of the Kabalistic tradition would be undocumented.]

Today I begin a three year curriculum of concentration exercises. Murshid gave his OK on Tuesday. He said we have a long way to go. "Of course, I've been through all the disciplines," he said. The first year's practice is to concentrate on objects. The second year, the student may concentrate on Murshid. In the third year, one may concentrate on Christ or Buddha.

In a sense, I've been concentrating on Murshid since day one, but I don't skip concentrating on objects. According to Hazrat Inayat Khan, "this practice is given only to those persons who are deeply interested in the personality of the Murshid, who have perfect faith in his spirituality, and who through the thought of Murshid will be able to accomplish the course of love and devotion."

Among the benefits I have already experienced are the enjoyment of all of Murshid's ecstasies and his emotional conditions of joy, intoxication, and peace.

July 4, 1968, Thursday

This is Jemila's and my first anniversary of meeting Murshid. It's also the day Murshid chooses to begin celebrating Hazrat Inayat Khan's birthday (July 5th) by talking about him. Murshid relates how Hazrat Inayat Khan summoned him to the Beverly Hills Hotel in Los Angeles, California, in 1926 and said, "Samuel, I am no longer Murshid and you are no longer *mureed.* We are going to talk man to man. How many faithful disciples do you think I have?"

"I'd guess at the very least 100," Murshid answered.

"No," he said, "Guess again."

Murshid said he'd guess again, but that it really wasn't his guess, and then he said, "20?".

"No!" Pir-O-Murshid said in a loud voice. (Pir-O-Murshid means "teacher of teachers.") "I wish I had. I wish I had as many faithful disciples as I have fingers on one hand."

Turning to those of us in the room, Murshid asks, "And who do you think bears the brunt of the Sufi message?" His rhetorical implication is that he, Murshid Samuel L. Lewis, bears the brunt of the Sufi message. And I believe him.

Murshid tells how Hazrat Inayat Khan said that Murshida Rabia Martin ["the first mureed on my arrival to the west," according to a section called "Autobiography" in *Biography of Pir-o-Murshid Inayat Khan*] shouldn't defend herself in public or handle the organization's money. Murshida Martin did both. In addition, Murshida Martin was instructed *not* to have an operation. She did, and she died "in agony." The message I derive from these tales is that there is danger implicit in disobeying a teacher's guidance.

Before Rabia Martin died of cancer in 1947, she became convinced that a living Sufi named Meher Baba should receive the followers and properties of Hazrat Inayat Khan's organization, which he had created in the 1920s and which she had nurtured. Rabia appointed Mrs. Ivy Duce her successor and gave Mrs. Duce the task of delivering the sacred papers, property, and all the people she could to a newly established group, rooted in Meher Baba, called Sufism Reoriented.

Returning to the matter of Vilayat's return, Murshid instructs me to record Vilayat's lectures at the ranch to play for the other disciples. "Show Vilayat," Murshid says, "the picture you took of Reps and me. And give Vilayat love, even veneration, if necessary." Murshid quickly explains, "He [Vilayat] has had much pain in the last two years. He knows I know about the pain."

Murshid said before, and repeats today, "If Vilayat and I don't make friends, I'll have to live for forty more years." [I believe he said this because previously the European Sufis rejected any prowess on the American side. Pir Vilayat is European, although it's nothing personal as they've never met before. Murshid means the friendship will help him accomplish his life's purpose in a timely manner; otherwise, he'll have to hang around a lot longer.]

Murshid tells us that his commentaries on the works of Pir-o-Murshid Hazrat Inayat Khan were dictated by Pir-o-Murshid himself, from the other side.

Murshid also relates a dream. It goes something like this: When Pir-o-Murshid was en route to the U.S. in 1926, Murshid saw him coming in a train to the Townsend Station. Murshid went down to the station, and his subtle body flipped out of his physical body. Inayat's subtle body did the same, and this wasn't all.

Murshid's heart shot out of his subtle body. Up and out of the smokestack of the train shot Inayat's heart. Their hearts dashed together and exploded in a flash. They became one and expanded out over the entire universe. "This," says Murshid, "is the real attunement with your teacher."

After Inayat heard this dream—presumably during The Six Interviews in Los Angeles's Beverly Hills Hotel—Murshid relates that he said, "No man has ever had such a dream!"

July 5, 1968, Friday

The last several mornings I have awakened and stayed in the semi-sleep state following my breath with my consciousness. During many naps on the living room floor at Murshid's after lunch, I utilize the following practice.

At the point of sleep when sleep has not yet come and external wakefulness vanishes, at this point *being* is revealed. (*Zen Flesh, Zen Bones*, p.201)

One result is a consciousness, or wakefulness, it seems, even as I sleep (a contradiction, no?).

At breakfast today Murshid hints that I might write his biography. I say, "I know," because I've had a similar feeling for some time. This feeling is intensified by my having Murshid's scrapbook, which contains writings copied from his 1925 retreat notebook and other works Murshid calls his "workshop poetry." When Murshid began his 1925 retreat,

He [Murshid speaking about himself in the third person] was too weak to carry books with him, so he only brought copies of the works of the Sufi poet Hafiz, a notebook, and foods.

On the third day, he completed the reading of Hafiz as the sun was setting. The rays of the sun fell on the book, and as he finished the last page two doves suddenly appeared, circling his head, cooing.

That night, as he was doing his spiritual practices, he felt a presence, and he was sure it was Khwaja Khizr... There was a recurrence of this appearance of Khwaja Khizr on the following night and on the next also. He offered poetry or music. Sam chose poetry. (*Sufi Vision and Initiation*, p.29)

On the sixth day of his 10 day seclusion, Murshid wrote in the notebook:

"Hafiz." What a joy to utter the name! What a thrill in the heart. I have never had a vision of him, and hardly read a line of his poetry, yet—picture him and what do I see? Smiles! One big smile, bearing joy to all who greet him. He is like sunshine, bringing comfort and courage. In my days of darkness he was with me, guiding me, encouraging me, showing me the way. Always smiling, always cheerful. When I look at the beautiful trees and pleasant meadows of sunny California, I picture him in his rose garden at Shiraz and feel that Hafiz, had he *not* been born where and when he was, *this* country with its lovely scenery and beautiful weather would have brought inspiration to his heart, and ode upon ode would have resulted. Allons, Hafiz! To study your works together.

> I hear the blue birds twittering in the trees,
> The leafy branches fluttering in the breeze,
> While I sit here, musing at my ease,
> Thinking of thee, Hafiz.
> The trees around me spring has clothed in green
> On hillside and in lovely vale between,
> A typical lovely California scene,
> Reminding me of thee, Hafiz.
> And now to study and to ready thy book,
> 'Neath shelt'ring trees and in this lonely nook,
> For though alone, God has not forsook me,
> Nor thee, Hafiz!

Hafiz is always young. Not a boy or youth, but in early manhood. He has the spirit and enthusiasm of the child and youth with the wisdom of experience. Written March 16, 1925, at 1:30 P.M. (*Sufi Vision and Initiation*, p. 33-34)

Today is Inayat Khan's birthday. I go with Murshid and others to Fairfax, where Inayat Khan's first disciples in the U.S. had their *khankah* named *Kaaba Allah* years ago. Murshid says the existing home at the site was built after 1949 when *Kaaba Allah* burned. Murshid shows us the outline of the face on the big rock at the curve in the road before the site of the house formerly named *Pir Dahan*. I fail once again to discern any significant atmosphere at this place. (see September 23, 1967)

As I drive him past the redwood forested area of Forest Knolls, Murshid says, "This is a place I thought I might live if I were going to be a writer." Another time in this place, gazing at the redwoods, Murshid said the trees here produced an atmosphere as holy as any church. I heartily agreed. The sacred manuscript of nature is the holiest book.

Later, Murshid assigns Moineddin to copy *Glory Roads: The Psychological State of California*, a book about California politics he wrote in collaboration with Luther Whiteman, a man I know nothing about. I have yet to read it, I don't know why—even though Murshid says my career is taking off where his coauthor left off. I don't look back, I guess.

Starting tomorrow, my new job will be typing notes Murshid gives during the spiritual dance class.

July 6, 1968, Saturday

I wake at 4:40 A.M. from a dream: There is a dispute with Murshid, I don't remember why. Based on Murshid's experience of me, he calls me "Reverend." The threat of our separation is implied. I cry in his lap at a restaurant counter. In dream, I remember his instructions—from real life—to lie in the sun and observe the color changes you see with closed eyes (the color denotes the element active at the time in the breath). I awake doing a concentration on the Earth, looking for yellow, the color of the earth element.

Murshid is frustrated with the Diner's Club and writes his attorney Theodore C. Lachelt, "Why they even dunned me once for an unpaid bill when they had not sent me the bill!" Murshid has talked to customer service reps who "let the matter hang" when he explains whatever anomaly he was calling about. But then it all starts up again. So Murshid tells Lachelt, "If they put my name on the 'list' we are in excellent position to bring some kind of counter-action whether they bring suit or not for a hypothetical amount due them."

Murshid advises me during work in San Francisco that what he calls "excitement" will be less near Vilayat. Therefore, I should stay close to Vilayat while attending his meditation weekend starting later today at the ranch. Murshid is not commenting on "adulation" near Vilayat, but is rather suggesting that people doing drugs would be doing so on the outer fringes of the gathering.

The Olompali ranch, the site of the meditation weekend, is located a few miles north of Novato, on the west side of Highway 101. The mansion grounds are surrounded by acres of wooded hills and pastures for grazing horses: a relaxed setting for the expected gathering of perhaps 100 people. [In 1996 I see by chance on CNN that the ranch is now Olompali State Park, and that it is being promoted for historical preservation for, among other reasons, the past tenancy of The Grateful Dead.] The weather today is California's best. There is sunshine with no rain forecast to torpedo our planned overnight stay.

My interview with Vilayat is mostly business. First, with intense interest, Vilayat asks about Jemila. Although aware that he is more interested in my wife than in me, I answer calmly. I give Vilayat the papers on *wazifa* that came from his father through Rabia Martin to Murshid, and also the photo I took of Murshid and Reps. He asks about Murshid's use of *wazifa*. I tell him that it is to some extent public. Any controversy remains unmentioned, although I allow that we chant *Allah* at public meetings, and that we do walking concentrations, chanting *wazifas* with *mudras*. Vilayat tells of being "practically excommunicated" by longtime Sufis when he gave *wazifas* out publicly. I appeal to Vilayat's progressive nature and show Murshid's loyalty when I report Murshid as saying, "Vilayat says he's made some innovations. Let him make any innovations he wants to. I will support them."

Then I start to tell Vilayat the story of Murshid's last interview with Inayat Khan, when Murshid was asked how many loyal *mureeds* he thought Inayat Khan had. Not wanting to bore Vilayat by repeating a story he has already heard, I stop after a brief intro and ask him, "Have you heard this story before?" Good stop on my part. Vilayat knows the story—I can't imagine how. "It was characteristic of my father that he always let people see his true self," Vilayat says. This response disappoints me by not addressing the punchline of the story. While acknowledging that Murshid had enjoyed an extraordinarily intimate moment with his father, it leaves out the implication that Murshid might have been one of Khan's three or four loyal *mureeds*.

Jemila has her mind blown when Vilayat tells her at a break about three angels that are hovering around her. This tells me Vilayat sees angels where others see nothing. I'm impressed. When Vilayat says he used music to recover from a motorcycle accident, I ask my only question: "What music?" "Bach's High Mass in B" is Vilayat's answer.

July 7, 1968, Sunday

Murshid and Gavin Arthur venture the thirty miles up from San Francisco to attend the Universal Worship Service at the ranch. In his talk at the end of it, Vilayat says he was ordered to attend this gathering by "the world government." It is, Vilayat says, a "possible impossibility. It is important not only that this is happening," Vilayat says, "but that *the place* where it is happening is also important."

Many incidental happenings raise the pitch. A guy comes into the assembly on acid and speaks incoherently but from the depths of his heart. He calls Vilayat "Val." He is very sensual but hostile, saying, "That's why I command you to get the hell out of here," right after speaking of love and telling Vilayat he is "made in His image."

Another person sings, "Get Together," a song recorded by Hamilton Camp with the chorus, "Come on people now, smile on each other, everybody get together, try to love one another right now." I go very high. During the singing, Murshid is behind me with his arms around Katherine and another woman, and I have my arms around Jemila as she stands in front of me.

When Murshid is invited to speak, he talks of the Universal Worship Services held years ago, where Inayat Khan used to slip in without fanfare. He would sit in the back, Murshid says, and while he would consent to speak when the *cherags* (the conductors; literally, "lights") importuned him to do so, Inayat Khan would be careful not to cast his shadow over anyone.

Murshid tells of visiting Fathepur Sikri near Agra in India, the city built by Emperor Akbar. Akbar's openness toward all religions demonstrated a tolerance and ecumenicism unique in its time. The Sufi Universal Worship, which Vilayat just conducted, reminds Murshid of Akbar, who welcomed to his court representatives of all the religious factions in India. The Indian guide Murshid had during his visit to Fathepur Sikri was whining about his poverty, so, ever dramatic, Murshid said, "I'll give you $10 more than your regular wage if I can prove to you that I am crazy." One can only imagine the guide's reaction. First Murshid asked the guide where Akbar's chessboard was located when the guide was standing on it. There was a second and a third demonstration that I can't remember. Fourth, Murshid asked the guide where Tansen lived when the guide was leaning against the door of Tansen's house. Murshid flabbergasted the guide with his craziness!

I understand Murshid had read history and had the psychic ability to know where at Fathepur Sikri these attractions were grounded. Murshid calls this capacity "reading the akashic records." (At another time, he tells us of doing the same dance at the same place at Fathepur Sikri where Ruth St. Denis and Ted Shawn danced it.) Then Murshid performs his flute of Krishna for the assembled crowd. It is a demonstration of effacement in Sri Krishna. Picture Murshid holding an imaginary flute with a big grin on his face while he hops sideways. He closes by reciting a poem from the *Vadan* of Inayat Khan:

> Let Thy wish become my desire,
> Let Thy will become my deed,
> Let Thy word become my speech, Beloved,
> And Thy love become my creed.
> Let my plant bring forth Thy flowers,
> Let my fruits produce Thy seed,
> Let my heart become Thy lute, Beloved,
> And my body Thy flute of reed.

Gavin Arthur is invited to speak. He, too, speaks from his heart and moves all present when he confesses that it was written that he would learn his lessons late in life. He says he feels that what he has seen here is a manifestation of the Aquarian Age. His stance before today in public debates with other astrologers has always been to prove that the Aquarian Age is *not* here yet. With great emotion, Gavin says that he is very impressed with what he has experienced today, implying that he has been wrong: the Aquarian Age *is* here.

July 8, 1968, Monday

I am very high this morning. I just got through calling Murshid to say, *Boy, how everything fits together.* Vilayat gave me his meditation papers, and on the second page of the introduction is the heading "International School of Meditation." This is exactly what Reps called for—a school. In response to my excitement about the unity of Reps's vision with Vilayat's International School of Meditation, Murshid says everybody is getting the same vision.

Talking to Murshid on the phone makes me high, because he is also high. Murshid says he sent off a battery of letters. When he says that he has Vilayat's "inheritance" for him, I don't know what he's talking about. Except next he tells me that he brought a robe to Olompali last night, and leaves it at that, leaving me to wonder if the robe was for Vilayat.

Fascination about doing Murshid's biography continues to recur, today in the form of coming up with chapters on the subjects that attract me most. These subjects include Murshid's memory of past lives, his possession of a bright light, and his ability to see into things. This last should be called *kashf*, or insight. I'd have to include Murshid's mastery of breath and his knowledge of the occult, which includes the astrological information he presents. All of these things are one level or more below the level of miracles. To me they are like magic, which is not Murshid's area of expertise. Nor does Murshid command the spirits like a medicine man in a Native American *yuwipi* (calling the spirits) ceremony. Most important to include in his biography is Murshid's functioning as a mystic, a state Hazrat Inayat Khan takes an entire book (*Mysticism*) to describe without ever quite defining it. In another book, *Sufi Mysticism,* he calls mysticism "the essence and the basis of all knowledge, science, art, philosophy, religion, and literature." Then there is also Murshid's functioning as a horticulturalist, politician, poet, humorist, psychiatrist, as well as a scholar in the tradition of French mystic and Hebrew scholar Fabre d'Olivet.

Whoa, this is enough about the roles. Murshid's theme, as I perceive it now, boils down to human consideration: *That ye love one another.*

Chapter 6

Tawajjeh (Presence)

Murshid wears his Buddhist robe.

Nothing can help study or meditation as much as the mere presence, the contact, the association with the teacher. By this means the pupil understands how the teacher would act under various circumstances. It is true that sympathy itself is a very great thing, because by it the pupil intuitively knows what the answer is to this problem or that...

It must be learned by contact. How can you learn it by contact? Well, you see this in your daily life. If your sensibilities are delicate, you can tell whether a person is pleased or displeased, without him speaking a word. You can tell if he is inclined favorably or unfavorably to you.

When this is so, there is an exchange of thoughts between yourself and the other person. More than this, there is an exchange of spiritual vibrations. Just by study or practice one cannot realize that truth, that feeling, that peace, that joy, that is beyond words, which belongs to being ourselves, our natural self.

In the east we call this tawajjeh, *which means presence, contact, association with. It is in that way that one learns what cannot be learnt any other way. (Unpublished teachings of Hazrat Inayat Khan)*

July 13, 1968, Saturday

This is like a book of myths and it will become a "myth" in the real sense. For no other purposes was I born, and for no other purpose do I live and die. And now the wheel-of-the-law turns, and even the "good karma" operates [Murshid was a "good" person most of his martyred early life] and this is written with as much joy and optimism as one has ever had.

Thus begins Murshid's letter today to the Temple of Understanding in Washington, D.C., which is convening a conference this month in Calcutta, India. Disciples Sheila and Dara (who, Murshid said, "received this name on account of the Moghul Prince martyr, Dara Shikoh") "have been prepared to go to India, first for the TEMPLE OF UNDERSTANDING, and then to see...President Zakir Hussein; then to call on Julie Medlock, bringing with them such things as she wants."

Murshid continues his letter, "It is significant that the scrolls [diplomas from a recent examination by Grand Master Seo, confirming Murshid's achievement as a Zen master] should arrive just as I was giving instructions to Dara." Murshid gives the Temple of Understanding no information about the "scrolls." No matter; this is about Dara, and more.

Dara's principals and associates are very wealthy... It was Mr. Paul Reps, who first requested me to contact Judith [the Temple's founder] who presented the idea of a SCHOOL for spiritual teachers of all faiths, actually, not poseurs and PhDeists to whom God is an afterthought if a thought at all. And I ran around mad saying, UNLESS THE LORD BUILDETH THE HOUSE THEY LABOR IN VAIN WHO BUILD. But if the Lord do build... [the ellipsis is Murshid's] Then Sam went to the place [Olompali ranch] and gave the spiritual dedication. Then Sufi Pir Vilayat Khan offered his services and dedicated the INTERNATIONAL SCHOOL OF MEDITATION which is not based on privileged me's and thee's but on the actual schools of Meditation...

It has taken forty years to have Vilayat meet this person face to face and he found more love, spirituality and brotherhood than he found anywhere else. The New Race, predicted by Sri Aurobindo, but not yet accepted by the followers of Sri Aurobindo, is here. They are all for the TEMPLE OF UNDERSTANDING and with heart, minds, members and money, God willing we are on our way.

Murshid goes on to list a host of eminences presently visiting or about to visit San Francisco, including Roshi Soen Nakagawa, Lama Anagarika Govinda and Dr. Huston Smith. He concludes:

On Christmas Day we [Murshid] merged into Lord Jesus and when the Sufi Vilayat was here into Lord Krishna. Someday we [this culture] shall accept the spiritual teachings objectively and impersonally and that will mean the end of wars and this nonsensical "excitement" which rules and ruins. I am not here to talk, but to do; not to promise, but to act. I have so far not asked for any material help for this ego, but first God, for God in the form of the TEMPLE OF UNDERSTANDING.

The fact that Murshid and the Temple have an on-going communication is in itself huge, a breakthrough, a change from the past when he was ignored. The process of merging Murshid's letters with my journal entries sometimes reveals an uncanny relationship. Keeping in mind Murshid's letter to the Temple of Understanding, consider my waking dream this morning about Murshid: He was in our bedroom, walking back and forth from wall to wall, hitting his head on the wall (breaking through obstructions). He was showing me how to walk! His instructions were to walk on the earth as if at every step I had reached the top of a mountain, with someone on each side of me, and we were stepping out into the air (reminiscent of the not so grounded tarot card of "The Fool"). I was slightly alarmed by Murshid striking his head on the wall.

This waking dream sends me to the passage in *A Sufi Message of Spiritual Liberty* about dreams. Inayat Khan writes, "Dreams have their effect sooner or later... The dream seen at midnight is realized within one year, and the dream of the latter part of the night within six months; the dream of the early morning is realized soon after." (*The Sufi Message of Hazrat Inayat Khan*, vol.5, p.29) Indeed, Murshid wrote the breakthrough letter the same day I woke up with this dream.

Among the five types of dreams described by Hazrat Inayat Khan, I would say this was the type of dream called "*Naqshi*—in which the real meaning is disguised by a symbolic representation which only the wise can understand." (Anyone becomes wise, given the thirty years it took me to ponder the meaning of the dream.) The other types of dreams are "*Khayali*—in which the actions and thoughts of the day are reproduced in sleep; *Qalbi*—in which the dream is opposite to the real happening; *Ruhi*—in which the real happening is literally shown; *Elhami*—in which divine messages are given in letters or by an angelic voice."

Resting after a 4:30 P.M. dinner, I remember a dream of several days ago in which Murshid taught me to do a dervish dance. In the dream, I am hopping around fast on one foot. Reinforcing these affirmations from my dreams, reading the following in *Mental Purification* further pointed to the possibility of physical centers opening.

As the organs of our senses can experience life that is around us, so the nervous centers can experience life that is within us. But when these centers are not used for many years they become blunted, not destroyed but blunted, and can no longer be

94

put to the use for which they exist. Many who embark upon spiritual work guided by a proper teacher begin to feel a sensation in the middle of the forehead, as if something is awakening there. After some time they begin more and more to notice a sphere of which they were quite ignorant. There are some who begin to notice a feeling in the solar plexus which they did not have before. If that feeling is awakened they naturally become more intuitive. Some feel a certain sensitiveness on the top of their head, or in the center of their throat. With their growth they feel it more and more. Among these people there will doubtless be found some who are intuitive by nature. (*The Sufi Message of Hazrat Inayat Khan*, vol.4, pp.130-31)

Indeed, the concentrations on centers that we do in class while walking have produced awakenings in my forehead and crown centers.

July 14, 1968, Sunday

Driving over the Golden Gate Bridge, I recall a rumor that the Beatles are coming to the ranch in Novato. The thought of such an occurrence produces a tremendous surge of power and urgency in my being. When this happens, it reminds me to get moving. Murshid's *tawajjeh* (glance) the last time he was our house had the same effect. So far, we have seen Murshid refer to his Six Interview experience (see January 13, 1968) in a letter to Dr. Nasr as "the *tawajjeh* of Hazrat Inayat Khan"; and, in the epigraph to this chapter, Inayat Khan chooses the word "presence" to define *tawajjeh*. Here Murshid conflates the two. Murshid formalizes *tawajjeh* or *darshan* by having the one receiving sit before him. In an unpublished paper, Murshid explains what he's doing during this process.

Not every person is capable of performing *Tawajjeh* or *Darshan*. There are those who make a ceremony or play and then there is often an exchange of magnetism. A searchlight does not seek anything from anybody. It throws out its power in the form of light and this is true of the seer also. If he has not the illumined soul, then it is a game and a very false game.

People talk about Christ-consciousness, and they neither have the power nor the wisdom or the compassion nor the self-sacrifice (especially the last) which demonstrates this in actuality. For the Light is not merely light; it is Light carrying the Divine Rays, the Divine Wisdom, the Divine qualities.

To perfect the *Darshan* one must make of oneself an instrument of higher powers, actually, not in thought. Indeed to think this here [that one is an instrument of higher powers] can increase illusion. The ordinary self must stand by and the light will then shine through the true self as it is called, or the higher self.

The seer has a certain faculty of discrimination and discernment through his ability to efface himself, and thus his own shortcomings. In a sense we can say that the Light of Wisdom shone through the Hindu sages; the Light of Compassion through Lord Buddha; the Light of Purity through Zoroaster, etc. But there is also a close attunement to each one; Rama confers ability to rule or control, executive ability, fearlessness and justice. With Sri Krishna it is endless love with joy to the point of ecstasy. With Jesus Christ it is compassion, self-sacrificing tender love.

In Mohammed is the synthesis and balancing, of all these perfections; the perfections of all qualities then blend as if in a single personality. Therefore

Mohammed has been called *Khatimal-Mursaleen*, the Seal of the Divine Messengers. And by effacement (*fana*), the seer becomes the instrument for all those who form the embodiment of the Master, the Spirit of Guidance. (Murshid's *Commentary on Insight* [*Kashf*])

July 15, 1968, Monday

Last night Murshid has me sit next to a new person who asks if he can see me after the meeting; I can't imagine what about. When we meet, Melvin tells me that it's Murshid who told him to see me. Why? After he reported to Murshid that he heard his voice giving him instructions, Murshid said, "See Mansur and he will tell you what will come next." I am baffled; all I can say is, "I don't know"; but since Melvin said the voice gave instructions, I ask, "What instructions?" They were of a general nature, so I give my best guidance: "I would say to keep listening to the voice and to follow the instructions." In three days, Melvin Meyer will receive initiation.

July 20, 1968, Saturday

Some weeks ago I began looking at the Ten Sufi Thoughts in an attempt to memorize them. The fourth thought is, "There is one religion, the unswerving progress in the right direction towards the *ideal* [emphasis mine], which fulfills the life's purpose of every soul." The meaning of "ideal" escaped me. My study of Hazrat Inayat Khan's writings suggested that the ideal must be constructed in the imagination as a preparatory step to mergence in the divine spirit.

I think about asking Murshid to say something about the construction of the ideal—a concept I derived wholly from my study of Hazrat Inayat Khan. But I seek no help from Murshid. I answer my own question. Murshid is my ideal. The concept is *fana-fi-sheikh*. In December of 1970, the last month of Murshid's earthly life, Murshid completed 150 elaborations on the subject of *fana-fi-sheikh*. A few selections follow.

(1) *Fana-fi-Sheikh* means assimilation or ego-self effacement in the living personality of the teacher.

(13) On receiving *Bayat* (initiation), devotees are not directly placed in *Fana-fi-Sheikh*.

(97) From the Sufi point of view, there is a union with all the Illuminated Souls Who form the Embodiment of the Master, the Spirit of Guidance. Progress in *Fana-fi-Sheikh* enables the disciple to become more aware of that.

(100) Progress in *Fana-fi-Sheikh* is evidenced in the actual experiences that the disciple has. It may be inner or outer. Outer growth is often characterized by intensities in love or pain or both; sometimes in breath, joy or ecstasy. The wise teacher therefore watches the mysteries of the disciple with great attention.

(101) Manifestation of holy beings is very determinate of itself. When there are many of these it does not always mean a growth from *Fana-fi-Sheikh* but that the disciple also is experiencing greater depths of consciousness and not apart from the teacher.

(129) When the disciple feels the teacher speaking through his mouth, using his mentality and emanating in and from his heart, he can truly be said to be in *Fana-fi-Sheikh*.

Reading tonight in volume 9 of *The Sufi Message*, in the section called "God-Ideal," I have several insights. One is that for me, this word "ideal" has been connected with illusion. Although utopias like the ones portrayed in Plato's *Republic* and Aldous Huxley's *Brave New World* are called ideal worlds, I know (through the accumulation of trivial knowledge that accrues to that rarest of birds, a graduate student in English) that *u-topos* in Greek literally means "no place." I have to cut the connection I hold between "utopian" and "ideal." Later, in the seventh section of "God-Ideal," Inayat Khan speaks of perfection. "Perfection" and "ideal" are linked in a passage that sheds light on my problem with the meaning of ideal.

We should begin by worshipping the personal God, and we should allow our soul to unfold in the abstract God... The worship of the personal God is the art of *idealizing*, [emphasis mine] the greatest and best art there is.

We idealize the object of our worship as the perfection of all things, of love and justice and forgiveness and power and beauty. In the idealization of our object we offer all the appreciation and admiration we have, and when we have humbled ourselves before the object we have created, we have begun our journey on the spiritual path... In the end it is this path which helps us to efface ourselves entirely in that object of worship, that object in which we see God. And by doing so, in time a door opens, and then we enter into the abstract qualities of the Spirit, to realize the ultimate truth. (*The Sufi Message of Hazrat Inayat Khan*, vol.9, p.90)

For me, practically, it comes back to Murshid as my ideal. It has been my practice since the beginning—an involuntary but compelling concentration on Murshid, or *fana-fi-sheikh*.

July 24, 1968, Wednesday
Murshid's abstruse letter to Vocha Fiske today begins: "*The Eyes of the World*. Do you remember this book by Harold Bell Wright of many years back? A society matron who considered it her duty to lay down all the rules and regulations was finally exposed by somebody tearing her clothes off in public and revealing a tremendous scar?"

Earlier (July 13, 1968), I mentioned Roshi Soen Nakagawa without directly quoting Murshid's remark that "today my closest friend has gone off to meet Roshi Soen Nakagawa, the great Zen Master who also accepts the credentials of this person." Not until considering Murshid's letter of today to Vocha Fiske do I realize that Vocha is the "closest friend" Murshid was referring to.

Murshid continues to Vocha, "Do you realize that your mere mentioning you are going to see Soen tears off the clothes of Don Hayakawa whose blind insistence that 'Zen' was a creation of certain Englishmen whom he once admired and anybody who contradicted him was out?"

"Barred," Murshid says after setting up the scar metaphor and bringing Vocha into the disrobing of Don Hayakawa, "from the top echelons of Harvard University because I have defended General Semantics, it is time to bare the scar of Don who has the audacity to proclaim certain friends of his as the top Psychiatrists of the world [Fritz Perls of the Esalen Institute] when they have not been able to heal the scar in his own family [the dysfunction caused by mental retardation]..."

"I feel like Alice at the end of the *Wonderland* when she finds she has been dealing with 'only a pack of cards.' Everything is bursting."

Not only is Murshid "about to edge into the seminars of the Philosophy Department of the University of California," but he has reached a gossip columnist. "Art Hoppe of the *Chronicle* here has used my 'reality versus realism,' and he understands fully the difference between observed facts and the pompous editorial 'facts' proceeding from everything but the cortex."

These quotations are Murshid to his "closest friend"—not class teachings—and what good gossip it is, long simmering and not muted.

In the same letter Murshid introduces Sheila to Vocha. "Sheila has been a most faithful disciple from before I was ill last year... [She] has one tremendous asset, which is a$$et, and that is going to squelch the whole gamut of value-judgment rejections of whomsoever."

Yesterday, Murshid and Sheila ran errands and "met real Asians. People with flesh-and-blood and not figments of Englishmen and others passed off as 'Asians'." They hit the Indian Consulate ("some of which staff is in bad repute with 'experts' because of the high esteem they hold this person"), two schools of Asian Music ("to each of which I gave a donation in the name of my late departed 'Godmother', Miss Ruth St. Denis"), a Persian bazaar, and an Afghani restaurant.

I can relate to this kind of errand filled day, because I've done it many times. Murshid sums it up by telling Vocha that "Sheila saw first hand that Universal Love which is beyond the ken of mind and yet which is so close to Wisdom—and one demonstration after another."

During class tonight at Sheila's Murshid says, "The Sun allows you to go directly to your goal. If you are the Moon, you can follow others. Mars likes to take orders. For Saturn, every detail has to be right. If any detail is amiss, the whole thing is wrong. Jupiter has the broad view, and is the executive type. Mercury can hardly wait to finish one thing before going on to the next. Venus is gentle, delicate."

In another lesson, Murshid relays something he learned from Alan Watts on the hierarchy of expressions (my term). A low touch is copulation; a higher touch, the embrace; the use of the hand, refining the embrace, which represents advancement. Exchanges through the eyes and the mind are examples of higher, more refined communications.

Murshid gives my privately assigned personal walk, the walk of the saint Mian Mir, to everyone tonight. To introduce it, Murshid says it is adopted from the rhythm of the saint as he knows it. Murshid wrote in his unpublished book *The Lotus and the Universe* something about Mian Mir. It was published in *Sufi Vision and Initiation*:

> The tomb of another Sufi, Mian Mir, was visited many times [in Lahore, Pakistan]. There is a close personal attunement with this saint who taught the children of Shah Jehan [the builder of the Taj Mahal]. They learned to "love" Allah, but not one another. The great lesson learned from Saint Mian Mir is that *"Allaho Akbar"* (ordinarily translated "God is Great") may be interpreted as "Peace is Power", in such a way to explain the whole of physics and metaphysics alike. (p.248)

In a manic mood after class I abandon the deliberate rhythms of Saint Mian Mir's walk. And as soon as we get in the car, I offer Murshid some berries. I'm embarrassed and rebuke myself for getting out of the rhythm of the walk so soon. Although this incident looks fairly innocuous on the page, you have to realize my humiliation was caused by Murshid's surprised look rather than the apparent inappropriateness of the action. No one continued the rhythms of the Saint beyond the class, nor was expected to. But no one caused him to look the way I did.

July 25, 1968, Thursday

Murshid is just leaving with Jehanara. He makes me confront my own selfishness by confiscating my finished copies of Vilayat's meditation papers, recorded at Olompali ranch, that I have been transcribing since Monday. Murshid says he is going to copy them (by retyping them, not by photocopy) to get them into his consciousness. He takes "The Introduction and Instructions in Meditation," "The Training of Breath," and "Introduction to Vision." During this transaction, I also receive instructions to copy the in-depth discussion of the spiritual practices called *Ryazat*. These papers are organized in three series, ten papers to a series. I have been studying them since the 19th, when I first received them.

When we join Murshid in San Francisco for Sufi Night, he gives a lesson on The Lord's Prayer—a prayer as familiar to a midwestern Presbyterian youth as is the Pledge of Allegiance. Murshid goes to work semantically on the end of the prayer, "For thine is the *kingdom*, and the *power* and the *glory*, for ever. Amen." He explains the words "kingdom," "power," and "glory" to expose meaning never imagined by this young Protestant.

Murshid says that "kingdom" corresponds to the sphere of the *jinn*, from which our word "genius" is derived. Sufis call this realm *Malakut*. He says that "power" corresponds to the world of the angels, *Jabrut* in Sufi terms. And "glory," Murshid concludes, corresponds to the source, or *Lahut*. These are associated with inspiration, love and luminosity, respectively.

Especially noteworthy, since it feels so harsh, is a correction Jehanara and Hassan receive for torpor tonight. Murshid rebukes them publicly for not being active enough. For a shy person like myself, to witness this and imagine myself on the receiving end—it seems both harsh and noteworthy. Murshid gives more than blows, however; Fatima receives the Mother Krishnabai walk. Krishnabai is the enlightened disciple of Papa Ramdas. All the rest of us get the Ramdas walk.

I stay up late reading the life of Abu Sa'id Fadlallah (b. Muhammad al-Mayhani), known simply as Abu Sa'id.

He was the sultan of his age and the ornament of the Mystic Path. All his contemporaries were subject to him, some through their sound perception, and some through their excellent belief, and some through the strong influence of their spiritual feelings.

He was versed in the different branches of science. He had a wonderful religious experience and an extraordinary power of reading men's secret thoughts. Besides this he had many remarkable powers and evidences, of which the effects are manifest at the present day.

On one occasion Abu Sa'id set out from Nishapur towards Tus. While he was passing through a mountainous ravine his feet felt cold in his boots. A dervish who was then with him said, "I thought of tearing my waist-cloth (*futa*) into two halves and wrapping them round my feet; but I could not bring myself to do it, as my futa was a very fine one."

When we arrived at Tus I attended his meeting and asked him to tell me the difference between suggestions of the Devil (*waswas*) and Divine inspiration (*ilham*). He answered, "It was a Divine inspiration that urged you to tear your *futa* into two pieces for the sake of warming my feet; and it was a diabolic suggestion that hindered you from doing so." He performed a whole series of miracles of this kind which are wrought by spiritual adepts. (*Kashf al-Mahjub*. London, 1970, pp.164-66)

July 26, 1968, Friday

After a day like today, I feel it will take a letter to my closest friend to get it all down. So, my dear friend, let me begin. There is so much activity, so much experience, a veritable *Ulysses* (I'm thinking of James Joyce's massive book, which takes place in one day and which is full of errands and people). I experience so much joy. There is the joy of planning a journey and fulfilling it; this accomplishment of short term goals in everyday life has to be good preparation for accomplishing long term goals. There are several stops to make, the first at the glass shop in Mill Valley, to get a piece of glass for Murshid's refrigerator. Then on to the radio store in Tam Valley, I can't remember what for. En route to Mill Valley, I pick up a young woman hitchhiking, and in Mill Valley, I see Barbara and give her a short ride.

From there it's on to San Francisco, where my first stop is Cleary's art gallery on Columbus. I know exactly what I want, and Mr. Cleary appreciates me finding more than I want; my find, a reproduction of a Persian miniature featuring an elegant couple sitting in a pavilion, is now hanging in our living room. After this, it's on to Murshid's for the dance class. I feel great joy seeing Murshid and giving gifts to people ("Christmas is every day" is a favorite psychedelic aphorism I coined). The engraving of Akbar from Cleary's goes to Akbar; I give Murshid the pictures I took of him, Akbar, and Amin; and Rene gets a transcript I made of Vilayat speaking at the ranch.

While walking with Murshid around Precita Park in front of his house, I ask him when I am not to practice walking like Mian Mir. Murshid says, "I didn't say when not to do it. I said to do it when it is convenient." Then Murshid says, "I'm going to change my walk. Tell me what you see." Murshid does the walk, and I immediately say it looks as if he were up in his crown center. "Look closer before you speak." I look again and say that it seems to be a combination of the Sun and Jupiter. "That's closer," Murshid says. "It was 'Toward the One.'" "Oh yes," I say. "That's obvious." "This walk," Murshid says, "is the most difficult. It is the walk Mian Mir did to get his distinctive walk." I ask what the difference is, and Murshid says that is for me to find out. I suggest that in the "Toward the One" walk the arms don't swing and that in the Mian Mir walk they do. But as my guesses are all in my head—an intellectual stab, rather than from deep feeling—there is no answer from Murshid.

On the way with Murshid and Shirin to buy vegetables at the Farmer's Market and register at the University (they're closed), Murshid is speaking about the way that Debbie's chart harmonizes with his own. (see April 13, 1969 for Murshid's introduction of Debbie.) He adds that there are several other people like this, including Shirin. Shirin contributes her observation that it is as if people who have been together before in a former life are coming together again. Murshid often said in public meetings that many of us were reincarnated Indians, and he was telling the same to his correspondents. (see the epigraph to Chapter 5)

The conversation strikes a note in me, because I have just read Inayat Khan on "Reincarnation." I ask Murshid if this means that his soul and Shirin's soul, on their way to manifestation, had met the same souls (this is the way Inayat Khan explains the phenomenon of past-life memories: Souls coming to manifestation pass souls going the opposite way, and they exchange information). Murshid answers with what seems like a non-sequitur. "Possibly, but Ramdas was my teacher in a former life." "Well," I say, "I've been reading Inayat Khan, and he does not speak well of those who speak of former lives. He makes fun of them in his play *Una*." Murshid says Inayat Khan's reluctance to speak much about reincarnation was out of respect for his students' process. Inayat Kahn "wanted people to advance and not get hung up in intellectual things. But once a disciple cornered him on the subject and got him to admit his belief in reincarnation." I ask Murshid if he was the disciple who cornered Inayat Khan. Murshid says, "Oh, no," with the same emphatic tone he used when I asked him if Inayat Khan and he had ever played bridge. My impression from this tone: Inayat Khan did not stoop to card playing ("Oh, no; he never played cards, so far as I know"). And Murshid could never be so disrespectfully impertinent as to corner his own murshid. Hazrat Inayat Khan answers more fully the question about reincarnation in his unpublished teachings:

People have often asked me: "What has the Sufi to say about reincarnation?" And my silence at times, and "Yes" and "No" at times has made it vague. Some perhaps thought that I did not believe in it, and that if I did not believe, then the Sufis do not believe, naturally. This is not the case. Every Sufi is free to believe what he understands as right and what he can understand. He is not nailed to any particular belief. By believing in any doctrine the Sufi does not go out of his Sufism, as by not believing he does not go out of the Order of Sufis. There is perfect freedom of belief. For my "Yes" there was a reason, for my "No" there was a reason, a reason not for myself, but for the person who asked me the question. People in the world wish to make things rigid, which are of the finest nature, which words cannot explain. It is just like wanting to weigh the soul or photograph the spirit, when a person describes the hereafter. I, personally, think that you must yourself be able to realize what is the hereafter. You must not depend upon my words. Self-realization is the aim. Beliefs in doctrines are pills given to ill people for their cure. (Hazrat Inayat Khan, Candidate's *Gathekas*.)

For a Chinese dinner Murshid and I drive to the Starview Restaurant on Mission, even though it is within walking distance from his house on Precita. We have their shrimp special. Then I go on to Bolinas for the *Gatha* Class reading.

July 27, 1968, Saturday

I am awakened this morning from a dream in which I am discoursing about a saint—or I am a saint, discoursing? Perhaps my recent reading of Abu Sa'id challenging the arrogant ascetic has something to do with this dream. Abu Sa'id challenged the ascetic to eat for forty days and not go to the toilet. This was immediately after Abu Sa'id had won a forty day fasting contest. I do not record the outcome (no doubt another victory for Abu Sa'id); but I flash on what Murshid said last Thursday: The adept can transmute bodily wastes. Ram Dass (Richard Alpert) gave his guru LSD to no effect, proving that present adepts, as well as those of the past, may transmute substances.

An extraordinary realization occurs during the dance class. Only somebody unlocked from years of uptight constriction can appreciate this one. *I relax for the first time.* The letting down of my shoulders makes me understand that I have been tensed up most of my life: shoulders ratcheted up close to my ears, chest stuck out. Afterwards, I understand the meaning of Murshid's round shoulders. He is relaxed as a baby. This knowledge makes me smile; bittersweet, but grateful to escape from my own uptight prison.

July 29, 1968, Monday

Murshid writes to Rev. Harold Priebe in Ojai, California. "Priebe," he later tells Jack Austin in England (August 1, 1968), "is concentrating on Peace efforts and apparently making some headway." Murshid's letter to Priebe ridicules the obtuseness of Buddhists. He uses the same phrase—"anybody not a Buddhist"—five times in different contexts. One example: "I did not intend to introduce Buddhism to the Hippies but there is a process called *PRAJNA* [insight], also comprehensible to anybody not a Buddhist." Just as *"darshan"* and *"tawajjeh"* were conflated earlier, now *"prajna,"* the Indian term, and *"kashf,"* the Sufi term, are conflated. They are both "insight"—in different languages.

In a letter to Paul Reps, Murshid begins, "I am enclosing copy of a letter to Julie Medlock who is directing the construction at Auroville, near the Sri Aurobindo Ashram in India. Some day when we get out of 'realism' into objective honesty some people will listen to the history of Julie as she revealed it to Sam but just now that is the last thing the various 'East-West' centers want to hear. And really this letter and the enclosure is for Sri Haridas Chaudhuri for one has still the hope that he will get into the actualities of cultural exchange and stop this nonsense of promoting self-important people of previous generations as the 'Suez Canals' of the age." Murshid follows this opening with an exclamation that he punctuates with a period, "Why he has associated with men who have the audacity, the damnable audacity, to consider themselves as representatives of 'Universal Religion,' which is nothing but the defiance of the Living God Himself."

July 30, 1968, Tuesday

Slept over at Murshid's last night and after breakfast he dictates a three page, seven headline letter (JULIE MEDLOCK; ZEN: ASIAN VERSUS SEMANTIC; SHEILA; INDIAN PHILOSOPHY; TOMORROW;

AMERICAN PHILOSOPHICAL MOVEMENT; SOCIAL ACCEPTANCE)
to Dr. Oliver Reiser, Department of Philosophy, University of Pittsburgh.

While we are out doing errands, Murshid talks of not touching people for years. He did this, he says, so other people would not steal his magnetism. Lately, in order not to be a slave to this habit, Murshid has changed his behavior. He touches people and allows them to touch or embrace him. "I broke the habit" sounds masterful, with overtones of altering addictive behavior, and it is intended to. A master masters himself, and Murshid is teaching by example.

Murshid says it was with God's permission he borrowed money to take me out to dinner this week. Also, God told him it is all right to pay for me to take a course with him at UC Berkeley in two weeks. He doesn't mention that it is Huston Smith's class. I don't ask what class, since I am conditioned now to rely on what happens, not on what is said—not to mention that I'd go anywhere with Murshid. He sharply criticizes Vilayat's breathing practices that he finds in the talks I transcribed, saying they are opposed to those Inayat Khan gave. Inayat Khan taught the refined breath and the heart center; Vilayat gives heavy breathing and the solar plexus. These observations are sent in a letter to Reps with no carbon copy. He muses that he lost lots of help because people had to take jobs, and talks about taking some time off himself. Murshid saying this is out of the ordinary, so I note it. He doesn't take any time off. Today I record information (Murshid was born at the corner of 16th and Guerrero in San Francisco) that was omitted from Murshid's skeleton biography in *Sufi Vision and Initiation*. We register at the University of California Extension on Laguna Street. These are the classes God gave Murshid permission to borrow money to pay for. It will be a week long presentation by my old friend Dr. Huston Smith, to be held at the Berkeley campus.

July 31, 1968, Wednesday

Tawajjeh makes my heart beat. Or, to say it another way, Murshid's gaze accelerates my heart rate. What is going on today between Murshid and his good looking women disciples, only Paul Reps knows. He writes Reps from San Francisco (August 2, 1968). "And on Wednesday night there was the manifestation in walk (there has already been manifestation in sound) of Rama, Krishna, Shiva, Moses, Jesus and Mohammed. It is so obvious and so effective; only in the Krishna effacement Sam fell in love with all the young women and how beautiful they are (or are becoming), that he was glad to get out of it. But said God: 'You need it. For you this experience is good, for others it would be dangerous'." Later, Murshid tells Reps that "the main lesson of the week was the extension of Concentration on *Salat* [the Sufi prayer] but now Sam is able to efface the ego and demonstrate the prayer."

August 1, 1968, Thursday

Today Murshid writes a diary entry letter with a Buddhist slant to Rev. Jack Austin in England. After mentioning a disciple (Brian, who was "asked to contact you"), and health matters ("Had my check up with Dr. George Fung today"), Murshid takes up mostly Buddhist issues. My typescript of Chinese Buddhist Master Tai Hsu's manuscript is finished, and Murshid plans to distribute it to Jack and local Buddhists Iru Price and Eugene Wagner. He also intends to send it "to Tuttle for possible publication." There is another manuscript, by Shaku Soyen, that Murshid says he has to edit "merely to see that either Pali or Sanskrit terms are employed throughout"; he asserts that he has "no intention of doing anything more..." Coming up is a Semantic Conference headed by Dr. Abraham Kaplan, who is Daisetz Suzuki's pupil. Murshid comments: "I was much surprised at Kamakura to be informed that I was then two grades in Zen over Daisetz, a point since corroborated both by Master Seo [who examined Murshid and presented the "scrolls"] and also at least indirectly by the records."

August 2, 1968, Friday

Paul Reps's letter today annoys a hard working Murshid who doesn't have time to deal with the inspirations that "a number of very good friends (you among them)...are constantly sending...disregarding constant remarks that I have been working 16 hours a day six days a week, and now I am working over 16 hours most days." The first line tells Reps, "This is being written very rapidly," and the concluding line of the paragraph is a fragment: "It is only due to the fact that I have now three secretaries and that they see sides of me that other people, for the most part, have a priori rejected, God bless them." It goes unsaid *what* we secretaries see, until the last sentence in the letter. "The secretaries all realize where Sam stands in the real mystical life and that is something. We do not walk alone." The most important thing Murshid has to share with Reps is that in the same mail, letters from Shamcher in Washington state and Shemseddin Ahmed in Lahore arrived. Both "have declared that the understanding between Vilayat and Sam will have world effects," Murshid tells Reps. "There was no question, Vilayat wanted the world (the circle) and Sam was instructed to lead the Hippies (the dot). And there is no question of inferiority, superiority, but only of complement and supplement."

The meeting of Vilayat and Murshid affected me, too. To me, the relationship between them is like that between Shams-i-Tabriz and Jelal-ed-din Rumi, as recorded in an undated, pirated edition of an ancient work published in Mexico.

At this time Master Jelal-ed-din was teaching science as Professor of four colleges. Students walked at his stirrup. Shams-ed-din arose, came forward, and grasping the bridle of his horse shouted, "O teacher of Moslems, was Abu Yezid or Mohammed the greater?" Master Jelal-ed-din replied, "Mohammed, God's envoy, is the greatest of mortals. What of Abu Yezid?" Then, said Shams-ed-din, what does it mean that Mohammed said, "We have not known Thee as Thou shouldst be known," while Abu Yezid said, "I am exalted, my dignity is upraised, I am the sultan of sultans!"? Our Master replied, "When Abu Yezid managed to reach God, he was satisfied; God's Elect [Mohammed] sought each day further, and from hour to hour and day to day saw light and power and divine wisdom increase." Shams-ed-din gave a cry and fell. Our Master got down from his mule, sent the imams away, and gave orders to raise the Shaikh. Until he came to himself, our Master held the head of Shams-ed-din upon his knees. Then he took him by the hand, and returned to the college on foot. Thereafter none had access to them. (Aflaki, *The Lives of the Gnostics*)

My constant thought with Murshid today is a phrase from Abu Sa'id's biography: "Being thoroughly acquainted with the thoughts of his disciple..." That the spiritual teacher can be "thoroughly acquainted with the thoughts of his disciple"—the familiarity inherent in this kind of relationship reverberates as I consider the meaning. Murshid says that Jemila and I and someone else who is interested in spiritual dancing might make a trip with him. Sometime today Murshid says I can try on his robe. Try on his robe?

Murshid pushes Nathan in the yard of our cabin on Bolinas Lagoon.

Chapter 7

The Robe

Dr. Huston Smith. This man is regarded as America's greatest authority on Asian faiths and philosophies. Twice, when self-important people turned down papers from Sam he accepted them. He is connected with the Massachusetts Institute of Technology, one of the most advanced groups in the whole world. But Ram is full of humor, as Papa Ram Das used to say. Sam's esoteric secretary [Mansur] was the star pupil of Dr. Huston Smith!

Huston Smith is regarded as the supreme authority both by all those who are taking psychedelic drugs or involved in forms of psychiatry which lean toward the Orient. In the class he told Sam that Sam would be given an "A." And Sam also brought him poetry rejected by the very "nice" East-West people whom I shall not name. (Murshid's letter to Anandashram, August 18, 1968)

August 5, 1968, Monday

What happened this morning impressed Murshid enough to tell his friends at Anandashram about it in his letter of the 18th.

Two weeks back on Monday morning a convocation was called by a very, very wealthy and powerful man of this region. [This unnamed mystery man, I guess, is Jeremy Ets-Hokim.] He is known as a politician, a successful business man and a "high liver." Underneath he is an advanced initiate and hides this. He goes around to spiritual and metaphysical places and they treat him in their usual manner...and churches too full of self-respect disregard St. Paul's "Show kindness to strangers for many have thereby entertained angels unawares." This has been his career. He called a spiritual meeting and in the end gave very determined instructions to Sam's disciple Sheyla [Sheila has been to numerologist Louise], to get ready to go to India. He was very adamant and first Sheyla and now another disciple, Dara, is being prepared. They will aim first at the Temple of Understanding which will hold sessions at Darjeeling (Calcutta)...

Sheyla and Dara are getting ready for India. They are both deeply in love with Mother Krishnabai. Sam has assigned to Sheyla the working title, "Spiritual Women in the World of Today." They may first stop at Madras where India Air Lines enters your country with a letter of introduction to Dr. Radakrishnan [President of India] who always answers Sam's letters, with whom there is deep understanding. The visit to Pondicherry [Julie Medlock] will depend on timing but they should visit there and even the Radho-Soamis before returning home. For they are connected with a growing movement in this land for communal living based on spiritual, not on political premises. This movement is growing very, very rapidly and is, on the whole, unled.

Sometimes, I feel very unreal, not myself. Jemila's pictures show me appearing heavy, a lifeless being, joyless. I must go get Abu Sa'id (*The Life of Abu Sa'id*) and copy a section that struck me the other day, especially the part about falling "into despair" and feeling "no joy."

Abu Sa'id was asked, "When shall a man be freed from his wants?" "When God shall free him," he replied; "This is not affected by a man's exertion, but by the grace and help of God." First of all, He brings forth in him the desire to attain the goal. Then He opens to him the gate of repentance *(tauba)*. Then He throws him into self-mortification *(mujahada)*, so that he continues to strive and, for a while, to pride himself upon his efforts, thinking that he is advancing or achieving something; *but afterwards he falls into despair and feels no joy* [emphasis mine]. When he knows that his work is not pure, but tainted, he repents of the acts of devotion which he had thought to be his own, and receives that they were done by God's grace and help, and that he was guilty of polytheism *(shirk)* in attributing them to his own exertion. When this becomes manifest, a feeling of joy enters his heart... (*Life of Abu Sa'id*, p.51)

Copying this presentation of process reminds me that everything changes. For example, last night while swinging Nathan in the swing and contemplating the biblical phrase, "Who by taking thought can add a cubit to his height? Or change the color of his hair?" I had the realization of the inability of thought in comparison to the greatness of God, the process of God. This afternoon, I was inspired to copy Jesus' Sermon on the Mount. When coming to the words, "Ask and it shall be given, seek and ye shall find, knock and it shall be opened..." weeping commenced; it was wonderful, and led to the inspiration to write a *Commentary on the Sermon on the Mount*, based on Murshid and Hazrat Inayat Khan's esoteric interpretations. My commentary begins:

GATHEKA (literally, sacred song; elsewhere, Sufi study paper): And seeing the multitudes, he went up into a mountain, and when he was set, his disciples came unto him, and he opened his mouth, and taught them, saying,...
TASSAWUF (in this context, commentary; elsewhere, Sufism): The mountain of Christ is a symbolic mountain, representing the high stage of consciousness to which the master attained before giving his teaching.
GATHEKA: Blessed are the poor in spirit for theirs is the kingdom of heaven.
TASSAWUF: Spirit means breath. Those individuals such as practice the refinement of breath in everyday life are practicing this...

When you consider the following piece of Hazrat Inayat Khan's commentary on "Blessed are the Poor in Spirit" that inspired the above, realize that the Sufi word for "ego" is *nafs* and the Sufi word for "breath" is the same word, "nafs."

The words "poor in spirit" are an unsatisfactory translation, and do not convey the real meaning of the text. There are certain words in the original which cannot be accurately translated. In Sufi terms this poorness of spirit is called *Halim Taba'*, and means mild-spirited. The more true meaning of the words is, "Blessed are the mild in ego," and this is the teaching of Jesus throughout. He himself is spoken of in the Bible as "the Lamb of God", conveying the meaning of the mild in ego, like a lamb... There is a verse in the Qur'an which says, "Arise in the midst of the night, and commune with thy Lord... Bear patiently what others say." This is not only a command to arise in the night and pray, but it also means that by rising in the night we crush the ego, for the ego demands its rest and comfort, and when denied, is crushed. The mystics fast for the same reason. The Sufis base the whole of their teaching on the crushing of the ego which they term *Nafs-kushi*, for therein lies all magnetism and power. Jesus Christ meant this power of magnetism when he told his disciples that they would become the fishers of men. This can be acquired by developing the personality in poorness of spirit. (*The Sufi Message of Hazrat Inayat Khan*, vol.5, pp.194-96)

August 6, 1968, Tuesday

After midnight, moon almost full, walking on the hill behind my house in Bolinas, I remember the spiritual practice *Allaho Akbar* to deal with the terrifying appearance of a skunk on the path. Murshid repeated this phrase when confronted by a mad dog. I shout, *Allaho Akbar!* three times, and the skunk scoots off through the grass. Perhaps I overreacted.

Tuesday is my day to help Murshid. Sheyla comes. Surely she reports about the convocation (with the wealthy, powerful man) yesterday, but it is my practice to stay out of Murshid's business with other students unless he brings me in. I take a letter to Paul Reps asking for money. My impression from things Murshid had said, although we never discussed it is that if Reps responds, his contribution will guarantee Murshid's secretary's income. I wasn't aware that Murshid had expressed a "What—me worry?" attitude about money to Reps. But, indeed, on July 29th, Murshid wrote to him, "The last thing I am worrying about is money. There are wealthy men and plenty of funds on the horizon, and apparently publicity too. And when the mature as well as the young experience expansion in real Love, real Joy and real Peace, no further argument is needed." But even here, Murshid allows his need for additional funds to show as he continues, "Why I am even supporting two secretaries from the collections which I never touch!" And Murshid gets by. Although additional funds could fuel a full time secretariat, and Reps is rich.

Murshid and I go down to the India Tourist Bureau for travel information folders. Not only is Murshid preparing Sheyla and Dara for India, but Olompali ranch's Don McCoy has asked for the same preparation. "In turn, Don has asked Sam when he wants to go to India and has promised to finance the trip," Murshid tells Reps on the 30th. Referring to Monday's meeting, Murshid refers again to finances: "There is considerable pressure of wealthy men behind efforts to get Sheyla to leave for India. It is Sam who does the work and he is going to suggest some financial cooperation from one of them who is one of the wealthiest and most powerful men of the region."

August 7, 1968, Wednesday

Phillip Davenport, editor of the newly resurrected *San Francisco Oracle*, uses my tape recorder to interview Murshid at Amin's house in Corte Madera. Jemila, Nathan, Katherine, Amin, and Akbar are there. The interview lacks flow, but Phillip is going to do more on Friday and, with editing, it could become a good thing. Says Murshid to old friend Vocha Fiske in a letter on August 17th: "Soon my picture, my history, and my

Phillip Davenport

knowledge of several subjects will be out on full display, and as soon as my personality is better known—and it will be and is becoming so—the next steps will be taken. Amen."

Next stop Sheyla's, where I have the feeling Murshid is my *father.* Not actually—it is the musing of a fatherless child imagining how a real father might feel. But actually, it is Murshid's experience (as he will write September 8, 1969 to Oliver Reiser), "The career of being a Pied Piper is accompanied by one of being father, mother, grandfather and spiritual teacher."

Murshid is staying with us tonight and tomorrow. When he and I return to Bolinas, two year old Nathan is playing with Summer. (Summer is the daughter of Barbara who is a friend of Jemila's.) Jemila says, "There are two angels at home." Murshid responds, "There's one more." "Us!" I pipe up. "That's almost what I meant," Murshid answers. I can't disregard anything Murshid says. His not so subtle suggestion that I am an angel sends me to read in Hazrat Inayat Khan's book *The Inner Life* about angels:

The Hindu word *deva* denotes an angel-man, and the Sufi term for this is *Farishtakhaslat.* Every soul has as its first expression angelic life, and therefore it is not surprising if man shows angelic traits in his life, for it is in the depth of his soul. The soul coming through different spheres and planes of existence partakes of different attributes; and the attributes of the lower world become so collected and gathered around the soul, that it almost forgets its very first experience of itself, its purest being. The soul that through all the worldly experiences has a tendency to turn towards its origin, its angelic state, shows a different character from the general characteristics of human beings. This soul shows the tendency of the compass, that always points in a certain direction, whichever way it is moved or turned; and it is the same with a soul whose nature it is to be pointing to the origin and source from which every soul comes. Now this soul may have the same tendency from childhood and through youth, and when grown-up it may still have the same tendency; it may develop it more and more, but this tendency is born with the soul and its magnetism is great. It attracts every other soul, because it is in contact with its real self, and that real self is the real self of every soul which it contacts; and therefore it acts as a magnet towards these souls. *Deva* is the name of this pure kind of human soul. (*The Sufi Message of Hazrat Inayat Khan*, vol.1, p.98)

August 8, 1968, Thursday

Murshid and I hike down Steep Ravine on Mount Tamalpais. I am impressed when Murshid says he expects to die in the orient. Reading the lives of various saints has taught me that mystics die consciously; obviously, then, they can choose where they die.

Today at Jehanara's I learn something about controlling myself. The after dinner coffees are all served with cream. Murshid and I like black coffee. We both politely drink the already creamed coffees. There is a class; then after, more coffee is offered. Mansur says, "Black, please." Murshid says, "I'll take mine any way it comes." Slap. I am reminded by the attitude in Murshid's answer not to speak at such times. The coffee comes black. Murshid doctors his by adding water and honey. I get my black coffee, and more. At other times I see others answer differently from Murshid on points of personal preference, and not go through the changes I go through. Somehow Murshid's contrasting answer to a situation we both face prompts me not only to feel Murshid's disapproval of my answer, but to reevaluate my response. Indeed, I assume Murshid hears in my answer a condemnation of the host for serving coffee with cream without asking first, and he is chastising me for it.

At Jehanara's I dance Greek dances with Murshid until the babysitter brings Nathan. Murshid says he wants to take two men and one woman on a trip with him. Murshid asks me, "What do you think of that?" I say, "It's OK if one of them is me," imitating—actually—Murshid in my boldness. Shirin told me yesterday that Murshid said several times Mansur was going to travel with him. (You notice I am beginning to use the third person in my journal. This affectation comes and goes, and I allow it.) When somebody says they feel funny today, Murshid says, "I feel funny all the time."

August 9, 1968, Friday

I drive Murshid back to San Francisco and take the opportunity to give a personal report. I have found if I focus on my breath while concentrating and doing *fikar* exercises, my eyes and mind don't fatigue. My revelations lead to a question. I ask Murshid if the breath of a master is *always* in rhythm. "No, but it is a kind of rhythm, controlled. It is controlled," Murshid says emphatically. Apparently, my report inspires Murshid with a realization. He says, "There are two kinds of states: one, very simple, like listening, when attention is focused on hearing words; another, the deep state, when attention follows breath, coordinating with the heart beat." Murshid adds, "I can usually tell what is wrong with each disciple before they tell me their problem."

At the dance class, I remind Murshid that Julie Medlock said Murshid was beginning to sound like a nine dimensional Gurdjieff. "Possibly I am, possibly I am," Murshid muses. "Julie reminds me of Shirin." Mansur says. Murshid comes back with: "Julie was very nice about most things, but she was slow to recognize Sufis. Do you know what happened when myself and two other men called on her?" Mansur guesses that they played bridge. "No." Mansur guesses that they hugged and kissed. "That's very close to what happened," Murshid says.

Phillip, in his capacity as editor of *The San Francisco Oracle,* asks me to schedule an interview with Huston Smith, whom Phillip knows as the

author of *The Religions of Man* and instructor of the course Murshid and Mansur are taking at Berkeley next week. After the dance class, Murshid and Mansur go to the Big Bonus supermarket. This inspires me to write:

Huston Smith

> It was Murshid's example that was the teaching. One time walking back from the grocery store, I said to him, "Murshid, I would rather go in shopping with you than hear you lecture." It says

in the teachings that a mystic is one who can do without doing and say without speaking. What could he have taught me this day? Concentration as he walked in search of some cranapple juice. Friendliness as he spoke to the checker. Positivity as he led me across the street. Silence as he walked in the presence of God. (*In the Garden,* p.21)

August 10, 1968, Saturday
Last night I dreamed of Murshid and woke up laughing and laughing.

August 12, 1968, Monday
Going to Huston Smith's class with Murshid is no more or less exciting than going to Big Bonus. Murshid considers himself among the "wise and awakened," not "the wealthy and intellectual" (letter to Anandashram, August 18, 1968), and it is a marvel to observe the everyday actions of this "awakened" person, wherever we happen to be. As I am parking the car before class, busting myself silently for failing to think about God while doing it, he says, "Don't be too hard on yourself for stealing somebody's parking place." It is another instance of the spiritual teacher "being thoroughly acquainted with the thoughts of his disciple."

Huston Smith is tall and lanky. His massive forehead, the hairline receding slightly, bespeaks intelligence. He has thick lips and an engaging smile. It is great to greet him again, less than two years after our meeting in Michigan. In chitchat before class, Smith is interested to know if Lama Govinda is speaking at the Esalen Institute's San Francisco branch as well as in Big Sur. Murshid doesn't answer directly—he doesn't know—but says, "Rev. Iru Price is Lama Govinda's host. I hope Lama Govinda will speak to the public, rather than to a privileged elite." Smith smiles and says enigmatically, while making the gesture that his words describe, "No more closed fistedness," then explains why he asked. He has time to drive across the Bay Bridge and connect with Lama Govinda in San Francisco, but not to drive to Big Sur.

During class breaks, Murshid works the halls striking up conversations, engaging whomever he catches in his net. After one of these enlivening breaks, Mansur says to Murshid, "When I watch you out there in the halls, I feel like I'm seeing a *Bodhisattva* in action." The *Bodhisattva* vows not to rest until all people are fully enlightened. Murshid laughs.

August 13, 1968, Tuesday

Picture a large classroom at Berkeley. There is the usual preclass hubbub. The teacher has not appeared. Students are turned in their chairs, conversing with others near and far. There is a question, directed to no one in particular, "Does anybody know if the test is going to be multiple choice questions or essays?" Without missing a beat, Murshid answers: "The Buddhists are meeting Friday, and there is no relation between what you find in the so-called Buddhist churches and the class material." The only connection between Murshid's non sequitur answer and the question is that Murshid had something to say about the efficacy of some local Buddhists's practice, and he took the opportunity of someone's question to express it.

Only I know what Murshid is talking about. The class material he refers to includes Philip Kapleau's *The Three Pillars of Zen*, a manual of experience and practice that Murshid admires. No one probes Murshid for more information,

Murshid at the Smith interview

but someone picks up on Buddhism and poses a philosophical question about suffering. "Was there more suffering in the sixth century B.C. or the twentieth century A.D.?" Answering everything that comes up now, Murshid says, "If we practiced the four *Jhanas* [meditations] of Lord Buddha, we would find that we would get more joy." With this, Huston

Smith enters and class begins. Murshid presented the *Jhanas* of Lord Buddha in his classes as follows.

After asking everybody to just be conscious of their breath, he would say, "Take a long breath and be conscious you're taking a long breath." Then after several breaths, two or three only, he would instruct, "Now take a short breath and just be conscious you're taking a short breath." It was similar to a dog panting. Seconds later, "Now take a heavy breath and be conscious you're taking a heavy breath." And two or three or four audible breaths later, "Now take a light breath and just be conscious you're taking a light breath." After a signaled pause he would say, "Now refine that breath as fine as you can make it." There would be no sound in the room as breaths were refined. "Now breathe in all the LOVE that you are capable of breathing in—love in and love out, love in and love out," and then he'd do it. "Alright, now breathe in all the JOY that you are capable of breathing in and breathe out all the joy that you are capable of breathing out—joy in joy out, joy in joy out." And when that had been practiced for a few moments, moments only, he'd say, "Alright, now with the breath very refined, breathe in all the PEACE that you can breathe in, and breathe out all the peace that you can breathe out—peace in, peace out." This would be practiced. "Now expand that peace to fill this room." This would be practiced. "Now expand that peace over the whole city (country, world)." These were called the *Jhanas* of Lord Buddha. (Adapted from Mansur's piece in *In the Garden*, p.137)

Murshid's July 29, 1968 letter to Rev. Harold Priebe, postulating the obtuseness of Buddhists, included a reference to the *Jhanas*. "The complete success of the applied *JHANAS* seem to be comprehensible to anybody not a Buddhist and not only the young but some mature people began coming here and are getting Buddha's Yoga [the *Jhanas*], also comprehensible to anybody not a Buddhist." Murshid and I eat at the Khyber Pass, an Afghani restaurant at Fortieth and Telegraph Avenue in Oakland—a restaurant owned, Murshid likes to write, by "brethren" (Sufis).

August 14, 1968, Wednesday

Huston Smith shows his documentary about Tibetan Buddhism, *Requiem for a Faith,* which highlights the ability of chanting monks to produce simultaneous tones and overtones, an apparent impossibility. Murshid explains to me that this Tibetan harmony is accomplished the

same way birds produce sounds in their chests. After the film, Huston Smith inquires about possible audiences for it. Mansur offers, "We'll make an occasion for the showing of your movie," but Murshid, standing alongside, says, "I have connections with the local Buddhists who brought Lama Govinda to town. We can possibly show your movie to them and that crowd." Like the time when I spoke for black coffee, Murshid's answer in contrast to mine shows me something. Today, I hear the difference between a good intention and the wisdom of offering a Buddhist audience a Buddhist film. Murshid and I dine at the Cairo, an Armenian restaurant at Fourth and Mission. Mansur and others stay overnight and play bridge with Murshid.

August 15, 1968, Thursday

Mansur never meets the Taoist masters Murshid speaks about today in class. Murshid says they are alive in San Francisco but that he can't give their names until they are dead. They don't want to be known. After class, Murshid says that maybe he'll introduce Mansur to one. He says he received a tiny bit of advice from one once, but that usually they don't speak. "From the little bit that you get from them, it can keep you going for a long time," Murshid says.

Monday and today, Mansur eats dinner after class at Murshid's. Murshid will write Vocha Fiske on Saturday (August 17, 1968) that although he spent "five days with Dr. Huston Smith, Sam had still to carry on interviews, classes, etc." At this evening's meeting, these activities come to fruition in spades for Mansur. Murshid initiates me into the fourth grade of Sufism. Hazrat Inayat Khan explains the fourth initiation as follows.

Initiations, according to the mystics, are twelve in number, divided into four stages; just like the semitones in the octave, or the twelve bones in the ear. The first three initiations are the first three steps, taken with the help of a guide whom one calls in Sufi terms a *Murshid*, a teacher. In Vedantic terms he is called *Guru*. He will be someone who is walking this earth, a human being placed in the same conditions as everyone else, in the midst of active life, and subject to all trials and troubles and difficulties. The help of such a friend is the first and most important step in these first three stages of the path... The fourth initiation the seeker gets from his ideal. And who is his ideal, who can give this initiation?... Even perfect man [Buddha, Zoroaster, Christ, Krishna] is limited in the imperfect garb of humanity. The human limitation covers perfection... A man cannot make himself as his pupil imagines him. Imagination goes further than the progress of man; the imagination of every person is his own, and therefore one can only make one's ideal oneself... So in this fourth initiation there is this ideal of man's imagination... Once this initiation is received man begins to radiate, to radiate his initiator who is within him as his ideal. (*The Sufi Message of Hazrat Inayat Khan*, vol.10, pp.62, 66-67)

During an interview afterwards, Murshid assigns Mansur all of Vilayat's practices and some additional Sufi prayers—*Saum, Salat,* and *Pir*—to be done in the evening. In dream tonight, Mansur dances like Murshid doing the Hare Krishna dance.

August 16, 1968, Friday

It's the last day of Huston Smith's religion workshop in Berkeley. Murshid claps his hands twice in class. One clap is for Kapleau's book and one for Miura Roshi and Ruth Sasaki's book, *Zen Dust*. It happens when the class is going over Dr. Smith's bibliography.

Mansur is taken aback when Murshid contradicts Smith's statement that Zen didn't come from Korea. Willing to concede that perhaps Zen had a different name in Korea, Smith asks, "What then was Zen called in Korea?" "Zen," Murshid answered, having the last word. Murshid and Mansur eat at the Minerva, a Greek restaurant on Turk Street. "A mystical week" is how Mansur describes this week in his journal; a feast week is more like it, considering the fine dining enjoyed by all.

Huston Smith at his interview

August 17, 1968, Saturday

Friday, Murshid said he was ready to go to Europe to defend Vilayat. "I'm in a fighting mood," he said. This mood shows when Murshid writes Vocha Fiske today. He begins, "It is not yet light. The Law of Compensation, human justice and Scipio [Publius Cornelius Scipio Africanus Major, 236-183 B.C.] is carrying the Punic war over into Africa."

I have your splendid letter of the 10th, having passed a most successful, vigorous week with human beings excluded by "humanists." It is impossible to give all details... Out of courtesy and human consideration copies are being sent to Lloyd [Morain] and Russ... [Joyner] Dr. Huston Smith who has accepted two papers rejected by Don [Hayakawa] told me I get an "A" in his course regardless of my examination... It is all over. It is almost twenty years since Don Hayakawa, too busy with a seminar of his own asked Sam to address a group of scientists meeting on the San Francisco State Campus studying G.S. [General Semantics]. Sam went and spoke on *The Use of General Semantics and Keyser's Rigorous Thinking in the Modern Laboratory*. The scientists asked Sam to write it up. The paper was sent to Don...and in the presence of a mutual acquaintance the paper was deposited in the wastebasket. From that point on, all one got was "The trouble with you Sam is..." This is "liberty, democracy, humanity and *peasants, shut up*", but particularly the latter. Now there are too many *peasants* and they are not going to shut up.

August 18, 1968, Sunday

Tonight Murshid questions Moineddin about Vilayat. Moineddin's loyalty to Murshid comes through to me as he diplomatically but repeatedly utters highly qualified appraisals of Vilayat's presentation. When Murshid speaks of his sympathy for workers because of his own job experience, Mansur becomes defensive (thinking Murshid is criticizing Mansur's lack of an outside job) and answers, "I have a job" (meaning the work he is doing for Murshid). Situations that Murshid has faced in everyday life often inspire his public pronouncements. Those who understand this realize that a pushy visitor must have imposed himself upon Murshid at dinner when he says, "When somebody comes to a Pir-O-Murshid's house, they just can't expect to eat with him. When people came to Ramdas's, Ramdas didn't eat with non-disciples. Disciples ate with him, and Mother [Krishnabai] served them." Tonight Mansur tapes two hours of Murshid's private interviews and *darshans*. In a letter today to Anandashram, Murshid speaks about the *darshan* process.

Sam is presenting spiritual, not intellectual, methods. He had used the Sufi *Tawajjeh* but only for disciples. Now he does the *Darshan*, following a real, real universal method, not intellectual. In one of the prayers [*Salat*] of Hazrat Inayat Khan, Sam's first Sufi teacher it says: Allow us to recognize Thee in all Thy holy names and forms; Let us know Thee as Rama, as Krishna, as Shiva, as Buddha...as Moses, as Jesus, as Mohammed. Now Allah (Ram) speaks to Sam and told him to perform first what is called *tassawuri*, a Sufi expression meaning outward attunement and effacement. But Sam must have satisfied Allah (Ram) for He next told him to perform *Darshan*. And one reports in a spirit equally scientific and devotional: Ram brings courage, fortitude, nobility, faith, honesty, one-pointedness, and is very effective for and with men. Sri Krishna is the most difficult for Sam. It makes him fall in love with all the women and they with him. And Sam has around him some of the most beautiful young women he has ever seen... Sam's best balance was the *Darshan* of Jesus which brings all love and tenderness for everybody and is something like the Buddhist Avalokita. Actually, this would be his favorite but one serves Ram, not himself. The *Darshan* of Shiva is like the Sufic *Akhlak*

Allah, that God is in, around, through everybody and everything. That of Moses is firmness, concentration, much of what the Indians include in *Artha Sastra.* And that of Mohammed is the total integration of all before him, and to Sam is that of Maitreya [*sic*] Buddha. But the "highest" is the *Darshan* of Buddha. This is "active peace." No movement here, and Sam has had his picture so taken and it may be published soon.

Sometimes, especially during the Krishna *darshan,* I vanish in light. It's getting to the point where I can really say that. It has been happening for some time, but it's so subtle, you're not sure.

August 20, 1968, Tuesday
Mansur goes to Mill Valley early with the car to get the generator fixed, and learns a lot about surrender and self will. When Mansur calls Murshid, he "tells" Murshid that the car is in the shop, and that he'll have to hitch back to Bolinas. Murshid replies, "I told Daniel not to come because you were coming." The tone of Murshid's voice tells me that my proposed solution will ruin Murshid's day. Mansur becomes self conscious about telling Murshid what he is going to do. The correct action would be to report what happened and let Murshid comment. Unwilling to shoulder responsibility of such magnitude, Mansur hitches to San Francisco and Murshid dictates a letter to Dr. Radakrishnan (the President of India) and the beginning of the *Gathekas* on reciprocity. It is high times for all. Murshid says to Mansur, "I've taken you on some real trips with me. And that's the way I'd rather teach you." Sheyla drives Mansur back to Tam Valley, where he picks up his revitalized van.

August 21, 1968, Wednesday
Murshid called the robe he is giving Mansur the "transmitted robe." What does this mean? To transmit: "to transfer from one person to another; to convey, as if by inheritance; to hand down or cause (as light or force) to pass through space." *Webster's New Collegiate Dictionary* gives these explanations. Mansur didn't think much about what it meant or try to analyze. He did consult a book.

Strictly speaking, the rite of transmission from one vessel to another cannot be confined to any particular set of forms. Its form may depend, in exceptional cases, on the inspiration of the moment. For example, in addition to the Shadhili initiation which the Shaikh ad-Darqawi received from his Master Shaikh Ali al-Jamal, he also received one from an aged Saint at the point of death who made him his spiritual heir by the ritually unprecedented yet highly significant act of placing his tongue in the Shaikh ad-Darqawi's mouth, and telling him to suck. (*A Sufi Saint of the Twentieth Century,* p.72)

Is this all you're going to say about "the robe"? the reader asks. This had never happened before at Murshid's. I am the first to receive a robe from him. Of course, I've read the *Sutra of the Sixth Patriarch* and know what a big deal transmissions are. But that was then, this is now.

Mansur has set up an interview with Huston Smith for tomorrow, and my idea is to limit questions to those concerning Smith's experiences. Sufism is based on experience. I don't want to elicit speculations. However, Huston Smith hasn't called to confirm our interview. It may not happen. Murshid decides not to come out to stay at our house in Bolinas tonight; Jemila's brother is here. Mansur realizes he should have told Murshid we have a house guest, since Murshid was planning on staying with us. Where was the consideration? It was not polite. Murshid says three different times, "I guess I'll stay at Sheyla's." I am speechless; guilty.

August 22, 1968, Thursday

In an exalted state, Murshid calls Mansur from San Francisco this morning to tell what changes in his program "have come to me very clearly." His weekly routine will shift so he stays Wednesday nights and Thursdays with Sheyla until she leaves for the conference in India. Murshid says he wants "to help Sheyla get to know Sheyla." Murshid will come out to Bolinas with Mansur on Friday, and stay Saturday and part of Sunday. Finally, next Sunday's open house will be the last for a while. In other matters: The lawsuit with brother Elliott is going on now. "I may lose," Murshid says, "unless I give it some time." Disciple Marcia, I am told, is beginning to work again on the Shaku Soyen materials. "It is all right for these people to want to help me," Murshid says, generalizing what is obviously his experience of a particular situation, "but that's not all it's about"—implying, I believe, that having students work for him sometimes costs more than it benefits him.

August 24, 1968, Saturday

I go to Huston Smith's hotel in Berkeley with Murshid and Phillip to interview Smith for *The San Francisco Oracle*. Dr. Smith shares intimacy by saying that he and Michael Murphy spent two hours musing about the future of the Esalen Institute. "Esalen," Smith reports telling Murphy, "is beginning to ask people, 'Well, what's next? We have come this far, but where do we go from here?'" Hearing this, Mansur catches Dr. Smith's eye and points toward Murshid. Mansur's raised eyebrows exclaim loudly: This man could be the future of Esalen if they'd let him in the door! Just as Mansur used to think ingestion of LSD by world leaders could bring peace to mankind, he now believes the truth embodied by Murshid is the answer to everybody's question.

I don't know, until I see Murshid wrote (in a letter to Sharab and Paul, November 14, 1968) that some of his fellow students started the Esalen

Institute and "they are as afraid of real mystics and real mystical experiences as many whites now are of the coloreds." Mansur says to Murshid, "Sometimes a trip to the store is a better lesson than the lesson." "Yah," Murshid replies with vigor, "but don't tell anyone." Mansur is referring to a visit to the Persian shop on Telegraph Avenue in Berkeley, where we stop between the interview and the dance class. "I get a little bit in the *Madzub* state when I'm in a store like that," Murshid quips. Here's a definition of *Madzubs* by Hazrat Inayat Khan.

When I became familiar with the strange life of the dervishes I admired the best in them and was able to recognize the *Madzubs*, who are the extremists among them. These are so absorbed in the inner vision that they are absolutely unconscious of the external needs of life. Sometimes they are both fed and clothed by others; their neglect of the physical self and their irresponsibility towards the world makes it seem at first sight that they are insane, but at times, by their miraculous powers over phenomena, they are distinguished as *Madzub*. They are understood to be the controllers of the elements, some with regard to certain portions of land or waters and some even for the whole world. Their thoughts, words, and actions are truly found to be those of God Almighty. The word is scarcely spoken before the action is accomplished. Each atom of this universe seems to be awaiting their command. (*The Sufi Message of Hazrat Inayat Khan*, vol.12, pp.143-44)

Walking away from the store, Murshid says he has big jobs for me. "Not hard, big!" In later years I have to deal with an issue the therapist calls "grandiosity." I trace its origin to Murshid. No doubt, the distinction between functional genius working on world issues and clinical pathology is blurry. Murshid's letter of August 30, 1968 to Paul Reps reveals grandiosity in the line, "If God permits Sam to go to India with Krishnadas it will become a matter of great import."

The same Krishnadas, a disciple who teaches yoga, comes today and Murshid jokes about travel. Does Krishnadas want to travel "to the North Pole?" Murshid asks. "Yes," says Krishnadas. "Tierra del Fuego?" "Yes," says Krishnadas. "You want to visit the North and South Pole?" "Yes," says Krishnadas. "Then Mansur and I will go to India." "Aww," says Krishnadas, unaware he is about to be gratified in another way. Vegetarian Krishnadas is so hungry as he stands in Murshid's kitchen, he announces, "I could even eat a cheeseburger." Murshid immediately produces some cheese from his refrigerator. "I wouldn't have given it out if Krishnadas hadn't asked for it. You know I said we'd go to Starview for lunch." Murshid says. In the middle of Krishnadas eating the cheese, Murshid says, "This is all we'll have time for" [i.e., cheese but no burger].

As we walk back from a nearby bakery carrying a banana cream pie for dessert, Murshid refers to the cheese incident with Krishnadas. "That's the way you do things," he says. "You've got to listen to every voice as if it were the voice of God."

The dance class has developed from an outdoor "spiritual" (meaning "breath") Saturday walkabout for a few of us to a full fledged training session. First, we embodied in walks the qualities of high beings in *darshan* (see August 18, 1968); now we move to Murshid's "favorite," a concentration on Jesus. As we sit around the walls of Murshid's townhouse garage, he concentrates on Jesus and begins to walk. After several circulations around the oval of the single-car garage, Murshid invites us all to join in and do as he is doing. Make no mistake about it, concentrating on Jesus puts us all in a high state; no words, just concentration.

Later, when we walk concentrating on the solar plexus, Murshid says, perhaps answering a silent question, "It doesn't have to be in the heart." He explains that concentrating on the *hara* (the Japanese designation for the solar plexus) plus the Saturn rhythm produces an energetic deliberateness. Giving another lesson on the varieties of touch and the subtleties of communication, Murshid hooks little fingers with each individual in turn and promenades around the circle. At one point Murshid says, "Well, let's see who's intuitive. Does anyone know why this class is hard to teach?" Mansur interrupts Akbar, who has his hand up, and blurts out, "Because it's hard not to go high," implying it's difficult to teach when you can't stay grounded. "Exactly!" Murshid says. Then we go outside.

We use Precita Park, a several block rectangle of grass and trees with a few swings at one end, as a venue for the dance class. This serves several purposes. For one, it answers any possible neighborhood speculation about Murshid's activities. After all, an increasing stream of cars and people is coming to Murshid's door. Now all can see the old man wears a burnoose and does circle dances with young people who sing and chant foreign phrases. In San Francisco, this does not raise many eyebrows. Another purpose the park serves is that the blessing dance Murshid plans for today requires room for a large circle. Blessings are personal, one on one affairs. At this stage, the blessing dance is the dervish dance. In this, the outside circle repeats forms of the Sufi *ziker*, while inside the circle one person dances with Murshid, repeating different phrases. Murshid and his partner continue on in counterpoint to the chorus-like chant of the outer circle until Murshid chooses another partner; and so it goes on until everyone has received a blessing. A blessing is thus defined as sharing the energy and rhythm of the teacher.

After the break, Mansur reminds Murshid of somebody's question: *Why did Murshid's left arm rise as he walked doing concentrations?* Murshid reiterates some different blessings: the Bishop's blessing, which can be done with angles in the elbows; the healing blessing... Mansur impatiently interrupts, "The question was, 'Why did the arm rise?'" "Because I got high!" Murshid says, at a loss for a more analytical explanation.

As I finish writing the events of this day at 2 A.M., I contrast the depression I felt yesterday with the joy I feel today. There were high times that description doesn't convey. Saying it was so conveys even less. I go out for a walk with tears of joy. No wonder spiritual teachers in the East are so esteemed. Murshid gives us such joy. I am inspired to write a long ecstatic poem.

August 30, 1968, Friday

Before getting to the purpose of his letter to Paul Reps, Murshid reiterates what has already been written in these pages "about the forthcoming apparent successful ending to the 'war' against the General Semanticists"; that "those opposed to the G.S. people are starting two papers"; that "the alliance with Prof. Huston Smith of MIT is on firm basis"; that "Sam has discontinued several classes..."; and that Auroville (the Sri Aurobindo ashram) executives have been "expecting Sam to help them out both with money and errands." He comments, "It is ridiculous. They have refused... [to get import permits and have denied]...the existence of Sufis."
Murshid continues, "The basic reason for writing...THE SCHOOL."

There is now not a single cloud in the sky or anything standing in the way but action. I don't know where to begin... When Sam asked God—and Sam does just that—about living at the Ranch in Novato, God answered him in the negative but said Sam might be living near there. Now a group of disciples has selected a place for a *khankah* in the town of Novato just a little over two miles from the Ranch. Our first meeting showed we might raise the capital, and after that it would be easy. The rent would be less than Sam alone pays now. So there is a good chance that Sam will move near to Novato and then take over for the time the spiritual overseeing. It is too early but it looks fine.

Tonight at an Indian dance performance, Murshid tells Reps, he expects to "address the present Ambassador from India... Tuesday is the 'summit' Buddhist meeting and Thursday the Vietnamese Art Exhibit!" The dance class, he says, "is the best of all. There is no nonsense about the objective fulfillment of SALAT and the prowess in self-effacement is affecting an ever greater number of people... And there is a strange re-invigoration of body, heart and soul which one experiences without being able to understand."

August 31, 1968, Saturday

In summary, several things occur to me this week. Are they tests, or what?

In this [thing called] initiation, there is a great deal that is amusing...; sometimes the teacher gives the pupil such tests that he does not know where he is, or whether a thing is true or false. (Hazrat Inayat Khan, *The Path of Initiation and Discipleship*, vol.10 of *The Sufi Message of Hazrat Inayat Khan*, p.64)

All of a sudden, Murshid takes my teacup while we're sitting at his kitchen table and drinks out of it. Why? I dunno. Another time, Murshid takes my pen and pockets it, not hearing my barely audible objection. Or consider this one, which started last Tuesday. Mansur went with Murshid to Father Blighton's. He overheard Murshid tell Father Blighton that he was discontinuing some classes; then, Murshid said, "Be sure to take names when I come next time to your place [to deliver the weekly lecture on mystical Christianity]."

So today after Murshid's lecture at the Holy Order of MANS, the chauffeur Mansur sits in his chair for a while after the talk, then decides to leave without signing the guest book. "I've signed before, Father, I guess I'll not sign again," Mansur says as he ambles out. Suddenly, Father Blighton asks to see Mansur privately. Did Murshid put him up to this? Instantly uptight, Mansur tells Father Blighton that a group of us hope to move in with Murshid in Novato. My purpose is to broadcast loud and clear my loyalty to Murshid. Father Blighton is not moved, but says very seriously and intimidatingly, "Do you want to realize the Self? You haven't, have you? You people act like it takes five years or something." The pressure is on. It's the Christian conversion thing. Born again or mystical Holy Order of MANS, it doesn't matter. They put it to you. I can feel myself start to get warm. Mansur gathers himself and says, "I'm realizing all the time. No, I haven't realized yet." I don't know what to say about my overdue enlightenment. The whole thing just makes me feel very self-conscious. None would say, "Yes, *I* have realized," and put themselves first like that, would they? The Bible begins, "In the beginning, God..." and in the world of realization modesty should forbid one saying, "Yes, I have got it," shouldn't it? Even though Murshid himself said it in the story he tells about his spiritual brother, Phra Sumanglo (Robert Clifton), who said, "We ain't got it Sam." "Well, we got it," Murshid boomed in the retelling, giving me unwavering confidence in the one I followed. I reject the implied invitation to "realize the self" at the Holy Order of MANS under the guidance of Father Blighton.

September 1, 1968, Sunday

I guess I passed the tests. Tonight Murshid bestows his green robe upon Mansur. It's the robe that Jehanara made for Murshid. It's the one he has been wearing to teach classes.

Chapter 8

The Witness

It is time for somebody to present Indian Cosmic Metaphysics. I have. It works... Indian Cosmic Metaphysics—and I have to use some very poor English equivalents—has the "super-worlds" of "mind", "intelligence" and "love." Mind is above the manifest, Intelligence is above and beyond analytical mind, Love is above and beyond Intelligence (but not always separate) and Cosmic Unity is above and beyond and yet absolutely penetrating the others. This is the simplest way to put it. Our dualistic, Aristotelian culture does not understand interpenetration. Love operates in the physical as gravitation, adhesion, cohesion and keeps the cells of the body together. An exceedingly particularized, analytical selectivity has made a certain derivative aspect of this Love appear as the whole... A New Race is manifesting to whom Intelligence and Integration are as natural as analysis, separation and dialectics were to the old... The New Race is here—[the one] Bulwer-Lytton, H.G. Wells, Sri Aurobindo and others predicted. Evolution does not stop with the physical, it includes the psychic... And beyond the psychic there is another tremendous sphere, the super universe of Heart. (Murshid's letter to Dr. Oliver Reiser, September 8, 1968)

September 4, 1968, Wednesday

As chairman at a meeting of Buddhists held yesterday, Murshid was a reluctant referee. Murshid wrote, "You must remember here that Sam's position is schizoid: in his ego capacity he sees both sides: in his initiatory capacity he sees only the initiatory side." Igniting a display of local spiritual political fireworks, Iru Price, Lama Govinda's host, set off Neville Warwick, a practitioner of Vajrayana (esoteric) Buddhism, when he announced himself as Govinda's chief local representative. Warwick, who was Price's initiator, challenged the appointment.

We learn from Murshid's four page letter to Warwick today, which is short on facts and long on nuanced statements, that at one point during Warwick's blistering attack on Price, Murshid asked Warwick, "Where is the Compassion?" Murshid then suggested that "your answer should have been and will be in the presence of the Lama and Iru: 'Where is Fudo? What is Fudo doing?' And Iru would be compelled to affirm or deny the initiations of another person. ["compelled", presumably, because Iru was present when Master Seo initiated both he and Murshid.] If he does not affirm I shall tell the Lama that the American people are not going to accept any egocentric as his representative, no matter how many ceremonial ordinations; that the *Dharma* is not based on ordinations but on attainment."

Murshid discusses at length the importance of hierarchy and the processes of initiation ("The democratic pseudo-psychological attitude has nothing to do with cosmic law, or cosmic principles."), the way of Dharma ("Dharma is based on Truth and not on the position of ego-individuals."), and the meaning of Sufism ("Sufism is presumably the integration of all the teachings of all the Perfect Personalities of all times."). He also refers to the curious business of having received the "Bodhisattvic Vow" from his Sufi teacher Hazrat Inayat Khan, "after he [Khan] had accepted initiation from Nyogen Senzaki. This was based on the actual experience of common participation in Enlightenment." He mentions further his recollection of a Buddhist scandal in 1915. Seemingly emboldened by the recitation of this ancient tale, Murshid writes, "And Iru is now forced to face the very, very hard fact that his oath to the Sangha is useless because we both were under oath to Master Seo and he has refused to accept the valid testimonials of a fellow *Sangha* (community of Buddhists) member so far *on anything connected with the Dharma.*"

Additionally, Murshid writes, "I should like the Lama to compel Iru to listen to the words of Phra Sumangalo when he entered my rooms in Clementina Street on his last visit. I should like him to have to listen and I should prefer your being there. According to all Hierarchal, Dharmic and Patriarchal Law, he would be compelled to do what he has never done: ACCEPT ONE SOLID TEACHING OF ONE SOLID BUDDHIST SCHOOL! Any one."

Murshid concludes by suggesting that Warwick treat Iru Price as Murshid treats Alan Watts. "You are only taking the position with regard to Iru I have taken to Alan Watts. I cannot be a hypocrite and demand or even request you act different toward Iru than I have toward Alan, but I see today all possibilities of Alan some day, somehow, reaching the door to humility (not humiliation) and becoming a devotee." The issue churns in Murshid's mind; another amazing letter to Warwick follows tomorrow.

September 5, 1968, Thursday

There was an initiatory bond between Murshid and Neville Warwick. Murshid spoke yesterday to Warwick of his obligations to him "as Initiator and as fellow spiritual traveler." Regarding Warwick's fight to oppose Iru Price as Lama Govinda's chief representative in the San Francisco area, Murshid notifies Warwick in a letter today that "you must not fight without weapons and you are to be given all the weapons." What are these weapons? Nothing less than the Dharma transmission, which Murshid defines in an article published in *The Western Buddhist* (Autumn, 1959) as "something more than philosophical truth. We have [with Dharma transmission] living truth. Buddha-transmission goes from enlightened person to enlightened person and this has been from the time of Sakyamuni [Lord Buddha] to now. This is also called 'transmission of *Dharma*' " (see the entire article in *Sufi Vision and Initiation,* pp.125-29). Murshid has Nyogen Senzaki's private papers, which include the Dharma transmission line of descent. Murshid tells Warwick,

> It has the complete line of Patriarchal Descent from Buddha to Hui Neng [the Sixth Patriarch] to Shaku Soyen. And I am not only empowered by the descent from Nyogen Senzaki but also by the letters from Soen Nakagawa to Paul Reps to offer the same Dharma Transmission [that I have] offered so far only to Senzaki's last private secretary [see September 25, 1967]—and it worked. This will both satisfy your stand the other night but it will be given to you personally *through* not *by* me, in both hierarchal and patriarchal capacity.... It has to be made clear that this is one line of descent, called Patriarchal which also Master Seo said I have. It must continue and you must not fight without weapons and you are to be given all the weapons.

September 8, 1968, Sunday

In yesterday's letter to Dr. Oliver Reiser at the University of Pittsburgh's philosophy department, Murshid complained about their mutual friend and Reiser biographer, Julie Medlock. Julie's apparent refusal to obtain import permits continues to frustrate Murshid's ability to send her supplies. Does Murshid hope Oliver will prompt Julie? It's a method Murshid often uses to deliver a message to a student. The letter ends with, "I do know this will be my last semester at the University of California here." The coded message is: *I'm getting too busy now to study.* Today's letter to Reiser has a headline: THE OBJECTIVE REALIZATION OF PROJECTS. In the week ahead Murshid anticipates "a week of financial and legal transactions ..." He is easing into this. Murshid describes Auroville's practice of "getting prominent people on the bandwagon and letting the 'peasants' contribute." Then he quotes Sheyla, who said, "Those people do not belong to Sri Aurobindo, we are Sri Aurobindo's people." Afterwards comes the discussion of Indian Cosmic Metaphysics, which appears in this chapter's epigraph. Under the headline AUROVILLE, Murshid announces:

> I am now compelled to manifest my own Auroville which may (or may not) be called the GARDEN OF INAYAT. We are seeking no further outside help. We have the money, the intelligence, and such mutual Love as I have not yet seen in a group. This person is the Guru-Murshid and the others are disciples. But we shall be near one large new type of commune and in touch with others and our efforts can lead to [the] adaptation of principles.

Months later (in a letter to Sharab and Paul, November 14, 1968), Murshid finds fresh ways to describe the occupants of his newly established

128

commune. "They are alive, and having had some kind of 'high' experience with Psychedelics, they welcome rather than shudder when one has the real mystical insight."

September 10, 1968, Tuesday

Jehanara and Mansur provide the funds to purchase the Garden of Inayat. Jehanara uses the proceeds from her father's Rudolph the Red-Nosed Reindeer royalties (seriously) and I cash my $3,000 life insurance policy. We buy the house at 910 Railroad Avenue in Novato for $27,000. My altruism blunts my self interest, and I omit inserting my name on the title. Murshid does not guide me otherwise, but describes my offering as like a contribution to a church. [It does not remain a "church," however, and as the house's value nears a million dollars I repeatedly remind myself that that was what it was supposed to be.] During the purchase, while negotiating with a hostile coven of real estate people, Mansur silently invokes Murshid. Reliance on the teacher helps Mansur succeed in conducting this difficult business transaction. Just after Mansur invokes Murshid at the real estate office, Murshid gives Hassan—Jehanara's husband to be—the practice to feel Murshid, to talk to him, to act as if he were in his presence; in short, the *tassawuri Murshid* practice I had spontaneously adopted.

September 11, 1968, Wednesday

Murshid speaks during the meeting at Sheyla's tonight of the pain and joy he experienced at the hospital while visiting disciple Vashti, who broke her leg and suffered other injuries in an auto accident. Murshid uses these hospital visits to illustrate his compassion in a letter on the 14th to Buddhist Eugene Wagner. Mansur feels what Murshid feels when visiting Vashti. It is an increase in sympathy for me to feel what Murshid feels. Each time we visit Vashti at the hospital, Mansur practices *Ya Shafee, Ya Kafee* (God is the Healer, God is the Remedy) from the moment we head toward the door until we leave her room. After the second visit, I notice my hands are highly charged.

What most impresses Murshid at the meeting tonight is the presence of Esalen psychologist Fritz Perls's secretary. Murshid writes (in a letter September 12, 1968 to Jeremy Ets-Hokim), "There was an event in Sheyla's house which was a demonstration of real Love. If I did not catch Don [Hayakawa] I certainly had a retired secretary of the famous psychiatrist, Fritz Perls, and this was, perhaps, a bigger and more important 'fish'. She found a 'family' which operates as a family with mutual love and joy and togetherness and no nonsense." To Vocha on the 25th, Murshid notes, "The visit here of one of Fritz Perls's secretaries was amusing. She was suffering from one of the very type of problem for which he [Perls] is *an expert* and therefore a representative of *Etcience* [a pun on a General Semantics publication]." Mansur is busy as always during the Mill Valley meeting at Sheyla's, and after, Murshid comes home with us, altering his expressed plan to stay with Sheyla. Tomorrow, Thursday, Mansur will probably drive Murshid back to San Francisco.

September 12, 1968, Thursday

It's 2 A.M. I'm still up. My mind's alert. I think of Murshid here a week ago telling me while we walked, "During my early morning walk, the whole hierarchy was with me." My desire to learn more takes me to the teachings published in *The Unity of Religious Ideals*.

According to the Sufi conception, there are seven degrees in the spiritual hierarchy, which can be distinguished as different stages of responsiveness, in other words, of higher initiation... They are: *Pir, Buzurg, Wali, Ghauth, Qutb, Nabi, Rasul*... The work of the *Pir* is helping individuals toward the unfoldment of their soul, and that of the *Buzurg* is to help by the power of his soul those who wish to advance spiritually. *Wali* is the initiate whose will has come close to the divine will, and he shows it in the harmony which reigns in his own life, not only with his friends, but he will also be in harmony with an adversary... He may control a community, keeping it on the right track... *Ghauth*...gives up his personality wholly to the divine guidance, and wherever this Ghauth may be there will be created an atmosphere of protection from all kinds of dangers such as floods, storms, plagues, or famines. *Qutb*...governs a country or a nation spiritually. *Nabi* is the apostle, called in Sanskrit *Bodhisattva*, whose spirit reflects the Spirit of Guidance. His work is mainly the giving of the message in the form of warning, awakening, preaching, teaching, and inspiring those to whom he may be sent. *Rasul* is the world messenger, who comes for all people at the time of the world's need, and brings with him that inspiration, influence, and power which will harmonize humanity. No man in the world has the power to give these higher initiations. They are given by God Himself, and the initiates prove their initiations not in their claims, but in their works. (*The Sufi Message of Hazrat Inayat Khan*, vol.9, pp.128-31)

I think of Murshid making allusions to himself as a reincarnation of the Tibetan teacher Marpa, vis-à-vis Dr. Warwick in the role of Milarepa. These allusions were expressed publicly, especially after Murshid wrote Warwick (September 5, 1968), "It has been made clear in extending the consciousness into the unseen, or in the descent of this consciousness to the seen that it was no game that you replied of your being Milarepa to my statement that for practical purposes I function as Marpa here. If it is not 'real' it may become real." Marpa was the guru who worked like a miller, grinding Milarepa's ego to shreds. The story, in a nutshell, goes something like this.

Milarepa, the great Buddhist saint and poet of Tibet, was born A.D. 1052 and died in 1135. Following the early death of his father, his relatives seized his inheritance. After many years of humiliation, he was persuaded by his mother to take revenge upon the wrongdoers through magic. He succeeded, through his sincere devotion and service to a teacher of sorcery, in obtaining a powerful spell which he used to assassinate many of his relatives. Afterwards, he repented, and determined to seek salvation by devoting the rest of his life to the practice of the *Dharma*. When Milarepa came to Marpa, Marpa relentlessly put him on trial by imposing upon him severe mental and physical tasks. Milarepa was ordered to build, single-handed, one house after another on a desolate mountain, then to tear them down again for no apparent reason. After years, Marpa finally initiated Milarepa as a disciple. Then, for eleven continuous months, Milarepa meditated alone in a cave. One day, while meditating in the cave, he fell asleep and dreamed that he returned home and saw the bones of his mother lying in the ruins of his house, and his only sister as a vagabond beggar. He awoke weeping bitterly, and longed to see his mother. He left Marpa and went back to his home village, where all the premonitions of his dream were confirmed. He made a solemn vow that he would meditate on a remote mountain uninterruptedly until he reached the Ultimate Enlightenment. For twelve consecutive years he meditated alone in a cave, living on nothing but nettles, until his whole body became greenish in hue. Finally, he earned his reward—the realization of Ultimate Enlightenment. (Condensed from *The Hundred Thousand Songs of Milarepa*, pp.xv-xvii)

This whole business recalls Murshid making allusions to Vilayat as Jelal-ed-din Rumi and himself as Shams-i-Tabriz. I see something about this phenomenon I didn't see earlier: these relationships are cosmic and day to day functional.

Three times in a short letter today, Murshid tells Jeremy Ets-Hokim about the commune he's starting, "which may (or may not) become an example for others to follow." The *khankah*, Murshid reiterates, "could be an example to the *Esquire*-utopias which seem to be growing in number. There is no opposition to them, only they do not seem to be building manhood and womanhood." There's a lot of throwaway wisdom in this letter; for example, when Murshid says, "It is forbidden to me to ignore the criticisms of others. That is an opportunity to explore both oneself and the Divine Wisdom which is in the sphere." And the answer to my big unspoken question: *If we're starting a commune, can everybody use my stuff?* No, writes Murshid. "If we are going to have a commune it should begin with communion on the spiritual plane and then a willingness to share in the thought world. The common sharing of things should come later. This is my position."

Mansur describes Sufism in a letter to his mother's Sunday School teacher and does *tassawuri Murshid* when he writes, "There are more Sufis than Jews; the last President of India, Dr. S. Radhakrishnan is a Sufi; the present President of Pakistan, Zakir Hussein, is a Sufi; but as far as the United States of America is concerned, these 40 or 50 million people do not exist." These are things Mansur heard Murshid say.

Friday, Jemila and I will go early to the City for breakfast with Murshid. Barbara is babysitting somewhere, and she will keep Nathan for the rest of the day while we go to the dance class. We don't know Murshid anticipates an acrimonious Buddhist meeting after the dance class. Murshid told Ets-Hokim yesterday, "The test of Love comes when one has to face enmity. I shall have to do this, in a sense, tomorrow night but there I shall be facing enough intelligence as to feel optimistic."

Lois Robinson and Barbara Moffat

September 14, 1968, Saturday

My guess is that Iru Price didn't show up at yesterday's Buddhist "summit" meeting, and the dramatic scenarios Murshid rehearsed in his letters to Warwick didn't happen. Following up today, Murshid writes Buddhist brother Eugene Wagner, "But people who have had Enlightenment and *Satori* (a sudden awakening) experiences are on the one hand by-passed by so many of the persons present and absent last night..."

"Last night," Murshid continues, "at one time knowledge of history was considered a virtue, at another time ignorance, and sometimes both of these views came from the same *anatta* [no self] -person." After the meeting, Murshid tells Wagner, what happened was that "in my night meditation my whole history of connections with Buddhist-Buddhist causes came in a flash." He lists M.T. Kirby (aka Sogaku Shaku), Rabia Martin, the Rhys-Davids, Paul Carus, Ashvaghosa, Scherbatsky, and Zoso Fernandez. "By that time," he writes, "I had had the *Alaya* [short for *alaya-vijnana*, universal consciousness] experience. The whole depository of mind comes at an instance without any of the processes covered by analytics or dialectics." In another revelation, similar to the one about his Sufi teacher administering the "Bodhisattvic Vow" (letter to Neville Warwick, September 4, 1968), Murshid tells Wagner that he learned Indian Cosmic Metaphysics from a Zen man. "Where and how did Sam Lewis learn Indian Cosmic Psychology? HE LEARNED IT SUDDENLY FROM THAT FORGOTTEN ZEN MONK, SOKEI-AN SASAKI. Sam learned more Indian wisdom from this Zen monk than from all the Indians he ever met..."

While Murshid wrote Wagner, Mansur visited psychic Lois Robinson at her home in the East Bay, an hour and a half from Bolinas. Murshid knew about Lois, had been to her, and recently went again. Murshid's renewed interest in Lois motivated me to make an appointment to see her. It is like a two hour *darshan*. Lois tells Mansur he was clairvoyant and had healing power. The past lives Lois enumerates for me were: a Pharaoh in Egypt, a Christ-conscious shepherd near Jerusalem, a spiritual teacher in India with many disciples and a dove that stayed on my shoulder, an American Indian with love and a feeling for nature and God, a samurai who knew killing, and a political prisoner in France. As an inflammatory journalist, I

had written and published humanitarian papers, for which I'd been imprisoned in a French castle tower, ball and chain around my ankle; hence, my present life weak ankle.

The visit to Lois explodes Mansur's idea that being a spiritual teacher frees one from the cycle of rebirths. It is news to me that I had been a spiritual teacher before; secondly, if I were a spiritual teacher in India in a past life, my idealistic assumption would be that I was fully enlightened. If I were fully enlightened, what was I doing back here now? I answer: *striving for God-consciousness*. But why again? It puzzles me. Do you have to keep accomplishing this thing? Lois's revelations rock my conceptions.

Lois Robinson

All of us in Bolinas—Moineddin and Fatima, Jehanara and Hassan, Mansur and Jemila—are invited for dinner in Sausalito, a town on San Francisco Bay just north of the Golden Gate Bridge. Our hostess is Nancy Fish: Murshid's goddaughter, an actress in John Korty's second movie and a guest recently on television's *The Dating Game*.

September 15, 1968, Sunday

Jemila and Mansur, who was on the crew, are supposed to drive into the City for the 11 o'clock premiere of John Korty's third movie, *Riverrun*. Wrong. It is cancelled and rescheduled. The premiere will be Friday, September 27th. A corollary to yesterday's reading at psychic Lois Robinson's is my feeling today: *Murshid was my disciple in India*.

After spending the day at Murshid's waiting for the open house he has here every Sunday, I think: *Mansur is being tested for stress by the hustle bustle atmosphere in this house*. Also, Mansur is sure Murshid is giving him timidity tests (to develop manhood?). They are little things that require me to stand up to Murshid, talk back, *treat him as an equal*. No example yet, but there will be. Tonight Murshid speaks of two men he has absolute trust in; of course, Mansur thinks he is one. Murshid explains, "This means we can rise in consciousness together."

It is very high here. The class learns *tassawuri Mohammed*, instruction in how to attune to the being of Mohammed. To the question: *How did you feel after the walk of Mohammed?* Mansur answers, "Tall, majestic." Excellent!" Murshid responds. Murshid asks Mansur to lead three *OMs* and Murshid plays some music after class. There has been the feeling that if Murshid travels inside the U.S. before the India trip, Mansur will accompany him. This comes to pass. "The India trip" is spoken about so frequently it seems a fait accompli. It doesn't happen.

September 17, 1968, Tuesday

Unless I am mistaken, Murshid's four page report today to his old friend and spiritual sister, Vera Van Voris, is an invitation to reconnect. They were both pupils of Rabia Martin and Hazrat Inayat Khan. Murshid ends the letter, "We still have open house on Sundays and Thursdays, although you would be welcome any time excepting when one is out of town." Murshid's report pointedly notes the growth of his following "to about 60 initiated disciples," and mentions the interest of three of Van Voris's contemporaries: "At least Gavin Arthur and Gina Cerminara investigated. They were curious and now they are happy. Things went bang-bang and Paul Reps came to an overflowing meeting..." Included in the report is the story of the creation of the *khankah*. "We held a preliminary meeting and decided to meet again in ten days to see how funds could be raised. We did not meet again. Within the allotted time we were oversubscribed without Murshid Sam putting up one cent!" Murshid reports his creation of spiritual dancing. "It has many offshoots. The first is Astrological-Occult walking and breathing... The next is the Mystical Walk based on knowledge of the Elements... [and] dervish dancing. This is the synthesis of living dervish dancing of many schools.... But the highest phase is the Spiritual Dancing based on the names of God, and it has brought more Joy than any of the methods used so far, tremendous response and it is difficult also for the Teacher because if he goes 'high' there is no control."

Gavin Arthur

Not until Murshid dies does Vera Van Voris make contact with Murshid's group, receive the title Murshida from Pir Vilayat at the Garden of Allah one Thanksgiving in the early seventies, and begin to teach Murshid's disciples.

September 18, 1968, Wednesday

A very special training session this morning occurs when Murshid takes me to the park. We are in San Francisco—I had slept over. We walk together doing the Sun, Moon, Mars, Venus, and Mercury walks. After that warmup, Murshid gives me a breath concentration: the astrological conjunction of Jupiter plus Saturn, to approximate the walk of Prophet Mohammed called *tassawuri Mohammed*. All this is a continuation of the work begun last Sunday.

After Mansur drives Murshid to Sheyla's, thirty minutes away in Marin County, the ranch kids come in with a rush. Murshid can see I am susceptible to this agitation. He calls me aside, has me sit in front of him, and tells me to do the Mohammed breath that he showed me this morning. Later Murshid says, referring to *tassawuri Mohammed*, "This is good protection for lots of things."

September 20, 1968, Friday

It is late Friday afternoon. Just as Murshid finishes telling me how people come to his house just before class late in the afternoon, a time he wants no visitors, long-time disciples Clark and Ernie walk in. They don't come that often, and are probably ignorant of Murshid's wish for privacy at this time. They expect to stay and eat with Murshid. How coincidental that Murshid is talking about something just before it happens. Now I understand it wasn't a coincidence. Murshid felt them coming, and what Murshid said to me were the words that their approach prompted him to say. When Clark comes into the room, Mansur is overcome with nervousness, as at the real estate office, or when in the presence of the disapproving born again Christians. Mansur needs to learn to deal with such vibrations.

September 21, 1968, Saturday

When Mansur stayed overnight Friday at Murshid's, Jemila rode back to Bolinas with Moineddin and Fatima. This allows Murshid to fully utilize Mansur and his vehicle to run errands Saturday. We hit Haig's, a gourmet shop on Clement, the Pakistani Consulate on Pacific, and a stationery store on Fillmore. We come home via the freeway to meet Frank (Halim, his future treasurer), who stays for lunch. After lunch and before dance class, Murshid dictates a letter to commune leader Lou Gottlieb, the bass player for the Limeliters, a popular 1960s folk trio. Gottlieb made headlines recently for deeding his land to God. Gottlieb's commune, Morning Star Ranch, north of Novato, uses a symbol that Murshid thinks is ill-chosen. There is no carbon copy of today's letter, but next year, Murshid writes from Lama Foundation, "I have explained [the consequences of] the ignorance of symbology and that hard fact [is] that Lou Gottlieb is in jail [for drug possession] because he is a master of 'humility' and closed ears. He is receiving the natural outcome of his own ignorance-egotisms on symbology."

At his house tonight, Murshid asks Clark if he will take him to the library to get some Sufi books. "There will probably be some work to do typing," Murshid says. "Many of the books are out of print." Mansur thinks: *I'm the typist. Why does Clark get to do it?* Sensitive to my thoughts, Murshid looks at me, smiles, and tells me, "You'll have more work. I want to see you afterwards." The moral is: *Do not be envious of others. There's plenty of work for everyone.* After the dance class, which concentrates more on walk than dance, the group does dervish dances. Then Murshid dictates a letter to Vilayat and Murshid and I go for a Chinese dinner at the Starview.

September 24, 1968, Tuesday

Murshid notes important events of the day in a letter to Vocha Fiske. Sheila and Dara left at last for "a summit conference in real Asia where certain leaders of the really real world will meet to study international problems"; the mail brought a copy of *The Bamboo Basket*; and Murshid "was surprised to see that a lot of his words, taken down on a tape recorder, have been published." In the evening, Saadia Khawar Khan calls. Murshid has given Saadia *Science and Sanity*. She likes it, so Murshid tells Vocha, "Now with her in the country Sam will go to Powell St. [Fields Book Store] with his check book and start buying." Murshid describes the General Semantics bunch as "a small group of people utterly without scientific training." He mentions Don Hayakawa: "You would think that a part Asian, part Occidental personality would be the first to champion such an amalgam, but it just ain't so, darling, it jest ain't so."

September 25, 1968, Wednesday

Mansur is present at Murshid's when Murshid gets Mansur's postcard, which isn't signed. I selected four verses (28-31) from Chapter 40 in Isaiah because they alluded to walking without fatigue. The last concludes: "But they that wait upon the LORD shall renew their strength; they shall mount up with wings as eagles; *they shall run, and not be weary; and they shall walk and not faint* [emphasis mine]." Mansur figured his omniscient Murshid will know who sent it. But Murshid doesn't know. Murshid says, "I think I know who this might be from: one of my old disciples, who was always preaching." Yikes, this wasn't my intention. Mansur says, "I confess. I sent it."

Mansur experiences a conflict of a new type at Murshid's today. He catches himself *not* surrendering to the teacher. Rather, I finish what I have started before responding to Murshid's request. ("Finish what you start" is a behavior freshly learned from Murshid.) "Take the typewriter off the table," Murshid says, while Mansur is en route to get an envelope to address. It is necessary to balance maintaining my concentration with responding to the will of the teacher. It is hard.

Murshid and Mansur are one hour's drive north of the City, in Marin County. Mansur forgot to bring Shamcher's letter to Murshid and a copy of Murshid's letter to Shamcher, which Murshid dictated to me in San Francisco. The forgotten letter begins, "It is Wednesday afternoon. Within two hours we shall be in Marin County. *Sam will show your letter and a carbon of this* [emphasis mine] to two different disciples..." Even though I typed those words, I required a direct order to remember to bring the letter. The two disciples who lose out because of my forgetfulness are Hassan Herz, who is opening a print shop, and Phillip Davenport of *The San Francisco Oracle*. But the real loser is Shamcher, who is looking for somebody to publish his memoirs.

That is not all I forget. There are some phonograph records as well. It's another instance of failing to respond without a direct order. It is a bad day, unless you have the attitude that problems are opportunities. At the time, Mansur writes: A wonderful day that reminds Mansur to be attentive to the desire and will of Murshid and to forget himself. Wake up, lad.

September 26, 1968, Thursday

In dream this morning, there is a buck deer [innocent aspect of self] that runs up to me. I face him fearlessly and am even thinking about trying to ride him like a horse, but I discard the idea. The image of a deer is what Hazrat Inayat Khan uses in *The Inner Life* to introduce the notion of *vairagya*, or indifference.

The characteristic of the deer, as described by the poets of India, is that when it is thirsty it runs about in the forests looking for water... And so is the thirst of a fine soul in this world. The soul of the spiritually-inclined man is constantly thirsty, looking for something, seeking for something; and when it thinks it has found it, the thing turns out to be different; and so life becomes a continual struggle and disappointment. And the result is that instead of taking interest in all things, a kind of indifference is produced; and yet in the real character of this soul there is no indifference, there is only love. Although life seems to make this soul indifferent, it cannot really become indifferent; and it is this state working through this life that gives a man a certain feeling, to which only a Hindu word is applicable, no other language having a word which can render this particular meaning so adequately. The Hindus call it *Vairagya* from which the term *Vairagi* (one who is indifferent) has come... When the *Vairagi* is still more developed in this feeling of *Vairagya*, then he becomes a lion... It is in this way that the lion-like soul of the deva, the angel-man, comes to the rescue of humanity. What is called the Master or Saint or Prophet or Sage is this developed *Vairagi*... (*The Sufi Message of Hazrat Inayat Khan*, vol.1, pp.99-101)

Another dream about feeding pizza to the birds is no doubt a result of Murshid's story of watching birds choose whole wheat Olompali ranch bread over Bimbo white bread. Such a dream gives me occasion to write: *Murshid and his small band of followers eat whole wheat breads and use brown rice as a dietary staple.*

In his archives, Murshid has a file for Rev. Cecil Gibbings of Longthrope Vicarage in Peterborough, England. Gibbings is a Sufi initiate and supporter of the Sufi Movement, the rival organization of Vilayat's Sufi Order. Both of Murshid's letters to him are written this month. On September 6, 1968, Murshid's theme—repeated eight times, like a mantra—is that he (Murshid) functions without permission from any corporation. Murshid reminds Rev. Gibbings that "God alone is the founder of Sufism." He continues, "I am amazed that you take the view that this is wrong and that a Sufi is now one who adheres to some modern corporation [the Sufi Movement] just organized in Holland. What this has to do with God I do not know; what it has to do with the actualities of Crucifixion and Resurrection I don't know." Murshid then taunts Rev. Gibbings with the fact that a local publication (*The San Francisco Oracle*) used the Sufi Invocation and "they did not ask permission from any corporation on the face of the earth and I do not believe any corporation is going to dare to do anything about it... The idea that one must join a corporation to become God-conscious is a challenge to Lord Solomon, that 'there is nothing new under the sun'."

Gibbons must have answered and told Murshid that Vilayat cast him off; hence, his embrace of the Sufi Movement. In his letter today, Murshid responds, "Of course I do not know anything about Vilayat casting you off. Well he cast me off. But then there is God and God lifted the veils. Besides Vilayat demonstrated proofs, proofs to the mystic, and they have been confirmed by members of other Sufi Orders..." Murshid continues in defense of Vilayat and suggests Gibbons's experience with him may have been a test: "My dear Brother, there is nobody that has turned this person down harder than his own present Pir-O-Murshid in Pakistan and it proved to be a test." But with what may forever preclude further correspondence, Murshid challenges the Christian reverend to consult Jesus. "If you are in touch with Lord Jesus Christ, why don't you ask Him and reply, instead of replying from another base? This would bring us together. If you are in *fana-fi-lillah*, then why won't you write, 'In the Name of God'?" Murshid ends where he began his first letter, which announces his lectures on First Corinthians, and suggests by example the path for Rev. Gibbons. "One returns to the chapter on 'Love' in the First Epistle to the Corinthians. One will continue to lecture on this splendid work."

138

September 28, 1968, Saturday

The Panoramic Highway winds through old growth redwoods on the way from Stinson Beach to Highway 101 and San Francisco. Experiencing an ecstasy with nature is how my day en route to Murshid's begins. Of all the letters I take in dictation today—Mohammed Cassim in Ceylon; Anandashram in India; Ruth, a disciple in New York; Shamcher—only a copy of Shamcher's remains. When Murshid receives a letter from Professor K.T. Merchant in India, he takes it as a sign he is to give Shamcher "full cooperation" in publishing his manuscripts. Merchant and "his Guru, so to speak," A.P. Wadia, "India's greatest economist," share "outlooks and experiences" with Shamcher. "So taking this as a sign, I have written to my disciple, Ruth...and enclose carbon herewith."

These typing sessions are consciousness altering experiences. Murshid goes high, I follow. Afterwards, eating or errand running grounds us. Today, we go to Fields Book Store. On this trip, Murshid announces that my role in the Astrological Dance Pageant, which he is formulating will be the Sun. Up until today, all I knew was what Murshid had said, "You're either going to be Sun or Jupiter, I must watch carefully." The eating ecstasy comes after the dance class. Murshid and Mansur go—for me, the second time this month—to Nancy Fish's in Sausalito for dinner with her and boyfriend Ralph Silver. As I drive away, Murshid says, "I am making you a witness to all of this." All of what? I'm satisfied, exhausted, happy, high. This? Yes.

September 29, 1968, Sunday

Today Mansur receives a warning from inside—*kids*! They are playing out in front. He runs thirty yards to the highway, where Nathan's playmate sits in the middle of the highway. It is the spur from Route 1 that runs along Bolinas Lagoon to Bolinas. Breathless, I scoop Summer up out of the road. Before going to Murshid's tonight Mansur opens volume I of *The Sufi Message* to the place he wants to read. After reading there, I look somewhere else. To what? *To a section about Guardian Angels.*

The Guardian Angel is a term known to many. This angelic protection comes to some souls on earth; souls who are walking on the earth, and yet are linked in some way or other with the heavenly spheres. Often one sees an innocent child being saved from an accident; and often a person is warned to save a child at the moment when it is in danger.

Contemplating the highway incident, I muse: *When you start listening, life becomes magic—miraculous—with God.* Intuition—always working, seldom heard—gets heard and...Bingo! Sometimes really dumb questions obsess you when you are on the spiritual path. You don't know they're dumb, you take them seriously. Such a question is on my mind tonight when I go to Murshid's, wondering: *How do you do fikar all night long,*

Summer and Nathan in Bolinas

even while sleeping? The idea behind this question is that of thinking of God "constantly." If I were rational, I could reason as follows: *Since doing fikar is to <u>consciously</u> attend to your thought, it's not possible to do fikar when you go <u>unconscious</u>.* I don't. To answer my dumb question, it takes Murshid reading the part in *World Is God* where Ramdas is asked, "How many hours did you spend sleeping when you were beginning your search for God?" Ramdas says he stayed up all night because he was afraid he would forget God's name. After the meeting Murshid gives me two letters to read. Both contain mention of people going without sleep. Mansur finally gets it: There is no esoteric way to be conscious when you are sleeping. Stay awake.

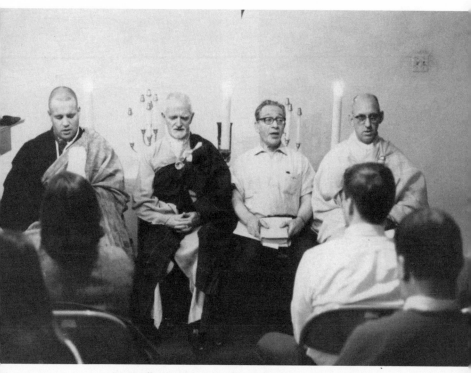

Dr. Neville Warwick, Joe Miller, Murshid, Rev. Eugene Wagner

Chapter 9

October and November 1968

In discussing these new developments with the housekeeper here, Fatima, Sam said, "I do not like to talk to you. I am your senior by many years in age. I am your spiritual teacher. But when I look into your eyes, I see nothing but Mother Krishnabai. Then I feel terrifically small." Fatima replied, "But I am Mother Krishnabai!" (Murshid's letter to Anandashram, November 7, 1968)

October 1, 1968, Tuesday

The news Murshid shares with Shamcher in a letter today is wholly about disciples. Some are moving to the new *khankah* in Novato, some are in India (Sheyla and Dara), Hassan published Murshid's poem *The Rejected Avatar* and will marry in two weeks. Murshid also mentions Phillip. Shamcher has asked Murshid for Phillip's address in order to pursue his own publishing agenda. "He [Phillip] comes to this house at least twice a week and I go to Larkspur at least once a week so we see a great deal of each other," Murshid writes.

He also works on projects at San Francisco State College... [one such project being] a big meeting for me for Thursday night the subject being "Sufi Philosophy"... In addition Phillip has already arranged that the next issue of *The Oracle* will be devoted more fully to Sufism. Last issue had the Invocation and "The Purity of Life" [a talk by Inayat Khan]. The reactions must have been good to warrant such a procedure. Or as Hazrat Inayat Khan said, "The Message is in the sphere; if I had not brought it somebody else would have." This is becoming objectively true.

October 3, 1968, Thursday

When Hazrat Inayat Khan appears in my dream tonight, I am deeply moved, feeling honored by a visitation of the highest guidance. Perhaps my psyche was prompted by Murshid staying at the house. In dream, Murshid is on the phone with Inayat Khan and I pass by. Murshid gives me the phone. At first, I don't say anything, and a long silence passes. Afterwards, Inayat Khan commends me on my silence. I don't remember his exact words; I remember feeling ashamed of mine. I experience a warm feeling, much like the one I got from Vilayat during the private interviews described in Chapter 5. (*Then, Vilayat, seeing the woman couldn't speak said, "Oh, the soul through the eyes." Yes, very nice, always talking to make them feel at ease, with an undertone of heart.*)

Referring to yesterday's visit by Moineddin and Mansur to the psychic Lois Robinson, Murshid says he sees Lois and him working closer together. Lois said she could see Mansur cutting his hair and beard on the spur of the moment. Mansur, indifferent to his hair and beard, kept them to play Prospero in *The Tempest.* Murshid says, "What would you do if we decided to put on the passion play, and you were St. John?" I don't remember how I respond, but of all the apostles, I like John best, so I begin copying The Gospel According to St. John today.

October 6, 1968, Sunday

During the meeting this evening, Murshid and Mansur simultaneously remember my fish in his refrigerator, and Murshid mentions it. This happens a lot. When Murshid eats at my house, he reads my mind that I want grace to be said, and he says it; or Murshid reads that I want an embrace when he leaves, and he gives me one.

Then there are times I wish Murshid wouldn't know my thoughts, like the night we celebrated his birthday at the Minerva Café, the Greek restaurant where I first encountered Greek dancing. Murshid saw my reticence to dance in public. He promptly had me stand and dance with him the Greek dance I'd taught him in private.

October 7, 1968, Monday

Intuitions keep coming about making an index for the writings of Inayat Khan. [An index was completed in 1969 and revised in 1979.] The depth and scope of the stories scattered throughout the twelve volumes of *The Sufi Message of Hazrat Inayat Khan* inspire me to collect them, like Arberry did for Rumi's. [*Tales: told by Hazrat Inayat Khan* was completed in 1975 and published by Omega Press in 1980 and 1991 and translated into Polish in 2005.]

October 9, 1968, Wednesday

During the day at his house, Murshid shows me how to support a friend. A certain Miss X has stolen disciple Renee's husband. Miss X is giving a party for Faune, Secretary Daniel's wife to be, and Murshid will not attend.

Later, when I ask the reason, Murshid says, "I am tired," but I know this isn't the whole truth. Murshid allows me to see what he is doing and shows me the virtue of standing by someone. Murshid wrote Neville Warwick September 4th, "Buddha did not say to speak 100% truth. He (whose words are by-passed by so many 'good' Buddhists) said, 'Speak the Truth with discretion.'"

October 11, 1968, Friday

Murshid tells why Murshida Martin failed: She was a hypocrite. She preached the psychic value of long hair, and then later cut her own. "Of all things," Murshid says, "*Sufis cannot be hypocrites* [emphasis mine]." Politicians everywhere say one thing and do another. Sufis must set a higher standard for themselves. Practice what you preach.

October 15, 1968, Tuesday

A British Buddhist is speaking on reincarnation at the Association for Research and Enlightenment. We argue about the route to take to the auditorium. Mentally, I am saying to myself: *Be firm! Be certain!* As outwardly uneventful as it sounds, this is my assertiveness training. The more I travel in everyday life with Murshid, the more I am confronted with situations that test my willingness to stand up to him. (see September 15, 1968)

October 16, 1968, Wednesday

My effort to constantly remember God is still foremost in my mind. I am a *fakir*, one who practices *fikar*, or who wants to, constantly. The oft-quoted Sufi saying, "The only virtue is to remember God by paying attention to the breath, and the only sin is to forget to pay attention to the breath," has had the effect of making me unequivocal about trying to remember God all the time, no matter what I am doing.

Tonight, thirty people celebrate Murshid's October 18th birthday at the Minerva Café, and Mansur dances Greek dances in public.

Afterwards at the meeting, Murshid asks me to explain what happens at the Sunday meeting to some folks. Inside, I am saying to myself, "Get high, handle this situation," while feeling proud to be called on. Proud like when Murshid noted that there were no questions at his lectures and I quoted a line from the prayer, Pir: "All ignorance vanishes in thy illuminating presence." My pride is showing. Catching myself basking in this glow of self-importance tonight, I experience how the feeling of pride robs attention from God and places it on oneself. Self-congratulation deprives God of attention. A *fakir* affirms God.

October 17, 1968, Thursday

Immersed in Sufi lore for over a year, I begin coloring my associates with qualities from the classical literature. I recall when Bob McKendrick, Sheyla's husband, came around with Sheyla and I compared his behavior to Abu Sa'id's when Abu Sa'id visited al-Khurqani, a great Sheikh praised by all the saints of his time. Al-Hujwiri, the author of *Kashf al-Mahjub*, narrates.

I have heard from Hasan Hu'addib, who was the servant of Abu Sa'id, that when Abu Sa'id came into the presence of al-Khurqani, he did not speak another word, but listened and only spoke by way of answering what was said by the latter. Hasan asked Abu Sa'id why he had been so silent. He replied, "One interpreter is enough for one theme." (*Kashf al-Mahjub*, p.163)

Why this comparison? Bob let Sheyla do all the talking.

October 19, 1968 Saturday

Murshid is here tonight for prayers at the *khankah*—910 Railroad Avenue, Novato. Murshid defined a *khankah* in *Spiritual Architecture*, one of his unpublished books, as a place of Sufi prayers.

October 20, 1968, Sunday

It is open house at the *khankah* and over 100 people show up. I ask Hiro Narita [director of photography on *Honey I Shrunk the Kids* and *Never Cry Wolf*], whom I worked with on *Riverrun*, to come and take still photos of the Opening of the Khankah Celebration.

October 22, 1968, Tuesday

Murshid writes today to Fred and Corinne (Reinhold) that Sheyla and Dara made it to Auroville. "After intensive efforts to have two way communications Sam received a very cordial letter from Julie Medlock. His friends have visited Auroville and been able to put over the hard truth that a blue-print is not a building."

Murshid uses old friends Fred and Corinne to reflect sarcastically on his success, comparing his career to that of Samuel Morse. "The whole change in circumstances reminds one of Samuel Morse, but, although revenge is sweet, humor is sweeter. And although Morse went to the law courts and won every case (which anybody not a 'realist' can accept) one's career is to concentrate on the positive side..."

Murshid ridicules realists, "people [who] pride themselves on the words 'democracy', 'liberty', 'humanity', [and] ... semanticists who verbalize that *words are not things* which their lives belie"—the usual suspects. The letter begins and ends with references to a contemporary, unknown to me, named Hugo. [Hugo Selig was a poet from the Dunes who foresaw Murshid's success.] "All the predictions of Hugo concerning this person are coming true," Murshid notes.

Murshid visits Laura, whose husband was busted; sees Vashti in the hospital; and visits a sick friend, poet Margaret Albanese. In my estimation, he is manifesting the meaning of the prayer *Nabi* [prophet], which contains the lines, "Comforter of the broken hearted, support of those in need."

October 24, 1968, Thursday

Today Murshid addresses the inability of a large organization to deal personally with him. He announces in a letter to American Friends of the Middle East's Washington, D.C. office his policy of giving a little money, but no more,

Because the average American, joining a "big" organization is a phantom to sign checks, otherwise he does not exist... As a person I am no longer trying to reach organizations and institutions; and as a person I am reaching the young, teaching them spiritual ways to Joy and Love without drugs and beyond drugs; drawing together those of former different faiths and presenting them a God quite outside of establishments of any kind.

Murshid adds that he seeks merely "verbal recognition"; that he is working toward the same goal they are. He concludes, "The easiest way to open up the check book would be the common recognition of hearts."

October 25, 1968, Friday

Murshid opens a letter responding to Buddhist Eugene Wagner's letter of October 22nd with a story. "Last week we heard a British Buddhist speak on reincarnation," he relates. "A young man who is very close to me [Mansur] asked whether it were not possible to die and be reborn without leaving the flesh. The speaker demurred. Sam arose and shocked both the old ladies in the audience and the speaker by saying it had happened to him."

The resulting chaos at the meeting, Murshid points out, was typical when Buddhists want to take the doctrine of selflessness (*anatta*) both ways. "I am sorry when so-called 'Buddhists' verbally adhering to *anatta* see only separations," Murshid writes. A *sangha*, Murshid reminds Wagner, is like an organism. "Cells are born, live and die. *Sanghas* persist." (Murshid talking about *sangha* to Wagner reminds me of a beautiful image he included in that September 4th letter to Warwick: "We are specks of dust which, when we enter a stream, no longer exist as ego-individuals but presumably as *Sangha*-members. And no person has any oath to any *Sangha* when he insists on placing his ego-life in any aspect as separate and private.")

"I cannot agree to any philosophical dispute based on personalism and personality," Murshid concludes, closing the door to taking Wagner's side against Neville Warwick. (Murshid threw away all letters from other people, so I don't know what Wagner's viewpoint was.) Murshid does not take sides; rather, he presents himself to Wagner like this: "True here I am trying to practice from Jesus Christ, 'Love ye one another' and 'I am the vine and ye are the branches thereof'. I always thought this to be Buddha's teaching, not necessarily Buddhist teaching."

October 28, 1968, Monday

This is the first diary entry written on my new Royal typewriter. Murshid has me bring mine into the City today to be cleaned, and I end up with a new used one. The used one costs $135, less $25 trade-in for the old one. Murshid pays.

In dream last night I saw Vilayat's form. While giving a group dance instructions, he asked me a question: "Did I teach you this when I was here last?"

I purchase thirty-six yards of cheap, dark cloth for my photo darkroom in a long, narrow storage area at the back of the *khankah*, just outside the door to Murshid's room.

I bring home a piece of driftwood that disciple Sibley gave to Murshid, and a new used file cabinet for the office.

When I hear Murshid define "Neptunian" types ("they know all the answers, but have difficulty manifesting on the earth plane"), I think about work. Would I go get a job and stop working for Murshid? The answer I get from inside: *Do what you are asked to do to cooperate with the county welfare people, and continue to serve your Murshid.*

From an unpublished treatise on *Breath*, dictated by Murshid to Moineddin, the numbered item that impresses me most is Number 170.

The extra-physical sounds which one sometimes hears are often psychic. Then they can be destroyed by *Fikar*. When *Fikar* increases these sounds, then they are important warnings or inspirations and spiritual disobedience to the same is more than breaking the pledge of *Bayat*; it is a refusal to listen to the Voice of the Living God, and thereby destroys the whole scheme of one's initiatory process. But blessed is he who listens to the Father's Word and performs His Will.

The effort to remember God constantly goes on, but remembrance is spotty. Ramdas's statement about staying up nights to remember comes to me. I put this possibility to myself. In reply comes: *When you can remember all day unceasingly, then is the time to worry about forgetting at night.* I can hear the voice of the silence just by focusing.

Murshid mentions an invitation from Master Seo, his Korean Buddhist Zen master, to visit Pittsburgh, where Master Seo is working as a professor at Temple University. [It doesn't happen.]

Wagner and Warwick are "feuding" now. Murshid's comment is succinct: "Those selfless Buddhists." I like the way Murshid uses the rejections in his own life to avoid taking sides in this one. I mean, if you support one side, you are rejecting the other. Murshid had been there and didn't want to dish out what he'd received. In his October 25 letter to Wagner, Murshid destigmatizes the word "occult"; defines *Dharma Dhrishthi*, usually translated "right views"; and shares his latest "occult" inspirations.

My life in the inner worlds—call it occult or otherwise, has led me to present dervish dances to young America. My program of eat, dance, and pray with people is now winning adherents among the young more rapidly than sneers among the elite! When the Universe opens up one has no choice. Dharma Dhrishthi means to me universal outlook or cosmic superpersonal view. It does not, to me, mean any "right" as against any "wrong" view. People who have not experienced samadhi, not having developed bodhi [awakening or enlightenment] simply do not know the truth of the Eight Fold Path [the Buddha's path to liberation]. The dervish dances are in a sense a synthesis of dances seen by me in the flesh. This is almost a useless statement for they will be rejected by the same people who reject the possibilities of the occult. I have to mention this because the inspirations of the dervish dances were followed almost immediately by the inspirations of Yogi dances. Needless to say the young have been equally enthusiastic in accepting the Yogi dances. The next inspirations while "occult" will demonstrate in dance or ritual form the numbers 1,2,3,4,5,6, both as numbers and as cosmic symbols. The dances of 6 include both the six-pointed star and the Shiva, Shakti. The next inspiration beyond that showed tantric vajrayana forms in dance and ritual beyond which I dare not look now.

October 29, 1968, Tuesday

Murshid calls this morning and begins the conversation by saying, "Pir-O-Murshid says pleasure blocks and pain opens the way for inspiration.

Last night we had a most spiritual walk." What Murshid means is that the pain of witnessing the feuding Buddhists (remember, he is "the vine" and they "are the branches thereof") produced "a most spiritual walk."

The subject of hypocrisy has been up for me since Murshid suggested that Murshida Martin failed because of her hypocritical nature. (see October 11, 1968) God led me this morning to read the first chapter in Hazrat Inayat Khan's book *Mysticism*. Khan says that a mystic "must continually speak and act differently from what he feels and knows." Then he asks, "Is it not a kind of hypocrisy?"

Khan explains that the practice of worldly mystics is to feel and know the truth, while speaking and acting as everybody else does. And if someone says that this is not right, the answer is that in the case of other people most things are wrong—knowing, acting, as well as speaking; whereas, in the case of the mystic, only one thing is wrong. The mystic at least feels and knows rightly; that much is to his advantage. (*The Sufi Message of Hazrat Inayat Khan*, vol.ii, pp.147-48)

The most recent example of hypocrisy I notice comes from disciple Marcia's boyfriend, Jack, not a disciple, whom Murshid considers his organizer. Some agreement must have been made, but the organizing work hasn't happened. Jack first appears in Murshid's correspondence October 22, 1968, when he tells Fred and Corinne, "Sam received a long-distance call from a scientist who is in love with one of Sam's disciples. He wants Sam to hold everything, to organize him and to help with our common researches to help human kind solve problems without dialectics, editorials and opinions of the 'more equal'."

Then—jumping ahead—on November 3rd, Murshid tells Shamcher, "Jack, the man who has planned to organize my efforts and who is also a salt-water conversion engineer [Shamcher's specialty] should be here by

Wednesday." But no. On November 13th, again to Shamcher, "The one who would help with the scientific research is caught in his own complexities."

What Murshid hoped Jack would help him organize is *"ordinary* Sufi Work"; "commentaries leading to the proper coordination of The Complete *Ryazat* of Hazrat Inayat Khan"; "piles of materials, published and unpublished from other schools of spiritual development"; and "scientific research in the fields of water and food production problems, covering mostly desert reclamation and the food problems of real Asia." (Murshid's letter to Suzanne D'Mitrieff, November 3, 1968)

October 30, 1968, Wednesday

While blacking the windows of the darkroom, I conclude: No one on the spiritual path escapes tests, and my tests have been entirely and delightfully thorough. One may read in *The Path of Initiation and Discipleship* about the discipleship of Khwaja Moinuddin Chisti, namesake of our Chisti Order who brought Sufism to India. He distinguished himself by sticking with his teacher when thousands of his teacher's followers split. What happened? Moinuddin's teacher pulled the Indian equivalent of visiting a whorehouse. The teacher watched a thousand disciples disappear and had ecstatic revelations and inspirations about the strangeness of human nature. Meanwhile, young Moinuddin saw no problem as his teacher bowed before the hideous Goddess Kali. When the teacher asked him why he stayed, Moinuddin answered, "There is nothing in what you have done that is against my convictions, because the first lesson you have taught me was that nothing exists save God. If that is true, then that image is not Kali; it too is God." (*The Sufi Message of Hazrat Inayat Khan*, vol.10, p.65)

October 31, 1968, Thursday

Murshid and Mansur go to the Novato office of *The Independent Journal*, the San Rafael newspaper. Why? To give them a news piece about Murshid's return to Marin County. Return from where? From San Francisco! Three times previously, Murshid has been featured in this paper. First, on May 13, 1957, it carried an article headlined "Marinite Tours Orient: Leaves as a Gardener, Comes Back a Dervish."

Sam Lewis, 60-year-old Mill Valley bachelor, was a gardener for the state highway department a little over a year ago. Now, back from a tour of the Orient, he is a member of the mystical dervish orders of Chisti and Nakshibandi. The tale told by this wandering Marinite approaches the fantastic at times. Lewis says that his father did not believe in college and as a result took him out of school and made him go to work. "However, when I was 52," Lewis adds, "my father evidently changed his viewpoint and although it meant dropping a regular job, I went to San Francisco City College, taking courses in floriculture and chemistry. I took a degree in 1951." After working as a gardener for the state until 1956, he received a sizeable inheritance from his father's estate, which immediately sent him flying to the Orient.

The second *Independent Journal* article was published on January 21, 1961, under the banner, "Science is stirring in the Middle East."

The last time wandering Marinite Sam Lewis of Mill Valley made headlines in the *Independent Journal*, he was just back from a tour of the Orient where he became a member of the mystical dervish orders of Chisti and Nakshibandi. Today, he is in another distant country—Gamal Abdel Nasser's United Arab Republic. Based in Cairo, he is carrying on a campaign with two general aims: 1) To assist the country in increasing its food supply. 2) And in so doing, to boost American prestige and reduce communistic subversion.

Third, *The Independent Journal* excerpted a letter from Murshid while he was in West Pakistan on another leg of this same trip. All three articles may be found in *Sufi Vision and Initiation*, on pages 105, 211, and 246.

Murshid doesn't mention any of these articles to the city editor. Curiously, the city editor doesn't ask Murshid why his return to Marin County merits a news story. After some conversation, Murshid says he is cultural advisor to the Temple of Understanding, a group that promotes world peace by sponsoring world conferences of all religions. This prompts the editor to decide that Murshid's information is a social item. I don't know if anything ever appears in the paper.

November 1, 1968, Friday

Murshid writes goddaughter Saadia today that Sheyla and Dara have written from India, but that they have not met with Pir Vilayat, nor with Iranian born, Harvard educated Dr. Seyyed Hossein Nasr, Saadia's friend and Sufism's most prestigious representative. Saadia is not only under Murshid's care as his goddaughter, she also accepts him as her Murshid, a role he emphasizes in this letter with six sentences beginning, "Your Murshid." Speaking like this, Murshid prepares Saadia for contemporary U.S. religious reality, where "religious people...are not concerned with Allah (God)." He warns her that "your Murshid is not on good terms with local Muslims. The question is whether these Muslims are accepted by Allah." Murshid wants Saadia to understand clearly his position relative to Muslim traditionalists, of whom Saadia is one, lest she be shocked at his unorthodoxy or his rejection by the locals.

November 2, 1968, Saturday

The Saturday dance class is closed to all but disciples. This is the class where Murshid chooses to introduce new inspirations. Dances and pageant forms based on Sufi studies called *nakshibandi*, or symbology, are up for Murshid now. The first lesson tonight is a pageant of the Sufi Symbol—a five-pointed star resting in a crescent moon within a winged heart. (Murshid will mention this lesson in a letter to Suzanne D'Mitrieff tomorrow.)

November 3, 1968, Sunday

Murshid's sudden abundance of secretarial help has been busy filing and sorting, and in the process, Julie Medlock's letter has disappeared. Murshid recalls that Julie had requested "certain types of agricultural and technical machinery." He answers her, "One of the problems Sam faces is that there are at least four organizations in the Near East collecting funds for equipment such as you wish." Nevertheless, Murshid intends to go forward and "seek funds not for ourselves (everybody does that) but for AUROVILLE." Fine, except that by the end of the letter, Murshid writes, "As we have our own new center I am holding back on dollars until it is permanently established." There is no mention of the required import permits, and direct help appears to be temporarily foreclosed.

Pir Vilayat is in India at the Temple of Understanding conference, and the secretary of the Sufi Order, Suzanne D'Mitrieff, is in Los Angeles. Murshid informs Suzanne, "One had about 30 disciples when Pir Vilayat came here and God, so to speak, said the number would be doubled. I have now reached an absolute of being unable to direct any more persons and am holding back..." (He changes his position on this when Vilayat names his hierarchical representatives from among Murshid's disciples and Jack shows up to organize the center.)

Don McCoy, director of the Olompali ranch (which "the Pir dedicated [as] the International Meditation Center") is in India. Murshid writes Suzanne that "he [Don] is going to be compelled either to accept Pir Vilayat or lose both the Ranch and his following; he is not a man to face realities." Murshid describes McCoy as "not very affable, but the generality [others living at the ranch] were." Pir Vilayat's blessing of the ranch was corroborated, Murshid tells Suzanne, by "the compounded visions of at least six persons, plus the direct Guidance from the Living God" that Murshid received. Murshid underscores McCoy's relationship with Vilayat as more important even than Vilayat's choosing representatives.

In the past, Shamcher and Murshid both functioned as Hazrat Inayat Khan's secretaries. Murshid mentions in his letter to Shamcher today that, like him, he was an amanuensis for Khan and recorded lectures in 1926—now published—which anticipated "that the New Age will have the group manifesting as an individual entity." [This is an extremely important New Age concept. The Buddhist word *sangha* is used in this chapter with this meaning.] The mission Murshid received from Hazrat Inayat Khan during his first interview in 1923 was "on the need to present mysticism to the intellectuals; it was rejected all over." One time, the rejection took the form of confusing Murshid with Khan. Murshid writes, "Among the papers seized by Mrs. Duce were the papers on *Zavaliat* [relating to the downward cycle; expiration as opposed to inspiration] which she thought Hazrat Inayat Khan wrote (while she returned to me the highest *Ryazat* assuming the opposite!)" Elsewhere, (in a letter to Sharab and Paul, November 14, 1968) Murshid describes Ivy Duce's discernment in this matter as "the insight of the unwise." Murshid feels compelled to tell Shamcher in detail what he's up to, as "it brings together all the items of the 1923 long interview (rejected by the 'good' people)." Most immediate was yesterday's dance class. "The work yesterday consisted of THE FIRE WALK; the receipt of blessings from the Murshid in the dervish dance; the Whirl; the Dance of Love and Brotherhood, very mystical though it may appear otherwise; and certain miscellany." Murshid tells Shamcher,

We ended by programming the pageant of THE SUFI SYMBOL, the second lesson, with four men as wings, three women as hearts and a man and woman, who happen to be husband and wife, as star and crescent. It became clear that the men, as wings would make up-and-down, therefore *Jelal* and *Jemal* movements; while the women, as Heart, would probably walk in a circle or curvilinear, therefore *Jemal* movements.

This was the day program. The nights are full of inspiration.

At night, it was revealed why God-Allah wishes Sam both in the capacity of Guru and Murshid to dance sometimes exclusively with the men, and sometimes exclusively with the women, in *Jelal* and *Jemal* movements; and when they join in *Kemal* (perfection) Murshid-Guru dances alone. This incidentally produces a higher ecstasy.

The inspiration and ecstasy connected with looking in the mystical manner sometimes has to be modulated. When Murshid speaks of going over his Dervish and Yoga dances "regarding the sciences of Electricity and Magnetism both in the Static and Dynamic forms," Murshid realizes that "this semanticizes the whole subject of 'Music of the Spheres'. One dare not look. This brings the transformatory experiences." This is a letter from a mystic to a mystic, and by the end Murshid is flying high. He writes, "There is now a potential staff, needed so badly. Melvin is working on the poetry, absolutely prophetic and one can say with assurance that in the future generations Sam will rank far beyond any Nostradamus or Edgar Cayce, etc."

November 4, 1968, Monday

When Murshid receives the announcement of a seminar on "The World of Indian Thought and Art" from Dr. William M. Brinner, chairman of the Department of Near Eastern Languages at Berkeley, he writes to acknowledge the flyer and offers to sponsor disciple Frank Tedesco. "Money is not my basic problem, time is," Murshid writes.

November 6, 1968, Wednesday

"This is the first letter being dictated at the new *Khankah*," is how Murshid starts his letter to Shamcher. After three paragraphs supporting Vilayat ("It is quite evident that the spirit of his Blessed father, and beyond that, the Divine Spirit Itself is inspiring this much abused and underrated man"), Murshid goes on to tell Shamcher how he knows when his inspirations are divine.

Sam is now receiving multitudes of dances, dance-forms, rituals, and pageants, faster than they can be recorded. However, the difference between a divine and ego-inspiration is that the divine inspiration or vision acts as if it were crystallized in the *akasha*. It does not change; it remains as if solid in vision.

I think Murshid writes this more for his secretary's edification than for Shamcher's. It is Wednesday. I am taking dictation. Murshid is at the *khankah*, a short distance from the Wednesday night meeting. This meeting serves in the same way as the Saturday dance class: as an outlet for Murshid's creativity.

Sam instituted the Sun dance and the Moon dance. The forces and factors involved make one feel that there is something like the restoration of Vedic and Mystery dances. So far the high point comes when Sam is merged into Sri Krishna. The difficulty is not in the merging but in the control of the ecstatic state. (Letter to Anandashram, November 7, 1968)

November 7, 1968, Thursday

The father function I sometimes feel vis-à-vis Murshid is not exclusive to me—goddaughter Nancy calls him "Daddy Murshid." Murshid demonstrates a similar connection with Sheyla, who is somewhere in India, when he notifies Anandashram today that he will be responsible for any debts Sheyla might not take care of.

Sam may have to ask you a favor. His disciples Sheyla and Dara are traveling in India. They report they have not too much money. Sam wishes them to visit Anandashram. While we believe they can cover their expenses there, if not, please let us know and we shall send the proper funds for their sojourn.

Later in the letter Murshid says, "Dara and Sheyla report the resemblance between the hippy communities, American and non-American, with Indian customs and traditions. This confirms Sam's belief. It is almost impossible to convince seniors that the soul has no age, and that those of young bodies may be far more advanced than they are."

After taking dictation from Murshid today, Mansur writes in his journal that he has the sense of watching Murshid draw from the cosmos. Perhaps "receive from the cosmos" is a more accurate image, but Murshid himself spoke of it in the active sense: drawing out of the cosmos.

November 10, 1968, Sunday

Murshid leads dervish dances this afternoon in San Francisco's Golden Gate Park. He tells columnist Art Hoppe that the location is just "below Hippy Hill." In the evening Murshid visits Paul Reps. What Murshid sees there inspires an unflattering comparison between Reps and Vilayat.

Says Murshid to Shamcher on the 13th, "Paul Reps has found neither love nor peace for one series of facts and reasons; Vilayat has not for quite a different series, he being in a sense a sainted martyr although he might object to this terminology." But, Murshid continues, "Vilayat sees the Universe and Paul Reps writes *Ask a Potato?* [and] ... oozes venom [toward] everything Pir-O-Murshid Hazrat Inayat Khan gave." Reps receives a carbon of this letter, demonstrating that Murshid does not say terrible truths about people behind their backs.

November 11, 1968, Monday

Murshid changes my concentration from the heart to the Sufi symbol. He does this after I ask, about my concentration practice, "Am I supposed to be retaining the image with my eyes closed?" Murshid says, "Always." Mansur, empowered by the importance of this task, begins to look at the symbol for one exhalation and one inhalation, and retains the image for slightly less time. Before Mansur drives Murshid to Olompali ranch, I ask Murshid when to do *kasab* (or *pranayama*, breath work). The practice given in Pir Vilayat's book is:

BREATHE IN FOUR BEATS,
HOLD THE BREATH EIGHT BEATS,
BREATHE OUT FOUR BEATS.
REPEAT FIVE TIMES EACH SIDE:
IN RIGHT NOSTRIL, HOLD, OUT LEFT.
IN LEFT NOSTRIL, HOLD, OUT RIGHT.

IN BOTH NOSTRILS, HOLD, OUT BOTH. (*Toward the One*, p.667)

Murshid tells me to do this practice "in the morning." I had been doing it at night. Murshid and Mansur go for a walk at the ranch. I am conscious of stepping where Murshid steps as a way to receive the teacher's blessing. It's funny how meaning is conveyed on the spiritual path. The phrase, "The Murshid is determined by his *mureeds*," is familiar to me. But not until today, walking in the steps of Murshid, does the meaning come to me. I understand how in the unity of teacher and pupil, the pupil affects the teacher. I understand how the Murshid allows himself to be determined through this association.

Murshid mentions a book on the shifts of the *tattvas* (elements), a deep and sacred subject not taken up until the fourth grade in the esoteric school of the Sufis. As in my earlier mention (July 6, 1968) of waking from a dream in which I looked for the color yellow in my breath, we have been trained to observe the regular, elemental changes in the breath. Secret? Yes. Jesus says not to cast your pearls before swine. Hidden? Yes, for subtle changes in the breath may be overlooked by those who don't care. Either Clark or Howard has this book on the shifts of the *tattvas*, but Mansur never sees it.

The Rejected Avatar, one of Murshid's epic poems, is the inaugural publication of Hassan's new publishing enterprise in Novato, called Prophesy Pressworks. Murshid asks me to send Huston Smith copies of *The Rejected Avatar*, and I enclose my review of Philip Kapleau's book (*The Three Pillars of Zen*), which was published in the *Oracle*. Just for fun I send a copy of the review to Kapleau. Kapleau answers me. That is a thrill.

November 13, 1968, Wednesday

Murshid deeply appreciates Shamcher's response to his letter of the 3rd and acknowledges his generosity.

Such letters have been received on rare occasions: two from women who were partly in love and rejected Sam spiritually and now have changed; the others from the very top Masters of the living world, whose very existence knocks the props out of all those metaphysical lecturers who talk in glib generalities about masters and saints and seers without naming them.

The love and affection between *mureeds*, which is so contrary to Murshid's experience when he was a *mureed*, is an ongoing condition Murshid feels compelled to tell Shamcher about, while admitting, "there are still some terrible clouds." One of these is his workload, exacerbated by the failure of Jack to come through as an organizer. Knowing that Shamcher wrote Phillip (Davenport), Murshid lets Shamcher know that "he [Phillip] is about to become a father and he has been caught pell-mell in all the dramas on the San Francisco State campus, caught in the middle and unable to do anything amid warring factions."

In addition to having the love of his disciples, Murshid recently met Swami Ranganathananda's disciple, Swami Swahananda. "It was like two lovers," he says.

I thrilled his disciple, the aforesaid Swami with living stories of a tremendous living human being. He must receive a treatment in my city as I received from him in New Delhi many times, "when two strong men are face to face though they come from the ends of the earth." Swami Ranganathananda is one of three very real "kings" of the orient coming soon to San Francisco; the others, Grand Master Seo (He regards Sam as a sort of *Khalif*, and perhaps rightly.) and Vilayat (We simply cannot let Vilayat down.).

Mansur has many copies of letters to mail. Paul Reps gets a copy of the letter to Shamcher. Shamcher and Reps get copies of the letter to Suzanne D'Mitrieff. Shamcher, Reps, Huston Smith, Dr. Chaudhuri, and the Indian Consulate get copies of Murshid's letter to the Temple of Understanding. This is a typical day. No wonder many of Murshid's letters don't appear in his files: He sends out all the carbons.

November 14, 1968, Thursday

It's doubtful Murshid knows that the Asia Foundation has been, according to William Blum, "the CIA's principal front in Asia for many years." (*Killing Hope*, p.343) Murshid writes them to make an appointment for Friday, November 22nd. Why?

Our good friend, Dr. Thich Thien An, instructor in Vietnamese Culture and Buddhism, expects to arrive in this city on the previous night. I think especially in view of the many complications involving his country, a Vietnamese should *occasionally* be given some consideration.

(Considering our hindsight knowledge of the CIA's complicity in the invasion of Vietnam and its direct involvement in more than fifty thousand deaths from the program code-named Phoenix alone, it is interesting that Murshid addresses a CIA front in the following manner: "My whole antipathy to our Asian policies is that we grant objective existence to powerful countries and persons with whom we do not agree—often are extremely antipathetic to—while we disregard the civilizations and persons of small, but often important, lands.")

Politics figures heavily in Murshid's answer to a letter from older Sufis Sharab and Paul. On Vietnam, Murshid writes, "We pay no attention to Asian cultures and there is nothing for the weak but to await who is going to destroy them and their culture." On the New Age and the press:

The New Age is being mishmashed by the press. Somebody said that the Black Panthers consisted of 500 Negroes and 10,000 newsmen. Even the old leaders of the Berkeley Free Speech Movement are against what is going on now. We start with non-violence and end with extreme emotionalism, bodily harm and all else. The conservatives want that so they can stop real free speech and the gangsters want it because this gives them free play....

My disciples and colleagues have drawn much larger audiences than the Black Panthers but you never hear about them. The New Age demands collectivism but the rioting Negroes are extreme individualists with no social consciousness whatsoever. Nor any morals. And that is what the press wants and certain power structures want. They use the situations as excuses to lower the booms, and do.

Mansur notices difficulty with rhythm in his breath while typing the letter to the Asia Foundation. What escapes me is to attribute my upset to Murshid's uncharacteristic anger at American war criminal activity by American individuals who remain on the loose at this late date, or who have died of natural causes.

Murshid gives Mansur *all* the *wazifas* to practice and master. Mansur asks Murshid some questions related to his spiritual practice. "What shall I do with my mind during *ziker*? Sometimes I hear sound, sometimes I see the words, sometimes meaning."

"Whatever you want," Murshid says.

"But I am confused about this. Am I supposed to remain in confusion?"

Murshid responds, "*Ziker* can be compared to a car. You have trouble starting it in the morning, but when you get it going, it goes smoothly."

"What is the difference between *ziker* and *wazifa*?"

Murshid defines the terms: "*Ziker* deals with God, and *wazifa* with the attributes of God."

"Several times I have asked you for practices—various concentration exercises, such as to see everything as God. But later I quit doing them. I think my lack of sustainability is from asking for assignments rather than waiting for you to give them."

"Let them go. I have given you this," Murshid says, pointing to the *wazifa* material.

November 15, 1968, Friday

Murshid's furnace goes out, and the landlord is delaying fixing it. After reading Murshid's commentary on *The Inner Life* by Hazrat Inayat Khan, I am again reminded to be concerned with the *rhythm* of my breath in *fikar*, as well as with thinking about the phrase. This is not the first time this realization dawns. (see August 9, 1968) Again, the emphasis is away from *thinking* about a phrase swinging on the breath to *feeling* the rhythm. The feeling coming through the rhythm broadens the experience. Isn't it true that what the universe wants us to know, we get over and over as recurring thoughts, dreams, and realizations? That's my experience.

Chapter 10

The Khankah's First Test

There is no time to write up the dances. Where is the secretarial help coming from? My esoteric secretary Otis Johnson, Mansur, is not only "going upstairs" with me, he has the economic problem. He has been on relief and the officials want him to take a well-paying job so he is mostly spending his time in taking examinations and interviews. In the few hours we have together he is able to accompany me on spiritual journeys, of a type none of the "experts" and "ladies" have accepted but we don't care any more. We are going to be as objective and impersonal in mysticism and the inner sciences as we must be in the outer sciences. (Murshid's letter to Paul Reps, January 27, 1969)

November 16, 1968, Saturday

"A Sufi teacher," says Murshid to Fatima during a walk at the bottom of Bernal Heights, a steep hill behind Murshid's house, "would not ask a disciple to do anything he would not do himself." Both are tired after a few times up and down hills. Murshid says it to point out the difference between a guru and a murshid. Murshids are willing to do what they ask others to do.

After the class, Shirin and Mansur are honored with a joint birthday party. Murshid has anticipated the party for weeks in letters; for example, he wrote to Shamcher [November 13, 1968], "We are having a party at KHYBER PASS RESTAURANT Saturday. This is owned, and I think I have told you, by the son of a Sufi and we meet brethren there occasionally. Even this party is a joint birthday celebration of two of the finest disciples. It will be followed by a work party at the *Khankah* on Sunday."

November 17, 1968, Sunday

In his letter on the 19th to Anandashram, Murshid uses the work party at the *khankah* as an example of the difference between verbal *karma yoga* (work practice) and real work.

Disciples and friends came, worked in joy without supervision, without homilies or sermons and in living brotherhood, such as Sam has not seen in his already long life in this land. Long work hours were followed by Dervish and Yoga Dances, which awakened and strengthened joy and love among the participants. We are putting the Brihadaranyaka Upanishad into practice and actualization among the living devotees, nearly all quite young, but many far more spiritually advanced than more or less famous sermonizers and intellectuals much better known.

When the crowd is gone, Murshid tells the following story: "Inayat Khan asked Paul Reps to call him 'Inayat,' and Reps wouldn't do it. Years later Reps realized he had made a great mistake." This story of a great soul being rebuffed when he sought to be more familiar with a close associate touches a note in me that causes tears to come to my eyes.

Later, we go into the meditation room—the antique house's original living room, now with no furniture—and Murshid does the Buddha breaths

and stops on the joy breath ("breathe in all the joy that you are capable of breathing in, and breathe out all the joy that you are capable of breathing out"). This again brings tears to my eyes, and reminds me of the night in Bolinas when I walked along the roads weeping and saying over and over again, "He gives us such joy!"

Back at the dining room table for

Goddaughter Saadi Khawar Khan   postmeeting tea and coffee, Murshid announces that he plans to retain

his house in San Francisco. This corrects a misimpression I have held, perhaps from hearing over and over variations on what Murshid wrote: The establishment of a *khankah* "would cut down on overhead, meetings, office work, everything." (letter to Sharab and Paul, November 14, 1968)

When Murshid began pushing for a *khankah* where we could all live together, my picture was of Murshid committing absolutely, like we were. We burned our bridges, abandoned our prior residences. When it becomes clear tonight Murshid isn't abandoning his house in San Francisco, I feel disappointed and deceived. Comparing notes years later with Fatima to see if I am the only one who feels this way, Fatima says, "I was relieved. It was really hard living with Murshid."

Nobody is prepared for what comes next. Murshid blasts us all—I mean blows us away with the energy of his upset—for allowing a nonresident to hang out after the work party. Drew, a nondisciple neighbor, was invited by a nonresident to stop by and hang out. Everyone leaves and Drew's still at the house, invading Murshid's space. Murshid goes bananas about this and another issue: He had no place to hang out during the work party. Murshid's doorless bedroom is right inside the rear entrance. There was no privacy when he wanted to take a break from workers going in and out of the house.

November 18, 1968, Monday

Tonight the *khankah* handles the test presented yesterday at its first family meeting. At the close of the meeting—how timely!—Drew calls to inquire about coming over to watch TV. No matter what is at stake with this individual as far as feelings are concerned, we at the *khankah* are like Caesar at the Coliseum. It has to be thumbs down; death to the practice of a nondisciple coming to the *khankah* for recreational purposes.

Goddaughter Nancy Fish

We fail to agree upon a refuge room. Candidates are the TV room, the sewing room located above Murshid's room, and my darkroom. It is agreed to meet the day before the next open house to decide. Murshid's upset has impressed us all with the urgency of his need for a refuge.

I say to Murshid at Nancy Fish's, "You can't compare a Murshid with a lecturer." My comment pertains to a discussion about the work of Paul Reps and himself. When Shamcher comes in December, I tell Shamcher the same thing. It comes out later that he puts our conversation in a manuscript eventually published by the Sufis in New York City. (see January 31, 1969) I suspect as much when Shamcher says cryptically, "You're a witness that what I wrote about Sam is true."

November 19, 1968, Tuesday

It's been twelve days since Murshid voiced concern about Sheyla and Dara, even offering to pay their rent if they arrived penniless at Anandashram. Posting his "monthly contribution" to Anandashram today, Murshid writes, "He [Murshid] is concerned over the whereabouts and financial status of two of his disciples now in India, Mrs. Sheyla McKendrick and Mr. Robert Dara Rowell. He has written that if they are in difficulties, they may proceed to Anandashram and would receive help in an emergency from him through you."

Murshid's letters to Anandashram tend to be summaries of his activities—with an Indian slant. No different today: "Sam has been writing and also receiving very cordial letters from AUROVILLE, Sri Aurobindo Ashram. After writing yesterday to Auroville, Sam returned to San Francisco and was *given hints of actual methods* by which tractors and other equipment can be sent to ashrams in India." Mother Krishnabai and others on the receiving end have to guess what these "hints of actual methods" might be. Surveying Murshid's subsequent correspondence with Julie Medlock (December 9, 1968), I would guess that "it is not only Rockefeller Foundation but a number of corporations large and small, known and not so known, who have offered Sam free models or machines for demonstrative and teaching purposes" that was the "hint."

As far as teaching is concerned, "Sam is now instructing through the sciences of Breath, Dance (*nirtya* yoga), Art (*yantra* yoga etc.), and other means which the living God is manifesting to and through him." Visitors are anticipated this week. "Sam is preparing to greet the Vietnamese, Dr. Thich Thien An, an advanced real Buddhist, with a knowledge of profound Buddhism hardly known in the western world," and Paul Reps. Lama Govinda ("Sam does not know how far this is a heart-man") may be in the vicinity, and arrangements are being made for a greeting party. "Sam has then to prepare to meet the Sufi Vilayat Khan...all preliminary to the coming here of Swami Ranganathananda Maharaj, whose very name and personality make it difficult for Sam to continue without entering an ecstasy."

November 21, 1968, Tuesday

It is not the arrival of the magnificent Dr. Thich Thien An today that I record; rather, the personal changes I go through "shouting" at Murshid during an afternoon bridge game. I suffer agonies of conscience during highly animated verbal exchanges over the card table. Afterwards, the saying "A mystic's work is to awaken the heart, man's ego stands in the way" comes to mind, as both my ego and my heart are exercised today.

Since Mansur goes back to Novato for classes tonight and misses Dr. An, I depend on details from several letters Murshid writes after his visit to put together a portrait of Dr. An: a gourmet and a holy man with a marvelous atmosphere you can feel, who considers each person a Buddha. His only stop in San Francisco is to visit Murshid. In a letter to disciple Howard, Murshid is most expansive about Mr. An's visit.

We had a real Buddhist Master walk in suddenly last week. It was nothing like your self-righteous Me-Big-Shot Roshi, you little nobody insignificant. Lots of people like that and that is what they will get. The Master was the very embodiment of Love and Peace. He did not have to speak on these, he was these and it was obvious to everybody. As the Master was deficient in "humility" he let the "Guru" present the Yoga of Lord Buddha [the *Jhanas*] which is shunned by Me Bigshot Buddhists of all schools. The Master accepted what is obvious and went on from there. There was complete unity. We did not even have to say "Love, Harmony and Beauty"—it was totally obvious. The Master had one moral teaching: Remember everyone you meet may be a Buddha in disguise and, if not, a Buddha in potentiality. This is, of course, totally contrary to prevalent "Buddhism" or any other religion. (November 26, 1968)

November 22, 1968, Friday

The gist of Murshid's letter to columnist Art Hoppe is, "You can pay $10 to hear a German named Lama Anagarika Govinda speak on something he calls 'Buddhism' to a veddy [sic] select audience. Or you can come here and hear an Asian [Dr. Thich Thien An] speak on his religion, also called 'Buddhism' at nothing per. This, of course, is contrary to our *culture*."

County welfare workers facilitate an interview for me in Oakland about a job as a group counselor. The juveniles in detention pending trial are rowdy, and I discern from the job description the interviewer gives me that I would have to break up fights and maintain discipline among the inmates. The interview is not a success, as I confess my unsuitability to police juveniles. Then, it is off to lunch at Murshid's and my real job.

First thing after lunch, a possessed woman appears at Murshid's house with her husband. Murshid and I chant "Allah" at this woman, kind of like born again Christians witnessing for an unwilling convert, giving her an in-your-face dose of "Allah, Allah." The woman, who is married to the Moslem son of a Sufi, cannot stand hearing the Name and she flees. Her husband returns twice to talk about her. Here I learn that possessing entities cannot stand the name of God.

Inayat Khan's book *Moral Culture*, included in his twelve volumes of published Sufi teachings, was initially a Sufi study paper (*Gathas*, Series 1, 2, and 3). I love these teachings, presented in three levels: dealing with ordinary relationships, the law of reciprocity; relationships on a higher level, the law of beneficence; and higher still, the law of renunciation. The commentaries that Murshid dictates today on this work will become part of the advanced teachings on morals.

Murshid and Mansur go to dinner at Starview and order two "Friday specials," a shrimp dish we both favor. After dinner, back at the house, we play cards and rest before going out.

Without fanfare, Jack, Marcia's boyfriend and Murshid's alleged organizer, comes to town. Our first stop tonight is over at DeHaro Street to deliver a letter to Jack, which comments on his plans—which, so far as I can see, never materialize.

Next, I drive Murshid over to Eighteenth Street and Dolores, where disciples Renee, Krishnadas, and others have a place across the street from the Good Karma Café. They don't live there, but use the space for Renee's theater and Krishnadas's Hatha Yoga classes. We go so Murshid can bless the space, and this pleases Renee.

Gavin Arthur holds open house on Friday nights. Gavin's house is littered like a museum, with every available inch of wall covered with memorabilia, books, clippings, and bizarre artifacts. Everyone is just chatting when we arrive. Gavin has Murshid come sit by him and introduces him as the head of the Sufi Order in the Bay Area.

The meeting is on hold until 9:30, when Gavin is scheduled to be on KPFA-FM Radio. To pass time, Gavin talks about "the Negro problem", which today directly impacted him and Cappy, Gavin's male consort. A group of Negroes who call themselves "The Cannibals" entered Gavin's apartment and "took a bite out of Cappy."

This story is so absurd Mansur can hardly contain himself when Gavin keeps repeating the bite line as he embellishes the story. "Why, one girl even got her tit bit off," Gavin reports with such emphasis that I *feel* it. Now it's not so funny. Gavin says he told Herb Caen, Art Hoppe, and other *San Francisco Chronicle* notables (as well as the police). The newsmen answered, *Yes,* they knew, but they were not publicizing it.

November 23, 1968, Saturday

In the afternoon I drive Murshid to Amin's, a seldom used venue for the dance class. After a long session, we are scheduled to go on to a meeting with Paul Reps in Sausalito. Murshid wants to give Reps a copy of his newly published poem *The Rejected Avatar,* and he doesn't have one. How can this be remedied?

Hassan has copies in Novato—too far. Amin has one in Corte Madera inscribed to "My beloved Amin," which isn't appropriate to give to Reps, so Melvin and I drive Laura to San Anselmo to get her copy.

What could be a blurb on the back cover of the poem, but isn't, is what Murshid shared with Anandashram (December 18, 1968): "Some people guessed that *The Rejected Avatar* was the blessing Sri Krishna gave to Sam because he, Sam, was not permitted to present his mystical and spiritual philosophy and knowledge to others."

At the meeting, Melvin has an exchange with Reps that leaves me puzzled. Reps makes me think of the *pranayama* practice (see November 11, 1968) when he uses the term "blow your mind" to describe the effect of holding one's breath without the guidance of a teacher. When you breathe in, Reps says, "the pause at the top releases energy. The pause at the bottom, what do you think the pause at the bottom does?"

"Radiates energy," Melvin says.

Reps answers, "No. Discharges energy. So if you hold the breath in without knowing what you are doing, you'll blow your mind." I am puzzled. Isn't a discharge a radiation?

Murshid's only comment on this evening is in a November 26, 1968 letter to an errant disciple, Howard Mussell. "Paul Reps was here," he writes, "and was amazed at the crowd—just grapevined that is all. He came and went. The only mature people there were friends of Dr. Warwick, all the rest young. No respectable people, not a single one!"

November 26, 1968, Tuesday

In writing Mussell, Murshid reminds him that when some disciples "returned to the fold" the other night "they saw what they have been missing [and] they felt very sorry." Spiritual teachers don't scold; they prefer "to point out one's potentialities," Murshid says.

Further, Murshid refers to Mussel's friend Clark, in prison for cultivating marijuana.

This person differs from *Advaitins* [making a sarcastic use of the Hindu term *advaita*, which means the doctrine of non-dualism]. He [Murshid] sees no differences. He is in the prison with Clark... Now you get put in jail, so to speak, if you "flunk in Botany", grow the wrong plants. While Clark is in prison his teacher is in prison. That is where Sufism differs from the "good" forms of Oriental philosophy still prevalent but on their way out. There are only two traditional religions: "I am as good as you" and "I am better than you." Sufism is so different; it is: "I am not different from you." This is also what the Buddhist Master [Dr. An] taught. So we are concerned with Clark.

This is the letter in which Murshid describes Dr. An's visit and, playing off his account of the evening, declares "war on 'Infinite Compassion'. We have oodles of that, all around," he continues. "Being Infinite it cannot touch us nor we it. So this one has come out for finite compassion."

I can hardly count the instances between now and January 26, 1969, when Govinda finally leaves the area, that Murshid uses the term "finite compassion" to describe his work relative to Lama Govinda's "Infinite Compassion." (see December 17, 1968 for Murshid's account of a Lama Govinda meeting)

November 27, 1968, Wednesday

It's Thanksgiving season and Murshid will be here at the *khankah* until the weekend. This morning I work in the office typing with Murshid. This afternoon I get into the gutter replacement project, using my new drill and new power saw, specially purchased to accomplish this project. It is necessary to bolt two by four extensions on the rotted rafter ends to provide solid nailing surfaces for the new gutters.

166

November 29, 1968, Friday

Dinner today is yesterday's Thanksgiving dinner warmed over. Murshid says, "I hope you don't mind if I say about dinner what the Germans said about Schlegel's translation of Shakespeare, 'It's better than the original!'."

Tonight we go to the Olompali ranch. Moineddin is giving Friday night classes in Sufism there now. Murshid leads dancing. "While the dance affects the group," Murshid writes Shamcher (November 30, 1968), "the Walk affects the individual, but the two go together."

December 1, 1968, Sunday

A helper comes and we get started on the garage at the Garden of Inayat (the *khankah*). We pull junk from the loft and pile everything in the center of the room. After sweeping the walls and pulling nails still stuck in them for providing hangers for tools, we put plastic up on the inside walls to keep out the weather. A wood stove will be installed. Murshid asks when it can be done. He says he is just asking for my son, Nathan's sake, imagining that this will be a playroom for Nathan. Actually, it becomes the nexus for the pottery concentration, once plans are formulated to build a kiln outside.

December 2, 1968, Monday

What Murshid finally articulates in today's letter to University of California Alumni Association director Richard Erickson is an insight first stirred by campus unrest at San Francisco State, when African-Americans demanded a Black studies program. It takes several letters to the International Society of General Semantics's Russell Joyner and columnist Art Hoppe for Murshid to clarify his thinking. He makes the following points to Erickson: There are already Black studies programs on various campuses; they aren't well known ("I do not agree with the absence of publicity concerning their actual existence and often very successful functioning"); there is no need to duplicate programs on all campuses; and they aren't well attended by Blacks ("I have enrolled in two courses in African Anthropology, no Negroes in the class. One in African Archeology, exactly one Negro in the class").

December 3, 1968, Tuesday

Murshid points out that California normally get lots of rain in January, so the push is on to finish the remodeling work on the *khankah*. Moineddin gets his first taste of scraping the old paint and puttying holes in the siding. The prep work to paint this house will take as long or longer than the painting, the paint is so chipped and the siding so compromised.

December 4, 1968, Wednesday

The statement Murshid makes today to "universal man" Paul Reps (the term is from a letter to Diane Ferry, December 8, 1969) provides me with proof positive that Murshid will live a long life. Murshid says, "There is little doubt but I shall live on and in the Grace of Health until all the messages of Hazrat Inayat Khan are given to the world. It may still take a long time."

December 7, 1968, Saturday

Not counting carbon copies of letters sent to Sri Haridas Chaudhuri of the Cultural Integration Fellowship, Murshid writes Chaudhuri five times during this chapter's time span. Murshid was the first to welcome Chaudhuri to San Francisco. He sat at his feet and assisted him, all for nothing but good karma. Now Murshid wants "slight recognition of our actual spiritual work and social undertakings." (December 7, 1968)

Chaudhuri responds to Murshid's letter of November 26th by sending his latest brochure, which includes a fundraising request. Thanking him on December 7th, Murshid says, "This matter will have to be taken up by my own Board now. We find ourselves in a delicate position that, although we should like to cooperate in full, our interpretation of cultural understanding, global perspective, and East-West Integration is somewhat different, not only from your efforts, but from the efforts of many groups operative in this region from time to time."

It doesn't take the "Board" long to decide. The next day, with copies of letters to disciple Diane Ferry and writer Paul Reps enclosed, Murshid says, "I wish to have my name dropped from your rolls. We have decided the money can better be used at Pondicherry."

Unfazed, Chaudhuri invites Murshid to attend his Christmas party. On December 19th, Murshid "regretfully refuse[s], suggesting it is bad manners to summon someone senior in years to your house. When the Chassid Saint came to San Francisco and asked me to call on him, I said I would but he would lose face, because I was nearly 50 years older. He took a taxi immediately and we embraced, exactly as one has been embraced by holy men of all faiths."

Haridas Chaudhuri's inability to placate Murshid inspires one monster letter, four pages long, filled with vignettes of Murshid's spiritual journey. It is to disciple Diane Ferry but aimed squarely at Chaudhuri, who gets a copy. Featured in one story is famed Roshi Yasutani. Yasutani's teachings are the central focus of Phillip Kapleau's *The Three Pillars of Zen*. Following right after that is a story about Sokei-an Sasaki's wife, Ruth Fuller Sasaki.

When Roshi Yasutani was in California he came to San Francisco to meet your Murshid, just to meet your Murshid and nobody else. We each took a single glance, the real *SAMMA DHRISHTI* [right sight] and the Roshi said, "Let us have some tea." For mystics know each other and half-mystics are often very ignorant and do not know it.

After that the Sufi Vilayat will come and it will be *TAT TWAM ASI* [Thou art that] and one hopes this will be true with Phillip Kapleau. When Murshid was taken to Mrs. Sasaki, she asked, "What did Sokei-an teach you?" "I *cannot* tell you. I do not mean to say *I may not tell you*. I may. Nothing esoteric, nothing secret but if I began telling you and talked on and on without stopping for ten years I would not finish." Murshid then gave some illustrative material which the "half-gods" call egotism. She ended: "I believe you." Of course she did. Universal Consciousness is Universal Consciousness.

December 9, 1968, Monday

Dara is back from India; Sheyla is not. Murshid informs Julie Medlock today, and it's not a pretty picture: "Sheyla has disobeyed all instructions and will have to bear some sorrowful consequences when she returns." Murshid's introductions for Sheyla to the conference's organizers, to Anandashram—all for naught. Dara attended the conference and "is very enthusiastic about AUROVILLE", Murshid tells Julie, but Sheyla spent all her time stoned in a village outside Calcutta where the conference was held. Sheyla and Don hooked up and are reportedly bringing back a dope-smoking holy man they discovered living in a van down by the river. Nobody visited Anandashram and Mother Krishnabai, whom Murshid describes as the most spiritual person in the world.

Murshid puts the best face on the lack of communication with Dara, telling Julie Medlock on December 13, "Buzz (Dara) is back and we had little to confer on. For those who function—and I mean function—with the Higher Mind do not have to talk a lot." Anandashram is informed December 18th, "The disciples in India did not follow their projected paths." The Temple of Understanding finds out on December 23rd that "we heard Dara Rowell's report and it will be taken seriously by the young." But by January 6, 1968, Julie is getting a different message. "Dara has not yet had time to report"; same message to Master Seo, on January 26, 1969—"I did not get a very full report on the meeting of the great religions of the world in Calcutta but Her Serene Highness, Princess Poon Diskul, seems to have played a leading role."

With Suzanne D'Mitrieff, Pir Vilayat's secretary, Murshid doesn't pull any punches (January 10, 1969).

Mr. Don McCoy, founder of THE RANCH, is at the moment in custody... Dara has left this state, apparently totally disgusted with the affairs of the RANCH... With regard to Mrs. Sheyla McKendrick... All signs point to mental derangement due to drugs. This soul needs love, tenderness and consideration, and at the moment is totally impervious to love, tenderness, consideration and response to anybody whatsoever. She is at the same time in an extreme case of egocentricity, and falsely imagines herself to be God-conscious.

In fact, Murshid doesn't let the Sheyla situation derail his program of support for Auroville, taken up in the first of two letters to Julie Medlock today. It includes his allusion to the Rockefeller Foundation as a source of machinery. After Murshid writes this letter, a letter from Julie comes and Murshid writes again, "Sam has gone into the whole field of simple and slightly complex machines. He has already taken up the matter of supplying you with fertilizers—at his own expense."

Plus, Murshid has been talking. "I have had several conversations with Craig Wallace... He lives in the rather opulent city of Ross. I shall ascertain whether he knows Mr. Russell Smith of the same city. Mr. Smith, Sr. was the top Vice-President of the Bank of America, long associated with the World Bank, retired President of ASIA FOUNDATION, and President of its Board of Directors. He was once my employer too and we are on excellent terms." It comes out here that Murshid is in debt "due to loans made to disciples and the new house at Novato." I learn later the debt is $1,000—and there is a surprise benefactor. Stay tuned.

Lama Govinda will not meet Murshid Thursday as proposed. Murshid was hyped last Sunday, writing Paul Reps, "The challenge this week will go to Lama Govinda and we shall challenge him with 'Finite Compassion' against his 'Infinite Compassion'." The same day, Murshid told Diane Ferry, "It is necessary to meet a great Buddhist leader (Madison Avenue style) soon. His name is Lama Govinda Anagarika. He was born in Germany." According to Moineddin, Lama Govinda has been meeting with Alan Watts and he is too tired to meet with anybody else. Murshid was building up a head of steam to meet him. It's probably just as well for Lama Govinda that he's tired. Murshid was talking about challenging Lama Govinda to *Dharma* combat, where the loser becomes the winner's disciple. "I'm not afraid of becoming his disciple," Murshid crowed. "I'm tired of bowing down to somebody to please a crowd whose teacher is below me spiritually."

December 12, 1968, Thursday
The energy Murshid built up for the cancelled meeting today with Lama Govinda gets transferred to a letter to Govinda ally Rev. Eugene Wagner. What Murshid planned, he'll do next Sunday instead. "Sunday night I shall read a paper from Her Serene Highness Princess Poon Diskul, given before the assemblage representing the real religions of the real world." When this reading happens, Shamcher is there, and Murshid's reading of "a fiery manifesto" gets mentioned in Shamcher's book. (see January 31, 1969)

Tonight after *Gatha* class, given by Murshid at the *khankah*, we have champagne and champagne flavored grape ice to celebrate Marcia's birthday party, compliments of her boyfriend Jack, who sent money to Murshid to buy these treats.

Murshid says he is going to cook four chickens for the party he is throwing to celebrate Clara Davenport's birthday on the 27th. Murshid cooking the food blesses the food and makes what the Indians call *prasad*. This is up for Murshid now; he's been eating Fatima's cooking and writing, "This body is now well in its seventies but functioning beautifully when there is the love-potion, so to speak, in the food as at the Garden of Inayat." (letter to Diane Ferry, December 8, 1968) Murshid continues giving instructions for the party. Jehanara is to make bread for stuffing and sandwiches. (On the day, when Jehanara bakes rye bread, Murshid cuts giant, two inch-thick slabs, and insists Fatima put bitter lettuce from the garden on the sandwiches.) At first, Murshid says, "There will be health food sandwiches with olives and creamed cheese." Then I hear him say to two different people that the sandwiches would be olive and *cottage* cheese.

I can hardly keep from laughing. It is contagious. Fatima catches the bug. She has been constantly amused anyway, everywhere—today in the meditation room, tonight at the champagne party, and now with me. When Murshid tells a story about Paul Reps and Mansur says, "That doesn't sound like the Reps I know," Fatima bursts out laughing. "Mansur is like Murshid's wife," she says. "He reminds me of my mother when he says stuff like that." The laughter dies. Murshid finishes giving birthday cooking directions. We learn there will be a potluck at Amin's house, the Garden of Allah, on the 24th. And Christmas day will be a family only celebration at the *khankah*, the Garden of Inayat.

December 14, 1968, Saturday

Jemila comes back Monday after visiting her sister for a month in New Hampshire. Murshid is anxious for her return. He has seen her in vision, and she figures in Murshid's dance manifestations. "Next week my chief dancing disciple returns," Murshid wrote to Eugene Wagner (December 12, 1968), "and then we shall begin the Symbolic and Tantric dances... These dances are in the *Alaya-Akasha* [the space, the unseen] which the intellectual-social people cannot accept at the mystical functional level." Two weeks of rain have prevented my working outside on the *khankah*. Murshid was right about the rain; and it came early.

December 16, 1968, Monday

In San Francisco, Murshid is having fun at Don Hayakawa's expense in a letter to columnist Art Hoppe. Murshid's theme today: Prof. Hayakawa, a Japanese-American, elevates British Zenists like Alan Watts and Aldous Huxley and neglects the Japanese; but Hayakawa, an excellent African culture scholar, has more interest in African studies than in rioting Black "non-students who themselves have never shown any interest in African Studies and are demanding courses in subjects just to put up a show of power."

A fire breaks out in Moineddin and Fatima's bedroom closet at the *khankah*. There were no combustibles in the closet. When Murshid comes on Wednesday the 18th, I take a letter to Clark. Murshid writes, "We have just had a fire here at the *khankah* in Novato. There proved to have been much more smoke than fire. The greatest damage was done to Fatima Patricia's personal effects and personal work. However, this will now give her the opportunity to redecorate her own room and possibly much of the *khankah* and so make it spiritually beautiful."

The Jablonskis are forced to lodge temporarily in the guest room. Smoke does damage to the hall, the guest room, and Jehanara and Hassan's bedroom—both across the hall from the fire. It is generally understood that the fire is elemental retribution against Fatima for getting angry at Murshid. Murshid will be analytical when he writes Paul Reps on December 21st: "A fire took place at the GARDEN OF INAYAT. It was soon put out. But the cause for the fire was exactly the same as that which destroyed *Kaaba Allah* and caused a forest conflagration where Meher Baba was supposed to come and did not."

Fatima's error of omission was that she didn't tell Murshid what she expected of him, yet chastised him for not adhering to her unspoken expectation. Mansur pictures Murshid's unexpressed anger as producing the fire in the closet. It is the most supernatural happening to date.

December 17, 1968, Tuesday
The following account of Lama Govinda's meeting tonight, attended by Murshid, is part of Murshid's long letter to imprisoned disciple Clark. (November 18, 1968)

We heard Lama Anagarika Govinda. He has all the "credentials" for an instructor in oriental philosophy in America... He was born in Germany... We had a chance to find out what infinite compassion is. Finite compassion takes into consideration men, women and children, their wants and needs, sorrows and pain. Infinite compassion does nothing of the sort. To illustrate: the Lama took up enough room for twenty people. His chief associate [Iru Price] would not permit any of the young to sit on the floor or indeed to approach his ?holiness? [sic] lest he be desecrated.

The doors were shut [shutting out Dr. Warwick], and apparently infinite compassion permits its advocates to be rude, inconsiderate, and even hostile. As I had no idea of infinite compassion before, it is now clear how it differs from finite compassion... The Lama is suffering from constant fatigue. Apparently everything fatigues him and everybody. Murshid having not reached infinity does not so suffer. Indeed, catching four of his young disciples suffering from fatigue he gave them *the works*: They all got Sufi mantras, which work, not esoterics which do not. Then Murshid had them all repeat the mantras in a dance. Then he gave them some *zikr* [a variant spelling of *ziker*] *practices* in a dance, sometimes held on to their hands, sometimes not. The fatigue disappeared. This is one of many examples of how finite compassion differs from infinite compassion as it is called, whatever that means.

December 18, 1968, Wednesday

Murshid doesn't always dictate to a secretary. He bangs one letter out unassisted, to Ruth Cook at Fields Book Store, the spiritual book store Murshid frequents. "Sam is blowing off steam," Murshid begins. Ruth, Murshid's contemporary, is probably some kind of initiate. Murshid informs her about the international contest for papers on Mahatma Ghandi's interpretation of the Bhagavad Gita, sponsored by U.S. journalist Vincent Sheehan: "One of my basic sins was that I won first consideration from a celebrated writer with my essay on the Gita."

Murshid shares his terrible vision [more wars and killing] upon hearing the U.N.'s U Thant call for a "moral and spiritual revolution." Then he goes on at length about the Lama Govinda imbroglio. "Sam was already [*sic*] to start something before the Lama," Murshid declares. "He [Sam] had a paper [by Princess Poon] which contradicted everything in the [Lama Govinda] brochure."

Murshid mentions his speaking engagement at the Aurobindo Ashram in San Francisco, which was not attended by any ashramites, and reveals—to me anyway—the significance of his frequently repeating, "the nephew of Judith Tyberg is attending my lectures." So what?

It is explained when he writes that Haridas Chaudhuri, Judith Tyberg, and one Dr. Zitko "and their 'elite' allies," Murshid tells Ruth, "joined in whole-hearted in a project in Arizona...which did not have Sri Krishna and flopped. They never refer to that." If Tyberg, who was a friend of Murshid's enemy Chaudhuri, has a nephew at Murshid's—to Murshid, this is a kind of victory.

When Murshid calls me in to take a letter, it's after lunch. Murshid tells Clark, still in prison, that a lot's happening. "If the loans made are paid back to me, there will be a temporary place [for you to stay] on your return. If not, provision can be had only on the payment of rent. Murshid is caught between desires to help others and others taking advantage of him beyond his means." I didn't know at the time that Murshid was out $1,000 dollars, "the beginning of the year found me a thousand dollars in debt." (letter to Paul Reps, January 27, 1969) I can only wonder whether Murshid grubstaked Clark when he went off to grow marijuana. I doubt it.

Murshid mentions Father Blighton's disciple Matthew, but the story is told best later (in a letter to Paul Reps, December 21, 1968): "Today Sam goes to a wedding. Matthew is the groom. When Sam [first] met him he asked, 'What is your name?' 'Matthew.' 'Why aren't you?' 'What?' 'Matthew.' Today he is, which will undoubtedly annoy all the sermonizers and lecturers on Zen and transformation." Murshid refers here to the Biblical Matthew. Spiritual names are given to support one's development. Matthew had a spiritual name when Murshid first met him and challenged him to, in effect, become his namesake, which he did.

My intimidating experience with Father Blighton notwithstanding, Murshid appreciates him tremendously. The above is followed by, "He [Matthew] has a teacher and this teacher has had more disciples having illumination than all the rest of us, spiritual and intellectual together. While the rich and powerful and elderly sit charmed at sermons on spiritual transformation, this teacher is effecting it."

December 19, 1968, Thursday

Still busy doing rain delayed gutter replacement and readying the *khankah* for a coat of white paint. Murshid dictates letters today to Haridas Chaudhuri and Huston Smith, adding a personal note to Smith's with the remark, "Tomorrow the Johnsons and I shall visit a shop in the city of Berkeley operated by a Sufi."

December 21, 1968, Saturday

Back in San Francisco today, Murshid expresses a variety of political views to African-American godson Norman McGee, as valid today as they were then. "There is no excuse for slums and I refuse to look at the Apollo space rot. If we have money to try to reach the moon, we have money to quit litter bugging the earth. This outside our maintaining a war economy. I believe the power-structures want this racial war, just as they like to see Arab and Jew fight and Hindu and Pakistani fight."

In Murshid's letter to Paul Reps, an additional detail of the Lama Govinda meeting emerges. "The stock of Reps [who gave the public practices] went way up," Murshid writes. "The Lama was asked to give a simple practice and it knocked him for a loop. He had to stop and ordered a silence... It was this that prompted this letter."

December 23, 1968, Monday

Murshid writes to Steward W. Holmes, coauthor of a study on irony and Zen at the Castleton (Vermont) State College English Department, and includes the fact that Huston Smith failed his *koan* practice. Smith revealed this to Murshid during his course at Berkeley. "But Dr. Huston Smith whom one is privileged to write told me he failed in his *Ko-an* efforts and this person has not so failed—i.e. he has been recognized by Japanese, Chinese, Koreans and Vietnamese, but not particularly by Westerners, excepting the young who are in revolt." Murshid's point: "Why don't you try to come closer to living Zen masters? There are plenty of them and some can speak English quite well." Or as Jon Levitz used to say in a skit on *Saturday Night Live*, "Get to know me!"

What Murshid does tomorrow night in Corte Madera is clearly in mind today, when he answers a "gracious letter of the 18th" from staid, Eastern-establishment secretary of the Temple of Understanding, Finley Dunne, Jr. Murshid's response shows that such nights are prepared well in advance.

The year ends tomorrow night when we shall celebrate CHRIST (not Christmas) by a *DARSHAN*, or whatever name we may call it, with a manifest experience of transmutation if not transfiguration. The Sufi practices *fana*, self-effacement, and in the state of *fana-fi-Rasul* effaces himself and actually effaces himself in the divine ideal. Beginning with Mohammed, one is now the instrument for Rama, Krishna, Shiva, Buddha, Moses and Jesus as well. The great Ramakrishna could see "God" better than he could see his fellow-men. This one has not reached that stage but he is able to practice and demonstrate self-effacement and bring blessings...

In these cases of *fana* and *Darshan*, one becomes the living instrument of the divine qualities which manifested in each of these Perfect Men, maybe only momentarily but really real. So one has been writing "When the Gods arrive, the half-gods go." One welcomes the dialecticians and metaphysicians but the corresponding practice is not observed. Now the young know it.

A very simple example is this: Stand as the *Five Pointed Star*. This represents the Birth of Christ, the Star of Bethlehem. Stand as the *Cross*. This represents the Crucifixion. Then the devotee does a sort of jumping jack: "Christ is born and Christ is risen."

Chapter 11

Tassawuri
(Attunement)

Murshid pulling Nathan in the wagon in the street in front of the Garden of Inayat in Novato.

Tassawuri is an advanced practice and requires a teacher, usually a living teacher. One does best by performing tassawuri either in the Presence of a living teacher, or when one has a firm impression of the teacher in mind, it can be done in his absence; or when the teacher manifests and brings a great blessing, tassawuri can be performed easily. There are several ways of acquiring tassawuri. One is to see the teacher and even follow the teacher while he walks. Another is to be deeply impressed, so that one is aware of the teacher's rhythm. (In the Garden, pp.110-11)

January 2, 1969, Thursday

It's the New Year, and Murshid tells Paul Reps, "The New Year's Eve Party might indicate the way for the year. It was the largest gathering, more than when you were here, with many disciples absent. We had to have three circles and this means I shall open up another item of real occult teaching

soon, using the Fire, Earth, Water and Air types separately, making their rhythms, etc."

Dr. Warwick and his disciples performed a Vajrayana Buddhist fire ceremony, or *puja* (devotional ritual). Murshid confesses to Reps he has been "somewhat skeptical," but "this puja is operative and it was very hard to keep the external consciousness." In Warwick's favor, he accepted Murshid's spiritual history, and he healed him.

Warwick's healing work on Murshid is revealed in Murshid's letter to Howard Mussell, November 26, 1968.

> Once this person was very sick. It was good because he has lived many years with little illness. Dr. Warwick came and repeated some mumbo-jumbo. This person could not understand a word. But one thing he could understand—the next day he was well and has been well ever since.

In addition to the Buddhist stuff happening on New Year's Eve, Murshid led Dervish and Yoga dances and "gave a very high type of *Darshan* absolutely excluded from all the so-called 'academies' of ???Asian Culture???" [*sic*] (letter to Julie Medlock, January 6, 1969)

The ground level, single car garage in Murshid's townhouse is being cleaned, swept, and emptied of junk, in order to create a larger dance space. Thirty people have been accommodated comfortably in Murshid's upstairs living room; fifty have squeezed in. The garage—Murshid calls it "the basement" in letters to Reps and friend Bill Hathaway—can handle eighty, and does when Pir Vilayat arrives Sunday.

January 5, 1969, Sunday

"We had no time to prepare for Vilayat," Murshid writes to "Erica, Bill (Hathaway) and boys." (January 7, 1969) "He had to call four times because of problems and when he arrived it was fortunately on Sam's regular meeting night [today] ... with only a few hours time to prepare and no advertising or anything, over 80 people showed up here!"

During his talk, Vilayat promotes his Los Angeles weekend titled "Methods of Meditation in the Great World Religions." The program is enough to make an English Department universalist like myself drool. Literary Criticism, my major, allowed me to dabble in literature from Aristotle to the present. Pir Vilayat's L.A. program has six topics: 1) Hindu practices; 2) Buddhist practices; 3) Practices of the Hermetists; 4) Contemplative practices of Plotinus; 5) Unfoldment doctrines of the Kabala, Proclus, and Avicenna; and 6) Unfoldment doctrines of alchemy, with emphasis on transmutation and regeneration. I was determined to be there, and, before sleeping, calculated a Thursday departure would get me to the Friday night lecture.

Between taking phone calls from Vilayat, Murshid writes a New Age group in London called Gandalf's Garden about the next meeting of the Temple of Understanding. Murshid knows somehow the next conference, called for Istanbul, will probably be moved to Geneva, and has already talked to his travel agent. Rev. Jack Austin, a Buddhist friend of Murshid's, lives in London. Anticipating stopping in London "either enroute or afterwards," Murshid, attracted by the New Age artwork in Gandalf's Garden's publication, opens communication with them. Taking note of the fact that Shambhala in Berkeley is Gandalf's Garden's distributor, Murshid offers to help. "We may also try to get your publication on the market both in San Francisco and in Los Angeles. This would come in the natural and normal order of our own private business."

January 6, 1969, Monday

Naturally, when Murshid was stoked to meet Lama Govinda in *Dharma* combat, he wasn't about to give away his secret, the knockout punch. Now it doesn't matter. Govinda, too tired, won't meet Murshid. He refers to the Lama's visit in a letter to Julie Medlock today.

Recently the German Lama Govinda and the English Alan Watts held a top level "Buddhist" conference. This is typical but "only in America." On the other side I have the latest material from Her Serene Highness, Princess Poon Diskul of Pismai who is not a PhDeist but is a really great sage and lady, despite and not because of her royal blood. The PhDeists have declared for "Infinite Love" and Sam for Finite Love. The PhDeists have written that the "Enlightenment Experience" (which apparently none of them have had) is the heart of Buddha's teaching, and Sam says it is pain and suffering, their cause and cure.

Sure, Buddha's enlightenment under the Bodhi tree was central to Buddha's spiritual unfoldment; Murshid is suggesting that it is not the heart of his teaching. Murshid seized on Lama Govinda's sloppily written brochure, but unfortunately for drama lovers, never got a chance to make Govinda his disciple by winning the *Dharma* combat. A copy of this letter to Julie, sent to the local Aurobindo ashram, serves a dual purpose.

Through this letter Sam is offering to put on another AUROBINDO program at the ashram but if the ASHRAM people do not show up—and they do not show up when Sam lectures there, he will get off the platform and walk away. It will be a test how much Sri Aurobindo's teachings really touch the hearts and minds of those who claim to be his followers.

January 7, 1969, Tuesday

I met good natured Bill Hathaway once when he came to Murshid's. According to Moineddin, Bill, who translates Russian scientific texts, is the source of the rumor that Murshid's hospitalization for "ptomaine poisoning" in 1967 was really a heart attack. Murshid greets Bill with a "Happy New Year!" in his letter today and quickly summarizes his recent past.

Coming out of the hospital one began working with the young. Vilayat came and it was necessary to make a rapid decision. As the Western world is not made of people who believe in the Living God, it is only the young that can accept that God speaks directly to man, through man, in man. A decision was made and one knew one's following would double, which it certainly did. Putting it drolly one said that one's effort to become a Pied Piper failed—only the young showed up. And when we needed money for a Sufi *khankah* we did not go around begging from everybody else. We turned to the living God and in a week had a house.

Then there was "the coming of Professor Huston Smith, the top American Orientalist [which] turned another page." Murshid acknowledges, "it is queer" to have an American expert on Asia, especially one who is "unable to solve *ko-ans.*" But in Smith's favor, as in Warwick's, "he has accepted both Phillip Kapleau and Sam Lewis... Besides Huston's star pupil is Sam's esoteric secretary [Mansur]. He is going south now to tape record Vilayat's speech."

About this time Ed Hunt, Murshid's elderly roommate, leaves. This opens space for students to live with Murshid. Melvin was one of the first. Another change for smooth-faced Murshid: "Sam has grown a beard. So has Vilayat. So has Gavin."

Somehow word got out that I was driving to Los Angeles to hear Vilayat in my like-new 1966 Volkswagen hippie van. One by one, they approached me. I wanted to slip out of San Francisco like a State Department diplomat on a secret mission to Los Angeles, but it was impossible to say no. First, there was David, a polio victim, who had a short leg and rocked when he walked. Next came Gwen, an acid and speed casualty, very spaced out but beautiful. Last was Greg, a long-haired Jewish barefoot hippie from New York.

This is the day Murshid sent the Tai Hsu manuscript I copied to Charles E. Tuttle Co., Inc., publishers in Rutland, Vermont. Murshid points out there was previous correspondence between them on November 6, 1967. He includes with the manuscript one of Reps' postcards, signed with a calligraphy brush. Tuttle had published Reps and Senzaki's *Zen Flesh, Zen Bones*. No doubt, Murshid hoped his association with Reps, one of Tuttle's authors, would help him publish.

January 9, 1969, Thursday

The link established by initiation is a serious matter, at least to the teacher who is connected back to the source of the line. When Murshid pursues errant pupil Howard Mussel by letter today, it is clearly in his capacity as teacher. He opens with: "The purpose of a Sufi is to awaken the light and life latent in human beings." This first sentence defines Murshid's function.

The second sentence, written non-dualistically, summarizes Murshid's estimation of Howard's current situation: "Occasionally he has to take in some side trips, no doubt, but these are not germane to his purpose."

In conclusion, the teacher speaks with compassion. "There is no compulsion in Sufism and so long as you are satisfied with your present program, please go ahead with it. And when you feel you really want full self-fulfillment you will be welcomed and no questions asked."

Howard and Clark are friends. Murshid told Clark (in a letter dated November 18, 1968) that he saw Howard at the Lama Govinda meeting. After his recitation of current events in that letter, Murshid presents this shocker: "I do not know how long I shall maintain my present program. Too much is expected and not enough returned." That is all about that—for this letter.

It all comes out in a second letter, to Paul Reps. "Samuel is in a deep difficulty today," Murshid stays philosophical, "and it is for the sake of wisdom that this has occurred. And if one were to be helped out, it might also be that the karma not being completely fulfilled, another difficulty would arise until the fundamental problem—which is not yet clear—was solved." Murshid continues, "No doubt one has almost superhuman power and superhuman faculties but one still is human, has to pay rent, meet social and financial obligations, income tax, etc." The topic of money is inevitably taken up in every letter to Reps, who lives comfortably in Hawaii on funds gained, let us say, by astute investments. Reps is generous with advice ("start a school"), but not with money. "One gets plenty of advice, no end to advice, advice, advice, world without end." Murshid continues,

On New Years evening one performed the *Darshan* that not even the greatest teachers who come this way can give. And yet one is supposed to sit around and wait for appointments with this one and that one. This will not be done. And tonight *one may make a farewell address because the people who come to Samuel's meetings are quite capable of paying admission fees to all sorts of meetings before all sorts of speakers on all sorts of subjects but for spiritual instructions, they have not been paying and one cannot stand this burden any more.* [emphasis mine]

Mansur and company head for Los Angeles today and go straight to Suzanne D'Mitrieff's house. We discover from Suzanne that a mountain retreat to be held in the days after Vilayat's weekend talks is unavailable to us, as advance reservations were required. We aren't concerned, for the cost is beyond our means and the bulk of the attendees are older people.

Pir Vilayat later tells me our entourage was responsible for his chief organizer disassociating from him. Pir Vilayat tried to dissuade him, reminding the man, "After all, we say 'Raise us above the distinctions and differences which divide men.'" Not persuaded, the organizer said, "Yes, but we own houses in good neighborhoods."

January 10, 1969, Friday

After reporting the worst to Suzanne about Sheyla and Dara, who were scheduled to hook up with Pir Vilayat in Calcutta, Murshid adds in his letter today, "Several of the local disciples may be appearing at your meetings." Pir Vilayat's audience fills a large school auditorium that has folding wooden seats. I place my battery powered tape recorder on the stage next to the dais where Pir Vilayat stands to speak. The routine, established by Pir Vilayat, of kicking off a weekend seminar with a Friday night program is later adopted by the next generation of seminar circuit Sufis, myself included.

January 12, 1969, Sunday

Murshid reports our presence in Los Angeles to Reps. "Another group of absentees are those who have gone off to hear Vilayat in Los Angeles. Nothing could be more pleasing. We hope to have tape-recordings and more." It's only been three days since it appeared Murshid might be shutting down operations. Now there's a sudden turn of events linked by Murshid to Reps's idea for a school. Murshid writes to Reps,

Hazrat Inayat Khan spent some time with Samuel in 1923 outlining his hopes, a matter not stressed because of the seemingly more important interviews of 1926... The real follow-up of 1923 came when Paul Reps proposed a SCHOOL, a School of learning and techniques, not of important and self-important people to bring East and West together. Evidently this must be in the Sphere because *yesterday a special delivery registered letter arrived with the first endowment* [emphasis mine]. I don't know how it got around. I do not even know the name of the donor...

Neither do I, but I find out later she's with me in L.A. It's Gwen, "our Cinderella turned out to be a fairy princess in disguise," Murshid reveals in his letter of January 16, 1969 to Reps. "She and several disciples have been with Vilayat and the date of their return is uncertain and perhaps unimportant." Unaware of Murshid's good fortune in San Francisco, my mates and I are exploring the San Gabriel Mountains behind the Rose Bowl in Pasadena. Under an oak tree beside the San Gabriel River, the thought of Murshid once again produces tears of joy for Mansur. The recording sessions are successful. We hook up with a meditator, Anon (for Anonymous), who is enrolled in the correspondence course of the Vedanta Center. He lets us use his small house as a base.

January 13, 1969, Monday

My request last Friday of Pir Vilayat to know the address of a man named Chuck produced a response that puzzled me. Pir Vilayat said, "Whenever I want to find anybody in Los Angeles, I call the East-West Center." When I call the East-West Center today, much to my surprise, I get the number. Chuck, when I reach him, says that Vilayat had him phone in and leave his number at the center. I had blindly followed Vilayat's bizarre suggestion and my success pleases me so much I find myself crying tears of joy at Diana's in Santa Ana, grateful for Vilayat, whose return to San Francisco inspired this trip to Los Angeles.

January 14, 1969, Tuesday

Murshid's mood is puckish today as he informs columnist Art Hoppe, "I am working on the petition to the students at Brandeis [allegedly a Jewish school] that they should march on Howard University [allegedly a Negro school] and demand a department of Jewish studies."

Gwen, David, Greg, and Mansur are en route north to visit Sheikha Bhakti Engle, widow of Hazrat Inayat Khan's secretary Fatha Engle, in Camarillo, California. Dictating a letter to Bhakti a week after we get back (November 22, 1969), Murshid pats us on the back for the trip.

One cannot help contrast the short trip of a few disciples from this region with the long trip of others, also from this region, to India. Those who went to India had long instructions which they promptly ignored and have, if anything, caused some confusion for Vilayat. Those who went to southern California had few instructions and did everything excellently.

The gift of a candle that I present to Bhakti not only pleases her, but strengthens my reliance on intuition. Before leaving San Francisco, I stopped at The Candle Shop and saw myself giving Vilayat some Persian

Rose incense, so I bought some and gave it to him. "What else have you got?" I asked the clerk, who came back with a beeswax sage honey candle. Without thinking, I said, "Sure, I'll take it." Moments later, it comes to me: *Give it to Sheikha Engle.* Much later, the rationale of giving holy people gifts of respect, something I read in Paul Brunton, comes to mind. "Beeswax! How did you know I have been wanting a beeswax candle? Why I just told Bob that we have to get one of these," Bhakti swoons.

Along with the tears of joy ecstasies on this trip I realize, being with David, Gwen, and Greg, that when you give up being alone, it is easy to enjoy those you get to know.

January 16, 1969, Thursday

Meanwhile, in Novato today, Murshid reflects in a letter to Paul Reps on last Sunday when he and new roommate Melvin enjoyed New York Jets quarterback Joe Namath's audacious prediction of a Super Bowl victory. "There was an important football game on last Sunday. The New York quarterback intuited the game excellently and all his predictions came exactly true. So he was accused of egotism, bombast and braggadocio. My disciple Melvin, who lives with me, tuned in with this man and sometimes we called the game play by play." Murshid tells Reps of the love evoked by his own being, and provoked by Wednesday night's reading of a poem that includes the lines "The world stands out on either side/ no wider than the heart is wide."

As there are so many pseudo-messiahs and self-praising cosmic-consciousness (?) people, last night Sam read "Renascence" of Edna St. Vincent Millay. He got two jolts: a) the young in the audience, not *mureeds,* who had this experience; b) the love, veneration and warm heart-feeling between the "guru" and the audience and the various members of the audience one with another. "Love ye one another" is a fact with so many young people.

January 17, 1969, Friday

Murshid and his "ersatz family" here in Novato visit Seth Wood, "an old buddy from Marin County" and Charles and Miriam Lindstrum, Murshid writes to Rudolph Schaeffer today. Murshid has written to Reps, "The rejection of intuition is the cause of all our trouble." Operative insight is up for him today. He references quarterback Namath's "foresight, insight and intuition," and adds,

The visit to the Lindstrums also exemplifies the practicality of intuitive foresight—which the dialectics of the "New" left and "New" right, and of the old, and all dualists shun—for one of the disciples had been assigned to list the trees of the region with the hope of encouraging wood-carving—and this is exactly what Charles is doing. Communication in zero flat.

Murshid's description of the Lindstrum home is so lyrical, his appreciation approaches aesthetic overload.

The "Sonoma Palace of Fine Arts" is at the head of a high valley road. There is a gully to the right with a stream, most lovely and musical at this time of the year. But the house itself dominates the formation... I am simply stunned for everything attracted me and by everything I mean "every thing"—rocks, scenery, garden, "Frank Lloyd Wright" architecture; the "union of the within and the without", the use of wood, stone, ceramic materials, painting, etc. It was too much and it must have stunned and attracted my family... I think this was one of the most wonderful days of my life.

January 18, 1969, Saturday

Murshid finally has a chance to assimilate all the impressions he receives from those of us who tripped to Los Angeles to see Pir Vilayat. I report, "Seeing a devotee of Swami Vivekananda named Anonymous made me want to meditate more." Murshid says, "Nobody should be allowed to come between you and the teacher!" His response stuns me. My immediate impression is that this comment refers to Vilayat. I feel Murshid is testing my loyalty. I know it is no good to argue with the teacher. Teachers don't always make sense logically. The issue is not always explicit.

If something disturbs Murshid, there is a flurry of words—they won't necessarily relate to the immediate situation. There will be a feeling, an atmosphere created by the uproar. It demands consideration. Hazrat Inayat Khan explains the phenomenon I am experiencing.

A real teacher is only an instrument of God. It is his presence, his wish for you that helps—not the words which he is saying. When I asked my teacher, "What is the sign of a real guru?", he replied, "It is not his form, it is not his appearance, it is not what he says, it is his atmosphere, it is what his presence conveys to you, it is what his atmosphere tells you. That which he may say, that is nothing." (Unpublished teachings of Hazrat Inayat Khan)

It touches my heart when Murshid's next comment is, "I don't want you to be an office manager; I want a spiritual companion."

January 21, 1969, Tuesday

All of Murshid's students know Swami Ranganathananda Maharaj is a spiritual giant. Murshid told us so. A large number of friends and disciples turn out to verify the claim today at a lecture hall on the Berkeley campus of the University of California. As Murshid relates to Reps (in a letter January 24, 1969), "Fortunately nearly all the young people who came to test Murshid's statement that Swamiji was a real Master, having had actual Divine experience, accepted it. And instead of being out on a limb, one's stock went up." My experience in Berkeley with Swami Ranganathananda is a knock-out, literally. In the beginning, the hall contained the usual invisible volumes of boredom and fatigue. Later, as a result of intense spiritual energy, I go from losing the Swami in light to being rudely awakened as my head bounces, unconscious, off my chest. I agree with Murshid's assessment in a letter to Bhakti Engle (January 22, 1969) that "Mansur has also had the great privilege of hearing and meeting Swami Ranganathananda Maharaj, one of the truly great men now living on earth."

January 22, 1969, Wednesday

Murshid introduces himself to Pir Vilayat's summer camp coordinator, Margaret Leach in Illinois, like this, "I am one of the last direct disciples of the late Hazrat Inayat Khan." Murshid requests "application forms and details, because we wish to cooperate in every way." Margaret learns that:

> We have got a thriving and growing School, mostly young people... When Pir Vilayat was here, I designated one of the disciples, James Pickard of Corte Madera, California, as my representative... James lives with Amin Quance who is a Sheikh designate and who has lived also in Nepal and traveled far and wide... The Esoteric Secretary, Mansur Johnson, not only wishes to go but has a station wagon which can accommodate several persons... Esoteric Secretary Mansur has been tape-recording the Pir's lectures.

January 26, 1969, Sunday

Korean Grandmaster Seo seeks Murshid's help landing a teaching job in the San Francisco Bay area. Too busy, and with no action to report until today, Murshid apologizes for his delayed response to Seo's letter of the 15th and writes, "This week I met one of the heads of Departments of Asian Studies in Berkeley and we have already agreed to meet. So when I try to fulfill this engagement, I shall bring your credentials and also tell more about you."

Swami Ranganathananda holds another meeting today, and (in a letter January 27, 1969) Murshid tells Huston Smith, "Otis and I did not go to yesterday's meeting in order that some of our group could go and I do not recall a single person who has not been impressed and enthusiastic—this after a long line of sometimes very questionable characters."

January 27, 1969, Monday

Early Monday morning, a letter to Paul Reps serves as a diary entry for Murshid. There are three paragraphs on Swami Ranganathananda and an unemotional rehash of two interviews.

> It was necessary to interview an expectant mother and a psychotherapist after the meeting on the theme, "Loving Father" with quite satisfactory results. The girl wants Murshid to adopt her. The psychotherapist is a friend of my San Francisco secretary [Melvin].

Attendance at University of California classes is not finished for Murshid—yet. He tells Reps, "Saturday the class in 'Influences of Ancient Asian Religions on Contemporary Society' began. We are using Huston Smith's book. Mansur has been very close to him." Even though it's old news, Murshid mentions the information that appears in the epigraph for Chapter 10: the bit about the job interview hoops that county officials make me jump through in order to continue receiving Aid to Families with Dependent Children. But it's a Paul Reps letter, and money talk is required, so once again, "The beginning of the year found me a thousand dollars in debt. We had rescued a 'Cinderella' and she proved to be a princess in disguise. That was liquidated and there are signs of receiving help, really for the first time in my life."

Murshid has reminded me several times lately to keep an esoteric journal. Maybe he senses I haven't written much since November. It's true. Since starting the *wazifa* practice in mid-November, I've spent a lot of time daily in practice. By December 3rd, my five times a day practice schedule had me involved daily for four and a half hours. Also, the writing presents a problem. What I wrote in the beginning were peak experiences. Now, there are so many, noting them all is impossible and redundant; I would be writing all the time.

January 28, 1969, Tuesday

Murshid sends "another fifteen dollars for postage" to Julie Medlock and comments to Reps about the women in Vilayat's life. (Vilayat doesn't live with his wife.) "Vilayat is very strong despite the women in his life. I have told him so and naturally all the young ladies wish he were free. Somebody put his picture on my altar; it has not been taken down. He is there with Mataji Krishnabai of Anandashram, Nyogen, Shaku Soyen, his father and this vociferous chatterbox."

January 31, 1969, Friday

This particular Friday, Mansur drives Murshid, Gwen, and David to Gavin's for his open house. Gavin honors Murshid by telling the story of how they became neighbors. Once when Gavin concluded a lecture, Murshid came up to him, congratulated him on his talk, and asked him where he lived. Why? Murshid wanted to live near him. Says Gavin, "Sam moved into the apartment next door and I never had to use the encyclopedia again. Anytime I wanted to know anything, I would just ask Sam." Gavin has stories about Walt Whitman and Whitman's teacher, Edward Carpenter, and stories about the silent Sufi Meher Baba and the poet William Butler Yeats. They are personal stories about his meetings with these remarkable men.

At first I think, "What a big ego." Then I realize, no, this is Gavin accepting himself as real in his life's situations. The meaning of what Murshid teaches made sense. "Sufism is based on experience," Murshid says, quoting al-Ghazzali, "and the first step is: We've got to accept the reality of our own experience." Gavin accepts his own experience. I actually felt like Gavin the other day when I said to Lauri, one of his disciples who came to Murshid's house, "Please feel free to come here any time." Gavin is free and open like that. Hugging her, I felt like Shams-i-Tabriz, who met Jelaleddin Rumi in 1244. Shams was the ecstatic saint who would embrace and even kiss women he didn't know on the street, according to a man named Ahmad who came to Murshid's over a year ago. This, in a culture where women weren't allowed to mingle with men. I embrace women at meetings more and more, following Murshid's example.

The other afternoon I joined Murshid at the breakfast table after a sleep on the floor in the front room. He was saying sleepily that he'd had a nice sleep. I said so did I. He said, "Well, you passed your spiritual test." "How?" I asked. "By doing what your teacher did."

A word for this rhythmic, sympathetic openness to the teacher is *tassawuri*. The trip to Los Angeles was *tassawuri Murshid*, in that from the moment I left the *khankah* and visited Vashti at the hospital before going to the City to pick up the others, I operated with feeling. I made plans by feeling and broke them with consideration, while being open to new inspirations. And this was how I understood Murshid operated.

Leaving Gavin's, I recall my last visit in mid-December with Shamcher, whom I took there for lunch. Shamcher, when you first meet him, has a way of deflecting all your attention back on you. While blinding you with his light (*Shams* means sun) and charming you with his smile, Shamcher will notice some thing about you and comment on it. This keeps you off balance and is a charming defense mechanism. It is unsettling to have so much piercing attention directed at me, but my discomfort does not keep me from noticing Shamcher's greatness. After meeting Shamcher and spending time with him, I feel that I have been in the presence of hierarchy. Murshid has spoken of "hierarchy," and Pir Vilayat has introduced me to terms like "the spiritual government of the world." I also discovered definitions of seven degrees in the spiritual hierarchy in the teachings of Hazrat Inayat Khan. (see September 12, 1968) Chauffeuring Shamcher around to Murshid's, to a restaurant, to Gavin's Friday night, to the Olompali ranch, and back to Gavin's for Saturday lunch allows ample time for Shamcher to interrogate me, and for me to probe this mysterious Norwegian myself. It is while driving Shamcher across the Golden Gate Bridge to that luncheon at Gavin's that I make the offhand remark about the difference between a lecturer and a murshid that finds its way into Shamcher's book. It appears in the context of Shamcher's sketch of Murshid.

Samuel L. Lewis was a native San Franciscan and a horticulturist. Early he had an urge to find truth or at least find something. The theories offered him in religion and science interested him but did not satisfy him. In 1910 Eastern mystic, Inayat Khan, a Hindu musician of the Moineddin Chisti order of Sufis, came to San Francisco. In 1923 Sam became his pupil. Though born of well-to-do parents, Sam's independence of spirit shaped for him a tough working-man's life, and it was only in his seventies he could afford to travel. To cover the greatest distance for the least funds, he relinquished all comfort and studied at the feet of many teachers, Buddhists, Hindus, Arabs, Japanese. He did not leave his old teachers as he acquired new ones but coalesced them into a whole. One of his Sufi Teachers in Pakistan dubbed him *Sufi Ahmed Murad*, meaning he who is endeavoring to fulfill his life's purpose, and when Sam's earth life had been completed, the same teacher redubbed him *Sufi Ba Murad*, meaning he who has accomplished his life's purpose.

Sam had already acquired a considerable following in San Francisco, and each time he returned from his trips he threw himself into his work as teacher and organizer with renewed energy and a wider vision. One of his young pupils [Mansur] told me about the difference between Sam and another would-be teacher, a Zen Buddhist who incidentally was an old friend of Sam's... "And this Zen Buddhist travels all over the country lecturing to mass audiences telling them about the futility of talk, in line with Zen theory or idiosyncrasy, yet he talks and talks and that seems to be all he does, while Sam remains with me. He cares. This other fellow moves on and on to new audiences, new triumphs, forgetting the old ones, while Sam stays with me whether he is here or abroad. Sam is like my father, or brother, or son or, perhaps I should rather say, like myself, myself as I want to be. He knows when I am hungry and feeds me. He never argues, never criticizes or preaches. He's just there. I'm taking up my responsibilities in society again because of him, though he never told me to. He just has that confidence in me, more than I have in myself. When I took those drugs I enjoyed the feeling of unity, I loved the weird visions but I lost my feeling of responsibility. I didn't care what I did or didn't do. I had no roots. Now I have roots and for the first time in my life I am enjoying them."

[Shamcher says] "You are working now?" He [Mansur] flashed me a grimace, "I am trying to. I am applying in the fields I knew before all these things happened. The employers ask me uncomfortable questions. My past is all that seems to matter to them. Sam comes to my aid every time, telling them I am the finest in the world. So far that hasn't helped, except to keep up my self-respect." "Missing the drugs?" "No. With Sam I am enjoying all the same visions, and more of them, without the hangovers." "How do you eat?" "Sam has taken care of that. I'm a fixer and custodian in one of the community houses, so my wife and I and our four-year-old eat well and proper every day, and feel as worthy of our keep as the other residents, most of whom work on the outside."

That same evening I watched Sam and a fragment of his crowd jubilate through a Shiva dance routine, accompanied by the rarest instruments from many corners of the world. *Then Sam read a fiery manifesto,* [emphasis mine] sparkling with wit and fury, from the then-leader of the Buddhist World Fellowship, Princess Poon Diskul of Thailand. Suddenly Sam turned to me, "Pir-O-Murshid Inayat Khan just appeared to me, telling me to share all my experiences with you." Inayat Khan had been my teacher as well as Sam's. He had left this world forty years ago. Was Sam's remark just a friendly joke to an old fellow-pupil? To him it meant more. Was he right, then? Today practically nobody can tell. To assert one or the other version would be just plain superstition. For we have carelessly neglected certain promising and even essential aspects of living, searching and training, for generations. Sam, along with a few others, has at least taken steps to regain the lost kingdom.

The financial history of Sam's enterprises shows a gradual change. Some of the teachers Sam had met lived off gifts from their pupils. This is customary in the Far East, but it was anathema to Sam in the beginning. He would rather give food and even clothing to his pupils, spending of [from] his modest earnings. When later he inherited money he spent it all on his crowd. Then businessmen among his pupils pointed out that this could not continue; there simply wasn't enough to run the enterprise this way. Sam went along and fees were set for entry into his classes and for instruction. (Bryn Beorse, *Every Willing Hand*, pp.85-88)

When not questioning me, Shamcher told me stories. Some people had criticized Vilayat, Shamcher said, for "getting into politics." What politics was Vilayat criticized for engaging in? Vilayat had fought in World War II. Shamcher exemplified for me a saying in Hazrat Inayat Khan's *Gayan*: "The truly inspired answer uproots the question." This was operative the time I asked Shamcher, on the way to Gavin's for lunch, "Could you tell me when and how you obtained enlightenment?" Shamcher said, "Oh? Am I enlightened? Thank you very much. But I think it is really you who are enlightened. It's true; I had an experience when I was eight years old which made me feel very lonely. Yet, perhaps I was enlightened last year when I was seventy-one years old. My parents didn't understand what was happening to me when I was small, but they knew something was. I became interested in the yogis and began experimenting with their practices. You know, a word like 'Beloved,' which begins one of the Sufi prayers, 'Beloved Lord, Almighty God, through the rays of the sun, through the waves of the air,' has a meaning which goes far beyond any meaning that you find in the dictionary."

Before lunch, Shamcher tells Gavin about my question. Gavin is seriously puzzled by it. "I never heard of such a thing," Gavin says. I can't believe he said that. Never heard of enlightenment? Gavin asks me to say a grace before eating and Shamcher chimes in, "Yes, let Mansur say it, because he is enlightened." I am mortified, and regret I ever brought it up. So we are all enlightened but not conscious of it all the time, I think, falling back on my understanding of Lord Buddha's basic teaching.

Once Vilayat was tested, Shamcher says, with the question, "If there were a war, would you fight?" Vilayat replied, "I would consider whether it were a just war or not." The answer came, "That's not good enough.

You eat the food of France; you fight the wars of France." Who was the questioner? It was his father, Hazrat Inayat Khan.

Shamcher tells of attending Hazrat Inayat Khan's summer schools in Suresnes, outside Paris, in 1925, 1926, and 1927. After a few days the first summer, Shamcher said to Pir-O-Murshid Inayat Khan, "I don't feel that I belong here, I believe that I must leave." "I do not care if you leave," the teacher said. "You may do that if you want, but it would be too bad for the others, for you are such an inspiration for them."

I think Shamcher wanted to leave the summer school because he had a problem with hierarchy—he didn't like titles. But he was also a trickster, who played a joke on Murshid once, asking Murshid to accept him as a murshid. "For 30 years I have accepted your economic theories," Murshid wrote back. "I will not accept this title." Shamcher wrote back, Murshid said, and apologized. Others do accept Murshid Shamcher.

Leaving Gavin's, Shamcher steps into a mud puddle as I hold open the door of the car for him. Shamcher, being wherever he is, appears not to notice the puddle or the water on his shoe. The image of Shamcher's shoe in the puddle sticks in my mind. Draw what conclusion you will; contemplating it takes more than a few moments of my time.

Chapter 12

Playboy
Discovers Murshid

Playboy magazine for March will be out in a few days [price $1]. It has a long article about the "cults" of California with considerable attention to one "Sam Lewis." The article shows that it is based on actual verbal reporting of somebody in the audience. This publication was a surprise to me and it starts out with a false statement—not a false premise, but a false statement about this house. Followed by a quasi-false statement that this person does not know how to breathe and was "wheezing" which is an assumption of medical knowledge on the part of the writer. And it is sarcastic because the subject was "Breathing" and he openly states that "Sam Lewis" shows he did not know how to breathe himself. Ted, I don't recall in my whole life any occasion wherein I wheezed. Even my medical history—there are not many records because on the whole my health has been excellent—shows no such indication. All bronchial and other examinations by the Federal authorities, etc. show that at least my chest has been always in excellent condition and the way I climbed the adjacent hill just before I read the article would bring forth a lot of witnesses. Also the article states I had shown a prize-fighter how to climb Nob Hill without losing his breath, which I have and he would testify in my behalf.

I had to contact a colleague on another matter (concerning ORACLE magazine) and he told me he had been a professional in this field of publication-legality and wants to do something. (Murshid's letter to his attorney, Theodore C. Lachelt, February 11, 1969)

The Murshid regards the disciples as part of himself. One says in public: "The difference between Sufism and other spiritual movements is that in Sufism Murshid and Mureed are one." Hazrat Inayat Khan put it also, "It is the mureeds who make the Murshid." This one has been more fortunate than Hazrat Inayat Khan or Murshida Rabia Martin in having wonderful mureeds. (Murshid's letter to goddaughter Saadia Khawar Khan, February 16, 1969)

February 1, 1969, Saturday

Murshid's successful presentation of how to correct an afflicted Saturn at Gavin's last night inspires him to promulgate a new policy: "If places are offered for lecturing, they will be accepted, provided my actual backgrounds and history are accepted." His acceptance at Gavin's inspires Murshid to address historical slights of his prowess by the locals. He writes Fritzi Armstrong, a local mover and shaker on the spiritual scene, about what happened at Gavin's.

There was a discussion going on at Gavin Arthur's on the subject of "Saturn." I am not an astrologer. I was initiated into esoteric occultism almost 50 years ago... I was permitted to demonstrate how to correct defects arising from persons with afflicted Saturns...something I have wished to do for years.

The "little event" at Gavin's that triggers this policy is Murshid's success in presenting the Saturn teachings. Old friend Vocha Fiske also learns of Murshid's new willingness to expand his teaching activities in a letter today—and of how it has triggered old resentments about rejections by "mature people." "This has been a very 'exciting' period," Murshid writes in a letter to Huston Smith. Excitement for Murshid consists of visits by Pir Vilayat and Swami Ranganathananda Maharaj, and a class by a woman, Dr. Nottingham, "The Influence of the Traditional Religions of Asia on Modern Movements." Murshid has to put his use of the word 'exciting' in single quotes, since he rails elsewhere against society's addiction to excitement.

February 2, 1969, Sunday

Murshid slams Acting President of San Francisco State College Don Hayakawa in a letter to Raymond Jaffe of the Experimental Collegiate Program at UC Berkeley today, and sends carbons to Hayakawa's associates. What new tidbits about Hayakawa does Murshid serve up today? For openers, "Several delegations have been approaching this person anent Dr. Hayakawa. They all have the same programs, reading over his books to show he is a man of no principles whatsoever, grasping each situation to further his ego and social standing." That's not all. "When I was living in Mill Valley his [Hayakawa's] name was proposed for the Marin Rod and Gun Club. He was rejected. He shouted it was because of his race!? The hard fact is that he was an atheist and the members of the Marin Rod and Gun Club are *good* people, and they did not want any atheist." What else did Hayakawa do? "Besides he had rejected any idea of any article on Zen coming from Japanese sources but accepted articles from Englishmen [Watts, Huxley] whom he admired... This shows the complete lack of principles on the part of power-structured persons."

February 6, 1969, Thursday

First, there was a fire in Fatima's closet; now, a fire destroys the ranch house at Olompali ranch. While Shirin and I ride up to take a look, Murshid writes a letter to Mirza Begg, author of *The Holy Biography of HAZRAT KHAWAJA MUINUDDIN HASA CHISHTI*, in Ajmer, India.

It is interesting to follow Murshid's defense of his unorthodoxy to an orthodox Muslim.

Knowing that the best defense is sometimes offense, Murshid launches into his first critical comment about Begg's *Holy Biography*: "It assumes much, too much for the scientific age." Yes, Murshid says, I've had the experience in your book, only for me it happened "at the cell of Bakhtiar Khaki,"[d. 1236, one of the successors of the subject of Begg's biography, spelled Moineddin Chisti in this book] but "If they [the holy ones] are relegated to the past only, they [modern critics] deny that Allah is AL HAYY and no argument has any value."

Moineddin and Murshid observe the rotation of the *tattvas* (elements).

Then, Murshid shares his present spiritual practice: "Every day I repeat a number of times YA HAYA WA KHAYYUM and this has been realized which keeps this body and mind in fine fellow [*sic*] and constantly confuses the critics and enemies, for they are unable to explain the vitality."

Murshid demonstrates his familiarity with two personages pictured in Begg's book. He describes one, Hazrat Pir Zamin Nizami Saheb, as "my host in my visit to Ajmer"; and the other, Fiyazaddin Sahib of Hyderabad, Deccan, as "my host and friend, and in many ways my spiritual brother." Murshid finds Begg's "Criticisms of Emperor Akbar" "inconsistent and not proven," given his loving dedication "to two of the Presidents of India who were not 'Muslims' in the traditional sense" [like Emperior Akbar who also was an untraditional Muslim].

This is all preamble. Murshid confesses at this point, "I realize in writing this letter and also in my societal and intellectual functions here that I shall be subject to criticism," the reason being that "my introduction of dance patterns into spiritual matters will be met with rages and ranges of hostilities from people who verbalize good-will." This, even though Murshid adds that he has received "the good-will and blessings from the Inner Planes of the Great Saints whom you justly admire."

Murshid presents the Prophet Mohammed's acceptance of his unorthodox predecessors: "The Prophet David gave us both Music and Dancing as ways to spiritual realization. And there is no doubt that Mohammed himself really accepted the contributions of his predecessors though the majority of his followers dissented." Just then, Murshid abruptly terminates this line of thought and continues to criticize Begg's *Holy Biography*.

"Nor is there any valid discussion of *WUJUD* [often used interchangeably with *hal*, "state of consciousness"]. A book [Begg's] is written in English, ostensibly for the Western world and terms are assumed, not explained. The non-Muslims can hardly understand what you are writing about and the majority of the orthodox in what is called 'Islam' (which has little to do with any surrender of any kind or any peacefulness of any kind) will criticize your work."

Finally, there's "the proclamation (which is very dear to me) that Allah has sent His Messengers to all peoples" —this from the holy *Koran*. There's a whole new class of Divine Messenger, Murshid asserts, "who brought codes but not written scriptures and their teachings are most wonderful though confined to Anthropologists and Archaeologists."

It all leads to the grand conclusion that "the Heart full of love is not concerned with doctrine." The no nonsense presentation of Murshid's dance program and its success has led to further developments: "We are now introducing Dancing and rituals based on the *Sifat-i-Allah*. One will be accused of making 'innovations' and absolutely pleads guilty. But these 'innovations' are winning the admiration of a growing number of young people who have given up religion in almost every sense of the term, but they have not given up God, and they certainly are accepting ALLAH at a rate no missionary has succeeded in."

Taking the discussion up another octave, Murshid challenges the reality of the past with the reality of the present. "It is so easy to write about the *Auliya* [meaning, the saints themselves, as Begg does about the Chisti saints]. But are they realities? Are we referring to living men? To those that lived only in the past? Or to some abstraction which wins our admiration and convinces nobody else. This is the way of the Orthodoxy. The way of Reality is to accept the experiences of others and do this without condemnation. *When it became evident that an ever growing sector of the human race was demanding experience beyond the material and took to bizarre ways to experience—and I mean experience, this person began JOY WITHOUT DRUGS."* Anticipating an awakened world of self regulating moral humans, Murshid professes,

We have no "moral" teachings. We repeat the *SIFAT-i-ALLAH,* not as epithets and characteristics of some Abstraction named "God" or "Allah" but the epithets of Life Itself, that Life is God, *al-Hayy.* And we find all these Attributes in the Living God, and so they belong to man, made in the Divine Image, actually, not abstractly or symbolically. Thus, man has within him all the Beautiful Names, the Beautiful characteristics, and by repeating *Wazifas,* the *Sifat-i-Allah* begin to manifest in human beings, with mostly Strength stressed for the men and Beauty for the women, always remembering that Allah is One and in Him all Attributes are found together, separated by the minds of men.

When we become aware of the Living God (Allah, *al-Hayy*), we promote Peace and find Peace, and out of that fountain all the other good and beautiful characteristics [flow] through mankind made in the Divine Image. I am not concerned with traditions, I am concerned with the human experience and I see ways out of the turmoils of the day. Those who join in recitations and dancing experience this and their questions are answered. It is a New Day, my brother, a dance of universal love and brotherhood and not of sham words masquerading as eternal verities and values.

This is not the end of the letter. Another half page follows; then:

The Prophet, on whom be peace said, "My words can never abrogate the words of Allah but the words of Allah can abrogate my words." Nonsense! Who accepts that? Only a few Sufis perhaps, not otherwise. [sarcasm intended] And so legal codes, very valuable for certain times and places, and institutions very valuable for certain times and places are fostered on the world and fail, because they do not come from the Throne of Allah. What comes from the Throne of Allah is Infinite in all respects and this Throne is found in the heart of man.

Shirin and Mansur, on the way back from the burned Olompali ranch, talk about the karma created there and about spirits being set free by the fire. Shirin had the experience of an entity attaching itself to the left side of her face right after the fire, which she released by invoking Allah and leaving the premises. We spoke about the disaster as a sort of purification by fire. Then our conversation turned to Don McCoy, the benefactor of Olompali ranch. Shirin's close relation to Olompali made me feel there was a karmic connection between her and Don. Shirin had told me of a vision of herself in a cottage, taking care of him.

I say to myself, *I'd like to ask Murshid what the past life relation is between Don and Shirin.* I am focusing very intensely on this question, and it comes to me slowly, with a sensation, full of feeling: *Shirin was Don's mother, and she*—I got it in feeling before I could even put it in words—*abandoned him.* When I tell Murshid, he says, "I can understand that."

In this vein of past-life tales, Vilayat told Greg, my L.A. traveling companion, that he was Trotsky in another life. I said, "That's funny, I keep seeing you as John the Baptist." Greg went to Vilayat and asked Vilayat if my sight was valid, and Vilayat said, "Yes." I see Vilayat as a sort of Saint Francis character, saintly and robed, but cringing under his robe.

February 7, 1969, Friday

Murshid spends the weekends in San Francisco. While driving Ruth and Murshid to the City along Marina, the northern section of San Francisco fronting the bay, Murshid tells me to go straight. I intended to turn, but I do *fikar* and erase the agitating impression of ego activity, which doesn't want to follow Murshid's direction.

My effort to keep the breath balanced or rhythmic is only conscious sporadically. However, while I was driving to Los Angeles, the phrase *Ya Hayy, Ya Haqq* was a nearly constant chant for me.

Ya Hayy is a very powerful practice. I said that [another phrase] is to be repeated only eleven times, and the same is true of Ya Hayy. Ya Hayy is so powerful a practice that I think if one repeats it more, one would do less well... And Ya Haqq is even stronger. You can't say that a lot because you'd blow your vocal chords, and it would disturb your neighbors. And you can't say it weakly or it won't have any meaning or effect. (Unpublished teachings of Pir Vilayat Khan)

I chanted this phrase all the way down and all the way back from L.A. I didn't have the above at the time of the trip, so I was unembarrassed by my over-indulgence. My three thousand to nine thousand times a day repetition of *wazifas* is my self-prescribed response to Murshid's assignment to master all the *wazifas*. I no longer attempt to concentrate on a phrase every minute of the day, as I did a year ago when I focused on "Toward the One" for six or eight months. Now, I choose certain times. I pull out the beads when driving, for example; and sometimes I don't *say* a phrase, but rather *feel* the rhythm.

Murshid speaks this evening at Brother Juniper's, the Holy Order of MANS restaurant down in the Haight-Ashbury district, run by Father Blighton's disciples. He says something about an embrace and a kick in the pants being the same expression of love. To illustrate, he refers to a Zen story about a disciple, Obaku, and the master, Hyakujo.

That evening Hyakujo gave a talk to the monks and told them this story about the law of causation. Obaku, upon hearing the story, asked Hyakujo, "I understand that a long time ago because a certain person gave a wrong Zen answer he became a fox for five hundred rebirths. Now I want to ask, If some modern master is asked many questions and he always gives the right answer, what will become of him?" Hyakujo said, "You come here near me and I will tell you." Obaku went near Hyakujo and slapped the teacher's face with his hand, for he knew this was the answer his teacher intended to give him. Hyakujo clapped his hands and laughed at this discernment. "I thought a Persian had a red beard," he said, "and now I know a Persian who has a red beard." [If the reader is puzzled by this exchange, a perusal of Nyogen Senzaki's book of 100 Zen koans, *The Iron Flute*, might make it clearer.]

Murshid also tells the story of a letter he got from his teacher Murshida Martin, accusing him of all kinds of things. Murshid wrote back quoting Hazrat Inayat Khan: "Poison from the hand of the beloved is as nectar to the lover." The whole affair, Murshid said, "was all a test."

A recent test that needled me was when Murshid confused me with Moineddin. Murshid and I were at the hospital visiting Vashti when he said that Moineddin had asked him the night before about his beautiful disciples. It was I that asked that, but I let it pass. Later, I overheard Murshid talking on the phone. He referred to me as his "best friend." As I experience slight because he confuses me with Moineddin, or pride because I am his "best friend," I'm learning to accept praise and blame with equanimity, as all in the realm of ego activity.

Murshid gives a practice to Jemila and Mansur: Imagine you are looking at your heart reflected in a mirror. It will be like a sun and, in the beginning, a little rough. Make it smooth. Sometimes when my breath is strong in the left nostril, the left half of my head feels clear or in light. "In light" is not visual light, but felt light.

February 8, 1969, Saturday

At the dance class, Murshid begins reviving the mystery dances, which means teaching about the elementals—earth, water, fire, and air—to all these women: Jemila, Fatima, Shirin, Gwen, Gypsy, and others, who dance together. Watching, I get such a feeling from them. It is an Isisian feeling about women and the meaning of femininity. It is as if this were a dance designed to make women become Women. When I see Shirin with her sleeping bag leaving Murshid's, I tell her my thought that "since we can't all live together, I feel that I should travel around and stay with everyone." She immediately says that would be fine with her. I can stay with her. "But please," she says, "no jealous wife. I hate that." "I'll work into it gradually," I say. But I never do—until 1994.

February 9, 1969, Sunday

Unless I write every day, I forget impressions of every sort. Unless I note my practice of imagining Murshid present, even when I'm alone, I overlook recording this detail. This practice helps me keep my attention high; I tend to relax when he's not around. It is time to say that I can see auras. No doubt my confidence increased after Lois Robinson said I was clairvoyant. (see September 14, 1969) I sit in the office with Gypsy, and we look at each other. Gypsy has green hands and yellow around her head. I see Murshid Thursday nights with purple between his head and shoulder. With him, however, I feel, not see, a vast aura of white light. This afternoon, reading L. Adams Beck's *Dreams and Delights*, I become aware of a *yellow* shadow cast by my hand on the pages of the book. Is the sun coming through the window doing it? Someone who came to work at the *khankah* is reading in the room with me, but I don't mention it until Jemila calls me to admire her paint job in the dining room. She follows me back and looks. She doesn't see anything. Right now as I type, I *see* a purple spot on both my hands. Two Thursdays ago, Murshid gave the class the practice, *Look at the sun and see colors.* I couldn't see any, at first.

> But now you will say, "What experience does a mystic have? Does he see colors, does he communicate with spirits...does he read thoughts?" And the answer is that to a mystic all these things are elementary. And those who do these things are quarter-mystics, half-mystics. A mystic who is a thorough mystic, for him these things are children's play. These are not beyond his power; they are within his power. But the power of a mystic can be so great, and insight can be so keen, that the ordinary man cannot imagine it. And for the very reason that an ordinary man cannot imagine it, a mystic who looks not different from an ordinary man, cannot profess to see or know or feel any better. Naturally therefore, the real mystic, who has arrived to a point of understanding, makes the greatest effort to keep his power and insight covered from the eyes of all. (Unpublished teachings of Hazrat Inayat Khan)

I blab about these things in the privacy of my esoteric journal. They are new to me. They are published here because this is a sharing of my process. Hazrat Inayat Khan's caveat above puts it all in the proper prospective.

February 11, 1969, Tuesday

For the next week, the article "Cultsville, U.S.A." in the March *Playboy* figures in Murshid's correspondence: twice to his lawyer, Theodore C. Lachelt; twice to his U.S. Representative, Philip Burton; to Anandashram; three times to columnist Art Hoppe; to goddaughter Saadia Khawar Khan; to Shamcher; to the Temple of Understanding's Peter Dunne (twice); and to friend Vocha Fiske.

Of primary importance for Murshid in his communication today with Ted Lachelt is the disposition of "a very large increment" in the annual report of his father's trust at Wells Fargo Bank. Murshid's longtime concern is: *Whom is this trust set up to benefit, the trustees or the beneficiaries of the trust—namely, Samuel and Elliott Lewis?* Murshid says to Lachelt, "I have felt that we should be entitled to 50% of this increment which would still leave a very large amount for the trustees, etc.," showing a willingness to settle for half and give the trustees something to watch grow. "If we received this amount it would be considerably more than what we are now getting and [would] still leave the original capital not only untouched but receiving a regularly increasing addition." Then Murshid gets down to brass tacks,

Elliott had told me that with his present expenses he is just making ends meet. I have been taking the stand that moral issues are not important—I have been beaten every time on this—it was simply a question of getting as much as possible, so if he gained I, Samuel, would gain. But without my consent or knowledge he [Elliott] telephoned Mr. Slosberg of Wells Fargo and inferred or more than inferred he was acting in my name—which he was not. He has no right to act in my name especially since his burdens are due to his inability to pay the expenses for the old family residence on Ninth Ave. in San Francisco from which he eased me out entirely, and which if there were morals, I should be joint owner. I am not. I am out. I cannot both be out and in and my name being used to support his claim on the house is very questionable. But again, it is not to me whether it is questionable, but how I am, Samuel L. Lewis, going to benefit in an imbroglio between Wells Fargo and Elliott. When my father died the representatives of Wells Fargo supported every statement and every lie of Elliott, cutting me out of all the heirlooms I wished, and should have had. So my policy has been to stand off and stand off entirely.

Finally, Murshid gets to the *Playboy* part of his letter to Lachelt, which begins this chapter. Here is the offending portion of the article Murshid is referring to.

In the scruffy Mission area, south of Market Street, an old Jew named Samuel Lewis sits under a portrait emitting "blessings from Ruth St. Denis," the disciples of mystical Islamic Sufism spread round about him. "I'm applying Sufi to the solution of the hippie problem," explains Sam, the self-acknowledged Sufi sheik of San Francisco. "They know there are states of consciousness other than the physical. I teach them, meditation and love." Just now, he is giving a lesson to eager youngsters in "the science of breathing." "The New Testament says God is breath," he confides. "Breath and life are one, but breath is more than oxygen and chemistry. It draws in the life force. It brings in life for health, for courage, for fearlessness, to overcome sleep, for longevity—of which I am the perfect demonstration. It needs a master—it cannot be learned from books."

Sam tries to show a prize fighter how to walk up Nob Hill at full speed without losing breath. "The soul is the divine breath," he says, wheezing as if he could use a little more of it himself. "And Sufism is the reality, the universal outlook, in which you can reach such an attainment that you can have the peace of awakening. Sufis use love—they believe in God as *experience*. Love means self-surrender. Self-surrender, which is different from self-denial, is getting guidance from a teacher, from God or from yourself. The Kingdom of God is *within* you—that's an *actuality*, not metaphysics."

Sam Lewis turns to a young female acidhead and asks her if she would be interested in "the joy without the acid." She nods wanly. "Look into my eyes, then. Your eyes are *shouting* unhappiness. I want to teach you happiness. His animated face freezes into a Keatonesque mask and he fixes her with the eerily hypnotic gaze of the big Buddha in Gump's... A scruffy young man with a gentle, abstracted air and cataracts of flaxen hair (courtesy Lady Clairol's "Born Blonde") is confused about Vedanta, a highbrowish Neo-Hinduism offering a modern interpretation of the classical Vedas, and Sufism. "The difference between Sufi and Vedanta," says Lewis straightaway, "is the energy the Vedantist uses to conquer his passions, Sufis use to find God. If you have a hundred units of vital energy and ten are sex, it's an important part of your life. Suppose you have a thousand units and fifteen are sex—sex has gone up rather than down, but it becomes so small compared with the whole—that's Sufi!"

"When you say don't use your penis, you're paying attention to your penis. We don't waste time with that. In Sufism, as in Zen, the devil is the ego, not sex. The question is not whether you keep up sex, but if you keep up God. Sex should be divinized, not forbidden." (*Playboy*, March, 1969, p.151)

Addressing a staffer in Phillip Burton's San Francisco office named Susan Kennedy as "My dear Susan," Murshid begins by leaping right into the *Playboy* issue.

There is something in my private life that may become public and once it becomes public may prove to be a veritable powder keg. *Playboy* magazine for March 1969, out in about two weeks, has a long article on the cults of California... A leading article almost begins with reference to "Sam Lewis" they call me by this name, no objection. They also give the residence but refer to this house in a most untrue, unfair, and misleading manner... Part of the article is quite true being almost verbatim what I actually said but scoffing at this and referring both to myself and to certain persons in the audience in manners to which the medical profession could take offence... I do not know about many of the cults referred to. I am described as a SUFI, which is true. I belong to the same movement as the Presidents of India and Pakistan and to notables of other countries generally referred to as Islamic.

Murshid, the Sufi, is about to construct a scenario in which his appearance in *Playboy* has the potential to ignite an international incident. Let's follow his argument.

There are more Sufis in this world than there are Vietnamese Buddhists. There are more Vietnamese Buddhists than there are Israelis... At the moment the Iraqis are deliberately persecuting and I mean persecuting Jews—I mean Jews per se and not just Israelis. The center of Sufism for all practical purposes is in Baghdad. Sufis had much to do with the establishment of this country (vide Gertrude Bell) I know what I am talking about and I know far more, regrettably, than too many men in the foreign office holding high positions... BUT if and when a copy of *Playboy* gets into the hands of any Iraqi or for that matter Arab. Or if there is a suit against *Playboy* on this matter there will be hell to pay.

I am in Novato oblivious to all of the above coming out of San Francisco, musing moments before I write in my journal, *What wazifa should I commence with the new moon February 16th? Perhaps I should ask Murshid.* No sooner have I posed the question than the phrase *Ya Azim* (the Most High) pops into my mind. This is remarkable.

So is Murshid's remark to me, which I must record. *You have peace,* he said. This impresses me. I never imagined I would be acknowledged for possessing peace. In *Vadan* it says, "Perfection is attained by five achievements: life, light, power, happiness, and peace." (*The Complete Sayings of Hazrat Inayat Khan*, p.145) I'm on my way.

February 12, 1969, Wednesday

I have read twelve pages of Iamblichus's *Life of Pythagoras*, have taken copious notes, and can hardly continue reading I am so intoxicated. Now I take a walk to try to calm down. The following from page three is a long sentence, so take a deep breath before beginning.

But, when Mnesarchus considered with himself that the God, without being interrogated concerning his son, had informed him by an *oracle* [emphasis mine] that he would possess an illustrious prerogative and a gift truly divine, he immediately named his wife Pythais from the Delphic Prophet [oracle], instead of Parthenis, which was her former appellation; and he called the infant, who was soon after born at Sidon in Phoenicia, Pythagoras; signifying by this appellation that such an offspring was predicted to him by the Pythian Apollo [oracle].

The reason this turns me on is because it is an ancient text speaking about what Murshid talks about: oracles. Murshid is always talking about oracles. A whole chapter stressing the oracular function of women in *Introduction to Spiritual Brotherhood* is called "The Place of Womankind in the New Age." It is one thing for Murshid to write prophetically about "the new type of oracle," another thing for him to begin "the restoration of the oracular function" at the Saturday dance class. It comes full circle for me to read about a society where oracles are used and then to see Murshid continuing an ancient mystical tradition. What Murshid gives me through his living example is an appreciation and understanding of historical tradition.

Pythagoras was sent to Egypt by his teacher Thales to study. He spent twenty-two years in Egypt. The soldiers of Cambyses invaded Egypt, captured Pythagoras, and took him to Babylon, where he studied with the Magi for twelve years—a thirty-four year discipleship! When the 56 year old Pythagoras returned to Samos in Greece, he could find no one interested in what he had to teach. To remedy this, he persuaded a needy young man to attend to him and learn from him in exchange for room and board and some spending money.

This stratagem shows the lengths a spiritual teacher will go to enlist a pupil. It is still used today. Mansur is on Murshid's payroll. Murshid pays me for "helping" him. After that initial payment of $200, Mansur is hooked, always well fed, and never again given money. If you have something beautiful that you can't give away, you might try satisfying the immediate need of the person, as Pythagoras demonstrated, to get their attention. Ancient Sufis used to carry water in the desert to give away. The gratitude of those whose thirst was quenched made them receptive to hear a word about God.

Murshid begins his letter to Anandashram, "This is really a *funny* letter and it is written very early in the morning, long before daylight." By the end of the third paragraph, Murshid has defined "funny" three ways: as a shocking law suit in paragraph one; having received no help, only suggestions, in paragraph two; and rejection if he "tried to lecture on Sufi Poetry" in paragraph three. Is this laughter to hide the tears? "Many copies are being made," Murshid continues to Anandashram, "and some of the recipients are going to be *shocked* because it looks as if Sam has to go to law to bring a lawsuit. And people will be *shocked*, but they will not *help* Sam in the way he wants it." Only to Anandashram could Murshid use the phrase "Sam's private Kurukshetra" (a reference to the *Bhagavad Gita*) and be certain he would be understood.

It is fortunate that in Sam's private Kurukshetra with Sri Krishna on his side battles are won. And there are many people who glub-glub *Prajna* but most reject it. Only to practice what is in the guidance is always a cause of *shock* to good people who are still attached to their egos... The Mystical Experience when God said to Sam: "I make you spiritual teacher of the Hippies" is fast manifesting, and it is as Sam has been telling everybody, "Sam's campaign to be a Pied Piper has failed miserably, only the young show up." And they do every week more. Only Sam has practically no *help* and the more he succeeds the more suggestions he gets, not help but suggestions. So this is a very *funny* letter.

Playboy, a very well-known off-color magazine, has written about Sam, and they say some things which are entirely untrue. They have written about him without his consent and they call him a "Sufi" which is all right. But the article has to do with the cults of California and the Sufis are not a California "cult."

Murshid temporarily leaves the *Playboy* issue with one last laugh. "It is all very very *funny*," he repeats; then goes on to describe what he is doing. The class where Murshid recites his Christ poetry on Tuesdays is "growing in attendance every week." He found at his Friday night meeting in the Haight-Ashbury district "not a few had spiritual experiences." The only good thing in his life, Murshid jokes, "is that three out of four people who make appointments don't show up." Last week, Murshid reports, after he presented the *HARE KRISHNA* dance, a disciple suggested cymbals. Murshid found finger cymbals and writes, "This was a good suggestion."

For not the first time, Murshid tells a correspondent about the visit by the Jewish Sunday school class, with kids more interested in Sufism than Judaism, with parents interested in neither. Murshid finds it wonderful "that there is an awakening toward the reality of the God-Experience." With this, Murshid invokes a new standard, distinguishing "God-people" and "Church people" from each other.

So many go around claiming God-experience and when they ask Sam, he always says: "Never mind their claims. Show me their disciples." And we hear stories of the rise and fall of this great personality and that but never a sign of any great disciple. So many churches and so many cults but only the young experience God, so we shall have a new age in which the God-people may be separate, in a certain sense from the Church people.

Murshid's contemplated lawsuit against *Playboy* comes up again in terms of Sri Krishna's battle on the field of Kurukshetra. "So Sam is ready for the KURUKSHETRA in the law-courts and this will shock the good people. They avoid Kurukshetra." Murshid alludes to money coming twice in the recent past to help him with bills, and fairly shouts with exaltation, "Now Sam feels he has Sri Krishna with him. He is going to compel the Americans by strange ways to accept the possibility of the God-experience and even more of the Love-experience—not thoughts, not emotions and not even PREMA [divine love] but the All-Embracing Love of Christ and Krishna, of Mohammed and Buddha as an actuality."

As if suddenly aware he's shouting, Murshid interjects, "Well, all this looks like bombast," and segues into what it's like to be a spiritual teacher with a disciple who phones in his illumination experience. "But in the midst a disciple of Sam [Dara Rowell, now in Ohio], twenty-five hundred miles away long distance in the middle of the day: 'Sam! OM! SRI RAM! JAI RAM! JAI JAI RAM! I have had IT, the illumination!' This is worth all the criticisms and suggestions and comments and enables Sam to again resume his program of seven days, 12 hours a day."

Recurring in my life are women with attributes of women from the past I've loved or wanted to love. Gypsy, whom I saw last night, is like Kay Peterka. Shirin, a double Scorpio with a Sagittarian moon, is like Marty Finney. Gwen has the voice of Judy Starbuck, exactly. When I ask Murshid what this means, he says, "If you looked at their charts, you would probably find they were very similar." I ask whether it has anything to do with them being soulmates. Murshid says, "No, just being tuned in on similar frequencies."

February 14, 1969, Friday
The last three weeks, I've taken Murshid back to the City on Fridays. First thing upon arrival today, Murshid wants to dictate a letter to his brother Elliott. This is a followup to Elliott's phone call, which prompted Murshid's letter of the 11th to attorney Lachelt. Murshid informs Elliott that according to his reading of "the last detailed report," laws governing wills notwithstanding, "we are entitled to the full income of earnings." Additionally, Murshid tells Elliott that the trustees denied his request in 1958 for medical assistance, claiming it would reduce the principal and

mean lower payouts when, in fact, the principal has grown. "So, I paid for the illness," Murshid writes. "Unfortunately, my physician of that time is dead." To Elliott's request for an estimated budget Murshid states, "I am now compelled to have both cook and housekeeper... The only reason my ends meet is that I am getting some outside assistance through paid lectures. I am compelled to do this."

Murshid and Mansur have been going to the home of Gavin Arthur for his Friday night sessions. Tonight, Gavin characterizes the Piscean Age as one of nautical exploration. Habits are hard to break. Gavin's still arguing that the Aquarian Age is not here yet. Following his logic, I say, "What about the exploration of space?" reasoning that if ocean exploration characterizes watery Pisces, space exploration might match airy Aquarius. It comes off as a kind of challenge. On the way home, I ask Murshid whether he thinks that Gavin's ascriptions of rulership of our age are correct. Murshid answers, "There's no point in disputing with the speaker." He says we should "go with the speaker." I take this as confirmation that my earlier comment was inappropriately challenging.

February 15, 1969, Saturday

Last night, fully conscious, I dream I see Murshid and myself coming out of a shop. I follow Murshid, who is leading, and Vilayat, who has long hair, into another house [the self]. This morning, I sleep two and a half hours at Murshid's. I've been taking the sleeping bag that Shamcher gifted me when he visited the *khankah* and sleeping in it when I stay at Murshid's. There are many dreams. The dream state is very casual for me. *I experience the reality of dream as I experience a daydream or imagination.*

Today Murshid dictates the second letter to his attorney on the *Playboy* issue. For openers, Murshid names the writer, C. Robert Jennings, and indicates that Jennings made an appointment he didn't keep to see Murshid, "but quite evidently was at one of my public meetings. Too many of the words and items are exactly correct but not others."

After an introductory paragraph, Murshid has me insert the first paragraph of the *Playboy* article. His exegesis sounds legalistic—he is willing to back with witnesses his allegations that "non-Sufis have been able to exclude this teaching [that Sufism is not "exotic" when actually "there are far more disciples of Sufism than there are perhaps of all other mystical movements combined"] from curricula and conferences." This has nothing to do with the *Playboy* article. Murshid's willingness to "swear on oath" that he "never wheezed once since early childhood" is the strongest case he can make for libel. The danger of riots resulting from the *Playboy* article is still an ever present danger, Murshid says, because

I am listed as a Jew in such a way as to propose an inference. No corresponding inference appears in later names. This is only important because copies falling into the hands of highly emotional political quasi-religious groups can lead to riots and disorders. Also possibly incendiary is the fact that Jennings ends this paragraph with "Allah'ha, Allah'ha." I never use such a phrase; Sufis never use such a phrase. It does appear as a part of certain formulae, but alone one either uses the term ALLAH or ALLAHU. There is nothing illegal in it, but knowing how easy it is to flare up ignorant mobs, it could very easily start something. And I am not talking nonsense.

Murshid says he can produce a dozen witnesses to the fact that "Saturday afternoon last I walked up Bernal Hill full speed to catch up with Mr. Simmons [Akbar]," the prizefighter mentioned in the article. Also, Murshid questions how Jennings can know a female in his audience is an "acidhead." In conclusion he writes, "I am a member of a number of Sufi Orders whose combined membership has been estimated roughly at 40 million. I am taking up with my colleagues whether we want a corrective letter, or [to] take stringent action [a lawsuit] or do nothing at all."

Art Hoppe, columnist for the *San Francisco Chronicle*, receives a postcard summary: "*Playboy* it is. They got some facts correct. See the March issue, they did not put me down as a giant—I mean in physique. They even said what I said, but when it comes to medical and psychiatric diagnosis, *Playboy* is flayboy. Evidently they have to do it... Le Femme present were all young, some very beautiful. Ergo, she was called an 'acidhead'. (I have yet to meet an acidlip.) So I am going to tell my lawyer, I am guilty by association. The association is only geographical which makes it worse." ["The inference from much of this article is that because I am a Californian I am automatically a cultist, the movement being exotic."] It is business as usual at the Saturday dance class.

February 16, 1969, Sunday

Continuing work on my book of tales, I find in *Sufi Teachings* this definition of perfection:

One may ask how sages and thinkers have distinguished the divine impulse among the different impulses that arise in the heart of man. First we must understand what the word "divine" means. Divine means a state of perfection. This state is experienced by God through man; in other words, when a man has risen to the stage of development where he can be the perfect instrument of God, when nothing of his own being stands in the way of the direct impulse that comes from within, that spirit may be called perfection. When a man has reached this stage, he at first begins to realize God only at certain moments; then as he develops he does it for a longer time; and those who develop still further pass most of their time in that realization. Then their feeling and thought no longer hinder the divine impulse, for it rises freely and reveals the divine purpose... One can distinguish a divine impulse from others just as in music one can distinguish the true note from the false, the harmony from the discord. It is only a matter of training the ear... The divine impulse is an impulse full of love; it gives happiness, it creates peace. The difficulty is that not every man observes the beginning of the impulse; most men only observe the result. They are like an intoxicated person, and so in time, as with a drunken man, they become confused and depressed, and there is struggle and strife. (*The Sufi Message of Hazrat Inayat Khan*, vol.8, p.148)

Murshid writes today to Saadia, who is studying at Cornell University in Ithaca, New York.

We may keep a phrase as a motto or we may weave it into our lives. Religion has failed because sacred words have been turned into mottos often in self-defense or otherwise and have not become the measurements of our beings... Your Murshid is going to cancel some engagements. He has not had a day off this year... If it had not been for the instructions from Pir Sahib Sufi Barkat Ali, this one could not have possibly held up. And there is no doubt that his instructions enable one to be a *Pir*, a *Wali* and an *Abdal*. These are each tremendous functions, in which one plays a role far transcendent to ordinary or even extraordinary human roles.

Then Murshid works into the subject of *Playboy*.

It is among the young, called "Hippies" that most Messiahs appear—and disappear. Now your Murshid is among them trying to present Love, Joy and Peace as actualities. Instead of asking them to repent for sins he is trying to bring out the perfections. This attracts no attention among the important people, the press, etc. But a publication called *Playboy* has written about your Murshid in an article called "Cultsville, U.S.A." There are four universal groups mentioned—Sufi, Vedanta, Zen and Baha'i. We are placed alongside all kinds of strange movements and persons which arise chiefly here in California.

The article is not particularly scurrilous about your Murshid but the implications on Sufism mean that your Murshid may be going to court. The matter has already been placed in the hands of my attorney at law but no action will be taken without full consultation with colleagues. In the past, without exception, your Murshid has always lost when succumbing to advice and always won when doing the contrary.

Murshid describes his condition while working on his *Inner Life* commentary. "During this time," he says, "one ceases at the human level, and all the consciousness of *Malakut* [the mental plane] becomes his." Some stories that Murshid tells in *The Inner Life* commentary are familiar to me from talks he gave. I am very impressed. There is something of the supernatural about them. Consider these four tales. How do you explain the experiences of Murshid, the commentator?

When the commentator was visiting the port of Aden in southwest Arabia there was one merchant who was so fair that everybody began patronizing him. And also in that store there was a dervish, very intent upon his devotions. The commentator was attracted also to this dervish and when his devotions were over asked if he could meet the Sheikh. Everybody pointed to the store-keeper. It was his store, he was a business man, he employed the others. And yet he was a sheikh of the Rifai Order.

When the commentator visited Luxor he was met by a registering clerk in the hotel. The clerk wished his *tashbih* [prayer beads] which was very expensive. He did not wish anything else. The commentator said that was impossible because he himself was already a teacher and was using that *tashbih* but was also saving it for a Sheikh. The clerk said, "I am the Sheikh."

When the commentator arrived in Port Said he hailed a taxicab because something about the driver attracted him. They discussed Sufism and both found they belonged to the Rifai Order. When the commentator asked the driver who was the Rifai Sheikh, he would like to meet him: "I am the Sheikh."

When the commentator arrived in Alexandria, in UAR, he went to the travel bureau. The manager came down. "Oh there you are. I have been waiting for two hours for you." This manager of the travel bureau was sage and seer and yet performing a public function. Even his own underlings did not know this until the foreign visitor arrived and it was necessary to speak openly.

Murshid tells Saadia some more stories.

Years ago your Murshid went out for a morning walk. When he was nearly home a great wolf-hound appeared in the way and would not let him proceed. There was no stick or stone available and to return the way one had come would mean being an hour late. But Allah, the All-Being and Praiseworthy, suddenly inspired your Murshid. He put his hands behind his back and growled tremendously at the hound-dog which fled. But your Murshid is sure some being or beings were standing by his side. Then he heard from the Heavens: BY PEACE YOU SHALL BRING WAR AND BY WAR YOU SHALL BRING PEACE. Not only has this come from heaven but for years it was never followed; one did what the *good* people advised and always lost. Murshid was a thorough Gandhian and absolutely uselessly. It never came the way the *good* people wanted.

Once your Murshid was near the Mall in Lahore, surrounded by communists. They were offering all kinds of allurements and inducements. Murshid stood quiet and repeated endlessly within: ALLAH! ALLAH! ALLAH! Murshid has won more victories [in this case, escaping the fury of a communist mob] by ALLAH HO AKBAR than all other means together and combined. Years passed and it was necessary to bring one's brother to court. Murshid did ALLAH HO AKBAR. Suddenly his brother changed his plans, the matter was settled satisfactorily out of court and now his brother is fighting for him. And it was and is necessary to stop silly ego-advice and even Gandhi, though he had *satyagraha,* which is *kemalic,* and non-resistance, which is *jemalic,* overlooked the *jelalic* aspects of creation. So India without the *jelal* is also in turmoil.

The Shias have asked whether Sufi Ahmed Murad [Murshid] thought Ali was as great or greater than Mohammed. He said, "Ali was always aware of Allah. Mohammed was aware of Allah and also of mankind always. Thus he was the Perfect Man." They accepted this explanation.

One last opinion of Murshid's from today's heavy letter to Saadia, loaded with teachings, is about pork, white bread, and Coca-Cola.

Now as to pork. We eat little meat of any kind. My own physician has explained the harm from the kind of protein in it, and it does cause many ills or rather factors in them [the protein molecules in pork]. While the important people are accusing tobacco and cigarette smoking for cancer, your Murshid has been asking, Why not investigate white bread? Why not investigate Coca-Cola? No, the important people have made up their minds and cancer will continue and continue and continue.

Mansur gets the impression when looking at Jehanara standing at the kitchen sink: *pregnant woman*. Tonight Jehanara reveals she is uncertain as to her condition. I say, "You are pregnant, I am sure. If you hadn't been unsure, I would not have trusted myself. But since you yourself aren't sure, I am sure." Fatima agrees: She knows she is!

February 17, 1969, Monday

Tonight I decide to go back to San Francisco and spend time working closely with Murshid next week. Tuesday there is open house at the Garden of Inayat. Wednesday we go to Amin's in Corte Madera. Thursday there is a special class at the Garden of Inayat for Novato and Corte Madera people. In April, Jemila will be attending a special three day course in Raku pottery, and I will be going to a philosophy course at the Berkeley extension with Murshid. Is it a coincidence that Murshid's schedule appears in my journal (as above) after Murshid's letter to F. Clive-Ross, Bedfont, Middlesex, dictated yesterday, put it out in its entirety?

But praise to Allah, with the spiritual practices one has received from one's Pir-O-Murshid, one is now capable of drawing the atmospheric energies and *baraka*, and [able] to assimilate the *Sifat-i-Allah*, so that the proclamations of religion become realities, all the time. I am on this occasion enclosing a small cheque, but it is my intention to send further moneys, inshallah. This is a new day and age. One has a program thus:

SUNDAY NIGHT, the Dharma. This includes the Yoga methods of Lord Buddha, sometimes slightly modified by Sufic additions, sometimes not. Also teachings in the Upanishads and Swami Ram Das.

MONDAY NIGHT. Sufism and elementary dervish dances.

TUESDAY AFTERNOON. Christian mysticism drawn from the scriptures with spiritual techniques. Class progressing very rapidly. Actualities, not pseudo-devotional attitudes to "saints" of the past. "Ye are Gods."

WEDNESDAY NIGHTS IN TOWN 15 MILES NORTH, a compendium of teachings and both dervish and Yoga dances. Very large group, beautiful young men and women, constantly growing in attendance.

THURSDAY NIGHT AT THE KHANKAH, NOVATO. Special instructions in Tassawuf—dervish dancing (advanced), the sciences of Breath and Contemplation (Mushahida) and Tawajjeh.

FRIDAY NIGHT. To the "Hippies", Haight-Ashbury district. A program so akin to your policies and article [Clive-Ross's practice is to publicize eastern philosophies] that nothing need be added excepting now the introduction of techniques, a mélange of Lord Buddha (not "Buddhism") and Sufism.

SATURDAY. Spiritual dancing. Dervish, Yoga and Mystery dances depending on mystical and occult teachings and awakening. Very well attended and excellent response, but for initiates only.

In a letter to Finley P. Dunne, Jr. of the Temple of Understanding, Murshid shares that he is canceling some speaking dates this week and next for various reasons, including "having my name mentioned in

Playboy." Dunne met Sheyla, Don McCoy, and Dara in India, so Murshid reports that Don and Sheyla "are in trouble, constant trouble. With Dara Buzz Rowell, it is the opposite. He has gone to Ohio. He has had the illumination experience and so telephoned me."

When Murshid mentions next week's planned *darshan*, he recalls the way he was characterized in *Playboy*: "In the *Playboy* article, the writer, otherwise the usually sophisticated newsboy outlook, says Sam put on a look like the Buddha at Gumps. I cannot see myself but I know how one feels." Murshid defines the terms *prajna* (insight) and *mushahida* (contemplation) in this letter for Dunne's edification. "Daisetz Suzuki and Sarvepalli Radakrishnan both proclaimed the supremacy of *PRAJNA*. But the former showed no signs of having and the latter all signs. It means the immediate grasping of a situation in its fullness with cause, movement and effect together, and the seeing of every event as a cosmos and every cosmos as an event... Finally I began giving instructions in *MUSHAHIDA*... It means complete vision of the whole world, over time and space."

February 18, 1969, Tuesday

Having been given a *mushahida* practice recently, I am glad to find an allusion to it in *Kashf al-Mahjub*. When Murshid sent *Kashf al-Mahjub* to the *khankah*, I asked him to keep it in the office, not in his room, so I'd have access to it. I begin reading the life of "The Caliph Abu Bakr, the Veracious (*al-Siddiq*)."

He is placed by the Sufi Shaykhs at the head of those who have adopted the contemplative life (*mushahadat*), on account of the fewness of the stories and traditions which he related; while 'Umar is placed at the head of those who have adopted the purgative life (*mujahadat*), because of his rigor and assiduity in devotion. It is written among the genuine Traditions, and is known to scholars, that when Abu Bakr prayed at night he used to recite the *Koran* in a low voice, whereas 'Umar used to recite in a loud voice. (*Kashf al-Mahjub*, p.70)

This is interesting as well since my feeling lately has been: *Recite in a low voice*. In three letters today, Murshid puts the *Playboy* affair to bed. To U.S. Representative Philip Burton: "There is an article 'Cultsville U.S.A' in the March issue [of *Playboy*] and I am mentioned in it. Our first impression was to seek some emolument for derogatory remarks. But considering the fact that in foreign affairs, Asian ones in particular, we are so far from the objectivity Rand-McNally must have that the mere fact of being mentioned is something." To columnist Art Hoppe: "I have thanked *Playboy* because they recognize I am alive, but from their description you would not otherwise recognize me or my audience!" To friend Vocha Fiske: "On advice of friends I shall not go to war with *Playboy* but instead have thanked them for even mentioning my person and background."

Chapter 13

Intuition

The next step of inspiration after impression is intuition. Intuition is a distinct feeling. It is not only a convinced feeling that perhaps it will happen so, but a distinct feeling that it must happen so. An intuitive person feels if somebody is writing him a letter from a distance. The intuitive person thinks about somebody and meets him in the street; he had thought about him. The intuitive person may feel when going to table that fish will be served him. He felt by intuition what was going on in the mind of the cook, and he has foreseen this. An intuitive person becomes a kind of thought-reader, what they call clairvoyant.

Although today there seems to be such a lot of that clairvoyance, it has become a business, there are so many clairvoyants! The most amusing thing is this: that it has become such an ordinary thing to have clairvoyance that very often friends ask if you have some clairvoyant power, if you are psychic. It is just like asking a person, "Have you a pen or paper?" Neither the one who asks nor the one who answers realizes how sacred the subject is, and how that subject may be treated. It is amusing to see how many people in these days talk so freely about having that power; if they only knew that when there is such a power one has to be modest about it, to close one's lips and look down. (Unpublished teachings of Hazrat Inayat Khan)

February 20, 1969, Thursday

Having cancelled classes at the *khankah*, Murshid enjoys his first day off since Thanksgiving. He's in San Francisco working hard, he tells astrologer Gavin Arthur, "in the most inspired fashion." And his inspirations are astrological: "I believe that the uncovering of the distant planets also brought with them the awakening of the corresponding psychic and scientific faculties in man."

Murshid continues by saying that the development of the piano with its octaves of sound followed "the uncovering" of Uranus, but he steers clear of weighing in on the subject of whether the Aquarian Age has come or not. "I am not imposing or proposing any Aquarian Age but I am definitely presenting that the subtle factors of both Uranus and Neptune are now part of the *mise-en-scene*."

Today Murshid proffers a gift subscription to F. Clive-Ross's *Studies in Comparative Religion*, sent previously to Peter Dunne of the Temple of Understanding and several professors at UC Berkeley, to Huston Smith. Murshid writes to Smith that he likes Ross's journal, "for here we have the same objectivity, the same impersonality, the same use of human experience as in the sciences but in another direction."

To Shamcher tomorrow, Murshid adds (after noting that he is distancing from universal religion organizations), "It is enough to work with Clive-Ross... He is my British counterpart and no nonsense. The work of his principals, Burckhardt, Schuon, Pallis, etc. is marvelous."

Smith also receives along with his letter a carbon copy of "The Awakening of Faith," which is "among a number of other things rejected by Dr. Hayakawa, the atheist, who has rejected his paternal heritage and is parading himself off before the public as a 'semanticist'."

February 21, 1969, Friday

Before dawn today, Murshid headlines a letter to Shamcher THE SPIRITUAL HIERARCHY, WAR, AND SUFI AHMED MURAD. He begins, "I have again been aroused from sleep and 'commanded' to write this to you and copies will be sent to Pir Vilayat, Vocha Fiske, Saladin Reps, Dr. Huston Smith and perhaps others. My esoteric secretary, Mansur Otis Johnson will be here some time today and will make also suitable copies." Most telling, concerning Murshid's state at this time, is his revelation, "And again [there is] the strange elevation taking one beyond sleep."

Murshid's persona in this letter reminds me of the protagonist in the movie *Powwow Highway*, who takes his inspiration from what he sees on TV, and is then led from adventure to adventure by following various signs. The first sign, for Murshid, was Dr. Nottingham of Long Island University, who spoke on Vietnam from a Vietnamese point of view.

Ordinarily, one might have let this go, but in a few hours a phone call from Professor An The of the government school of languages asking Sam to come to Monterey to speak on "Zen"; and the finding of a picture of General Edward Lansdale. One must explain.

In 1931, I was in Cleveland reading Aflaki in French and was amazed that one's own mystical experiences, practically rejected by this culture, were all in line with the Mevlevis. This did no good at the time but the reverse, the almost absolute acceptance by Asians of all kinds has placed one in a strange position.

On arriving in Japan we took a taxi and stopped at Tsurumi monastery between Yokahama and Tokyo (Sojiji). My friend Okudo-san asked me how I felt. "Very strange." "That is not strange. You are in a strange country." "Oh, that is not the reason I feel strange. I feel strange because I do not feel strange. I feel strange because nothing is strange. I know everything that is going on. I know these trees, the ceremonies, the teachings, everything, everything but the language."

About six weeks later we called at the monastery and had an interview with the Roshi. There were a number of notables, several translating. It was not necessary. As one stayed a while, one became aware of ALL SEVEN PLANES OF EXISTENCE AT ONCE, the only time I have ever been so multiple-conscious. The longer together the easier the communication, and then he took me to a secret shrine (not the only secret or sacred shrine Sam has been brought to) and tried to explain the UNIVERSAL BUDDHISM which I already knew and accepted.

The mystical experiences in Japan continue to the present. "In this city [San Francisco] one has had almost the same kind of greeting from Master Seo, Dr. An, Princess Poon Diskul, Swami Ranganathananda Maharaj, Sidi al-Alawi and Rabbi Schlomo! All the same story, over and over and over."

Finding the picture of General Edward Lansdale triggers Murshid's war memories, from when he worked with G-2, as U.S. intelligence activities were known during World War II.

During the War, I did some pseudo-research for Colonel Harris of G-2. He tested me and I passed and he, with his subaltern, Edward Lansdale, had a laugh on me. But two years later, when I wanted a release, I had to go to Colonel Harris and showed him my esoteric notebook with the precise predictions. Most of these notebooks were destroyed in a fire... ALL PREDICTIONS came through with a precision not found in any Edgar Cayce or Eileen Garrett or Nostradamus or Blake!...

When Colonel Harris saw my notes [on Jews perishing in Nazi prison camps] and my explanations of the Sufi Hierarchy he accepted my position. The only other person was the then Captain Edward Lansdale. This man is now Lieutenant General of the U.S. Army and has been one of the tops in Viet Nam. My letters to him were returned. But Allah is great, no doubt about it. I saw a "Lieutenant Edward Lansdale" living in Novato, where the *khankah* is, and mentioned this to Mansur Otis. Then we found the picture which Lansdale gave me—he was my one war hero. So I am again going to find him and see whether an American who can get along with Vietnamese, etc. may help bring understanding.

Though Lansdale was Murshid's war hero, he was also, perhaps unknown to Murshid, "the head of CIA clandestine and para-military operations" (*Killing Hope*, p. 42) in the Philippines in 1950. Lansdale ("a major and the chief of a group known as the Intelligence Division of the staff of the G-2, Armed Forces/Western Pacific," *In the Midst of Wars*, p. 4) worked to crush the Huks, an indigenous nationalist movement started to repel the Japanese invaders. While the Huks routinely aided the Americans in their common struggle against the Japanese, they were defeated by General Lansdale, who, among many activities, turned native superstitions into weapons of war. The Americans, with their agenda to bring the Philippines, its leaders and people under U.S. control, succeeded. And Lansdale was one of the major players.

Murshid correctly notes Lansdale's presence in Vietnam and his ability to get along with native peoples. Lansdale took his Philippine campaign of military and psychological warfare to Vietnam in 1953, as the U.S. was beginning to try to extend its control to mainland Southeast Asia. Lansdale published his memoir *In the Midst of Wars* (N.Y., 1972) too late for Murshid to review.

Lansdale aside, Murshid tells Shamcher that "two disciples have had the Great Awakening. One of them is referred to in the article in *Playboy*. He happens to be the prizefighter whom I taught to walk up a steep hill full speed and he is an adept at it. But he has had the Awakening again and again and copy of this goes to Vilayat because I have at least two disciples worthy now to be *Khalifs*—one you have met, Moineddin."

February 22, 1969, Saturday

Phillip asks to publish my poem "Ithaca" in *The San Francisco Oracle*. While I ponder this question, another question comes up: *Should I ask Murshid?* An answer comes—in Murshid's words—which addresses both

Fatima and *Khalif* Moineddin out behind the *khankah*

questions. *They asked. You didn't seek it. Give it.* Experience shows me now that when a question is forcefully presented, an answer comes with equal power.

The great understanding for me today is that *all* that comes is real. It is to be paid attention to. All those impressions. All those intuitions. Being guided to allow publication of my poem in the *Oracle* is not the end of it. It doesn't seem correct for me to receive this kind of recognition before something of Murshid's is published. My strong guidance is: *Do not permit my poem to be published until Murshid has something published.* I share this with Moineddin, and he is inspired to speak with Phillip, the editor.

February 23, 1969, Sunday

I am at Murshid's, having slept over Saturday night. Barbara calls Murshid about a ride for her sister from the bus station. Murshid puts me on the phone. When I talk to Barbara, she says the matter has been settled. Her sister will walk. *But I see myself picking her up!* I am listening to the intuition. I don't mention picking up the sister. Later the call comes requesting a ride; I go get her.

On another day, I set out with Murshid during rush hour. Murshid says I could take Folsom Street to Ninth Street. Then he suggests the freeway, if

Khalif Akbar Jim Simmons

I want to chance it. I don't. Besides, he also says there is a chance the freeway will be busy. Later, on Sutter Street in heavy traffic, Murshid says, "I see my negative intuition is working." "That's a question," I said. "What do you do with negative intuitions? Do you change your plans, or watch them happen?" "We didn't take the freeway," he said, "but we got it [the traffic] down here anyway." Sometimes, you can't escape, I thought. Today I read this passage in Murshid's unpublished book *Spiritual Architecture:*

Of course there is another extreme, and that we see in the restaurants where all may be methodical and mechanical, but without feeling. It is too business-like, and there is no spirituality in that. The food is not prepared for anybody in particular; there is no connection between the cook and the patrons. That is why spiritual people are discouraged from eating too much in the restaurants.

Murshid said once that spiritual readings are no good unless one can experience what they teach. The other day after the yoga class, I wanted to stop and eat with Jemila somewhere between Novato and Larkspur. But when I considered the quality of various eating places along the way, I didn't *want* to eat anywhere until we got to the *khankah.*

Murshid's passage above is followed by, "Something is lost [eating in restaurants] and although very often the food is nicer or tastier and there is a certain kind of enjoyment in eating it, it should not be done too often." This reminds me of the time Murshid took me to eat at a large restaurant with "nice décor," located a few blocks from Folsom on Army Street. Murshid called it an "adventure"; he'd never eaten there before, either. I had not been his disciple very long, and the only meals he had treated us to were at either Chinese, Japanese, Indonesian, or Mexican restaurants. Anyhow, this place with the "nice décor" was not good and it was expensive. In my heart, I wished we had eaten Chinese food. I tried to be discreet, but my unhappiness was all over my face.

Murshid overlooked my displeasure and commented, "nice décor" again when we left. He was teaching me a version of the lesson on restaurants that he had articulated in *Spiritual Architecture* and, of course, he knew everything I was feeling.

February 24, 1969, Monday

Murshid's letter to Mrs. Earl Hubbard, wife of the editor of *The Center Letter* in Lakeville, Connecticut, begins, "You have placed me in the strangest quandary I have ever encountered in a long life." Murshid doesn't want to be dualistic, but he can't help himself. "I was all set to make some remarks on *The Center Letter* which remarks would be dualistic. The very basis was that I felt that Earl's statements do not conform to the principles (or revelations) of the late Sri Aurobindo." Murshid goes on to say he's too much under the influence of Aldous Huxley's *The Perennial Philosophy* to accept the *Center Letter* statement. "All Societies in the past have been dominated by the need for food, clothing and bodily security. The bull's eye of human endeavor was the production of enough material goods to survive from day to day."

Why does he say this? Because "today I am addressing a slowly but steadily increasing number of younger people who think our over attention to material wants and lusts is absolutely absurd." While he wants to comply and fill out a questionnaire that accompanies the newsletter, he demurs "until we are willing to sit down and listen to other outlooks, other potentially wise people, either the aged of Asia or the young of America."

In conclusion, Murshid "leaves the matter of membership unsettled." Even though he wants "to cooperate," he rejects "anything that even by innuendo suggests one group of people is more equal than another"; though he hastens to reassure Mrs. Hubbard, here, that "I don't think this is your intent." Such communications embody what discipleship with Murshid is like. There is a blowup of sorts, and one is left looking for the meaning of it all. I think the letter to Mrs. Hubbard reflects something like that.

It is not unusual for Murshid to tell a correspondent: A carbon of this letter is going to be sent to another person or persons. Murshid's letter to disciple Shemseddin Ahmed (aka S. Ahmed), who is in Saudi Arabia performing the Islamic pilgrimage, the *hajj*, is unusual. He seems to think better of his decision to send a "copy of this to my friend, F. Mawlawi Sahib, head of the Bureau of Arab Information here; he is a descendent of Maulana Roum [Rumi] , and we are very good friends." He writes an extra page to Shemseddin, beginning, "This is a post-script dealing mostly with Sufism and no copy to the Arab Information Bureau," seemingly intended to reassert intimacy. What Murshid tells S. Ahmed is that Sufism in the U.S. is "either in the hands of non-Sufis [Meher Baba's Sufism Reoriented] or of legal organizations [the Sufi Movement], usually corporations...

The corporations have money and following but no prestige. One group had accepted Meher Baba. Another is just a corporation with legal sanctioning, derived from the incorporation of Hazrat Inayat Khan's office force to ensure the publication of books.

Murshid's unemotional critique of the Sufi Movement is a serious indictment of a spiritual movement.

By "democratic" processes, they have *elected* at will "Pirs", etc. with no regard to spiritual enlightenment or even initiation. They have even changed [Inayat Khan's] esoteric constitution and have radically altered his *Confessions*, omitting sections and introducing others. This is fine for the ignorant, but they practically deny the existence of higher levels of consciousness and direct functions therefrom.

In the body of the letter, Murshid tells a good story.

After leaving Ajmer, I contracted dysentery, the only time in my life. When I reached New Delhi, Hazrat Inayat Khan appeared to me and said I should visit the UAR Embassy. So I went and nobody was there (it was lunch hour) but one man.
"What do you want?"
"I am interested in Moineddin Ibn al-'Arabi and in Egyptian art prior to the Mameluke dynasty."
He dropped his papers and stared at me in astonishment. "How did you find me? Why I am the world's greatest authority on those two subjects."
That is how I became friend of the late Mohammed Hussein of the Faculty of Arts, Cairo, one of the most beautiful friendships of the [my] life... The dysentery disappeared.

Murshid's guidance is: Pay attention to the first impulse. On my way to San Francisco, the impulse to go to Mill Valley for incense arises. Mentally, I assent. Later, another thought comes: Go to the Candle Shop in San Francisco. Why? I question. *To arrive earlier at Murshid's,* my reason answers. I resist this in principle, remembering the importance of following the original impulse. It pays off. At the Sundancer in Mill Valley, there is a sale going on. The sign says, "20% off on all purchases over $1."

In addition to following first impulse as a practice, there's just plain intuition. Consider three examples.

Stopping at a stop sign at Market and Laguna in San Francisco where there is a angular intersection, I foresee a car turning off Market and pulling past me. It does.

Later I get the feeling, driving toward Murshid's in Golden Gate Park, that I will have to pick up Debbie. The idea comes into my consciousness, and I notice it. That is the great thing: To pay attention to all that enters. I let it pass. There is nothing I can do about it. I don't know where she lives. By the time I get to Folsom Street, the thought comes again, and I feel I *should* do something about it. I stop at a phone. I lose my dime. Taking this as a sign, I drive on to Murshid's. I'm not there five minutes and the phone rings. Guess who? "Would it be too much trouble for someone to come and pick me up?" Debbie asks.

After the adventure with Debbie, Murshid and I arrive outside a brown building in Berkeley. I suddenly feel the need to join in Murshid's concentration in order to promote success. Accordingly, I allow myself to see an office with receptionists greeting us cordially. Moments later, we enter an office where there are three young women, one very cordial. The result is a successful meeting. What's a successful meeting? Here's disciple Halim Frank Welch's answer to that question.

On another Monday outing we [Murshid and Halim] went to the Pakistani Consulate which is located in Pacific Heights in a very fine mansion. Murshid was dressed in his gardening clothes. We walk right into this place, a very formal, uptown office. Murshid walked right in and said to the receptionist, "I want to see the Consul. I'm Samuel Lewis."

"Oh, very good, sir. Do you have an appointment?" "No, no. I want to see him. It's very important." "Alright. I'll see what I can do." She got one of the secretaries to come see us. So we went to the secretary's office, and Murshid sat down and said, "I'm Samuel Lewis, Sufi Ahmed Murad Chisti." And his energy was so strong that the secretary couldn't even relate to what he was saying. So she went and spoke to one of the aides to the Consul. She showed us to the aide's office and Murshid sat right down and said, "I'm in a constant state of God-intoxication. I'm constantly saying *ziker*."

The aide said, "Oh, *Alhamdu Lillah*! [Praise be to God] Wait right here." So he went and brought the Consul into the office, and Murshid said, "My teacher is Sufi Barkat Ali, lower Pakistan, and I'm in a constant state of remembrance. I'm teaching the young; I'm teaching dancing." "Alhamdu Lillah," the Consul said, and he told us who his Murshid was, and they swapped Murshid stories. And that was that. They kind of embraced and said good-bye.

At the filling station on the way home, something says, "Pull out three quarters to go with your two one dollar bills." The tank isn't empty. Gas is 30 cents a gallon. The tank holds ten gallons, and the bill should be much less than $3. But the man gives me ethyl—the expensive stuff—and the tab comes to exactly $2.75. I give him that exact amount when he comes to the window. He says, "Did you look at the pump?" "No, I just pulled it out." He goes into a little ecstasy, and so do I.

February 26, 1969, Wednesday

I am at Murshid's taking dictation. Murshid toys with the California Alumni Foundation, telling them he's "honor bound" to make a $50 donation, since he was in the class of 1918, fifty years before; however, he tells them, he has calculated he will spend over $1,000 in class enrollments by year's end, so why pay more? Just "a rhetorical question," he assures them with a mischievous grin they can't see. "I shall shortly be dictating another letter in regard to matters of general interest and should support my proposals with an additional financial allotment."

The next letter is to the Temple of Understanding. As with the Alumni Foundation, there is to be no check enclosed. "I am unable at this writing to vouch any exact sum due to income tax obligations on the one hand and further family litigation." But the withholding is a kind of tease, for Murshid goes on to say, "However, the ides of February indicate, *inshallah*, the joint possibilities of a lesser tax payment on the one hand and an increment of estate allotment on the other. Naturally, I intend to share this."

After someone at Berkeley asks him about the merits of so-called "experts" Watts and Huxley, Murshid, solemn as a judge pronouncing the death penalty, shares his judgment with the Executive Secretary of the Temple of Understanding. "My judgment compels me to issue a negative. But now with the decision making in my hands, I can no longer permit any vetoes on the historicity of Fathepur Sikri or President Z. Hussein, etc. etc. etc. [The connection here with Watts and Huxley is that the putative "experts" on eastern religion didn't acknowledge the Sufi connection in either religion or politics.] The world cannot remain half free and half dialectic."

February 28, 1969, Friday

Murshid indicates his program for today in the first paragraph of a letter to Professor Oliver Reiser. First, he will go "to address the young in the Haight-Ashbury District—and back to Marin to the College [of Marin] to attend [a] meeting where Senator Church will address the audience. I have a question for Senator Church." I don't go, and don't know the question. Murshid also attends a party he will describe in a letter to Vocha Fiske tomorrow.

March 1, 1969, Saturday

Last night attended a party. It was at the house of my only Mulatto disciple. The audience had a fair sprinkling of "blacks", and was of three groups—my disciples, the actors from *The Committee* and various personal friends. In the absence of disturbing elements it was marvelously integrative and harmonious. *The only thing is that one finds the lonely and heart-hungry people, and one doesn't like to "answer" their inquiries too much* [emphasis mine]. It is so easy to break the veil with the young, so easily easy.

Murshid "doesn't like to 'answer' their inquiries too much" because his capacity "has now expanded to the limit of personal endeavor." (letter to A.B. Patel, March 3, 1969) The significance of what happened at Berkeley is still up for Murshid when he writes Vocha Fiske today. "The fact that some top officials of the University of California asked one for advice concerning the various so-called 'experts' on Asian matters and that Sam only confirmed them is going to lead to the gradual withdrawal of the importance of the European and English 'experts' on Asia."

My question this morning is: What should I do while Murshid and Melvin are at the class on the effect of the traditional religions of Asia on modern progress? The answer: *Go to Fields Book Store and Gavin's.* I see myself doing both things, but I don't accept it at first. I haven't yet found Ralph Waldo Emerson's guidance in his essay "Self-Reliance": "To believe your own thought, to believe what is true for you in your private heart is true for all men—that is genius." While waiting to drive Murshid and Melvin to class, I copy out something from Paul Brunton, which inspires me to consult Emerson and find the above. Brunton wrote:

> If he [the reader] prefers prose there are some delightful essayists to serve him, writers who raise the divine spark of creative art and set fire to the tinder of man's imagination. Emerson's essay on Self-Reliance, for example, holds at least a hundred quotable sentences. (*The Secret Path*, pp. 183-84)

Scanning Emerson's essay for quotable sentences, Mansur compiles an article celebrating Emerson for the May *San Francisco Oracle.* (see May 5, 1969) At Fields Book Store, I put *Pistis Sophia* on layaway. The subtitle's suggestion that the book is Jesus's wisdom teachings given eleven years after the Resurrection attracts me. At Gavin's, Alice, one of Gavin's helpers, emerges to get the mail when I arrive. She lies, saying Gavin isn't in. I know he is. When I get back from a meditative walk about what to do with this contradiction, Alice is back. We chat, and the sudden appearance of Gavin in the hall solves my dilemma.

Gavin fixes tea, and we talk. He tells about getting food and drink spiked with LSD at a place I don't know, called Harbinger. Gavin says he went to hear Gina Cerminara, the author of *Many Mansions* which is about reincarnation. He's been busy lately translating a book on astrology from many cultures. He got an invitation to go to a society cocktail party. I listen, fascinated. I think of telling Gavin I'm compiling my own book of tales by Inayat Khan, but I don't mention it. This is one of those situations when I think my purpose is to be receptive. It takes a lot to turn the attention of an egomaniac away from himself and on to you. And for what? Recognition that I am doing something? It isn't worth it to me. But listening to Gavin gives me the idea to be more human, more expressive, not so closed up. To be, in fact, a little more like Gavin—gabby. In fact, in a recent dream I have done just that.

So I open up and mention going to the fish restaurant outside Berkeley and seeing all the unhappy people. Gavin's disciple, Ed, shares a similar perception of a party he went to Sunday at the Zen Beat poet Gary Snyder's house. I tell of hearing Ansel Adams at the College of Marin, and Gavin goes to get the leather bound issue of the *Dunes Forum*, which has one of Adams's photos in it. Ed gives me a letter for Murshid from Dr. Fung, the Chinese minister of the Buddhist Universalist Church in Chinatown that Murshid helped build. We shake hands. Ed says, "Come back." Mr. Uptight, who loosened up a bit today, says, "I will."

I pick up Murshid and Melvin at class without incident. Murshid reports to Vocha that in class, "the teacher accepted each and every contribution" he made, the first being about the word "Confucianism." "My final point was on predictability," Murshid continues to Vocha with copies going to G.S. officials Lloyd Morain and Russ Joyner.

As the "important" people in G.S. [General Semantics] especially the parlor and bedroom "scientists" do not accept predictability, I mentioned conversations in Hong Kong with a Chinese savant. From the Yin-yang standpoint we predicted that the next Nobel Prize in science would go to a Chinese. Sam, who has studied organic chemistry in the laboratory and not in the parlor or bedroom, at that time pointed out the similarity in principles between dextro and levulo rotations in sugars to the Yin-yang polarities. We agreed. Before Sam returned to this country, a Chinese won a Nobel Prize on this very point.

March 2, 1969, Sunday

Murshid tells the story of Sogaku Shaku (The Rev. M.T. Kirby), Murshid's early Buddhist teacher and a disciple of Shaku Soyen. Early in life, Kirby was involved with Catholicism. He lived in a monastery for a while, but they used to feast all the time. Even on fast days, they used to eat as much as a normal person. This turned him off. Being of a monkish temperament, Kirby went to a Zen monastery. One day he got a terrible beating from his master and was sent out of the monastery. He fled from the place of his torment and threw his arms around a tree "and sobbed in utter despair. In that instant it happened—the *satori* experience, the reality."

Later, I ask Murshid about the meanings of some astrological aspects. He says a sextile (a relationship between planets of 60 degrees) between the Sun and Venus means a "good heart." He says a sextile between the Sun and Neptune means "far reaching mystical vision." Murshid says someone with Neptune and Pluto sextile is "either cosmic or delusional." Gavin said (according to Melvin, who got it from Murshid) that Neptune square Jupiter produces "either insanity or genius." (A square is a 90 degree relationship.) Venus conjunct Uranus "makes it difficult for a person to find a mate, because of their tendency to idealize love." (Conjunct planets are within a few degrees of each other.)

March 3, 1969, Monday

I am at Murshid's, about to leave for the *khankah* after helping with last night's initiations. I have an interview for a six day a week job, forty-five miles south of San Francisco. I live twenty-five miles north of San Francisco. My feeling about the interview is that it is *absurd*. I recall Murshid saying that our relationship has been "remarkably free of psychological problems." I decide to ask for Murshid's guidance regarding this absurd job opportunity.

"You shouldn't ask me things like this," Murshid says. "You should concentrate. I'll solve this for you; then there will be another and another. Concentrate!"

As I gather my things, Murshid plops down in front of his typewriter and begins to answer a letter from Professor Alfred Bloom at the University of Oregon in Eugene. For openers, Murshid announces he is sending Bloom a copy of Master Tai Hsu's book, which "has been sent to Tuttle & Co. in Vermont, and not being returned we presume it is being kept for publication." After listing four additional Zen works he could send to Tuttle, Murshid lays out his bona fides.

Dr. Seo is my present Roshi. He was also a disciple of the late Master Tai Hsu... My first teacher in the Dharma was one Dr. M.T. Kirby (Sogaku Shaku). He was a disciple of Shaku Soyen. He told me the whole story of his enlightenment. (March 2, 1969) This was rejected by all the "experts" on the ground that people attaining *satori* never told. He taught me the Sanskrit terms and the Theravadins have never forgiven me for that. He became the teacher of Dr. Malalasekera. He introduced me to Nyogen Senzaki early in 1920.

When Melvin arrives to take dictation, Murshid has three more letters to write. Each is to an organization: A.B. Patel's World Union International Centre in India, John Stockwell's American Humanist Association in San Francisco, and Frank Kelly's Center for the Study of Democratic Institutions in Santa Barbara. In Patel's letter, Murshid connects an incident from last night's meeting with a slogan ("Discovering Oneness") from the World Union's newsletter.

Last night according to my program, I was speaking on [about] Julie Medlock when the telephone rang. The call was from Schatsie (Charlotte) Wallace. I had never met her but know the rest of her family. She came in later and we asked her both about the Temple of Understanding and Auroville. Her face lit up—beautifully lit up—when Julie's name was mentioned. This must have had a deep impression on the audience—all young people. Most of them, perhaps all of them, are interested in *putting into practice* "Discovering Oneness."

At the end Murshid coins an epigram: "When hearts accept hearts 'Discovering Oneness' will manifest by itself."

Murshid's explicit problem with Stockwell's Humanist Association is that "my person is held to derision by important [Hayakawa and company] or self-important Humanists."

The third organization, Frank Kelly's Center for the Study of Democratic Institutions, sounds to me like a CIA front organization set up to channel funds to U.S. client states, known as "emerging democracies." Massive infusions of U.S. cash are used to buy U.S. control. Murshid begins, "I have abstracted your name from *World Union Focus* [a publication of Patel's World Union]. I do not know what democracy means and so have no clear idea as to what is meant by Center for the Study of Democratic Institutions." Murshid tells Frank Kelly, "Years ago I was connected with the Roerich Museum in New York. They called for a world congress, not too different in form and theme from various world congresses which your Center and other Centers seem to advocate. I sent them a report with the theme *that a man did not become a superman by being an official of his government* [emphasis mine]."

Does Murshid know Kelly's organization is a CIA front? I find his closing words curiously reflective of my suspicions about it. In the last paragraph, Murshid reprises this theme. "I believe that people may be transformed by experiences in the 'Realms of Existence Above and Beyond' [quoting from *World Union Focus*]. I would like to see some evidence that they are transformed by becoming officials of some international organization." Murshid reports that "I have been to your Institute several times and the reaction is that a person's experiences should not interfere with another person's importance." Murshid also tells a story of his meddling in foreign policy by having the audacity to act as a citizen peacemaker—or, dare I say, a representative of the Hierarchy.

I was sent on a peace feeler mission from Pakistan to India. Although it was just before India's Independence Day and even the most important foreigners could not obtain interviews, I saw in rapid succession the Chief of Protocol, the President, the chief Vedantist, and the Chief Sufi. Then I left Delhi in further pursuit of this mission. When I returned and called on the American officials, Embassy and USIS [United States Information Service], I was berated and derided. The Hindus and Pakistanis then called in Kosygin [i.e., the Russians]. This is typically typical and I can give many other instances.

March 5, 1969, Wednesday

At the class tonight at Amin's in Corte Madera, I feel that in the next round of the *Ramnam* dance I'll be coupled with a certain girl. I am. While at Amin's, I recall my Iowa City psychedelic drug ecstasies and the subsequent comedowns. They seem like an outward illustration of my chart, with its green Neptune-Pluto-Uranus midheaven and a black Moon, which translates as a lovely inner life with trouble on the outside. When I ask how to master that, the answer always comes, *Seek ye first the kingdom of God.*

I take Murshid to a speaking engagement at Sonoma State College. The lecture is on tape. I think the deepest feelings are the most important, but I wonder about that when my deepest feeling today is that I am out of harmony with Murshid.

March 6, 1969, Thursday

Murshid today addresses Art Hoppe, a columnist for the *San Francisco Chronicle.*

This is some more not-news which ought to become news. In any event we are sending a copy to Herb Caen, to the associates of the acting President of San Francisco State [Don Hayakawa] and to others, and *I am not fooling in the least.* Yesterday I was in the 21st century, the real one. I was a guest speaker at Sonoma State College. The subject itself is unimportant, excepting that unless there has been a complete change of heart and mind, the acting President of San Francisco State would either have forbidden it or sneered...

There was a very aged gentleman in the audience, an official of the college. He was very delighted to hear somebody talk on Whitman, Emerson and James, three very American personalities who are either sneered at, ignored or absolutely derided by the Generals of Semantics so-called. [This is another blast at Hayakawa, who made his academic reputation in the field of General Semantics.] Evidently the talk must have gone over, for not a few of the audience came all the way from Cotati to Corte Madera to hear me at night. My efforts to introduce the Asian philosophies of Asians are slowly penetrating the minds and hearts of the young wherever I meet them.

In the midst of campus unrest and the resignation of the President of San Francisco State, Professor S.I. (Don) Hayakawa was made acting President of the university. The main issue behind the riots was the demand that a "Black Studies" program be provided as a part of the regular curriculum at the university. Professor Hayakawa's law and order stance was a huge popular success. During the dictation of the letter to Art Hoppe regarding S.I. Hayakawa, I get the feeling: *This is the beginning of the documentation of the past.* I say this to Murshid, and he responds, "Yes, that's exactly right." As Murshid's secretary, I am privileged to share his joys and participate vicariously in his battles. One such ongoing battle is this one with "the acting President of San Francisco State." Here Murshid repeats to Art Hoppe information the reader first encountered back on August 17, 1968, including:

Toward the end of the speech [covered in a Ron Moskowitz "article on page 14 of today's paper"], the acting President is quoted as having said, "that happiness is a man who is thoughtful, educated, rational and reflective." Every time this man has faced me, he has used nothing but derision and personality, nothing but the sneer, the scoff and audience appeal. This is bad enough in private life, but in public, coming from a man who has pretended to present the [General Semantics] philosophy that words are not the things they represent, it is either ignorance, hypocrisy or risibility at its utmost...

Murshid's aggressive stance to Art Hoppe this morning is a demonstration of his rejection of the Gandhian passivity that he first mentioned in a letter to his goddaughter Saadia last month. (February 16, 1969) It reminds me of a question I have. Says Mansur, "That's something I've been wondering about. Do you recommend people to follow Gandhi because you did?" Murshid answers, "I don't recommend anything. Inayat Khan says, 'Follow your meditation, not principle.'" "You mean that you followed your principles and not your meditation." "Yes. My intuition told me to do one thing, and I *didn't* do it. I followed my principles."

Less than a year before (June 26, 1968), Murshid wrote to Hayakawa himself, seeking a remedy for the history of personality rejections. Referring to another occasion, Murshid said to Hayakawa,

Instead of being permitted to introduce a Keyserian interpretation of G.S. (General Semantics), I was attacked personally by a group of presumably devotees of G.S. And why was I attacked? Because of efforts on my part to reconcile our mutual differences, and forget the personality and work for a cause... But as this person has found the answers to a number of scientific problems in Alfred Korzybski's and Keyser's work; and, as these answers have previously been rejected or ejected by your colleagues and yourself, what is the answer to this dilemma?

Hayakawa never answers this question, or the letter. Murshid goes on to reveal his vision of General Semantics's potential to problem solve.

In closing I list some of the problems I have tried to present with G.S. [General Semantics] solutions: the Mendel-Lysenko dispute [genetics], *Silent Spring* [environmental pollution], Viet Nam [international conflict], What is "Zen?" [spiritual], collaboration with Dr. Chandrasekar ["who is perhaps the best demographer on earth and who specializes in population problems and their solution" (*Sufi Vision and Initiation*, p.188)], and the solution of problems by "Integration."

Other officials besides Hayakawa in General Semantics are steadfast in their refusal to accept Murshid's utilization of general semantics as a valuable tool. Murshid is interested in solving problems, and frustrated and disappointed over what personality rejection means in terms of the failure to do so. After writing to Art Hoppe, and before we go to Egger's Nursery, Murshid writes another letter, to Lloyd Morain, the office manager at General Semantics's home office, aka the International Society of General Semantics (I.S.G.S.). Fresh from addressing a large audience at Sonoma State College and the strong letter to Art Hoppe, Murshid is uncompromising.

My dear Lloyd, There is the policy of "negotiation from a position of strength." I do not believe that the International Society of General Semantics movement is in the hands of persons who have any moral standard or believe in Emerson's "Compensation" or anything like that...

It is most unfortunate that we could not have been friends... I am no longer appealing to senior citizens of any kind. I am going before the young who have open ears, as well as open minds and hearts, and succeeding. I believe that ultimately there will be a semantic movement which will give the world positive non-Aristotelian systems of thought, both in its depth and in its actions.

Murshid and Mansur often work in the office in the morning and then unwind by going out in the car to do errands after lunch. Today in the afternoon, we go to the bank, the library, and Egger's nursery. On the way back from Egger's Nursery, after buying three bags of fertilizer, Murshid speaks of his feeling of freedom after being repressed all his life. He remembers the time he bought twenty tulip bulbs. The other people at *Kaaba Allah*, the Sufi house in Fairfax in the twenties, bought 100 tulips at the same price. All twenty of his came up, and only ten of theirs came up. You can come up with your own meaning for this one. Mansur comments to Murshid regarding the inner freedom he felt in Iowa City and his external hangups, as objectified by the green, well aspected planets and his black, not so well-aspected Moon, which have been on his mind since last night at Amin's. Mansur asks Murshid how to harmonize these things. Murshid says ominously, "You have three things in front of you: A spiritual teacher, a wife, and pain and suffering."

Chapter 14

Ecstasy
in Everyday Life

Father Blighton's place where Murshid lectured

It is with great joy that one has received another packet of books. But it is also in greatly changed circumstances. These books are definitely in demand. The whole world is outwardly changing. One does not expect others to adhere to any moral standard, one expects oneself, but now there is a whole generation of young people here in America, totally different from those of the past. Sam has "reasons" to believe many are reincarnated personalities who have lived before in Indian bodies. There is too much evidence of it. (Murshid's letter to Anandashram, March 11, 1969)

March 7, 1969, Friday

When Murshid interviews Hassan, Jemila, Fatima, and Jehanara, I write down the practices they receive. Before that, I do my practices in the office, but leave the room early when Murshid notices me in the room. I think Murshid wants to use the typewriter—but he doesn't use it. The desire to make my experience real by paying attention and recording what I do now is operative.

Murshid and I drive to San Rafael where he sees Theodore Lachelt about the family will. Murshid suspects his brother is dying. His concern is whether his brother's share of the estate, $700 a month, passes to him when his brother dies, "or whether I would and could be cut down to the income only of the estate, a considerably less amount, leaving the capital to increase indefinitely for the final beneficiaries who are institutions, not blood relatives." Murshid explains to me that it is a human question: Should a member of the Lewis family benefit? Or should the trustees of the will be able to tilt in favor of the final beneficiaries? Murshid puts these concerns on paper in a letter tomorrow to Lachelt.

Continuing to San Francisco, we go to Nancy's in Sausalito, the village just north of the Golden Gate Bridge on the bay. Murshid talks about Fatima's feeling that the *khankah* is too small. I think, *I don't feel anything about the khankah*, and condemn myself for feeling like this. I think also that I don't want to work as a group counselor, which the employment counselor has been testing me for. What do I want to do? The answer I get is do research on Emerson and look for references to oracles in Plato. Phillip comes to the *khankah* on Sunday. I will present the idea of using Murshid's group ideals, as presented in *Introduction to Spiritual Brotherhood,* as criteria the *San Francisco Oracle* could use for picking communes to do articles about. Nancy gets some new practices before we leave her house.

Then I drive Murshid to Toraya, the Japanese restaurant on Fillmore in San Francisco, for lunch. I tell him, "If you're going to read the menu,

Father Earl Blighton

I'll use the bathroom." He asks me what I want. I say, "I give you permission to order for me." Harmonious answers like this may have impressed Murshid with my suitability as a traveling companion. He says he's seen me traveling with him. Returning from the washroom, I learn Murshid ordered me scallops and himself swordfish.

After Murshid buys fish and chicken wings at Onorato's, I ask him, "Is there any excuse for breaking the rhythm of the breath?" I am thinking of sudden movements that you have to make to escape accidents. He says, "That's hard. Each thought, each emotion breaks *a* rhythm of *a* breath. But if you breathe right, you'll have right thoughts."

After a short nap, I wake up at 3:30 and drive Murshid, Melvin, and Gwen to Brother Juniper's, Father Blighton's place in the Haight-Ashbury district. When a stoned and loud-mouthed black guy, who was really being disruptive, interrupts Murshid, I help one of the brothers named Eric show him to the door. I could put him out without guilt, because I had "no malice aforethought." Where did I read warriors are trained to kill without anger? I read it in one of Inayat Khan's tales.

Remembering the business with Hayakawa and the General Semantics people, I ask Murshid for an example of "semantics." Murshid answers, "Considering and integrating all the facts."

Murshid predicts again that he will be world famous. I flash "obsession." Is Murshid obsessed with fame? Ever since living in Bolinas, I've had the impression: *I will help Murshid gain fame.* Murshid's response to this sentiment has been, "You can help me most by developing the most."

At the table tonight Murshid says, "I've got it from God two times, two [different] years that is, that I'm to leave [to die]. But don't worry, the nearest is over twenty years." I think, *Moineddin Chisti and Abu Sa'id both served their murshids twenty years. I will serve twenty-one.*

Murshid has another interview after supper. Melvin shows me his daily journal of life with Murshid. It brings tears to my eyes, it is so beautiful. Melvin and I embrace. Then we take Murshid to Baskin-Robbins, his ice cream store of choice. What we bring home will serve the Saturday dance class.

March 8, 1969, Saturday

My practice is still remembering what I do and recording it—all for the purpose of objectifying my experience in written form—to make it more real.

I stayed Friday night at Murshid's. Shamcher's sleeping bag on the floor in the front meeting room was my bed. I get up at 6:30 and do my practices. As I walk past Murshid at the typewriter, typing his letter to attorney Lachelt, he says, "When you're ready, we'll go to the Farmer's Market." I'm ready any time, I tell him. On the way to the market, Murshid relates that when everyone gathered for the reading of the will, he was criticized for not being familiar with it or able to interpret it, even though he, unlike everyone else, was not given an advance copy. At the Farmer's Market, Murshid buys oranges—half a box is sent to the *khankah*—some Swiss chard, carrots, and onions.

This done, Murshid dresses in his brown dervish robe, a burnoose with a hood, and he wears a Turkish prayer cap. A week ago Murshid announced his intention to dress like this in a letter to Vocha. "Next week I shall probably put on two 'scenes'," Murshid wrote. "One will be at the University where I shall come, no doubt, in the guise of a dervish. As dervishes are excluded by the 'only in America' East-West Congresses, it is time to make a scene... The other will be with the young."

Now bearded, Murshid looks very impressive in his robe, so I take a black and white portrait of him by the windows in the room where I slept. Hassan publishes the result on page 2 of the Prophesy Pressworks (Novato, CA, 1972) edition of *Introduction to Spiritual Brotherhood*.

I take Murshid and Melvin to the University of California extension for their Islamic studies class. David and Gwen, my fellow travellers to Los Angeles, who live with Murshid, come along for the ride and errands. The parking lot is full. I enter anyway and am met by a University security man. As he approaches, I shout, "I'm just a delivery boy." Security answers, "You want me to sign for them?" When he sees my package is Murshid and Melvin, he says, "What's this?" and makes a few wisecracks.

Then David, Gwen, and I embark on an exhausting round of errands. I deliver four *Oracles* to a friend of Murshid's. We park on Polk Street and walk to Fields Book Store, only to find that they don't open until 11. We go on to Cost Plus, and then I stop at Tower Records at the corner of Bay and Columbus, just to price records. We go back to Fields. I buy *Pistis Sophia* for $7.50 (big mistake; I never do read it). We have three more errands: returning typewriter ribbons (the store's not open), buying stamps, and Gwen's pickup at the shoe repair shop. We stop. I space out what happens. Later, I see her boots in the car. I go back to Murshid's house long enough to dump Gwen and David and pick up Mother Krishnabai's *Devotee's Diary*. Then I drive back to UC, read, and sleep a little before class gets out.

Murshid's voice wakes me up, and I sit up and wave to him, coming across the parking lot. We three drive back to Murshid's house for lunch. The dance class is scheduled for the afternoon.

At class, someone asks what I have done the last few days. I blank. I simply cannot say anything about what I did this morning or the night before! Not until then do I realize how high I got in the class. Murshid gives the following practice to all at the meeting: *Watch your own ability to predict.* He gives Jemila the practice, *Refer to your thoughts as a text you have to look up.* Murshid gives Jehanara a practice: *Watch a thought placed on your breath.*

Murshid goes to bed at 7 P.M. and sleeps until 6 in the morning. He tells friend Vocha Fiske in a letter tomorrow, "This week has been so pregnant with events."

March 9, 1969, Sunday

I get up late—at 8 this morning. After breakfast, I begin to type—too soon. My stomach is upset. I lie down and shut my eyes. *Oracle* inspirations start to flow.

The *Oracle* is a vehicle for me to externalize many things Murshid has been teaching, not to mention making Murshid better known. Eyes shut, I get high on the possibilities: New Age principles can be articulated and disseminated in this newspaper. A section concerned with communes can promote cooperative living. A Psychic page, featuring interviews and articles about actual psychics, can give validity to subtle faculties. A Solutions page can begin to remedy setbacks to problem solving that Hayakawa and the General Semantics crowd set in motion with the personality rejections of Murshid.

Why am I telling this here? Because Murshid inspired all of it. Murshid wrote in Part 2, Chapter 5, of *Introduction to Spiritual Brotherhood*, "While a group may function as an individual, it should be in such a way as to give the individual greater, not lesser, scope for the fuller expression of his personality." Mansur is finding greater "scope."

My stomach upset settles. I begin to type Misra's *Buddhist Texts* article, which Murshid has recommended to Vocha Fiske, Professor Alfred Bloom, A.B. Patel, and Paul Reps. It wasn't the need for copies to distribute that won me this typing assignment. Rather, I told Murshid that *Buddhist Texts* was boring. In response to this, Murshid had me copy it. Surprise. I like it. It shows me that following a piece carefully as you copy it can change your perspective. It was the same with *Introduction to Spiritual Brotherhood*. In the beginning, I said the style of *Introduction to Spiritual Brotherhood* was bad. "I had to punctuate the damn thing before I could understand it," was my line. Murshid had me copy it as well, and now I appreciate its profundity.

Today I type the rest of *Introduction to Spiritual Brotherhood*. *Oracle* editor Phillip Davenport comes and I give him his copy. Phillip accepts my proposal that the communities we feature illustrate the ideals embodied in *Introduction to Spiritual Brotherhood*. Talking to Phillip in Moineddin's room, Murshid has a blue-green ball of color over his left shoulder.

Thanks to Phillip I realize years later that I joined Murshid in *samadhi* during his *darshans*, when while sitting next to him he looked at the person in front of him. "When the image vanishes," Murshid told Jemila, "that's it." Swami Vivekananda agrees, writing, "When *dhyana* [meditation] gives up all forms and reveals only the meaning, it is *samadhi*." Vivekananda expresses the process leading up to this experience.

We have now come to the chapter in which the powers of yoga are described.

1. *Dharana* is the holding of the mind to some particular object. When the mind holds on to some object, either in the body or outside the body, and keeps itself in that state, it has attained *dharana*, concentration.

2. An unbroken flow of knowledge about that object is *dhyana*. When the mind tries to think of one object, to hold itself to one particular spot, such as the top of the

232

head, or the heart, and succeeds in receiving sensations only through that part of the body, and no other part, it has attained *dharana*; and when the mind succeeds in keeping itself in that state for some time, it has attained *dhyana*, meditation.

3. When that [i.e., *dhyana*] gives up all forms and reveals only the meaning, it is *samadhi*. This comes when in meditation the form or the external part is given up. Suppose I am meditating on a book; I have gradually succeeded in concentrating the mind on it, and then in perceiving only the internal sensations, the meaning, unexpressed in any form. That state of *dhyana* is called *samadhi*. (*Raja-Yoga*, p.183)

In fact, the way I realize that I joined Murshid in *samadhi* is when I read Phillip's report of one those darshans. It was Moineddin and Mansur that Phillip described as "two of his advanced murids [*mureeds* who] sat at either side" in the incident I quote below. Mansur doesn't realize the light he is experiencing is visible to others until he reads this account.

My first formal darshan with Murshid Sam occurred during the course of a Sufi Dance meeting at Scott Hall in the San Francisco Theological Seminary, which is located in San Anselmo. Murshid's darshans consisted in gazing into his murid's eyes, while he concentrated on one or more of the prophets. I had much shame in my being and was not looking forward to this experience. As I walked into the darkened room, I was unexpectedly blinded by a great sphere of light. Murshid was in the center of the light and two of his advanced murids sat at either side. I was just barely able to see their outlines through the light. Far from being reassured by the light, it added to my fear—until out of the light Murshid's voice came, saying, "Do not be afraid. We have come not to condemn you, but to praise you." ("Memories of Murshid Sam," by Vasheest Davenport in *The Sound*, no. 92, January 1991)

Tonight, I make the decision to put letters and notes in my journal. This marks a shift. Now everyday activities will be considered grist for my esoteric journal, a sort of Zen is everyday life realization. The amount of this material being generated produces an ecstasy for me. And what produces ecstasy seems important.

March 11, 1969, Tuesday

I drive two *mureeds*—Faun, Daniel's wife, and Barbara—to Murshid's in San Francisco. We stop at Gavin's to pick up my astrological progressions. With my level of understanding, they tell me next to nothing.

At Murshid's, I clean out his Indian bookcase. Murshid dictates a letter to Russ Joyner at the International Society of General Semantics. He writes that he told an audience of young people last night that he hoped to solve many of the world's problems when Alfred Korzybski's *Science and Sanity* appeared in 1933. "Instead most of the problems of the year 1933 remain and a lot more have accumulated." Murshid cites Dr. Anatole Rapport, who said "a small group has taken hold of the General Semantics movements. These people seem quite incapable of indulging in what Cassius Keyser called 'rigorous thinking'." Murshid continues,

I am not going into this more here, but instead I am enclosing a copy of *Logical and Scientific Method in Early Buddhist Tests*, by G.S.P. Misra. I have already discussed this subject matter with a number of leaders of the so-called "third world front." I have not been particularly sympathetic with these people, but find on talking with them, they are complaining about the American inability to accept Asian cultures. This is all the more marked when your principal [Hayakawa], part Asian himself, has adamantly and absolutely refused to look into the cultures of his ancestors and kindred peoples.

There is an excellent shrimp and oyster lunch. After a rest, I take Murshid on two errands. First we go to Rudolph Schaeffer's School of Design and then to the University of California Extension. Next, there is a stop at the Holy Order of MANS. What impresses me in his talk at the Holy Order is Murshid speaking about the creation of a "scientific astrology," whereby— and this is Mansur's view—astrological blueprints of individuals could be used to explain energetic interactions between people.

Back at Murshid's, I call The Switchboard for addresses of communes for a trip I am planning. I also call Larry, another of Gavin's helpers, to check an astrological point.

Murshid and I go to pick up Parisa—another disciple—at Amin's in Corte Madera for dinner at San Rafael's Basque Restaurant. We take Parisa home before I drop Murshid at the Garden of Inayat. Then Jemila has to be picked up at Novato High School and taken home. When I return to the Garden of Inayat, Shirin needs a ride to the ranch. I get back from taking Shirin after 11 P.M., free at last to begin my evening practices.

March 12, 1969, Wednesday

Russ Joyner, office manager of the International Society of General Semantics, has received many of Murshid's letters and carbon copies. Today he calls Murshid.

Murshid dictates a letter to columnist Art Hoppe. "A few minutes ago I received a telephone call from the office manager of the I.S.G.S. asking me to call off my private witch-hunt. He further asked for a manly interview, something I've never been able to obtain in this direction over the course of many, many years."

There are more breakthroughs. "The last two weeks have seen a number of breakthroughs in my private life including those great American virtues, social and financial improvements. More important than this is that all the professors on Asian subjects whom I have met in the last month have accepted without question my personal experiences."

I dream after lunch there is a white bird (spiritual freedom), maybe a pigeon (a message is coming to me), on the water, and two birds come along and begin to kill it by pecking a hole in its head. Then, I am the bird. (Spiritual rebirth is a death of the old self.)

Remembering the part in *Devotee's Diary* where Mother Krishnabai speaks about devotees telling Ramdas their secrets, I give Murshid my journal to look at—my way of baring all.

March 14, 1969, Friday

At the *khankah*, I am up at 5:30, finish my prayers by 6:30, and go back to sleep on the office couch. Murshid comes in and types something at 8:30 and wakes me up. Appropriately awakened, I transcribe some Inayat Khan stories for my book of tales and battle with my son, Nathan, to put on his coat before going outside. A hot shower at 10:30 awakens me fully. Murshid and I leave shortly after, in time to get to his place for lunch.

After lunch I lie down until Murshid is ready to dictate letters. The first one is to Philosophy Professor Archie Bahm at the University of New Mexico in Albuquerque. Bahm sent Murshid a copy of his recently published book, *The World's Living Religions*. Why did Bahm, an unknown to Murshid, send a copy? University of Pittsburgh Professor Oliver Reiser gave Bahm Murshid's name.

In Murshid's first communication to Professor Bahm, he moves quickly from expressing appreciation for receiving the book, which he notes resembles Huston Smith's *The Religions of Man*, to an implied question: "I do not know how far you have advanced in your comprehension of Hinduism?" Murshid adds several provocative statements. "In India I was not permitted to enter certain gatherings without first giving a comprehensive *and acceptable* dissertation on the *Gita*. In this country I have been barred not only from the table, but from the audience, in gatherings dominated by several well-known persons you have named." One of Bahm's authorities on Sufism is A.J. Arberry, the English translator of oriental texts. Murshid has more to say about Bahm's authorities.

All my stands in all religions are based on including in them "varieties of religious experience" insofar as it affects them. Thus, al-Ghazzali has said, "Sufism is based on experiences and not premises." It is unfortunate that the men you have selected as your authorities in Sufism are men who have not had any of those experiences which would validate them, in the scientific sense, to be spokesmen for anybody but themselves.

As a positive example, Murshid holds up F. Clive-Ross's journal.

There is today a publication, *Studies in Comparative Religion*, most of the articles of which have been written by savants who have had the valid experiences. In other words they affirm al-Ghazzali's, "Sufism is based on experiences and not premises."

After describing the difference between debates in India and the West, Murshid indicates he is not without credentials.

In India, debates are held so that we might find that Truth from which various views have been derived. In the west, debates are only too often between "right" and "wrong." But in the field of comparative religion, *credentials have been more important than knowledge or wisdom*. So far as Buddhism is concerned, this place is known as the MENTORGARTEN, a name bestowed by the Zen Roshi Shaku Soyen on earlier efforts [by his disciple Nyogen Senzaki] to bring East and West together. I have inherited at least the name, and when the world stops relying on "experts" and goes to sources, *they will find proper credentials on the walls in this house*, etc. [emphasis mine].

Carbons of Bahm's letter are sent to Huston Smith, Oliver Reiser, and F. Clive-Ross. For some reason, Murshid's letter to Clive-Ross is not in the files. In lieu of reporting what the missing letter said, let me summarize Murshid's history with Clive-Ross.

As the editor of *Studies in Comparative Religion*, Clive-Ross engaged Whital N. Perry "to devote a series of articles [which became *Gurdjieff in the Light of Tradition*] for the review that would pierce through the obscurity and get to the real fact of the matter"—about Gurdjieff. So far as I know, Murshid wrote the first letter to F. Clive-Ross on June 12, 1968. It was initiated when one of Clive-Ross's celebrated writers, Seyyed Hossein Nasr, asked Murshid to support Clive-Ross. Nasr was one of Murshid's long-time correspondents and was known also to Saadia, Murshid's goddaughter.

"The writer," said Murshid in that first letter, introducing himself to Clive-Ross, "is both a real Sufi mystic and a real disciple in Zen, having sat at the feet of well-recognized masters in each; he is also a realized disciple of the late Swami Ramdas of South India." This is Murshid presenting his credentials, no nonsense. Not spiritually timid, Murshid reported his recent success. "During the last year an ever-growing audience of young people has been attending the lectures and sessions given here and elsewhere." He expressed appreciation for articles Clive-Ross had published in *Studies in Comparative Religion*. "The writings of Frithjof Schuon are especially appreciated... The articles by Henry Corbin and Seyyed Hossein Nasr strike recordant notes." However, Murshid's critical review of one article in Clive-Ross's journal seemed calculated to show he was learned enough to write articles for such a journal.

I must, however, write in other terms of the article on "Jonah" by D.M. Deed. Years ago I did considerable research on this subject. Unfortunately a fire in 1949 destroyed all my records. There was also a book or article holding that the myth of Jonah was based on initiatory rites. Although it was not included in my thesis, written before encountering the book, there is much to support such a claim. Dr. Deed has overlooked many excellent Jewish writings and commentaries on this subject, especially the *Parke of Rabbi Eleazar*. I believe there are some materials available at the Royal Asiatic Society on this subject.

My personal contribution was to collect and select a number of Puranic items which come so close to the text [the *Parke* mentioned above] that one may conclude they were both derived from the same general source. Indeed there are many parallels between ancient Hebrew and Hindu literature, especially from the standpoint of *myth*, so that there is still work to be done in this field. As most of this research deals with the first parts of the Book of Jonah, it does not necessarily contradict this article. But I am inclined to believe we have still much to learn from myth, folklore, Purana and mysticism.

In spite of his show of erudition, there was no answer forthcoming from Clive-Ross in England by January, 1969. As reported above (January 15, 1969), Murshid wrote Clive-Ross again and purchased three subscriptions for himself, Reverend Warwick, and Reverend Wagner. A four page letter accompanied the $42 check.

Not reported were the words Murshid spoke when he sent that check: "Now, Beloved Ones, I am very satisfied with your publication, but I am not satisfied—and this seems to be most common under the so-called 'Judeo-Christian ethic'—with letters never answered, inquiries ignored, and articles shunned."

Still verbalizing his frustration, Murshid indicated that he had more money, "and more will be sent *when I am considered as a flesh and blood human being and not merely as a check-writer,* the usual custom!" After giving sketches of Father Blighton, Rev. Warwick, and Rev. Wagner, Murshid shouted, "I am using all your articles and all books by your contributors. I haven't a single criticism of anybody excepting that *the only existence I seem to have is when I write a check.*"

Returning to the letter accompanying his check, Murshid spent a page and a half writing about his prowess in mysticism, Islam, Hinduism, and Buddhism. His conclusion:

In the Orient I was called upon to lecture on the depths of their religions and philosophies. My goddaughter won first prize in an international philosophical contest for which the writer did not have "credentials." But he wrote the paper which won the first prize! The same took place here when none of the Orientalists could answer some complex questions put by Dr. Singer of the University of Chicago. There was one person in the audience who could and did. He was never invited again. This thing is very annoying. Love and consideration do not mean being negative. The Christ that I have seen—and I certainly believe that it was pure vision—is identical with that of Khalil Gibran. But pure vision is not wanted, only *articles...*

Nevertheless I have nothing but the warmest admiration for Dr. Schuon and Marco Pallis [a contributor] and your chief writers and your writers not so important, yet. But *why not more consideration to the living experiences of the living, sometimes, somewhere!* "Lo, God is here, let us adore," is fine for a hymn. "Allah is closer than the neck-vein" is wonderful—to quote! From Paul Brunton, I inherited the Way-of-Breath, the Way-of-Heart, the Way-of-Eye. They are demonstrable and demonstrated. *I wish that some time a person so far away could be given objective consideration.* But I am not buying space. I love you all and *hope that this may be more than mere cheque-book consideration.*

After writing today's letter to Clive-Ross, which I am sorry is missing, Murshid asks me to write a cover letter to Huston Smith and send it along with copies of his letters to Archie Bahm and F. Clive-Ross.

Lunch and naps over, I am inspired to take notes at Murshid's afternoon talk today at Brother Juniper's. My intention is to capture Murshid's shotgun approach in lectures, and to note the variety of subjects he ranges through. In my experience, Murshid never spoke to more than a handful of people at the café. Sometimes, out of this handful, one or two would leave as he began.

Murshid begins by mentioning the play *Frogs*, by Aristophanes (circa 448-380 B.C.). The chorus in that play speaks about vain repetitions, which means to repeat mantras that have no mantric value. Murshid gives a weird example: The word "hullabaloo" means "Praise the Lord." "We don't believe in superstitions, but we go to football games and say, *Ra! Ra!* And that is the ancient Egyptian name for God," Murshid says. *Allaho Akbar* is prominently mentioned in *The Thousand and One Nights*. In *The Sorcerer's Apprentice*, the water, representing the mantra gets out of control, meaning one loses one's balance. The idea, Murshid says, is to control the mantra, not to let the mantra control you. In France and in Russia before their respective revolutions, it was discovered that excitement leads to boredom; a mystical idea, Murshid says, but asserts it is a physiological fact.

Murshid speaks about his "walk work." It is customary in a dervish school "to follow the path"—literally—both on pilgrimages and while doing practices in a group. Murshid cites a book written by Havelock Ellis, called *Dance of Life*. "Ellis says you can tell everything from the way people dance," says Murshid.

He alludes to another book, *African Dances,* by Jeffory Borg (no such title or author is in the Library of Congress). Murshid challenges the audience to grasp the proposition that either all Blacks are crazy, or all Whites are crazy. In some African cultures, Murshid says, the sleeping stage is more important than the waking stage. Then, he veers into foreign policy: "In some cultures, foreign policy is determined by dreams. Ours is different. Our foreign policy," Murshid says with a dose of truthful sarcasm, "is determined by not knowing the other fellows."

Shifting abruptly back to the subject of his walk work, Murshid describes the condition of one disciple who was wasted after walking a number of blocks, "and couldn't protest anything"; meaning, the person's overactive mind was fatigued, to the point where their mental activity was diminished, and their receptivity increased. Still on "walk," Murshid speaks about the relationship between walk, the breath, and muscles. He describes a very delicate girl who developed prowess in mountain climbing by cultivating these elements. Speaking about prowess in athletic ability makes Murshid think of boxer and disciple Akbar, whom the *Playboy* article referred to as a "prizefighter." Mention of Akbar and *Playboy* draws Murshid off, briefly, on those tangents. Murshid regrets not having been able to climb the Washington Monument in Washington, D.C. It was closed when he was there, he says, implying to the audience that the seventy year old man in front of them is not intimidated by going up a thousand stairs. No, he relishes the challenge.

Does Murshid have a comment about unemployed Pakistanis just hanging around? Yes, and it would be good business to sell hammocks in Pakistan, Murshid says. I take this as a foreign investment tip. Besides understanding that Pakistan has no hammocks, I draw the conclusion that there are a lot of people hanging around doing nothing in Pakistan. "They need to revitalize themselves," Murshid says. "God in the self is all energy. All energy is in the breath. God is the breath. They need to learn to transmute the spirit."

Murshid triggers my associative powers. I speak, out loud, the phrase that epitomizes my justification for following the spiritual path: "Seek ye first the kingdom of heaven." I throw it out like punctuation for the preacher. Murshid answers me and says we need to find in ourselves the techniques for joy. I don't expect Murshid will take the occasion of me blurting out a comment to say something I've never heard before. "The stage where the breath is real—and you are not—is a very important stage," Murshid says. This information makes my day.

"And next week we will do some dervish dances," Murshid says, "because when you participate, you have a communion. You can experience joy." Someone asks for the title of the paper Murshid said he wrote for the course entitled "The Effect of the Traditional Religions of Asia on Modern Political Movements." The answer is "The Effect of Islamic Culture on Pakistan, Present and Future." William Donkin's book *Wayfarers: Meher Baba with the God-Intoxicated* (Myrtle Beach, S.C., 1988) comes up. It is about *madzubs*, God-conscious crazy men. According to Murshid, Donkin wrote it at the behest of Meher Baba. Speaking about *madzubs*, Murshid says, "When they get serious, they get into the depths of consciousness. Then they can answer any question, solve any problem. Spiritual people have strength and power. You can tell it from their atmosphere."

Murshid repeats what he told Clive-Ross in January about how author and adept Paul Brunton taught him three methods of realization: the way of the breath, the way of the heart, and the way of light, or the eye. This leads Murshid to mention that the oracle was a respected institution in certain countries like Japan and Greece, but that politicians have subverted it.

Murshid reminds the audience that the requirement for oracular function is inner sight and honesty, and suggests the consequence for ignoring this function by quoting the Bible (Proverbs 29:18) where it says, "A people without vision perisheth." Elsewhere (in Acts 2:17—Murshid doesn't quote chapter and verse), it says, "Your young men shall see visions, and your old men shall dream dreams."

Murshid refers to a man named Trebitsch-Lincoln, also known as Dr. Ruh. Dr. Ruh was in the habit of changing religions as he searched for truth. Ruh made predictions, and they came true. On the other hand, Boake Carter was world famous for his predictions, and none of his predictions came true—like the one that denied there would be World War II. When the war came, Carter committed suicide. Culverson, the bridge expert, got a lot of publicity on this subject, but Murshid does not elaborate, and no one asks for clarification. (Are you mystified? Why would a self-styled predictor's death result in publicity for a bridge expert? This stuff is coming at me a mile a minute, and, after a while, I just take it in, write it down, and let it go. I have no clue.)

Once, says Murshid, he wrote a paper on the Book of Jonah, and his interpretation was based on the Indian folk tale where gold, jewels—all possible wealth—are found in the belly. A Jewish work, the *Parke of Rabbi Eleazar*, has the Jonah story in it. (Interesting how Paul Brunton's teachings and this Jonah story from a letter months before to Clive-Ross, whom Murshid addressed today, appear in Murshid's lecture today. That these ideas associated with Clive-Ross in the past, should appear in a lecture on the day when Murshid wrote to Ross seems perfectly natural to me, knowing Murshid's mind the way I was getting to know it.)

Murshid points out that the Jewish Kabala may be interpreted on four levels: the literal, the parallel, the figurative, and actual experience. "Sanity," Murshid says, moving on, "is a balance." He doesn't describe his own condition as "controlled schizophrenia," as he often does. Then he calls for questions.

Someone asks about a communication barrier. I don't understand the question, and Murshid's answer seems to be a non sequitur. "In Chinese culture you pay the doctor when you are well," says Murshid. The Chinese doctor's interest in your health is subtly reinforced by this cultural tradition of paying for health, not sickness. When you get sick, he cures you for nothing. "I lived with a spiritual healer," Murshid says, thinking of Major Sadiq in Lahore, "who never charged anything."

"Does your faith have a text?" someone asks.

"What we do is based on the development of inner consciousness. This development throws light on the texts of all religions that exist."

"What book can I get at the store?" a questioner asks Murshid.

"Your own self," Murshid answers.

Someone with a smattering of Indian philosophy asks, "Were the Sufis the first to recognize avatars?"

"Sufis don't teach avatar. God made man in His image. Sufis would never call a God-conscious man an avatar. They say, *La illa ha el il Allah*, 'There is no God but God.' There are a lot of avatars. There was the Mahdi in the nineteenth century. He died in glory. There is the Ahmadiyya movement, they say you must be kind, good, gentle. You must lean on your own self. *Ye are Gods*, Jesus said. *When Dharma decays, I come*, is a Hindu teaching, spoken from the point of view of the Messenger. I didn't say it [believing in avatars] was wrong," Murshid says.

"Where is God at?" somebody asks.

"There is no place He is not at," Murshid answers.

"As a Being?" they persist.

"He is," Murshid affirms. "He is not separate from His creation, but these are just words until you experience. That was a good question." He thanks the five people present and we leave.

Out on Haight Street, as we wander amongst street people, I wonder, just as *Oracle* editor Phillip has wondered: Who will buy an *Oracle* devoted to topics like community, psychics, and solutions that Murshid has gotten me so excited about? We find the car and go to the New Age health food store. The Buddhists who run New Age are forming a nonprofit corporation. The corporation will lease the store, with the profits going to their new community. I imagine the *Oracle* as a vehicle like the store, with profits going to our community, the Garden of Inayat.

Pir Dewwal Shereef of Islamabad gave Murshid the name *Islamia Ruhaniat* (the spirit of Islam) for his organization. Somehow, I think it will become the umbrella entity for all our activities. Overeating all day, I feel drowsy after dinner. Murshid goes to bed right after dinner. Smelling the air, which is not so fresh, while walking up Bernal Heights behind Murshid's house with Melvin, Gwen and Marty, I feel the unhappiness of the city. Or is it my own unhappiness?

Chapter 15

The Diamond Sutra

"King" (Gavin) Arthur, March 23, 1969   Timothy Leary

Next week, we are going to have a series of birthday parties, both here in San Francisco and in Novato. They will largely center around my old friend Gavin Arthur whom you met. He will have what we call "a ball," hundreds and hundreds of people. My own affair at Novato will center around both a huge curry dinner which I am cooking myself and around dances, my own choreography. It has not been known, and a lot of people would not accept, that the late Ruth St. Denis was, as I call her, my "fairy God-mother." I am now giving to the world what she taught me. (Murshid's letter to his uncle, Harry Rosenthal, in Vancouver, B.C., Canada, March 15, 1969)

Introduction

Murshid received initiations in Japan at temples in Kamakura and at Sojiji. The Roshi at the Sojiji Monastery in Tsurumi, Japan, Murshid says, presented seven levels of experience: 1) words 2) meta-linguistic 3) telepathy 4) unified telepathy 5) and 6) there are no two persons (that's what he said) and 7) there is no anything. In January, 1920, Murshid began studying Buddhism with a disciple of Soyen Shaku (whom he refers as Shaku Soyen). The disciple's name was The Rev. M.T. Kirby, also known as, Sogaku Shaku. In March of 1920 when Kirby moved to Hawaii, he introduced Murshid to Nyogen Senzaki, another disciple of Soyen Shaku. Soyen Shaku, teacher of both Kirby and Senzaki, came to the United States in 1893 and, like Swami Vivekananda, attended the World Parliament of Religions at the Columbian Exposition in Chicago. In 1905, Soyen Shaku returned to San Francisco with Senzaki and left him there to teach. In 1923, Murshid introduced Senzaki to Inayat Khan, and the two went into *samadhi* together (see April 30, 1969 for more). The name Mentorgarten, which Murshid gave his place at 410 Precita Avenue in 1967, as mentioned earlier (March 14, 1969), was an inheritance from Senzaki, who got it from his teacher, Soyen Shaku.

March 15, 1969, Saturday

Murshid got up before dawn and wrote his oldest and dearest friend Vocha Fiske that he "had to go to bed early last night because of a slight case of the flu." More importantly, he said, "I got a surprise phone call from Russ Joyner," responding to Murshid's letter (see March 11, 1969), "and have called off the warfare, at least temporarily." The article on *Buddhist Logic* was to be Murshid's ammunition in the war. He tells Vocha, "I was ready to circulate it far and wide and tell the world that it was a terrible thing that the Generals of Semantics would have nothing Asian despite that the Generalissimo is half Asian himself." About Joyner himself, Murshid writes, "Only Russ is very fair and fair-minded," and sends him a copy.

Pennsylvania professor John Shover, who used to teach in San Francisco, is notified today that Murshid is going "to hear a Prof. Williams, who used to be connected with Penn., give the concluding talk in a series on: 'The influences of the traditional religions of Asia on modern developments'." Murshid tells Vocha he writes Shover because "four professors in a row have accepted my verbal reports concerning Asiatics and one comes from Penn."

When I reveal Jemila and I might travel in May to visit communes in the southwest to do research for an *Oracle* article, Murshid is upset, which means he talks in a loud voice. Jemila is already committed to going to yoga classes, he points out. This and other absences leave the *khankah* not properly staffed. Like all ego-activity scenes with Murshid, my pervading feeling is that the immediate issue isn't the real issue. At such moments I contract, cool it, and try to discern what's what. I especially avoid arguing with the teacher. According to *The Path of Initiation and Discipleship*:

Dispute with a spiritual teacher is never any good. For the pupil may be speaking one language while the teacher speaks another, and when there is no common language, how can the dispute be profitable? Therefore in the path of mysticism there is no dispute. (*The Sufi Message of Hazrat Inayat Khan*, vol. 10, pp.73-74)

Thus, Mansur goes through his changes, unaware that Murshid's loud voice signifies more than he thinks it does. Tomorrow, Murshid will write another letter to Vocha Fiske. "I was amazed to find my chief secretary telling me he could not give me so much time because of an opportunity which makes him in every way the successor to Whiteman and Lewis!"

During the break at dance class, Murshid poses some questions and begins surveying everyone in turn. He asks Parisa, whom he hopes will become his dance secretary, what she felt when she did the Avalokiteswara walk. "I feel a tremendous magnetism and power in my hands," she answers. "Do you think you could get that magnetism down into your feet?" "I could try." "Exactly," Murshid says in a firm voice, to underscore all that is involved in the teaching to balance her manifestation, and all that is involved in her willingness to give it a try.

Having no answer myself, and witnessing Murshid asking everyone to answer in turn, I begin to feel uneasy. I can't say why. Then, my uneasiness becomes conscious; it is self-consciousness. What is going on with me is captured perfectly by the saying from *The Bowl of Saki*, by Hazrat Inayat Khan: "Everybody feels, fewer think, fewer still express what they think." My ability to express myself is not there.

"What did you feel when you did the Avalokiteswara walk?" Murshid says when he comes to me. I answer by saying, "I felt very tall." For the second question, "What did you feel when you did the Jesus walk?" I flash on my feeling when I try the Krishna walk, get tired of smiling, and become aware of the strain. Again, self-consciousness. I don't remember what I say. As I record these experiences, a philosophical explanation of this incident comes to me in Buddhist terms: Mansur was experiencing self-consciousness as a sort of suffering. With suffering defined as being conscious of your self, the concept of suffering is no longer an abstraction for me.

March 16, 1969, Sunday

Murshid's second letter to Vocha Fiske in two days begins, "Sam woke this morning like Alice at the end of 'Wonderland' when it appears that her erstwhile enemies were nothing but a pack of cards. This is my diary entry and copies are being sent to Russ [Joyner], Bryn Beorse [Shamcher], and the Reinholds [Fred and Corinne]."

Diary entry letters like this are most revealing. The fact, mentioned earlier, that Oliver Reiser referred Archie Bahm to Murshid comes out in this letter. The basis for Murshid's change of heart regarding Mansur's trip to Lama is shown here to be that "secretaries, loyal, devoted, helpful...

also have two obligations in life, to add to their earnings and to give full expression to their faculties." In addition, Murshid touches on *Playboy* ("no time or energy to consider a suit against *Playboy*"), the *Oracle* ("the acquisition of a publication by my friends"), Olompali ranch ("may fall entirely in the hands of my friends"), pictures taken of the dance class, a review of Paul Reps ("he really knows but is acting"), rowdies on Haight Street, future parties, his class at the university. That's not all: Murshid mentions Senzaki's works, the possibility of his (Murshid's) predictions being published, a disciple's practice of numerology, Murshid's introduction of a "new type of spiritual singing" ("in line with 'angelic' music heard by me years ago"), the goodwill amongst disciples, and the possibility of a future trip to the orient from Murshid's increased stipend from the family estate.

The family estate and brother Elliott are the reason Murshid has for writing Theodore C. Lachelt this Sunday morning ("no different from any other for Sam"). "Now the Estate has asked me to submit a budget and Elliott is demanding I send it to him first." Elliott got the family house and the heirlooms, and Murshid tells Lachelt, "I had to fight even to get my own library out of the house." But now Murshid is adamant.

I cannot submit my budget to Elliott because I know what he will use it for. If he offered me the family heirlooms I might do that, but I shall make no such dicker. I need $800 a month, and the allotment was raised to $775, close enough with my outside endeavors. But there has been no proper provision for medical assistance or a housekeeper.

Murshid focuses later today on an enclosure "that Archie Bahm sent along with his book, *Organicism: The Philosophy of Interdependence*." Murshid is ecstatic about what he finds: "I am so delighted with this work I can hardly read it. One gets almost into an ecstasy. Of course the Upanshads teach that with each grade of consciousness the capacity for Ananda is multifold increased." Murshid discovers Bahm is presenting integration. ("Since childhood I was involved on the one hand with the Mathematical Philosophy of Cassius Keyser and the profound teachings of the Upanishads. I sought an integration and from the standpoint of fluxions and calculus worked in that direction.") He may also have noted in the book blurb that Bahm had studied Buddhism in Burma and Hinduism in India. Bahm, like him, is another American willing to sit at the feet of, and learn from, foreigners.

March 17, 1969, Monday

Mondays Murshid lectures at the Holy Order of MANS community house. He opens by telling what his dances are and what he demands. The disruption at Brother Juniper's on March 7th is still with him. "The dance is devotion and prayer in action," Murshid tells the audience. "Attention and respect are demanded from someone coming to learn the dances. This is contrary to what many people think. They see here's a man that talks about love. They think: Love means he is indulgent. They may not pay attention or act respectfully." In the aftermath of that disruption, Murshid writes friend Vocha Fiske, "the possibility of expansion in the Haight-Ashbury district...means putting the foot down... I don't mind teaching dervish dancing for nothing but I shall have discipline, or else. For instance, no drunks, under no circumstances." (March 15, 1969)

Murshid's ongoing topic for these Monday talks is *the Gospel of St. Thomas*, which he accepts as an eye witness report. This Coptic text, from around 140 A.D., is supposed to be the actual spoken words of Jesus, as recorded by his disciple Thomas, also called Didimus the twin (of Adai). It was recovered from a ruined tomb near Nag Hamadi, Upper Egypt, in 1945. Murshid says the continuing study of the Dead Sea Scrolls might shed light on the Gospel of St. Thomas. He mentions the Greek word *hermeneia*, meaning a deep explanation that you don't get by intellection, from which we get "hermeneutics," the study of the methodical principles of interpretation. The word *pistis*, Murshid says, means "heart reliance." It has been incorrectly translated as "I believe" (*credo*), instead of "I have faith" (*fideo*), implying that the ancient meaning of "faith" was "heart reliance."

After the lecture, Father Blighton makes Murshid an offer he can't immediately accept or reject: accommodations for Murshid's students and Murshid's use of some classrooms at the Holy Order of MANS house, located at Potrero and Twenty-Fourth. Basically thinking out loud, Murshid answers that he might give one event a month in Novato and the rest here in San Francisco, or give all classes for one month in Marin County. When Murshid gets home, he writes Saadia at Cornell that with an offer of "a place in San Francisco for a *khankah* and a school..., one does not know whether to consider it or not."

But it is Saadia's invitation to speak at Cornell and at Harvard before the Muslim Student Association's national meeting that inspires a fresh round of letters to Saadia, Samir A. Hoodbhoy, Executive Secretary of the Pakistan Students Association of America, and Professor Oliver Reiser. In his letter to Saadia, although Murshid expresses overwhelm ("so far as time is concerned the difficulties are so great as to be insurmountable"), he surrenders. "If Allah wishes me to travel I shall do so."

Accordingly, to conference coordinator Hoodbhoy, Murshid simply tells about himself in a straightforward way and indicates, "I understand you would pay my expenses if I took such a trip... Will you please advise at once if you wish to make any arrangement, so my schedule can be properly adjusted."

To Reiser, Murshid says, "I am in an utter state of bewilderment," then summarizes some recent bewildering successes: Joyner's call, errands for Master Seo, family money, appreciation for turning him on to Archie Bahm, and "the surprise invitation to visit Harvard and Cornell as guest speaker. I have not at this moment any ability to get on my feet." With that last, Murshid presents an interesting image of his current condition.

March 18, 1969, Tuesday

Murshid's only letter today is to Master Seo, who wants to teach in California. "I have visited the Department of Nearest Language in Berkeley," Murshid writes, "but there is some uncertainty about timing." The best approach, Murshid suggests, might be through the Extension division. He also mentions doors opening for Seo with "Professors of Buddhism in Oregon and New Mexico" (Alfred Bloom and Archie Bahm), as well as his connection in the Department of Far East Languages at U.C.L.A.

March 19, 1969, Wednesday

When I show Murshid my *Oracle* work just after his nap, he says, "It's so revolutionary, I'm astonished." Murshid dicates a letter, "The dormant career of WHITEMAN AND LEWIS is also now in operation... It is very curious, and also to me very marvelous, that my chief secretary, Mansur, to whom I am dictating this letter, is taking up exactly where Luther Whiteman and I left off. No doubt this is because certain things are written in the ethers."

Murshid gives me the errand of leaving a letter at his lawyer's office in San Rafael. I see the building and my car parked three spaces from the corner in my mind's eye when I think about the chore. As I come down Fourth Street, I can see there are no parking places. Still, I don't doubt for a second I will park there. As the light a block before the building changes from red to green, a yellow car pulls out from my envisioned space, and I park in it.

The *Oracle* interview with former Harvard professor Tim Leary is arranged for tomorrow in Berkeley. I am excited to meet this LSD guru, because he indirectly affected my life. While living in Mexico City in 1963, I hooked up with some LSD evangelists named Thad and Rita Ashby. The Ashbys ended up in Mexico City after they had aborted their trip to join Leary and Richard Alpert (Ram Dass) in Zihuatenajo, Mexico. According to them, the local authorities sent Leary and Alpert packing. To pass the time waiting for a shipment of Owsley acid coming from California, the Ashbys and I drove around Mexico City smoking marijuana. In the

Tim Leary at his interview

meantime, they converted me. Since running naked and hollering like a banshee in a residential area in Mexico City is frowned upon, I spent a week in jail before being given a free ride in an airplane to San Antonio, Texas. After hitchhiking north, I enrolled at the University of Iowa to get a Ph.D. in English. I introduced psychedelic drugs to Moineddin, Murshid's successor, and my wife, Jemila, amongst others. All the time, I followed the career of Tim Leary and subscribed to his scholarly journal, *The Psychedelic Review*, which also published articles by Huston Smith and another Harvard teacher, Richard Evans Schultes, renowned expert on the medicinal uses of plants.

March 20, 1969, Thursday

Who impelled me to be an *Oracle* editor? Emerson, with his notion of many careers.

If our young men miscarry in their first enterprises they lose all heart. If the young merchant fails, men say he is ruined. If the finest genius studies at one of our colleges and is not installed in an office within one year afterwards in the cities or suburbs of Boston or New York, it seems to his friends and to himself that he is right in being disheartened and in complaining the rest of his life. A sturdy lad from New Hampshire or Vermont, who in turn tries all the professions, who teams it, farms it, paddles, keeps a school, preaches, edits a newspaper, goes to Congress, buys a township, and so forth, in successive years, and always like a cat falls on his feet, is worth a hundred of these city dolls. He walks abreast with his days and feels no shame in not studying a profession, for he does not postpone his life, but lives already. He has not one chance, but a hundred chances. (Excerpted from Ralph Waldo Emerson's essay "Self-Reliance.")

First thing in the morning, Fatima and Mansur go to an *Oracle* meeting at Phillip's on the boardwalk in San Anselmo. After an errand in San Rafael for Jemila and a stop at the Lucky Grocery in Terra Linda, we're back in Novato, just long enough for me to putter in the darkroom and change my pants.

I leave with Murshid for Phillip's—again. There is a delay while we wait for Phillip's wife Clara to get Jeremy Cave (Shirin's boy friend) to babysit her son Kevin. David Sapp, a friend of Phillip's joins us for the interview and Murshid takes us all to lunch before we go our separate ways. We eat lunch at the Japanese restaurant Toraya on Fillmore. Murshid orders scallops for me and seafood *nabi* for himself. Phillip gets prawns, and David sushi.

After dropping Murshid off, I have to buy gas and a tape before heading over the San Francisco-Oakland Bay Bridge to 1230 Queens Road in Berkeley. As we approach Timothy Leary's house high in the Berkeley hills, memories from my past come flooding back. Phillip, David, and Mansur arrive at four in the afternoon—on time—and a note on Leary's window says, "Sun enters Aries at 11:08 A.M." My first impression of Leary, who is sitting on his bed, is *old man*. He winks a lot at first, which I understand as a friendly gesture to put us at ease. When I ask him if he minds if I photograph him while he telephones, he winks.

Later, sitting in Murshid's kitchen, I have to laugh when I remember asking Leary twice if he could be "more general"; this, while he was already talking in broad theoretical terms about astrology. When I tell him about Thad and Rita, Leary says, "You don't know Thad's sun sign, do you?" I guess Gemini because Thad was so talkative. Leary says his own Sun is in Libra, his Moon in Capricorn, and that he has Sagittarius rising. I tell Leary my strongest impression of Thad is that he had abandoned me in jail after my "bad" acid trip and that he didn't answer my letter. Leary says, "He probably didn't get it."

Leary seems annoyed by my first question, "What time do you go to bed at night?" "Depends how high we are," he answers. "We tend to go to bed when we start coming down." I feel he is an anachronism, continuing to ingest so much acid, the ravages showing on his face.

"He's got a good heart," Murshid says, when I share my judgment. What's more: "He's a Neptunian type." This means he knows all the answers but has difficulty manifesting the solutions. I feel Leary is still preaching drugs, and I am done with them—well, done with LSD. Leary gave us some pretty good grass during the interview, and we all left with smiles on our faces.

March 23, 1969, Sunday

What happens today is disclosed in a retrospective letter Murshid writes Shamcher next Tuesday.

We had a glorious Sunday, celebration of five joint birthdays and a work party in Novato. The weather was wonderful and an enormous amount of work accomplished. Sam cooked dinner for a hundred people and about a hundred showed up. We kept well within the time limits. Gavin was King and a girl named Gypsy was Queen. We had some dedications and a number of my dances. Twice small delegations came from Sonoma State College and both said they have never witnessed such joy and beauty.

What a shift Murshid makes from opposing my trip to New Mexico to telling Shamcher in this letter, "I may send Mansur on a trip to one of Oliver Reiser's colleagues (Archie Bahm), and this can have important results."

March 26, 1969, Wednesday

In a gesture that I interpret as approval for my trip, Murshid says, "And when you go to New Mexico, you're me!" While I'm on the trip, Murshid writes Huston Smith, "At times he [Mansur] acts almost as if my 'reincarnation'."

March 27, 1969, Thursday

Today I learned: *Never express a do-gooder fantasy in front of your Murshid at the dinner table with the rest of the family present.* I created an uproar and Murshid literally roars it was the Devil who made me think about living at the gate of the Olompali ranch and charging visitors for camping privileges. What's up at Olompali ranch? It's always overrun by visitors. There's been a fire. Several people have died there; one drowned in the swimming pool, another rode a horse out on Highway 101 and was struck and killed by a truck. Recently (March 16, 1969), Murshid summarized it for Vocha.

Within a few hours after Russ called, one received the news of great changes at Olompali ranch, two miles away from my Novato home. It is an old historical place and was occupied by a group of far out people under one, Don McCoy, who put up a lot of money and just allowed things to happen, mostly parasitism and psychedelics, under the name of a commune. The parasitism and "drug" scene dominated but change of land ownership, accompanied by a strong effort on the part of those who want a commune to establish one almost throws the whole thing in Sam's hands.

Don McCoy, who provided the money to support the ranch, has been separated from his money. His relatives, who branded him crazy for bankrolling a commune, went to court and had him declared unfit to manage his affairs. Murshid thinks about taking over the ranch, but decides otherwise, for the curious reason that he's not "objective" enough. He tells Vocha,

Sam cannot work here without two colleagues Shamcher Bryn Beorse and Vilayat Khan, the real leader of Sufism in the western world—i.e. one whom the Sufis of the Orient accept. The size of the ranch, the possibilities, etc. while in full accord with my visions and forebodings, require a more objective person (or persons) to take over.

It is the presence of disciple Shirin at Olompali that compels Murshid's attention to the ranch and, hence, mine. Without naming her, Murshid writes Vocha, "The girl who is taking over is a Math whiz, and one of the most beautiful blondes I have ever met. We do not have to telepath or commune or anything." How does Shirin see Murshid? "Murshid was in love with me," Shirin succinctly puts it.

So when Mansur proposes being gatekeeper, Murshid has to blow up. Others are present. It is necessary to produce a corrective impression, an object lesson, when a key member of the team blunders publicly.

Tomorrow I have to transcribe the 7,550 word Leary interview. There is also darkroom work, developing the pictures I took during the interview and previously, of Murshid.

March 29, 1969, Saturday

The March report of California State Assemblyman John Burton is in Murshid's hand. In a letter to Burton, Murshid acknowledges the report ("I am in full accord and agreement with you on every single subject, down to details..."). He calls for equal time for students: "I think some legal means must be had that every radio and television station which provides any time to any non-student in regard to any subject under discussion on any campus should be by law compelled to give equal time to some student."

Murshid today acknowledges additional material sent by Professor Bahm, but defers saying more until he has a chance to go over it. Instead, he tells Bahm about his new beard. There is deep meaning—to do with Murshid's sense of self and identity—and the kind of intimacy you might risk with a new friend in the exchange.

I am having an experience which may seem simple to you and is simple to others, but still persists. I have lived many years with a clean face, shaving regularly. Then at the urging of some young people I left my hair to grow both somewhat long on the head, and also in full beard. I look in the mirror every day and cannot identify this as myself. I have had many pictures taken but always seem to regard them as pictures of a stranger.

I know that it is, but I do not know why it is. I simply cannot establish what some would call "self-identity." Indeed sometimes I do not feel any identity at all, either with my former pictures or present visage. Nor can I reconcile myself either with the acceptance or non-acceptance of being. I feel that I am, but there the feeling stops.

Saadia's invitation to speak in the East is still on Murshid's mind. He cautions Saadia, "One hopes you are not disappointed at this time if your Murshid does not travel now. Even if a free ticket was sent and expenses, there is the danger of moving according to man's will, not according to Allah's will." Later, in the same letter, considering if there was a free ticket, Murshid says, "one would go but preferably at some later date. One also has a living brother here who is ill."

March 30, 1969, Sunday

It's Sunday, and Professor Williams's course on the modern impacts of religion requires a paper. Murshid referred to this paper on March 17, 1969 in a letter to Saadia: "One has decided to present a paper on Pakistan, mostly from field notes and some from correspondence."

Murshid's letter to Williams begins, "I am impelled if not compelled to write a letter at this time before submitting a properly annotated paper on the position of contemporary Pakistan, based on the principle that traditional religion does often play a part in the social and political movements of the day." Not knowing if Murshid submitted "a properly annotated paper," my guess is that this letter is in lieu of a paper. By Murshid's admission, the letter is "rapidly written and not annotated." He returns to the class paper theme again and again: "I know from the *inside* the place that Islam plays in the universities of Peshawar, Islamabad and Punjab." His inside information is inconclusive: "All the officials [I] met were from West Pakistan... I could never get any expression whether they wanted independence, to join their Indian relatives, or be with the 'Islamic brethren'. They were ambivalent..." There's familiarity with the great: "Professor Durrani is one of the top physicists for the whole continent of Asia and during my stay was regarded also as the top electrical engineer of Pakistan. We could and did discuss the principles common to the deeper phases of certain sciences and mysticism." Murshid concludes, "My final paper should have names, dates and events..." *But if it is never submitted,* Murshid seems to be saying between the lines, *I hope this letter will suffice.*

To his diary letter a few days from now (April 1st) Murshid acknowledges as much. "I had to rush off a paper on 'Pakistan'...without waiting for a properly annotated essay which no doubt will come later."

I cannot let go by without comment another letter with the story of Saadia submitting a paper Murshid wrote and winning first prize. The story appears again here in Murshid's letter (in lieu of a paper) to Professor Williams.

I came near being the speaker for one of the conferences going on this week on the east coast. My goddaughter, Miss Khawar Khan, is now enrolled at Cornell. She won first prize in an international philosophical conference. She read a paper. The paper was written by an "ineligible" American!

There is a moral issue involved in this transaction, but I am not able to define it. Each time this incident comes up, Murshid's spin on the event subsumes the issue of submitting another's work as your own.

March 31, 1969, Monday

The letter Murshid writes today to his living teacher, Pir Barkat Ali in West Pakistan, is especially clear. It is written the way you speak to communicate with someone who speaks English as a second language, tempered with the high regard and respect Murshid accords his Pir. "One does not know what the supreme practices of a devotee should be?" Murshid begins rhetorically. "There is an almost constant *ziker*, the practice of *ahklak Allah* (see July 12, 1969), and the conscious realization of the noble *daroods* (affirmations) which by grace of Allah you assigned to me." One purpose of the letter is to explain Murshid's innovations.

It has been necessary to find out how to communicate with my fellow Americans... The great *innovation* that this person has introduced are the dervish dances. They are compilations of the Mevlevi, Rifa'i and Bedawi practices. Having been a guest of these various dervishes at times, before Allah, there is no reason not to use these methods.

In describing the "Ya Mohammed Abdul La, Mohammed-ar Rassul Lillah" *ziker* he created, Murshid says, "This is based on Hadiths." Later he confesses, in a manner typical of a man of God, "Sometimes one does not know oneself why one says or does things."

April 1, 1969, Tuesday

When Murshid addresses Pir Vilayat Khan today, he implies that my trip to New Mexico is a job, rather than the speculative venture it is. "My two esoteric secretaries Mansur Johnson and Daniel Lomax have been both offered outside jobs. This is going to be fine financially but may mean seeking help from other disciples." Murshid's primary reason for writing is to present to Pir Vilayat with a report on the changes at Olompali ranch. "Olompali ranch—this is the place which you have dedicated... I do not know what your intentions have been, but I can assure you that all external and some internal obstacles are being removed. Both on the spiritual and material side, the influence of my very beautiful mureed Shirin Doyle has gone up."

Before hitting the road for the *khankah*, Murshid concludes a diary letter to Shamcher. "I am now in a quasi-dilemma of my secretaries getting outside jobs, but this will add to my emoluments and things look very bright."

When Murshid arrives, he assembles us all in the meditation room for a special lesson. I get so busy after this, I don't write again until Saturday, when I make the following notations about the intervening days.

April 2, 1969, Wednesday

Murshid gives *darshan* at Amin's, where we meet every Wednesday.

April 3, 1969, Thursday

At the *khankah*, Murshid blows up about Nancy's friend, Ralph.

April 4, 1969, Friday
There is another blowup at breakfast, about cultivating the cornfield next door.

April 5, 1969, Saturday
I have a dream in which I am embracing Murshid. I experience complete ego loss with that hug. There is a blowup at breakfast again about the cornfield next door. Some people want to grow corn. Murshid thinks it is biting off more than we can chew. I'm not involved.

April 7, 1969, Monday
An "autobiographical entry" letter is addressed to Rev. J. Eugene Wagner in San Francisco, with copies to three others: Professors Bloom and Bahm in Oregon and New Mexico, respectively, and Dr. Warwick, locally. For Bahm, this carbon is a second installment of Murshid's previously reported identity crisis. "Self-identity has become very difficult. Daniel Lomax, one of the secretaries, has long had a leonine appearance and has had both beard and hair trimmed. And this person, looking so long like an imp or leprechaun, now has the hair on both head and face long and looks at times almost like a holy man. Neither of us is reconciled to any self-identity. Both look strange to ourselves."

Two days ago, Murshid received a copy of *The Buddhist Revival in China*, by Holmes Welch. The book mentions Venerable Tai Hsu, whose papers Murshid submitted to Tuttle, the publisher of *Zen Flesh, Zen Bones*. Tuttle rejected Tai Hsu's papers. Murshid tells Wagner that Welch's book "has a picture of Dr. Trebitsch-Lincoln, and I have some knowledge—quite direct too, concerning the time when he was supposed to have 'disappeared'." (For more, see April 9, 1969)

The upcoming Mystical Experience class evokes a question for Murshid: *Are we going to depend on books or on human experience?* Daisetz Suzuki became known for his books—better known even than were his fellow-disciple Nyogen Senzaki or their teacher, Soyen Shaku. Follow Murshid as he expresses his position.

It was all right to be told at Kamakura in 1956 that one was already two grades above Daisetz Suzuki. The whole subject of "grottoes" [shrines] mentioned by L. Adams Beck and Sokei-an, complicated by the information, "Daisetz has never been here" [what Murshid was told at certain grottoes] brings up this question on how far literary authorities will be accepted seriously above "those who have crossed to the *other shore.*" One is also problemized by The Diamond Sutra because one does not affirm directly, but one has to express and now get out into the open. [Plainly speaking, Murshid "does not affirm directly" because in Buddhism's Diamond Sutra there is no person, yet he is. Suzuki, the literary authority, did not have Murshid's realization and was not honored, as was Murshid, by being invited to the special shrine.]

April 8, 1969, Tuesday

To the Temple of Understanding's executive secretary, Finley P. Dunne, Jr., Murshid writes,

The dream of a TEMPLE OF UNDERSTANDING is most marvelous. To cast a negative note might be unfortunate, but "unless the Lord buildeth the house they labor in vain who build..." In America...there has been a substitution of calling in famous or select people instead of the representatives of these religions and...when you accept as important, persons, who do not believe in prayer or call to prayer, to support the TEMPLE OF UNDERSTANDING, there is in the inner worlds a negative note. We cannot both have "God" and not-God at the same time and achieve an aim. There must be the utmost devotion, concentration and consideration.

No names are mentioned, not until tomorrow. Writing to A.B. Patel's World Union, Murshid looks back on the letter just written to the Temple of Understanding. He tells Patel:

One is now in an awkward position that one has had to take to task another world movement because while its ideals are perfect, in its practices it has fallen back on the same procedures of appealing to name-and-form to lead, and the "important persons" are given important places regardless of their integrity because of the supposition that this will draw membership and masses. In this case they have summoned a man inimical to most of the real leaders of the real religions of the real world and evidently there is no way to stop it. Or maybe there is.

April 9, 1969, Wednesday

Murshid doesn't beat around the bush in today's letter to Reps, which he dictates to me. After describing the Temple of Understanding as a "very beautiful inspiration...now coming dangerously near to self-destruction," Murshid writes:

In the same letter [from the Temple of Understanding] which gave one a detailed report, praise is given to Alan Watts, a man of absolutely no integrity and of no faith, and they're using his pictures... I am sick and tired of having important persons bypass karma and moral laws. I see nothing but destruction, as I have both seen and foreseen in the past from such misbehavior. To have a universal religion led by a man of sex, alcohol and drugs is hardly a way to salvation.

I perceive a mixed message when Murshid dictates the next part of the Reps letter. He tells Reps, "My financial situation is peculiar. There has also been a steady increment of remuneration. But it means carrying several persons and a constant danger of them abandoning self-reliance." Murshid's way to balance these opposing concepts, in my case, is to feed me on every occasion when we are together at mealtimes. I receive food, but no money. Murshid has some afterthoughts on the Holmes Welch book and the Tuttle rejection of Tai Hsu. Continuing his letter to Reps, he complains,

This same Tai-Hsu whose manuscript they rejected is a dramatic hero of this work [*The Buddhist Revival in China*]. I refuse any more to accept any snubs or rejections that I did not sit at the feet of this Master. I am sending the Tai-Hsu manuscript to Harvard along with a suitable letter to Holmes Welch, the author. While this is a commendable book, I must factually differ from the author on one small point, and that is concerning Dr. Trebitsch-Lincoln. Welch says he disappeared, but during that period in which he is supposed to have disappeared he was in touch directly and indirectly with both Senzaki-san and Zoso [Fernandez, Senzaki's chief disciple], now both deceased. While this is a minor point, I have been constantly speaking on Dr. Trebitsch-Lincoln, whose cosmic predictions invariably came true. He was no Jean Dixon, Edgar Cayce, Eileen Garrett, or Alice Bailey. He was very unpopular, totally honest, and invariably correct. He died on Mt. Omei-Shan in central China. In fact, anent Omei-Shan, Holmes Welch is very weak. He mentions Harry Frank who had been there most unfavorably; he does not mention Fleming, author of *Tibetan Marches*, who also spent some time at Omei-Shan. This may not be important of itself, but I am no tyro, and I do not care any more what people think of it.

Murshid corrects a pessimistic false impression he's given Philosophy Professor Oliver Reiser in a letter today. It begins, "Sometimes life is full of wars and battles and sometimes life seems comparatively free from them, but the overall picture of the moment is so favorable that one is liable to create—and one has created—wrong impressions if there is pessimism hinted." A summary of upbeat news includes the detail, "My secretary [Mansur] will be visiting New Mexico in May and much may come of it." At Amin's tonight for the Wednesday night meeting, when Amin's dog Caesar gets up or Fatima changes position, I see a gold imprint on the floor.

Every soul radiates an influence which charges the atmosphere all around... The character of this influence is light or heat, which silently spreads its warmth, according to its power of radiance (Unpublished teachings of Hazrat Inayat Khan)

April 10, 1969, Thursday

What I find interesting in the "campus disputes" letter, the first of two letters Murshid dictates through me to Russ Joyner today, is Murshid's support for a law ensuring that TV stations give equal time to all parties when covering "the affairs of any campus... I have suggested to Senator Moscone that there might be a law...that gives...equal time...to an official of the student body and also to an official of one of the teacher's or professor's groups." While the first letter to Russ Joyner deals with "campus disputes," the second seems to be Murshid's mellowed response to Joyner's telephone call, which proposed a truce. "In one sense, maybe in more than one sense, I owe you a profound apology," Murshid begins, perhaps recalling the numerous carping letters and carbons sent Joyner. Please understand, Murshid conciliates, that "in another sense, I am fighting, so to speak, for my life. When a person is brushed aside, when he offers solutions to problems, perhaps it does not matter; but when the problems remain, one may ask: what has been gained?"

After this introduction, Murshid gives the example of how the U.S. ignored Robert Clifton's warnings on Vietnam. Even more relevant is an example of what might have been accomplished if Murshid's letters had not been ignored. Pir Dewwal Shereef is the unnamed "guru" in the story Murshid tells Joyner.

The "guru" of Field-Marshall Ayub Khan has had many conversations with me, and he has put aside funds for a chair at the University of Islamabad wherein semantics or its equivalent could be taught. This "guru" at least solidly believes that the word "Islamic" should be semanticized. He has the money, the organization and the backing. Letters written at his request have been ignored—I don't want to go into this anymore; we want to *do*, not gripe.

April 12, 1969, Saturday

Writing before the Mystical Experience class at the university extension today, Murshid's admiration for his Uncle Harry's "adventurism" comes through in a letter. Murshid tells Uncle Harry he has "been a guest of honor at the Royal Palace Grounds in Japan and Thailand and had teas in the Presidential mansions of India and Pakistan." Then Murshid writes, "There were certain streaks of adventurism in both [your brother] Walter and yourself, and I have had the same streaks and maybe still have them." In the Mystical Experience class, I see the professor's light; his aura, if you will.

Some noteworthy incidents Murshid mentions during the dance class: Murshid searched for *soma* in India. He says it exists in a sap or as a mixture of saps. (See more on this, February 8, 1970) Murshid explains how the dances came: "First I see them. Then I feel them. Finally, I think them." Murshid says pants evolved because of horseback riding. The sari, he says, is totally feminine, because it wraps around. He asserts that the Mogul men and women dressed completely opposite than we are used to: The men wore skirts, the women pants. Murshid says Krishnamurti separates himself from humanity. He sits in a chair and is brought questions. You might as well read on existentialism—a subject Murshid associates negatively with Hegel, Marx, Nietzsche, and "super verbalisms with the label 'semantics'." There are four words for "love" in modern Greek, Murshid says. And there are eight ancient Greek words for "love," suggesting there's more to love than our language can encompass. Murshid says the way to tell a mystic from someone with "peak experience" (a term from modern psychology describing a high state) is that a mystic answers letters. Murshid has written 106 letters since the first of the year. That number includes, I am sure, answers to every letter he received.

"What are the powers?" someone asks. I perk up. "The Diamond Sutra," Murshid says. When the teacher recommends something, I want to check it out. "Powers" evokes stuff like teleportation to me. To teleport means to me to transport the body from place to place, but the word's not in the dictionary! I consult The Diamond Sutra. The editor of Shambhala's version of *The Diamond Sutra* writes, "The reader who has heard the fame of this Buddhist scripture and quickly reads in the hope of finding arcane knowledge is likely to be disappointed." (p.9) True enough. Consider this:

After the Venerable Subhuti asks Lord Buddha, "World-honored One, if good men and good women seek the Consummation of Incomparable Enlightenment, by what criteria should they abide and *how should they control their thoughts?*" Lord Buddha answers cryptically. "Subhuti, all the Bodhisattva-Heroes should discipline their thoughts... Yet when vast, uncountable, immeasurable numbers of beings have thus been liberated, *verily no being has been liberated.* Why is this, Subhuti? It is because no Bodhisattva who is a real Bodhisattva cherishes the idea of an ego-entity, a personality, a being, or a separated individuality [emphases mine]." (*The Diamond Sutra*, pp.23-26)

Murshid's Zen teacher Nyogen Senzaki gave a talk on The Diamond Sutra in San Diego on May 19, 1946. At one point during the talk, he must have held up his beads, because he said,

I have here a commentary on The Diamond Sutra which is, I think, the best of all commentaries. It is hidden in these Buddhist beads. Those who wish to read it, step inside any bead and study it to your heart's content! I am not talking of some sort of magic or miracle. I am not going to monopolize this particular commentary by myself. Any one of you can enter into a marble or a bead, if you learn how to do it. It does not matter whether you are stout or slender. Some day you will do it easily and freely in the same graceful manner as you entered into this room. Then you will read the best of all commentaries of The Diamond Sutra at a glance—nay, you will be graduated from the whole course of the teaching which The Diamond Sutra discloses." (*Like a Dream, Like a Fantasy*, p.54)

Moineddin seated with Murshid facing Fatima, Van Beasley, Akbar Simmons, and Daniel Lomax at the beginning of Van's initiation, May 4, 1969.

Chapter 16

Zen Is
Everyday Life

So far as permission is concerned, nothing but yes. Murshid [Hazrat Inayat Khan] said: "What I teach you, you should teach others." It is a question when we can have a proper secretary. (Murshid's letter to disciple Marcia Pavolic, April 13, 1969)

April 13, 1969, Sunday

Murshid's question, above, about "when we can have a proper secretary" explains why I feel conflicted about not doing *enough* to serve Murshid. On another day, I am impressed with what Thoreau and Murshid call self-reliance. Back and forth I go, and it is necessary for me to embrace both service and self-reliance to be around the man with Libra—balance—as his birth sign. Marcia sends a dues payment, and Murshid responds by discussing some problems relating to money and help.

The establishment of dues and at least an informal organization brought, on the one hand, more people and more money, but also came near to producing more laxity. It was necessary to point out that, it must be understood whether the *khankah* is to be a living entity or merely a sort of cooperative boarding-house. Each one having his own path and supporting it by ego-reasoning resulted in several financial set-backs [a reference to Hassan's printing business].

The situation became worse because Murshid was getting outside jobs. Murshid's outside jobs brought money and the others got promises [a reference to Mansur's wished-for remuneration from the *Oracle*]. But this involved another problem that with the people at the *khankah* getting outside jobs, with or without pay, there has not been a proper secretariat... Daniel is now working for the City of Novato, part time. Hassan may get a full time job. Both Fatima and Mansur are now depending on the *Oracle*, the publication of which has been constantly delayed. If it brings in money Murshid should have a secretary well equipped to work on the music and dance themes; i.e. Ruthie whose name is now Parisa (fairy-like).

Murshid makes a flattering comparison between himself as a young man and Mansur: "Mansur has worked out a career for himself which is very much in line with Murshid's work at the same age and he may be going to New Mexico next month. And then to Colorado to join Vilayat in June."

Mansur's involvement in the *Oracle* meetings allows Moineddin to fill in for him with Murshid. What happens? "Moineddin now understands my work because he has been functioning as the esoteric secretary at the highest level. We cannot do more than three hours of this a day," Murshid writes.

In the second sentence of his letter to the President of India, Dr. Zakir Hussein in New Delhi, Murshid describes himself using a word I've never seen before. I guess from the context that *tanasukh* means "reincarnation." "I am known here even among your colleagues as a sort of *tanasukh* of Prince Dara Shikoh." The purpose of the letter is to introduce "disciple... Miss Deborah ("Debbie" in earlier chapters) Churney." Debbie "has been urged to come to India and pursue the career of spiritual and Indian dancing... She is a beautiful young girl, a fine disciple, and especially adept in devotional dances. She is now studying with a somewhat famous teacher here named Janaki." Murshid sketches for President Hussein his success in Vincent Shean's Gandhi interpretation contest, and his rise from a hospital bed two years before to successful spiritual leader today. Murshid implies that his "slow but steady increment of money" allows him "to send at least one person to India (*inshallah*) whether it be the aforesaid Miss Churney or more." On this subject, to Marcia, Murshid writes that Debbie's "father is becoming interested enough to at least proffer her her fare. We shall have to take this up tomorrow if not before."

Murshid uses the receipt of material on the Experimental College Program at UC Berkeley from Joseph Tussman to promote more integration and to critique the suggested curriculum. Murshid writes Tussman,

I have been advocating a "grill organization" so that different departments, even different sciences and subjects on the same campus but covering the same geographical or historical area should be integrated more and the same program used to cover all the campuses... The same amount of brain-power which could be used or misused in studying classical Greece or 17th century England might be used on the "problem of the day", especially where answers to these problems are to be found on one or more of the working campuses.

April 14. 1969, Monday

Last night I was several places in dream with Murshid, getting teachings. Once he demonstrated his ability to go through walls and change clothes instantly. He went into a garage. I followed. He was gone, and his clothes were hanging from a light fixture in the center of the room. He was outside in his dervish robe.

Anandashram has sent Murshid more books. Friends at the ashram, addressed as "Dear Ram," receive Murshid's check for $25 and a letter. Anandashram's Mother Krishnabai, also known as "Mataji," figures in an anecdote Murshid tells.

Both in the university and the class in Christian Mysticism we are studying the *Gospel of St. Thomas*. This proclaims the majesty of male over female. One of my young lady students questioned this so last night we presented material on Mataji. You can tell Mataji that Sam considers her the greatest of saints but will not be her *bhakta* [devotee] both because she does not want any *bhaktas* and because he is Papa's *bhakta*. We went over this point last night in both extreme reverence and extreme humor, the way I am sure Papa would have liked it.

Dancing disciple Debbie's name is not mentioned, but her possible visit to the ashram is foreshadowed.

This brings up another subject. Two of Sam's disciples [Sheila and Dara] went to India but did not fulfill his requests. Now another young disciple has been won over to the idea of going to India to study spiritual dancing. We understand that this would involve a visit to the general Travancore-Cochin area but do not know yet. It is our hope that then she can visit Anandashram. This matter may take several months to settle but [we] wish you to be informed ahead of time.

Murshid opens his letter to Saadia, "There have been constant delays in writing," and goes on to give his sanitized view of one of many family meetings, possibly the one of April 2nd.

One's burdens have increased, necessitating a "family" meeting at the *khankah* in Novato to make the disciples realize we are uniting for the sake of Allah, and if that comes first all other things will follow. There I have very good help in the *khalif*-designate Moineddin.

April 15, 1969, Tuesday

Today, Murshid's letter to the Alumni Association is a follow-up to the Joseph Tussman letter of two days ago. Murshid succinctly plugs one of his pet projects on "how the University of California may help to solve some of these [poverty producing] problems, instead of the proposal to look into ancient history or medieval England." It's not that Murshid dislikes historical studies; he's more interested in solutions for contemporary problems.

The same efforts, the same thoughts, the same research could bring out some most interesting and wonderful answers... We live in a day of "problems" when we could equally be living in a day of "solutions." There are many near-solutions to the above and other real or pseudo-problems found in the present and past work on the campuses, fields and laboratories of the University or Multiversity.

April 17, 1969, Thursday

At dinner, I remember another dream. I am embarrassed in dream because I am smoking at one of Murshid's meetings. Interrupting my mealtime reverie, Murshid mentions that Daniel is late. I say, "I should call him." Murshid says, "Don't call. This is Daniel's test." I think: This just came to Murshid. Murshid got this guidance in response to my comment!

April 18, 1969, Friday

Murshid is in a fury when W.D. Begg, Topdara, India, sends him a brochure featuring Saint Sathya Sai Baba.

Why should Adi K. Irani, quondam secretary to the late Meher Baba, be concerned with another supposititious Saint or Avatar? I personally am sick and tired of the long parade of so-called super-personalities. I do not see the problems of India solved, nor do I believe they will be solved by homage to fleshly beings... I understand we are soon going to have one Sai Baba come to this land. No doubt he will be welcomed. I should like to see one of these saints or holy men do something to stop war, to mitigate poverty, to extend a loving hand to those in need, lead in worshipping and decry those that worship them.

After going on for a page on this subject, Murshid explains he's been rebuked (on the inner planes, I would guess), for not using strong language. "This no doubt is strong language. I have been called to account here for not using strong language. I think this is the only way to awaken those who regard other than God (Allah, Ram) for worship."

Knowing that Begg has complained of financial problems in the past, Murshid challenges him to get relief from the new avatar he promotes. "I would like to help you, but God Himself says that you must turn to Saint Sathya Sai Baba for help now, and not to me. This is your test and not mine." Murshid shares another view of this exchange with Begg in a diary entry letter to Paul Reps.

But yesterday I broke out in fury. A brochure came from India from a purported Sufi. It came out for an avatar, a new one. This was bad enough. But who published the brochure for a new avatar? Why the cousin and secretary of the late M.B. [Meher Baba] and it had the declaration that this man was still in the flesh and had actually resurrected from the dead; ergo, was the *real* Sadguru! Coming from M.B.'s chief associate! And I bet Lady Duce will get copy if she has not already. So I have written: LA ILLA HA [In the Middle East there is no consistency in the transliteration of languages.] EL IL ALLAH [the last words in his letter to Begg].

April 19, 1969, Saturday

At the University of California Berkeley Extension, where Murshid is taking a course called "Mystical Experience," I hear Professor Needleman read the 137th Psalm, about bashing children's heads against rocks. "Happy shall he be, that taketh and dasheth thy little one against the stones." I ask myself, what is this all about? The answer comes, *The children are thoughts.* This is a symbolic description of the process of mental purification undertaken by mystics. This surely would never have occurred to me if I hadn't heard Murshid's interpretation of the battle of Kurukshetra in the Bhagavad Gita; namely, it is not an external battle: it is the inner battle mystics fight to purify their own hearts.

from left to right: Fatima, Moineddin, Murshid, Rev. Eugene Wagner

My thoughts in this, the second meeting of the Mystical Experience class, are, no doubt, colored by my association with Murshid. I think, *What value are ideas about mystics compared to knowing a living mystic?* I think, *Why are mystics always long ago and far away like in this class?* Murshid is more positive about the class. In a letter to Dr. Zakir Hussein, President of India, on the 13th, he reported being "in a seminar on mystical experience wherein mystical experience was discussed more than the opinions of great men about it."

The difference between priests and prophets occurs to me: Priests perform priestcraft, meaningless rituals; prophets, inspired by God, perform miracles. I think of the Holy Order of MANS, whose seminary requires mystical experience in order for an aspirant to become ordained as a priest. Someone in the class asks, "What happens between thoughts?" I answer—to myself—*awareness.* Someone says, "Mystics are empirical." I think, why doesn't the class ask Murshid to give them the *experience* of awareness with Reps's first practice in *Zen Flesh, Zen Bones?*

Radiant one, this experience may dawn between two breaths. After breath comes in (down) and just before turning up (out)—*the beneficence.* (p.193)

I am feeling a lot of tension from my thoughts and impatience with the academic experience. This is a class about a concept, mystical experience, and Murshid's life *is* mystical experience. Mystics are rare, and here he is. With difficulty, I still my mind and focus on the class.

With a published talk in hand by Seyyed Hossein Nasr, Department of Islamics, University of Tehran, Iran, Murshid calls attention to his unorthodoxy by indicating he "agrees thoroughly and absolutely" with the talk. Yet, "it is this very agreement which produces some differences or misunderstandings." The problem for Murshid is: "I do not accept that Mohammed is the Seal of the Prophets from those who do not accept his teachings." The implication is that there are Muslims who do not accept the teachings of Mohammed. Murshid's example is the saying of Mohammed's which is "contrary to 'Islam' that 'My words cannot abrogate the words of Allah, but the words of Allah can abrogate my words.'" Generalities aside, what Murshid means is what he wrote.

There is no place in books by so-called "Muslims" for a *feringhi* [foreigner, i.e., Murshid] to whom the Messenger appeared long before he studied [the] Holy Quran. And neither any place in "Islamics" at all for a *feringhi* who never met an Imam until he was well over fifty years of age! So this being so, the teachings one gives do not follow traditions at all, but may follow (Allah knows best) the type of "revelation" suited to Americans. It is overlooked—a "good Muslim" may overlook anything—that Holy Quran distinctly says it was given in Arabic so that the immediate audience could understand.

At the dance class during the Neptune walk, with his concentration at the crown center, Murshid recalls a conversation at a party with the daughter of the famous Russian dancer Nijinsky. Nijinsky's daughter said over and over, "I can understand everything, but I cannot understand Papa." Murshid said, "I can understand Papa." "Tell me," she said. "I told her," Murshid said, "and we became friends." Murshid explained Nijinsky's madness to his daughter in terms of centers. Nijinsky was too much centered in the crown center, just as Isadora Duncan was in her sex (second chakra) center. Each became unbalanced in a different direction. Nijinsky went crazy.

April 22, 1969, Tuesday

Murshid writes Shamcher, "Yesterday, one visited the Berkeley campus and three departments accepted 'The Rejected Avatar' and at least one library the works of Swami Ram Das." Here, as well as to Reps, Murshid mentions Alan Watts. "I shall mention only one name, Alan Watts. I am terrified that the Temple of Understanding has called him in, a man of no faith, who does not believe in anything but his ego and who has publicly and privately flouted four of the five moral principles of [Buddhism, the] *Pancha Sila*." [The precepts are, roughly: don't kill, steal, lie, misuse the senses, or get intoxicated.]

After the early morning letter to Shamcher in San Francisco, Murshid is all business when he arrives at the *khankah*. He takes me into the office and outlines what he calls his "priorities." First, there is the music, dancing, and walk work. Second, fabrics—cloth for robes and costumes. Third, there are the aesthetic aspects of drawing, fine arts, and ceramics. Fourth, Murshid has his literary work. This is divided into creative, research, and Sufi (esoteric) writing. The Sufi writing concerns 1) commentaries on the Gathas and Githas; 2) commentaries on the elementary and advanced literature published in the twelve volumes of *The Sufi Message*; and 3) commentaries on scriptures. Fifth, Murshid is concerned with the financial organization, dues, collections, the bank account. I feel honored that Murshid has shared the scope of his work with me, but the information does not inspire me to action of any kind. I receive the information and await further orders.

At the now routine family meeting the first day Murshid arrives, he brings up the subject of absences from the *khankah*. He enumerates trips; for example, Mansur's New Mexico trip coming up May 5-20. Murshid reports that Parisa, Shirin, and James are planning on going to Pir Vilayat's camp in Colorado June 18-31. He brings up Jemila's cutting yoga classes and indicates his desire for the *khankah* to be covered by someone in addition to Moineddin. In all these instances, Murshid demonstrates his foresight, the quality he has of looking ahead. He speaks at this meeting of wanting to have a map of the yard. He wants to know where the squash will be, where the corn and beans will be planted. The beans will have to be staked out with chicken wire. We'll need some Adena fertilizer for the corn. Possibly some irrigation.

April 23, 1969, Wednesday

When Murshid sits with me today and says, "I'm going to look inside," I have no idea what I am about to receive. I get a piece of paper and write what comes up. Do not let the banality of what follows suggest that this is not some kind of spiritual transmission.

There is a woman named Elizabeth Yeager who has psychiatric trouble. Murshid will see her, but a gift offering from her is necessary. I have to tell her that. "There is Nathan," Murshid says, "who has to be looked after during the three days Jemila will be away—Friday, Saturday, and Sunday, May 9th, 10th and 11th." Between Mansur and Daniel, who is "the Assistant Esoteric Secretary and Financial Secretary," Murshid wants us to compile a list of candidates for initiation. This never materializes. I keep a list of disciples who attend dance class. I keep an esoteric notebook where every disciple's practices are recorded. I never list candidates in this notebook. "I want to make a special effort to help clairvoyant disciples," Murshid says, but he needs to know who they are. Clairvoyant disciples reveal that faculty to Murshid in private interviews, and I am not present. Still, he is asking me, because he is practicing non-dualism.

The May Day celebration is on Murshid's mind. He thinks out loud. "Should we have a Maypole? Can we get fruit from Fred? Should Dr. Warwick be invited? Should we have cheese sandwiches or what?" In general, should he take charge or shut up? It's a rhetorical question to me; Murshid will take charge. Murshid's comment about the *Oracle*, which is late coming out, is, "If the *Oracle* doesn't get out, I'm going to get in another logjam." He has been trumpeting its arrival to myriad correspondents at home and abroad. I tell him it is due out Sunday, April 27th. Murshid repeats the need for chicken wire for the bean plants. The field has to be plowed before planting, and a careful plan made of where things are going to be planted. It is "a minor point," Murshid says, but he asks me to put the Gospel of St. Thomas on the table. At the *khankah*, Murshid wants us to read *The Bowl of Saki* aphorisms for the day at breakfast every morning, along with the prayer blessing the food. Finally, Murshid asks me to put the Walk Papers and Dance Manual typescripts out tomorrow morning before I leave. When the dictation stops, I realize Murshid has just written a letter—to me.

Tonight, we hold our first Wednesday night meeting at the seminary [not the Holy Order of MANS] in San Anselmo, a large circular space with a dome, great for dancing and the bigger crowds that are coming.

April 24, 1969, Thursday

One of the practices Murshid has presented is the use of the word-sound ALLAH for the alleviation of problems. Two nights ago, I practiced what I read in *Irfan* by Faqir Nur Muhammad Sarwari Qadri before visiting Norman, the printer, on *Oracle* business. Qadri writes,

> The pious slaves of Allah draw an augury (i.e., read some supererogation [means the act of performing more than is required by obligation] and text and go to sleep) whenever they desire to know the good or evil end of a thing or future incident or state; they receive a clear and true answer in the dream. Some practice bibliomancy from the Quran or some other book. Sometimes the augury comes out to be true and favorable. Some live-hearted Gnostics attend to their minds during wakening and are informed in the twinkling of an eye.

There was a dream after I practiced this, I forget now, but the outcome was favorable. So again, this morning, I practice *irfan*. Again, there is a dream: a tiring dream, like an escape, a long walk. I am carrying two cats, which I throw over the final fence before me. By the time I climb over, the cats have slipped back through the wire. Murshid reveals some of what *irfan* means to him in one of his unpublished commentaries, where he discusses how to remove deep impressions from the mind.

This is very difficult if man tries this with his personal will. Then we say we invoke God. But how do we invoke God? As many mystics tell us, for practical purposes GOD IS HIS NAME. And there is a Sufic science called *irfan*, which roughly interpreted means *gnosis*. By invoking the Name of Allah, one is invoking Allah, and then one does not have to consider "my will" or "Thy Will," because in *irfan* there is only the one will, and it is operative. One can place the Name of Allah any place inwardly or outwardly, and one can use one's own will to direct this Divine Force and Divine faculty. It is like exerting a counter-pressure. It may be quick; it may take a long time, but the pressure and counter-pressure of ALLAH has also with it the benefit of the Sound itself connoted by "Allah," so that all aspects of the universe unite here to man's benefit.

Parisa calls on Murshid at the *khankah*, and he honors her with a lengthy report. I love to hear Murshid's updates at the beginning of meetings or in his letters. It is an opportunity to compare my recollection of events with Murshid's account. Today I am nearby with a paper and pen.

Murshid tells Parisa he has to write letters to disciple Dan Taylor; Suzanne D'Mitrieff, Pir Vilayat's secretary in Los Angeles; and Professor Joseph Needleman, our Mystical Experience teacher. Murshid tells Parisa that Dane Rudhyar's and Henry Cowell's early books were important for him. Said Murshid to Reps, "When Dane Rudhyar was young, he worked on music and brought out some wonderful things." To Vocha, he said that "[when I presented] 'angelic' music heard by me years ago" to Rudhyar, Rudhyar "rejected it." I hear Murshid say to Parisa, "Someone is needed to write up the dances." This is an invitation to Parisa, I think. She doesn't volunteer. I never know or care— it's not my business—why some individuals stop and some others come forward when they meet Murshid. I continue to record Murshid's comments to Parisa.

Murshid says that the Saturday dance class is a "public dance." This puzzles me, since only committed disciples attend. True, Parisa doesn't attend, and this could be Murshid's way of inviting her. Murshid speaks further about the dances. He says, "In the yoga dances,

Moineddin, Murshid, Rev. Wagner

the postures and breathing are important. In the mantra dances, the sounds are important." Murshid says, "Susan's [possibly Gancher] return means something for fabrics." There are "long silences coming," he says mysteriously. Murshid says, "I don't want to keep people up late. That's my unselfish reason for leaving class early. The selfish reason is to go to the ice cream store." "There are no personal favors," Murshid says. "What is given is what is seen inwardly." Murshid explicitly says that he has typing for Parisa, having to do with the music, dancing, and walk work.

Parisa disappears after this interview, and next month, Murshid notes to a correspondent that Parisa "has disappeared, although I understand she is now back." After Parisa leaves, Murshid momentarily looks distracted. I ask, "What is it?" "Go ahead with what you planned," he says. "After the New Mexico trip, you may drop the commune trip."

By "New Mexico trip," Murshid means Lama. The Lama Foundation is just one of several communes or alternative communities I plan to visit May 5-20. Lama sent Murshid an invitation to visit; that's how I found out about it. In a few days (April 26, 1969) Murshid recreates the situation in a letter to Sitara, an old friend in Seattle: "The other day something funny happened. Mansur and I were having a Chinese lunch. The fortune cookie said that Samuel would go on a long distance business trip. We came to this house immediately after, and there was a letter requesting I go to New Mexico." Needless to say, I can't visit just Lama and not the others. It is part of my self-expression as a self-styled journalist to cover the new communities in the American Southwest.

April 25, 1969, Friday

I go to Gavin's Friday night open house with Murshid. What I like the most at Gavin's are his stories about the poet Yeats and other famous people he had encounters with. Tonight Gavin tells about speaking to Gurdjieff about Ouspensky, Gurdjieff's famous biographer. Gavin prefaces his remarks about Gurdjieff by saying, "It is the fashion today to call him Gur-GEEF, but when I talked to him, he was referred to as GURR-gi-eff. When I ask Gavin what he thinks of Ouspensky's books, which I read avidly in college, he says, "What can you expect of a petty Prussian aristocrat?" I think Gavin is San Francisco's version of Andy Warhol.

April 26, 1969, Saturday

It is Saturday morning in San Francisco, and Murshid begins a letter to Sitara, a Sufi lady his age in Seattle.

I am dictating this to Mansur my esoteric secretary. He has just copied the Sufi Thoughts. It is sadly remarkable that many persons after taking *bayat* forget these as being elementary. They are to some of us quite fundamental, and it is wonderful to find the young people practicing, "Draw us closer to Thee, every moment of our life," as the line goes in *Saum* [the Sufi prayer].

How do young people practice "Draw us closer to Thee, every moment of our life"? One way, as a *mudra* during the prayer, with the hands together like a screen moving closer to the face, and then washing over the body without touching it. True, this is but a movement representing the idea of closeness. It is up to the devotee to strive to realize it "every moment of our life."

Sitara's letter asked Murshid to pray for Shamcher. Murshid informs Sitara that Shamcher's letter also asked him to pray for her. Murshid gives Sitara the practice Pir Barkat Ali gave him. "Please do this practice: with *tashbih* (beads) 101 times *Ya Hayoo ya Qayoom*. This was given me by my living spiritual teacher. It has enabled me to work all the time and retain strength, vitality and inspiration." After telling the story of the fortune cookie (see April 24, 1969), Murshid writes, "Mansur is going to New Mexico himself shortly and on his return will arrange the cortege or caravan for Vilayat, in Colorado." It never occurs to me that Murshid is introducing me to Sitara in preparation for our journey to the Northwest in the fall.

April 27, 1969, Sunday

Murshid writes four pages to Paul Reps entitled THE CONFESSIONS OF SAMUEL L. LEWIS. Writing Shamcher right afterwards, Murshid's first line is, "There is something in the universe which compels one to write in an abbreviated form 'Confessions'." No doubt, Shamcher receives a copy. "Confessions" has been used as a literary term for autobiography since St. Augustine's Confessions in 400 A.D. It is telling that Murshid begins by referencing Lord C.P. Snow's scientific versus literary-humanist culture. The scientific and literary-humanist camps are what Lord Snow refers to as the "two cultures." Murshid's use of this idea is that scientists will listen to reports and humanists won't. "The former determine life by facts and events," he tells Reps; "the latter by their personal reactions to their reviews of the activities of others." The inference I draw is that Reps, as a witness to events in Murshid's life, chooses to react as the latter. Murshid's letter to Reps illuminates their relationship, if you read between the lines. For example:

> The first event of importance was the introduction [by Murshid] of Hazrat Inayat Khan to Nyogen Senzaki. Much of your own life has stemmed from this meeting and it is awful even to refer to the hard, hard fact that this grew out of the Khan-Senzaki meeting and so did a lot of other things, a lot of other things. [Without Murshid's introduction of Reps to Senzaki, the literary collaboration on *Zen Flesh, Zen Bones* would not have been possible.]

Murshid alludes to the time he was walking on the beach south of the ocean side Cliff House Restaurant in San Francisco. "Here I have the impudence, the imprudence, the audacity to tell—and it is hard, hard fact—that my first *satori* took place right here in San Francisco exactly where Shaku Soyen had walked." During the *satori*, Murshid writes, "one picked up from the cosmos—actually *alaya*–the place of Nyogen Senzaki, long known to Zoso Fernandez and myself and to practically nobody else." [By saying he picked up "the place" of Nyogen Senzaki, Murshid means he grasped Senzaki's cosmic importance.] This is an allusion to a situation in a story in Murshid's paper "Dharma Transmission." (*Sufi Vision and Initiation*, p. 87)

After Nyogen went to Los Angeles, this one said to Zoso, "Nyogen is not a homeless monk; Nyogen is a Master; he is more than a Master; he has the Dharma-Transmission." "Of course." We vowed to silence until one of us was left. Zoso is gone, Nyogen is gone, and when Nyogen was gone it was discovered—or rather uncovered—that he was the Dharma-Master of the Age.

The next high point was "the 1926 interviews with Hazrat Inayat Khan, six interviews, only one sought by SAM, five by Inayat Khan, and one [Murshid] has never been forgiven for that!" In other words, what should have been considered a blessing was treated as an offense. Why? It seems to have been a lack of generosity of spirit. Four more high points, in chronological order, are:

On February 5, 1930, three years after the demise of Hazrat Inayat Khan, SAM went into seclusion and as he sat down to meditate the "Astral Body" of the Pir came into the room, and he [Inayat Khan] sat down and meditated with him... In 1930 one met Sokei-an Sasaki, sat at his feet and returned to San Francisco in 1931 knowing all the scriptures of the world by Dharma-transmission... In the summer of 1946, while one was in the woods in South Carolina, one was initiated in *fana-fi-rassoul* [annihilation in the human ideal]. The results of this are in the poem "SALADIN"... When one went to Asia in 1956, one was amazed that one was always received at the highest levels everywhere, scorned and rejected in his own land. One will not relate here what is in the diaries [see *Sufi Vision and Initiation*]. But around 1961, one received the basis for RASSUL GITA which, if God permits, will be a companionate piece to *Bhagavad Gita*...

When Murshid brings the story round to present time and success with the youth, it is poignant to read.

But behind this is the sad story of all these beautiful young people: they have had sex, they have had comforts, they have had luxuries, but never true love and affection, and they long for these, because these are the realities belonging to the soul itself.

A disciple named Marc Gold, in New York, is corresponding with Murshid. Upon hearing about his studies, Murshid comments,

As a Sufi one is not concerned whether you take up hatha yoga or tai chi or any one of a number of excellent systems for partial development of the personality. One is in favor of them. But one is even more in favor of complete spiritual training.

Lest there be any misunderstanding, Murshid continues, "Of course, it is much better to be under the direct training of a Murshid."

April 28, 1969

This is the day Murshid answers the invitation to visit the Lama Foundation in New Mexico. He begins,

The brochure of LAMA FOUNDATION has been received and has either put me in a most delicate position or has solved some of the greatest complexities of my life. We are moving into a New Age where not only the philosophies are different but the faculties, functions and outlooks (abilities and senses) are different.

Murshid suspects correctly that Lama "may be one of the groups, even *the group* destined to herald in the New Age." The New Age "has been predicted by a number of real seers," Murshid writes, including Bulwer Lytton (author of *The Coming Race,* Calif., 1967) and Sri Aurobindo. A short history of community building by Aurobindo's followers in India and the U.S. follows, and Murshid gives the reason U.S. efforts failed. "The Sri Aurobindo movement in this land is almost entirely under personality leadership giving no scope for the very type of humanity predicted by the Indian seer." However, Murshid informs Lama,

I have been called on in several capacities and am illustrating this [community building] on a small scale, like a miniature Plato. Indeed Sunday we are having a joint May Day and Wesak celebration and are going to have Puja given by a local Lama.

Not only is Murshid involved in community building, he has impressive spiritual qualifications.

I am the first person in history, I believe, who has been validated as a spiritual teacher in Sufism, Zen and certain Yogas, chiefly Mantra and Karuna (sober Bhakti) and have knowledge of all the scriptures of the world, and also a good background in many of the sciences. I am a member both of the American Association for the Advancement of Science and the Royal Asiatic Society, and not a lip-service promoter of a dream called "integration."

In order to facilitate my trip, Murshid writes that "my secretary Mansur Otis Johnson will leave for New Mexico... He has been the star pupil of Prof. Huston Smith of M.I.T. and is absolutely trustworthy." Although Murshid received an invitation to visit Seattle just after getting Lama's invitation, he concludes with Lama by saying the other "invitation [is] refused until our mutual relation is established." It is instructive for me when Murshid defines universal consciousness in this letter.

There is another aspect and that is the *universal consciousness*, the reality of which is quite different from literature on the subject from those who have not had *satori* or *samadhi* or *wujud* [spiritual intoxication] or any of the actual cosmic consciousness states. In such states there is a breakdown of barriers of self and self, of race, religion, country and all barriers. They no longer exist.

Murshid continues with instructive definitions in another letter to W.D. Begg written today. "To me, science is learning through outer experience and mysticism is learning through inner experience, but both are ways of knowledge and in a sense, directly or indirectly ways to God." Begg's letter brings Murshid "joy and satisfaction." I think he is gratified just to receive a response, as he lambasted Begg in his last letter for promoting a new avatar. In fact, Murshid reveals (in a letter to Paul and Sharab May 3, 1969) that what really happened was:

Sufi Ahmed Murad Chisti wrote a letter excoriating a follower of Chisti for jumping on, then off the Meher Baba bandwagon with a long essay on LA ILLA HA EL IL ALLAH. It had just the opposite effect of our egocentric logic! It brought him to realize he is far from accepting God as the ONLY BEING and a beautiful response came. This is the true Repentance.

"But there is a strange note," Murshid says in response to Begg today. "It is as if you had the problems and Allah came and answered this person as if he were the one with the problems you have. Praise to Allah but every month, nay every week this year has shown an improvement over the last. The attendance at meetings grows, the number of mureeds and candidates grow and the collections at meetings increased."

April 29, 1969, Tuesday

The first impression Murshid gives Oliver Reiser in his letter today is "that it is evident there may be something in the universe like Emerson's 'Law of Compensation'..." It is Lama's invitation that has Murshid writing like this.

April 30, 1969, Wednesday

The dream this morning is as follows: There is a school setting, and I am moving around in it. Then I keep saying over and over something like, "The militant Black Panthers suffer from a lack of humor."

Now Vocha Fiske is visiting and has given Murshid many quotable quotes; including, "According to Fiske, Reps is a phony." My only hint of a Reps shortcoming is when Murshid said Inayat Khan made Reps Protector of Los Angeles—I capitalize the hierarchical function, as if it were a title— and Reps left the area. When I question Reps about this, he terminates our correspondence with a terse postcard: "Don't write to me again."

Murshid writes Vocha Fiske fifty-six pages of letters between April 26,

Murshid leads the Ram Dance, consisting only of men.

1968, and December 13, 1970. The first letter was addressed "My dear Vocha." Somewhere in between she became, "Dear Mother Divine." Murshid explained the title: "You not only come by this title rightfully, but with the passing of Ruth St. Denis also you inherit it." Vocha is a *grande dame*, a former actress, who came to know Ruth St. Denis through a different circle of friends than Murshid. At breakfast at the *khankah*, Vocha says, "When I awoke this morning and received [her way of saying she meditated], I felt that this house is a house of peace."

Murshid shifts the conversation to Buddhist matters. "I almost killed myself working for Senzaki," he says. "I had to threaten some Japanese businessmen with riot to save his library." Vocha tells how Senzaki delivered one word and a gesture from Goethe's *Faust* with great cosmic meaning. When Murshid tells her that Senzaki had a Ph.D. in German literature, Vocha says, "This explains why he was interested in such things." Murshid tells more about Senzaki in his unpublished *Commentary* on *The Inner Life*.

The Zen monk, Nyogen Senzaki, was sent to Germany and earned the title of Doctor of Philosophy. He could speak and read six languages well. His Master, Roshi Shaku Soyen, put him on twenty years silence with regard to spiritual matters. In the year 1926, he opened a Zendo in San Francisco, threw off all titles and disclaimed any knowledge. He would not let his earlier followers even refer to it. He just taught meditation and nothing else and only gradually reintroduced his learning and only secondarily. And he never referred to himself as "humble." He was humility and did not have to use words or play pretend. But during the time before he was a Zen monk in full operation, he also led in games and socials and parties. He was a social as well as intellectual figure. And throughout his life, he could change suddenly, and did.

Vocha tells more stories about the beginning of Buddhism in America. She says that Soyen Shaku had two disciples who trained with him for fourteen years. Then Soyen Shaku asked them what they wanted to do. One of them, Daisetz Suzuki, said he would like to continue with his Buddhist scholarship. The other one, Nyogen Senzaki, said he would "be a homeless monk." "Then," Soyen Shaku said, "you shall carry Buddhism to America."

Senzaki worked various jobs for twenty years, she says, and this helped him to understand the American people. She recalls him saying, "I believe you can understand the American people through their pocketbook."

Murshid keys on this and adds, "Alan Watts's greatest sin was to forbid those people who were writing on Senzaki to talk to me. I was the only person who knew Senzaki in that period. One of the greatest things I've ever done," Murshid continues to Vocha, "and I'm going to go down in history for it, is introduce Nyogen Senzaki and Inayat Khan."

This was the meeting later written up by Nyogen Senzaki, where Senzaki told Inayat Khan, "I see a Zen in you," and Khan told Senzaki, "I see a Sufism in you." This after both entered *samadhi* together. Senzaki concluded the article by writing, "Now Bodhisattvas... What do you think of Inayat Khan? If you wish to meet him today, just open the door and face the lovely shrubbery in front of the meditation hall."

Just before they parted company on another occasion, after having attended a koto concert together, Nyogen Senzaki said to Hazrat Inayat Khan, "All sounds return to one, and where does that one go?" The Pir-O-Murshid gave the proper Zen answer, "Goodnight, Mr. Senzaki." Murshid's comment is: "These were the last words between these two seers who loved each other."

May 1, 1969, Thursday

Talk about Senzaki continues. "Was there anybody Senzaki confided in?" Vocha asks. "Senzaki talked to God," Murshid says. "Senzaki, as you know, was a Buddhist, and the Buddhists, as you know, don't believe in God," Vocha retorts. "Sez who?" Murshid challenges. "Someone says it," Vocha comes back. "Buddha never said there was no God. He said there was no ego," Murshid corrects.

May 2, 1969, Friday

There was an article in a recent paper about "one of the Shankaracharyas of India protesting against the termination of caste." With that, Murshid opens his fifteen hundred word letter to the Temple of Understanding's Peter Dunne. Buried innocuously in the fifth paragraph is Murshid's continuing effort to jettison Alan Watts as a Temple of Understanding advisor.

There is already a sort of "revolution" in another field—the displacement of "famous" Englishmen and Europeans as mentors and "experts" in "Oriental Philosophy." Two of your closest colleagues who told me their stories are not going to be happy if you retain this type of person as associate and adviser, especially when this type of person does not accept the moral standards of the religion (or religions) upon which he lectures.

Murshid shares my excitement about the *Oracle* in this letter: "It is even possible that the *Oracle* will become an 'Oracle'." Murshid also expresses his intention to bring Halloween back to its original focus, the celebration of saints. "It is also our intention to restore All-Saints day and get rid of this horrible blackmailing by little children with their 'gimme' and no more Saints." Murshid doesn't live long enough to reap another harvest he sees coming; namely, big money.

A very large section of my present following is made up of run-aways from well-to-do families and there are possibilities of inheritances and even donations from these parents when they find their "drop out" offspring are finding themselves.

Shamcher informs Murshid in his latest letter that Fazal Khan, a successor of those who usurped Vilayat's Sufi Movement, may be visiting San Francisco during the summer. In response, Murshid tells Shamcher,

This legal trouble had been foreseen by Pir Dewwal Shereef of Islamabad [Ayub Khan's Pir-O-Murshid]. He has authorized me to establish either ISLAMIA RUHANIAT SOCIETY or KHIDRI RUHANIAT SOCIETY. This would make it possible to have a Sufi Movement which would not use the word Sufi in order to be an American legal entity. But because of the actual growing attendance, the actual increment of my own income, and at this writing, the very bright prospects for a much larger income to the GARDEN OF INAYAT, it has become necessary to organize legally in order to protect us against income tax obligations.

May 3, 1969, Saturday

Murshid's narrative voice in his letter to Sharab and Paul has an unusually personal quality and immediacy.

Peace unto you. This is probably my last letter before a certain fame or notoriety or even infamy descends. In a short while I shall be leaving for the *khankah*, called "The Garden of Inayat." We are celebrating the Buddhist Wesak and the traditional May Day together. The May pole is up and there will be dances around it. The first lectures of Hazrat Inayat Khan in the west were on "Yoga Dances." He had to leave off and hardly anyone has even an inkling. But today we are performing spiritual dances, and more and more with ever greater response...

The Oracle is out. This started as a Hippy paper dominated by Allen Ginsberg and Timothy Leary. Leary is still in the background but he is over concerned with Sex—not in the emotional manner in which it is treated in the press but still in a very egocentric manner. Every year while maintaining his "messiah-ship" he has a different cause. So his following dwindles but more young take marijuana, at least.

When Vilayat was here I saw the jump from 20 mureeds to 60 and then a following of about a hundred though I expect more people today. One is fighting a whole culture. One wishes to restore the innate spirituality of Nature, wherein people respected the Sun and Moon and seasons and Saints. We are far from that. But one has choreographed a large number of dances and every time there is any inhibition, any time there is opposition or insomnia, one receives a new Dance or dances, and the same will be true today. The Dances ooze out of one as aphorisms and poetry do from others.

There is another take on Sufi politics concerning Fazal Inayat Khan. "Now I hear [from Shamcher] that Fazal, misled by wealthy backers, may try to get at either Vilayat or myself or at Vilayat through Samuel." Murshid reveals how he encouraged the *Oracle* to be an "oracle."

SAM challenged *The Oracle*, asking why it was not an oracle. Then things began to happen. This American is a thorough pragmatist. He has an oracle [*The Bowl of*

Saki] based on *Gayan* and *Vadan* and uses it and gets disciples [see April 23, 1969] to use it. This has in turn awakened those disciples who are natural Oracles. And the other night the chief one said: "I saw everybody in light and you in the greatest light with Inayat Khan standing beside you and really directing everything." Of course this is so, and the work of 1911 is coming to fruition now. Mrs. Vocha Fiske, my oldest and best friend, is here now dividing her time between here and Novato and she has been amazed to find the objectification of everything held for years, and not only that, but there is Peace and Brotherhood and cooperation among the disciples.

At nine o'clock in the morning Hiro Narita, John Korty's assistant cameraman, takes a family portrait. (Hiro was at the Garden of Inayat to take photos of our opening celebration.) The whole *khankah* goes to the city at 9:30 A.M. We make stops at Phillip's to pick up some *Oracles*, in Mill Valley to buy some dry cat food, in San Francisco to drop off Vocha at Lloyd Morrain's house; and finally, at The Candle Shop for incense. Murshid serves curry rice for lunch with strawberry pie from the corner bakery for dessert.

The dance class begins early, so we can rehearse what Murshid calls "a yoga dance," the Shiva dance, a complicated square dance that utilizes two people to embody a sacred symbol. Each couple, facing each other, makes a swastika by raising their right arms, bent at the elbows, while lowering their left arms, also bent at the elbows, keeping their upper arms parallel to the floor. The center of the swastika is the heart. Hitler usurped a sacred symbol. The swastika is a heart symbol.

May 4, 1969, Sunday

Hiro Narita witnessed and photographed the May Day celebration, Wesak [Buddha's birthday], a Buddhist puja, and dedication of the pottery and printing establishments. Murshid later describes to Vocha Hiro's reaction.

There is a Japanese photographer who has become a sort of press agent. He has seen my work; he thinks it is wonderful. The idea of peace through religion and the actual acceptance of all faiths have impressed him.

After spending Friday and Saturday with Murshid, I am a moon, receptive. Jemila expects me to be the sun, expressive. A master would be able to shift immediately; me, I am slow. I use these esoteric terms to explain to Jemila why I am acting like a jerk.

May 5, 1969, Monday

This issue of the *Oracle* has a cover by Fatima, pictures of Murshid leading dervish dances, and Dennis H. McGinley's article on numerology. There is also a piece of Murshid's called *Towards Spiritual Brotherhood,* and Mansur's poem "Ithaca," which I allowed since Murshid's piece appeared.

There is an article called "Obsessed" by Shamcher, the interview with Tim Leary, and some artwork by Diane Ferry, a *mureed* who later settles in Santa Fe to study weaving. Murshid expresses his response to this issue in a letter today to Oliver Reiser.

The *Oracle* appeared with a large space given to this person, another to an article by this person; two articles by life-long friends [Shamcher and Reps], two more by my chief secretary, Mansur Johnson (friend of Prof. Huston Smith of M.I.T.) and the main art work which I esteem as excellent, by my housekeeper, Fatima Jablonski. The distribution of this paper will make one better known, or notorious.

The President of India, addressed only days ago, has died. "The ceremonials will consume the few minutes I have today," Murshid tells Reiser. He attends the memorial service in the interval between his class at the Holy Order of MANS, which ends at five, and the Sufi Dancing class at 7:30.

Tonight at dinner in Novato (Murshid is back in San Francisco), I mention Murshid's wish that we have someone "cover" the *khankah* when Fatima goes to Chicago. We discuss the idea of considering the *khankah* complement of six people as always necessary. Hassan wants to abstract it and consider the *khankah* covered if the absent people's roles and functions are delegated. I report that Murshid is considering the possibility of having another person, a girl, move in. I feel that when a person comes along who seems to belong here, it will happen. I work now on a project at Novato Builders Lumber Company, digging a ditch for some water pipe. It comes up just when I need extra money to replace my light meter, essential for the trip to the Southwest as a photojournalist.

Tomorrow, Tuesday, I go to Berkeley to do *Oracle* distribution. Wednesday, I'll work digging. Thursday, I have to go to the Civic Center for an Aid to Families with Dependent Children meeting. Friday, I am scheduled to take Jemila to an ancient Japanese pottery class in Sonoma, and afterwards to take Murshid to town. My esoteric journal has taken a "Zen is everyday life" turn. Grist for the journal is my program, not my latest psychic experience.

Chapter 17

The Lama Foundation

The simplest stand taken was that there are more Vietnamese Buddhists than there are Jews in the world. This is a hard fact we do not face. It does not mean that the Buddhists are noble or wonderful, although one does find a kind of peacefulness in them and perhaps a large amount of ineptness. One cannot help feeling for them every time one strikes a gong or cymbals or other brass instruments. (Murshid's letter to General Edward Lansdale in Alexandria, Virginia, June 1, 1969)

Mansur presents Sufi dancing for the first time outside California at Lama Foundation.

May 6, 1969, Tuesday

This week Phillip is in Los Angeles distributing the *Oracle*. It must have been at the meeting last week, when I volunteered to place some *Oracles* at newsstands and bookstores in Berkeley that it dawned on me: *No money*

Mansur at Lama

from Oracle sales will be available to finance my trip to New Mexico. There is no periodicals distribution syndicate working for us; it is up to us to distribute the papers. We owe $1500 to the printer, payable at $500 per week, and I'm leaving for New Mexico before that bill will be paid.

Murshid begins a heartfelt letter to India's Consul General, K.S. Baipal, at the Indian Consulate on Market Street in San Francisco. "It was genuine sorrow on my part to see the passing of my spiritual colleague, Dr. Zakir Hussein." Murshid reminisces about someone he saw at the memorial service.

You had on the platform my old friend, Dr. Lal. He will remember the late Ram Lal Channon. Channon was my "guru" almost in secular affairs. I began reading about Gandhiji [Mohandas K. Gandhi] in 1911 and knew all about him when he returned to India. So I was the only American, I believe, permitted to have an interview with the late Villabhai Patel when he came to this city. He spoke on the need of Indian Independence to lead the world spiritually.

He was ill on the day I visited him, and I asked him how could he accomplish it. He said, "I do not know." One replied: "This one may know." He put out his hands... [ellipsis by Murshid] There is no use going into detail; the late President Dr. Zakir Hussein illustrated the point. [He put out his hands as if to say: "My son, you are the one I have been looking for."]

Murshid ends his eulogy letter for his spiritual colleague, "The late President Hussein was none other than 'my self' in another body. I believe we stood for exactly the same things in all directions." Feeling this kind of unity with the deceased president, Murshid mixes his Indian experience with his prediction of real integration in further comments to the Consul General.

Sir, we are going to have Cultural Integration and no longer private selected groups carrying this name. In 1956, I was taken to the tomb of Humayun by Pir-O-Murshid Hasan Sani Nizami. He said, "This is the tomb of Prince Dara Shikoh." I walked around it seven times and said, "Let us go." He understood. The passing parade of Intellectuals will not understand. We are going to have Cultural Integration.

Murshid mentions his visit to the Royal Asiatic Society, his performance of the Dance of Universal Peace at Fathepur Sikri, and his ecstasy at being denied entry at a theatre showing an Indian film because it was sold out. The popularity of Indian films is proof, he suggests, of a New Age.

The purpose Murshid has in writing Richard J. Kozicki, professor in the South Asian Studies Department at Berkeley, is to express the following.

For years, I have been working on the theme how California can help Asia. Actually, this has come to mean at least in part, how the University of California can help Asia. I found my dream coming true when you showed me what you are doing. [Kozicki was working on Murshid's theme.]

Although Murshid and I won't call on UCLA's Dean Carroll Parrish in Los Angeles for many months, it comes out here that Parrish used to be Murshid's secretary.

A number of years ago an official history was written on Thailand by one of your colleagues at UCLA (David Wilson). I called on him and said, "You have written an excellent book. The facts are wonderful, but your chapter on problems is almost hopeless for every one of these problems has been faced by your colleagues on other campuses of the multiversity. I can name these colleagues. I can tell you what they have done, are doing."

He immediately sent me to Dean Carroll Parrish in the administration building at UCLA. Without looking up Dean Parrish said to me, "Do you know Her Serene Highness Princess Poon Pismai Diskul?" I immediately replied, "Who the heck do you think sent me here."

Now it seems that Carroll Parrish was my very first secretary at a time when I was trying to introduce Sufism into America. I then failed. I am now succeeding. I had 150 guests at my combined May Day and Wesak dance festival. We put on many dances based on the actual religions of actual Asia.

Also, Murshid informs Kozicki he has received a letter from Edward Lansdale.

This is the Lieutenant General who was second in command in Viet Nam. He was my war hero and no nonsense (I actually received a Washington Citation during the Second World War). When I met Edward Lansdale, he was a Captain soon to become a major in G-2. But by agreement with his superior Colonel Harris, I destroyed all my original documents etc. Because of my Asian backgrounds I wrote to him, but the foreign office refused delivery and returned my letter.

General Lansdale writes that he is now writing a book on his own direct experiences. A book which I am sure you will be interested in and which I certainly intend to get for you. [In the Midst of Wars was published in 1972—after Murshid's death.]

In a letter to Anandashram, Murshid says, "And now within one year, as Ram has shown Sam, his close following has jumped from 60 to a 100—it was foreseen and it comes. And this is the limit that Sam can do until he organizes."

May 9, 1969, Friday

Too much work and not enough help is the situation Murshid communicates today to disciple Marcia Pavolic.

My programs are not only more full than ever but there is an absolute dearth of help to the degree that unless a change is made the white flag shall have to be put up. For on the one hand, one is receiving larger and greater inspirations, and larger attendance with some increases in income, and practically no help excepting from Melvin who lives-in here. Mansur has three part-time jobs and is giving almost no help. Daniel, who is the Assistant Esoteric Secretary and part-time Financial Secretary, is also working part-time outside and has little time for Murshid. And everybody wants to join Vilayat in Colorado whether they have money or not.

Murshid is fresh from what he calls an "unfortunate meeting" at the *khankah*. What I've been describing as a "blowup," Murshid calls a "crisis." Here's how he describes the situation to Marcia.

We had another crisis at the *khankah*. I can only give the Murshid's point of view which is that the material livelihood comes first and then the spiritual work. Out of six disciples living there, it is pretty bad that only one has accepted this, and only after two failures in the business world, [projects] taken without Murshid's blessing and by pressure from outsiders. One still has to face these pressures of outsiders who convince disciples that they should do so-and-so, and I have seen endless failures. These are based neither on common sense nor on what Inayat Khan called "super sense" and I have just come from an unfortunate meeting. Even when they see that Murshid is receiving from God, so to speak, it is not yet the determinant.

It is the determinant for me—seeing that Murshid receives from God— in fact, for most of us. If we hear "Murshid said," that stamps whatever with an air of finality. But who really knows about the others? I speak for me. There is a new twist in Murshid's desire to organize himself.

Daniel says Vilayat does not wish it [organization]. Actually Vilayat has enemies who want to thwart him, and they have called for a conference here in San Francisco to tempt or to challenge S.A.M. The seriousness of this has not reached my family.

There is tension building around Olompali ranch's refusal to allow Shirin to move her kiln to the *khankah*. Murshid shares his assessment of the situation with Marcia.

Shirin built a kiln and we voted to have it at the *khankah*. But the Ranch family has refused to permit it to be moved; and God says that Shirin is to be told it was a slave camp where she did all the work and no pay and no thanks and there is no proper ownership.

May 10, 1969, Saturday

Murshid shares an example of divine will, more events in India in 1962—and, especially, his condition of not requiring sleep—with Shams-ed-din Ahmed, who is back in Pakistan from his *hajj* in Saudi Arabia.

In 1962, I visited the tomb of Amir Khusrau with Pir-O-Murshid Hasan Sani Nizami and one of his brothers. The spirit of the saint appeared to me and gave me the same robe which had been offered by Khwaja Khizr and Moineddin Chisti. He said: "I appoint you as successor to Mohammed Iqbal in the School of Jelal-ed-din Rumi." When I came back to Pakistan, Sufi Sahib gave that robe and I have it. [The careful reader will recognize this anecdote; it's been mentioned twice before. Receiving repetitious recitations of Murshid's history was part of my experience. Sharing that experience is one reason for repeating them. Another is to serve the reader who just opens the book and reads at random.] And all the famous and infamous people, all the authorities who preach without identification with their own words, cannot stop what is the Divine Will. It is in operation all the time, and one is now seriously considering also giving up sleep.

Murshid offers a different take on the memorial ceremony for India's President Zakir Hussein, which leads to a clear statement of his beef with Reps.

The other day President Zakir Hussein died, and I had to listen to dualistic and hypocritical *important* people speak about him. But the time has come, the hypocritical and important people are being found out and very gradually the name and prowess of Sufi Ahmed Murad Chisti is wending its way into the universities exactly in accordance with the blessings of Hazrat Inayat Khan. His disciples and followers refused to accept; even the man who was present [Reps] has refused to accept because they do not understand *nafs* [ego].

Later in the letter, Murshid has more to say about Saladin Reps.

The story of [Murshid's poem] *Saladin*, the outer story, is a shame. The person to whom it was dedicated refused to look at it. He is rich, famous and very, very lonely. He gets all his books published, he gets audiences everywhere, but they are audiences, they are not parts of himself and he has deserted Pir-O-Murshid Inayat Khan for his own fame and glory and he will go down in history unless he comes to the gate of *tauba* [repentance]. I know all about his private life and have kept quiet and probably will continue to keep quiet; but it is disgusting how so many pretended devotees defy [the line from the *Koran*,] *Allah knows all things*. They act as if otherwise. And I personally defy all so-called Muslims who do not accept: *"Act as if in the presence of Allah, and remember, if you do not see Him, verily He sees you."*

Although Murshid writes about his lack of a secretariat with a non-accusatory tone, I read the following as a condemnation of my failure to help more.

Last Sunday one had 150 and the daily attendance grows, the number of meetings grows and one has to visit the universities more and more and more, and no help. My chief secretaries are now engaged in their own pursuits and Allah is manifesting more and more and more.

Still writing to S. Ahmed, Murshid gives a picture of Sufi politics involving Pir Vilayat Khan and Fazal Inayat Khan.

I understand they [Fazal's camp] are instigating legal proceedings against both Vilayat and myself. Yesterday one of my disciples [Daniel], given *bayat* by Vilayat, told me that Pir Vilayat knew exactly what was coming, and he has taken all the legal precautions. We are preparing to send a caravan to him for [his forthcoming] mountain climbing [retreat in Colorado].

In what is Murshid's last letter to Reps, he begins:

Inayat Khan is dead; Inayat Khan slain by his living disciples, and slain by those who swore fidelity to him.
Inayat Khan is resurrected; resurrected because the Message is in the sphere and not in this ego or that ego.

Murshid believes Reps is culpable. But personally, for Murshid, the issue is Reps's nonacceptance and nonsupport over the years. This is what he has confided in today's letter to Shams-ed-din Ahmed. Today, Murshid is talking turkey to Reps.

It is a pity that you do not realize you cannot take wealth and fame with you and cannot avoid your own memories and karma. All the teachings have been dropped to support your Name and thus you will have nothing to take with you into the next world but a four-letter word identified with Ego and not with the Supreme.

Murshid precedes the words above with a couple of interesting sentences: "We do not all live in the eternity. This person has not asked for forgiveness of sins but trusts Allah enough that the punishment will 'fit the crime'." Understand that when Murshid writes like this he means to say that he lives in eternity. He said so in a May 6, 1969, letter to Consul General K.S. Baipal: "Those of us who live in eternity and who remember 'past lives' are now coming to the fore to help young people." Murshid's files do not include Reps's responses. His last words to Reps:

There is a Rinzai Center in the telephone book and we are taking pictures of Soyen Shaku and Nyogen there this morning (don't ask me whether the frames are of oak or chestnut or fabric, veddy [sic] important you know—real people may ask how one got these pictures!).
Wealth to the wealthy, fame to the famers, [sic] but those who live in Eternity, Eternity will live in them. God bless you, Sufi Ahmed Murad Chisti, He Kwang, Zen-Shi, Samuel L. Lewis, S.A.M.

May 13, 1969, Tuesday

Saadia seems to require considerable delicacy when apparently being advised on her requests for help, her tendency to give Murshid advice, and her expectation that Allah will fix things.

This is a very hard letter, to keep the heart alive and for love to be functioning and yet to advise, there is a limit to what one can do. And if there is any criticism it is that persons seeking advice or help for themselves say "take it easy" and when they say "take it easy" they do not see that that defeats the one whom they seek for help. For actually it is Allah that does, and it is Allah that Suggests, but many very good people think, and then they presume, Allah will carry out their plans and so there is plenty of confusion. Indeed, it is a part of human psychology and they trust and pray that *their plans* will be carried out, but do not realize that Allah may be depending on them to carry out His plans.

In this letter, Murshid regards the fact that his secretaries (myself included) have outside jobs as a "financial release." "The two chief secretaries have now secured outside jobs which mean[s] a certain financial release, but excepting Melvin here, one has nobody to fall back on with more *mureeds*, more applicants and more classes to teach and more mail to answer."

May 14, 1969, Wednesday

The term "attunement to the teacher" may be defined by four details from the Wednesday night meeting. Attunement is a kind of telepathy. First, I become conscious of the current in my breath *before* Murshid calls the audience's attention to it. Second, when Murshid poses a question, "What kind of walk do we do with the etheric breath?" I know the answer: *No walk.* A walk using the etheric breath is impossible, because an etheric breath is too refined for movement. Third, I know we'll stop twice at the same partners in the *Ramnam* Dance; and fourth, I know Murshid will choose me to do "Allah Hu" with him in the center of the circle. Could it be he chooses me because I am concentrating on him so hard?

May 15, 1969, Thursday

Sometimes, like today, Murshid asks me to write a letter for him.

Dear Josh, I write. Received your letter of the 13th and am sending enclosed two copies of the Oracle at Murshid's request... Now, on the question of Murshid finding you a room, his response to this was that this is the kind of thing he just did not have time to attend to with people who can't breathe correctly, or who have fear, or who are confused, coming to him for assistance...

Since disciples continue to ask Murshid for help of this nature, Murshid will write January 13, 1970 to his goddaughter Nancy,

I am not a marriage counselor. I am not a professional psychologist. I am a hodge-podge: a spiritual teacher, scholar in several fields, poet, and artist of sorts. The one thing I do not have is time, and I have failed—utterly failed—in impressing many people about this. I have again and again pleaded, warned, lectured, on please don't bring me your housing problems, and what problem do you think I have most today among my disciples?

Not sex, not employment, not disharmonies from others with others, not money, not, not, not, but: Where shall I live? and With whom shall I live? I have been able, perhaps by grace, to see the light increasing in many of them, but still the interpretation most unfortunately of the spiritual path seems to be: How and where to get a new landlord.

May 17, 1969, Saturday

"Your letter of the 14th announcing a meeting for June has been received and will be shown shortly first to Mansur Johnson, the esoteric secretary, and then to others," Murshid writes to Suzanne D'Mitrieff in Los Angeles. "Mansur is about to leave here shortly, and will return later to participate in the session of the International School of Meditation directed by Pir Vilayat in Colorado."

May, 18, 1969, Sunday

This morning Akbar, Hassan, James, Phillip, Jeremy, and Mansur leave at 5 A.M. for Olompali ranch to retrieve Shirin's kiln bricks. This is a serious commando raid. Shirin is leaving the ranch and isn't sure her fellow ranchers will allow her bricks to go with her. Our aim is to see they do. The kiln concentration is a *khankah* concentration, meaning it's something we all want to manifest, and space has been provided for Shirin to set up shop. She needs the bricks to build the kiln. Our raid meets no resistance, and we escape with the bricks.

Afterwards I vacuum the car, sleep from 8:30 to 10:30, and then read some of Marie Corelli's *Romance of Two Worlds* in the bath. She is one of Murshid's favorite authors.

Back in San Francisco, Murshid addresses Rev. Eugene Wagner concerning Lama Govinda's new book, *Buddhism and Modern Thought*. An incomplete review copy has come to Murshid, and he announces his intention "to be radically critical" for reasons that are difficult to discern from the language alone. It helps me to recall the feeling from Murshid's earlier correspondence to Rev. Warwick and Wagner about meetings with Lama Govinda.

[Murshid will be] radically critical here because in the reflection on two separate meetings of human beings not regarded as existent by our *"anatta"* friends, the inevitable conclusion was that today "Buddhists" do not believe in any God but certainly do believe in the human ego (their own).

In a short letter to Anandashram, Murshid differentiates between the young and their elders.

The young people are so different—they are objective and heart-seekers. Their elders are subjective and power-seekers. And whatever else be said, there are always young and more coming. There is another fact and factor that they are all seeking a

"Loving Father." Whatever Christianity has done, it has emphasized "Loving Father" but there are not many "Loving Fathers" and apparently from the present scene even less loving mothers. Sam has three God-children because they did not have loving mothers and loving fathers. And now he has what he calls "ersatz grandchildren."

May 19, 1969, Monday

Murshid begins his response to his uncle, Harry Rosenthal's, letter by correcting Rosenthal's misimpression about Murshid's contact with the Social Security Administration. It was "not so much to get money but to get a ruling: How much one over 72 is permitted to earn without this interfering with his general position. For my income has been going up from outside sources." The cost of living is of no concern, Murshid tells Rosenthal.

We go to the Farmer's Market or even buy from stands along the highways. In Novato I am now growing a number of crops and it appears we shall have more. Besides, I know how to buy very cheaply at good markets; I know this city. And also where to buy dinners, fine dinners at low prices.

A letter from Pir Vilayat has come, and first off Murshid responds by writing of his visions. "It is notable that when you spoke to me last I had visions, and the affairs of the last year have borne out these visions almost exactly."

I have placed in the hands of Moineddin Jablonski the material from Secretary D'Mitrieff. I am hoping that we may both go to Hollywood for that meeting. Secretary Mansur Johnson will soon be off to the state of New Mexico, and in August I shall personally follow up whatsoever he may have accomplished.

While unable to supply Vilayat with any contacts in Cleveland, Murshid assures him, "I shall be pleased to serve you in any capacity because this may be written in the Sphere (*inshallah*)." And Murshid tells Vilayat directly what he has already mentioned to Suzanne and Shamcher.

I should like to see both Moineddin and Akbar Simmons officially instituted as *Khalifs*. They have shown all the signs of spiritual awakening but I have been holding it off hoping that in your presence it could become more official. I have full authority from both the combined Chisti-Kadri-Sabri Orders in Pakistan and the Islamiya Ruhaniat Society of Islamabad to select and ordain *Khalifs* but should prefer to work in unison.

May 20, 1969, Tuesday

Murshid tells Shamcher, "With the receipt of a long letter from Vilayat it would seem a cycle is at an end." Mystic talking to mystic, he continues,

It comes while the *Oracle* is on sale, and indicates a movement into a wider dimension outwardly. This wider dimension has always functioned inwardly and it has taken some years, etc. to bring it out. And as everything followed exactly as Insight showed, I do not wish even to question this trend.

Word of our successful raid to rescue Shirin's kiln bricks has reached Murshid.

We had some trouble with regard to a kiln, built by one of my most beautiful and loyal *mureeds*. I asked the others to stand by her, and they did it so wonderfully that not only was this matter straightened out, but Murshid received a sudden wedding invitation from Olompali ranch which he could not accept.

On the eve of my departure for Lama, it is my good fortune to celebrate Fatima's birthday with the rest of the family at Oakland's Khyber Pass Restaurant, "the owner of which is related to important Sufis of Afghanistan (not the imaginary Idries Shah ones but real people)." A few weeks later (June 2, 1969), Murshid tells Viola Sharab Harris that he "inwardly cried" during this dinner. Why? "Pir-O-Murshid Inayat Khan, with all his magnificence, never gathered around him the souls who could establish spiritual brotherhood."

May 21, 1969, Wednesday

My trip to New Mexico begins with some trepidation. I drive first to *Oracle* editor Phillip's house to make sure he still supports my trip. That is: Is he still committed to publishing the results of my research? If not, I am prepared to abandon the whole thing, even though I am packed and ready to go. Phillip is unwaveringly committed, so I let him know I am on my way. The temptation is to bring a bunch of books along with me, but I only bring what is relevant to my specific mission. I wouldn't have been so concentrated before I met Murshid.

Driving south down 101 from San Francisco, I flash on the Whole Earth Catalog Store in Menlo Park, which retails products featured in Stewart Brand's *The Whole Earth Catalog*. The *Catalog* includes *The Dome Cookbook*, a Lama Foundation publication by Steve Baer, who designed the dome-shaped meditation house at Lama. Several of the places on my itinerary besides Lama—Libre and Drop City in southeast Colorado—have domes. Buying the *Dome Cookbook* at Stewart Brand's store is on my unwritten agenda. The time off route to locate the store is wasted, however. They don't have a copy to sell. Let your fingers do the walking. Call first. I don't follow this guidance. I want to see the store at any cost.

I drive straight to Henry Cowell Redwoods State Park, located north of Santa Cruz, California, my first night's stop. Despite the name, there are no redwoods here. Madrones are all over the place, and sand trails lead through pine forests. I set to work. I left books I wanted to read for pleasure at home, but not unfinished work. Vilayat's lecture, recorded at

Mentorgarten January 5, 1969, has to be transcribed. Murshid wants me to see Suzanne D'Mitrieff in Los Angeles and give her a copy. Vilayat's lecture transcription is a labor of love, but still, I will be glad to get the job off my mind. Typing it will give me an opportunity to reexperience Vilayat's presentation of paradox. He says, "We are tied up by all kinds of concepts. First of all the most fundamental of all concepts is that we assume we are the person experiencing something..." I've already transcribed eighteen pages of the lecture, and do six more today. This picnic table at site 48 costs $3. With my battery-powered tape recorder and Jehanara's portable typewriter on the picnic table, my outdoor office is a happening thing.

On first arriving, though, the strangeness of the place terrified me. I was frantic as I unpacked, ate, read, typed. I forgot to say grace. Once the area was magnetized by breathing in place for a time, I felt safe enough to venture down the path. It is a four-tenths mile walk to an observation point. Walking there at about five o'clock, I surrender to the beauty. I miss my family, especially Nathan and Jemila. The longing caused by separation, I think, is one of the meanings, and pangs, of love. I walk back from the observation tower chanting *Ya Rahman*—the Merciful—with hands outstretched to bless the ground, the way Murshid taught us in the Bismillah with Partners dance as Murshid and Mansur walked blessing the land at Olompali ranch.

May 22, 1969, Thursday

The transcribing is finished and I mail a copy to Murshid. I mail another copy to Lynn Wills, Vilayat's youth secretary in Los Angeles. I also send in my application for the Colorado camp. I was so impressed with Vilayat's brochure description of the Colorado camp that I copied it out for an old college friend whose letter came just before I left on this trip. What the brochure says will be the program at the Youth (ages 18-28) Seminar, June 21-29, is "an enriching experience...covering the learning of the most varied cultures and civilizations...to familiarize young people with all world religions and...to see what bearing they have on psychology, aiming at setting into motion forces of transformation."

I feel again a certain pang. What am I doing here? This fear I always equate with the way I felt in 1964, the last time I was driving off alone into the unknown, on the way to Mexico. *Why do you go on when you feel this reticence?* I ask myself. Turning back to the comfort of home would be too humiliating. This fear is not like a warning of danger. It's more like stage fright; and I have to perform. I think I pick up Jemila's thoughts of longing for me. My love intensifies. Even though the ego would like to write personal letters to Jemila, my orders from inside are to write to everybody, as Murshid did when he was traveling. My communal self, or persona as a guy on a mission with an extended family behind him, transforms me into a writer to all; and my wife is one of them.

May 23, 1969, Friday

Murshid uses his engraved stationery and calls attention to it, beginning a letter today to Charlotte Brautlacht in Bothell, Washington

This is written on official stationary just to show the spiritual names. One is usually called "Murshid" or SAM here but in the Orient mostly "Sufi Sahib." One is also being called more and more, "Dr. Lewis." One is not particularly attached or detached from names.

Murshid informs Ms. Brautlacht that "Vilayat expects to be in San Francisco on June 12, but we may not cooperate in this meeting, as it would interfere with our programs." Things change, though, and on the 29th, Murshid tells Vilayat that he'll greet him on June 12th.

As it grows dark, I start to do my practices in Oceano, California, parked in a picnic area across from the county campgrounds. The practices are my prelude to sleep. Signs all over the place say NO CAMPING. I drive fifty-five miles down the road, and the intuition says to prepare to pull off the road. Gaviota Pass is the next opportunity. There are signs there about how much power is used to pump water in the irrigation canal, up this hill and on to Los Angeles. I sleep in the car and use the public toilet in the morning.

May 24, 1969, Saturday

I am up at seven, off by eight, mail some letters in Camarillo, get gas at nine, and am at Mrs. D'Mitrieff's in North Hollywood around half past ten. After handing off my transcription of Vilayat's lecture, I'm driving east toward Arizona. At Cloudburst Summit, elevation 7,018 feet—the last pass in California before Arizona—I'm sitting in the shade of a fragrant pine tree 100 yards from a stream fed by a late spring patch of snow just above. I take off all my clothes and lie on a rock until it gets too hot, which takes maybe two minutes. My canteen filled, my face washed innumerable ecstatic times, my second cup of coffee—this time with mountain water— finished, a couple more pieces of baklava eaten, and I'm ready to begin work.

I write Murshid with a carbon copy to my extended family at the *khankah*: "The fearful magnetism that gripped me in Santa Cruz is now gone." Things not mentioned in my letter are the sound of the wind in the pines, the fragrance of the trees, the sound of the stream, the sky at sunset. I watch the fog, the cloud bank, and a few twinkling lights from Los Angeles showing through the cloud cover. I wonder if the clouds will come up this high and burst at Cloudburst Summit. "No doubt one is deliberate in writing," Murshid begins a letter today to Huston Smith.

> One has come to the end of negative protestations, and can now rather calmly watch certain movements follow the same roads to oblivion as their predecessors. They begin with universal appeals and sooner or later become caught in small issues with small persons. I have seen this so many times.

From the looks of this, it would appear that Murshid has decided to stop writing the Temple of Understanding concerning their use of Alan Watts for promotional purposes, but the Temple of Understanding will receive a carbon copy of this letter. Murshid shares with Smith his amazement about their common pupil. "Mansur Otis Johnson amazes me. He is becoming involved in the same type of activities with the same approaches and same points of view I had earlier in life. It is remarkable. He is on his way to New Mexico now. On his return he will lead a caravan to Colorado to be with Pir Vilayat Khan, the Sufi teacher, in a mountain climbing retreat." With regard to the letter Murshid wrote in lieu of a term paper, he tells Smith, "Prof. Nottingham recently gave me an 'A' without waiting for the term paper."

If it weren't for a remark near the end of a letter Murshid writes to Oliver Reiser today—"I have lost faith in the Sri Aurobindo movement which has fallen into the hands of traditional politicians"—I would miss the meaning of his letter to Mr. A.B. Patel, General Secretary of World Union, in Pondicherry, India. True, Murshid does ask rhetorically whether Sri Aurobindo's definition of a prophet includes politicians like "the late Woodrow Wilson or the late Jan Smuts, or any erudite politicians who could turn out delightful phrases like a mint turns out coins, but who showed no evidence of having attained *Vijnanavada* or *Anandavada*." But without the statement to Reiser, I would be hard pressed to know Murshid is protesting the takeover of Aurobindo's movement by politicians.

May 25, 1969, Sunday

Murshid's friend the Rev. Jack Austin from Barnstead, England says on his postcard, "Maypoles disappeared over here, in their original home, a couple of centuries ago now. I doubt if one has been seen, apart from exhibition pieces, since about 1780, so you are reviving an ancient English tradition!" This gives me the headline for the *Oracle*'s photoessay I am assembling on Murshid's Mayday celebration—RESTORATION OF ANCIENT CUSTOMS. After working all day, I sleep a second night at Cloudburst Summit.

Murshid, meanwhile, follows up on an earlier (unaccepted) invitation to his contemporary Vera Van Voris. Murshid reextends the invitation, but tempers it: "The invitation for you to visit the *khankah* is always open but things are happening. What is written in the heavens is bound to happen on earth and the opinions of mankind do not affect the holy inspirations." What's happening besides growth is the cancellation of the Sunday night meeting in San Francisco. Instead, "We shall soon have Sunday night picnics with dances in Novato and this should draw ample audiences... It is a new day and one faces it half in grandeur and wonder and half knowing that privacy may disappear forever."

To disciple Marc Gold in New York City, Murshid confides, "I had hoped Ruth [Parisa], whom you have met, would become my dance secretary but she has disappeared, although I understand she is now back. I need a secretary for music and dancing very badly."

May 26, 1969, Monday

God says I've had enough sleep about 2 A.M. up in my Cloudburst Summit nest, so I start driving east on Interstate 40. Eight hours later, I am parked just before the Route 64 turnoff to the Grand Canyon, next to some delicious pines east of Williams, Arizona. It has been hot, and I am road weary. The trees smell wonderful, and I think I might stop here. But after a little sleep and food, I drive another 125 miles and pull off at an unimproved rest stop. There are no trees for shade, only outhouses and trash barrels. I stop for the night.

May 27, 1969, Tuesday

Up at seven, I am off and driving soon after. The heat and the need to ground while driving increase my appetite. I consume five Dolly Madison powdered sugar donuts; three coffees; four oranges; sunflower and pumpkin seed, date, fig, and raisin trail mix; two hamburgers and two French fries from Henry's; seven ounces of Coors beer; two chocolate bars; more trail mix; and four more oranges to satisfy the need to drive on a full stomach.

The University of New Mexico in Albuquerque, near the junction of I-40 and I-25, is easy to find. Seeing Professor Archie Bahm is my immediate goal before turning north. I need to shower, but why? The heat is so intense; I'll be wringing wet, shower or no. My travel worn appearance is not out of place at the university. Bad news: Bahm isn't in his office, and today, he is not scheduled to be. While scanning a newspaper article about philosopher Alfred North Whitehead written by philosopher Bertrand Russell, I notice a secretary going into the hall where Bahm's office, D-4, is located. My plan is to borrow the secretary's pencil and copy Professor Bahm's phone number for later use. Surprise—the secretary says Bahm is in the library, next building to the left. There he is, just finishing a seminar on the Theory of Value. I introduce myself and say my mentor is Samuel Lewis of San

Francisco. "I want to give you greetings from Mr. Lewis and make your acquaintance."

Professor Bahm asks me what I am doing in this part of the country. I say I am out here doing research on intentional communities. He puzzles over the word "intentional" for a long time—as if trying to conceive of an unintentional community. This is surprising to me. I try to explain, "You know, people who go out on the land and live with other people in a communal arrangement." When Bahm understands where I am headed— north of Taos—he tells me about the scenic overlook south of Taos. At this place, you can see a basin cut for 100 miles by the Rio Grande River on the left, with the sacred green magnetic mountain (featured in Frank Waters's *The Man Who Killed the Deer*) in the Sangre de Cristo mountain range on the right. I thank him and tell him I am only incidentally sightseeing on this trip. I don't say I am on a mission or tell him that I didn't buy any color film, which is good for scenery but unnecessary in a black and white newspaper. Someone told me before I left that Murshid said: "As long as Mansur does what he goes there to do, he'll be all right."

Paving the way for Murshid's visit is my purpose in meeting with Bahm. Just exactly how one does this is never clear to me. I say, "Mr. Lewis will be in the area in August, when he comes to Lama. Lama," I explain, "has invited him to come and present his teachings." It seems important to show that Murshid had been recognized as a teacher. Professor Bahm is very affable. If Murshid drops by, he says, "I'll be happy to have a chat with him. It would easy to get together because my house is right on the campus." "Murshid is teaching spirituality through the dance," I blurt out before I can catch myself. I know I am pushing the envelope here, using the word "spirituality," so I back off. I don't want to explain this to a philosophy professor. "Murshid is integrating in individuals what Lord Snow calls the literary-humanist/scientific dichotomy by giving very short talks and then demonstrating joy—if that has come up in his talk—with a dance," I say, seeking to direct Bahm's attention away from my use of 'spirituality' by making a longwinded speech.

The term "literary-humanist/scientific dichotomy" is going too far, though. It doesn't fit here. In my zeal to accomplish *tassawuri Murshid* (attunement with the teacher), I almost get in deep trouble. Thankfully, Bahm lets these comments pass unchallenged. I don't have to explain what Murshid means by the literary-humanist/scientific dichotomy. At this moment, I haven't the slightest idea what it means. In conclusion, I present Professor Bahm with a copy of the *Oracle*. Bahm gives me his book. I leave and call Skip, the editor of *The Astro Projection*, Albuquerque's version of *The San Francisco Oracle*. He isn't home, so I get on I-25 and drive north—toward the Lama Foundation.

Will Lama be located in the high desert northwest of Taos? No, it's in the Sangre de Cristo Mountains off to the right, as I drive north from Taos. Look, there's the sign for the D.H. Lawrence ranch, next to the turnoff to San Cristobal, where Lama gets its mail. Lawrence, the literary man from England, found beauty here. "Taos has the most beautiful skyline of anywhere I have ever seen," he said. His view of the Rio Grande River gorge skyline was the same as Lama's. Both Lama and the Lawrence ranch look west at the vast expanse cut by the river. From this viewpoint on the side of the mountain, the gorge cuts a vast panorama from left to right. Dazzled by the awesome view, I collect myself to walk a quarter mile to Lama's main building.

May 30, 1969, Friday

In his letter today to Vocha Fiske—"Mother Divine"—Murshid writes,

[Murshid] just had a scene because of some obeisance to John Cage who is a sort of composer and has made a lot of notoriety with his far out arts. I see nothing in them but chaos and if it is "wrong" to oppose chaos then Sam is not only "wrong" but will follow such a "wrong" path.

Murshid mentions a Zen practice which is not to speculate—one of his inheritances from Nyogen Senzaki.

One is [engaged in] the constant diatribe against speculation, and the constant run-ins with those who love speculation and accuse you of lack of love and consideration if you do not assent to every speculation coming out of their egos.

Murshid's correspondence with Paul Reps is finished, but Reps is still on his mind.

The other thing inherited from Nyogen Senzaki has been his papers. It is all "right" for a Paul Reps or Ruth McCandless or Robert Aiken to become a joint author to Nyogen Senzaki by putting up money. That is just, noble and proper. But for Sam to make one step forward with Senzaki's papers, that is presumption, egotism and confusing.

Not hearing from Suzanne D'Mitrieff, Murshid writes again: "Recently a letter was written asking exactly what times meetings will be held in your house when Pir Vilayat is here."

June 1, 1969, Sunday

"I am very sorry that my position has not been made clear," Murshid writes Saadia.

One would like to help others but now one cannot even help oneself. There are more and more disciples and candidates to become disciples and less and less help.

The Chief Secretary is in the State of New Mexico. The second one is working full time here. Our housekeeper is away on another job, and with two homes to cover and multitudes of details, one did not have a single day off the whole month of May and not even many free nights.

Saadia is looking for information about courses at UC Davis and UC Santa Barbara, as well as housing information. Murshid tells her,

It may be possible to visit Santa Barbara in about two weeks, when we may have to go to Hollywood... But one is totally unable to give information about getting quarters. One has at least ten disciples doing that here and all appeals that one is overloaded have not been too successful.

Saadia has queried Murshid on his need for a cook, as her aunt may visit and would like to be useful. Murshid says,

If your aunt comes one will have to know the days. For we have also coming from different places my closest Korean friend and Pir Vilayat Khan, and each expects to be treated in the proper manner and each is quite unconscious of the fact that we may have other obligations. In addition to this, I have failed to write my term papers on *Arabic Art* and *Problems of Pakistan*. I am making every effort to do this today.

The Pakistan term paper is the first thing Murshid addresses in his letter to *Muslim News International* in Karachi, Pakistan. Writing Art Hoppe, Murshid notes,

I am writing today a number of serious papers: for East Asia to General Lansdale, copy enclosed; for the Near East, one on Nabatean Architecture; and for South Asia, one on Pakistani troubles, which will be shared with professors at San Francisco State and the University of California.

Like a true former intelligence operative, Murshid tells Hoppe, "I am not going to relate my relations with General Edward Lansdale. He was my war hero, but there are things one does not talk about." Murshid begins his serious paper to his war hero General Lansdale on a personal note. "You have no idea of how happy I have been to hear from you. Twice I tried to reach you during the intervening years, and the letters were returned." Murshid sets the stage for his revelation of personal experiences.

It is not very pleasant to travel in Asia and have the foreign offices of both the Russians and Americans against you at the same time, and the situation is worse because I know Americans who have been in worse positions.

As preamble, Murshid outlines the story of Rev. Samuel Brown, who operated a hospital in Pathan country and was asked to leave Pakistan when he reported Russian spies. Murshid mentions that he, himself, was saved in India "by the fact that the 'Edgar Hoover' of that land is also my spiritual brother." Preamble over, Murshid continues.

I must begin by telling you my heir is a chair! I am not fooling in the least... This chair was sat in years ago by Robert Clifton (Phra Sumangalo). He was my closest friend for thirty-five years and a noted Buddhist leader... I think Robert was the first person in history to have become a "prelate" or monk in Pure Land Buddhism, in Zen, in Chinese Mahayana, in Tantra and in traditional Theravada. He came to this country twice with warnings of what was going on within the Buddhist lands. He was excluded everywhere and a very top U.S. official issued a warning that anybody who gave him an interview would be summarily dismissed. So we have Viet Nam.

Lansdale, remember, was among the first CIA advisors to pave the way for the U.S. invasion of Viet Nam.

It was this incident [officials in the United States ignoring Clifton's reports] which caused Dr. G. Malalasekera to denounce the United States by saying: "How can you trust a nation which does not trust its own citizens"—unfortunately very true.

I had a teacher in Buddhism in common with Dr. Malalasekera. His name was M.T. Kirby. He lived in the Hawaiian Islands and could speak Japanese. He found out their plots on the islands. For this he was ejected. We got Pearl Harbor. Don't... think these have not weighed deeply on my consciousness, and then I followed in the same ways. God help the American who knows Asians and is anti-communist and non-communist.

After sharing more Asian exploits with Lansdale, Murshid concludes, "I think I am the first Murshid-Roshi-Guru in the history of the world."

June 2, 1969, Monday

Murshid tells the Temple of Understanding he plans to deliver *The Encyclopedia of Buddhism* today to the libraries of the Departments of Far East Studies and Southeast Asian Studies at UC Berkeley. "To some people this will be a great gift; it is not actually a gift, it is a protest, a cosmic protest. It is a protest against the current attitudes that important people are important and not important people are not important." I know right away where Murshid is heading with this, but it's unexpected, since Murshid wrote to Huston Smith on the 24th of May that he'd "come to the end of negative protestations." Murshid continues his letter to the Temple of Understanding.

The efforts for "Universal Peace through Religion" failed and this group was reabsorbed into its parent body, "The World Church Peace Union." Much of this failure was due to the rise of a rival institution which began with the theme of restoration of the world Congress of Religions and it also had its headquarters in Chicago. But they called in non-devotees (as most unfortunately you are now doing) and it ended in a series of brawls and nothing more.

Not content with this parenthetical allusion to the Temple of Understanding, Murshid comes back to them after mentioning the failure of the Roerich Museum.

There is no greater dream than the TEMPLE OF UNDERSTANDING but when God is not put first and famous men are paraded, especially men who have no particular beliefs and who are off in strange tangents, where is the divine vision?

Divine vision? "I am not here going into personal history, excepting that I SAW the termination of the World War II before it began." Knowledge of the world's religions gives Murshid a basis to criticize Israel. "The Jewish religion, in their prayer book, calls for the restoration of the Oracle. There is a so-called 'homeland' now in Palestine, but no temple and much less no oracle." Murshid returns to his theme.

Unfortunately you are now heralding a person who does not accept any such approach at all and if we are going to have a TEMPLE OF UNDERSTANDING, I think we must emphasize both TEMPLE and UNDERSTANDING and not repeat the same mistake of emotional appeal from some famous person who accepts neither Temple nor Understanding... A meeting becomes spiritual when there is spiritual realization among those in attendance.

Murshid is self-conscious about writing such a strong letter.

This is no doubt a firm letter. One has failed when one has presented views or even reports without firmness. And one has seen innumerable failure[s]. If we can stick to God and leave out the "famous people" we are going to have this Temple. But if we are repeating the same old programs of calling in "famous people" with strong but limited emotional appeals, it means a delay of bringing the peoples of the world together.

After delivering copies of *The Encyclopedia of Buddhism*, Murshid informs Senator J. Sherman Cooper in Washington, D.C., that he has placed two copies "in the libraries of the University of California." Murshid refers to Dr. Malalasekera's quotation ("How can you trust a nation that does not trust its own citizens?") and says, "It is a tragic mark on this country and its foreign policies that the small person does not count and the eye-witness who reports anything contrary to policy is not permitted to file his experiences."

June 5, 1969, Thursday

My clothes are drying on some fenceposts next to the laundromat in Questa, New Mexico. I just left Lama for the second and last time this trip. (What I've done between visits and after I leave—where I've been, whom I met, what they said—is outside the scope of this book.) My mission is accomplished, and the photojournalistic result of this trip is sixteen newspaper-sized pages long. I laid it out with my calligraphy and photographs, accompanied by transcribed text from tape recorded interviews with communal pioneers. It is destined for a special section of the *Oracle* called "New Age Life Styles: Southwest U.S. Communal Life." Eventually, this laundromat will be closed to the public every Tuesday morning to allow

Lama, exclusively, to do its laundry. The Lama Foundation will fully utilize all the washers and dryers and guarantee the owner's Tuesday income for many years.

I don't heed Murshid's suggestion to drop the commune trip after I visit Lama. The trip is hard, but what keeps me going is the principle assimilated from Murshid to *finish what you start.*

Yesterday, I was not very surprised to find photographer Dennis Stock, who visited the Garden of Inayat in Novato, at Lama with William Hedgepeth, a senior editor from *LOOK Magazine*. They are doing a book about communities in the southwest United States.

Before breakfast today is the first time Sufi dances are performed outside of California. I show Steve (later, Nur-ed-din) Durkee, his wife, Barbara (later, Asha Greer) and a couple of guys Barbara later calls "GI's," meaning former soldiers, the dervish dance cycle of three dances. I leave a diagram of these dances with Steve. Steve and Barbara, along with Jonathan Altman, are the founders of Lama. They hope to fill in the octagon shaped hole in the middle of floor of the dome before Murshid arrives. Many dances call for various combinations of people to stand in the center of the circle. Steve, Barbara and the community's enthusiasm for the small piece of Murshid they experienced bodes well for his pending visit. It is not an exaggeration to say they are ecstatic over this visit.

Come August, there could be twenty to thirty people at Lama. There are already two additional ones since I left the first time. It is possible the dances will be incorporated into their program and performed every morning before breakfast. The Lama people are waiting to hear when in August Murshid wants to come. They will send him a ticket for the airplane and pick him up in Albuquerque. All he has to do is say when and they'll take care of the rest.

It is a very auspicious omen for the success of the dances that Dennis Stock photographs this morning's dances. I have to sign a release to permit them to use my picture in their book *The Alternative: Communal Life in New America* (New York, 1970). This memorable occasion—the first performance of Murshid's dances outside of California—has been recorded and will be reported. It won't be the last time. Murshid's fortune is changing. It is a new age, and the dances have begun to spread far and wide.

Chapter 18

Murshid
or the World?

Before the Living God, it is very strange that you ask to be accepted while you yourselves do not show how to accept others. India is full of so-called Maharishis, Messiahs, Avatars, and me-ego-me-egos. The same problems persist that belong everywhere to samsara. The same or other, or even better programs and, perhaps, revelations have been offered, carefully packaged and preserved by "Us special representatives" of whom there are so many today I cannot count them. This is particularly true in India and California. I do not know any law or rule by which the rain and the sunshine and the eternal God is restricted to a certain geography, or the blessings thereof confined to certain individuals or groups. My secretary [Mansur] is away studying these NEW AGE EFFORTS. I myself am a veteran in this field. As a veteran I do not like to see the same mistakes repeated that I have seen repeated over and over and over. (Murshid's letter to A.B. Patel, World Union International Centre, June 7, 1969)

June 7, 1969, Saturday

Murshid wrote the letter cited in the epigraph above while I was traveling. It contains almost three thousand words. The recipient, A.B. Patel, was a leader of the Sri Aurobindo movement. His book *Towards a New World Order was published* in 1974, after Murshid's death. Without his letter I can only infer what he said by Murshid's response.

It is amazing that you my good friend, acting as if you were a spokesman for the super-mental evolution, should dare to assume that I have not been to Pondicherry, that I am not fully aware from both the inside and outside of what you are doing, or that I would dare to make a criticism or suggestion without such knowledge... Nor would I dare to speak holding to much of the point of view of Shankaracharya if I had not been initiated, ordained, and validated by actual Zen masters whom I can name and Sufi Pirs whom I can name and the late Swami Ramdas of Kanhangad— also by Paul Brunton during the lifetime of the late Sri Ramana Maharshi. If this background is not enough I can give you more but to do so means that before the living God Brahma Ishvara Allah we are accepting dualism and I mean dualism and *tat tvam asi* is hokum and nonsense and I mean just that.

In the middle of page two of this letter, which is also, indirectly, to the powers that be in the Aurobindo movement, Murshid speaks clearly to the point he confided on May 24th to Oliver Reiser ("I have lost faith in the Sri Aurobindo movement which has fallen into the hands of traditional politicians").

If you are daring to put on the same level with Sri Aurobindo, or the Mother, the work of any group, and I mean any group of *ahankara-manas* politicians, you leave open to a person that does not accept *manas-ahankara* the right and privilege to offer suggestions and criticism. And if you are going to place any of the work of the United Nations, its framers and founders, its officials and its dismal failures alongside *The Life Divine* [a book by Sri Aurobindo], you had better consider that the living God may not agree with you.

Murshid contrasts what he is doing with what he claims the Aurobindo Movement has done, "We quote the Names of God. We adore God. We praise God. We are putting into effect the *Brihadaranyaka Upanishad* by raising the levels of potentialities of *ananda* (joy). We do not need any documentary from the United Nations for this." At the bottom of page two, Murshid becomes self-conscious.

This is no doubt a strong letter. I want the same ideals and I have long had the same goals. I have seen one after another so-called world movement rise and fall. I have participated in many of them. All failed. No *one* accepted "Whatsoever ye do to the least of these my creatures, ye do it unto me." Not one accepted, "a little child shall lead them."

At the bottom of page three, the letter stops suddenly. "I pause at this point because I have been summoned to a meeting of other people who

believe they are also on the threshold of the super mental consciousness."
The next day, Murshid finishes the letter with a description of the meeting
that pulled him away.

Last night was spent at a colloquium of young people. Over a dozen seeking
answers. No bland or blind assumptions were accepted. All points of view were fully
expressed without any personal or personality allusions or recriminations.

Murshid's description of his behavior at the meeting appears to be as
quarrelsome as that in his letter to Patel.

Once during the evening it was necessary to bark and bark out loud. But the chair
having seen the celebrated Indian musician Asoka Faqir and the writer [Murshid]
rush up and embrace each other in a public place, ruled that this person had done
more than discuss love, he had expressed it.

Barking and hugging for all to see, Murshid is in a state here. His not
too subtle point: your organization is not utilizing awakened beings.

Real love does not decry intelligence or wisdom. One of my poems is entitled
One Eye, Two Eyes, Three Eyes, and a Thousand Eyes. The last two allude to *ajna* and
sahasrara [the third eye and crown center]. The world is not going to advance when
persons without awakened so-called higher faculties are denied and descried by those
without such faculties awakened. A gold-miner dare not ignore gold; a diamond
seeker would not overstep precious stones; but literati clinging to apparently noble
words have full right apparently to ignore, by-pass, and even deride the very ones
who exemplify what they are *talking* about. And this was the gist of the discussion
of these young people, and others.

June 9, 1969, Monday

Just as I am working on the fourth draft of this book, the S.I.R.S.
(Sufi Islamia Ruhaniat Society, headed now by Murshid Moineddin) is
considering whether to impress on the monument by Murshid's grave the
hadith, "In that day shall the sun rise in the West, and all men seeing will
believe." It is not generally known, except by a few readers of Murshid's
letters, that he used this phrase extensively. It appeared June 6, 1969, in his
letter to S. Ahmed, and today in his letter to W.D. Begg. In both instances,
the usage is in a context describing his success with the young. Murshid
is already planning to present his poem "Saladin," some of which was
dictated by Prophet Mohammed, in an upcoming poetry writing class.

I shall enroll at a University here in a course on poetry writing as the result of
study of Oriental Philosophy. I shall bring to class copies of *Saladin* or portions
thereof written in *hal*, in *fana-fi-rassoul*, whence the glorious Messenger often
dictated word for word, et cetera.

Mentioning that the *Oracle* and another publication, *Planet News*, have
given him attention, Murshid writes, "It is the living heart which rouses

life in the hearts of others. It is the living spirit which touches all souls."
Begg, who enclosed a paper he authored entitled *The Holy Saints of Ajmer*,
is one of the correspondents who receives Murshid's effusive statements
of belief.

I believe our mutual endeavors may do much to promote universal understanding.
I believe that the spirit of man, freed from restrictions and bonds that limit him, will
establish brotherhood on earth.

Murshid refers again to his embrace Sunday of the musician Asoka
Fakir of Bengal.

Love is not restricted, and those who saw the meeting with Asoka Fakir of Bengal
the other night recognized the mutual love and the mutual objectives of spiritual
realization thru music and dance.

June 10, 1969, Tuesday

Nobody can sum up Murshid as well as Murshid. In his letter to
Shamcher, he describes what he has presented in several recent letters,
especially his latest to A.B. Patel: "Now one is strong—which does not
mean that one is not also tender and wise." Murshid discovered somehow
that *Playboy* published his letter to the editor and concludes, "Evidently,
Playboy can show respect." One forgets Murshid was merely an aspirant
during his early days with Hazrat Inayat Khan until reading,

Our first and, for a long while, only work was *A Sufi Message of Spiritual Liberty*,
but spiritual liberty was hardly gained during the lifetime of Hazrat Inayat Khan
or for a long time thereafter. It was Paul Brunton who made for me the first big
breakthrough.

The first thing I record in my journal upon returning from New Mexico
is a lesson learned tonight about how to show respect for the teacher. I have
to ask two non-mureeds to leave. The family meeting is not open. Murshid
comments, "Whenever Murshid has to get angry at a non-mureed, all
disciples are to blame." All disciples are to blame, because they should
speak for Murshid. "When Murshid gets angry at a disciple, it is only him
[the disciple]... Murshid has three expedients: the worst is to take matters
in his own hands; the second, be silent; the third, to leave."

June 11, 1969, Wednesday

The first couple of sentences in Murshid's letter to Julie Medlock set the
tone for what's to follow.

This is a very sad letter. There is not a cloud on my own horizon, but it is
impossible to share the sunshine with those who will not accept the rest of the
personality and being... I have received a very nice and totally analytical letter from
brother A.B. Patel. It tells of all the "good" he and your colleagues are doing. But I

cannot accept [this] because "good" is restricted to what certain persons are doing and not to what others are doing.

This is getting to be a predictable refrain in Murshid's correspondence. He tells Julie Medlock:

Having partaken both inside and as a partial witness of so many movements with universal *claims* and seeing them all go down the drain, one notices that they all had in common an absolute refusal to accept even the gentlest and most kindly advice.

Murshid's first mention that Mansur is back occurs today.

My chief secretary, friend of Prof. Huston Smith of M.I.T. has done some successful research in visiting New Age communes. All of them start with the same general verbal platforms, some with the same principles, and some are actually practicing integration which is integration and not some traditional format verbalized as "integration."

There's a report that the spirit of Ruth St. Denis is visiting Murshid. "The other night there was a visitation from Srimati Ruth St. Denis, who began a series of the restoration of 'Mystery Dances' also." In response to a note from Pir Vilayat's headquarters in France, Murshid asserts, "One realizes that Pir Vilayat has a crowded schedule, but also this person has a crowded schedule." After reporting that it's been forty-six years since his first interview with Hazrat Inayat Khan, Murshid reports that "yesterday saw a marvelous manifestation of what he [Hazrat Inayat Khan] wanted— the mystical teachings presented to important intellectuals." Referring to Vilayat's visit on July 2nd, Murshid writes, "We should have a large meeting of disciples as well as of non-disciples. We have completed what was requested when he was here before."

The *Oracle* is out again, Murshid tells Huston Smith, and he will send a copy. Also, "more funds have been released from my family estate and this is enabling me to purchase copies of *The Encyclopedia of Buddhism*." Murshid informs Smith that "[Mansur] is away on a research trip and is expected this week. At times he acts almost as if my 'reincarnation'."

Moineddin and Murshid are driving to Los Angeles on Friday to meet with Vilayat on organizational matters.

While riding to the meeting tonight I talk to Jemila about using the $100 Murshid pledged for the Colorado trip for car maintenance. We decide I should wait until breakfast tomorrow to discuss it with Murshid. It would be inconsiderate to interrupt his concentration on the meeting with this kind of business.

June 12, 1969, Thursday

At the breakfast table, when I present the subject of using the $100 for car repairs, Murshid goes ballistic. I have to leave the table to get my breath back under control. Murshid keeps saying that my New Mexico trip was a private trip, and that the car needs repair because I took that private trip. I think this isn't relevant. Murshid is going to take my car to Los Angeles tomorrow, and it needs maintenance. He said he'd pay $100 toward the Colorado trip, which is scheduled as soon as he gets back from L.A. Money for maintenance, money for gas, what's the difference? Jemila takes the car to Sausalito for repair. Murshid doesn't pay.

In the afternoon after my nap, Murshid comes in the office, sits down, and says, "Do you want to see Vilayat at ten?" He doesn't say "tomorrow at ten," or "Friday at ten," which is when Vilayat is going to be at the Mentorgarten. I say, "Not particularly, but I'll consider." I remember this evening that last Thursday night Jemila came home from seeing Murshid with the impression that he wanted me to go to Colorado, and not her.

June 13, 1969, Friday

Early today Murshid informs me that the additional income he expects to receive from the family estate will benefit me in one or all of three ways: 1) as a paid official in the Sufi Order; 2) to use for improvements around the *khankah* (with me as paid handyman?); and 3) for my own expression (outright gift?). This, coming on the heels of yesterday's blowup, activates old thoughts related to the reliability of verbal expressions of financial support from Murshid; namely, I can't plan on it. I hear about these three benefits to accrue to me with the same detachment I receive other teachings. I'm neither happy nor sad. I'll believe it when I see it happening. Such remarks awaken the tension I feel between serving Murshid and earning my way in the world. For my part, *Oracle* work is fun. Since there is no income coming from the *Oracle* work, it's not work as far as the welfare people are concerned. No income means they won't cut my stipend. I proceed not by plan, but by constantly trying to feel the will of God.

Before we leave for the City, Murshid writes a quick letter to Vocha Fiske. He says he'll probably hand deliver this letter to Vocha at her address on Las Palmas in Los Angeles. Murshid recently expressed (June 10, 1969) that "one cannot help feeling that one may be called upon to be used in games." Murshid shows here what he had in mind, writing Vocha,

I have to see Vilayat Khan this morning before departure and can easily adjust to his plans. I am not interested in the politics but am interested in the legal moves. With a rising income, growing following and the possibility of considerably increased emoluments sooner or later, I must have legal protection.

I drive Murshid to San Francisco to see Vilayat. Afterwards (see June 18, 1969), Murshid writes Shamcher that the "meeting with Vilayat in this house was short and profitable. We did some short phases of our dancing and chanting, and Samuel performed the rhythms of the seven planets."

Murshid and I (and others) did *Allah Hu* together during a demonstration of dervish dancing for Vilayat.

The leader selects a partner, bringing him to the center of the circle, where they join right hands, and move clockwise around each other, chanting ALLAH HU (bringing head up on ALLAH and down to heart on HU). Repeat at least 4 times; leader then joins circle, or musicians, and his partner chooses a new partner. (Murshid's Dance Manual, unpublished)

There, in the presence of Vilayat, my breath is upset. The result is awkwardness. [Little do I imagine I am picking up Pir Vilayat's agitation at being in my presence because of his as yet unexpressed love for Jemila.] I speculate my unsettled condition is related to my indecision about going to Colorado because the welfare people have a series of weekly meetings scheduled. My presence is required if I want to continue to receive assistance. I do. This assistance allows me to work for Murshid, pursue my interests with the *Oracle*, and make ends meet. And it means I must stay home from Colorado.

June 14, 1969, Saturday
In the afternoon, Phillip, David Sapp, and I interview Richard Alpert, also known as Baba Ram Dass, for the *Oracle*.

June 15, 1969, Sunday
I make the final decision about going to Colorado. Rather than jeopardize my income from the county, I decide to stay home and attend their meeting. My respectful practice has been to honor their rules, as I would those of any boss. But as I have saved up for the camp, and as Jemila is itching to go, she will go. The caravan leaves tomorrow, Monday the 16th. Jemila gives me instructions for Nathan and the plants in her absence.

June 18, 1969, Wednesday
First thing in the morning, Murshid jumps on the typewriter and tells Shamcher, "We came in last night from a very pregnant and hopefully profitable trip south." Murshid and Moineddin stopped at Bhakti Engle's place in Camarillo on both the way down and back from Los Angeles. They went on to visit Ramdas's grandson "and one beautiful meeting led to another." They arrived late at the business meeting, but Murshid "had nothing to propose and much to support," including Shamcher's selection to the board of directors of the Sufi Order. Murshid reports, "Vilayat hinted that this new corporation alone will have the right to use the word 'Sufi'." Commenting on Pir Vilayat himself, Murshid says, "I myself like Vilayat's independence from authority and orthodoxy and his complete and marvelous universal outlook. The possibilities here are stupendous."

In the heady space between just arriving from Los Angeles and leaving San Francisco for Novato, Murshid writes Sharab Harris in Guys Mills, Pennsylvania.

There was a work *Between the Desert and the Sown* and one feels a little like that at the moment, waiting for the station wagon to go to Novato, with just a few hours before the caravan departs for Colorado, with several reports and a number of instructions, and dashing off this letter, because all the secretaries will either be gone or working at specialty jobs in this general area.

Murshid announces tonight that Moineddin will be vice-president; Mansur, secretary general; and Daniel, treasurer in the organization that he will head. My inner response is that to be appointed secretary general without spiritual experience is not a good thing. Such an appointment would only be a continuation of the kind of priestcraft that characterized spiritual movements of the past.

June 19, 1969, Thursday
This morning Murshid tells me that Vilayat has suggested a robe for me. I take this as a sign that I can drop my modesty about serving as an official in Murshid's organization. Murshid tells me he's noticed Jemila and I have been getting on better during the year. This is spiritually a good sign, as well as an indication of personal progress, in that more love and respect is showing in our relationship.

After the meeting, Murshid speaks about the "wide eye." He says Frank (Halim Welch—see his story in Chapter 13) already has it. Murshid says he'll turn on his own wide eye and watch who responds with the wide eye rather than with "the personal eyes." I'm not sure I know what he is talking about, whether the third eye or intuitive responses. Murshid goes on in his stream of consciousness way and says he has several strong men, having implied earlier there may be more. Then, out of the blue, he turns to me and says that *it will be helping him if I go out and earn a dollar, even if he doesn't see any of it*. This message couldn't be clearer if Murshid sang the country song *Get a Job* to me. Still, I can't compute working full time and helping him.

June 20, 1969, Friday
This morning Murshid refuses to come to breakfast until we agree to hold a special meeting, so he can report to everyone at the *khankah*. At the meeting Murshid makes several points. First, he announces that his three secretaries in San Francisco—Barbara, Linda, and Melvin—are in Colorado without his blessing. *How strange*, I think. I was present when Murshid asked Melvin if he wanted to go to Colorado. I assumed when he asked Melvin the question it implied his approval. Look at how my

assumptions are wrong. Another point is that the cornfield next door has been cultivated without Murshid's permission, and now there is no one to take care of it. I'm out of this one, too. Also, the circular tree seat built around the willow tree in the side yard was started without Murshid's permission, and it just sits there unfinished. According to my recollection, I started the tree seat after Murshid suggested it. I vow to myself to finish it. Unless the wisteria donated to the *khankah* is planted before next Sunday, Murshid says he is going to burn it. In this case, there has been inaction because nobody would be so inconsiderate as to act on a gardening matter without consulting first with Murshid. None of my energy is ever directed toward gardening. The article "Introduction to Spiritual Brotherhood" was published in the *Oracle* against Murshid's wishes. Again, I am responsible, but I note to myself that this is old business stuck in Murshid's mind. That was two *Oracle* issues ago.

Recalling that Murshid said yesterday it would help him if I made money, I think about arranging lectures in the communities I visited in Colorado and New Mexico. I think of Bernard Phelps, who was my speech professor and facilitator of the lecture series at Miami University, where I did my undergraduate work. I could write to him for advice on how to proceed, but I don't.

Murshid mentions again that no spiritual school gets up later than 6 A.M.; but it has not been established that this will be a hard and fast rule. There will be another new rule: Everybody must work at least two hours a day for Murshid. "Work" means working in the garden with him, or studying Inayat Khan's books. "Work" also means meditation. Murshid asks how many have read Inayat Khan's books. I am the only one. People don't seem to have time. Six weeks ago, I handed out Series I of Murshid's *Commentary on Moral Culture* and said that I'd distribute the second and third series when people were through reading the first. There have been no requests. Murshid asks who gave permission for Summer, Nathan's playmate, to be at the *khankah*. The question implies something's wrong with this, but no one challenges the underlying assumption. No one answers. Who can answer? No one asked permission for Summer to come to the house, so obviously no one "gave" permission. The matter dies—until tomorrow.

June 21, 1969, Saturday

Around half past five this evening, after Murshid and Mansur have picked up two three year olds (Summer and Nathan) at Ayesha's (Barbara's new spiritual name), Murshid tells me everyone is going out to eat, and I will have to stay home and take care of the kids! Why? Because I invited an outsider (Summer) to the *khankah* without the house's approval. Murshid says I am never to do this again.

It is a quarter to eight at night. I am thunderstruck; I've never missed a meal with Murshid before. I am trying to understand how it happened. I remember Murshid being in Los Angeles when the plans were made. I also remember that Murshid asked yesterday who gave permission for Summer to come to the *khankah*. I had missed Murshid's meaning yesterday. I went ahead and picked up the kids today with Murshid. Yes, something could have been said today before we picked up Summer. But who knew? I said nothing. I feel stupid and write, "I feel I have much to learn. This concerns consideration."

House members begin walking to their meal at the Peacock Inn just as Jehanara comes home. Murshid won't let them wait for her, and they walk away. But I imagine Jehanara picks them up after she puts away the groceries and drives off toward the restaurant.

After dinner, Murshid pretends the children bother him when they are playing in the bathroom. I am too uptight and inexperienced in such matters to diffuse his pique by saying, "What's the matter, Murshid? Are the kids bothering you?" Again, consideration, but, again, I don't speak. I see these tests as teaching devices. They call attention to one's faults. Superficially, it seems to be behavior. It appears to be a failure to speak; but it's more. It's remembering. This very incident recreates the *khankah*'s first test. It's respecting another. Consideration.

June 22, 1969, Sunday

I say to myself before the dance class: *Watch carefully.* This is a class. That means somebody is teaching and there is something to learn. I receive telepathically the changes in the dance the turn before Murshid changes from, say, a single turn to one and a half turns, and from one and a half turns to two. It happens twice. During repetitions of old dances, my effort is to concentrate on the phrase. Also, I focus intensely when Murshid gives concentrations. There are several, like "feel in the heart" or "breathe in the right nostril." I notice others in the group much less, even when I'm not walking myself, because when Murshid gives the concentration—for example, "Abraham walk, concentration in the eyes, with straight backbone"—I am getting into this as I sit, while others are walking.

June 23, 1969, Monday

The only letter Murshid writes today is to Richard O. Buxton, executive director of Alumni House at UC Berkeley, informing him that Samuel L. Lewis is donating two copies of *The Encyclopedia of Buddhism* to UC Berkeley and one to UCLA. I've never before seen a description of Murshid's accidental encounter with Mario Savio and the Free Speech movement that

Murshid shares with Buxton. It was December 2, 1964, on the steps of Sproul Hall on the Berkeley campus that Savio exhorted the crowd to "put your bodies upon the gears (of the university machine)...and you've got to make it stop." This made "world headlines."

On the day the original "Free Speech" outbreak took place, I was an unwitting witness having just come from a lecture on African Ecology. To the amazement of the professors over 300 persons attended, and I presume all professors and students! This was not news. And 400 persons—and no one knows how many were students—made world headlines.

June 25, 1969, Wednesday

When I read for the first time Murshid's fifteen hundred word essay, *Project Prometheus and the DDT Complex*, in the form of a letter to Oliver Reiser, I get that Murshid does not share the common belief that DDT is too harmful to use. Consider the following passage which prompted me to write in the margin, *Murshid likes DDT?*

And when we enter into the field of radioactive phenomena, we are facing reactions which are both vibrational and atomic at the same time. The atomic and molecular changes may or may not be dependent or independent on the radionic changes and certainly there have been fall-out measurements which I must temporarily accept as valid. But today the logistics of the fall-out phenomena is being applied willy-nilly to after-effects of DDT, *and* without any clear logic, to an ETC [General Semantics] series of verbal conclusions not based on anything in particular. Roughly speaking—and it is very rough—the spray poisons may be depending on contact or stomach narcosis. The chemistry involved in each case is different. But the newspaper logistics are all denials that "to every action there is an equal and opposite reaction" and carbon-chlorine, carbon-sulphur and other changes are discussed assuming at the *same time* there are and there are not radical chemical changes. While one reads a good deal about saturated and unsaturated fats, often written by people who do not know these terms, the possibility of closed and open chains, of the types of compounds used, is left up in the air. And it is now assumed that out of DDT comes a violent compound which continues on ad nauseam, affecting bodies and things without itself being changed at all.

No, Murshid answers me.

I am neither defending nor objecting to DDT but...before I personally would come to any conclusion I should like to see the complete formula, the chains involved, and the changes to these chains—or some evidence for the persistence of certain complex molecules before coming to any conclusion.

That last bit is the sticking point with Murshid, for he reiterates a few lines later, "The bland and blind assumption that active molecules do not lose their fervor or poison no matter what happens has to be proved and the deaths of crabs, birds, etc. a la *Silent Spring* [Rachel Carlson's book which launched the environmental movement in 1962 with its exposé of the effects of pesticides on wildlife] has to be studied more dispassionately." Although Murshid mentions in the beginning that "I had been a professional spray operator," it comes up in the end as well. "It is funny that I who worked a lot with DDT was ill only from one compound, a lead product, and never from any complex hydrocarbons." Since Murshid goes on to say, "Of course we used gloves, masks, etc. when necessary," the above cannot be construed as Murshid vouching for the safety of DDT.

To Lloyd Morain, who receives a copy of the Reiser letter above, Murshid adds the dig, "Problems are not solved, they are resolved, and they are resolved according to the importance of the persons entangled in them. And if you don't believe me all you have to do is to read the latest copy of *ETC.*, your own publication." In both letters, to Reiser and Morain, Murshid's opening image is "hopes...dashed, but...," referring to his wish that General Semantics might be used to solve problems.

Rev. Eugene Wagner has been providing copies of *The Encyclopedia of Buddhism* to Murshid. Murshid sends Wagner $50 and news that he received an emergency call from his brother. "Just as my father before, there is a death-bed contrition and it may lead one into a rather enviable (for me) financial position and the money would be used either for the establishment at Novato, or for traveling in the Orient." Fortunately, at the time, I am not confused by hearing today how Murshid plans to allocate his family wealth.

June 26, 1969, Thursday

The burning question for me before I go to bed after the Wednesday night meeting is whether Murshid will support a price increase for the *Oracle*. Phillip brought it up; I picked up on it and promoted doubling the price to fifty cents. Since there was no money for my New Mexico trip, it seemed necessary if working for the *Oracle* was to pay off for me. The point was raised: *We'll lose business.* I argued, "This is a test. We've put out two papers in the style we're advocating. If we raise the price and lose readers, let's quit. It won't pay. If we don't lose readers, great! Our income doubles."

The alarm rings at 5:30 A.M. I am not up until quarter past six, but begin interacting with Murshid almost immediately. Murshid says he does not favor a price increase for the *Oracle*. When I ask him about my work in general on the paper, he says if I put in four hours at the *khankah*, he doesn't care what I do.

Then, Murshid asks me, "Have you seen the magazine *Spiritualism*?" The name is not familiar. I say, "If you mean the magazine called *Psychic*, yes, I have seen it. I bought it. But a magazine *Spiritualism*, I have not seen. Do we have one?" In the cloud of smugness about correcting Murshid's slip of the tongue, I miss whatever is behind his question. Changing the subject, I ask if there are errors in the book called *Metaphysics,* which is included in volume five of *The Sufi Message.* "Maybe," Murshid says. "There were in the beginning," and he didn't know if they were corrected. I don't pull the book out and show Murshid the layouts below. I endow Murshid with a sort of mental omniscience, assuming he knows exactly what I am alluding to. I call your attention to "fear" and "sadness" below. I ask this of Murshid because of the apparent contradiction between Chapter 1 (number v) and Chapter 2 (number vi). In Chapter 1, page 234, we read:

Fear has the influence of the earth element; affection has the effect of the water element; anger has the effect of the fire element; humor has the effect of the air element; and *sadness* has the effect of the ether element [emphases mine].

Chapter 2 (number vi) says on pages 243-44:

There are nine different emotions which the soul experiences through the heart. These are influenced by corresponding elements, thus:

Emotions column	Elements column
Humor	air
Joy	ether
Sorrow	earth
Fear	ether and air
Pity	water
Courage	fire and air
Indifference	ether, fire and earth
Passion	fire
Anger	fire and air

The problem appears to be a dyslexic typist who switched the words in the second list. Fear is most definitely connected with the earth element. Practicing consideration, I ask Murshid if I can use the office until eight. He says he isn't going to get in before then. I ask Murshid, "How should I trim my beard?" He says, "Wait and see what Jemila says." [She is at the Colorado camp now.] I ask Murshid if I can bring Nathan to the Gatha meeting, or if he should play up in his room. Murshid says, "Not at the beginning of the meeting. There is going to be a silent concentration, and he would be a disturbance." Even though I drive everywhere with Murshid, a one on one interaction with the teacher like the one recorded above happens infrequently.

June 28, 1969, Saturday

After acknowledging a letter Murshid calls "friendly and moral" from Diane K. Pike of the Foundation for Religious Transition, Murshid delivers a closely reasoned, tightly worded, multipronged attack on psi (psychic) researchers who "turned down the possibility of Asians having prowess in their chosen field, much less superiority." His diagnosis of the problem:

"The importance of certain personalities is so great as to make honest, objective, impersonal research almost impossible." Murshid doesn't spare board members and sponsors of the Foundation for Religious Transition, characterizing them as "men who have given me the public lie and been accepted without any opportunity to present any case whatsoever."

There's an early warning in a letter today to Oliver Reiser that Murshid may go to the Lama Foundation sooner than August. "My program has had to be rearranged which may mean I shall call on Archie Bahm sooner than planned but will write to him first." It is possible to date from this letter the first hint Murshid has of the arrival of Saadia.

My affairs have become exceedingly complicated. My brother may be dying... And I am harassed in the time-processes not only with family matters but the sudden appearance here of friends from far-off places, including my illustrious (not here) goddaughter.

This letter to Reiser, his intellectual friend, only three days since the last, is partly a vehicle for Murshid to deliver some autobiographical ramblings.

One of the big influences in my life came thus: I was moved by Cassius Keyser, partly in person and partly by studying his works, to move into collateral fields, and at that time I was deeply in love with algebra. (There may be something Freudian here, for some of my relatives also seemed more in love with this sort of abstraction than with sex.) Independently I was studying Bertrand Russell and was moved by a number of his early works and thoughts which have long since disappeared from public attention. And the constant running into parallels prepared me for *Science and Sanity*.

In another way, this letter follows up on notions sketched on the 25th to Reiser, like:

The refusal of the dialecticians of all camps (by whatever name they are known) to consider Indian systems of logistics helps leave unsolved problems which are just as much problems of obscurantic minds as of objective validity.

Today, Murshid gets very specific.

As the present logistics are failing to solve problems, it is time to examine at least superficially the *Nyaya* and *Dignaga* non-Aristotelian logics. The *Nyaya* logic has for its virtue the compulsory need of referents demanded also by A.K [Alfred Korzybski] but not by many of his disciples; and in this seems more in line with a presumably "scientific" logic. *Dignaga* goes further in assuming or proving that facts are independent of the personality of the observer—and it was just this by which Einstein was able to resolve the dilemma of the Michelson-Morley experiments. (I read these reports many times before I studied Einstein and hate to have to make this public, but the young are looking for honesty and leadership and they are going to get it.)

Just as he did three days ago, Murshid wrote Reiser and sent a copy and a letter to Lloyd Morain, Today it is the same—and for the Morain letter, what a beginning! "In the last meeting with the late Hugo Selig, before he left Santa Barbara for Pismo [the Dunes], and his last days, he spent hours discussing you as his greatest failure." Referring to the end of today's letter to Reiser, where he lists applications of semantics to specific problems, Murshid says to Morain,

The carbon to Oliver Reiser indicates what I shall do, and perhaps must do, not only to vindicate life but to help humanity rise above some of our present day problems... I have written and will write more to Entymologists on DDT, etc. which I have both used and seen used on a larger scale than you can conceive and I mean just that. [Murshid witnessed Pakistan and India being "saved from famine by DDT."]

June 29, 1969, Sunday

In a letter to the author of an article Murshid read in the *World Buddhist Federation* news bulletin, he makes me laugh. After remarking that he has tried for years to effect a return to the policy of inclusion last exemplified by the 1893 Parliament of Religions, he says, "It is an excellent career if you want to be a martyr."

Murshid takes my hand to begin the Ram dance, which concludes *Om Hari Om*. This phrase impressed me the first time I read it in *God Intoxication*. When Ramdas entered a cave where he suspected there was a tiger, he shouted, *Om Hari Om!* This is a special formula to protect myself from tigers, I thought when I first read it. By now, the phrase connotes merely: peace exhaulted peace! Murshid mentions us going to Egypt. "I don't care if Mansur takes any clothes," he says, "as long as he brings his films." This is the first time Murshid mentions travel to Egypt. What the meaning of "films" is, I can only guess. I suspect he is referring to the latest *Oracle*, which published numerous photos of the Mayday celebration. Murshid asks me what his goddaughter Saadia brings (meaning, what quality does Saadia represent). I say she brings "the perfection of woman." I don't know what I'm thinking. I don't know what I see, but these are the words I use to describe an indescribable something.

June 30, 1969, Monday

Yesterday Saadia Khawar Khan brought news that Dr. Seyyed Hossein Nasr, a visiting professor at the Center for Religious Studies at Harvard University, might visit San Francisco. Murshid tells Dr. Nasr that Saadia "put on a fashion display which won the admiration of all." He offers his cooperation with Nasr's transportation needs or "in any way you desire, especially if we have some information as to dates." Murshid elaborates on Saadia when he writes columnist Art Hoppe.

She is working for a PhD in clothing, fabrics, design, etc. and she put on a costume show in my San Francisco home that was a wow. I thought I had some beautiful young girls in my entourage, but when they were costumed! their husbands and boy friends just went gaga.

That is the straight part of the letter. From here, Murshid finds several clever ways to slam Lloyd Morain's General Semantics organization, referring to "the various 'Liberty, Democracy, Humanity, and Peasants, Shut up!' Societies." Although Murshid says he'd "rather settle this peaceably," he concludes, "In the meanwhile I shall write another paper on DDT which will be considered by laboratory-scientists, but not, of course, by 'experts' who have never sprayed anything but people's reputations."

In the following letter to Lloyd Morain, Murshid calls the Hoppe letter (a carbon of which is enclosed) "presumably whimsical," and goes on to present his lose/win strategy for an article on General Semantics stemming from his early work "with and under the late Cassius Keyser of Columbia. I am not expecting any recognition of this and this non-recognition gives anything I write more validity."

Murshid's letter today to a Sufi lady friend named Hamidan records an event I witnessed yesterday that reverberates for years.

This is a tragic, comic letter written in haste. Yesterday, my Khalifa and goddaughter, Miss Saadia Khawar Khan reached this city for a short visit, and we took her to the meeting presided over by Fazal [Inayat Khan, Vilayat's nephew]. It was tragic. At the end we did a little chanting and a stranger said, "Why didn't you do that earlier, to put some life into this meeting?" About half the audience was composed of my young followers and many of the older people were also friends and associates. The general feeling was that it was a funeral service! There was no life of any kind... It is tragic indeed how this young man who has never either studied or faced life should dare to present himself, or have himself presented to the public as a "leader" among Sufis. Why the recent President of India, the late Dr. Hussein, was a Sufi and he never dared to say or do what this unfortunate young man has tried.

It takes Murshid over a year after Fazal's visit yesterday to write him, August 1, 1970, at Sufi Movement headquarters in Geneva. (This is the Sufi Movement Fazal's forebears usurped from Vilayat, as reported in Chapter 5.) Fazal answers Murshid September 25, 1970.

I have no doubt that you are doing good work although it might be mixed. It was a pity that in our contact in Frisco you were so tough, anxious and showed off this *Ishk Allah* (God is Love) group song which was not understood by all the square people present.

Murshid responds from Lonnie Less's apartment in New York City on October 4, 1970.

At San Francisco, I was told to get out of your meeting as soon as I entered the door, God is my witness, and perhaps your sacred grandfather [Hazrat Inayat Khan] also. How many times have you actually seen him? You are asking a validated Sufi teacher, whom you call by a nickname (Sam) to crawl at your feet.

Murshid writes again October 5, 1970, not satisfied with his response the day before, and answers numerous points from Fazal's September letter. These include Fazal's request that Murshid return teachings Rabia Martin had received from Inayat Khan; Fazal's insistence that only the Sufi Movement could publish teachings; and Fazal's assertion of authority over the Sangathas, some advanced spiritual teachings. It is one of Murshid's strongest letters, in which he functions fully as Defender of the Faith.

This issue is still alive for Murshid later on today. Walking outside with Suzanne, Krishnadas' girl friend, and me, Murshid speaks as if dictating a note: "Dear Krishnadas, although you were not with us yesterday in body, you were with us in spirit." Krishnadas got caught with some marijuana at an inspection station in Arizona and is residing at the Mojave County Jail in Kingman, Arizona. "You did not miss anything by not being with us when we went yesterday to see Fazal Khan, Vilayat's nephew, at the Canterbury Hotel, 750 Sutter."

After I leave San Francisco for Novato, Murshid pulls out a letter he received several weeks earlier from Harvard Professor Holmes Welch. Welch, a resident at the East Asian Research Center in Cambridge, Massachusetts, had the humility (Murshid might say) to ask for materials Murshid said he has that contradict Welch's published date of Trebitsch-Lincoln, or "Dr. Ruh's" death. First, Murshid regretfully reports that his records were destroyed in the 1949 fire. Then he places Trebitsch-Lincoln in China on the sacred mountain named Omei Shan (aka Emei Shan).

I do not recall the year but he was on the sacred mountain in 1936 [when Welch has said he was dead] when the defunct *Literary Digest* gave him a big write up, mostly concerning his warnings and prophecies, which came pretty well to objectification, far more than any superficial "Jean Dixon" stuff. [Murshid's certainty in the matter stems from the fact that Paul Fernandez, the chief disciple of Nyogen Senzaki and Murshid's spiritual brother, received letters from Trebitsch-Lincoln-Ruh until Ruh died].

When I get back to the *khankah*, Phillip calls to say he has arranged a meeting for tomorrow with Carleton Kendall and Norman, the *Oracle's* printer. I reluctantly say I will attend. Then I remember that there will be no price increase for the *Oracle*. The prospect of work without pay doesn't sustain me. My feeling is to fulfill my obligations, do what I said I would do, and get out of the *Oracle*—then do more work for Murshid and the Sufi Order, the cause of God. I call Phillip back and announce my resignation. When it comes down to Murshid or the world, I choose Murshid.

Chapter 19

Murshid's Ultimatum

Within a week I receive two excellent letters from the University of California, one in regard to Asian-Asian cultures, and the other in regard to my own research and logistics anent Spray-materials. Lloyd [Morain], who will get a copy of this, called me down in public for not accepting "Silent Spring" and the right of all big persons who cannot tell a "drug" from a "drug" to speak on this subject, but a poor workingman like me, even though a professional, has no business interfering with the arguments of important people. (Murshid's letter to Shamcher Bryn Beorse, July 9, 1969)

July 3, 1969, Thursday

Last night Murshid initiated me as a *nakib*. He told Jehanara *nakib* means "custodian." Much later I read in Murshid's book *The Lotus and the Universe* that a *nakib* is one "who acts as an external spokesman for the mystical brotherhoods."

This afternoon, after listening to Beethoven's Third Symphony, I weep. I realize the importance of beauty. We have been saying the Sufi Invocation, *Toward the One, the perfection of love, harmony and beauty...* Beauty makes me weep. And what does it say in Gayan? Love creates harmony, and harmony creates beauty.

July 4, 1969, Friday

Murshid exalts when W.D. Begg repents his promotion of a new holy man. Murshid has written repeatedly to the Temple of Understanding, urging them to turn away from their use of Alan Watts as a spokesman. If they had, Murshid might have described their turning away as passing through the gate of *tauba*, or repentance.

As Murshid, three year old Nathan, and I are walking to the wine store near his home in San Francisco I ask Murshid, "What is *tauba*?" Murshid says simply *tauba* is repentance, and that I can read more about it in *Kashf al-Mahjub*. The section about repentance in *Kashf al-Mahjub* concludes:

Dhu'l-Nun the Egyptian says: "There are two kinds of repentance, the repentance of return (*tawbat al-inabat*) and the repentance of shame (*tawbat al-istihya*): the former is repentance through fear of Divine punishment, the latter is repentance through shame of Divine clemency." The repentance of fear is caused by revelation of God's majesty, while the repentance of shame is caused by vision of God's beauty. Those who feel shame are intoxicated and those who feel fear are sober. (p.299)

This is truly wonderful to read after my experience of beauty the other day with Beethoven. The explanation in the book grows from the ordinary and culminates in love.

Repentance is of three kinds: 1) from what is wrong to what is right, 2) from what is right to what is more right, 3) from selfhood to God. The first kind is the repentance of ordinary men; the second kind is the repentance of the elect; and the third kind of repentance belongs to the degree of Divine love (*mahabbat*).

Love creates harmony, and harmony creates beauty. The detail in the repentance story below of Abu 'Amr b. Nujayd when he leaves his spiritual teacher surprises me. My projection is that no one would do this.

As a novice, I repented in the assembly-room of Abu 'Uthman Hiri and persevered in my repentance for some while. Then I fell into sin and left the society of that spiritual director, and whenever I saw him from afar my remorse caused me to flee from his sight. One day I met him unexpectedly. He said to me: "O son do not associate with your enemies unless you are sinless (*ma'sum*), for an enemy will see your faults and rejoice. If you must sin, come to us, that we may bear your

Jehanara, Moineddin, Fatima, and Murshid

affliction." On hearing his words, I felt surfeited with sin and my repentance was established.

July 5, 1969, Saturday

I set up an interview with Murshid and ask him, "What am I supposed to do?" What to do? How to live? They have been the recurring questions of my life since I took psychedelics at the University of Iowa in 1964. How to live has been answered by Murshid. Rhythm, balance, considering one's life a work of art—all this Murshid has presented, and I've gratefully received.

I'm still missing—and long for—the kind of guidance Frank Lloyd Wright received from his mother, who said, "You are going to be an architect." Murshid fields my question in terms of my secretarial work for him. He ignores my longing-for-definition thrust. Murshid says I can coordinate the people working on dancing—

Saadia, Melvin, and Gwen Bernham

Jemila, Marcia, and Linda. He says, "After the dancing work, there is work on esotericism." Murshid is thinking out loud. He practices non-dualism, which, in practice, means pupil and teacher are one. My question triggers a thought process that reveals his work and my place in it. He goes from the generalization, "After the dancing work," to a particular job for me, "there is work on esotericism." Murshid continues his stream of consciousness narrative: I should be familiar with his commentaries on (Hazrat Inayat Khan's) *Cosmic Language* and *The Path of Initiation and Discipleship*, which he is writing in the early mornings at the *khankah*. Melvin will probably do the typing on *The Path of Initiation and Discipleship*. Murshid suggests I look through the esoteric book in which we keep people's practices and see which people need their practices updated. This is something I don't do. How can I say they need their practices updated? This seems to happen when people find themselves in an interview situation with Murshid. Also, I can arrange interviews on Sundays while Moineddin leads dances. Again, even with permission, I don't feel comfortable establishing Murshid's agenda until he sets a time. I should feel free to ask about any of the practices that I have or don't have. I might check how many copies there are in the files of the "Waris" papers (a biography of a nineteenth century saint) and the *irfan* papers that we give out (see July 28, 1969 for Murshid's prescription for this practice).

The list goes on: I might be aware or even make a daily journal of what goes on at the *khankah*. I inaugurate this journal today, and it is the source of some remembrances for this book, like, "Jemila is making preparations (in Iowa) to go to Europe for Vilayat's Youth Seminar." This last bit is not a small event in my life, but it gets no play in my esoteric journal because it is *too personal*. Jemila returned from Colorado and left a few days later for her parents' home in Iowa. She said she wanted to go to the European retreat, to be held by Pir Vilayat in Chamonix, France. I saw her radiance and I thought: At last she feels the same joy for the spiritual path that I have been feeling. Murshid continues, no longer outlining things I can do, but rather sharing his vision of the future.

The Sunday food schedule should be arranged ahead of time. On the 19th, the dance class will be in San Francisco. There will be a dinner open to all—unlike the dance class—and Lois Robinson will be speaking at 420 Sutter that evening. There are things to be picked up at the ranch.

Thank you for sharing is my silent response to Murshid's presentation of a program like this. Other than gratitude for being included, I feel this concentration is Murshid's responsibility. I don't put my mind into how to bring it off. I'll be assigned a task on the day something needs to be done. Then Murshid gets back to something that more immediately concerns me, since I collect money for him at meetings. "Separate dues payments from general admissions," Murshid says. "Some dues money will go to buy things Vilayat requested for our chapel." Further, Murshid defines three roles for me: disciple, father, and official in his organization.

Somewhere along the way, I remind Murshid that he said we were not to think of any other projects until the house is painted. Murshid responds that we have our group concentration on the kiln, and the group can think of this, but I am not to think of any new projects. Murshid says he doesn't care if I do any more physical work around the *khankah* after I get the house painted. Imagining the gutter/house painting project completed is a relief for me. I was impressed early on with the notion that the one who suggests a project will be the one to do it. Opening my big mouth got me the painting and gutter job in the first place. Murshid reminds me of this and tells me that I am responsible for accomplishing any further suggestions I make. I won't be making any.

July 6, 1969, Sunday

In the early afternoon, Murshid talks briefly to Vilayat on the telephone regarding Jemila's trip. Vilayat feels it will be better for Jemila to go to New York rather than Europe. The discussion is couched in terms of how Jemila can spread the dances. Murshid begins work immediately writing a *Dance Manual* for Jemila to use. Subsequently, Jemila's parents call and volunteer to pay for her trip to Europe. Jemila calls it "a miracle." Vilayat also offers to pay. Murshid says he has an "emergency fund of $200" that he hasn't told us about, "besides my regular travel fund." Perhaps Jemila goes to both New York and Europe. Murshid describes these events in a letter to Shamcher on the 9th.

Sunday we felt it imperative to begin work on the Dance choreography but had an awful time: long distance phone calls, both from Vilayat and the parents of Jemila Johnson. Jemila is the wife of Secretary and now *Nakib* Mansur Johnson. She did well at Colorado, and Vilayat wants her to bring the spiritual dances east.

Murshid is glad for Jemila to go to New York to spread the dances. I am disappointed, sensing somehow that this success spells ruin for our relationship. When Murshid is dictating the dances for the first *Dance Manual*, he comes to *Allah Mansur* and translates it "God is strength and joy," giving me several looks while he repeats it.

July 7, 1969, Monday

When I walk in the door, Murshid is responding to a letter just received from Buddhist Jack Austin in England, who sent a magazine, *The Western Buddhist*. Austin is seeking suggestions for distributing the magazine and Murshid suggests New Age, the health food store "controlled by the followers of Lama Anagarika Govinda." Additionally, Murshid tells Austin, "one of my own disciples [Hassan Herz] works there" and "he is also a printer." In conclusion, Murshid writes, "[I] have to go over the rest of the articles with disciples, the most important of whom just came in the door." Then, Murshid proceeds to dictate letters to American Friends of the Middle East and his Uncle Harry. And that's OK. That's what I came for. Murshid is feeling expansive in an artful letter to American Friends of the Middle East as he contemplates the spread of his dances to the East Coast. The letter begins:

I am finding that there is one program on which nearly all contending groups in this country agree, that is that not only is one's own particular program superior to all other particular programs, but that success must come through certain individuals and that if it does not come through a particular group of individuals, it either will not come or should not come.

I call this the Great Stoneface Letter since, after this opening sentence, Murshid says that this "particularly American psychology" appears in the American novelist Nathaniel Hawthorn's short story "The Great Stoneface" and manifests itself in the attitudes of various California movements. Murshid rephrases his contention that groups are too exclusive. "The possibilities of either religion or psychology being based on the experience of God rather than on any theologies or doctrines have not been too welcomed." However, Murshid goes on to say, this is happening "among the young," and not only are the young experiencing God, but Israelis, Christians, and Muslims are dancing together.

Murshid has delayed writing his uncle Harry Rosenthal, hoping to communicate the dates of his visit to Seattle and coordinate a side trip to Vancouver to visit Harry. The unresolved issue of when Murshid is going to New Mexico holds up this letter. For now, what Murshid says is, "I am hoping to come north about the beginning of September."

Looking back, I glean the following information from a copy of a letter I write today to some friends in Mexico: Next Friday Jemila goes from Iowa to New York to be again with Pir Vilayat. I am still telling myself it's a deep spiritual connection.

July 8, 1969, Tuesday

Murshid reports in a letter today to *Studies in Comparative Religion* editor F. Clive-Ross on his generosity to the University of California at Berkeley. I have been on very good terms with the Department of Near East Languages, but have extended friendship by my presenting both the Department of South Asian Studies and the Department of Far East Studies copies of *The Encyclopedia of Buddhism* as my "golden anniversary" gifts.

Extending generosity even further, Murshid asks Clive-Ross, "Could you send them complete sets [of *Studies in Comparative Religion*] and charge the bill to me?" Murshid and Clive-Ross continue to correspond, and Murshid and Mansur find their way to Pates Manor on Hatton Road in Bedfont, Middlesex, England, in April of 1970. Murshid's last letter to Clive-Ross is September 20, 1970. Clive-Ross seems unimpressed when we visit him at home, as does Martin Lings when we visit him at the British Museum. Lings, quoted earlier, is the author of al-Alawi's biography, *A Sufi Saint of the 20th Century*. Murshid tells Clive-Ross in his last letter,

> It is unfortunately symbolic that Martin Lings does not accept what Sidi Abu-Salem al-Alawi [successor to al-Alawi, the subject of Lings's book] proclaimed here publicly. The writer [Murshid] was scoffed and derided by nearly everybody in this region, including the audience for Sidi al-Alawi. But almost immediately after he [Sidi al-Alawi] proclaimed that Ahmed Murad [Murshid] was a true Sufi things began to happen, happen as rapidly as it has been possible to assimilate.

July 9, 1969, Wednesday

I write three letters: to my mother, Betty Holzhauer; to my grandparents, Otis and Mabel Johnson; and to my cousin, Bill Wachob. In all three, I mention that I didn't go to Vilayat's Youth Seminar in Colorado. Jemila, I tell them, is going to New York to spend more time with Vilayat, who—for those who were not familiar with the name—is the director of the International School of Meditation. I think this sounds important. Actually, Vilayat is speaking in Iowa, and she will also be there with him.

Murshid shows today he is aware that his fixation with the "Generals of Semantics" is compulsive. He begins a letter to Baxter M. Geeting, "I must apologize if in writing to you it is like consulting a psychologist or psychiatrist." Murshid wants to contact J. Samuel Bois, the author of *The Art of Awareness, a Text on General Semantics*, which Murshid says he finds "delightful." Geeting, a professor of speech at a college in Sacramento, has no connection that I can discern with this author; nonetheless, not knowing how to contact Bois, Murshid writes to Geeting, "I am taking a sort of liberty to write to you." A four page letter follows. It makes points reiterated here before; afterwards, Murshid sends Shamcher a carbon copy of the letter, along with two more pages entitled "GENERAL SEMANTICS VS. GENERALS' SEMANTICS."

Murshid uses a diary entry letter to Shamcher today to speak primarily about Pir Vilayat and Paul Reps. Murshid notes that Hazrat Inayat Khan's story "The Spirit of Prophesy" in his book *The Way of Illumination* "was nothing but the predictions of what would happen to the 'Prophet's son.' You don't have to read between the lines to see that this has been the story of Hazrat Inayat Khan and Pir Vilayat Inayat Khan." In the story, the followers of the prophet reject the son. After alluding to the growth of feelings of love and brotherhood, Murshid writes,

I had a terrible time—not always successful—in controlling tears during our initiatory ceremonies and the marvelous lecture that Pir Vilayat gave. No wonder there is wonderful enthusiasm in singing aloud: Pir Vilayat Zindabad; Pir Vilayat Zindabad, Pir Vilayat Zindabad; Vilayat Inayat Khan... Paul Reps has now broken with me and it is just as well. He is attached to wealth, fame and loneliness and the latter is the only one of the three he can take to the next world. In this he is inferior to my brother, who is feeling the loneliness so strong that he telephones here more and more.

July 11, 1969, Friday
Today I am conscious all day that Jemila is traveling from Iowa City to New York city to join Pir Vilayat.

July 12, 1969, Saturday
Murshid is as conscious of Jemila's movement as I am, and he is thinking of what her journey to New York means for the future of his dances. I know this from what he writes Premanand Trikanand, Ramdas's grandson, who is living in Hollywood. "Yesterday morning Sam wrote up the *Ramnam* and Ram-Sita dances which, with the Dervish dances, are now destined to go all over the world." The spectacle of Jemila's blooming spiritual illumination has awakened my longing to be able to love more, which I express in the dance class today by "letting go." I free dance during *Ahklak Allah,* when you move as if in the presence of God.

July 14, 1969, Monday

Ayesha, one of Murshid's oracles, calls looking for a book about the centers in the body. When she hears me on the phone, she says I sound down. We finish, and I wonder if there is more to Jemila's attraction to Pir Vilayat than a powerful spiritual connection. Ayesha calls back, solicitous about my mood. I cover my real fears and tell her about failing to find a job today. Ayesha says she'll look for me and pronounces either oracularly or positively that definitely, yes, something will come in a few weeks, but she also gets "loss of determination" from me. Later, finishing L. Adams Beck's *Garden of Vision*, I am moved. I weep. I chant *Ishk Allah Mahbud Lillah* (God is love, lover and beloved). I long to be able to let go, to give in love. Jemila calls. She's going to make arrangements to go to Europe. I am to send her birth certificate to New York so she can get a passport. I don't tell her to check with Murshid.

In a letter to Helen D. Bruner, director of public relations for American Friends of the Middle East, Murshid turns a fundraising slogan back on the sloganeer.

I agree with you thoroughly. A "pat on the back" for a job well done *is* nice to receive... While you are asking for new attitudes, new approaches, etc. and never acknowledging letters of any kind, this person has, via the use of Dervish dances, had Israeli Jews, American non-Israeli Jews, Christians of part-Jewish blood, Muslims and Hindus join with many others in a Christian Seminary doing these and other dances. We would like an occasional "pat on the back." It might even loosen our check book.

July 15, 1969, Tuesday

Sunday Murshid dictated a letter to the Lama Foundation, but told me to wait until Monday to mail it. Monday a letter came from Lama, asking when Murshid is willing to come. Today I answer: Murshid has decided not to go to summer school, which will end August 10th. He's awaiting a visit from Professor Seyyed Hossein Nasr; however, since Dr. Nasr's arrival is not definite, please make the ticket for whenever you want Murshid to come. Lama's letter says interest in the dervish dance cycle has fallen off. I sympathize, saying, I know very well what you mean about waning interest in the dances. I have experienced that and remind myself each time that it's not the dance but the repetition of the sacred phrases that is important. In any case, Murshid will soon come to bring inspiration and many new dances.

Daniel, one of Murshid's regular guitar players for the music that accompanies the dances, reports to me that Murshid proposed Jemila and I move out of the *khankah*! Murshid will often leak his most unsettling news to one disciple, knowing that it will reach the person he wants it to reach without him having to say it directly. According to Daniel, we have to move out of the *khankah* if Jemila goes to Europe. When I ask why, Daniel says it's because Jemila is going without Murshid's permission, plus my recent bad attitude.

I sit in meditation breathing *Toward the One* for maybe forty-five minutes. Several times I see Vilayat's profile in light. I replay the whole sequence of events over and over: Jemila returning radiant from Colorado; Europe being mentioned as an impossible dream; the seesaw, back and forth about New York and Europe; my growing sense of helplessness to influence the process. If love is loss of control, then I am on the verge of a heart opening experience.

July 16, 1969, Wednesday

When I finally tell Murshid Jemila is going to Europe, he says, "For God's sake, stop her." Shortly after, we have a family meeting and Murshid says, "If Jemila goes to Europe, she can't live here any more." Once again, I seek the silence and chant *Ya Wahabo* (O inspiration). The state I'm in requires more than inspiration, but it's the best I can think of. An answer comes: Until your light is lit, you are incapable of considering deeply such a situation. Ask Murshid. I do, and the last thing he says is to repeat, "For God's sake, stop her."

Jemila, Pir Vilayat, and another young woman from the Colorado camp

Chapter 20

Enlightenment

I do not think any persons, real or actual spiritual teachers, have as yet collected the quantity and quality of devotees who come here. Our children's party was quite a success. The opening up of spiritual dancing has proven almost too much. It will go around the world in time and of course be denounced by those who have not had the great experience. They see only in and with and through the ego no matter what they proclaim. (Murshid's letter to Eugene Wagner, July 25, 1969)

My work with the young is increasing. Some of the ideas and methods are being copied. I have the assignment to have 50,000 Americans repeat Allah, and I shall not stop no matter what those calling themselves Muslims say. I cannot teach Shariat [the required rituals for Muslims] and I cannot stop saying Allah. Holy Quran tells us to say Allah. Besides this it works; believe me it works. (Murshid's letter to Shemseddin Ahmed, July 28, 1969)

July 17, 1969, Thursday
While painting after dinner, I feel Murshid will carry my coffee cup away full. This is telepathy. He does, and I call to him. He puts it back.
When I tell Murshid tonight that I talked to Jemila three times and told her we had a lot of work to do, Murshid adds, "both inner and outer."

July 18, 1969, Friday
Today I experience a silent teaching. It happens when I am in the kitchen getting Murshid a lemonade. The juice is in the glass; and when I go for some ice in the freezer, I see an empty ice cube tray. Instead of getting ice from the full tray, I get sidetracked and begin filling the empty ice cube tray with water at the sink. As I take it back to the refrigerator, Murshid comes out and gets some ice for himself! Even before Murshid gets up, I feel the heaviness you feel—but don't always recognize—when your conscience is telling you *not* to go off on your tangent. I am not responsive enough to drop what I am doing and get the ice. This shows how responsive and concentrated I have to train myself to be around Murshid. I can't allow myself to get sidetracked. When I'm in the middle of doing something, I must finish what I start. Another time, Murshid is scooping out hard ice cream. I ask him if I can lend him a strong arm. He says, "Attunement is what counts."

July 19, 1969, Saturday

I feel the significance of *grounding knowledge within,* when I get the feeling of Venus—and perhaps Saturn—during the dance class. At that point, I realize the meaning of Murshid's advice to "get the feeling inside your own self." The note I write to Jemila at her parents' in Iowa echoes Hazrat Inayat Khan telling Shamcher the other people will miss him if he leaves the summer school. How important your trip will be, I tell her, to those who were at camp, especially Jill and Ayesha, who, in a kind sense, envy you. Who wouldn't envy a woman so struck by a man's spiritual teachings, so ignited with love for those teachings, that she followed him for more? I did the same following Pir Vilayat to Los Angeles.

Murshid's letter to Pir Vilayat today is difficult to summarize. It's a laundry list of Murshid's activities, typed single spaced over one and a half pages. As a report by a subordinate to the leader, it must have been gratifying, if not somewhat frightening to the leader. The subordinate is certainly active, he might accurately conclude, if not out of control.

July 20, 1969, Sunday

While I am painting, Murshid calls me in to record Marcia's practices. Marcia is getting a lot of attention recently. ("And Miss Marcia Pavolic, a disciple who has been living at the extreme south end of the State [near San Diego] came up for particular instructions in dances," Murshid wrote yesterday to Pir Vilayat.) Murshid is grooming her for the dance work. Murshid asks when Jemila will be back. I say three weeks from when she left, July 10th. "That's too long," Murshid says, and shortly afterward gives Marcia initiation into the *Ra Keper Ra Atum Ra* Egyptian dance.

Several days ago, I felt I would be the one to introduce the Sufi Pir Vilayat Khan and the Zen Master Philip Kapleau to each other, much as Murshid introduced the Sufi Hazrat Inayat Khan and the Zen monk Nyogen Senzaki. It never happens. Does it serve any purpose to record delusions of grandeur? Only as proof that there were delusions of grandeur.

July 23, 1969, Wednesday

In an afternoon dream, the psychic reading my palm says, "I see death very clearly." And in dream I respond, "Spiritual rebirth."

I ask Murshid three questions today. I get at least three teachings. 1) "Should I be at the door [of the Wednesday night meeting] tonight?" Murshid says, "Whatever your function is." Much later, I remember our agreement with the people at the seminary in San Anselmo, that we aren't allowed to have someone at the door collecting money. Murshid probably knows this, I realize, but doesn't say anything. There is no judgment like, *Don't you remember what our agreement is?* He is practicing *no dualism.*

The pupil and teacher are one. If you blame or judge the disciple, you are blaming or judging yourself. He doesn't put his mind into it. Agreement or not, I just want to get the money for Murshid. 2) When Murshid asks me, "Will you take a letter?" I answer, "May I wash my hands?" Murshid says, "Yes, right here in this room. I'm going to dictate it to you." Confused, I don't know what he is talking about. Now I think he must have been in an abstracted state, concentrating on the letter that was coming through, and only heard a part of what I said; for example, when Murshid said, *Will you take a letter?* he heard, *Mumble blah my hands?* 3) When Murshid says, "Two or three had asked to be initiated," I ask, "Who?" I just wanted to put their names in the esoteric notebook. Murshid answers, "They just came up to me. I didn't get a chance to talk to them." This is about Murshid sharing an encounter that could have a significant impact on his workload.

July 24, 1969, Thursday

After a phone conversation with Jemila in New York, I have three impressions. First, I feel like I'm in a tragedy. Second, when I ask what she'll do in Europe and she says, "Go to his [Vilayat's] house," I say, "It sounds like you're going off to be with your lover." Third, I feel if she goes, she'll never come back.

July 25, 1969, Friday

Murshid is working away at the *khankah* and something Buddhist flies into his mind. (This is the impression I get.) And so he stops work and addresses "Bodhisattva" Eugene Wagner, beginning, "I am interrupting my work here which goes on incessantly." The climax of this letter is featured in this chapter's epigraph, but the subtext for Wagner, the Buddhist, is that all of Murshid's success demonstrates that "there is something going on and going on despite the ego. The attempts to present something called 'Buddhism' via the ego will fail."

July 26, 1969, Saturday

When I get to his house in the early afternoon, Murshid has me make a copy of a letter he wrote today to Shamcher. He does this when he wants to impress me with something or keep me informed of the latest developments. Murshid begins,

My dear Shamcher, I am on the last pages of the Commentary on *The Path of Initiation and Discipleship*. While this is labeled a "Commentary", at the same time it puts on paper the synthesis of various initiations I have had in different mystical schools without in the least making it an autobiographical undertaking.

Autobiographical parts in this just completed commentary are veiled in most places, such as when Murshid speaks knowingly about the

Upanishads ("There is a direct relation between spiritual growth and the experiences of ecstasy or bliss"), Zen Buddhism, Christian mysticism, ancient Egypt, Islamic esotericism, and Walt Whitman ("The efflux of the soul is happiness"). There is overt autobiography in the commentary when Murshid writes,

Once the commentator went into an ashram of a purported Indian saint—there is no assurance that she was not a saint—and he pointed out where she was in the meditation, and where in the lectures, and where she held audience. The disciples all took this as a sign of her greatness, but they did not take it as a sign of the Sufi having any special faculties. How could he know? He knew because there is a science of Peace. The commentator has lived in many wildernesses, in forests inhabited by wild animals. In America he only encountered snakes and in India and Pakistan not even them. He does not know how or why, but there was always a sense of divine protection.

The "commentator" shows up again at the very end, commenting on Hazrat Inayat Khan's statement,

If a man has that one strength which is faith, that is all the power he needs on the path. He can go forward and nothing will hinder him, and in the end, he will accomplish his purpose.

Murshid writes,

That has been the experience of the commentator. Maligned, cheated and robbed, he continued to pursue the path laid down by Hazrat Inayat Khan and especially fulfill the science of commentaries... It [The Path of Initiation and Discipleship] is first, foremost, and last a commentary as Hazrat Inayat Khan would have it. The work itself was an initiation. Much of the time there were struggles going on—all kinds of them. But the last week has been characterized both by more and more disciples coming to Murshid offering help, and more and more having mystical experiences of a considerably higher order than those that have occurred in previous years to anybody. One thing is certain about these experiences, that they belong to a cosmic harmony. One feels much more a guide than a teacher.

Classes have been started both in cosmic drama and in choral singing. I am not in the former at all. I am in the latter as a performer and not as a leader, and that more to encourage others. For at this writing, I am not at all sure of my geography, at least till the end of September. What I am sure of is the general and particular advancement of an ever growing number of young people.

Murshid goes on to assure Shamcher that nothing will affect his cooperation with Pir Vilayat. Speaking again of his own operations, he says, "At this writing the possibilities for radio, television, or cinema attention [are] considerable." (Two days ago, I started to do film work for Fred, a *mureed* who is employed by KQED, a PBS affiliate in San Francisco. Fred has among his credits a series of TV films about Krishnamurti and may at this time be giving thought to his film *Sunseed,* about Murshid and other spiritual teachers.) Continuing his letter to Shamcher, Murshid reports,

There are now in San Francisco at least four cultural integration groups, all mutually exclusive. Two rival ones, totally intellectual, have not only excluded this person and his efforts, but have had the audacity to give pseudo-lectures on Sufism—whatever that means."

Murshid and Pir Vilayat in the back yard of the *khankah*

One of these groups happens to be Haridas Chaudhuri's Cultural Integration Fellowship. We often go there for Sunday services, but Dr. Chaudhuri never accepts Murshid's prowess. Neither, at first, does Chaudhuri's teacher in India, Professor Chatterji. An amusing story of the relationship between Murshid and Dr. Chaudhuri's teacher is found in a letter Murshid writes to Professor Jacob Needleman, December 15, 1969.

On my sixtieth birthday I was given a special tea by Swami Ranganathananda Maharaj who was then stationed in New Delhi and also present were the then Vedantist leader of Bengal and with him Prof. S.C. Chatterji, then head of the Department of Philosophy at the University of Calcutta. Without waiting for an introduction Prof. Chatterji broke into a hostile diatribe against this land [the United States] and its selection of Germans as the spokesmen for their philosophy, Germans of high social and institutional repute and very, very high up in "Cultural Integration." Swamiji said, "Why don't you listen to him before you attack him?" Chatterji had attacked the long list of what I have called EPOOPS—there used to be a lot of them, a few still around—that is, European Professors of Oriental Philosophy. I turned to Chatterji and asked, "Which would you rather hear the

Flute-of-Krishna or have me discourse on the CHANDOGYA UPANISHAD? Right off, no preparation?" Swamiji said, "He means exactly what he says." Professor Chatterji apologized before noted witnesses. But you could never hear me present the Flute-of-Krishna or discourse on the CHANDOGYA or any other Upanishad before his pupil who heads "Cultural Integration" in these parts—not on your life, nor his! "Cultural Integration" has to be very selective indeed, and the more PhD degrees the better!!!!

Murshid never lets up on Dr. Chaudhuri. In fifteen letters between November, 1968, and August, 1970, Murshid's tone is as churlish as in the following conclusions from three of those letters. "I am very, very sorry you have substituted realism for reality." "In hopes that someday your operations may have some relation to your own words." "We hope someday you will come to recognize the moral worth of objective knowledge." Recounting the Chatterji incident above to Dr. Chaudhuri in a letter March 25, 1970, Murshid calls it "one of the most memorable incidents of my life." It is, he says, "going into my autobiography of course, or into my biography." And so it is. Murshid continues on to Shamcher, unloading on a couple of people who have money, and who collaborated with Nyogen Senzaki.

It was all right for an Asian, Reps, or a Mrs. McCandless to go before the public as "collaborators" with the late Nyogen Senzaki, when all they did was to put up the money. Each became famous (!) by such means, and each has been horrified that Samuel Lewis who has possession of many of the late Senzaki's writings should even try to get them published. This is actually amusing, because the actual Zen masters are all for it. They want Senzaki's work to get better known. This person wanted to turn over any financial benefits therefrom to Senzaki's successor, Roshi Soyen Nakagawa, while the Roshi wanted to turn any financial benefits over to us!

Murshid was even harsher toward McCandless and Reps in his diary letter to Vocha Fiske, written two months before today's letter to Shamcher. (May 27, 1969)

It is all right for Mrs. McCandless or Paul Reps to use Nyogen Senzaki's things— this is "good", but for Sam Lewis, this is illegal, mayhem, plagiarism and downright *stealing.*

Near the end of the letter to Shamcher, Murshid writes, "Attention must be paid to a paper on 'The Organic Gardening of a Sufi Khankah'." Murshid actually writes this article and submits it to *Organic Gardening* for publication. He hears nothing. He finally writes the magazine February 17, 1970.

Sometime ago I sent you an article for your publication entitled "The Garden of Inayat." You wrote saying that it was being considered, and I have heard nothing further for some time. If you are not planning on publishing this article, will you return it to me please so that it may be published elsewhere? Enclosed you will find some stamps to cover postage costs.

Relations with *Organic Gardening* grow ugly by August 20, 1970. Murshid writes,

Thank you for your notice "YOU CANT BE REPLACED."[This was some kind of patronizing reader appreciation cash solicitation.] This is certainly news to me. I don't understand it at all. One of your editors came out here, met the writer, and begged for an article which was written at his request. And then, following the usual "Judeo-Christian" ethic it was returned. I don't know which side you are on in your own editorial, so we are withdrawing; sending you no money nor any subscriptions, or anything. Our own garden is thriving magnificently. Our own people are prospering in New Age food concerns and in raising vegetables organically. I agree with your philosophy, but I totally disdain your ethics. There is nothing else for me to do but discontinue having relations with you after receiving such treatment.

Driving on the way to the dance class with Murshid sleeping in the car, I miss the exit to Corte Madera. Murshid awakes and says, "I know what you're doing when I'm asleep better than when I'm awake." I say, "You knew I missed the turn?" Then I think: Murshid knows what I'm doing even when he's sleeping!

July 27, 1969, Sunday

Murshid's clear message in his letter today to Dr. Seyyed Hossain Nasr, an Iranian born, Islamic expert in residence at Harvard University, is (to paraphrase) I have been distinguished by experiences just like those of Prophet Mohammed.

Allah, to Whom be all Praise, has chosen at His times and convenience to lift the veils of this person. But Allah to Whom be all praise, chose to lift veils and one was blessed by the manifestation first of Khizr and then of Mohammed.

In dream last night, I watched a cat-bird show. At the conclusion, my bird flew to the cat's head and the cat ate it. "Bird" in my dream symbol book signifies spiritual freedom; ability to soar to higher awareness; freedom from material ties. "Eat" in the dream symbol book suggests nourishment is needed, whether mental, emotional, physical, or spiritual. "Cat" is the feminine part of the self.

July 28, 1969, Monday

Murshid offers pain relief in a letter to Sharab, who wrote him on the 21st, suggesting, "Now you should breathe in often, concentrating on *YA SHAFEE* [God is the Healer] with the inhalation, *YA KAFEE* [God is the Remedy] with the exhalation. If the pain stays in a particular place, concentrate on it and breathe in and out with ALLAH, and also feel the sound ALLAH in the place of pain. This should be most helpful" [the latter being the *irfan* practice].

I just called Waterloo, Iowa. My suspicions are confirmed. Jemila has gone to Europe. The feeling is one of disappointment. As I lie in bed, I see

Vilayat seated, his right cheek showing its profile. Jemila is kneeling, Vilayat instructing her. Then she is crying in his lap. Next, I see her alone in sexual frenzy. Feelings of jealousy? I am confused. I have five jobs waiting to be scheduled: 1) a fence in Mill Valley for a woman named Smith; 2) Fred's film about Krishnamurti; 3) Phil Green's film on the Hopis (he works at KQED with Fred, and needs an assistant editor); 4) a retaining wall to be built with Jeremy; and 5) more ditch digging for a water line at the lumber yard in Novato.

Murshid reiterates his message to Dr. Nasr that traditional Islam (*Shariat*) does not produce the effect the Prophet wanted in a letter today to S. Ahmed excerpted in this chapter's epigraph. This letter also contains an interesting definition of Sufism (*Tassawuf*): "the science of the Being and Presence of Allah."

August 1, 1969, Friday

The chapter in Murshid's book *Toward Spiritual Brotherhood* on "The Individual in the Commune" introduces the concept of "dictator communes."

While the communal movements are verbally dedicated to efforts to enfranchise those hampered by establishments, they have only too often merely established new power structures, often *dictatorships*.[emphasis mine] These dictatorships do give ample opportunities for the leaders to have full scope for their own innate faculties but do not give ample scope to others. Therefore, many of the so-called new order and New Age efforts are only so verbally, not actually. (*Toward Spiritual Brotherhood*, pp.82-83)

The impression I had upon reading this passage the first time was that it applied to Don McCoy, who was running Olompali ranch north of Novato. Looking at it again today—a few months later, in 1969—I think it refers to Murshid himself. Odd that I should write this. The reason for my insolence may be obvious when I tell you that I am going to be forced to move out of the *khankah*. That aside, the idea is that the ideal commune allows the individual greater expression of his or her personality. I want to know how to express my personality.

A month from now Murshid will describe himself as a dictator. When addressing Shamcher about the continuing problem of "over-sleeping" by some members of the *khankah*, Murshid writes (August 25, 1969), "There is practically no time and every now and then I guess I get rather high or *dictatorial* because of the lack of energy among several who could be of great help."

Murshid asks me to write again to the Lama Foundation. I tell them Murshid's airplane arrangement: He leaves San Francisco Thursday, August 7th at 9:30 A.M. and arrives in Albuquerque at 12:45 P.M. Next, Murshid will fly Texan Air from Albuquerque (no more than an hour by car) to Santa Fe, but he doesn't give me the critical information—his time of arrival. I enclose the last *Oracle*, which contains Murshid's picture, so they'll have a clue what he looks like. I add: Murshid is short, doesn't act anything like a lot of people's ideas of how a holy man ought to act, and will more than likely be dressed in ordinary American clothes—not a dervish robe.

front: Melvin, Mary Sue Sitton, Benefsha Gest, Murshid, Vilayat, Jemila, and two unidentified females *Back row:* David Hoffmaster and Mansur

August 2, 1969, Saturday

"The feeling now is fear," I write today as the implications of Jemila's going to Europe without Murshid's permission sink in. It means we'll have to move out of the *khankah.*

Writing today to Archie Bahm, Murshid's first impulse is networking—specifically, as regards Oliver Reiser, a colleague of both men. "I have been going over your notes with a definite purpose in mind which may be of importance to the work of our good friend Oliver Reiser." Murshid has reread Bahm's book *The World's Living Religions,* and proceeds to discuss it from four points of view. In the middle of a rigorous intellectual argument ("In this sense science is true when the researches or laboratory work of one is corroborated by others"), Murshid segues into an example.

I once did work on Fuchsias and Primroses and was surprised to find that a whole research class at the University of California in Los Angeles was doing some research work on the same flowers at the same time with identically the same results. But this may not happen often and the search for "Integrals" in life is still worth pursuing.

In another letter he writes himself to Lama today, Murshid repeats the information he had me send them, and acknowledges receipt of their check for travel expenses. This is only Murshid's second letter to Lama. He sets them at ease about his ability to rough it, and introduces his program.

I have learned a little about your procedures from Mansur Otis Johnson; and having both studied and been disciplined in Oriental cultures as well as having lived "ruggedly," there is no problem here. But I am assuming you wish to know something about Sufism in some sense and am ready therefore. Sufism may be "taught" in one of several ways: a. Meditation, etc. b. Breathing practices, etc. c. Lectures d. Music, dancing, chanting.

Seek and ye shall find. This seems to be the answer to the question I posed yesterday, *How can I express my personality?* The answer I get is, *In everything.* I begin by cleaning my room and buying elemental colors to put around. I listen to Beethoven's Second Symphony in the kitchen for the second time today, after having taken another oracle by reaching into the jar with 365 *Bowl of Saki* aphorisms that Murshid has had us place in the rose colored dining room. There is a tiny piece of paper for each day of the year with a saying on it. I get: "Man's thoughts prepare for him whatever happiness or unhappiness that he may be experiencing." Last night the oracle I got was: "It is really a very high stage on the path of love when one can love another and expect no return."

August 3, 1969, Sunday

Appreciation of the teacher comes by the lack of judging the teacher. Because judging the teacher is the fault that very often manifests, it manifests even not knowingly. No *mureed* can say that he has not gone through it in some way or the other. I remember once having seen Murshid's golden shoes and wondering why Murshid must have gold shoes. It was not a lack of appreciation, but it was insolence on my part. My answer came very soon, from the lips of my Murshid, because there, everything is known. And his answer was that "the wealth of the earth is at my feet." Gold is the wealth; that at the feet; that is the symbolism. Therefore, a *mureed* who does not guard against that judging quality, which brings about lack of appreciation, may develop the tendency not to appreciate fully, and in that case, he cannot be fully benefited. (Unpublished teachings of Hazrat Inayat Khan)

In response to the dictatorial tendencies I am experiencing, I make a list of Murshid's faults. I do this in extreme disregard of the inscription above, which I only discover later. I seize upon this teaching to minimize my offense; it shows all *mureeds* judge other people, as I said before, "in some way or the other."

WHAT I CONSIDER BAD IN MURSHID
WHO IS MY EXAMPLE, PEACE BE ON HIM
+ The stupid tests, like asking me for a sheet of paper when Murshid knows I don't have it and Moineddin does.
+ The disharmony that results when Murshid sits at tea on Thursday nights after Gatha Class.
+ Murshid's sense of insincerity—his puckish tone of voice when you meet him in everyday life.
+ Murshid making people uptight by asking them, "What do you think? Eh? Eh?" about things which nobody either cares about or has time to think about.
+ Murshid's non-sequiturs.

After seeing what I have written, after judging Murshid so harshly, I am compelled to write a balancing list of:

WHAT IS GOOD ABOUT MURSHID
+ Murshid's personal sacrifice for the cause of God—giving so much time to teaching.
+ Murshid's devotion to Hazrat Inayat Khan's instructions to be Defender of the Message and, in another tradition, the loyalty shown by him naming the house—the name Nyogen Senzaki gave him—Mentorgarten.
+ The way Murshid mingles with people, although this is balanced by "insincerity" and "uptight" above.
+ Murshid's intelligence.
+ Murshid's awareness.
+ Murshid's wisdom.
+ Murshid's compassion.

With my inner eye, I see Jemila in France. This is the morning she is supposed to leave France. (Jemila offered Nathan the choice of going on this trip, and Nathan didn't want to go.) Since Jemila being in Europe reminds me we can't live at the *khankah*, there is an answering thought of my living at Murshid's in San Francisco. So many times Shaikh al-Alawi has been on my mind. He's the one who lost his wife as a result of his devotion to his Shaikh. As al-Alawi tells it in Martin Lings's book,

I was very much addicted to learning, and would sometimes steep myself in books the whole night long; and I was helped in these nocturnal studies by a Shaikh whom I used to bring back to our house. After this had been going on for several months, my wife took offence and claimed divorce from me on the grounds of my not giving her her rights, and she had in fact some cause to complain. (*A Sufi Saint of the Twentieth Century*, pp.49-50)

I'd say it this way: When Jemila and I lived in Bolinas I was occupied all the time watching my breath. I grew very detached from the earth plane, so that when my wife would speak to me, her words and thoughts would appear ridiculous. I was unable to answer in a normal amount of time. Sometimes

I would be pondering Jemila's statements for a long time. Sometimes I would dismiss them as too ridiculous to waste any time trying to figure out. Questions like, "Do you love me?" were so patently ridiculous. My love was expressed in the nonverbal fact that I lived contentedly with Jemila and entertained no thought of any other woman as my wife. Wrong.

August 4, 1969, Monday

On the eve of his departure Thursday for the state of New Mexico, where they might meet, it's as if Murshid is reviewing Archie Bahm's intellectual history. Writing again today, Murshid says,

The over-all outlook which was mentioned in the previous letter was fully justified by re-reading your *Organicism* [complete title: *Organicism: The Philosophy of Interdependence*] and I am unable to find weaknesses—they may be there but I have not found them.

August 6, 1969, Wednesday

Once again, Murshid addresses Dr. Seyyed Hossein Nasr, and once again, he questions *Sharia* (the Arabic for *Shariat*) the body of traditional Islamic law.

In men's minds, indeed in the minds of a lot of men, there are "thought-partners" to God. Among the Jews it is race; among the Christians it is doctrines; among the Muslims it is most often something very vague called "*Sharia*," something also vague called "consensus", and something not so vague, i.e. the historical, the very historical personality called "Mohammed" (on whom be peace)... I do not know what "*Sharia*" means. I do know what "Act as if in the Presence of Allah" and "Remember, if you do not see Him, verily He sees you" means. But this does not make a man a "Muslim"—far from it!

Murshid, who previously indicated to Nasr that he doesn't practice *Shariat*, ends by offering himself as an example for Muslim traditionalists to deal with.

Today one has a class in *Mushahida* [contemplation] and our good friend, Saadia Khawar, will be present and learn directly from the person whom she regards as a Murshid. This is a real method, a real outlook which opens up real facets of the real inner personality without any lucid or confusing metaphysics. It definitely exemplifies *La illa ha el il Allah*, and makes it practical for those *who have risen to the heights of direct perception* [emphasis mine].

August 7, 1969, Thursday

The day Murshid leaves for Lama, Jemila arrives home. It's the day I recollect a dream in which Jemila is in the middle of a lovemaking scene with someone I characterize as "our oriental teacher of *chi*."

August 8, 1969, Friday

When I ask Jemila to confirm or deny my intuition, my feeling, my inner sight and my dream about her relationship with Vilayat, she confesses. I am crushed. My concept of the purely spiritual relationship of Jemila and Vilayat—I finally realize—is not true. I become enlightened.

August 9, 1969, Saturday

I write to Murshid at Lama: The man who calls himself the head of the Sufi Order, into whose hands I entrusted my wife Jemila, has betrayed my trust and committed adultery with my wife. I address my letter to Murshid in my moment of heartbreak like I would address my own father if he were still alive: "Dear Father," I begin. I ask Murshid to forgive my ego interference with his loving warnings. I tell Murshid I'd seen Jemila with my inner eye in "sexual frenzy" and about the dream the night before she got home. I ask permission not to have to attend any of Vilayat's summer camps. In the following days, months, and years, my enlightenment will burn deeper.

Chapter 21

The Aftermath

I do not know whether you will recall the incident in your home in New York when I was asked to die in the name of [Meher] Baba in five minutes and to the discernment of all present, did just that. (Murshid's letter to Elizabeth Patterson, Myrtle Beach, South Carolina, August 25, 1969)

I once went to a New Year's Eve party given in a most fashionable home in North Hollywood. Three separate groups of so-called spiritualists came asking Sam where they could get money. They all claimed super-sensory faculties, but still they had to ask a stranger where they could get money. It was plain as the nose on the face—all they had to do was ask the host. He was very wealthy, and would have given, but none of the "clairvoyants" dared to approach him. It was very funny. (Murshid's letter to Julie Medlock, August 26, 1969)

A few years back Sidi Abu Salem Alawi came here. I was just told a Sufi teacher was coming, nothing else. But I brought a picture of his great Pir-O-Murshid, wore my dervish robe, and offended and astounded the audience by translating directly the third part of his speech although in the ordinary state I know no Arabic. When he was asked if he would establish a khankah here, he said no because a man in the audience had the baraka [blessing]. The audience walked out. But now the new generation is walking in and the blessings are given, actually given in my Ziker dances and no nonsense. (Murshid's letter to F. Clive-Ross, Middlesex, England, August 26, 1969)

Tears of joy are more precious than pearls (The Complete Sayings of Hazrat Inayat Khan, p.170)

August 10, 1969, Sunday

After staying at the *khankah* for three days, Jemila leaves today and flies to Boston, en route to her sister's home in New Hampshire, where she left Nathan. Then, I presume, because she doesn't tell me, she goes to France to be with Vilayat *again*. It is raining tears in the van after I leave Jemila at the San Francisco airport. I cry and cry and cry all the way back to the City. When I get to the place where the Farmer's Market is off to the left, I find myself saying, I dedicate my life to you, God, I dedicate my life to you, God. I have ecstasies of joy and weeping while driving to Lagunitas, a small town in the redwoods north of San Francisco, to do film work in the studio Fred Cohn has set up in his house. My mental themes, compulsively repeated, are variations on the thought: *I've got a real father and there is a father-son relationship higher than physical father-son.*

August 12, 1969, Monday

At the family meeting at the *khankah* without Murshid (who left August 7th for Lama), pregnant Fatima, wife of Moineddin, wants to know the answers to some questions. She asks, "What are we going to do to establish the *khankah* as a whole thing working together?" She fills the space after her question with two more questions. "Are we going to get somebody to live here and help?" Nobody knows. "Is Jemila coming back or not?" No one can answer her. Hassan, the husband of Jehanara, wants to know what Murshid was told. I share the gist of the letter I sent to Murshid on August 9, 1969. Hassan wants to know what Murshid said to me before he left. I tell him Murshid told me to meditate.

August 14, 1969, Thursday

Murshid writes a personal letter to me (which I consider so precious that I hide it and can't find it to this day) and tells me to think of Mother Krishnabai, the late Papa Ramdas's devoted disciple and spiritual successor. I take comfort in the thought of her unconditional love, and contrast her chaste relationship with her spiritual teacher with the promiscuity of Pir Vilayat. Murshid also suggests I think of Inayat Khan. This is confusing, since Jemila told me before she left that Vilayat said Inayat Khan sent her to him. Whose side is God on? My mind is blown, because how could the son of the man who wrote the sentiment below do this to me?

The heart of every man both good and bad is the abode of God, and care should be taken never to wound anyone by word or act. (Hazrat Inayat Khan, *The Bowl of Saki*, July 16)

I am feeing so sorry for my self I conveniently overlook Khan's guidance in *Gayan*, where it is written:

"One should take oneself to task instead of putting one's fault on another." "The human heart must first be melted, like metal, before it can be molded into a desirable character." "Pleasure blocks, but pain clears the way of inspiration." "The pain of life is the price paid for the quickening of the heart." "A worldly loss often turns into spiritual gain."

August 15, 1969, Friday

This afternoon Murshid writes the family at the *khankah* a postcard style letter from the Lama Foundation.

Funny experience at Albuquerque where met Frances [von Briesen] and Barbara [Durkee]. Overtaken by rainstorm—lots of rain this year. In the middle met Doyle [disciple Diane Ferry's boyfriend]. Things fine with him and he may remain here. Diane working. Both may come for darshan Sunday. Gave them [the Lama community] our *Om* last night and made them cheerful especially Cal who has been at my Monday night meetings [in San Francisco]. He arrived the day after Mansur left. But people work here and work hard. My hut [for teachers, which burned in the fire of 1996] unfinished but should be ready by Wednesday. Possible that I may come here later. Ram Dass' article in *Oracle* far better than expected. He has been here and will return in October. This much better than his New England seclusion. Much more harmony and work than expected. By next year (or before) should be good for article in *Organic Gardening* but already good for article in *Oracle*. May give them copies of *Oracle* at *darshan* Sunday. Tomorrow hope to visit new Morning Star community [located, like Lama, on the western slope of the Sangre de Cristo Mountains] in morning. Start *darshans* and Sufi lectures in P.M. Taught at least four dances this A.M. Very well received. Feel fine but sleeping on account of altitude. Like place, views and people. Next year, *inshallah*, we might send Moineddin and Fatima here to instruct parents. Tonight hope to add chants but will look over [the] literature [I have] with me. Then will ask what they want both spiritually and materially. They also have a room being constructed for meetings when there are squabbles. Around 30 people here. Love and blessings, [signed] Murshid.

August 16, 1969, Saturday

Murshid notifies the *khankah* in a letter of his pending arrival Thursday night (August 21, 1969) in San Francisco on TWA. Murshid is sometimes cooking for the Lama community, gardening, visiting nearby communities, and giving classes morning and evening, not to mention interviews. No wonder what comes through most strongly in this letter is Murshid's fatigue.

I sorely and sadly need a vacation. They say Murshid puts in more hours than anybody else... Will have to discuss "vacation" when I return. If Khawar's [Saadia Khawar Khan's] aunt comes I cannot get away so easily, but want a real vacation, perhaps with Mansur, perhaps with somebody else. Here they say I work harder than anybody else.

August 17, 1969, Sunday

The occasion of one lady at Lama wishing to go over Murshid's poem "Saladin" pushes Murshid's thoughts beyond work already done. Murshid tells the folks at the *khankah*,

There are too many book definitions of "Sufi" and too few who have had either the Divine Vision or its most important derivatives. The basis of all of these is in "Saladin" but one's real great work has not even started. It is possible, *inshallah*, before Saadia goes, that Wali Ali may help with the most important epic which will live beyond Murshid. One is more and more aware of the work to be done and it is possible that "in that day will the sun rise in the West and all men seeing will believe." As yet the inspirations are not so great as at Myrtle Beach [Meher Baba's place in North Carolina] or [at the tomb of] Mian Mir or the Garden of Inayat, but they will come when Allah wills. One feels that one will take a typewriter on future visits.

From a man who leaves such an extensive written record, Murshid's tagline from this letter is particularly intriguing. He concludes, "Everything does not have to be reported; some things may be told, some never told."

August 19, 1969, Tuesday

I have had no will power to get up early in the morning since Jemila left. I'm sleeping a lot. Murshid's letter from the Lama Foundation (see above, August 15, 1969) comes today. It impresses me with "work," and I have been typing all day. I'll paint some later, go to bed early and get up tomorrow.

August 21, 1969, Thursday

Last night I dream about traveling with Murshid. Today Murshid is scheduled to arrive from New Mexico.

August 22, 1969, Friday

The day after he returns, Murshid hits the ground running. In addition to delivering the predictable blast at Dr. Chaudhuri, Murshid takes A.B. Patel, the editor of *World Union*, severely to task.

I personally do not countenance the rejection of the teaching of Sri Shankaracharya [God and man are one] and the denial in practice that the Divinity is in human beings while asserting and asserting very strongly that this same Divinity may manifest in specialized institutions of this same imperfect humanity.

The "specialized institutions" are perhaps Mr. Patel's own *World Union* or the entire Sri Aurobindo Ashram. After listing what he considers well known spiritual failures like "the Baha'i Movement, the Theosophists, the Roerich Museum," Murshid says, they all placed "the institutions of man, or, as you are doing, the folk-lore of man above the Divine Inspirations and *prajna*."

August 23, 1969, Saturday

In Murshid's absence, the dreams are so frequent I put a piece of paper beside my bed to record them. As I prepare to put the sheet out today I think, *The dreams are not as vivid as last week.* Murshid's back. Murshid's diary entry for today is a letter to W.D. Begg.

The events of the past month have been fearfully active, but when one begins to make THE REALITY of Allah, then Allah not only walks to him but with him. This is demonstrable and has been demonstrated... The God experience has nothing to do with intellectual prowess... I have just returned from the State of New Mexico where not only was I sent for but the plans are to recall me and have me teach the Oriental philosophies based as they are, on direct mystical experiences with or without book substantiations... No more pretense of mystical or esoteric prowess but actual demonstrations and the communication of Love, human and divine; the performance of *akhlak Allah* [the manner of God], the chanting of *Ziker* with a single Indian mantra [*Om Sri Ram Jai Ram Jai Jai Ram*] opened hearts.

In Murshid's absence, Saadia received hospitality at both his houses. In sending a check to Begg, Murshid includes Saadia.

I am at the moment enclosing a check for Fifty Dollars, and ask that you make a contribution out of this of Rs. 100 to SYED ANVEEH AHMED, HAJI NISAH MANZIL, and DARGA SHARIF. One is rushing this in the hopes that it will arrive before the *Urs*. Both my goddaughter, Miss (Prof.) Saadia Khawar Khan and myself feel totally with you in Love, Joy, Peace and Divinity.

August 25, 1969, Monday

Last night in dream Jemila said she wants a divorce. Very flip. Murshid uses his letter to Shamcher today to vent frustration with close associates with low energy and a tendency to oversleep. Murshid writes he has "sufficient funds but very insufficient assistance. The people at Lama and the visitors to the *khankah* realize this, and when the disciples here at hand realize this, no doubt they [Moineddin] will desist from their long hours of over-sleeping." Shamcher need not read between the lines of Murshid's letter to discern the upheaval going on at the *khankah*.

Last night we had the most unusual "family meeting." For the first time there was no financial problem. But one woman [Jemila] has left the *khankah* with or without reason; her replacement [Marty] left only to discover she had no real cause for that; her replacement [Gwen] in turn has not been well; the house mother [Fatima] will soon become a real mother; and we had to consider very seriously inviting non-disciples who are applicants and need homes to replace the unfortunate disciples too concerned with their problems, or over-sleeping.

Murshid reminds Mrs. Elizabeth Patterson [see epigraph to this chapter] why he left the Baba movement. "I had to withdraw from the Baba movement because of the questionable ethical standards of personalities presumably high in his entourage." If this was a temporary setback, Murshid tells her, it didn't stop him.

Today, before God, I am still operating, tomorrow, before God if he so wills, I shall still be operating. I do not believe there can be any limitation imposed upon any human being by any church, sect, or legal entity.

Murshid is preparing the way for the vacation he sorely needs. He writes today to a former follower of Fazal Inayat Khan's in the Seattle area, Charlotte Brautlacht. Her Sufi name is Atiya. "The plan is to leave here on September 13—and one just remembers that that is *HEJIRAT DAY*, the anniversary of the departure of Hazrat Inayat Khan from India in 1910!

The situation is this: One needs a vacation and would like to travel with
Mansur Johnson, the esoteric secretary who has his station wagon."

I first saw Greek dancing at Murshid's birthday party at the Minerva
Café on Eddy Street in San Francisco. I wanted very much to learn to do it.
Those four waiters doing the dance Anthony Quinn did at the end of *Zorba
the Greek* touched my soul. Tonight I take Fred, my film boss, to dine with
me at the Minerva, a cavernous place with banquet rooms and a dance
floor. Pictures of famous patrons, presidents, and film actors line the back
wall. The four waiters, wearing red vests once again do the Zorba dance. I
am in ecstasy. After their performance, I offer to pay our waiter if he will
teach me. The waiter says, "Eat your dinner. The lesson starts at half past
seven. A regular class meets then. Anyone can join. Anna is the teacher."
Tonight I have my first Greek dance lesson.

August 26, 1969, Tuesday

Murshid's first topic in both his letters to F. Clive-Ross in England
and Julie Medlock at the Sri Aurobindo Ashram today concerns Saadia's
winning first prize with an essay he wrote. Near the end of Murshid's letter
to Julie, there is a particularly poignant short sentence: "There is still time,
but not much." Without speculating on whether Murshid is meaning his
time remaining on earth or his advanced age, I know with hindsight he has
a little over a year to live.

Anticipating teaching at Lama next summer, Murshid sends $25 to
Anandashram in India. "This is not an offering," he says; "it is to ask you to
send some literature, any literature, to LAMA FOUNDATION." Describing
Lama in Hindu terms, Murshid writes,

There are two types of communes arising, one of those who seek spiritual teachers
and are very *sattvic* [refined] in all respects but with a degree of *rajas* [activity] needed
for karma yoga. The other type is definitely *tamasic* [inactive] and need not concern
us.

Murshid has predicted the spread of his dances throughout the world to
other correspondents before. Today, he sees the eventuality of Americans
introducing spiritual dances in India, and he jokes with Anandashram,
"It will be very funny for Americans to be coming to Asia and offering
spiritual dances, but that is very probable, *inshallah.*"

August 28, 1969, Thursday

I cry at the table today. It's because Murshid tells of somebody giving
him instructions by whispering in his ear. I get a glimpse of worlds beyond
name and form. It melts my heart. This information—some mantra—is
what Murshid needed to get into the Nakshibandi Order, the Sufi order
focusing on symbolism.

Later, I ask Murshid to help me respond to something I have received from Libre, a community in Colorado I visited, where I interviewed cofounders painter Dean Fleming and Peter Rabbit. Murshid dictates my response, which criticizes the clarity of one of their brochures. The response, doomed to go unanswered, concludes with these damning remarks about Stewart Brand's Bible for new age communities, the *Whole Earth Catalog*.

What appears clear is that the words "whole earth" have no particular relation to the whole earth at all. Where anything definite is mentioned or implied it is clear; but when poetical phrases are used for actualities, we are confused.

I sign it, and afterwards have second thoughts, as I did when I was getting ice for Murshid's lemonade. But the letter is in the mail. Predictably, there is no further communication from my friends at Libre. In this instance, I feel for the first time a dualism in my relation with Murshid, as though his goals (to awaken others) are at odds with my purpose (to establish a friendship).

August 29, 1969, Friday

Murshid takes me in the office, and I reveal my feelings about the loss I am experiencing. I weep. Murshid tells me to feel assured. He says anything I do is right. I go to my room and weep some more. I read "Suras" (God speaking through the kindled soul) in *Gayan*, trying to get a feeling for Inayat Khan.

Blessed is he who has found in life his life's purpose.
Blessed is he who resteth in the abode of his soul.
Blessed is he who heareth the call from the minaret of his heart.
Blessed is he who seeth the star of his soul as the light that is seen in the port from the sea.
Blessed are the innocent who believe and trust.
Blessed are they who patiently strive in the cause of truth and do not weary.
Blessed are they who fear lest they cause another the slightest hurt by thought, word or deed.

I start to go downstairs and, halfway down, I hear Murshid weeping in the office. I stop and let him be. Then I feel once more, but in a way I have never experienced before, the sorrow of Murshid's whole life.

August 30, 1969, Saturday

Having read that having a life's purpose is a blessing, I reaffirm that I'm here to serve Murshid, to serve God, to do whatever I can do to help the message of God spread far and wide. At this moment, I decide the purpose of my life.

348

September 1, 1969, Monday

It seems there was a Pakistani feast, cooked by Saadia, at Murshid's over the weekend, with "a big houseful of guests." I know this from Murshid's letter to Irene, a person I do not know. Although Murshid has indicated to other correspondents he needs and plans a vacation, to Irene, he reveals that "it is still uncertain but if I go to Seattle it will not be a vacation in the true sense." (The next chapter, "On Vacation with Murshid," illustrates Murshid's premonition.)

I think seriously of divorce today, focusing not so much on Jemila's love for Vilayat, but on her lack of love for Murshid. The most serious ground for divorce is Jemila's lack of devotion for Murshid. If we can't agree on this focus for our lives, maybe marriage is not an option. When the phone rings, it is Jemila asking, "Do you want me to come back? Do you want to get a divorce?" "I don't know," is my reply.

When I seek Murshid's guidance, he looks at Jemila's letter and advises me to be courteous and indefinite when I reply. Murshid offers about Jemila, "She acts as if we were so many selves. You act as if there is a God." I say I don't know if I do. Murshid asks my feelings, and I begin by telling him about my decision to dedicate my life to God. "Didn't I just say so?" Murshid says. "Anything you do is right. You've got wisdom. Feel self-assured."

September 2, 1969, Tuesday

I write a letter to Jemila.

I have quite surrendered to God. I was thrilled to receive your letter the other day but puzzled by your questions, such as, "Do you want me to come back?" to which I can only answer, "Do you want to come back?" That is my feeling in the matter. I have quite surrendered to God. I am here; going forward, doing what I can to help the Message of God spread far and wide, and you must tell me as soon as you know what you plan to do.

September 3, 1969, Wednesday

For many months Murshid has been cultivating Charlotte Brautlacht (Atiya), Fazal Inayat Khan's former disciple. Shamcher introduced him to her, and there have been correspondence, a discussion of Sufi study papers, and reports on activities. Murshid's words to Irene two days ago were that, if he should go to Seattle, "it will not be a vacation in the true sense." Well, oh my God, the quality of the typing in the letter Murshid writes today to Atiya, by virtue of its appearance alone, is enough to warn Atiya (although Shamcher surely already has) that something out of the ordinary is headed her way. Murshid types the letter himself. His touch is light, his mood is excited, and three or four letters on each single-spaced line are missing, fragments appearing above or below the line, sometimes half above the line, nothing below. The letter is visual chaos.

Murshid explains, "This is written in the middle of excitement." He talks about being greeted by old people upon his return from Lama and mentions programs with Saadia being "received gloriously." Saadia will leave after more programs scheduled for next weekend "and I for the northwest, riding with my esoteric secretary, Mansur Johnson. The reason for this is that Mansur has been going through a dramatic tragedy and we both need to get away." Murshid asks Atiya to send a road map! He hints—really incoherently, since besides the aforementioned typos, there are misspellings ('qua te s also' stands for 'quite often')—"I may even have another disciple [along with me on the trip] but we use the station wagon for sleeping quite often and there is no special financial problem at the moment from this end." The unreadable typing and misspelling must have created an impression one can only imagine. The inchoate message: I may be bringing two people, whom I can afford to pay for if you are unable to give hospitality.

September 5, 1969, Friday

In spiritual dances with Murshid, Jemila played both Rama in the Ram Dance and Krishna in the Krishna Dance. Her departure and indefinite absence from the *khankah* is something Murshid takes up in a letter to Marcia Pavolic.

Jemila has left the *khankah*, sometimes for noble, sometimes for "little girl" reasons. This means I must rearrange the leading dance work. This is not so easy as it sounds. Two of my young women disciples have passed the initiatory tests and I shall also have to go into meditation, or subject all of us to tests to ascertain because ego-feelings must not interfere. There must be a new Radha for Krishna and also a Sita.... (Radha was the consort of Krishna and Sita was the wife of Rama). It may just be that you will be asked to come to the *khankah* with Jemila away and Fatima soon to be in labor. The replacements are not available due to other complications. So I'll take this up soon. Gwen Zeinob [Gwen's new spiritual name] was to have gone to Novato [the *khankah*] but she is signed up for Art School and remains in San Francisco.

What has Murshid been telling every correspondent this week? Tomorrow and Sunday we are dancing here in connection with the Precita Park-Bernal Heights annual Fair. And Tuesday night a try-out at the Family Dog (a mass audience venue) at the beach. Both also in connection with Pakistani ladies' costume exhibit. After that I hope to leave. Today is Friday. We leave next Wednesday.

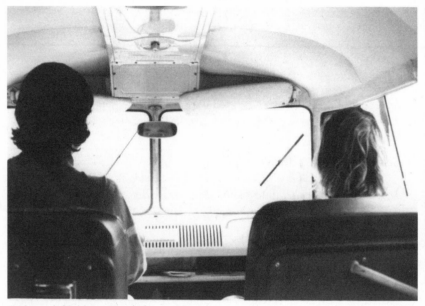
Saul Barodofsky drives Murshid on vacation.

Chapter 22

On Vacation
with Murshid

*In India, but not here, I was permitted to debate—in fact in some places
I was compelled to debate with the highest spiritual masters—before being
admitted into their companies, but Indian debates are not based on egotism and
dualism, and knowing this beforehand, it was a simple and easy matter to earn
the right to associate with them. And I know today a similar requirement is now
being established at our universities to determine whether or not a claimant is
a fraud or a sage. I do not think a man is any wiser because he makes a more
grandiose claim. I am not the least interested in any ego reaction to this letter;
I am interested in the rejection of the Gita by so many pretenders: they do not
demonstrate any acceptance of the Gita's teaching "equal-minded in pleasure
and pain." I am not interested in trying to prove or disprove—I am interested
in watching to see how and if claimants prove their sanctity, their humility and
their super-mental acclaims. (Murshid's letter to Walt and Magana Baptiste,
San Francisco yoga teachers, September 9, 1969)*

The Background

As mentioned, Murshid needs a vacation, and I am in the middle of a
personal tragedy. Somehow I feel like a Henry James character being sent
on a long ocean voyage to soften one of life's hard knocks. Accompanying
Murshid and me on this journey is Saul Barodofsky and his big, long haired,
black Labrador retriever. I have a clean 1966 Volkswagen van, which has
the middle bench seat removed. A plywood platform has been installed
with a mattress on top covered with a spread. You can sit with your back
against the backrest of the rear bench seat and stretch your legs forward.
I am forced to endure outrage after outrage as the dog, Wooda, from time
to time vomits, sheds black hair, tracks mud, or comes in rain soaked and
shakes himself.

I begin the journey chanting the Sufi *ziker* constantly, every mile that
I drive. Murshid endures this all the way to Seattle and around a bit,
until I get lost looking for one of our destinations. Then Murshid tells
me that Inayat Khan did not recommend repeating *ziker* while driving.
It's too dangerous. "What should I remember?" I ask Murshid, keying on
the literal meaning of *ziker*, which is remembrance. *Toward the One*, is

Murshid's response. He gives me the abbreviation of the Sufi Invocation to practice behind the wheel. It's in English, and more grounding, I think. You are not as apt to get lost in the practice and die in traffic as you might practicing the Arabic *ziker*.

During the visit with Atiya up in Washington state, the similarity between Shakespeare's history plays—which involve power struggles in the succession of kings—and current dramas in the Sufi Order repeatedly comes up for me. Atiya was at one time involved with Pir Vilayat's nephew Fazal in the Sufi Movement. Then she defected to Vilayat's Sufi Order and badmouthed Fazal. The picture I get of the goings on is nothing noble. It is Shakespearian, tragic. Or should I say, human?

I have the idea when I take notes on this trip that, someday maybe, others might want to follow in the footsteps of the master. That is, go where he went and even eat where he ate as a kind of pilgrimage. This explains my attention in this chapter as to where we ate and slept. Before we leave on Wednesday the 10th, Murshid leads a dance in the park, puts on a fashion show, and, of course, answers his mail.

September 7, 1969, Sunday

Murshid sends $10 for a two year subscription to a publication from India called *Darshana International*, telling them,

> It may be unethical to say that I happen to be perhaps the first American, the first Westerner and even the first human being (I do not know) that has passed all his examinations in Sufism before Sufi Murshids, and all his examinations in Zen before real living Roshis—not before "experts" and "credentialed"-professors or otherwise.

The dervish dances Murshid leads today in Precita Park, just outside the Mentorgarten, mark the first ever public performance of the dances. The occasion is a fair in the park. Our chants and dances blend harmoniously with the carnival atmosphere. The sun is shining, children are frolicking, and a large group of us is saying *Allah* in an American park. It is outrageous by contemporary American standards of propriety, and nobody looking on seems to care.

September 8, 1969, Monday

Murshid boasts with no exaggeration to his disciple S. Ahmed about yesterday's dance:

> Yesterday we performed dervish dances in public and not only our people but a lot in the audience were chanting ALLAH, ALLAH, ALLAH, when we left the arena. I do not think a single missionary coming to this country under any auspices, has ever accomplished that.

Atiya, apparently not put off by Murshid's erratic typing in his last letter, sends the road map he requested! Today Murshid thanks Atiya in a letter he dictates, so there are no typos. He is clear about the vehicle he is taking and his traveling companions—Mansur and Saul—but uncertain about the start time ("There has been a slight delay on our departure here.") and the length of stay ("The date of my departure south [to LA before going north] is at the moment quite indeterminate depending to some extent on plans you may have initiated."). "Anticipating a wonderful visit," Murshid concludes.

September 9, 1969, Tuesday

Holy cow! Murshid can't remember ever writing (with the help of Melvin) more letters in a single day. We have five: To Oliver Reiser, University of Pittsburgh professor of philosophy, Elizabeth Peterson, recent correspondent from earlier days with the Meher Baba people in Myrtle Beach, Virginia; Walt and Magana Baptiste (see epigraph for this chapter), yoga teachers and contemporaries of Murshid's; Anandashram; and Krishnadas, to whom Murshid confides, "Wali Ali Melvin Meyer [the first time Murshid refers to Melvin by his new spiritual name Wali Ali] has been of supreme help and *inshallah* something will be done for him when the occasion permits." We rarely get much in Murshid's letters about what his correspondents say to him—he receives their input and responds with barely a mention. Elizabeth Patterson, remember, was reminded how Murshid "died" on command. (see epigraph for Chapter 21) She must have added more, as Murshid writes to Ms. Patterson,

Among my researches have been the subjects of *baraka* and *cosmic language*. It is not necessary to comment on them as your letter itself is a commentary thereon. Some day, no doubt, the world will understand these things better.

Murshid writes so many letters today he misspeaks his latest destination, calling New Mexico "Colorado," as in, "Not only was my Colorado trip quite successful, but since my return, representatives of several institutions of learning have come to this house." (letter to Oliver Reiser) Unmentioned to me is Murshid's expressed intention to Reiser "to plan a trip to Europe and perhaps the Near East next year." This travel motif is reiterated again and again. To Anandashram, he writes,

The time has come for Super Action. So Sam is making the first steps to go to other lands to present the realities of divine vision and the operation of love-culture in a way adapted to the hearts of the day.

To Walt and Magana:

I am now making plans to attend a conference of the real religions of the real world where I shall be given ample time to support contentions based on hard facts of history and humanity.

Murshid fleshes out his latest travel idea to an even greater extent to Anandashram.

Sam's plans may take him next to the conference of the religions of the world, and he is going to present the standpoint of universal love and universal joy along with *prajna*, with or without the intermediation of dialectic cultures which are not necessary inheritants of divine wisdom.

Hence, the day before Murshid's departure to the Northwest—Seattle, Atiya, friends in Oregon, and Uncle Harry in Vancouver, B.C.—he decides his mission will be a world mission. I can't imagine what a presentation "of universal love and universal joy along with *prajna*, with or without the intermediation of dialectic cultures which are not necessary inheritants of divine wisdom" would look like. But I feel privileged to be able to watch from the front row and see for myself.

September 10, 1969, Wednesday

The dream I have the night before leaving signifies a new life and a renewed being. I dig a grave (the limiting depths one digs for one's self) in a kitchen (place for cooking up plans) and bury some garbage (discarded ideas). At the end of the dream, I take Fatima and one other to a new house (a new life). Then, I have to go out and push one car (me in physical life) with another car (Murshid).

We drive northwest from Novato on 101 to Eureka, on the coast about 284 miles from San Francisco. We eat lunch at the Eureka Fish Grotto.

Murshid has the seafood combination, I have oysters, and Saul has sole with crab meat. After lunch we make our way slightly southeast from Eureka to Redding, and go north 105 miles to the town of Mt. Shasta. Just out of town to the north is the 14,162 foot mountain which gives the town its name. Mt. Shasta has the same

Saul, Murshid, and Helen at Crater Lake, Oregon

sense of sacredness about it as do the San Francisco Peaks near Flagstaff,

Arizona. I photograph Murshid standing next to the highway north of Mt. Shasta with Mt. Shasta behind him (the cover photo).

The town of Mt. Shasta is where we planned to visit Saul's mentor, Mother Mary, but she is in Ashland, Oregon, seeking help for an illness she doesn't survive. Mother Mary dies January 4, 1970. We eat at an Italian place called Veneziano's, where Murshid has trout, Saul roast beef and ravioli, and I, ravioli.

We continue another eighty-two miles or so, cross the northern California border, and find Saul's friends, Helen and Ray, who live on Oregon Street in Klamath Falls, Oregon. After we arrive and Murshid says his feet are sore, Helen massages Murshid's feet. I sleep on the floor, unaware of where anyone else crashes.

September 11, 1969, Thursday

We drive 141 miles from Klamath Falls to Bend, Oregon. At Bend, Murshid tells me Allah revealed to him my future. Murshid says I will go with him to Turkey for the next meeting of the Temple of Understanding, scheduled for next spring. Last weekend only Murshid was going to Turkey. It was yesterday at Veneziano's, the spaghetti place in Mt. Shasta, that God first whispered something in Murshid's ear about this in relation to me. It was tentative then. It is definite now. I feel happy about this.

Murshid and a waterfall along the Columbia River

We eat lunch at the Skyline Restaurant in Bend, where we all have scallops, the dish Murshid used to order for me at the Japanese restaurant on Fillmore.

Continuing north, we arrive at the east-west flowing Columbia River, the northern border of Oregon. We drive west along the Columbia River and stop at several waterfalls. I take a picture of Murshid at the tallest. He says our arrival at this place is the climax of our trip. I am puzzled at this statement. I remember Murshid hustled us out of there before I was ready to go. I think: *Murshid would rather leave me wanting more than satiate me to the point of boredom.*

Going east to Portland, and then north to Tacoma, Washington, at the southern reach of Puget Sound, we eat a Chinese dinner at Wong's in Tacoma.

We arrive at Atiya's in Bothell, Washington, three days before the time Murshid hinted we might arrive, which is the day after Hazrat Inayat Khan's *hejirat* day. Murshid is drastically early, but no matter. We are received, and Murshid talks for two hours, giving Atiya a fantastic rap that touches on the highlights of his life's spiritual journey. I don't know that Murshid wrote to Atiya on August 25, 1969, "There is one policy which I pursue: The smaller the group, the more intense the communications. One is therefore not at all concerned with the size of a welcome or of an audience." This is Murshid's ever so sweet and subtle way of saying it would be fantastic if you could assemble a group of people to meet me. But there is no group, and Murshid gives it all to Atiya.

September 12, 1969, Friday

Murshid talks for two more hours after breakfast. It is more of the fantastic same as yesterday. What does Murshid talk about? It is similar to his stream of consciousness talk at the Wednesday night meeting (presented in Chapter 14, March 8, 1969), where he seems to jump from topic to topic, serving up personal experiences full of deep wisdom.

For lunch we eat rice and vegetables, plus fish, then nap. Murshid talks for two more hours, giving Atiya the answer to a problem she presents: *How do I prevent feeling the emotions of others?*

Murshid's answer for Atiya is to think the phrase *Toward the One* as she breathes in, and *Toward the One* as she breathes out. Atiya knows this phrase. She is familiar with the Sufi Invocation, which begins this way. It doesn't occur to me Atiya might be nearing her capacity for receptivity to Murshid after six hours of his one sided presentation. I am loving it.

We take a break and walk, eating blackberries we find on the way around the neighborhood. Atiya is very keen for Murshid to tell her if he feels anything special about the atmosphere in her well built stone house. She is fishing for a compliment. The vestibule, English Tudor or Gothic style architecture, has a dome ceiling and bow slit windows. Murshid is noncommittal. Atiya's pride is more evident to me than any special atmosphere. We watch *The Felony Squad* and local news on television before dinner. After, there is more talk.

September 13, 1969, Saturday

This morning at Murshid's request, I copy a letter he has written to Bibijan, heretofore called Suzanne D'Mitrieff. Instead of writing September 13, 1969, at the top of the letter, Murshid types, "Written on *Hejirat* Day, 1969, Bothell, Washington."

My dear Bibijan: *As-salaam aleikhum* [peace be upon you]. After a long time God has vouchsafed a vacation, for even a young man can not work seven days a week incessantly. I am here with Nakib Mansur Johnson and another disciple named Saul. We went up via central Oregon and the Columbia River highway, which they had never seen before, and wished to arrive here on the anniversary of Hazrat Inayat Khan's departure for the West. This has been so, and this afternoon we shall have a meeting to celebrate the event.

Murshid goes on to say that he hasn't signed any organizational papers to establish his group as a center in Vilayat's Sufi Order. Writing this book, I find out for the first time that just before leaving Murshid was really stressed.

For five nights in a row one was awakened from sleep by emergencies, which were necessary but were too much for the body and ego. Nevertheless one was directed by God (One can say sarcastically that membership in the Sufi Movement does not hinder Divine experience!), and one is directed to attend the next sessions of the TEMPLE OF UNDERSTANDING...and place my spiritual credentials before an audience, and then being recognized as Hazrat Inayat Khan wished, and not as various persons and corporations who have not had the inner initiations proclaim, the people of the West will have to under compulsion, regrettably but under compulsion and not under any surrender willing or unwilling, accept the SIX INTERVIEWS WITH HAZRAT INAYAT KHAN. What I am going to do, *inshallah*, is to attend the next session of the TEMPLE OF UNDERSTANDING.

To top this off Murshid speaks about his place in the hierarchy.

My work has been that of BUZURG and later changed, and it is only hoped that the people in the West, as the young are now doing, will accept the evidence of divine wisdom and not of ego. It is partly a question of whether one shall be called on to act. BEFORE GOD AND NO NON-WITNESS CAN HAVE ANY EFFECTIVENESS, I was made "Protector of the Message" and this has been confirmed by a multitude of Sufis of all schools.

There is a Universal Worship service at Atiya's this afternoon, and Shamcher is coming. I will give him four more chapters of Murshid's *Commentary on The Path of Initiation and Discipleship*, and photograph him. At the Universal Worship Shamcher gives a sermon. After pulling everyone available into the circle, Murshid shows Shamcher a few dervish dances.

Our stay at Atiya's is abruptly terminated. After Shamcher huddles with Atiya, he tells us it will be impossible for us to remain as Atiya's guests beyond tonight! It is like a slap in the face. Clearly, Atiya has solicited

358

Shamcher's help to deliver the eviction notice. I don't expect it, especially from him. But it isn't Shamcher really. It is Shamcher speaking for Atiya. I see something in this. I see how you can be harsh with one friend in order to help another friend. Our visit is cut short, but as we have no expectation to stay any duration, we leave. Neither Saul nor Murshid grumbles or appears surprised.

September 14, 1969, Sunday

We have been invited to visit Shamcher at his home in Keyport, Washington. To get there, we have to put my van on a ferry that motors across Puget Sound from Edmonds to Kingston, and then drive about ten miles to Keyport. If you want to drive to Keyport from Seattle, you have to circle Puget Sound, go about 137 miles south

Murshid and Shamcher talk in the yard in Keyport, Washington.

of Seattle through Tacoma and Olympia, and loop north, passing through Bremerton. Shamcher lives in Keyport, not to be secluded and near water like in his native Norway, but rather to be near the U.S. Navy Torpedo Station. This is where he works as an engineer; even though, like Murshid, he's in his seventies. Without prompting, Shamcher explains that he does his job of manufacturing without any troubled conscience about creating war materials. "If the Americans didn't have a mighty war machine," Shamcher says, "the Nazis might still control all of Europe and Norway."

Once while we are talking, Shamcher gazes fixedly at me without warning or explanation. My heart beats faster and my chest feels warm, even after we leave. That's the good part. Also during this *darshan* (blessing through the glance), Shamcher expresses that he sees a possible accident. He interrupts his staring at me and tells me something like: *If you don't have an accident, you'll be fine.* I am mystified and fearful. How do you avoid an "accident" someone predicts for you? I don't appreciate this information.

With Saul driving, Murshid yells, "Slow down!" Saul slows. "Slow down!" Saul gets slower. "Slow down!" Saul pulls the van out of traffic, stops the car and pulls out the keys. Murshid says, "No. *You* slow down." (Apparently Murshid senses Saul is inwardly hyper.) I think, *Murshid might have given clearer directives.*

Murshid himself gives *darshan* at the house of a lady named Betty later this evening. Betty, Jerry (a friend of Atiya's), and Atiya are there. These small gatherings of older people make me think of soirées Murshid might have attended before the young people arrived in his life. This is the first day Murshid talks of going home since we left four days ago.

We spend the night at Sitara's in Everett, Washington. Sitara, a Sufi widow in her seventies, lives alone. Her husband concocted an herbal eye drop, marketed as Dolphin's Eyedrops. Sitara gives us each a bottle. There is a large framed picture of Jesus Christ in her living room. In my presence the kindly lady points out to Murshid my resemblance to the picture of Christ hanging on her wall. I feel somehow special, humble to be placed in such august company. Murshid acknowledges her comment by saying, "We just have to convince one person of it."

Now that I am convinced, years later, I ask my mother: *How does it feel to be the mother of Christ?* Her response (after reading what I wrote above) is: "You have got to be kidding, but I guess that you aren't! I can assure you that there was no immaculate conception. Look-alikes are not the real thing. I've been told that I look like the Queen of England."

September 15, 1969, Monday

I had a dream last night of sex in a closet with Jemila. When Murshid hears, he says, "It means she may be coming back."

This morning, as we get on the freeway after leaving Sitara's house in Everett, Murshid yells at me, "You're going to have to face some tests of an entirely different kind." I shudder, remembering what happened yesterday to Saul. I recall Murshid's explosions after his return from the Lama Foundation, which foreshadowed Jemila's trip to Europe. Jemila's trip continues to cause me excruciating pain and suffering.

The first test has to do with getting on the freeway as we leave Sitara's house in Everett. Murshid has criticized me before on this trip for not taking the responsibility to find the right road. Today when I stop to ask somebody walking along the street, Murshid says I should listen to him, rather than to a stranger. Rather than allow Murshid to catch me in a "damned if you do, damned if you don't" situation, I tell him curtly that I am driving! When we get to Seattle, Murshid wants me to turn right. I do, and when I don't turn right again, Murshid berates me for not turning right the second time. After this second application of heat, I think: *Something heavy is coming!* (This is the point when Murshid says not to chant *La illa ha el il Allah* in traffic.)

Our goal when we leave Sitara's is the loop drive around the Olympic Peninsula, the core of which is Olympic National Park. Twenty-five years later, I would read Carsten Lien's book *Olympic Battleground*, which tells about the decades long, semisuccessful battle three environmentalists coordinated against Washington State timber interests to create Olympic National Park. Just as we start to circumnavigate the Olympic Peninsula, we stop to eat seafood at a café on 101, just off Route 410 that we are taking to Aberdeen, a town on the Pacific coast at the base of the peninsula.

On this loop drive, Murshid says my discipline is to do as I say. In addition to doing what I say I'll do, I vow to think or fantasize only about things I want to manifest. No time wasted on other stuff.

We eat seafood again in Port Angeles, on the north coast of the peninsula, and sleep in a Port Townsend motel, completing our circle around the Olympic Peninsula. I guess I am not bubbling over with optimism. Later tonight Murshid says he is going to give me a practice for positivity.

September 16, 1969, Tuesday

After breakfast at the Surf Café in Port Townsend, we ferry the opening of Puget Sound, called Admiralty Inlet, and arrive at Keystone, Washington. We drive north along the water on 525, 536, and 537 to Vancouver, Canada, and Murshid's Uncle Harry, the last and oldest member of his family. "There were certain streaks of adventurism in both Walter [Harry's brother] and yourself," Murshid wrote Harry Rosenthal, who once stole a train from Poncho Villa and sold it in Texas, according to Saul.

And I have had the same streaks and maybe still have them... Once I went to the Japanese Consulate here and was given the brush off. Then the chief cultural attaché came in, and bowed so delightfully that all the others lost face. And you can believe it or not, even the Prime Minister of Japan, coming here bowed to me. And when a former Prime Minister of another land came here, he got out of the line and made people come before this person. Which made them all mad. (April 12, 1969)

We find Uncle Harry at his apartment on East Fourteenth Street in Vancouver. Murshid takes us all to lunch at the Chinese restaurant called Dynasty. Uncle Harry's only warning we were coming was the line in Murshid's letter of July 7, 1969, "I am hoping to come north about the beginning of September." Murshid, who will never see him again, says goodbye to Uncle Harry, and we visit Mylora, an organic farm on Number 5 Road. We are given several giant squashes that we stash under the platform in the van.

Saul brought medicinal herbs at Murshid's request to take care of Uncle Harry, who hasn't been well. At the Canadian border returning to the U.S., U.S. Customs officials stare long and hard at Saul's various packets of green herbs, some of which have to be smelled to pass inspection.

Heading south, we arrive at Everett, Washington, and sleep at the Rip Van Winkle Motel. Today we skip dinner. Nobody cares, we're so well fed.

September 17, 1969, Wednesday

It takes twelve hours for us to drive from Everett, Washington, to Helen and Ray's house in Klamath Falls, Oregon. We eat lunch at a roadside café and have dinner at Faa's in Eugene, Oregon. Saul runs over a large rock while driving after dark. Both the right front wheel and the right rear wheel are hopelessly bent from the impact. The Michelin radial tires survive just fine, but it costs $30 to replace both wheel rims.

September 18, 1969, Thursday

After waking at Helen and Ray's in Klamath Falls, I record a long sequence of dreams. In the last, I'm with Murshid. There are two turkeys. I take a long shot at an old one with my cross bow (power to set goals) and hit it. The turkey turns into a young girl who dies. Before dying, she digs a grave (inability to take action) like a hole in the asphalt. The girl dives in after taking off her turkey suit, and begins to cover her body with wet earth (my feminine side needs to get free of my limiting situation).

With Helen along, we backtrack north about sixty miles to Crater Lake National Park. The elevation of the lake is 6,175 feet and its depth is 1,932 feet. The lake is obscured by fog. We take the rim drive, which circles the lake, and see nothing. Then halfway around, the fog clears. I photograph Saul, Helen, and Murshid all together, and Murshid alone.

Back at Helen and Ray's in Klamath Falls, Murshid phones San Francisco. "It's a good thing I called," he says. "Vilayat's sick. Now you've got to pray for your enemies, although he isn't mine in that sense." It is one of the few times Murshid explicitly mentions Vilayat vis-à-vis my personal drama.

One of the other times was when Murshid showed me Vilayat's answer to the letter he wrote when it became known that Vilayat slept with my wife. What remains with me is Vilayat's answer: It was that since I was young enough to start a new life, his destruction of my marriage was OK. This reasoning, and the moral code it represents, was another awakening for me in this entire enlightenment experience.

September 19, 1969, Friday

There are lots of dreams this morning, including a significant one where I find a man sitting in my parents' home and holding my wife's hand. I tell him to leave, then wake up.

After retracing the route we took coming north from Mt. Shasta to Klamath Falls, we detour into unfamiliar territory. Going southeast on Route 89, we stop and eat lunch at the Milky Way in McCloud, California. Another ninety-two miles takes us to the Mt. Lassen Volcanic National Park, one hundred thousand acres of evergreen forest, fifty wilderness lakes and nearly fifty mountains, dominated by the 10,457 foot Mt. Lassen. The brochure calls Mt. Lassen a "plug-dome volcano that sleeps at the southern tip of the Cascades." I walk gingerly there, feeling the vitality of the sleeping giant and of the land itself.

Dinner is at the Timberhouse in Chester, California. Murshid takes some old friends from Fairfax out to eat. Murshid rides with his friends, while Saul and I follow their car to the restaurant. It is very touching, accompanying these old folks.

All day I am foggy. I have a headache. Sometimes I can't talk with a normal voice. Murshid says, "Next year, not this year, I've got a job for Mansur: going around to all the colleges collecting good news. Solutions to problems." This goes along with what he used to say over and over to people in letters and during lectures: "The University of California has solved all the problems of the orient. What stands in the way of implementing these solutions is not knowledge, but the egos of people." This was what prompted me to initiate a "Solutions" column in *The San Francisco Oracle*.

September 20, 1969, Saturday

There are recurring dreams of yesterday's activities: taking people to dinner and following them in cars. Finally, a boy, a girl, and I are riding in a car. I go back to pick up Shamcher. The boy, somewhat puzzled about where to go, sets off to lead us on his motorcycle (the need for balance in my life).

Bob's Fine Food Fountain, about sixty-five miles from the Nevada border in Quincy, California, serves us breakfast. The elevation here is 3,423 feet. We have lunch at the Nugget Casino in Carson City, Nevada. Murshid thinks Jemila will realize she had a ticket for a train that went on without her. I take heart at this idea, momentarily believing things might magically revert to "normal." But my feeling at the end of the trip, which Murshid told Saul was intended to snap me out of the condition known as a "broken heart," is that I don't want to see Jemila. The afterthought that comes is about crucifixion. It is real, and there is life after death.

We arrive back home at the *khankah* at 7 P.M. I can't sleep, so I mark our route on some maps. It is 11:15 P.M. as I write. We planned to be gone two weeks. Our trip lasted ten days.

Chapter 23

The Present Cycle

*There have also been numerous problems arising out of the Summer Camps,
but I think many of them were tests for me, personally, and on the whole they
have resulted (with a little drama) in the spiritual elevation of several of the
persons concerned [Mansur and Jemila]. (Murshid's letter to Atiya, November
8, 1969)*

*The present cycle began when my esoteric secretary, Mansur Johnson, was
suddenly subjected to a great trial and I knew at once it was his initiation. As
Murshid and mureed are one, I had to go through the fires of purgatory with
him. But in the Egyptian initiation of the fires, while real, do not touch or harm
the person and I saw how the Love, Wisdom, Majesty and Benevolence of Allah
work. (Murshid's letter to Shamcher, November 19, 1969)*

September 22, 1969, Monday

Starting today, two days after returning from vacation, Murshid focuses
on his attendance at the next conference sponsored by the Temple of
Understanding. "The time is now," Murshid begins his letter to Finley P.
Dunne, Jr. at the Temple of Understanding headquarters in Washington
D.C. "The time is come when a mystic will not only be permitted to speak
on mysticism but will be permitted to function and [be] listened to."

It is an announcement to be repeated in multiple ways to everyone Murshid writes. He makes a typical comment today to Erich W. Bethmann, director of research of the American Friends of the Middle East, Inc., also in Washington, D.C. "I believe I shall be permitted to speak," Murshid says, "when the Temple of Understanding has its next convocations. I shall mention the careers and accomplishments of Emperors Suleiman the Magnificent [reigned in Turkey, 1520-1566] and Padishah Akbar [first Emperor of India, reigned 1556-1605]."

Was Murshid allowed to speak? Did he say these things? These are valid questions. In fact, Murshid did not ask to speak at the conference of the Temple of Understanding, so, of course, he did not say these things. It was not necessary. In the way of mystical economy, these comments were already in the space; they had been said already.

For Murshid, the end of his lifelong pattern of rejection is a momentous event. He trumpets this milestone in letters and uses the conference of the Temple of Understanding as a vehicle to announce his personal progress.

Murshid describes the process of his decision to attend the Temple of Understanding's conference to Finley Dunne, Jr., a tall, graying man in his sixties who always wears a suit and tie. It was tantamount, Murshid writes, to "a mystical-mystical experience" he had a few years back. At that time, "God, so to speak, told me I would become spiritual leader of the hippies." Now, Murshid says,

I had another mystical-mystical experience, not a dream-pantomime of a psychedelic, to now join you and Judith [Hollister, Temple of Understanding founder], and all your wonderful colleagues to attend the next session of the Temple of Understanding, no matter where it is held on the face of the earth, *inshallah*.

September 23, 1969, Tuesday

Murshid copies yesterday's letter to the Temple of Understanding to longtime nemesis Dr. Haridas Chaudhuri, contrasting his acceptance by others with Chaudhuri's rejections.

Now, that such a fine personal and personality relation has been established with the leaders [of the Temple of Understanding], they are quite willing to have a Sufi speak, something unheard of by the various competing schools of verbalized "integral studies" [meaning Chaudhuri's California School of Integral Studies].

Before Murshid left on vacation, Saadia Khawar Khan Chisti (this last being Saadia's new spiritual name) pledged financial assistance for Murshid if he needs it to go to the Temple of Understanding conference. Although Murshid doesn't need it, he publicizes the fact of Saadia's offer to both Dr. Chaudhuri and W.D. Begg in India, whom he writes today.

In another letter today, Murshid mentions to Saadia having receiving "a wire" [concerning her marriage!] from Sufi Barkat Ali, and sends Saadia a copy of his response.

As you have seen the wire from Sufi Barkat Ali, one merely encloses a carbon. On this point I have no view whatever. It will be as Allah wills, but to make this clear, I feel it proper to accept absolutely any advice, conclusions, or directives from Babaji [Sufi Barkat Ali]. I think you do too, although it does affect your personality much more than my own.

To Sufi Barkat Ali, Murshid writes,

Now on the matter of Khawar's marriage, this person has no views. He is trying to keep his mind clear, realizing that he might even benefit materially and otherwise from such an event. The only belief one has is that Saadia Khawar be permitted to complete her schooling, and inshallah, obtain the degree of Doctor of Philosophy (or some variant) for which she has been working so hard.

Reporting on his personal life, Murshid tells Sufi Barkat Ali, Saadia, and W.D. Begg that he begins "this morning the class on Asian Islamic Art" offered by a local university.

Just before dinner, Murshid calls me outside and tells me that the letter I have written to Jemila accomplishes the purpose of the practice for positivity he gave on vacation. (see September 15, 1970) I wrote this letter two days ago. It begins, "All right, let's get one thing straight at the start. You were meant for ME." It goes on to include such gems as, "If Vilayat ever comes to San Francisco, I'm going after him with a horse whip"; and, "What business has Vilayat got telling people they're from Venus?" As if that weren't enough, I asked, "What does Vilayat think he's doing estranging you and my son from me?" I understand from Murshid's comments that my anger, as expressed in this letter, means "positivity."

September 25, 1969, Thursday

At *darshan* during the *Gatha* class in the evening at the *khankah*, Murshid brings up "your problem" and says that I am doing right by facing the problem. Just for someone to speak to me about my "very complex personal problems," words Murshid used when speaking about my situation on the 23rd in his letter to Begg in India, comforts me somewhat. In the short talk that ensues, Murshid offers advice on magnetism. "Don't speak when you know, and it will increase your magnetism," Murshid says. I'm not known for small talk, so I assume this is guidance not to lose energy looking for sympathy. Murshid goes on—and now I feel he is speaking from personal experience—about karma: "You can't hate your enemies when you see what's going to happen to them." I know a little bit about Murshid's oppressors. Murshid will write Shamcher (October 13, 1969),

When I left [to visit Hong Kong, India, Pakistan, and Thailand] in 1956, I had ten sets of enemies. God, who does answer and commune, said, "Let your enemies fight your enemies." This is exactly what happened. When I returned these were reduced to three: 1) My brother, who is now my friend; 2) Alan Watts, who has lost his eminence and is even going around saying "Allah"; and 3) Mrs. Ivy Duce.

Murshid gives the "joy, love, and peace" breaths (the *jhanas* of Lord Buddha) tonight at *Gatha* class. Two days later, he writes about them to the former United Nations representative from Ceylon, Dr. G. Malalasekera, who provides Murshid with copies of the *Encyclopedia of Buddhism.*

Now I present the first two *jhanas* to all my audiences. I think exactly one other person in this vicinity presents the *jhanas*. I am not concerned. Americans are by nature pragmatic; they soon find out that the *jhanas* are real and operative.

I feel how sorrow and joy are connected when I do the Buddha breaths. I also feel the heat. *Tapas* is the Sanskrit word for this heat; the Tibetans call it *tumo*. A selection from the *irfan* papers, which Murshid had me type the first day back from vacation, will show in Islamic terms what I think I am experiencing at Murshid's tonight from the Buddhist practice. These practices may have different roots, but in the body, heat is heat. The author, Faqir Nur Muhammad Sarawari Qadri, writes,

When the concentration on His personal name Allah begins to influence the person of the meditator, first of all a sort of *heat* [emphasis mine] appears inside the seeker and he feels something like the heat of fever in himself. He cannot sleep at night; and especially he feels pain when he sleeps on his left side. If it occurs thus, the seeker should not get frightened. On the other hand, these are the signs of eternal perfect health.

September 26, 1969, Friday
It's different strokes for different folks. Murshid described the decision to attend the Temple of Understanding conference as "a mystical-mystical experience" to the American Finley Dunne, Jr. Writing to Seyyed Hossein Nasr, he calls the decision to attend "clearly indicated by *kashf* and, let us say, *mushahida* (contemplation)." Murshid adds, "And certainly Allah, to Whom be all praise, is quite willing to approve of the Hadith: 'In that day will the sun rise in the west and all men seeing, will believe.'"

This morning Murshid holds the first meeting of a new class in dervish dancing at his home; then, he attends Jacob Needleman's class at San Francisco State on contemporary spiritual movements. After dinner, Murshid attends Rabbi Schlomo Carlbach's gathering, "also based on spirituality through love dances."

September 27, 1969, Saturday

Murshid reveals why he didn't want to attend the Muslim Students' Association annual meeting in his letter today to F. Clive-Ross in England.

Along with my goddaughter and *Khalifa* Miss Saadia Khawar Khan, we had refused to attend the Muslim Students' Association national gathering on the grounds that they were too concerned with politics and superiority complexes and not enough with Allah and Hadiths.

Murshid tells Clive-Ross that he intends "to present some of the Hadiths at the meetings of the Temple of Understanding." At the conference so far, Murshid will present Hadiths, Emperor Akbar, Suleiman the Magnificent— and yes, universal love and *prajna*.

September 28, 1969, Sunday

Norman McGee is Murshid's African-American godson who lives in New York City. Sometimes Murshid speaks in the vernacular to Norman. Here the lead-in is, "Mohammed was not a prelate, not a land-lord, not a monarch, but a humble working man with God-consciousness." Then it comes—and I am always struck when Murshid reminds Norman in more than one letter—"Remember, Krishna means nigger-baby (i.e., Black)!" Murshid shares with Norman something not revealed to others: what he plans to take with him to Turkey. "I am taking such notes preserved from fire and tragedy during the years for this coming parliament." Indeed, Murshid instructs me to copy portions of his scrapbook, including a poem about the Parliament of Religions, to take to Turkey.

September 29, 1969, Monday

The Ali Akbar Khan School of Music is located in Terra Linda, an exit off 101 between San Francisco and Novato. The school was featured in the latest *Oracle* and is addressed today by Murshid. Murshid tells them that when he visited Fathepur Sikri in India, "I gave it out that I was a madman." Details of this episode are given earlier (July 7, 1968), but today we learn that when Murshid attends the Temple of Understanding conference, he expects "to address an assemblage of the world's great religious leaders on Fathepur Sikri, Akbar and Tansen," one of India's greatest musicians. Add "Fathepur Sikri" and "Tansen" to the list of various topics Murshid plans to discuss at the conference. "I have been twice to your college with the intention of making at least a small contribution," Murshid concludes to the Ali Akbar School, "and nobody paid the slightest attention to me." Murshid goes on, as he will with several other worthy recipients of charity, to postpone a contribution until after Turkey.

I am now not in the least offended but in view of the new situation that I am called upon to attend a Parliament of the world's religions next year, I leave it to your sense of justice to grant a reprieve, and can almost solemnly promise that on my return I shall be glad to cooperate in whatever ways may seem most feasible.

Commenting upon Finley Dunne, Jr.'s response to Murshid's announcement that he is coming to Turkey, Murshid enthuses: There is "a common enthusiasm. This has been so great that it was only by restraint I did not telephone." Grounding his communication with Dunne, Murshid makes an inquiry that could be construed as a suggestion. "We are presuming that we should be paying our fare to New York or Washington, and have a chartered flight thence on. This of course is just a presumption, but we shall work on this theory until we hear otherwise." There will be no charter flight.

September 30, 1969, Tuesday

Murshid is getting focused about the Temple of Understanding and asks from the American Society for Eastern Arts "a moratorium as to contributions until my return"—as distinct from the Ali Akbar School, who will not receive now and never received in the past.

The letter Murshid writes today to *San Francisco Chronicle* columnist Art Hoppe is interesting reading for the spin he puts on the Temple of Understanding: "They have also selected me as one of the top advisers." I would say Murshid selected himself; but in the world of unity, where is the ego? In mystical experience, who does what?

Here now is Murshid's answer to his Buddhist teacher, Master Seo. Murshid alluded to Seo's letter in his September 28 letter to Norman ("Last week I received a cablegram from my chief Sufi teacher [Sufi Barkat Ali] and an air-mail letter from my real Zen master"). Seo's letter advised Murshid that he was returning to the U.S. He didn't mention where in the U.S. he would be returning to, but Murshid isn't concerned. He tells Seo he is going to Turkey, gifting *Encyclopedia of Buddhism* volumes, and being busy, "very, very busy."

October 1, 1969, Wednesday

Sometimes it takes a subsequent letter to shed light on a previous one. Today's letter to Vocha Fiske illumines yesterday's to Lloyd Morain. "Yesterday I received a letter from Lloyd," Murshid writes Vocha, "and [today] have refused his protestations of respect." Murshid refused Morain's overture because he wanted a gesture, not words: atonement in the form of getting his article published. Murshid says to Vocha, "He has failed utterly to accept any contributory article." Moreover, Murshid pledges to work against Morain's colleague, S.I. (Don) Hayakawa, Murshid's longtime nemesis. "Owing to the present scene with the possibility of your fellow-general being named for high office, I own it as a duty to myself and my country to see that such persons are not permitted to reach such places." Alas, Hayakawa will be elected a United States senator.

Murshid writes an outrageous, three page, twelve hundred word response to the editors of *The Saturday Review*. It regards an article by Theodore C. Sorenson, a former advisor to President John F.Kennedy. Murshid rails at his government as it relates, and has related, to "CITIZEN SAM LEWIS." His complaint is as applicable today as it was in 1969. Implicit is a lament for the failure of democracy—where government listens to the people, where it is government of the people, by the people, for the people. In 1969, it is twenty-four years since 1945, when, emerging from the ashes of World War II, the national security state was born and national policy continued to be driven by agencies (State Department, CIA) not elected, and not responsive to the people.

A thought from Murshid's letter to Vocha today describes some of the fallout from this situation: "We [the United States] have the audacity to interfere with the private affairs of exotic nations and pay no attention to their history, religions, folk-lore and ideals." Referring to the war going on at this time in Vietnam, Murshid says,

We are now paying a terrible price, and we are going to continue to pay terrible prices until those in high places at least listen to Americans who have been to odd places, mingled with the populace, and who have information that could be of help to this land [in other words, when a very serious shift of emphasis occurs].

In response to the Sorenson article in *The Saturday Review*, Murshid gives an example of his treatment by the U.S. State Department.

In 1960, I had planned to go to the Near East. The State Department was interested. I had constant letters from them, fixing a date for a meeting, and showed up promptly at the hour they had selected. When I arrived at that office not a single person with whom I had corresponded was present. There were no notes around. In fact, there was only one person around, and he knew nothing about it. AND SINCE THAT TIME NOT A SINGLE PERSON FROM ANY BRANCH OF THE STATE DEPARTMENT HAS EVER ANSWERED ANY CORRESPONDENCE FROM ME ON ANY SUBJECT!

I enjoy how Murshid refers to his "love-attunement" with other great ones he has met and become one with. "I have had the doubtful experience of love-attunement with such various persons as the Hasid Rev. Schlomo, the late Rufus Mosley, the still living Dr. Radhakrishnan, Roshi Yasutani, etc., etc., etc."

At the big Marin County public meeting in San Anselmo tonight Murshid says, "You get the karma not from your acts, but from your intention." Obviously, I'm remembering lessons about karma because I feel Vilayat made big karma with me. Murshid says people attack others because they're lonely. I acknowledge that. I am lonely. My attacks on Vilayat are to bring Jemila back, to make her realize I want her exclusively. There is no malice.

Tonight I sing the *"Ya Vilayat Zindabad"* anthem Murshid created. I sing it to Vilayat when Murshid leads it. The meaning, in bastardized German, is "Long live Vilayat." Murshid introduced the song to welcome Pir Vilayat when he returned one time to San Francisco. Strangers used to think Murshid was singing, "Pir Vilayat's in the bod [body]," and Vilayat himself thought it was something else.

Murshid says to me, "You'll have to decide how long you're going to hang on to Jemila." "How," I ask, "does one decide such a thing?" "When you feel it," Murshid says. Then he uses the analogy of playing with the cat. If the cat doesn't go after the shoelace Murshid dangles, Murshid goes about his business. I get the message intellectually; but emotionally, it will take years.

October 6, 1969, Monday

Murshid reports today to Art Hoppe that he's received six apologies

...from VIP organizations, all having in common the general formula: "With your money and our brains we can save the world." No doubt this is sarcasm, but unless you have money or fame or a solid backing, all the logic and knowledge is of no avail.

Among the groups apologizing is the Muslim Students' Association. Murshid reports what he wrote to them: "I called them down on fourteen points and was amazed that not only did they answer but conceded many." Murshid repeats themes he developed in response to Sorenson's *Saturday Review* article. (October 1, 1969) Among the mass of autobiographical details in Hoppe's letter, the most grand are, first, "I have been sent on a peace-feeler mission between India and Pakistan to be berated by the Foreign Office and have the respective countries call in Kosygin. And," second, "that my 'peace program,' accepted by Arabs, Israelis, and especially the UN functionaries who particularly admired it was smothered by our own State Department and the *important* ?'peace'? [sic] organizations."

October 7, 1969, Tuesday

In poetry class today at the University of California San Francisco Extension,

Murshid went to get the criticism of his poetry. Instead the teacher [Lew Welch, an old crony of poets Gary Snyder and Philip Whalen,] came and sat at his feet and said: "I need spiritual help." This is in marked contrast to the receptions one has had in the past. Later he [Welch] mentioned the name of a certain predecessor [the poet Alan Ginsberg] and I said, "Now you know why I speak of myself as 'rejected.' For years that man saw to it that none of my poetry was published or even got a hearing." It is changing much. (Murshid's letter to Saadia Khawar Khan, October 13, 1969)

October 9, 1969, Thursday

Murshid's dance class has grown from a handful of us in his tiny living room to fifteen hundred last night at the Family Dog on Ocean Highway, south of the Cliff House, where seals and sea lions frolic on the rocks to the delight of patrons. Murshid's spoken message to the multitude is summed up later in two slogans: *Youth of the world unite, you have nothing to lose* and *We must dance together instead of march together.*

Art Hoppe hears from Murshid, "Some 1,500 young people welcomed this person, his disciples, his dances, and their chants before this audience. Many joined in the chants, and so far as available in the dances also."

It is not just braggadocio when Murshid will say to Shamcher (October 13, 1969) that getting over a thousand Americans to chant *Allah* "is something no so-called 'Muslim' has ever succeeded in doing in the West." The audience listened to Yogi Bhajan, Swami Satchitananda, and others. It is a prelude, Murshid says, for when we go to Istanbul in March for the Temple of Understanding conference.

Murshid's commemorative agenda of intentions for the Temple of Understanding conference grows today to include memorials for two additional people, Nearler Cram Cook and Harold Lambe. Murshid tells Art Hoppe, "I intend to memorialize both of these people at the next Parliament of Religions." Cook was "born in Berkeley; she spent her last days in India highly honored." Lambe was "more fortunate. He died recognized in the eastern part of this country."

When we go to Egger's Nursery today, I have to laugh remembering my dream: Jemila and I are in the back seat of our VW bus beginning to make love. We are parked somewhere in the City I thought was private. All of a sudden there are four cops (help is available) in the car, giving us a ticket for $60 (the number six means guidance). Murshid says today he is leaving me his unfinished epic poems. In his will, I presume. This doesn't happen. Does he think for a minute I might finish those poems? I don't know.

October 11, 1969, Saturday

Lamenting my fate, I write a song in imitation of Bob Dylan:

My gal's going to India [February, 1970]
She's going to leave her old man here.
My gal's going to India
Says she's going with her Pir.
I say my gal's going to India

She's going to leave me here.
My gal's going to India
Says her soul don't know any fear.
Yes, my gal's going to France
Going to camp 'neath old Mount Blanc [June, 1970].
My gal's going to France
The news hits me in the head like a plank...
There's nothing I can say to you,
My love is not enough.
There's nothing I can say to you,
It's not enough even to be tough...
But I'm not going to give up hope, babe,
A guy's got to see what he's got to see.
A lady's got to try to find her love in life,
And for sure, what's going to be is going to be.

October 13, 1969, Monday
Murshid tells Shamcher,

Since my return here I now not only do not have days off, I have a single night off, and have practically no assistance. This is not, however, a "sad" story. Mansur works a good deal; Moineddin, house manager and *Khalif,* also has a part-time job, and the main problem has been *the uncertainty in homes.*

One of the six apologies Murshid received (October 6, 1969) was from Lloyd Morain, representing the Humanists. "So Mansur and 'Sufi Sam' were invited to Humanist House," Murshid writes Shamcher, "to discuss communes last week. It was an excellent meeting from every aspect. But it is Mansur Johnson who carries the Whiteman-Lewis torch." I earned this characterization as a result of my trip researching communes, and I feel proud to unconsciously emulate Murshid's past actions. What it portends for the future, I haven't a clue.

Wali Ali is traveling with Murshid around San Francisco. "One finds it easier to see from the point of view of others and my disciple Melvin (Wali Ali) who goes with me says I do give non-dualistic answers and this very method has become impressive."

Murshid will celebrate his birthday in Novato and then, he says to Shamcher, "The open work in Novato ends...and more attention will be paid to San Francisco." I don't understand. Is this a seasonal decision? Fall is coming and it's time to retreat from the venue where there's a garden? Murshid doesn't say.

Later, Murshid writes to Saadia, whose marriage situation is foremost in his mind. Murshid juxtaposes tradition—meaning, in Saadia's case, an arranged marriage—and romance. "Tradition is tradition," Murshid says, "and very often tradition stands so much before the Divine Will that whatever Allah wants is not directly accomplished on earth." On the other hand, "There is hardly a valid alternative. The 'love' or romance is sometimes wonderful, sometimes terrible. The Jemila incidents are both complicated and very foolish. They destroy all basis for anything positive."

Murshid suggests that Saadia ask for marital guidance from Allah. Then, out of the blue in the middle of the second page, he says, "Excepting Moineddin when I first met him, and Mansur, since his trial began, there have not been many visions of *mureeds*. The visions are all of group-endeavor such as is taking place now."

This group-talk reminds me of Murshid's use of the term "group-unit" in five chapter titles of his book *Toward Spiritual Brotherhood* ("The Spiritual Significance of the Group-Unit"; "Inner Action of the Group-Unit"; "Outer Action of the Group-Unit"; "Formation of a Group-Unit in the Presence of a Teacher"; "Formation of a Group-Unit in the Absence of a Teacher").

October 15, 1969, Wednesday

Murshid says if Jemila comes back, there will be consequences. She'll be put back a class. She'll have to work harder in the garden. She'll not be able to participate in family meetings for six months, but she can attend. These are strong words from Murshid, which I appreciate.

I can see from the fact that Atiya corresponds with Murshid after we visit that she likes him (or wants something from him), even though she evicted us. Murshid waits a while to answer Atiya, finally writing today, "You must excuse this person. He has not had a single day off since returning and in going over the schedule, he has a single night, Fridays!" The value of Murshid's letter to Atiya is that years later, it informs us of his schedule:

Now Sunday night we have Dharma teaching; Monday night Sufism in San Francisco; Tuesday night poetry class; Wednesday night public meeting in Marin County; Thursday night intermediate and advanced esoteric class; Friday night free; and Saturday night dancing class.

I am doing Greek dancing every Monday night. Not included in the schedule above is the class Murshid is taking on Friday: Jacob Needleman's class on contemporary spiritual movements. In a letter on the 13th to Shamcher, Murshid anticipated hearing the representative of Meher Baba, Alan Cohen, this week. The whole class is dedicated to presenting Meher Baba. In advance, Murshid, Jewish himself, noted that here is another Jewish person representing a movement. "The situation is peculiar because people, and especially young men of 'Jewish' antecedents, have taken over many movements."

October 20, 1969, Monday

Over a hundred people gathered Sunday at the *khankah* to celebrate the Murshid's October 18th birthday, which he shares with disciple Sibley Cogswell. Murshid writes today to friends at Anandashram,

Sam has just had a birthday signifying he has been now 73 years in *jagat* [the body]. It was certainly the most marvelous of occasions. After 50 years enmity one received a greeting [by telephone] from one's brother; this proved to be an excellent augury.

Murshid thrilled to the singing of the choir, and effaced himself when, "Early in the celebration some friends gave Sam a memento of Sri Krishna and immediately he went into a Sri Krishna chant. People tell me it was very beautiful and moving."

One of Murshid's most cherished birthday presents was Fatima's twenty by thirty inch Persian miniature imitation drawing of Murshid and his court. Fatima, pregnant with Nuria, is a disciplined artist. The drawing is published in the *Oracle*.

Writing again today to Shamcher, Murshid clarifies an enigmatic comment a week ago, about the open work in Novato ending. "I have felt that the end of the 'family' days are over. I am sure it was God's wish that Hazrat Inayat Khan wished me to carry on his *exoteric* work, to present mysticism to the intellectuals. This is now going on apace." Also to Shamcher, we have Murshid's first reaction to Alan Cohen's presentation at Needleman's class.

Last week we listened to a representative of Meher Baba at the San Francisco State College. This week I have been called to comment... The very glib mannerisms of Dr. Cohen, the putative representative of Meher Baba and presumably Murshida Duce, have done much to expose the cult methodologies of charlatans.

October 21, 1969, Tuesday

Murshid writes a personal friend, Leonard Austin, that "Mansur is studying Greek dancing which pleases me very much." I don't overlook the joy of pleasing someone else in this activity. About mutual friend Gavin Arthur, Murshid says,

Gavin doing well but aging; me doing super-well and not aging. Maybe I have a secret Dorian Gray picture, but I think it is Allah.

Today Murshid shows the proper way to approach one's representative, or *Khalif*, in a letter to *Khalif* Akbar, the part Chinese prize fighter we seldom see. Akbar approached Murshid with a "very heart-cordial letter," and Murshid replies,

We understand perfectly that the Sufi sees life from the standpoint of another as well as of himself. [Seeing from the point of view of another, which Inayat Khan stressed, could be considered training for non-dualistic behavior.] I am certainly not going to throw any burdens on you, although I must note in general your program, your seriousness, your acceptance of studies, your outlook, and your endeavors, remarkably parallel those of *Khalifa* Saadia Khan.

To highly disciplined representatives like Akbar and Saadia, Murshid offers freedom, noninterference, and support.

In your case as in hers, compassion and the wide outlook encourage as much freedom as possible so as not to add to restrictions you have placed around yourselves. No doubt these disciplines, these self-disciplines, will help each of you to reach your goal.

Noting my recent experiences with Jemila and Vilayat, Murshid suggests to Akbar the spiritual value of difficulties. "Mansur has gone through some severe trials which are part of his spiritual awakening."

October 24, 1969, Friday

I feel fine today without Jemila. She says she feels fine without me. I don't sense any remorse on her part for her betrayal. I don't feel she wants to come back to me. From now on, I consider her my ex-wife. I decide to buy a do-it-yourself divorce kit.

Murshid told Atiya in a letter October 15th, "Note must be taken to have *Irfan* sent to you." Today, he's in San Francisco, far from the copies in Novato I'd made the day after we returned from vacation. Murshid reports to Atiya, "I have asked about *Irfan* and we have only a single copy here."

A few weeks ago, the buzzword in these pages (October 1, 1969) for enlightenment was "love-attunement." Today, in a letter to John Stockwell of World Union in San Francisco, it's "the grand awakening." "But the day is past when people of lesser spiritual development are going to be permitted to dominate over those who have had the grand awakening in some form or other." Tomorrow, it's "highest attainment." The concept of enlightenment intrigued me enough to allow Shamcher to make a fool of me. (January 31, 1969) From my perspective, Murshid can't speak enough about it. Stockwell is the local branch leader of a group that Murshid mentions to Atiya in the context of his conflicts.

Have had two "fights" on my hand: One with a group which is very modest, calling themselves "World Union." They have never permitted me to speak on any of the subjects on which I have been trained; and when Vilayat appeared, cut off the question period.

We'll hear more about Stockwell, as that fight turns to friendship.

October 25, 1969, Saturday

Murshid considers his attendance and contributions to classes like Jacob Needleman's "as *exoteric* work to carry mysticism to intellectuals." Murshid is in his glory doing "God's work that Hazrat Inayat Khan wished"—this work with intellectuals. The presentation by Alan Cohen on Meher Baba evokes a balanced, three page response today to Prof. Needleman on "messiahism." The subject is messiahs, sons of God, incarnations of deity, and avatars such as Meher Baba. In short, Murshid says that people promoting an avatar exclude other great ones, showing their shortcomings. The authority behind Murshid's words is himself and Sufi teachings.

I look at the India of this century as Sri Ramakrishna, Ramana Maharshi, and my own Papa Ram Das, with total inability to make any distinctions or differences between all of them with Sufi and Zen saints and masters whom I have met in the flesh. Or as Sufism teaches "Thy light is in all forms, thy love in all beings."

Murshid has the authority to judge, and he reveals, "Why even I was not bestowed with a robe until I had a disciple *who had made it*." Before that, he says,

The general exoteric doctrine is that a real or presumed teacher substantiates his claim not by ego-personality, but by the success of some pupil reaching the highest attainment. Certainly this was true of Sri Ramakrishna and Vivekananda. In a more dramatic and historical way by Marpa and Milarepa.

October 27, 1969, Monday

On the heels of Murshid's letter to *Khalif* Akbar, which was full of comparisons to *Khalifa* Saadia, Murshid notes in a letter to Saadia today,

There is an interesting side-line that your position and that of *Khalif* Akbar are remarkably similar in all the aspects and vicissitudes. Perhaps that is part of the test, or progress, or needs in the spiritual life, or more properly, the complete life which takes in all aspects... The difference between the Sufi and other devotees and mystics is that the teacher takes on, even deliberately takes on, the troubles of disciples.

After noting the many positives in his life, including more followers, a large attendance at his birthday party and meetings, and increased inspirations, Murshid shows that for him, as well as me, Jemila's absence is still affecting things. "On the hard side there are still strong aftermaths of the departure of Jemila Johnson and great uncertainties as to the residences of disciples." As you have read, this includes me.

A lot has been quoted in these pages about Murshid's access to political and spiritual leaders in the East. Murshid tells and retells this story, most recently to his friend Vocha Fiske. (October 1, 1969)

Years ago I said to my friend, Robert Clifton (Phra Sumangalo), "Grand Phra, you and I are mere nobodies. Together we have not been able to get 30 people to listen to us in this city. But I do not think there is a king or prime minister, or cabinet official or university president, or professor or holy man, or, for that matter, peasant from one end of Asia to the other whom you or I cannot meet, if we have not met them already. But who here believes us!"

And Clifton answered, "Too true, Samuel, too true."

Murshid reveals today just how he gained access to philosopher and one time president of India, Dr. Radakrishnan. In a letter to Art Hoppe, Murshid writes, "When he [Dr. Radakrishnan] was President of India, I phoned and came in and saw him, just like that!"

November 1, 1969, Saturday

John Stockwell, head of the Bay Area World Union Center, represents one of Murshid's current "fights": World Unions who won't permit Murshid to speak. Murshid's in-your-face-by-letter style got replies from Stockwell October 21st and 24th—and included, after Murshid spoke about it, a card from Stockwell pledging to visit the Family Dog. In earlier letters Murshid argued both personally ("It is possible that my very gruff tone today may seem out of line with a philosophy of love..."), and critically ("Any group can establish an organization and call itself world this or world that"). Today Murshid speaks not "on account of kindness, but rather to make a diary record to show the change from subjective pretense to objective honesty which is going on in our midst."

> In 1931, I left New York City to return to this state having studied Japanese Zen with one Sokei-an Sasaki and for that which is beyond reason, found myself capable of interpreting the basic scriptures of all religions excepting Zarathustrianism... The prowess of my knowledge—it should be called *dharma*-transmission—from Sokei-an Sasaki came in my first real test in Asian-Asian philosophy in 1945 when I was asked by the Chief Secretary of the first Indian embassy to give an essay on the Sufi Moineddin Ibnu-l'Arabi, and my paper was entitled "The Unity of Ibnu-l'Arabi and Shankaracharya." The secretary warmly embraced me.

The significance of the historical Akbar for the Temple of Understanding and Stockwell's World Union becomes clearer in this letter. After reminding Stockwell that Fathepur Sikri and the Taj Mahal "were not built by ghosts," Murshid writes,

> Any organization pretending to be a World Union or anything like that, that ignores the earlier efforts of the great Moghul Akbar, will have to face sooner or later the public accusation of fraud, and I mean just that.

To state the implied (and more): Akbar built Fathepur Sikri and encouraged religious tolerance. The Taj Mahal was the creation of Akbar's grandson Shah Jahan (1605-1627). The Moghul line ruled India for almost 200 years from Babar (1526-1530) through Humayun, Akbar, Jehangir and Shah Jehan to Aurangzib (1658-1707).

November 4, 1969, Tuesday

For the third week in a row, I audit Murshid's class with poetry instructor Lew Welch at the University of California Extension in San Francisco.

November 5, 1969, Wednesday

I decide while painting to let Murshid be the barometer for the plan I'm hatching to move out of the *khankah*. If he backs it, that will be a sign; if he opposes it, so be it.

November 6, 1969, Thursday

After the real estate man calls to tell me about a perfect house he has found for Jemila and me, I announce at lunch a proposal to move out of the *khankah*. The effect on Murshid and the family is horrendous. Why have I gone ahead with my plan to get another house without consulting Murshid? I remembered Murshid telling me, "I don't want to be involved in the moves of disciples." What I omitted to consider was my duty to him as his secretary. After my announcement and the blowup that follows, another meeting is scheduled. When this issue called the "housing situation" comes up, I am asked to speak. I say, "Due to the sense I got from everybody at the last meeting when I had a plan to move out of the *khankah*, I have abandoned that plan." As a result, I decide that if Jemila comes back and doesn't live with me at the *khankah*, I will file for divorce. What happened to my earlier resolve to divorce? Hope, dumb hope, intervened. Meanwhile, if Jemila doesn't come back, I will file for divorce. Don't believe me until I say I've done it.

November 8, 1969, Saturday

This morning at the *khankah* I finish repairing, sanding, and washing the screens; then I prime them for painting. This afternoon I go to San Francisco and finish waterproofing Zeinob's old room in Murshid's basement before I install a window and a glass door. Zeinob, formerly Gwen, who journeyed with me to Los Angeles to see Vilayat with Greg and David, has moved in upstairs.

There are thirty-two people (fourteen women and eighteen men) at the Saturday night dance class tonight in Murshid's single car garage under the Mentorgarten on Precita in San Francisco. Murshid indicated in a letter to Pir Vilayat (November 3, 1969) that having more than twenty-four people in the dance class precluded individual attention. In response to the overcrowding, Murshid plans to convene a class tomorrow for the new people to do what we started doing when this class began: walk around the block watching our breath.

Am I mentioned in the Pir Vilayat letter? Yes. "Why there has not been a single occasion when I could get Moineddin and Mansur and Daniel and myself together to have a proper business meeting to sign the articles of incorporation."

November 10, 1969, Monday

Murshid writes Murshida Ivy Duce today. As mentioned earlier, (October 24, 1969) Ivy Duce, Sufism Reoriented, and Meher Baba are on Murshid's enemies list: "Have had two 'fights' on my hand... [World Union and] the other is with the Meher Baba people." Wali Ali's interview after Murshid's death with Murshida Ivy Duce, founder of Sufism Reoriented, is relevant at this point.

Just to sort things out: Alan Cohen, who gave the Meher Baba presentation that Murshid commented on in his letter to Professor Needleman (October 25, 1969), is related to Meher Baba through Ivy Duce. Let's go back for the history.

Both Murshid and Ivy Duce were disciples of Murshida Rabia Martin. According to Duce, Martin was designated Hazrat Inayat Khan's spiritual successor. This designation was confirmed by Hassan Nizami, grand master of the Chisti order in New Delhi, India, who has thirteen thousand disciples. As reported by Duce, Nizami heard Inayat Khan name Murshida Martin his successor just before Khan died February 5, 1929. He was buried near Hassan Nizami's home in Delhi.

Murshida Rabia Martin, according to Ivy Duce, received a certificate from Hassan Nizami attesting to her appointment as Inayat Khan's successor. The European followers of Hazrat Inayat Khan did not accept Murshida Martin's certificate. They rejected her for being a woman, an American, and a Jewess. They rallied instead around Maheboob Khan, Inayat Khan's brother.

This rejection didn't deter Murshida Martin from functioning. She traveled to Iraq, Iran, and India, and taught in South America (Brazil) and Australia. But she cried, according to Murshida Duce, when telling about the election that denied her the position Hazrat Inayat Khan wished for her. The tears weren't self pity, Murshida Martin explained, but sadness because the Europeans had broken the hierarchic chain.

Ivy Duce told Wali Ali in the conversation, which she would not allow to be recorded, that when Murshida Martin traveled, she asked Duce to look after her students while she was gone. For the next bit, I quote Wali Ali's notes:

In New York I [Ivy Duce] saw her [Murshida Martin]. She said she was convinced Meher Baba was the *Qutb* [the highest Sufi hierarchical position] and she planned to go see him... Murshida Martin got ill and was never able to go. I was horrified when I was told that I was to take over. Felt unprepared. Thought it was a shame that the work would fail. I decided to go meet Baba. My daughter and I went to India. At that time asked Baba, and he said she [Murshida Martin] was the real successor. I told him, "I understand you're the *Qutb* and I've come for help." Meher Baba said, "It's your destiny to do this and I'll help you." I thought he would send someone to take over. But no, he said, "You do it. Be honest and make no claims. I'll do the work for you." This has always been the case.

When did Ivy Duce take over for Murshida Martin? Apparently, it was when Martin died in 1944. Murshid left California in 1945 for Myrtle Beach, a Meher Baba center. His recent letter to Elizabeth Patterson, still in residence at Myrtle Beach, shows an ongoing connection with this center. Murshid also spoke in the Needleman letter of October 25, 1969, about his Myrtle Beach experience.

As to Myrtle Beach, it was to have been established as a center. Land was acquired, buildings constructed, and I personally was summoned to prepare to give courses on Meher Baba as the Avatar of the age based on evidences from scriptures not studied by the emotionalists but which I had long studied [Ivy Duce said Murshid went to "fix grounds for them"]. And I [Murshid Samuel Lewis] was sent for to give lectures on the scriptures and their allusions to the manifestation of a coming world teacher. Nothing of the kind happened whatever. I was never permitted to speak on any religion. I was submitted to severe moral analysis which was nothing contrasted to that others were subjected to.

Ivy Duce said Murshid "couldn't say one kind thing about them. Intellectual criticism, after eating their bread." According to Duce, Meher Baba sent Murshid a telegram instructing him to return to *Kaaba Allah* in Fairfax, California, for two years (where Duce, presumably, was in charge), "as your working there will help my work."

Most annoying to Duce when Murshid worked under her was what she called Murshid's "transmissions" (again quoting Wali Ali's interview), "where he [Murshid] claimed to speak in the voice of Inayat Khan, Moses, Mohammed, or Meher Baba. In one instance when he had claimed to have a transmission from Baba standing on a balcony, I wrote to Baba about it; and Baba denied it. I read Baba's letter before the group with Samuel there, and told him to stop it."

On December 31, 1948, *Kaaba Allah* burned and, a week later, Murshid resigned from Ivy Duce's Sufi group. Sufism Reoriented was established in 1952. There was the matter of papers still in Murshida Duce's files which she offered to return in August, 1953 "if he [Murshid] would agree to stop sending me letters. I had received 100s of critical letters from him. He promised he wouldn't write any more. He received back the papers, but eventually he started writing letters again."

This brings us pretty much up to the present. There's one undated letter to Murshida Duce from Murshid. Murshid refers to the Sufism Reoriented sign on the hill behind his house. It faces south, so you see it as you're coming in to San Francisco from the airport. It reads, *HAPPINESS CONSISTS IN MAKING OTHERS HAPPY. Meher Baba.* Murshid comments, "Every time I pass that sign there is a vision of the reward or punishment to those who financed the undertaking accordingly as they accept or reject what they themselves have paid for."

And now today, a writing of Meher Baba's titled *Divya Vani* (*My Work*) comes into Murshid's hands. He quotes it and then chides Murshida Duce.

A few weeks ago one received a telephone call that you were ill, and [was] asked that we pray for you. Before God, I shall no longer accept that when someone rightly or wrongly says you are ill, that this person is any way to be blamed either for your illness or for such reports. And before God, and I don't care what your disciples lie to you, I have never said that you were not a Murshida, but I have said that you were not connected with the traditional Sufi orders.

When Murshid wrote Saadia on October 27th that the Sufi takes on the troubles of disciples, I didn't realize how literal that could be.

Murshid has been going through pains in his body for almost the last month. They all reflect the pains and sufferings of disciples near and dear to one. Murshid has not asked Allah to relieve him from such pains. Indeed he has used them as indicators that by looking into his own being he is discovering the trials and tribulations of the daily lives of others. This may not be very comforting, nor is it any solution to a person in pain to be informed that others also are in pain. Equally, it is not particularly beneficial to remind anyone that patience is a great virtue. So instead Murshid is getting these empathetic pains, and is quite willing to bear them. This covers of course your own situation as well as those of others.

November 12, 1969, Wednesday
There are advantages if you get your own place, as well as spiritual benefits, Murshid advises a young disciple, Debbie Churney, in a letter today.

The advantages of settling [are] that you can build your own atmosphere and be comfortable in it and go to it for refuge. What you do otherwise may be your own concern, perhaps must be your own concern. And if Murshid had any advice or instructions, it would be to do your prayers and practices there, perhaps burn a little incense, especially at the beginning.

Speaking self-consciously in a very gentle, fatherly manner ("Murshid has to be your father and mother and grandfather and spiritual guide but not the sheriff or boss man"), he recommends art dealers and friends Chingwah Lee and William Clary to artistically inclined Debbie. Besides advice, Murshid details some of his activities, including his recent visit to a new swami in town [Swahananda], and his performance of dervish dancing last Sunday in San Francisco's Golden Gate Park, followed by attending Paul Reps's public appearance in Sausalito. Murshid previews the next dance class for Debbie. There will be work on the Wheel Dance, which is an outcome of the Sun and Moon Dances. Afterwards,

> There will be a party for Shirin and Mansur in Oakland. Many may want to come, but they will have to pay for themselves. Murshid is paying just for the "family." Then Sunday we are going to have a great big work party and all these dances and maybe more. Hope you can come.

How could she refuse? Debbie, already a disciple and a dancer, continues to support Sufi activities in the Bay Area to this day.

November 13, 1969, Thursday

At the *khankah*, Murshid dictates a letter to poet/teacher Lew Welch. Murshid says he "can by a combination of two items look into the future." The first is the rhythm scheme Alfred Lord Tennyson uses in his poem "Locksley Hall," which begins:

> Comrades, leave me here a little
> > while as yet 'tis early morn.
> Leave me here, and when you want me,
> > sound upon the bugle horn.
> [The content of the poem has nothing to do with it. It is the rhythm.]

The second, "far more relevant being non-egotist," is *prajna*, or insight. For those looking for *The Answer*, Murshid gives it in this letter.

> So whether it is the problem of the suffering of humanity as faced by Lord Buddha and avoided by "Buddhists" or the problems of Lew Welch, these can be faced by rising above the sway of ego—not destroying the ego, but finding the "universal mind" in which we all live and move and have our being.

Easier said than done, right? It's three days since Murshid wrote Saadia about his pain. He's still hurting, telling Lew Welch, "I am in pain as this is being written and it has nothing to do with any dualistic pain."

November 16, 1969, Sunday

After all the delay about signing Vilayat's legal papers to formalize Murshid's work as a "branch" associated with Vilayat's Sufi Order, Murshid writes Atiya, "I had better begin by confessing some 'sins.' It has taken me a long time to get together the three men to sign the Articles of Incorporation, and after getting them together and having them signed, it has been misplaced." At this time, Shirin is building a kiln at the Garden of Inayat, and Murshid exults in his disciples' ability to act without direction. He explains to Atiya,

> As Hazrat Inayat Khan said, "The Message is in the sphere." Without particular conferences so many disciples seem to be seeing, so to speak, with their third eyes,

seeing the same thing, that a great deal of progress has been made without any need for conferences and discussions.

Murshid finds common ground with Atiya through spiritual disputes: Murshid's, with Ivy Duce; Atiya's, with Mr. Dickenson, a functionary in Fazal Khan's organization. Murshid notes in passing that the number of women seeking "power and leadership" is dwarfed by "the growing army of partially enlightened young people." And the mention of women reminds Murshid of his "relation with the Christian Father Blighton."

I met him years ago when practically all his disciples had left him and he was under attack by a number of prominent society "ladies." These women have made it their habit to invade, and annex or try to destroy every new quasi-spiritual movement. I said I would pray for him. At that time he had 6 disciples, 3 of them false; at that time I also had 6 disciples, only 3 of whom have withdrawn, but thank God not false. He now has a following of about 150. His financial assets have multiplied manifold. But the great thing is that he has had at least 20 cases of enlightenment in the past two months.

November 19, 1969, Wednesday

This is the day I finally act on my recurring notion to divorce Jemila. I was shocked to learn from my mother that Jemila returned to Waterloo, Iowa, and left Nathan with her parents there so she could go east again to be with Vilayat. When I talked to Jemila on the phone after that, I felt, *This person isn't acting like a wife ought to act.* That did it; I decided to divorce her and followed through.

The name of this chapter, "The Present Cycle," was taken from a diary letter Murshid writes today to Shamcher. He begins his discussion of current events with the paragraph that appears in this chapter's epigraph. Murshid continues,

It was during the war that when it was said that Hitler was going to call in psychic powers, I asked God what to do and He said: "Go upstairs!" I went upstairs and became an *Abdal* which means changeling [the image that Murshid used for this transformation was "chameleon," in the sense of a changeable person]... I am not going into that history which was rejected by the people of the West and accepted almost unanimously by Asian and Arab Sufis. But when Mansur came to his trial I was given the same instructions, to enter into a higher dimension. This instruction was, unlike the above, to do something on this plane, so we are planning to go to Istanbul in Turkey to the next conference of the great religions of the world under the auspices of the TEMPLE OF UNDERSTANDING...

Murshid goes on to elucidate what he meant when he told Shamcher on the 13th that I carry "the Whiteman-Lewis torch." "The next phase is very old. It was Luther Whiteman who put to me years ago the integration of occultists, religion, and social problems using basic mathematical logic. It was done and forgotten." Teaming up with Shamcher after Murshid's death to work for OTEC (Ocean Thermal Energy Conversion) was one direction that carrying the torch led me. Then, Murshid gives the historical context for *Toward Spiritual Brotherhood* and his reaction to its publication.

Years later I wrote several papers, such as "The Garden of Inayat" etc., either fallen into the hands of Mrs. [Murshida Ivy] Duce or destroyed in the fire of 1949 with a single exception. This, the [book length] paper on *Toward Spiritual Brotherhood* was given as esoteric instruction to disciple Phillip Davenport. He became editor of *The San Francisco Oracle* and without consultation began publishing it. I took it as the sign that God wished it so.

An offhand remark I made at poetry class last night has more significance to Murshid than I understood. "Last night Mansur and I at the same time in the same place individually had 'break-throughs' indicating that many of these people may be coming to our meetings, beginning tonight." It is flattering to be considered in the company of Murshid's top student, Moineddin Jablonski.

You may remember when you asked me about *Khalif*, and I indicated the prowess of Carl Moineddin Jablonski. This has been entirely successful because it came from the Sphere. Vilayat has approved of Mansur and Daniel here, and I have seen also this corroborated so to speak, by God Himself, or at least by and through the sphere. It is remarkable that Mansur, and by himself, has picked up exactly where Luther Whiteman left off and already Vocha [Fiske] knows this. We can learn that God alone exists, that the Sphere (or the *Alaya Vijnana*, to use the Buddhist term) is.

November 20, 1969, Thursday

Murshid is teaching, not preaching, no nonsense now. Beginning to Saadia, he comments at length on his opening greeting.

As-salaam Aleikhum [Peace be upon you]. When this phrase is uttered it is of itself a prayer. When it becomes a mere empty greeting of courtesy it loses all its *baraka* [magnetism]. It is the basis of meditation and devotion and concentration. It is the beginning and end of all things and not just a refuge to fall back on in times of trouble; it is a refuge and more than a refuge... *Fikar* is the special practice of most value—concentrating on LA ILLAHA as we exhale and EL ILALLAH as we inhale. Continue to do this with rhythmical breathing as long as we may, and to do this until it becomes continuous and unconscious, so to speak.

Murshid first told Saadia about his empathetic pains on November 10th. Today, still teaching, he adds,

Murshid is going to the doctor today. He believes that the troubles are psychic and mental, but there is a physical effect. No doubt all of us, breathing in from a disturbed atmosphere pick up these disturbances, and so affected by these disturbances, we are disturbed. It is universal and yet it is personal, but it is universal to a far greater extent than it is personal. Sensitive people are affected by these vibrations, by these atmospheres. The early verses of Holy Quran were meant to be protections against such events and eventualities.

After typing this letter himself, Murshid speaks to me about Saadia and says our marriage would bring him "tremendous personal advantages." This comment blows my mind! Without my knowledge, Murshid has been matchmaking. His letter to Saadia includes some observations about me.

Mansur is well educated. He graduated from university and for some time functioned as a college professor. He feels that life is sterile. He has many aptitudes, such as carpenter and painter. He was an orphan, of apparently excellent family, either scientists or in government service [grandfather Otis B. Johnson was the first Secretary of the Federal Trade Commission created under Franklin Roosevelt]. His foster-father is a fairly successful business man [biology teacher]. Several people have had the same spiritual vision as Allah has given me. It was not my personal vision or feeling but it must be potentially true for it keeps on coming back. As my own potential picture of this ego was always marvelous, one adheres to the same standard with others. Not only with Mansur but with several disciples here it seems to be foreboding: "In that day will the Sun rise in the West and all men, seeing, will believe."

Tonight I practice Gnosis (from *Irfan*) on the subject of my marriage to Saadia. The dream that comes in response to my prayer is merely a replay of yesterday's letter to Jemila. I said in that letter that I divorced her. That's how they do it in Islam: Just say it three times. Further, I said if she were here, I'd spank her and send her to her room—treating her as if she were a misbehaving child. In dream, Jemila is too tired to make love, and I begin spanking her.

November 21, 1969, Friday
The signed articles of incorporation for Murshid's branch of the Sufi Order are finally sent to Suzanne D'Mitrieff.

November 23, 1969, Sunday
Four days after Murshid's last diary entry letter to Shamcher, he writes him another today. Much is happening and Murshid is interested in recording the firsts, such as being called on in Jacob Needleman's class at San Francisco State to explain *Alaya Vijnana* [storehouse of consciousness]. "This is the first time, I believe, this has ever been done and one takes it as a sign of the end of obscurantism and '*an-atta*-ism' [no self-ism] which have passed for 'Oriental Philosophy'."

At this time, Murshid's meetings with a variety of exotic characters, both visitors to his house and encounters he has sought, are inspiring to him. There is Schlomo Carlebach, a Jewish mystic; Vietnamese Zen master Thich Thien An; and Swahananda, a teacher of Hindu spiritual dancing. And today he relates,

Yesterday one had in rapid succession a meeting with two Christian mystics and a visit to the new Zendo recently established here. There is a lady Roshi here... Kennett Roshi was, I understand, a disciple and friend of my life-long friend, Robert Clifton (Phra Sumangalo).

In the past local Buddhists seemed to think, according to Murshid, that "sitting is enlightenment itself." Yet Murshid says, "I have yet to receive any report locally of either '*satori*' or recognition of 'others' as themselves." In the presence of Kennett Roshi yesterday, Murshid felt comfortable enough "to report the second Sojiji visit at Tsurumi, between Yokohama and Tokyo." That's the report that, Murshid jokingly remarks, killed Nyogen Senzaki. The story goes that Murshid came back from Japan and asked Senzaki: "When Sam and Sogen Asahina met, were there two, one, or no people in the room?" It may have killed Senzaki in the sense that ofttimes when a student has the grand realization, the life's purpose of the teacher is accomplished. Then they choose to leave the body. In passing, Murshid notes the relationship of *mahamudra* meditation with the Sufi term *mushahida* (contemplation).

The *bhumis* [stages] and *paramitas* [perfections] of essential Buddhism are the same as the *Urim* [lights] and *Thummim* [perfections] of the Bible and, no doubt, of the *hal* [state] and *makam* [station] of Sufism. For years one has been arguing there is a single *DHARMA* [Buddhist teaching] which is reflected in the word *Ekayana*.

In practical matters, Murshid reports that an invitation has come from Boston (the East-West center, one of our hosts on our return from the Temple of Understanding conference) and a volunteer secretary has appeared who is willing to type some Zen manuscripts.

November 24, 1969, Monday

In a letter to Anandashram, Murshid uses the same words a therapist might use to describe his emerging vision. "Sam did not return to the United States with any grandiose schemes, but if we are to take visions and dreams seriously, he may have to play an important or dramatic role in the world." Murshid reiterates the oneness he has felt meeting other great souls.

Sam has found, when he meets these spiritual representatives of any faith whatsoever, there is no differentiation of personality. It is *tat twam asi*. There is no sense of meeting "somebody else," and this is true regardless of the person or faith involved.

Rarely does Murshid speak about spiritual phenomena, but here he does. Referring to an earlier report ("Sam told about the resonance which takes place in singing the *Ramnam* using the head as a dome"), he tells Anandashram, "Now the resonance has become more complete, using and vibrating the whole body, demonstrating what is taught, is taught but not studied in the Christian Bible, that 'The human body is the temple of the Holy Spirit.'" It is not just *Ramnam*; with the Sufi *ziker*, "it is happening exactly the same"—as also in some disciples, "sometimes more significantly in them than in Sam."

November 27, 1969, Thursday

The creative process is ongoing for Murshid. Tonight at the *khankah*, he introduces Dervish Square Dancing. "The Square dance is an American institution, four couples," Murshid will tell Saadia tomorrow. "We begin with *La illaha El Il Allah*, then add *Allah*, then *El Allahu*, then *Allahu*." This one just came through and will be presented Sunday at the Saturday dance class, moved a day due to today's Thanksgiving holiday being celebrated on Saturday. The dance evolves, and a square dance using *Ramnam* proves more popular.

November 29, 1969, Saturday

Murshid gives his retrospective on Thanksgiving—celebrated today—to goddaughter Saadia, who's back at Cornell University.

We had a wonderful holiday, both houses together. We have no more room here at the table so are considering adding another table if there is room for chairs. We had 13, with Mansur away. It also marked a period when some financial matters— relations with the disciples living with me—cleared up considerably. Mostly unconsciously, they were having Murshid carry burdens and worries, making all legitimate business hard. And add to that the pain one was carrying, now remarkably diminished.

Then Murshid looks back to Wednesday and speaks about the ecstasy generated by a couple of disciples who produced a musical rendition of *Allah*.

This was introduced by the choral master, Bill Mathieu, and Moineddin. It was all-powerful and was marked by the descent of the Holy Spirit upon this person so that his voice enveloped everyone's and from what I understand was also both the highest and lowest. I do remember it was the loudest by far. It took one up into spiritual consciousness.

We were a tolerant bunch, and, I think, everyone got a kick out of Murshid's singing.

November 30, 1969, Sunday

Disciples are working. That's good! There is no help. That's bad! It's a situation Murshid, as a balanced Libra, feels both stressed about and comfortable with. He needs help and disciples must work. It is harder for me being caught in this. Murshid emphasizes the positive in a letter to Vocha Fiske. "Of three others who have been my secretaries, it must

388

be said they are all working now, which has eased my financial burden somewhat."

Murshid introduces the word "realism" in this letter, and I want to note its first occurrence here. It will appear numerous times in subsequent correspondence, and frankly, it gets a little boring. But since it's Murshid's code word for others' subjective interpretations of what he considers to be objective reality, let it be noted how he uses it here, in one of its first appearances.

Fortunately I can laugh at some of my own dilemmas—for instance new correspondence both from far and near which shows that sooner or later what is objectively right will be accepted by more and more people. This characterizes more than anything else my present existence. There is also encouragement to write my memoirs, which will be a diatribe against the passing subjectivisms mislabeled 'realism'."

For reasons I will learn later, Murshid alerts Vocha of his intention to visit Los Angeles, where she lives, in the middle of January, 1970.

Chapter 24:

December 1969 and January 1970

Once I was teaching a group. They wanted to learn dervish dances. I said, "Repeat Allah." "We can't." "Why?" "We are Jewish." "I know that. All right repeat the Name of God given by Moses." "Oh, we can't possibly do that." "I knew that before I began, and that is why I have asked you to repeat Allah. I am trying to respect, not insult you." They repeated Allah. So the great name of God remains a mystery because pseudo-devotees [Jews] who claim their religion is THE RELIGION also claim they are such sinners that they can't do this and that. I accept no idea of sin; we have too much of it. I stress, "Be ye perfect" and try to follow Christ and Mohammed and Krishna but no nonsense, and it works. People in the end accept realities, verities. (Murshid's letter to William Arlock of Great Books in Los Angeles, December 6, 1969)

Here in San Francisco at the last meeting of the U.N., Honorable U Thant said, "What the world needs is a moral and spiritual revolution." Most everybody applauded and loudly. The Cardinals, the metropolitans, the chief Rabbis, the top representatives of all the worlds' faiths and unfaiths shook their heads in approval. I was horrified, and still am. I told my companion of the evening, we are going to see now so many bloodbaths that it will be impossible to take account of them. That ended my friendship with my companion of the evening—Brother, can you spare a dime for Biafra? Or is it for the orphans of Viet Nam? Or is it for the Palestinian refugees? Or is it...? (Murshid's letter to Art Hoppe, December 28, 1969)

December 6, 1969, Saturday

Murshid treats a letter from William Arlock (see above) as an inquiry for spiritual teachings, but only certain ones. Murshid discourages Arlock from pursuing Kabala.

I do not encourage interest in Kabala. This was a secret and sacred transmission among the Hebrew peoples. It was handed down basically in silence. What is known as "Kabala" today is a very limited and non-Jewish complex of psychism and occultism with almost no relation to the *Sepher Yetzirah* [*Book of Creation*, 2nd-4th centuries, the original Jewish mysticism based on the creation story and elemental alchemy] and very little with the *Sepher Ha Zohar* [*Book of Light*, written by Moses de Leon, circa 13th century]. Besides their inner sciences began and ended with the Sacred Name of God.

Murshid offers to send introductory Sufi papers or to give suggestions on studies in "devotion or mysticism." He coins the term "Grand Consciousness" in this letter ("others are also attracting the young and bringing them into experiences of the Grand Consciousness"), to go along with "love-attunement" and "grand awakening." I love these concepts.

Some other concepts that are the foundation of Sufi esoteric teaching show up in a letter to Shamcher today. Murshid revives the issue of a deletion of the Sufi method of realization from the 1914 edition of *The Sufi Message of Spiritual Liberty*.

The deletion from *The Sufi Message of Spiritual Liberty* that Sufism is based on *kalama, nimaz, wazifa, ziker, fikar, kasab, shagal* and *amal* [as the easiest, shortest, and most interesting path to spiritual accomplishment] still stands [in the most recent edition]. The fact that these words were not explained [or mentioned] in the text only indicates that they belong to traditional Sufis and no corporation has any claim here.

December 7, 1969, Sunday

Earlier (November 16, 1969) Murshid wrote his Korean Zen Master, Kyung Bo Seo, that he admired Dr. Neville Warwick's "mountain climbing approaches to spiritual awakening." However, the ceremonial aspect of Warwick's work, known as *puja*, comes under fire today. Murshid writes Warwick, "I have accepted *Vajrayana* as far as *Mahamudra* is concerned and rejected it as far as *pujas* are concerned. Buddha did not proclaim *pujas*, and I have not found any illuminatory experiences as the result thereof." Murshid is interested in awakening, not ceremony. But Murshid concedes,

Much as I may criticize *puja*, it is infinitely better than ego-ship and some of your erstwhile associates seem to have gone astray after egos with their empty aphorisms. At times I believe aphorisms cause more evil than wickedness; they spread endless confusion.

While Buddhist ceremony is one target for Murshid today, the popular Buddhist practice of sitting is another. Murshid writes Master Seo, "There is no doubt multitudes of Americans will become interested in the *Dharma* when it consists of something more than just sitting." How does one master speak to another master? However they are guided to speak.

December 8, 1969, Monday

Murshid considers today's position letter to Shamcher important enough to send copies to Vilayat Khan at Suresnes (a suburb of Paris where Inayat Khan made his home) and Vilayat's L.A. secretary, Bibijan. After saying he's not concerned any more with "the bypassing of the instructions given to me by Hazrat Inayat Khan," Murshid states diplomatically that he intends "to function in and with them fully, so far as they do not impede progress or cause needless confusion." Who could object? Furthermore, Murshid, unlike Vilayat's critics, wants Vilayat's teachings "incorporated into the Sufic compendium"; but Murshid, still the diplomat, doesn't want to do it without Vilayat's permission. What this means is that, unlike the Europeans, Murshid accepts Vilayat; therefore, whatever he offers would be accepted as part of the Sufic field of knowledge. Reiterating the previously mentioned omission from later editions of *The Sufi Message of Spiritual Liberty*, and with the 1914 edition of the book in hand, Murshid mentions another deletion: a sentence that said Hazrat Inayat Khan "attracted many disciples and founded an order of Sufism for America, the headquarters being at San Francisco."

We now know from Murshida Duce's interview with Wali Ali (see November 10, 1969) that the Europeans passed over Murshida Martin as successor to Hazrat Inayat Khan, explaining why they might want to obliterate all reference to the headquarters being in San Francisco. Acknowledging headquarters could give Murshida Martin standing. But what would the motivation be for leaving out the method of realization of the Sufis? The answer to this goes to the heart of this fracas that Murshid is joining: the attempt of a modern corporation to control ancient teachings. In the book, the method of realization was too public.

Murshid points out that before methods like *kalama, nimaz, wazifa, ziker, fikar, kasab, shagal* and *amal* appeared in the *Gathas*—which discussed all of these except *amal*—*The Sufi Message of Spiritual Liberty* was used as a textbook. Murshid knows about *amal* from letters Hazrat Inayat Khan wrote to Murshida Martin—letters presently in Murshida Duce's files.

December 11, 1969, Thursday

Murshid's lesson at *Gatha* class is that evolved people are like the sun. They give and ask no return. They are like the rain in the saying, "The rain falls on the just and unjust." This notion finds expression in a letter (December 21, 1969) to Shemseddin Ahmed.

Not only from legends and traditions, but from my own experiences, both Isa [Jesus] and Mohammed seem to have operated as if they were Sun in human form, not Allah in human form but the SUN in human form. The Sun gives, the Sun blesses, the Sun does not depend on human kind, the Sun does not depend on earth, the Sun does not depend.

The lesson jogs my memory, and I remember Murshid saying at some point, "Each person should be helping another person to solve his problem." That makes counselors of all of us.

After the *Gatha* class and during tea at the *khankah*, Murshid tells me he and I are going to Bibijan's for a Sufi Order organizational meeting in January. Going, that is, if I'm not working. I am glad. This is a change from this afternoon, when Murshid said he would take Moineddin because of the trouble I am having with Vilayat.

December 13, 1969, Saturday

A few days ago (November 13, 1969) Murshid offered poet Lew Welch advice on how to see into the future. On the same subject today, Murshid writes Vocha Fiske,

It is so easy and so provoking to really see into the future and it has nothing to do with any form of psychism, at least any I know. It requires an absolute honesty which few people have and even I do not particularly like or admire. It is the honesty of a football referee or umpire [illegible], cold, stern, and exceedingly balanced and straight forward.

December 14, 1969, Sunday

The American Council on the Middle East's call for "a just settlement" in the Middle East comes under fire from Murshid today. He notes, in response to their letter of December 11th, the absence of Arab and Muslim culture in U.S. institutions of higher learning.

Therefore, I do not know what you mean by "just settlement" until some form of *justice* provides for instructions in Arab culture in this land on a basis fairly comparable to instructions in European and Jewish cultures.

Murshid adds Prince Dara Shikoh to the growing list of topics to be presented at the Temple of Understanding conference, writing, "I hope to be able to present three names before that august assemblage, i.e. Sultan Suleiman the Magnificent, Emperor Akbar, and Prince Dara Shikoh."

Going beyond reporting what he is doing, Murshid sets himself up as equal to the American Council on the Middle East and challenges them to "consider our ideas, and our ideals and accomplishments as in accord with your own endeavors." Given that, Murshid says, "we shall be only too glad to send you the proper financial disbursements to this common end."

Murshid announces to Oliver Reiser that he's received a copy of Shamcher's book *Every Willing Hand*. He anticipates the book "will take my name and person not only out of ignominy, but into the very opposite direction. After all, my career has consisted in being rejected and having the rejecters gawk every time a great personality came here and we encountered in public."

Murshid is still excited a month later (January 18, 1970) and his reaction to Shamcher's book overflows in a letter to columnist Art Hoppe.

My friend Bryn Beorse [Shamcher], is publishing a book in which he gives a good section of a whole chapter ["The Communicators"] to this person and the world is going to be annoyed in taking a mere nobody and comparing him to the greatest figures of the day. But at least I can protest I am [meaning, he exists], and not a figure of the imagination. I certainly know the Jewish, Christian, and Islamic religions and the history of practically every country in Asia, to say the least.

Murshid is referring to Shamcher's comparison of him with Dag Hammarskjöld, Secretary General of the United Nations from 1953 to 1961. Shamcher says,

Sam's position and work were never a secret. Some say he shouted from the housetops. His contemporary, Dag Hammarskjöld of the United Nations, on the other hand, kept his mystic trend hidden from all but a few trusted friends. Many hail this attitude as the essence of wisdom, and in view of Dag Hammarskjöld's position it might well have been. Sam's open door and un-secrecy may stem from a different kind of wisdom, from a different sort of circumstances, for one thing realizing that if the mystic's goods be not now openly sought and coveted, our civilization may face a dim future. (p.77)

Exalted by the reception of his *Ramnam* square dance at the dance class last night, Murshid tells Anandashram,

Sam hears that his dances are now spreading like wild-fire. He has no monopoly, no copyright and if Ram wishes this it will come and not all man's organizations, not all the closed "Yoga" groups in the world can stop it, for heart calls to heart and soul to soul.

December 15, 1969, Monday

With the exception of a few revelations, it is not the content of Murshid's letter today to Jacob Needleman that is noteworthy; it is the format. Murshid omits writing Needleman's name and address in typical business heading format above the greeting. Instead of the normal greeting,

Murshid writes, "Dear Ram," explaining, "I am purposely omitting your name as several carbons are being made of this." No other correspondents are officially copied at the end of the letter, but from the letter's headline, TOWARD REAL CULTURAL INTEGRATION OF REAL PEOPLE AND REAL CULTURES IN THE OBJECTIVE WORLD, one could guess that Dr. Haridas Chaudhuri at the Cultural Integration Fellowship might receive one.

Readers of this book will be familiar with all of the stories and most of the concepts in this four page letter. Several new revelations include how Murshid ended up with the Sufis, and an early important teaching. Murshid shares that his deep study of "the real Upanishads and real sacred literature of real India" showed him "that there were deep parallels between certain intellectual and psychological processes in man, whether of the East or West, and this landed me in the camp of the Sufis." Further, at least two pages later, Murshid reveals a Sufi teaching that he has held like a principle.

I was trained from the beginning in Sufism: never discuss what you have not experienced, and the same standard and integrity used in discourses on the sciences is applied by me equally in the historical and mystical fields.

By setting for himself the standard used by scientists, Murshid points out, he excludes himself from integrational movements.

December 16, 1969, Tuesday

We have seen Murshid lecture a Muslim, like Iran's Dr. Seyyed Hossein Nasr, along the lines of, "We do many things here that do not please 'Muslims' but the question is, do they please Allah!" He writes in this vein today to Muslim W.D. Begg, the biographer of Sufi great Moineddin Chisti, in Ajmer, India.

Let's be clear, were Murshid to repeat what he says here in some Islamic countries, Muslims would come at him with knives ("Too much nonsense about the 'Five Pillars' of Islam. *The Pillar is Allah*"). Murshid's pillars of Islam, he writes Begg, are *ishk* (love), *ilm* (knowledge), *shahud* (bearing witness that God alone exists), *rahmat* (divine compassion), and Mohammed. (The traditional Islamic pillars are profession of faith, prayer, alms, fasting, and pilgrimage.) From Murshid's place of safety in San Francisco, he works to make attitude adjustments to others from a distance. Begg is an intellectual, who will perhaps gain some understanding when he receives Murshid's appraisal of Meher Baba.

Meher Baba either was instructed in or appropriated the intellectual side of Sufism. He failed miserably as to *fana* [assimilation in]. He called LOVE *surrender*, meaning mostly surrender to him. I call LOVE self-effacement in the Beloved.

After another statement expressing his openness to Rama, Krishna, Shiva, Buddha, Christians, and Jews, which "will shock Muslims," Murshid asserts his intention to outdo the Bhagavad Gita. How? In his as yet unwritten poem "Rassul Gita" ("It is within me and there are stacks of notes, but now the trance/vision is complete").

But all of this including your suffering and mine point to *Rassul Gita,* which is this compendium of my life based on *fana-fi-lillah* [absorption in God] via the *Bismillah* [in the name of Allah], for out of this comes everything, and the goal set for me is to outdistance even *Bhagavad Gita.*

December 17, 1969, Wednesday

Murshid and I go to the Windsor Vineyards in Sonoma County, where Murshid buys some cases of wine for Christmas presents—mostly for older friends, not disciples. When Windsor can't fill a case with the brand Murshid wants, we drive to their Sausalito distribution outlet and purchase what the vineyard didn't have. With journal entries like the following, you can tell things are getting back to normal for me.

1) Cleaned off my desk; 2) Gave Fatima her photo receipt (for buying photos of Murshid I was selling); 3) Collected 63 cents from Jehanara; 4) Started a "Places Murshid has taken us" section in the *khankah* journal; 5) Wrote out my rent check 6) Paid my VW insurance; 7) Took Murshid to Egger's Nursery, the bakery, and the bank; 8) Picked up Ayesha's typewriter and Ayesha, brought them to the *khankah,* and later took Ayesha home; 9) Went to the lumber yard; 10) Worked on a Subject Index for the 12 volumes of *The Sufi Message*; 11) Practiced the Zorba the Greek dance routine I learned in my Monday night Greek dance class with music in the family room. You see I am going my way now. This is the day Murshid is leading dervish dances in San Francisco; 12) Read some about King Arthur.

December 20, 1969, Saturday

Four days ago Murshid told Begg near the beginning of his letter that he had to "condemn [some] emissaries from India" for making "disastrous predictions, none of which have come true." Today, he writes A.B. Patel that he doesn't want to "deplore. We are out to act." How does Murshid act? "If one were to put the super-conscient into a word it would be HEART." And then, a page later: "I must repeat, to me the super-mental consciousness means the HEART consciousness... The awakened heart feels the sufferings of all mankind."

Lest anyone thinks Murshid gets stuck in a condemn/deplore mode, the same day he writes Patel he is writing a gracious letter of appreciation to Wallace Thompson, executive director of the American Society for Eastern Arts, which sponsored an Indonesian dance recital attended by sixteen disciples. The dance troupe is managed by a woman named Tandy, whom Murshid calls "one of our spiritual sisters."

To old friend Sharab, Murshid writes, "We are planning a Cross and a Manger [for Christmas] but no *tree*." This is one of those cases where a disciple took action without instruction from Murshid. Mansur formulated a plan to manifest the Cross that Murshid told correspondents he would have rather than a Christmas tree—without orders from Murshid.

December 21, 1969, Sunday

The challenge Murshid stakes out in his letter to S. Ahmed is to bridge the gap "between surrender to Allah and what passes as 'Islam'." As an example, Murshid cites the fact that "a 'good Muslim' does not even have to say any *kalama* [prayers]; he just has to require that others do it." This, of course, is the definition of hypocrisy. For S. Ahmed, whose address is simply "The Mall" (Lahore's main street), Murshid condenses his purpose at the upcoming Temple of Understanding conference to bringing "a message of spirituality and universality based on direct experience and wisdom." I appreciate Murshid's careful qualification of his acceptance of all the world's scriptures "not contradicted by Holy Quran." He goes on to S. Ahmed,

I do not accept that Quran was the only sacred book. Holy Quran does not say it is the only sacred book. But bigots have made it "the only sacred book" and by so doing have taken away its value.

Murshid indulges in feigned ignorance regarding some children in the park. Surely one who can see into the future can see (if he were to look) that the children saw us all dancing and chanting when Murshid led us in this very park a few months back during carnival. Yet he tells S. Ahmed, "Recently to my amazement, as I was crossing a square in front of this house a group of young children came to me, surrounded me, and chanted ALLAH, ALLAH, ALLAH. Whence this inspiration?"

December 22, 1969, Monday

On November 10, 1969, Murshid writes Murshida Ivy Duce, "Don't think I am not going to have this prayer [prayers of Meher Baba] published." This is a ploy Murshid explains today in his letter to Elizabeth Patterson at the Meher Baba Center in Myrtle Beach, South Carolina.

In a way a request to use the Prayers of Meher Baba was a test. If a Prayer be copyrighted, it is no longer a Universal Prayer... If the persons I had approached were spiritual at all, they would have been thankful that I even mentioned Baba; more thankful that I would be broadcasting his prayers. Instead a rude rebuff. I have thrown away most of these rebuffs.

Echoing what he told A.B. Patel a few days ago, Murshid shares with Elizabeth Patterson the secret of his success: "I have been so many places where western man has not gone, and *this was possible because the doors of the heart have been opened."*

December 24, 1969, Wednesday

I wake up weeping. In dream I was sitting facing Murshid. He was giving *darshan*, and tears were coming to my eyes.

> Though there are grades and though we may even know how much these grades differ from one another, they do not have common denominators; you cannot always express the awareness of one grade in the language of another. You can make others feel it. And therefore sometimes there is the practice of TAWAJJEH or DARSHAN to enable others to learn by feeling. But in this there is no speech communication. When speech is used, it is for quite other purposes. (Murshid's *Commentary on The Inner Life*, p.25)

There's a subtle shift in Murshid's attitude toward A.B. Patel at the World Union. He writes Patel again today, refraining from blaming Sri Aurobindo's World Union for excluding unknown people, and instead expressing the spirit of Christ on this day before Christmas.

> Deep down, we have to come to human understanding and love. I cannot demand that mankind accept my mystical experiences. It is in my poetry, it is in my *darshans*, and it is in manifestations of using Universal Mind in operation.

For me, Murshid's history of rejected mystical experiences is always something of a mystery. I value mystical experience. Doesn't everyone? When Murshid opens this letter by telling about a Christmas retreat where "the heavens opened and Jesus Christ manifested with a world mission... concerned with bringing peace in Palestine," this sounds impressive! A visit from Jesus, a world mission—one might think all the Christians who value Jesus would give support, if they only knew! What Jesus advised, Murshid shares later, was "the internationalization and de-politicalization of all holy cities; I stand [and say] before the Living God that the divine inspirations, which originally brought this to both my inner and outer consciousness, stand." The internationalization and de-politicalization of Jerusalem, whether you characterize it as an idea from anybody or an idea from Jesus, remains to be accomplished.

December 25, 1969, Thursday

Christmas Eve there was a party in Murshid's garage. The room was decorated with tie dyed sheets, colored paper lamp shades, many scented candles, soft mats on the floor, and a cross, which I crafted out of some rugged six by sixes I found somewhere.

After Murshid's gathering we went to the Church of Man for the midnight service. A girl with bright eyes I'd seen at talks Murshid had given there was there again. I gave her Murshid's present to me, the still-wrapped votive candle, one of which Murshid presented with blessings earlier to each of the eighty or more people at his house.

After sharing presents with Murshid and the family this Christmas morning in Novato, we all go to Nancy Fish's house in Sausalito for a party.

December 29, 1969, Monday

No, there is no telephone call from Finley Dunne, Jr. in Washington informing Murshid the Temple of Understanding conference has been moved from Istanbul to Geneva. Rather, Murshid calls them. He writes afterwards,

> I was very glad to have your news this morning. My own recent experiences with the Turkish visitors to this city fully confirmed your report. As a side issue, it will be far more comforting to be meeting in Geneva, where I can not only present any program or talk in conformance with the general purposes of the Temple of Understanding, but where I shall be in a position to cooperate even more fully with Pir Vilayat Khan.

This is the most overt Murshid has gotten with Finley Dunne, Jr. about actually making a presentation at the conference. The remainder of this short half page letter is a glowing endorsement of Pir Vilayat. Murshid makes the incredible claim "that consciously or unconsciously Pir Vilayat Khan is promoting the program of universality in spiritual dancing much better than my own ego could have." At this point, I don't think Pir Vilayat ever led a dance, so his ability to promote universality through dancing eludes me.

Before that, Murshid writes, "I have dared to compare a meeting with Pir Vilayat Khan some time back to that between Gornemant and Parsifal." Is this the reason a week ago I was researching King Arthur? In the *Encyclopedia of Arthurian Legends*, I read that Gornemant de Goort taught Parsifal chivalry and knighted him. In other words, Gornemant was Parsifal's mentor.

In a letter to Shamcher, Murshid effuses about the change of location of the Temple of Understanding conference. "I am glad it has been transferred *from* Istanbul for our recent experiences show that the present Turkish regime is extremely narrow and reactionary." I am disappointed, having already devoured a big book about the Sophia Mosque (The Church of Divine Wisdom—*Sancta Sophia* in Latin, *Hagia Sofia* in Greek, *Aya Sofya* in Turkish). It isn't until I follow the footsteps of Alexander the Great (1998) that I visit this mosque.

December 30, 1969, Tuesday
Murshid threw down the gauntlet to accept his ideas, ideals and accomplishments in his letter (December 14, 1969) to the American Council on the Middle East. Today he characterizes A.C.M.E.'s response as "your very fair letter of December 27th." Murshid adds, "We *may* [emphasis mine] be working closely with you." Remember, Murshid offered "proper financial disbursements" if "you can consider our ideas, and our ideals and accomplishments as in accord with your own endeavors." But what further elements does Murshid add? First, he makes "potential cooperation" contingent upon a long awaited visitation by an Arab from Israel. Then, Murshid gives several concrete suggestions for Middle East peace solutions, using the royal "we." It's a daunting mix of practical suggestions and affirmations of beliefs for Frank C. Sakran, executive secretary of the American Council on the Middle East, to digest.

We believe there should be, indeed there must be, neutral recognition of various religions and holy places. We see in desert reclamation infinite potentialities for the solution of many of the problems of the day. We practice the brotherhood of man, without verbal nonsense. We welcome all peoples. We have a mass of materials both on the religions of the world, and the potentialities of development of the Near East. We believe there is a God; we believe as Quran teaches that He always has His vicegerents on earth. We do not accept the outworn method of pious appeals. We consider the resolutions passed by both Muslims and Israelis, vanity and useless.

Finally, Murshid suggests that all the above might require "great power" intervention in the area in order to bring peace.

Although any actual suggestion is controversial, when the Greeks and Turks fought some 140 years ago, the great powers took it upon themselves to bring peace by intervention. We believe this may be necessary now.

December 31, 1969, Wednesday
I work all morning with a terrible toothache, assembling new hospital beds for the convalescent hospital in Greenbrae. I seek emergency dental care in the afternoon, and the root canal costs $185. The crowd at Amin and Amina's New Year's Eve party in Corte Madera, including Dr. Neville Warwick's Vajrayana Buddhists, numbers around 100 people.

January 4, 1970, Sunday
Murshid's attitude softened in his letter to A.B. Patel on December 24, 1969. The reason, other than the Christmas season, is not apparent until today, when Murshid tells correspondents Anandashram and Haridas Chaudhuri that he's received a "retraction and apology from Mr. Patel, one of the leaders of the Sri Aurobindo movement." The karma the Aurobindo movement faced, Murshid tells Anandashram, was being excluded "from

the convocations of holy men [for example, at the Family Dog], and from considerations in the class studies of our colleagues and [at] universities [Murshid's class studied Meher Baba, but not Sri Aurobindo]."

The Asia Foundation published a picture of the Mangla Dam on the Jhelum River in West Pakistan in their December 27, 1969, weekly newsletter, *The Asian Student.* Murshid writes the Asia Foundation and says, "I cannot over praise you." In the twenty-first century, Murshid's praise would not be politically correct. Starting back in 1994, the World Bank's awful record of financing development projects that promote environmental destruction and the dislocation and impoverishment of local communities spawned the "Fifty Years is Enough" movement. Murshid, however, is interested in "pragmatic outlooks" that solve problems. He explains:

My whole life—not very successful as yet—has been dedicated to an unnecessary war between *reality* and "realism." The example I have used the most, and to no avail, has been the successful construction of this Mangla Dam, and the now hush-hushed reports on Aswan Dam [under construction in Egypt with Russian help]. To me there is such a vast difference between American accomplishments and communist programs that it is impossible to arrive at any satisfactory logical conclusions... I am not engaged in any crusade against communism. I am personally against any form, against all forms of dialectics. And perhaps my American background makes me sympathetic to pragmatic outlooks. But I believe these pragmatic outlooks and their successful adaptations to the problems of the day can and should make all of us optimistic.

Murshid notes cryptically in a letter to Bibijan that there has been some resolution of the threat of a lawsuit by Fazal Khan mentioned in the beginning of this chapter. Murshid writes, "I understand that those who try to start some disturbances in the Northwest have been properly taken to task." No further details are available. Continuing to Bibijan, Murshid says, "I have made preliminary arrangements to fly south [for Pir Vilayat's business meeting] with Mansur and to cover all the functions necessary or advisable in your region."

January 5, 1970, Monday

A letter today from Pir Vilayat in France tells Murshid that Vilayat will come to San Francisco for just one day, but omits details, so Murshid doesn't know the day or time of his arrival. Murshid is also in the dark about whether he is expected to be in Los Angeles for a business meeting, or even if there is a meeting scheduled. Murshid confides to Shamcher his need to clarify with Vilayat as to "our program [at the Temple of Understanding meeting], whether [it is] the same or mutual or distinct."

The transfer of the meeting from Istanbul to Geneva signals to Murshid the likely attendance of Pir Vilayat himself at the conference. This—along with an inquiry from another man in Los Angeles, whom Murshid characterizes in a letter to Bibijan as "a good contact" and to Shamcher as one who made "a complete inquiry into my spiritual dancing"—prompts Murshid to limit the number of courses he takes at the various universities. "I am discontinuing my university studies," Murshid writes. "They are going to be restricted to an attendance at a class on Vietnam on Saturday morning, for which I shall enroll but not seek credit, due to questionable attendance."

January 6, 1970, Tuesday

William Arlock is the "good contact" in Los Angeles. Murshid uses Arlock's offer to help as an opportunity to "give some background to be a platform from which to work" in a letter to Arlock. What follows, among other details, are the dates 1916, 1919, and 1923, associated, respectively, with the years that Murshid read the Upanishads, met Rabia Martin, and encountered Hazrat Inayat Khan in person. Arlock's request for guidance is answered. Murshid recommends *The Mysticism of Sound* by Hazrat Inayat Khan. Murshid invites Arlock to "charge it to my account" at Books in Review in Los Angeles, which happens to be Vocha Fiske's mail drop. Murshid says, "I know them very well and a visit to them at an early date is imperative for a number of quite private reasons." Murshid has requested a meeting with a dance faculty member at U.C.L.A., Dr. Alma Hawkins. He volunteers to call on Arlock "at your convenience" while he's in L.A. In one part of the letter, Murshid mentions learning from Ruth St. Denis "how to read the *akashic* records." In another part, Murshid tells a story intended to show his interest in the mysticism of sound.

> I was lecturing at the Theosophical Society in Oakland, when I was explaining a certain combination of fire and earth, and gave out the sound of what I called a war-chant. A man standing near jumped way up into the air and said, "Who did that? For goodness sake stop!" "Why?" "That is the Zulu war chant; where did you learn it?"

In closing, Murshid dictates a funny mistake—"I shall let you know further when a trip south is impossible"—then writes, "When there was a test to determine who was most advanced in Mahayana given by the Grand Master of Korea, this 'Sufi' surpassed all the various Buddhist *leaders* (most of whom are not on speaking terms with each other!)."

All the above is quite serious. This kind of shameless and confident self-promotion is what has attracted me to Murshid. I wanted to see what was behind all this bravado. Dear reader, I'm sorry I couldn't express this for you earlier. Unfortunately, in the beginning, such an understanding was only a deep stirring within me. As the Sufis say, expression develops in stages, which are: feeling, thought, and finally speech.

January 8, 1970, Thursday

During the lesson tonight I have a vision of each of the assembled disciples creating a pocket of influence, as in the days of old, making Murshid a very great *Shaikh* by virtue of the influence of his spiritual descendants.

January 9, 1970, Friday

Shamcher sends me the first of several checks for $5 today, each accompanied by some comical explanation for his generosity. I thank him and add, "Your wonderful check is exactly 1/6 of my entire treasure hoard but it lacks the all-important signature." Then, I return it for signature.

January 10, 1970, Saturday

Murshid almost blackmails my old employer, the PBS TV station KQED in San Francisco, for an interview with the Arab Sufi citizen of Israel "expected here hourly." A pledge to contribute in exchange for an interview is promised, and then withdrawn. If the man "expected here hourly" doesn't arrive by the end of February (Murshid has gone from hourly to bimonthly), Murshid promises, "you will get a check anyhow. I am not a blackmailer, I am not an expert, I am just one of a multitude of little Americans, 'ugly Americans' if you will, who have been there. And someday we are going to be heard."

The scene Murshid describes in a letter to Julie Medlock takes place in Professor Needleman's class. When Murshid declares, "What is needed is humility," someone challenges him. Murshid tells the rest of the story. "When one asked, 'What is humility?' Sam replied, 'Ability to listen.'" The point Murshid is making to Julie is that A.B. Patel, Auroville, and the various World Unions and integrational movements have no humility. They will not listen to others. Just to make sure Julie gets the point, Murshid summarizes the class attitude toward a few contemporary movements.

Krishnamurti and Meher Baba were certainly rejected; the Subud movement was ignored; Zen Buddhism was greeted "neutrally"; Tibetan Buddhism with some warmth; Sri Aurobindo not even mentioned; Sri Ramakrishna with considerable warmth—and I ask, "Why not?"—he achieved God-consciousness and passed it to Swami Vivekananda and others and this stream of spiritual consciousness is still functioning.

January 11, 1970, Sunday

Murshid has a meeting with the Consul General of Indonesia during the day, and initiates six young men and one young woman in the evening.

January 12, 1970, Monday

Murshid's output today is five letters. I cite the one to columnist Art Hoppe, with copies sent to a U.S. congressman and a state representative, simply to show Murshid's shrewd use of language. Remember his "blackmail" letter to KQED (January 10, 1970)? This thrust evolves into today's remark: "One of the big broadcasting companies is actually considering investigating these dances!" Murshid can say they are "considering investigating [my] dances" because Murshid himself wrote the letter asking for consideration. Murshid tells goddaughter and newly appointed *Khalifa* Saadia today,

I am so short-handed that, even with growing financial betterment, I have not been able to get proper help. Mansur is more concerned with financing his own way, and I think this is wonderful. His life has been complicated by the return of Jemila, and there is no question that each has a large role to play in the spiritual life. Murshid is making no endeavor to reconcile them, and Jemila is split between a desire to establish a home, a career, and spiritual life.

Jemila's return is in no way related to her former connection with me, but—no coincidence—seems to have been timed to coordinate with the return of Pir Vilayat to the San Francisco Bay area. I know it is finished with us now.

Saadia floats the idea of an import business in Pakistani dresses past Murshid. Murshid agrees to pay the freight charges, "but I would then leave them [to sell] to Amina, because it is beyond my capacity and time to be concerned with anything more."

January 13, 1970, Tuesday

The essence of Murshid's strong letter to Nancy Fish is her failure to discern who he is. Identifying himself as "a hodge-podge, a spiritual teacher, scholar in several fields, poet, and artist of sorts," Murshid tells Nancy, "I am indeed sorry you have not tried to find out anything about what I am doing, or what I am trying to do." When Nancy, who is contemplating leaving her husband Ralph, equates her situation to Jemila and Vilayat's, Murshid explodes. He gives never before revealed commentary on Vilayat, Jemila, and his role as a spiritual teacher functioning in ways that impact on the lives of others.

The worst excuse, the positively worst, is to find any parallel in the acts of Jemila and/or Pir Vilayat. Pir Vilayat has done what a man like Ralph is utterly unable to do—he has laid before me all his *weaknesses*, shortcomings, etc. This takes a great heart, a great soul. But I am equally aware of his visions, his insight, his mission in this world. There are no parallels here, none at all. In the case of Jemila, it is even harder to explain, that is to a non-mystic. People who know nothing about mystical experiences cannot be expected to have any respect for them...

A spiritual teacher, a murshid, is one who is expected to bring disciples toward God-realization. God, to me, is reality, and although I do not see Him, He permits me to see. So when I have gone to Him with, let us say, the problems of Vilayat, the problems of Daniel, the problems of Fatima, the problems of Jemila, the problems of Mansur, the veils are lifted and one sees. But there is no room for argument here; what is seen is seen and cannot be touched.

This may give you a glimmer or a glimpse of my almost compulsory silence of what I have seen concerning Jemila, her purpose in life, her immediate and not so immediate future. It is not in accord with my personal views. It is not in accord with any traditional or personal or other ethical standards. But it is in accord with vision and with cosmic karma, and purpose in life. Each one of us has his purpose, his own fulfillment, and in our Sufi Thoughts there is a phrase, "Constantly leads his followers toward the Light." Whatever has happened to Jemila, there has been a marked increase of light.

Murshid concludes the letter to Nancy, "The next two years the doors are open to working on a world scale, and I mean a world scale... You therefore have no choice but stay away or *accept*." He signs the letter "Daddy Murshid."

January 14, 1970, Wednesday

I have had to face financial emergencies coming in the form of an automobile breakdown and a root canal. Fortunately, I had a cushion to meet these emergencies, but my cushion is gone and the lack of a job still troubles me. A temp agency is helping me look for secretarial work. I can type. An employment counselor from the Welfare Department is on the lookout for jobs in their sphere. An application is on file at a San Rafael factory due to hire within the week. It would be difficult to find an employer who understands the need for me to fulfill my secretarial duties in the Sufi Order. Murshid and I are going to Los Angeles sometime soon (February 24-27), for *more* than a weekend—probably during the week. I am worn out looking for work! The rent remains unpaid, and I want to attend the Greek dancing class ($84) at UC extension in San Francisco with Phillip's wife Selima (Clara's new spiritual name received April 19, 1969), my dance partner.

Murshid notices all this effort, noting, "Mansur is really trying." (in a letter to Vocha Fiske, January 17, 1970) He also cites Moineddin and Hassan's expected raises at the New Age health food store. A few days later (January 19, 1970) Murshid tells the Lama Foundation, "Mansur is now working outside most of the time." To Saadia, he writes, "Mansur is more concerned with financing his own way, and I think this is wonderful." Murshid's approval reinforces my course of action.

January 16, 1970, Friday

The connection between Ruth St. Denis and Murshid's friend Vocha Fiske was first revealed to me when I read his fan letter of January 6, 1970, to Walter Terry, author of *Miss Ruth*, a biography of St. Denis. Vocha is mentioned in that book. Murshid writes Oliver Reiser today, "I did not realize that Vocha Fiske was so close to Ruth St. Denis. I knew them both in roughly the same regions, but they were in different social groups." It should be noted that St. Denis's pictures, a signed one of her alone and another with dance partner Ted Shawn, share space in Murshid's home with photos of Hazrat Inayat Khan, Papa Ramdas, Mother Krishnabai, and Nyogen Senzaki.

January 17, 1970, Saturday

We meet every Wednesday at the seminary in San Anselmo; it was no big deal to obtain the space to use yesterday to accommodate Pir Vilayat's return visit (he also came on the 7th). Yet for Murshid, writing in a diary letter to Vocha Fiske, the meeting "was in some sense the most tremendous *outer* event of my life." Murshid begins this letter, "It is the New Age. Last night Vilayat Khan came to San Anselmo and without any fanfare, we had at least 150 persons, and I doubt whether there were ten over 35 or even over 30 in age." Murshid describes the meeting in a letter to Shamcher (January 19, 1970) as the best ever.

It was not only the size at an unadvertised, unscheduled affair, but the whole program was of a New Age typology. The chief difference perhaps to me was that there was no occasion to weep. I don't know what struck the Pir most—our singing of Maheboob Khan's [Hazrat Inayat Khan's brother's] compositions, my own *Azan* [call to prayer], the general program, or his having complete liberty both for [leading] singing and talking. While it was a long affair, it was not drawn-out. And I believe it was perhaps the best Sufi Meeting ever to be held in this country.

In the audience was the Arab Sufi from Israel, long heralded by Murshid as an expected visitor. Murshid segues from mention of his arrival to editorial comment: "As usual, we listen to everybody but the people themselves." He doesn't mention what he will tell a correspondent named Luckman tomorrow, that he "will listen to this Arab" Sunday and meet with him Tuesday.

In preparation for the class today on Southeast Asia taught by Professor Richard Kozicki, who lived in Burma and Malaysia, Murshid copies some of his notes from former U.N. official Gunnar Jarring to bring to class. Professor Kozicki has elaborated everything that Murshid once told his former boss Russell Smith that he "long wished for": namely, desert reclamation, arid land culture, salt water conversion, and soil and crop adaptations—all details from Murshid's project "How California Can Help Asia." (letter of January 19, 1970)

Recently, Murshid condemned some prognosticators from India whose negative predictions were false. (see December 12, 1969) It is helpful when Murshid gives an example of what he means by "prediction." Today in this letter to Vocha Fiske, he does.

And my World War III, [which I] *predicted* and I mean predicted *in 1920*, that the real world war would come between the professor and the commentator, is not only on the horizon, it is here.

In a letter to Mrs. Doris Hosea in Oakland, Murshid records the flood threat in Novato that had him digging emergency drainage ditches at the *khankah* while the rest of us men were away working. He doesn't mention Vilayat by name here; instead, he refers to him as "my best friend from France [who] showed up without notice and expected me to make arrangements for him." Why did Vilayat show up? Murshid answers: "Because he is trying to sell 'Dances of Universal Peace' to a large corporation." It's no wonder that to some people Murshid is a strange bird. Imagine, a corporation buying dances.

I write to Vocha Fiske, who has befriended and communicated with me since her several visits, that we are doing gas and electrical work at the *khankah*; that the dining room and Murshid's room are getting space heaters; and that the barn, where Hassan and Shirin are developing cottage industries in printing and pottery, is being rewired.

January 18, 1970, Sunday

Murshid's output is five letters today. Pir Vilayat asked Murshid to write up the dances. He tells Richard Harvey of Boston's East-West Center, "Pir Vilayat is trying to get a national hook-up for these dances, and this also requires them being written up in a literary form."

After a man who represents Dr. Richard Alpert (Baba Ram Dass) visits Murshid, he writes to Anandashram, "There is already a sort of legend that this Ram Dass and Sam are the leaders of the New Age." Reading the Sufi saint Shah Latif of Sind, Murshid finds a theme that he will articulate over and over: "God is not your jailer, He is your Lover."

In a letter to Buddhist Jack Austin, whom we visit in London after the Temple of Understanding conference, Murshid identifies University of California Professor Lancaster as "one of Nyogen Senzaki's last pupils." Murshid recently gave Lancaster Kennett Roshi's "material." He informs Jack about Kennett Roshi's plan to establish a Zendo near Mt. Shasta.

What pleased Murshid most in his encounter with Kennett Roshi was being bettered in "a tête-à-tête with Kennett Roshi, who proved her prowess in adopting the witticisms of H.S. Gilbert to some of the common complications of the day." For a Gilbert and Sullivan buff like Murshid, he's a gracious loser. Murshid writes to Art Hoppe,

> In 1928, in this city of San Francisco, I met the late Dr. Henry Atkinson, most of his life Secretary of the World Church Peace Union. He looked over my plan for Palestine and said: "Mr. Lewis, I have been around the world three times. I have met every king and prime minister on earth, and you are the first man to have brought me what I want."

This passage, though quoted by Murshid innumerable times the last several months in correspondence, has been omitted from summaries to avoid repetition. It appears here because this meeting, which Murshid cites repeatedly, was central to his study of religion. Atkinson was a mentor for Murshid.

January 19, 1970, Monday

A new wrinkle in Murshid's persona is his financial independence. This comes up in a letter to American Friends of the Middle East, a group that historically took money but rejected reports. Murshid allows that "It may not be a virtue that one is heard simply because he is independent financially." After noting that there are many "rival or parallel" organizations competing for money, Murshid concludes with his hope that they'll accept "the report which I may be sending in on conversations with this newly arrived Israeli Arab." The Sufi Arab from Israel has a name; he is Azam.

January 20, 1970, Tuesday

In five out of six letters today, Murshid mentions Azam. Although he writes Vocha Fiske, "Azam immediately felt that Sam is the person who can help promote real peace in the real Near East," Murshid has been promoting Azam as the peacemaker. Azam has emerged for Murshid as a symbol of those without a voice in Palestine; so he has championed him, sight unseen, as a stand-in for himself. By promoting Azam, Murshid can support a separate ego doing what he, himself, wishes to do: that is, force the corporate media and State Department to accept information from citizens.

That is the reason for Murshid's announced intention to his correspondent Luckman (see January 17, 1970) to accompany Azam with a secretary and "write down all the reasons or unreasons why the 'peace' people and the press and the clerics, who adhere to different aspects of 'Judeo-Christian ethic' (whatever that is) turn us down."

After a three hour breakfast meeting with Azam, Murshid determines that their projected visits to important people about cooperation between Jews and Arabs in the Middle East will have to be postponed. Azam must finish the semester at a college in Fort Worth, Texas. Then, Azam will continue his studies at San Francisco City College.

Azam is the fellow one organization's financial contribution depends on. What will Murshid say to the American Council on the Middle East now? Not another word. There is no further correspondence between Murshid and the American Council on the Middle East.

And what was a former boss living in Ross, California, named Russell Smith, told yesterday? "It is certain this week that I shall increase my allotment to the Ross Art and Garden Center, and perhaps to the California Academy of Sciences, and conservation groups. As for others, I am either maintaining the same dues or withdrawing." The American Council on the Middle East is one victim of Murshid's withdrawing.

January 21, 1970, Wednesday

In a dream just before waking, I am present at a dinner party. Many guests are seated at a large table. The host is explaining how on his right (the future), burners and things would be placed, and on his left (the past), the corridor from the kitchen (cooking up plans) would be blocked with a sliding partition, which he could open with a magnet. Then the guests begin to sing Auld Lang Syne (signaling a passing). Murshid is there. With the words of the song, "Should old acquaintance be forgot" and phrases from the *Prajnaparamita Sutra*, I begin to weep. Murshid walks across the table on his knees to the host. I break a dinner plate. It falls on the floor.

On January 15, 1971, less than one year from now, Murshid is dead. I have no idea at the time that this dream foreshadows that. Later I have a vision. I see Murshid walking like a cartoon character with extreme seriousness along a desert road, looking from side to side—a caricature of him doing the Mercury walk. I feel with certainty the location is in the Near East. The sensation is as if Murshid has bilocated, and he is really there *and* here, accomplishing something very important.

January 23, 1970, Friday

In a gesture reserved for special occasions, Murshid responds to a letter from the Lama Foundation on his letterhead stationery. Top center is his American name, address, and phone number: Samuel L. Lewis, etc. To the left, in full caps, is his Sufi name, SUFI AHMED MURAD CHISTI, with "University of Islamabad" in script underneath. On the right is his Zen name, Reverend HE KWANG, with the title *Zen-shi*, meaning "Zen Master" underneath. The occasion for this letter is Lama's invitation for Murshid to participate in its summer, 1970 program. Murshid lists what's up in the air: no date for the Temple of Understanding conference; his brother in the hospital; his intention to send "my lieutenant" Moineddin to Lama while he's in Europe (impossible now due to Moineddin's good job at New Age foods); Vilayat's visits and the dance write-up he requested; no secretary available ("Mansur is either working at odd jobs or in line for 'something big'"); plus other prospects. In summary, Murshid says, "At the moment I have no calendar at all, and so cannot either except or refuse but will file your letter and let you know later."

In a letter today to Saadia, Murshid provides a retrospective on Azam, giving details not written elsewhere. He suggests that, even though Azam left, it may just be the beginning. During their breakfast last Tuesday, Azam told Murshid he was "a *talib* [disciple] in Sufism" and "intends to have his Murshid, who apparently lives in Jerusalem, contact me." According to Murshid, Azam "has a peace program based on spirituality." He continues,

> His general over-all approach to both religion, especially the spiritual side, and politics, so to speak, are the same as my own. We both want to get rid of wholesale murder justified by something called by selfish people either "religion" or "politics." He has had to witness mounting hatred and murder. His whole concern is with Allah and not with human devices and institutions.

Twice in this letter, which Murshid dictated to me at the *khankah*, he laments his lack of help ("the office work has, with few exceptions, devolved upon Wali Ali and Murshid"; and then on the next page, "the call upon this person has been enormous, with no secretary available and only desultory help"). It is stressful to hear Murshid's calls for help, especially as I am at the moment helping, yet both of us know I cannot be a full time helper.

It is a difficult choice for me to decide whether to go with Murshid to the Indian Independence Day celebration in Berkeley or with Selima to the special Greek dance class. I choose Murshid, and Selima will stay home.

January 24, 1970, Saturday

One characteristic of Murshid, which describes his way of living, is his responsiveness to everyday events, such as an article in the newspaper. We've seen him respond to articles in magazines and write Walter Terry, author of *Miss Ruth*. An article called "Church's Failure with Teenagers," by *San Francisco Chronicle* Religion Correspondent Lester Kinsolving, provokes a wry response: "Your article...is sadly amusing." Today, Murshid informs Kinsolving he has "just started my fourth class on *The Gospel of St. Thomas*" at Rev. Earl Blighton's, where religion "is based on definite teachings *of* not about Jesus Christ." Finishing by talking about his students ("we all love each other"), Murshid says, "Very few older people have this conception of love—all they think of is sex or infatuation. That is not what Christ meant. I leave off in mid air."

R.C. Zaehner of All Souls College in Oxford, England wrote *Hindu and Muslim Mysticism*. What provokes Murshid about this book is that it's "backed by deductions from writers of other ages, having practically nothing to do with the objective world or humanity of the day." The contents of this book—together with the fact, revealed in Murshid's first sentence, that he "is a Sufi Murshid (i.e., a Muslim) going this morning to sit at the feet of the Vedantist Swami Swahananda (a Hindu)"—inspires these critical comments.

I arrive sometime after these letters are finished and drive Murshid, Zeinob, Saul, Ed, Michael, David, and Wali Ali over the Bay Bridge to the Indian Independence Day celebration at the First Baptist Church at Haste and Dana Street in Berkeley.

Murshid has to skip his Southeast Asia class today with Richard Kozicki, who gets a letter report of the celebration in lieu of Murshid's presence in class. We hear three excellent speakers: a Swami (Swahananda of the Vedanta Order) whose very presence makes my heart beat faster; a newspaperman, Lal, who speaks on science; and a scientist, Perry Stout from UC Davis, who speaks on food problems in India. All are excellent in their way. Murshid is pleased and notes the absence of English and German (European) professors of oriental philosophy, or EPOOPs, as he calls them.

After lunch with some disciples, I go without my dance partner, Selima, to the Helmet Club, where my Greek dance teacher's teacher is giving a special class. Murshid returns home after the Indian celebration and answers a letter in today's mail from an old friend, Sharab Harris.

After writing two paragraphs, Murshid is interrupted. "You will pardon me; at this moment my goddaughter's husband phoned (Nancy's husband, Ralph); he is in severe difficulty, perhaps for the first time and wants help, but read on." So, Murshid's letter to Nancy (January 13, 1970) shook things up!

Alluding to his brother Elliott's illness and the possibility of becoming a wealthy man should Elliott die, Murshid concludes, "The time may come *inshallah*, when I will be relieved from all duress." When he writes this I mistakenly think he's going to die, but he means money may come. "At the moment the pressures are so great it is difficult for me to think and write as clearly as I might. You may not notice this, but it is so."

After dancing I go to Murshid's for dinner. I have very close communication with Murshid today. He says at dinner, "I think I'll make something we don't have very often for breakfast next Thursday at the *khankah*." I get 'pancakes,' and it is pancakes! Then, Murshid speaks rhetorically, as if to the spirit of the food, "You've done something to me that doesn't happen very often." It is easy for me, with a full stomach, to feel "satisfied." He says, "I'm satisfied."

After dinner, there is the Saturday night dance class, held, as usual, in Murshid's garage. There are seventeen men and fifteen women. The men include Wali Ali [Meyer], Moineddin [Jablonski], Krishnadas [Duncan Pierce], Phillip [Davenport; yes, in Chapter 14, he was Vasheest, because I cited an article he wrote years later under that name. At this time, he is still Phillip.], Frank [Welch], Doyle [Wegner], Sibley [Cogswell], George [Matthews], James [Pickard], Paul [Rognlie], Hassan [Herz], Jelaleddin [Cave], Wayne [Jaekel], Drew [Langsner], Saul [Barodofsky], Amin [Quance], and me.

The women in attendance are Basira [Updike], Vashti [Morgan], Jehanara [Herz], Fatima [Jablonski], Jill [Cogswell], Zeinob [Bernham], Marcia [Pavolic], Mary Sue [Sitton], Marty [Peller], Shirin [Doyle], Laura [Mathison], Jemila [Johnson], Debbie [Churney], Ayesha [Moffat], and Amina [Erikson]. At dance class, I know the holy walks will come next. They do, and my intuition has been working like this all day.

January 25, 1970, Sunday

Anticipating Indian Independence Day back on January 17, 1970, Murshid wrote to Vocha Fiske, "Meeting *loaded* for me this time. Old friend Lal among the speakers. No more 'expert' nonsense." Dr. Lal was disappointing, but being in the presence of Swahananda brought tears to Murshid's eyes. All this emerges in a letter to Dr. Sarvepalli Radhakrishnan, former president of India. Murshid begins by telling Dr. Radhakrishnan that Indian students have taken over the Independence Day celebration, and it is better because of it.

The first speaker yesterday was Swami Swahananda. He is a direct pupil of our very good friend Swami Ranganathananda Maharaj. *I have a very difficult time listening to him, seeming to become all tears, and all heart in his presence...* The next speaker was a Dr. Lal of this city, a very old friend, who has also been a guest of your country. While he spoke on science in contemporary India, he failed to answer my question as to whether he had been to Poona or knew about the contemporary progress in certain sciences in your country. This was most unfortunate, as he was making a plea for humanism and he failed to recognize the very high intellectual standards of the majority of the audience. Many in the audience knew far more of this subject matter. His plea for humanism failed therefore.

In his letter to Vocha Fiske, Murshid offers another reason for Lal's disappointing performance. "He [Lal] lost the audience; he spoke on humanism. As the organized humanists do not recognize Indian cultures, the Indians in turn are very cool to it." Thinking about Lama and other East Coast invitations, Murshid tells Vocha, "I wish to get over a scheduled trip to Europe so as to fulfill those invitations." He asks her indulgence if the letter is not too clear, as "I am utterly swamped." Murshid writes five letters today. He'll write three tomorrow, three Tuesday, four Friday, and two Saturday.

Murshid's letter to Master Seo today is his last, ever. Considering that Murshid delayed answering Seo's letter of December 27th "because of several uncertainties," Seo may have determined that Murshid is too busy to help him. Still, Murshid pledges "a very suitable financial donation" for Seo's proposed zendo in Virginia should his brother pass away.

January 26, 1970, Monday

In a diary letter to Pir Vilayat in France, Murshid reveals his expectation of one or two legacies "if his [Elliott's] words were correct, and I am not yet counting on that." What might Murshid do with inheritance money connected with his brother's death? He explains to Vilayat, "This would mean the establishment of a good secretariat here, and possibly of a print shop and organic farm."

January 30, 1970, Friday

In his letter today to Vocha Fiske, Murshid lightheartedly adds to his list of projects he contemplates if he should inherit money: "If my brother leaves the world...the publication of *Eye Not-Witness* or something of the sort." The big news, Murshid shares with Vocha, regards "a 'conspiracy' to make me famous." Clarifying what he means by "conspiracy," Murshid tells Vocha that when he attended Baba Ram Dass's public talk Tuesday the 29th, Alpert "[came] out flatly in public for this person. This at a time when another person [Fred Cohn] is ready to film one both in class and in public efforts." Without naming Kinsolving, Murshid praises his article. The reason for Murshid's high praise: He's frequently quoted the biblical line, "a little child shall lead them," and Kinsolving gives young people a voice.

This last week one of the editors of the *San Francisco Chronicle* published the outlooks of young people on their own problems. With all the experts and authorities, someone thought it would be a good idea to let the young speak for themselves and they did.

As with Azam, Murshid found an alter-ego with Kinsolving.

The Australian publication *Contact* impresses Murshid because as he says to them, "You have not adopted the general formula: 'With your money and our brains we can save the world.'" Rather than making a claim of some grand awakening, Murshid *defines* the viewpoint of God-consciousness.

The spiritual realization of God-consciousness brings with it more than expansion. It brings with it love, compassion, mercy, harmonization, and consideration. It brings with it the central worthiness of others.

Universality aside, Murshid parades his Christian beliefs ("I believe that the Kingdom of Heaven is within. I believe with Jesus Christ that 'Ye are Gods'"); his tolerance ("I do not believe in forcing my beliefs upon others"); and the secret of his success ("When love is radiated, when joy is radiated, when calmness is radiated, they attract"). Murshid has no idea how *Contact* got his name, so he asks them, "What do you want from me? I should appreciate an answer." If you were seeking counseling from Murshid, one of the first questions he would ask you in a private interview is: "What do you want?"

January 31, 1970, Saturday

What do you want? is a question Murshid asks Saadia today when she dumps problems in his overloaded lap. "It is right that you tell some of your 'troubles' but what do you want?" By offering his example, Murshid suggests indirectly the correct course of action for her. "This person takes refuge in Allah and often Allah comes to his rescue, praised be He." As an example for Saadia of his workload, Murshid cites "the most complex situation with Nancy." I find out details unknown to me: Nancy left San Francisco to visit family in New York, "abandoning her own baby"; Ralph, her husband, came to Murshid, cried, and blamed himself, and "is undergoing repentance." Further, Murshid revives the circular-tree-seat-I-built issue.

Last year I went out with an axe. "What are you going to do?" I am going to destroy that seat. Why was it built? Murshid said he did not want it. Murshid said he did not want any more ideas from outsiders. [Murshid often would soften his dissatisfaction with you by storming at others not present.] It has been done and the things he has asked for are not done and all kinds of excuses are given.

After telling the tree-seat story Murshid tells Saadia, "This jolted Moineddin [who was on the receiving end of the encounter]." And what is the purpose of this communication? How might it relate to Saadia? All is revealed at the conclusion of this cautionary tale.

There has been some caution not to be involved in a lot of "beautiful" ideas which throw work on somebody else. And when this "somebody else" is the spiritual Teacher, it can only produce difficulties.

Saadia's problem letter could be construed as throwing work on Murshid. Or is it the tree seat? The ways of a spiritual teacher are sometimes puzzling. Saadia is not alone in bringing Murshid aggravating situations. This week, he tells her, "Only two persons placed before me the problem of where they should live. And this week one had to put the foot down on any question of acquiring the land next door to the *khankah*." Furthermore, the extended period Elliott is taking to die has shown Murshid the downside of his death.

If he passes away I shall have to do a lot of clean up work and this will mean the cancellation of those things being done for Allah. My work here is to get people to recognize and praise Allah.

The stressful issues are on page one of Saadia's letter; on page two, solid achievements and others with great potential to blossom. Murshid is currently creating the famous Greeting Dance (*As-salaam Aleikhum*) and Love Dance (*Ishk Allah mahbud Lillah*). There is Shamcher's book. Pir Vilayat is not only "selling the dances to a corporation," but also "trying to get a contract with a national broadcasting company for the Sufi dances." Murshid also mentions Ram Dass's public support and Amertat's (Fred Cohn's new spiritual name) feature film project. Overall, he seems to be saying: Now do you understand why I began this letter, "Your latest...has found a very tired old man"?

The "something big" Murshid hinted at for me (January 23, 1970) manifests tonight. The feature film project is beginning. Amertat offers me a job assisting him. We'll shoot a few minutes showing Murshid leading the dances Wednesday night in San Anselmo; then, in the kitchen and dining room at the *khankah*; and finally, in San Francisco, dictating letters while playing solitaire. The film we shoot will be shown to investors to raise money for the documentary feature eventually titled *Sunseed*, on the subject of new age spirituality, featuring many teachers.

Chapter 25

February 1970

Years ago I personally had some mystical experiences which ultimately Baba himself gave instructions that I was to prepare to give lectures on all the religions of the world; he asked me to make copies of references which could be used to support his mission. (Murshid's letter to Alan Cohen, February 2, 1970)

February 2, 1970, Monday

When I read the epigraph above, I want to know if Baba did this on the inner planes or whether there were witnesses. When Murshid says "Baba himself gave instructions" and "he [Baba] asked me," my guess would be this all happened on the inner planes; consequently, there would be no witnesses to verify this mission that came out of "mystical experiences." Earlier (November 10, 1969), Murshida Duce checked with Baba to see if Murshid's expression of Baba's wish was really Baba's wish. It wasn't; and Murshida Duce chastised Murshid publicly. With respect to the lectures Baba asked him to prepare, Murshid tells Alan Cohen,

I gave up a comfortable job, went east, became a veritable slave under the assumption that this was necessary for "karma yoga"; never once was permitted to speak on my knowledge of the scriptures of the world, or on mystical or other traditions, or the facts of mystical experiences, etc., etc. Never once.

To paraphrase Murshid's words about Jemila to Nancy (January 13, 1970), some things are hard to explain to a nonmystic. Murshid doesn't explain to Cohen why he went to Washington, D.C. He simply tells him, "I then had some mystical experiences and had to go to the city of Washington, D.C. and try to establish peace in Palestine." "To establish peace in Palestine" was Murshid's mission. This kind of grandiosity is typical for mystics; it rubs off. When I tell my therapist later that Shamcher and I, lobbying for solar energy (especially the form known as ocean thermal energy conversion, OTEC), aim to help change the energy future of the U.S., he describes our goal as "grandiose." After he was so enlivened by the mission of peace in Palestine, imagine Murshid's confusion when his effort produced the following effect.

Oh, I was successful all right by the diplomats, but then was told most emphatically that Baba wished war. If I had retained the letters sent, especially with remarks that "Baba said this, or Baba said that" a lawsuit would have been a pushover. I had been a poor man and rejected socially, and every advantage was taken of it. You can imagine my consternation many years later when I came upon the words of Baba, approving many of the very projects with which I have been concerned as a person, as a devotee, and even originally from his own instruction. This sort of thing compelled me to seek in quite other directions.

Murshid goes on to describe another episode in this vein.

When I sat before Princess Matchabelli, she constantly told us that Baba wanted his name to be presented to everybody. It did not matter if it was favorable, or unfavorable, that to him friendship and contention were alike, and the only thing he objected to was hush-hush about him. And when I returned to San Francisco, there was nothing but hush-hush about him. I had nothing more to say.

What I like about this letter to Cohen is the way Murshid can tell his mystical story of victimization, persecution, and response without rancor. He comes to an entente with Cohen. "I have perhaps as much background in sacred literature as you have in your own profession," Murshid writes. "It does not make me any better or worse." To arrive at this attitude of equality, Murshid went through the wringer, got his edges milled; he suffered. His life demonstrates that the spiritual path is not a bed of roses.

Only two days before, (January 31, 1970) Murshid portrayed himself as "a very tired old man." He represents himself to Oliver Reiser today as bubbling over with optimism: "This month has opened with far more optimism than one has ever had."

The cast of characters Murshid writes letters to expands, as new names and different organizations fill his epistolary life. This month he writes fifty-nine letters, consuming roughly 102 single spaced typewritten pages. In one of two letters in January to Murshid, Richard Harvey of the East-West Center in Boston asked him about George Gurdjieff. Murshid answers today,

My main differences with Gurdjieff, and I cannot necessarily justify myself for these differentiations, seems to be the lack of high moral ideals and human consideration in his methods.

February 3, 1970, Tuesday
The death of British philosopher and mathematician Bertrand Russell (1872-1970) evokes Murshid's thumbnail obituary in a letter to Julie Medlock.

I know you had great admiration for him, and I certainly had for his work in mathematics, logic, the literary side of science, and his early social works. But I do not approve, and did not approve, of his work on psychology, sex, and that humanity which he never had the privilege of joining.

Murshid elaborates on his putdown of Russell's sociology and sex writings in a letter to Vocha Fiske (February 3, 1970): "His stuff on sociology and sex and philosophy showed him as a leader of the literary-humanist group"—i.e., an unscientific commentator. Murshid had an intuition and his instruction to "the secretary here" was to hold Oliver Reiser's letter of the 2nd, "because I expected something was coming up." (This letter was either mailed or misplaced.) The "something" that came up was the death of Lord Russell. Commenting about his intuition, Murshid says,

This was a manifestation of prajna. Our other, to me, great philosopher of the century, Dr. Radhakrishnan, has been an intense advocate of prajna. This might be translated as cosmic insight and foresight, and it never fails.

Once again today, the press of opportunities opening up causes Murshid to describe the Temple of Understanding as more of an obligation than an opportunity ("if I ever get the Europe trip off my back").

February 4, 1970, Wednesday
While Murshid dictates to me a letter to Pir Vilayat, Fred and Julie Cohn are in the office, answering Murshid's call for someone to write up the dances. Murshid announces to Vilayat, "The Dance Department opens with this letter." He sends Vilayat a copy of Fred's film proposal and elevates Fred's inspiration to film him and other spiritual leaders to the level of a divine inspiration, "Now my position is this: that Allah (God) may be speaking through many people." Along with Fred's proposal, Murshid

gives Vilayat the methodology he uses to evaluate his participation in such projects. The interesting thing here is Murshid teaching Vilayat, or at least sharing a practice with the son of his teacher, the head of the Sufi Order. Murshid says,

> There are two ways in which to react: 1) a personality feeling; 2) the practice of fikar and if there is no change in the stream of the breath when an idea is presented, that idea is in tune with the universe.

Ram Dass spoke last night. Murshid went, and tells Vilayat, "He is one of those who wishes [to have] materials on ryazat." Ram Dass wants the Sufi practices for *Be Here Now*, a book being put together at the Lama Foundation. Murshid got it from Ram Dass, "the chief spiritual teacher there," that "he [Ram Dass] intends to put all his time and effort into a publication" and that "because of his concentration on the book, they want me down there to become chief guru and also to organize a Sufi Center." Little remains for Murshid to tell Vilayat except that the gas and electric work at the *khankah* is almost finished, "We are almost through here at the *khankah* with problems related to gas and electric installations, including the pipes etc. needed for Shirin Doyle's kiln."

February 6, 1970, Friday

Although the letter from the *khankah* titled "Tentative Plans for Spring Festival" is for Gavin Arthur, there is no name, address, or greeting on page one. The typist taking dictation, probably Moineddin, does as Murshid tells him, and only on page two indicates the letter is Gavin's. This is a case where Murshid, focusing on the message, omits the preliminaries. He begins: "One has passed through the stages of 6 disciples to 30, and 30 to 60. One is now progressing to the next stage of 60 to 100 disciples, not counting followers." This is confirmed by the esoteric notebook I keep, which includes Murshid's disciples' names and practices. It has seventy-seven names (Julie Cohn being the last), and isn't much utilized from this point on, for several reasons: growth and expansion, and my changing function. As a come-on for Gavin Arthur to attend the Spring Festival Murshid is arranging for March 21st (which happens to be Gavin's birthday), he offers Gavin a throne.

> Two thrones will be set up, one for you and one for Basira, the young lady seeress who was enceinte [pregnant] last year. She has since given birth to a beautiful boy named, and I hope aptly, Samuel Vilayat. If you cannot possibly be present, "your" throne will be occupied by disciple David Hoffmaster who has a physical deformation... This may become a publicized event. Plans are afoot to have cameras and even sound equipment. This is not in my hands; this is in the hands of some very fine and faithful disciples.

If the throne and the publicity aren't enough, the ultimate come-on for the astrologer is Murshid's summary of the astrological work, as it's progressed since Pir Vilayat first witnessed the group demonstrate "the whirls of the seven planets."

Since that time I have presented the walks of combinations, of Saturn and Jupiter, and then Saturn, Mercury, and Jupiter, the last indeed is full of potential mastery and self-fulfillment.

Here, Murshid is describing the type of work that is done at the Saturday dance class, where participants are instructed to breathe and walk in a certain way. This so-called occult knowledge helps disciples master themselves. Murshid gives Gavin a preview of tomorrow's class.

The next lesson will include the dance of Sun and Moon together and Venus and Mars together. While all these walks and dances are based on the science of breath, the Venus-Mars dance is the only one which is absolutely and essentially a woman-man affair. We shall also go over the Sun ritual; the moon ritual; the wheel dance and others, some partly presented and some not yet offered.

A letter from the Temple of Understanding settles Murshid's uncertainty about the date of the conference. First off, as a courtesy to the Temple of Understanding, Murshid reminds them that he's not traveling alone. "I am hoping to have with me my secretary Mansur Otis Johnson, who as I have told you before, has been a pupil of our good friend Dr. Huston Smith, and also became very close to him." Acknowledging the featured speakers and the program sent by the Temple of Understanding, Murshid writes that he is "delighted." This is followed immediately by one of Murshid's original aphorisms for attaining peace: "I only know two ways to bring about peace (there may be others), love, and business or trade." Shortly after, Murshid reveals that "one is functioning continuously in a high state of consciousness." Thinking, perhaps, about the conference program, which does not include him, Murshid says, "If I have anything to say it will be to mention the Great Mogul Emperor Akbar who did so much to endeavor to bring recognition between one faith and another."

That Akbar worked all the time and "seldom slept at all" is new information for me. I'm happy to know what a manifestation of super-consciousness looks like. Just as he anticipated the Saturday dance program for Gavin, Murshid previews his Sunday night program for the Temple of Understanding.

I am lecturing this Sunday on the Taiteriya Upanishad, having in view the actualization of the super-conscious or super-conscient, if you are a follower of Sri Aurobindo, and no nonsense, actual experience.

February 7, 1970, Saturday

There is a big family birthday party for Hassan (Herz) this weekend at the *khankah*. After this, no more birthdays of house members occur until after the Spring Festival.

Despite being in receipt of the Temple of Understanding program that doesn't list him, Murshid characterizes his role in Geneva in a letter to Vocha Fiske like this: "My 'plan' is to go to the international conference in Geneva where this time I shall be permitted the floor before being attacked—if indeed I am attacked."

Murshid doesn't wait for Gavin Arthur to respond to his invitation, but in the middle of the letter to Vocha—he gets the inspiration to do it at that moment—Murshid calls Gavin, who accepts.

In a letter to General Semantics's secretary, Lloyd Morain, Murshid proclaims, "With the writing of this letter comes the end of a long period of darkness [Murshid's relations with the General Semantics movement] to which I hope I don't have to refer much any more." Dear Lord, my fervent prayer is that it may be so.

February 8, 1970, Sunday

The subject of Murshid's diary letter today to Anandashram is Milton Singer's book *Krishna: Myths, Rites, and Attitudes*, which Murshid recommends, even as he writes, "It is not often that one would dare to recommend a book to a spiritual center." Murshid met Singer at a conference at the Sheraton Palace Hotel in San Francisco once and answered some of his "abstruse questions." Murshid identifies with "the notations in this book" and this makes him feel it should be better known. It's really deeper than this, but to get to that Murshid speaks about his present state of mind.

The amazing thing is the flash and rush of inner inspiration coming to this person at the present time. One is actually overworked—nothing like a day off this year so far, and no sign of any. But it is just at this time and under these circumstances that the heavens themselves seem to open up and the Divine Mother in the form of the Goddess of Creative Imagination and Direct Insight keeps one busy, even in the midst of dreams, meditations, and relaxations.

Ordinary language does not fit what is happening to Murshid. He is not talking about ancient Egyptian pyramid texts when he coins the term the Goddess of Creative Imagination. What Murshid really wants to express here is the relation between his inspired existence and what he's reading.

What is remarkable is the very close concord between these inspirations and the whole tenor and methodology of the Bhakti mentioned in this work. Sam is not especially a Bhakti. He is a Sufi, or may be called a Sufi, but in the universal sense, and perhaps in the sense that he is like a reincarnation of the Mogul Prince Dara Shikoh, which has been mentioned before.

This, again, is a mystic trying to find words to describe the connections one makes in an exalted state.

Judging from Murshid's opening, his correspondent W.D. Begg must be having troubles: "The easiest thing in the world is to give a sermon when another is in difficulties." But this doesn't mean Murshid will not give a sermon. He goes on for two full pages, more or less, about reliance on Allah, and concludes with a short story. He is suggesting, perhaps, that Begg should pray for a miracle.

Some years back a very dear friend of mine, a leading Buddhist, wished to go to Australia. He had no funds but some golden statues which he was ridding himself of. Suddenly Tengku Abdul Rahman, the Prime Minister of Malaysia, came suddenly [sic] to him; said he knew about his troubles and gave him a round trip ticket. This is Sufism in action. What will happen when the world comes to know of this method?

Murshid sends *Studies in Comparative Religion* editor F. Clive-Ross $10 today in response to invoice number 01013, along with a copy of the Begg (sermon) letter, which also contains assertions of prowess.

In the traditional sense one has the *baraka* and *silsila* [transmission], again both from the Sufis of the "East" and "West" but the blessing from Mohammed himself, and it does not matter what all the scholars and orthodox "think" from their ego-consciousness.

Just as Murshid identified with Singer's book on Krishna, he identifies similarly with Frithjof Schuon's article in Clive-Ross's journal. Murshid tells Clive-Ross that the article, "Nature and Function of the Spiritual Master," absolutely exemplifies his present life.

I realize that claims in this direction may be subject to criticism, but something more is needed than endless abstruse articles and lectures not supported by living evidence. The quotation from Schuon, "No one will meet Allah who has not met his envoy [Mohammed]", has long been illustrated by my poetry, nearly all of which has remained unpublished.

Murshid's direct experience of the Prophet Mohammed, explicit both in his letter to Clive-Ross and in the enclosed copy of the letter to W.D. Begg, fails to impress Clive-Ross, who just happens to publish "abstruse articles." Murshid, who wants to visit Clive-Ross in England after the Temple of Understanding conference in Geneva, writes, "I am assuming it will be possible to call on you early in April, after the conference of THE TEMPLE OF UNDERSTANDING." Clive-Ross agrees to allow us to visit him. We do, but our reception is chilly.

Parapsychology Professor Charles C. Tart is featured in a program on television titled "Altered States of Consciousness," and Murshid is impressed. After identifying himself in a letter to Professor Tart as a mystic who had all the experiences reported by LSD advocate Timothy Leary, Murshid assesses Leary's experiences as

comparatively low... All the deepest schools of mysticism present that there are seven planes of consciousness, and the most I could get out of Leary were variations of the second plane.

Murshid sends Tart a copy of "The Rejected Avatar," and comments about the making of the poem.

[It] came in a blending of dream consciousness and active *prajna*, or direct cosmic insight. The poem wrote itself. There are many instances of this. I have not been able to get anything accepted by the literati, but I am not troubled.

Further, Murshid has this to say about the creative process that is bringing in the Dances of Universal Peace.

What is more important at the moment is the combination of the dream and super states of consciousness, introducing dances which are being communicated to quite a number of young people; all these dances come very quickly and manifest on three higher states of consciousness before they come to outer form; usually the dream consciousness is the last, where I see these art forms before presenting them objectively.

Later on in the letter, Murshid tells Tart that his "report of psychic events," written up after his return from the orient in 1962, was rejected by psychic researchers, even though these events "were generally at a somewhat higher level than those reported by drug takers." Immediately recognizing that it might sound like he's putting down drug experimentation, Murshid adds,

But if you think I am condemning anybody, part of my work has been a search for soma and other vegetals used in ancient times to raise the state of consciousness. I have also attended Arya Samaj ceremonials where natural derivatives were employed to produce a super-mundane effect through the smoke coming from chemical action.

Unlike United States President Bill Clinton, Murshid inhaled. I digress here somewhat, in the belief that Murshid would have been deeply interested in Swami Rama's chapter on "Soma" in his book *Living with the Himalayan Masters*. Early in the book, the author mentions that "the soma creeper comes from the succulent family and grows at the height of 11,000 to 18,000 feet" in the Himalayas. Then later, Swami Rama tells of meeting Vaidya Bhairavdutt, a famous herbologist, who brought him a pound of the creeper. Swami Rama and Bhairavdutt experimented with it on some *sadhus* (renunciates) who were in the habit of using marijuana and hashish, and they found that it made them fearless. When Swami Rama and the herbologist took some later on, the herbologist "started chanting and singing and ultimately threw off all his clothes and started dancing. But I had a severe headache," Swami Rama writes. The herbologist shouted that "he was Shiva, the Lord of the Universe and cried, 'Where is my Parvati [Shiva'a wife]? I want to make love to her.' This disturbed all the students who came to visit me in the morning," says Swami Rama.

They tried to restrain him, but he became so strong that five people could not hold him down. Though he was a slightly built man, he threw them off, one after another. I saw what was happening from a window, but I did not come out of my room because of my heavy head. Another Swami brought three quarts of warm water and told me to do an upper wash, a yogic technique for cleansing the stomach, which involves drinking a large quantity of water and then vomiting it up. This relieved me a bit. This experience, which occurred during my stay at Ujaili Ashram in Uttarkashi, disturbed the whole routine of the ashram and I did not know how to explain it to my students. After a careful study of the use of psychedelic preparations over a number of years, I have concluded that the harm they can do far outweighs any positive benefits they might have. Those who are not psychologically prepared will have negative experiences either when they ingest the intoxicant or later. Those who are prepared don't need such drugs. (*Living with the Himalayan Masters*, pp.276-77)

February 9, 1970, Monday

Thinking organizationally, Murshid informs Suzanne D'Mitrieff that practically speaking, he has three centers—in San Francisco, central Marin County, and north Marin County—under the aegis of one legal entity; and that he anticipates establishing centers in New Mexico at Lama, and in Massachusetts and West Hollywood, where Richard Harvey and William Arlock have expressed interest in his activities.

Murshid tells Congressman Paul McCloskey, Jr. a story today about a peace organization he resigns from when they solicit money in exchange for the opportunity to meet some famous people.

They asked me to send ten dollars so I could meet the famous people of the world. I wrote: "You are asking a man who has been a guest of honor at the royal palaces of Japan and Thailand; and had teas in the presidential mansions of Pakistan and India to send you money."

February 10, 1970, Tuesday

Noteworthy in a short letter to Saadia is Murshid's explanation for the phenomenon manifesting now: His energy seems unquenchable and, like Akbar, is giving him some sleepless nights. "People marvel at the energy, but man does not possess such energy. He makes of himself a vehicle for the divine energy which may pass through his personality and bodies."

February 11, 1970, Wednesday

I remember this day very well, because I disobey Murshid. We begin working on the esoteric writing at 6:30 A.M. with Murshid dictating his commentaries on the Gatha study series called Symbology (*Nakshibandi*). How he does it is to review his earlier commentary and then dictate a new version. After Murshid completes Series II, he tells me to throw the old ones away. I do, but later, with some trepidation, I go back and get them out of the wastebasket. The scholar in me wants to compare the old ones with the new version. Another reason is that these old papers have a lot of Murshid's magnetism. To choose a sample to present here, I open at random to a paragraph that begins "*Tawajjeh*."

OLD: *Tawajjeh* is a practice whereby the teacher enables the pupil to receive the divine faculties which are his; also by the use of his glance he communicates life and blessing to pupils.

NEW: *Tawajjeh* is a practice whereby the teacher uses the glance both for the purpose of communication and also for arousing latent potentialities in disciples.

After breakfast, Murshid dictates a long letter to the Lama Foundation. He begins by saying it is "a very difficult letter."

But the difficulty may be in my mind only. It [the letter] is being written under harassment, and therefore, may not be entirely clear or justified. At the present moment, I am taxed to the utmost. I do have a very faithful secretary in San Francisco [Wali Ali] as well as Mansur here. We are just beginning to get additional office help, far less than needed but still real. Everything being done now, everything in the offing has been seen in vision.

After speaking about the multiple constituencies he will represent in Geneva (Korean Buddhists, Asian and American Sufis), Murshid recognizes his ability to play a part, even if he isn't on the program.

I shall have so many "credentials" that I can easily stand aside for others and still fulfill any role. I already know what that role is: It is the integral harmonization of all the diverse religions, sects and cults. I am neither presenting words nor personality here. I am neither capable of making a long speech on silence nor maintaining silence at this convocation. Not only has Jesus Christ taught that in such affairs one may be opening his mouth that the word of God comes through it, I must fulfill—this is my dharma—the words of Hazrat Inayat Khan: "Open our hearts, that we may hear Thy Voice which constantly cometh from within" and "Speakest the word that is put into thy mouth, as the Light filleth the crescent moon."

No doubt, bombastic claims are inferred here. That is right, they may be bombastic. But the time of the fulfillment of my life's effort is come.

Twice in this letter to the new age community, Murshid uses the word "crap."

I would not dare to write this letter unless I had on the one hand the divine approval from within and the approval of an infant from without. I mean a suckling infant [Nur-un-nisa Jablonski] and no nonsense about it—no more crap, no more hyperbolic obtuse harangues but realities from the worlds within and without.

The second time Murshid speaks in the vernacular is when he refers to a line from Walt Whitman.

> I am not offering any crap hypocrisy of Whitman's "In all men I see myself." This has to be functional, this is functional. I have not only had no days off this year, hardly any hours, and in my final state of my preparatory work for God, the stage of advancing from 60 disciples to 100. And I mean 100 human beings not thought forms, not audiences considered as brainwashed peasants without throbbing hearts—but all aspects of myself, and I mean actually and not symbolically, every one of whose pains I feel, can feel, do feel; every one of whose difficulties I can share, do share, must share; every one of whom is more than a sleeping giant, but God Himself trying to come to manifestation while functioning in the human body.

After writing this, Murshid directs me to drive out to Lake Nicasio in the center of Marin County where the Spring Festival is going to be held. There, amazingly, a few miles from San Francisco and the *khankah*, are wide open spaces and reservoirs of fresh water.

After that, we visit Hans ("the number two man from Lama Foundation") and Frances (von Briesen), who are visiting relatives in the San Francisco Bay area. Describing Hans tomorrow in a letter to Oliver Reiser as "a drop-out, electrical engineer and physicist... [who] has not given up his allegiance to the scientific methodologies," Murshid enjoys the discovery of one who shares his disaffections. "He [Hans] has been unable to straddle the two cultures as depicted by Snow and Korzybski. He is sick of the misuse both of the word 'science' and the social, to him, misapplications of it."

February 12, 1970, Thursday

Look at today's date. Murshid describes the California weather as "spring time out here" in his diary letter to Oliver Reiser. There is a "totally bright outlook," with two exceptions: The *Oracle* died and Elliott continues to live. Exaggeration might characterize Murshid's count of his disciples ("in the neighborhood of 100 young people"). And grandiosity might characterize Murshid's role vis-à-vis spiritual communes ("I may be taking over the leadership in the new age communes"). I say this because he writes "communes," plural, and I only know about Lama. Lately, Murshid's reception from professors in university classes has been a sign of change, but seldom has he given details from a class. Today he does.

> I am enrolled in a class on Problems of Southeast Asia, a very odd class; the professors and most of the enrollees have lived in Southeast Asia. I think among and between us we have covered every country of that region. There is none of the old age "what do you think"; the discussions are based almost entirely on what do you know. Many in class have been totally frustrated, never being permitted to

present their first-hand research and experiences to others. It is this sort of polluted nonsense which stands in the way of the solution of problems.

It is amazing that with classes like that there is no paradigm shift more than thirty years later. Why not? The forces that control these things are very strong. Even when the enemy disappeared following the collapse of the Soviet Union in 1989, Cold War level military expenditures continued. These matters were out of the control of the electorate, the town meeting, the town council, or any board of supervisors. Our national engine is driven by the corporate money of the military-industrial complex, as Eisenhower warned in the early 1950s. And Murshid died before he could fully orchestrate against the antidemocratic forces who refuse to accept "first hand research." Murshid is enjoying vicariously another class, which disciple and roommate David Hoffmaster attends—Professor Lancaster's class on Zen Buddhism.

One of my disciples who also lives with me in San Francisco is studying what was originally known as Zen Buddhism with Prof. Lancaster at the University of California in Berkeley. Prof. Lancaster has presented the *dignaga* system of logic [that recognizes perception and inference as the only means of valid knowledge] and is turning down all answers to all questions based on Aristotelian methods. He says they do not work; they cannot be applied to Asian cultures. I believe he is absolutely correct.

This four page diary letter may be mined by future students for Murshid's views on many subjects, including economics, sound, Bertrand Russell's contemporary Rufus Mosely, cell theory, trends of the early seventies, and ecology. Here's a piece on ecology.

We had a definite ecology, that is biological ecology, in San Francisco. Eucalyptus trees were imported from Australia, planted everywhere and destroyed the natural ecology—that is "ecology" as defined by scientists. The Eucalyptus or gum is a fast growing tree, good for wind-breaks but not for fuel or usage as hard wood. It kills out all other plant life around it and in this sense is individualistic—contrasted with the oak which is quite social. The oak is a "climax" tree in the part of Marin County around here, but the sociologists, the press, the literati, not only do not know about ecology as a natural science, they can't even understand it. They have stolen the word, and everybody is discussing the word without solving any problems.

February 13, 1970, Friday

"Australia is now being added to my correspondence," Murshid writes his cousin Marion, who, when we pass through New York in March en route to Geneva, invites us for paella. Murshid accepts her invitation to stop, but says "I can't promise whether to stop long." Murshid wrote to Australia January 30th and does so again today, after having received an issue of *Contact* and a letter from R.L. Adamson of the Aquarian Arcane

College in Liverpool, Australia. The letter to Adamson is a diary letter, but it contains more teachings than it does personal information. Sufis use the term "master" for "one also who has passed through experiences of cosmic union and attunement. Such persons often go around in the most humble guise. Adulation, popularity, and social prowess mean nothing to them."

No more fitting words could be chosen to describe Murshid himself. Murshid offers Adamson an example of such a being in Sokei-an Sasaki. "After six months with him," he writes, "I found I could understand all the scriptures of the world... he showed me (and others) how to tell the spiritual grades of everybody up to one's own status." Murshid goes on to say that the teachings he received from Sasaki are available in the Upanishads and some works of Mahayana Buddhism.

According to Indian cosmic metaphysics, there are innumerable grades of evolution with all sorts of outlooks which we might verbalize as mineral, vegetable, animal, *asura* [demons], *manusha* [man or rational being], human, and so on until one becomes THE GRAND MAN.

I quote the above to contextualize Murshid's otherwise abstruse definition of God-consciousness.

Thus God-consciousness can be conceived either as the consciousness of the fullness terminating our perfectibility; or it can be regarded as all the varieties of grades and form from the most hardened material to and through the most sublime of sublime.

This definition emerges from Murshid's discussion of the two forms of Zen Buddhism: the one form based "on persons and institutions," which Murshid discounts. The other, "based on the personal experience of *Samadhi* which is sometimes, but not always, connoted by the Japanese term *Satori*," is of interest to Murshid. He finds this form among the Japanese, Vietnamese, Koreans, and Chinese. Murshid's contact with Tibetans is minimal. In Geneva, he calls my attention to the profound capacity for peace exhibited by the Tibetan representative in attendance. Regarding the Chinese, Murshid writes that "their Zen is one of cosmic attunement and attainment, not of ritual, not of important names, not of books, but of Being."

Masters or teachers are recognized in all the mystical schools Murshid knows when such a person has had "one or more pupils who have experienced spiritual awakening." On how to identify a saint, Murshid says, "I have also met many whom I regard as living Saints among Christian monks and nuns. One can tell this by the Light that emanates from their eyes and by the feelings that come from their hearts."

428

Parts of this letter read just like a talk Murshid might give between dances at a public meeting, especially when he speaks about what love means to the Sufis and what his work is.

With the Sufis in particular, love is regarded as most important, love that is living, communicable and sharable. As the Bible teaches us, although it is not part of religion at all, how can we love the God whom we have not seen, when we do not love our fellowman whom we have seen. Therefore my work is to elevate this love-consciousness, and apparently there is now some acceptance of this in the lives of a growing number of young people.

Elijah Mohammed, leader of the Nation of Islam, uses this same biblical reference in a speech I view later on C-SPAN, a cable TV financed channel without commercials.

February 15, 1970, Sunday

After the kind of letter Murshid wrote Nancy (see January 13, 1970), which bluntly ended, "stay away or accept," one looks with trepidation to see what happens next. Again, we only have Murshid's side of the correspondence, but it sounds as though Nancy protested against conventional morality. Murshid devotes almost a full page to discussing codes of morality, enough to make anyone feel uneasy about defying conventional morality. Then, in response to Nancy's offer to help, Murshid bends her positivity in the opposite direction with a suggestion that she receive "advice or [counsel]." Nancy is not a disciple. Murshid relates to her as "Daddy Murshid." He explains what a murshid is: "A spiritual teacher, a murshid, is one who is expected to bring disciples toward God-realization." Earlier in the letter, he says, "It is the mission of the teacher to help transform and transmute disciples." Murshid tells Nancy there are two types of souls.

There are types of souls, expressive and responsive, and there are others who are entirely negative. The negative ones are not responsive. They may believe they are responsive when they condemn the expressive ones. That is a teaching; it is not a personal matter. It comes from studying and understanding types.

It is not coincidental that Murshid writes on expressive and responsive types. Nancy is an expressive type who has angered Murshid for not receiving his guidance. He turns her offer to help in the direction of receptivity. The truth is that Murshid is interested in awakening humanity, and he is using his position as godfather to awaken his goddaughter, just as he would a disciple. Murshid continues to talk to Nancy about what a spiritual teacher does.

It is the duty of a teacher to help all disciples toward perfection; to help them with their virtues and good qualities; their hopes and aims and wishes. Whereas the negative types do nothing, the positive types may seem to be trying to do too much, but in this trying to do too much they do do; the expressives do not do so much but harmonize. But the negatives, whom the Hindus call tamasic, they do not contribute at all.

Murshid hopes Nancy will come to class and tells her that "to understand you will have to come to either the dance classes, or the public gatherings— Sunday and Monday here and Wednesday in San Anselmo; or to a Gatha class." I never see Nancy at a class. But her career as a Hollywood actress doesn't falter.

Murshid's letter to columnist Art Hoppe begins, "I have never considered it my mission to rise and defend the great corporations." But Murshid has promoted American interests and had run-ins with communists in foreign countries. The following happened in India.

Before me, we [the U.S.] sent [to speak to the crowd] three newspaper "experts." The communist hecklers stopped them. They [the "experts"] wrote books which sold. They also got mobbed. I haven't written any books that have sold, so far lots of rejections which do not bother me at all. But there I was on the platform defending Carnegie and Rockefeller and the Duponts especially. And when I was through, the audience set out to mob the communist hecklers. It was all against the rules. I had to save their lives. I did not gain anything by it. And of course, this was not mentioned. Wrong man. The wrong man can never solve anything, it ain't in the books. So we keep problems. [What happened simply was that Murshid found a way to speak to the crowd. He succeeded in turning the crowd against the hecklers when some diplomats—I'm guessing—got heckled. What rankled him was the failure of his government to recognize his kind of prowess and use it for the benefit of the nation.]

February 16, 1970, Monday

Murshid gives notice ("One's chief *Khalif* is ill") to Atiya that Moineddin's kidney failure, which will keep him busy fighting for his life through several transplants over the years, has begun.

Sheikha Vera (formerly, Van Voris) Corda is the woman Rabia Martin made a *Sheikha* at the same time Murshid was Martin's Khalif. Vera is a contemporary of Murshid's who experienced *Kaaba Allah* in Fairfax in the 1940s. Her letter of the 15th reaches Murshid today. Murshid responds to the cancer information included in the letter, "I shall pass the cancer information over to my *Hakim* [leader of healing] here." To one of her questions— Do you know anything about manzanita?—Murshid answers, "I know some things about the manzanita. My own theory is that practically all plants are either edible or medicinal or 'poisonous' and the last term has a definite esoteric meaning." *Sheikha* Corda wants to know: What about those old original writings of Hazrat Inayat Khan?

Murshid says, "As to Murshid's works, at one time they were all handled as you suggest by the late Mustafa [a character from the past I am not familiar with], but after Rabia Martin died her successor ignored them

and they finally perished in the fire of 1949 [when *Kaaba Allah* burned]."
Then Murshid remembers I'm working on a subject index for the twelve
volumes of *The Sufi Message of Hazrat Inayat Khan*, and says, "Some of
his works have since been annotated or indexed by the young disciples."
Finally, Murshid informs *Sheikha* Corda that he's surrounded by beautiful
women and men.

Once Rudolph Schaeffer said, "Sam, where did you get all these beautiful boys
and girls"; I had hardly given it a thought, but certainly there is an Alchemy at work,
only now it is not only Alchemy but beautiful young men and women come here
for study and *bayat*.

What makes Murshid designate this letter as a diary entry? I think it is
to record events like last night's initiations.

Seven received *bayat* last night. The hardest thing in life is to have to deal with
each and all as if everyone was the Beloved One of God. This is very time consuming,
but I am required to sleep; that is about my only recreation. Nevertheless, health is
pretty good for an old codger. I have at the present time my chief Khalif, my close
associate Bryn Beorse, and my brother, on the sick list.

February 17, 1970, Tuesday

Today, writing to the Temple of Understanding, I think Murshid simply
wants to know if they'll book a double room for two persons at the Hotel
Intercontinental, or whether he should. Murshid opens,

Having the news from Peter Finley Dunne, I realize you may be very busy, but
I am hoping the request for two persons, one double room at the Intercontinental
Hotel, will go through. Does this have to be confirmed by us? Or by a travel agent?

February 18, 1970, Wednesday

I know well the situation that leads Murshid to write a four page letter
to Saadia and her Aunt Bibijan at Cornell University. I, too, have provoked
Murshid many times to inspiring answers by doing things he disapproves
of. Saadia said and did two things: She concerned herself with the problems
of others, and she indicated to Murshid her interest in studying Buddhism
to understand more about the nature of the suffering which she was just
now experiencing.

Murshid drives home a number of points in this long letter that are
important illuminations of Sufi teachings. As far as studying Buddhism is
concerned, Murshid counsels Saadia he is "not sure that this is the will of
Allah at all. A Murshid is not a *hakim* [healer]. A Murshid is not a *Shifayat*
[a conductor of healing ceremonies]. Hazrat Inayat Khan definitely laid
this down." What this means is that among the Sufis, the function of
one who awakens people is different from that of one who heals. Saadia,

presumably, as a *Khalifa*, is on the path of awakening others, so the way she's showing her concern for others is inappropriate for one on her path. Murshid identifies another problem with Saadia's approach.

If you remain concerned with the small you will be entangled with the small. When your Murshid came into Karachi in 1956, he saw in one place 600,000 displaced persons; not that many displaced persons but that many displaced persons in one single city. It is to the eternal glory of General Ayub Khan that almost alone he cleaned this all up. When your Murshid saw this tremendous poverty, he gave up his career of working with ornamental plants and concentrated on food growing. He is still engaged in this pursuit and evidently Allah so wishes it, because all kinds of doors are opened not only for Murshid but also now for his chief disciples. *Alhamdu Lillah.*

Saadia, a Muslim from Pakistan devoted to the Holy Quran and the Hadiths, has not shown any interest thus far in studying the teachings of Hazrat Inayat Khan. Murshid wishes otherwise. "Your Murshid would have liked you to have studied some of the teachings of Hazrat Inayat Khan, not those in books but in the sacred lessons." Murshid suggests by what follows next that the sacred lessons, which we know as *Gatha* classes, could elucidate the states he experiences; but it is with indirect suggestion that he teaches this.

Your Murshid is constantly receiving from Allah in *fana-fi-sheikh, fana-fi-rassoul,* and now *Alhamdu Lillah* in *fana-fi-lillah* itself. It is the true work of a Murshid and the work of a true Murshid to listen always to Allah. It is not true that *Bismillah* means "in the name of God"—it means "from the sound of God"; it means "in the supreme light of Allah"; it means much, much more.

In the *Hadith* is said, "Holy Quran was given in seven dialects and each one has an inner and outer meaning." I am not concerned with Muslims, I am concerned with Truth. There are seven planes of existence as Lord Mohammed said; they are [i.e. they exist.]. From each we get an outlook vastly supernal to and transcendent over the one below. So *fana-fi-sheikh* is stupendously transcendent over the human outlook. *Fana-fi-rassoul* is almost inconceivably stupendous over *fana-fi-sheikh. Fana-fi-lillah* is in common language "far-out" and trans-verbal.

Murshid mentioned the "seven planes of existence" in his letter to psychologist Charles Tart. (February 8, 1970) He begins this letter to Saadia and her Aunt Bibijan with a lesson on the "three distinct meanings of the word Islam." As in his letter of the 13th, in which Murshid discussed two forms of Zen Buddhism, here he takes apart Islam and reveals a mystic's understanding of both Mohammed and Jesus.

There are today at least three distinct meanings of the word Islam: peace with Allah; a religion theoretically or actually based on FIVE PILLARS [see December 16, 1969] with some additions; whatever Muslims do. If you examine these three aspects as human institutions you may find them totally different and confusing. Even in the FIVE PILLARS, four belong to human behavior and one with certain qualifications to Allah. In the third type of "Islam," it all has to do with human behavior.

Lord Mohammed presented the truths proclaimed by other faiths. Mohammed differed vastly from the vast number of so-called Muslims when he said that Allah sent prophets to all peoples. It is a delusion that Muslims believe in this—they do not. They definitely do not, excepting of course, saints and Sufis.

Mohammed did not come to teach everything; he came to unify what had been taught. So long as Muslims are concerned only with the unification and not what has been taught to the world by the wise Allah who existed long, long before Mecca Sherif [the governor of Mecca], we are going to be concerned with problems, the problems of ourselves and of others. Allah presents peace and so Islam; the *nafs* is the spirit of agitation.

Jesus came to awaken mankind to the fullness of human and super-human possibilities. This mission was not entirely successful. But Jesus came to the wise and Mohammed to the ignorant, a more difficult undertaking.

Where does Murshid go with all this? It comes down to one sentence.

It is by our efforts to reach the stage of *nafs-i-selima* [refinement] that we attain the peace within ourselves; that we become MUSLIMS in the sense that Mohammed meant; and then, we can be of the greatest assistance to ourselves and to all the world.

Murshid dictated this letter to me before breakfast. For historical or other reasons, I pay close attention to how Murshid spends his time today. He arrived last night (Tuesday), spends Wednesday at the *khankah*, and usually conducts the open meeting Wednesday night in San Anselmo. Thursday, Murshid is at the *khankah* all day with a Gatha class, for disciples only, in the evening. Friday, Murshid returns to San Francisco. This week, the schedule changes.

After breakfast Murshid writes a three page letter to Dr. Hashim Sharabi. Murshid spoke with Sharabi at some U.N. anniversary held in San Francisco. I send copies of this letter to *The Saturday Review*, Admiral Evenson (American Friends of the Middle East), and The Arab Information Center. One interesting story speaks of Murshid's mission to get fifty thousand Americans to say Allah.

I came back from Pakistan with the instruction that my life mission was to get 50,000 Americans to say "Allah." It looked impossible. But I have had those mystical experiences which mystics have and which the literati disdain. I arose from a hospital three years ago with a vision of what was to come and it has come. I now have almost a hundred disciples. I now have succeeded in getting even thousands to repeat "Allah."

Fred and Julie (Cohn) come after this, and Murshid starts dictating dances to Fred, while I process the Sharabi letter. Finishing with Fred, Murshid rings up Roger Sommers, an unknown to me; and then, Lew Welch in Marin City. Lew, our poetry instructor, isn't home, but Murshid speaks with Lew's wife. She asks about Sufi meetings. Hanging up, Murshid says, "It was good for that." Murshid speaks once with Moineddin and Fatima in the meditation room, in what I would describe as a private interview. Murshid has just written Saadia,

> Up to this time, Murshid has been very tender not to let you know all that is going on. Do you think the above is all that is going on? Murshid cannot get an hour off and is on the verge of a breakdown.

This detailed presentation of a day in the life fleshes out what Murshid alludes to. At least twice, Murshid takes Julie into the office. I am not present. It is another private interview. George Matthews comes during lunch. I ask him, using Jehanara as an intermediary, to wait in the TV room upstairs. Shortly after lunch, Murshid meets with him, in another private interview. Before we leave on errands, Murshid and George speak again in the yard.

Somewhere between breakfast and the arrival of George Matthews, I drive Murshid to Eggar's Nursery, where he buys six rhubarb plants and says hello all around. We stop at a new bakery on the way back. Murshid buys Moineddin a peach coffee cake and me an apple tart to show his gratitude for our service.

After we get back from the bakery, Murshid and I go next door to see Phillip. He just moved into the house across the street with his wife—and my dance partner—Selima, and their kids, Kevin and Shirin. Murshid speaks to Phillip about when we could move the playground equipment we have over to his yard. This brings up questions of where the boundary of his yard is. Also, if and where planting is allowed to take place, as his place is a rental property.

I learn from Murshid's exchange with Phillip. We are there because God said: Go see Phillip. If you get a command from God, and you follow it, it is an adventure to watch what comes. It's especially exciting and safe when you are shadowing the actor like I am doing. The person of God can be detached, because you're on a mission from God. There's no attachment. It isn't from you. When Murshid asks questions of others, I see his receptiveness to answers and his willingness to accept whatever comes. At that point, it's God speaking through Phillip.

After lunch I drive Murshid to San Anselmo, where I tape a sign on the door of the seminary: DERVISH DANCING TOMORROW THIS WEEK ONLY. The purpose is to notify people who mistakenly come tonight that the Wednesday night dance will be tomorrow.

Next Murshid and I journey to the Ross Art and Garden Center. Murshid pays $25 for a new membership. He paid $10 last year, and he says he wants to "up" the amount this year. "But," he says, "since I bought a membership for Jemila last year [$10 and $10 or $20 total], I'm not upping [increasing] it as much as it seems."

Murshid directs me to Terra Linda, another suburb, where the travel agent is busy, so we go next door and get ice cream. Murshid gets two dips of raspberry sherbet, and I choose two dips of cherry cheesecake.

Murshid pays the travel agent $200—$100 from the Sufi Order account and $100 from his own account—and books us a flight to leave San Francisco March 30th. The Swissair flight to Geneva, Switzerland, leaves New York at midnight on March 31st. It arrives in Geneva at noon on April 1st. We are booked to stay six days in Geneva, ten days in England.

A little bit later, back at the *khankah*, I see Murshid with a bowl of potato peels in his hand, roaming around outside. When I ask what he's doing, Murshid says he is going to put the potato peels in the compost.

Between 5 and 6 P.M., Murshid watches Perry Mason on TV, a ritual for him, here and in San Francisco.

February 19, 1970, Thursday

Murshid cooks breakfast today. It is a welcome breakfast for Phillip and his family. We are fifteen people in all, including Van, Shirin and Jelaleddin, Mary Sue, and the seven family members at the *khankah*—Moineddin and Fatima, Jehanara and Hassan, Mansur, [baby] Nur-un-nisa, and Murshid.

Murshid starts the day with a letter to Art Hoppe; then follows with letters to friend Rudi of the Rudolph Schaeffer School of Design and Lloyd Morain.

Murshid calls Ayesha and asks her to return his typewriter. He calls Zeinob to say he is not coming tomorrow, but he's going to have Mansur drive her to the federal prison where Gary, her future husband, is in jail.

Murshid plants potatoes today and goes to the bank to discuss a loan for the trip to Geneva. He has private interviews with George Cameron, who will be Pir Vilayat's secretary after Bibijan steps down, and with Jehanara about her practices.

February 20, 1970, Friday

Looking to smooth the way for us in Los Angeles, Murshid writes Papa Ramdas's grandson, Premanand Trikanand, who lives in Hollywood.

Secretary Mansur and Sam will be leaving here sometime next week for a very quick trip to Los Angeles and Hollywood. At this writing it is difficult to give details for the time will be determined by events which have not yet transpired. There are two opposite factors for this sudden journey. One is that Sam has hardly had an hour off much less a half-day, much less a day off, this year, and there are no signs for any spare time unless by such a radical geographical move. So we are going to take this radical geographical move.

Dialogue continues with another representative of the Temple of Understanding named Dorothy Rapp. Murshid seeks guidance from Rapp about the hotel room in Geneva: "We have assumed that you may be booking our room and we will be paying for it." Murshid is not giving up on a possible presentation either.

We are also arranging to copy notes accumulated over a number of years originally intended to be presented at a conference of the World Church Peace Union many years past. The conference never took place. The notes still hold good, and many more have been added. All of these should be of interest to the Temple of Understanding whether they are presented at the conference or not.

Through a remark in Murshid's letter to an old friend in Gay Mills, Pennsylvania, I find out that Vilayat answered Murshid regarding Geneva. Vilayat said that he may not be there, and that Murshid should carry on without him.

February 21, 1970, Saturday

When Murshid answers his cousin Marion, he is so generous as to acknowledge that "Mansur also has been very devoted to the ideal for which we are working together."

Doing a bit of networking, Murshid writes P.K. Gupta, an Indian friend of W.D. Begg in Arlington, Massachusetts, that Richard Harvey "would welcome any Indian who has a mystical background, and especially one in Sufism, and especially one in Chisti methods." Then Murshid writes Richard Harvey at the East-West center in Boston and sends him a copy of his letter to Gupta with the comment: "One trusts you will find this satisfactory."

February 24, 1970, Tuesday

Murshid and I take Route 132 to Modesto. Ruth Mossman, an old friend of Murshid's, lives there. We stop at a Cowboy Bar-B-Q to phone her when we get within the city limits. I pick up a street map of Modesto, find her house, and admire the large tree in the front yard. This monster tree reminds me of the large tree in Santa Rosa, in Luther Burbank's front yard. Burbank, who talked to plants and is known for developing a spineless cactus, was visited by Hazrat Inayat Khan.

Arriving in Fresno about 1:30 P.M., I am really hungry. Murshid and I eat at Rustigan's Iran Restaurant, corner of Talerie and U Streets. They specialize in Armenian food. We share our dishes, eggplant with ground beef and lamb and potatoes in a sauce. I learn from a pictoral history of Rustigan's lining the walls that Mr. Rustigan's first restaurant job was at Omar Khayyam's in San Francisco. Lunch costs $3.89.

The speedometer reads 83,432 miles on my 1966 VW bus when it is filled with gas in Bakersfield at 4:30 P.M. Since the last fill up before Modesto, we have gone 243 miles.

A little after the fuel break, we stop and Murshid phones Bibijan in North Hollywood. The result of the call is that Bibijan comes over to our residential hotel (where Vocha Fiske also lives) at 1738 Las Palmas. It costs Murshid $7.88 a night for a room with two single beds.

I don't know why Bibijan comes or what Sufi Order business, if any, is accomplished. I'm paranoid and imagine that Atiya in Seattle has warned Bibijan that Murshid might stay indefinitely, so she should under no circumstance allow him to come to her home. After a short meeting, Bibijan leaves. Is this the highly touted meeting Murshid had on his mind in so many letters? No, the need for that organizational meeting becomes unnecessary, possibly after Murshid finalizes the Sufi Order branch papers.

February 25, 1970, Wednesday

Murshid and I have breakfast at Benny's, a greasy spoon at the corner of Wilcox and Hollywood Boulevard, and eat lox and eggs.

I call the Volkswagen dealer, because the starter has been working intermittently since yesterday. The service manager says sometimes rust gets in that little electromagnet called the solenoid and nothing happens when you turn the key. The thing to do in such a situation is to bang on the solenoid or get someone to push the vehicle. With the car rolling, you drop the clutch, which jars the starter gear into engagement with the teeth of the flywheel, and with luck, you start the car.

I have been parking on hills and letting the car roll to start whenever this happens. Today, I forget. When I turn the key and nothing happens, I look at Murshid. "We need a push," I say.

"You want me to push? All right," Murshid responds without batting an eyelid, and the 73 year old gets out and pushes the three thousand pound hunk of metal until it starts.

We find Papa Ramdas's grandson, Premanand Trikanand, at home on North Cherokee Avenue in Hollywood. Premanand lives with his wife Sheela, and they have turned a small study off the living room into a room for their devotions. There is an altar with life sized—yes, bigger than life—pictures of Papa Ramdas and Mother Krishnabai on the wall behind it. Murshid says Mother Krishnabai has the highest realization of anyone he has ever met. Krishnabai came to Ramdas as a seeker and achieved the deepest realization.

Murshid and I join in the Trikanands' devotions and sing *Ramnam* (*Om Sri Ram, Jai Ram, Jai Jai Ram*). Some Indian musical instruments—

sitar, tamboura, tablas, harmonium—are arranged elegantly in the room. Premanand plays a squeeze box harmonium, which has a small piano-like key board. Sheela plays a tamboura. We sing a version of *Ramnam* with a different melody than the one we usually use. Ah, sweet India.

Murshid fails to reach Fred and Corinne Reinhold by telephone from Premanand and Sheela's. "In my last rather hurried visit to the Los Angeles region, we found your telephone had been disconnected and made no further effort to contact," Murshid will write to them the day before he leaves (March 28, 1970) for Geneva.

Murshid and I return to the Las Palmas Hotel and talk to Vocha until after 10 A.M., when the Bank of America at 6780 Hollywood Boulevard opens. Then I drive Murshid there, and he withdraws some money. Murshid has a Bank of America identification card that facilitates his use of any of the three accounts with Bank of America that he maintains at this time.

Johnny Weismuller's health food store (the same Johnny Weismuller who played Tarzan in the movies) catches Murshid's eye after the bank visit. What Murshid learns there, he shares with the Reinholds in the letter mentioned above. "Johnny Weismuller's health food store on Hollywood Boulevard is prospering, limited only to the degree that they are able to get organically grown food." Murshid knows this because he talks to the store clerk, and asks her how they are doing. Business has tripled in the last five months.

Next we drop by 9021 Melrose to see Mr. Arlock, a recent correspondent and representative of Great Books of the Western World. Arlock's sincere expression of interest in Murshid's works inspired him to consider Arlock a candidate for a Sufi center leader. We're told that Arlock is elsewhere, at the University of California in Santa Barbara. Murshid stops to call an old friend named Nusi McLellan. She, too, is unavailable. Everybody gets one chance on this trip, and that's it.

It is time for a trip to the Baskin-Robbins ice cream store. This is our substitution of ice cream for lunch. I get two dips of cherry cheesecake ice cream. My psychological state at this time is that I am preoccupied with food, always eagerly anticipating the next meal. I am gratified to find that Swami Rama was similarly preoccupied as a young aspirant.

My master told me, "If you really want to learn from a genuine swami, go to this man and live with him." I was directed to go to a place near Gangotri where I found a swami sitting in a cave. Never before had I seen such a beautifully formed body. At that age, I was interested in body building and physical strength and was envious of a body like his. He had a broad chest and a very small waist, and his muscles were very solid. I was amazed to learn that he was eighty-five years old.

After I greeted him, the first thing I asked was, "Sir, what do you eat here?" I was preoccupied with food. After my experience at the college, I had become like a Westerner in the matter of food. Each day a variety of meals was available, and I was always anticipating the various dishes to be enjoyed at the pending meals. (*Living with the Himalayan Masters*, p.437)

Ice cream in hand, Murshid and I motor back to the hotel at 2 P.M. for a rest. After napping, we rise and return to a quite satisfactory Chinese restaurant called the Cathy Host. We select Combination Dinner #3 for two or more persons. For a mere $2.95 per person, it features an appetizer (choose one) of chicken egg roll, Sui My (paper beef), fried shrimp, or a special soup, and a main course with two dishes: Chinese peas and water chestnuts with tenderloin of beef and chicken subgum chow mein fried rice.

Stuffed with extra servings of rice—as usual at Chinese restaurants—I drive Murshid down to Santa Monica's Ocean Palisades Park, and we walk around a bit. Then we swing by the Chapel of Light, where the Koan of the Cross branch of the Sufi Order conducts the Universal Worship service the fourth Wednesday of the month. This place is just four blocks from the beach, at 1245 Fourth Street in Santa Monica. Murshid and Mansur sleep their second night at the Las Palmas Hotel.

February 26, 1970, Thursday

Premanand invited us for breakfast today; but before going there, Murshid points out the house at 1752 Hudson where he used to live. Then we swing by the Vedanta temple, located at 1946 Vedanta Place, a very difficult to find road behind the famous "Hollywood" sign, high in the Hollywood Hills.

After breakfast, I take Murshid to visit with Vocha at the hotel. Then we stop at Hudson's on Hollywood Boulevard so Murshid can buy a fingernail file and some tooth powder. We choose the Corsican Italian Restaurant at 1312 N. La Brea for lunch. I have a Shrimp Louis, and Murshid has a Spanish omelette. We both have an excellent onion soup, and spumoni ice cream.

I have a realization: It is possible to stand up straight with a full stomach. I also have a perplexing remembrance. I remember wondering when I was small: How do you win wars? Kill everybody on the other side?

Murshid and I look unsuccessfully for David Wilson on the campus of U.C.L.A. I have no idea then or now who he is. Murshid wrote to him six years before. At U.C.L.A., we do see Dean Parrish, Murshid's secretary years ago. I don't remember much about this meeting. After some shuffling around from room to room, we track Parrish down in an administration building. Murshid summarizes his present work and that is it. There are no emotions or bad vibes from Dean Parrish; nothing, really. He seems politely stunned, as if our unscheduled visit temporarily interrupted his plan for the day. From the campus, Murshid rings up Dr. Alma Hawkins in the Dance Department, and we look unsuccessfully for her in Room 205 at the women's gym.

With Murshid's encouragement, I pick up three different hitchhikers, two noteworthy. One shouts, "Murshid!" His name is Charles, and Basira, a disciple, was his first love. Another man gets in the car, listens to Murshid for a while, and says, "Mr. Natural. He's Mr. Natural." In fact, the cartoon character Mr. Natural, in R. Crumb's stable of cartoon characters, is a bearded guru who sounds very much like Murshid.

We leave for Jelila and Bob (Muni) Fraley's in Camarillo after finishing at U.C.L.A. They have a marvelous avocado orchard next to their home. Bhakti Engle, Jelila's mother, lives in a guest house among the avocado trees. Muni and Jelila are vegetarians. I am amazed, watching them serve themselves dinner. They each have a huge bowl of salad, one of which would normally be used to serve a family of six or eight.

Bhakti sees me sitting stiffly mute and remarks kindly, "Look at how Mansur just sits there taking it all in. That's what a *mureed* is supposed to do: receive and assimilate the teachings. Chew them up like food and digest them well." Much later, when I look at myself in the movie *Sunseed*, straight backed and concentrated at the Saturday night dance class or sitting at the table in the *khankah*, I think: How serious he looks. I sleep on the floor at the Fraleys in my sleeping bag.

February 27, 1970, Friday

After waking up at the Fraleys', Murshid and I find the Sun and Earth Health Food Store on the University of California Santa Barbara campus and get some breakfast. Murshid talks up the health food movement with the employees.

The only other stop worth mentioning before we arrive in San Francisco is at the town just north of Aptos, California. We stop at the Peterson Nursery, 2500 Porter Street. Murshid calls someone there his teacher. A horticulture teacher perhaps? I'm too abstracted to ask. With no idea beforehand of what Murshid's agenda is in L.A. —it is all in Murshid's head and I don't pry—I'm really spaced out.

The following, written March 2, 1970 to his cousin Marion, who feeds us at her home in New York the night before we fly to Geneva, is Murshid's retrospective of our trip to Los Angeles.

We had to rush to southern California to see Mrs. D'Mitrieff the Secretary of the Sufi movement, for we are preparing to go to Geneva. Every minute was occupied by business, and we even had to skip some meals. Our work with the Fraley's was entirely of a spiritual nature. We did stay over night, but not even for breakfast; that was all. All the conversation was about spiritual matters, and even there, we could not fulfill our common efforts... Our trip was marked, not marred but marked, by strange events in picking up hitch-hikers, each of whom had some spiritual message for us.

February 28, 1970, Saturday

Murshid's last letter of the day (to Russ Joyner) reports that he "started in the morning by writing a diary letter to Oliver Reiser, then sundry letters, personal and philosophical." Always looking ahead, Murshid indicates to Reiser that I will be accompanying him to Lama, where special housing will be provided. "If the present outlook continues, I shall be taking my secretary, Mansur Johnson, with me to New Mexico where we shall have our own 'shack'."

The sundry "personal and philosophical" letters include one to Gandalf's Garden, a hippie group in London. Murshid tantalizes these seekers by presenting his good self as a mixture of a Sufi, Buddhist, Muslim, and tarot card character.

I shall be going to Switzerland wearing at the same time a Sufi robe and a Korean Buddhist robe. The reason for two robes can be seen in the number 5 tarot card called THE HIEROPHANT, which is my present line of life. But the robes also signify, as the Quran teaches, "The Light is neither of the West nor the East."

T.D. Lingo, who represents the Adventure Trails Survival School in Blackhawk, Colorado, writes Murshid an appreciative letter with questions. Murshid gets philosophical and invokes the periodic table of elements to preface an answer to a question about the transmutation of sexual energy.

I am going to mention the subject "sex" here because you have mentioned it. I have no answers. There are anywhere between 92 and 108 chemical elements, and they seem to display various kinds of polarities, from oxygen which I call the great whore, to the predominant silicon which, although the most prevalent of all elements, seems to act like a monk.

The answer Murshid gives affirms transmutation of sexual energy with a qualification that is very difficult to understand.

My present conclusions on the transcendental side are that transmutation is wonderful and totally different from repression or even sublimation—a term which is not entirely comprehensible to me. But at the same time there are transcendent values according to our states of consciousness, and in the higher states of consciousness (as I have experienced them to date—and I mean directly experienced them—no borrowed knowledge), it is possible to utilize sex energies to promote health and vigor and longevity, even by utilizing polar magnetisms which are associated with one's personal physiological sex.

This is a branch of Murshid's knowledge I have never heard him explain. Just how Murshid uses his sexual energy to promote his health and vigor is a question I never ask.

Chapter 26

Movie Star

Some day, no doubt, my autobiography or biography will be written. It will either be called I More Than Accuse or When Man Bites Dog It Absolutely Mustn't Be News. (Murshid's letter to Jeremy Ets-Hokim, March 4, 1970)

I have gone over many books on Theravadin teachings; I think the jhanas are IT, but just as iron exposed to the atmosphere, exposed to moisture, exposed to acid, becomes an iron-compound adding something to its presumable essence which was not there before, so a devotee performing a jhana becomes altered by such practice or practices, and is no longer the same personality. This is Lord Buddha's teaching. (Murshid's letter to Rev. Jack Austin, March 10, 1970)

One has spoken with both exaltation and sadness of having to abandon, at least for the time, anything like a stable family. Problems are not solved by our refusal to attend to them, and my whole life has been so bound up with the hopes for peace and good will in the holy lands of the world...

The heart above all is concerned with the pains and pangs of others. (Murshid's letter to Saadia Khawar Khan and her Aunt Bibijan, March 13, 1970)

March 1, 1970, Sunday

Murshid's correspondence increases: sixty-seven letters consuming 109 pages is his production this month. General Semantics's Russ Joyner gave Murshid a book, *Civilization at the Cross-Roads of Destiny*, by the Vice President of India, His Excellency V.V. Giri. In addressing V.V. Giri today, Murshid focuses not so much on the book when he writes, "I am not going to review this book; I am going to put it into action," but on his analysis of India's problem. "The trouble with India," Murshid writes Giri, "if one assumes the right to criticize any nation, which no sane man can logically do, is that India has been so afraid of *rajas* [action] it falls into *tamas* [inactivity] constantly." Murshid ties this observation to Gandhi.

> Gandhiji did accomplish, and this is more important than any rhetoric about him. The above criticism that India has been afraid of *rajas*, so afraid of *rajas* that it has fallen into *tamas*, partly applies to him.

The *satyagraha* (reliance on God) aspect of Gandhi's teachings, according to Murshid, has not received enough attention, with everyone focusing on nonviolence. But it is Murshid's personal belief that "the *satyagraha* of Gandhiji and the *prajna* of Dr. Radhakrishnan are ultimately one."

It is in this letter to Vice President Giri (before the month is out Giri becomes President of India, which causes Murshid to tell Art Hoppe "some of my best friends have been president of India, and some presidents of India have been my best friends," March 15, 1970) that Murshid lists four eminent Indians with whom he has had interviews.

> The late Villabhai Patel, your magnificent retired President Dr. S. Radhakrishnan, your congressional leader Sri Surendra Mohan Ghose, and most of all...your noted demographer Dr. Chandra Sekhar, whom I have met many times in many separate parts of this world.

Murshid mentioned Surendra Mohan Ghose when he wrote R.L. Adamson in Australia on February 13, 1970. It seems that Ghose recommended Murshid to Adamson. This is further evidence—there is correspondence with Radhakrishnan as well—that esteem flows both ways, and that Murshid's claims are more than bluster or braggadocio.

March 2, 1970, Monday

The question about our hotel room in Geneva is answered today. "We received word that our hotel reservations have been accepted," Murshid tells his cousin Marion.

Murshid reflects on the brief meeting in Los Angeles with Suzanne D'Mitrieff (Bibijan) that was so mysterious to me (see February 24, 1970) when he writes Atiya in Seattle.

I did have time to discuss matters seriously with Secretary Bibijan. We both feel (and do not like to be critical) that Pir Vilayat has given too much time to travel and not enough to organizational settlement.

Additionally, Murshid says his collections of money for admission by disciples and non-disciple alike to meetings which I collect are ample, but that there is "no provision for distribution." Nor have spiritual papers been provided, "and again no provision made for this. It is very awkward. We should like to share our material blessings with Bibijan in an orderly and legal fashion."

I get from Murshid's letter to Saadia his reason for staying two weeks in Europe: It's practical. The additional days in London after the conference are "to fulfill a period of two weeks, so as to obtain the minimum tourist rate." To Saadia, who has offered financial support to Murshid in the past, he focuses mainly on money. Citing his brother's illness, Murshid says a prolonged tour—for example to Ithaca, New York, where Saadia is a student at Cornell—is not possible. "I do not have the money." Murshid reveals his acquisition of a loan "to cover the expenses for Mansur and myself," and justifies the extra expense of a companion.

If I were to travel alone, there would be no financial complications, but I am no longer able to handle all the financial and commercial transactions needed for such a journey, and also to carry on my main missions social, spiritual, and intellectual.

This is not the end of it. If Murshid were to remain on the East Coast, he claims, "there would have to be in my hands funds not now available." Still, it's not finished. After an optimistic report about the filming due to begin, he says, "All of this makes very uncertain any visit to universities in the Eastern states without some financial support and other arrangements for this now elderly person." We know from the letters that Saadia offered to help Murshid with travel expenses and that he acknowledged a check from her. What Murshid drives home today is: *Make a financial commitment if you want me to visit.*

March 3, 1970, Tuesday

Murshid invites some of his correspondents (yoga teachers Walt and Magana Baptiste) to the Spring Festival; others, like columnist Art Hoppe, are merely informed, with copies to PBS TV station KQED and radio station KPIX.

March 4, 1970, Wednesday

In 1967, just before Murshid planned to visit England "to make some studies in problems of pollution and ecology," he became sick and landed in the hospital. It seems obvious to me, but perhaps not all would understand this experience the way Murshid did: "I took that as a sign not to be involved in such matters." Not many details are available about that aborted project, except that Murshid found in San Francisco "a most complicated system or total lack of system of sewage outlets." He saw "that money could be made from waste products of all kinds." (letter to Shamcher, March 24, 1970)

March 6, 1970, Friday

Murshid has big hopes, emerging from his contact with Gandalf's Garden, to establish a Sufi center in London. "On the surface, the Geneva convention will make history, but to us, our coming to London will affect humanity much more," Murshid writes to Gandalf's Garden. This letter, dictated in San Francisco to Wali Ali, frees me to express myself in Geneva. "Personally, I intend to give Mansur, my secretary, full scope for expression and not waste any time myself chittering and chattering about the 'youth' to whom I am superior in age." This is an opportunity I only think to exercise once, but don't. That moment comes at the end of the conference when someone stretches a string, row by row, for all to grab, symbolizing our unity. Why not hold hands? I think. But I don't wish to express myself like this. I defer to Murshid. Let him jump in. He's surely thinking just what I'm thinking. He isn't. And so we are both good followers, going along, grabbing the string.

March 7, 1970, Saturday

In another letter, to Professor K.T. Merchant in Bombay (dictated in San Francisco, which means that I don't read it at the time), Murshid goes beyond giving me scope for expression at the conference; *I will represent youth.* "My secretary and I are now preparing to go to Geneva, me representing various sectarianisms which, one can be sure, will be presented; he representing youth." Literalist that I am, all the times I hear Murshid quote the Bible's "and the lion and the lamb shall lie down together and a little child shall lead them" passage, I don't get that for Murshid, my generation, the youth, is a child. In this letter, Murshid makes that clear. "My point of view is that not only the lamb and the lion must lie down together, but also a child, that is youth, must lead, and on this point all elders suddenly seem to close ranks."

March 8, 1970, Sunday

I sang in a dream last night, "You are beautiful and sweet; you have eyes of combed gold."

Murshid braces for the film crew to invade his life. He tells Saadia, "*Kashf* is a great faculty; it often operates contrary to the wishes and whims, but it is never wrong." Murshid gives what he considers his farewell address to his family at the *khankah*. It is not an address of departure; it is an address of complete change of function. This change immediately comes into being, for this week this home is to be "invaded," so to speak, by cameras and sound equipment. The equipment will record, not only what we are doing in dervish and spiritual dancing, but also Murshid's whole private life and the objective presentation of Sufi mysticism in and to the Western world.

In other words, it is actually the end to a form of peace and quiet so longed for, but which must be surrendered for the sake of Allah. As one has foreseen it, there can be no comment. There can only be acceptance of the Divine Will, in operation, in actual operation in the external world. There seems little doubt as to the outcome, although there is always a danger of self-pride, especially when forms of success long foreseen are vouchsafed.

Murshid goes on, summing up in a sentence the radical change he's now experiencing.

It is not especially easy for a man whose whole life has been passed in being rejected almost everywhere and anywhere, to becoming accepted in an equal and opposite fashion which is now going on.

With confidence born of acceptance, Murshid takes on a heavyweight of world class caliber, Nobel Prize winner in physics Charles H. Townes, who published an article called "The Convergence of Science and Religion." I can find no record of this article, only a 1996 videotape of a lecture, "Logic and Uncertainties in Science and Religion." Townes's most popular book *Making Waves* (Woodbury, NY: American Institute of Physics, 1995) is held by 362 libraries. Murshid commends Townes today on his article, then offers his understanding of Dalton's 1803 theory (each chemical element has its own kind of atoms), which is highly personal when we remember that Murshid uses the biblical verse "The stone that is rejected becomes the corner stone" to describe himself.

I have long felt that the Daltonian atomic theory came out of influences derived from Aristotle and invented in Christianity. It seems up to a point all the basic elements accepted this theory but thorium. Then with the discovery of radioactivity it would seem that nature had some built in Buddhists, and that the stone that was rejected had become the cornerstone... Working on an analogy, one felt also that the cells might be a function rather than a thing, and that many cellular theories were also derived from the same Aristotelian-Christian outlook.

There are too many undefined concepts thrown together for me to get Murshid's point. It is little help when Murshid adds,

One can almost say that the present bases of our fundamental sciences were Buddhistic rather than Christian, and certainly bear out the teachings of Lord Buddha (Buddhism is not any more necessarily the teachings of Buddha than Christianity is necessarily the teachings of Jesus Christ).

When Murshid tells Jack Austin that he is "involved in a philosophical controversy" (March 10, 1970), I am hopeful he will elaborate on the relationships of atoms, cells, Christianity, and Buddhism. He does, to a certain extent.

> As I have seen it, the discovery of radioactivity was a demonstration of the Teachings of Lord Buddha. [But which teaching?] By analogy I presumed that the *cell* also might be functional, and not a thing. [This doesn't help me understand.]

I do learn it is Vocha Fiske who gave Murshid two books by disciples of Ernst Haeckel "supporting the functional as against the thing-essence of the *cell*." This specialized discussion shows Murshid flexing his intellectual muscles. His intent, no doubt, is to arouse the Nobel Prize winner's curiosity, in hopes there might be a meeting. "As I am preparing to leave the country now I hope that accomplishment on my part may lead to the value of our meeting after our return." There is no meeting that I know of.

March 9, 1970, Monday

The loss of privacy occasioned by the film crew covering Murshid's life is the reason he gives for the end of family in a letter to Julie Medlock at Auroville in India. "The idea of having a family, even an enlarged family, is out of the question any longer." Murshid also announces to Julie that he received his passport today.

More to announce his arrival than to request a seat, Murshid writes and asks the Universalist Unitarian Church in New York to reserve him a seat for Easter services.

March 10, 1970, Tuesday

In dream, I'm doing saints' walks up and down the hills of San Francisco. Upon waking, I am amazed that this practice has impressed me this deeply.

Murshid reminds F. Clive-Ross that he expects to be in London by April 7th, and again sounds the end-of-privacy gong. "Whatever the outcome of this forthcoming journey may be, it is certain that my own private career is at an end."

Murshid acknowledges Richard Harvey's letter of March 3rd, and asks Harvey if hospitality with him is possible—while keeping open his option not to accept. "We are assuming at the moment that you will arrange quarters for us, although at this writing we may also have other proffers."

Murshid sends his cousin, Marion Martini, a confirmation of our expected arrival on the 29th. He tells her, "For many years I have longed for a happy family. I now have a happy family, or rather, two happy families, one in San Francisco in the Mission district, and the other in the city of Novato 30 miles to the north." Good things—long sought, it seems—don't last. Murshid adds,

But my Pied Piper efforts have caught up with me. A local radio-TV station had a preliminary filming of my meeting in the central part of Marin County about 20 miles north of here, last week. Wednesday and Thursday will be spent at the Novato home, and the technicians will be there. Friday, Saturday, Sunday and Monday will be spent here, and the technicians will be here.

The result of this publicity, Murshid tells Marion, "may mean a very revolutionary change and one can well become a public figure." Belief in this certainty prompts me upon our return from Europe to write the *Tonight Show*. I tell them about Murshid's appearance in Geneva. I am certain my notice will propel Murshid even more into the national spotlight, as augured by letters such as the ones above. The popular show, which caters to movie stars promoting their latest films, ignores my announcement.

March 11, 1970, Wednesday

Murshid begins his letter to Anandashram by saying,

Sam was influenced to maintain a diary after reading the works of Thomas Jefferson, Ralph Waldo Emerson, and Papa Ramdas. But in retrospect it must be said that the more one considers it, there is no diary; there is only the fulfillment of the divine life in and through what would appear to be an ego-personality which is nothing but a mode of God Himself expressing Himself outwardly. And daily Sam seems to find that there is really nothing else but this divine life.

Addressing those at Anandashram as "Dear Ram," Murshid tells them:

Three years ago when Sam was flat on his back in the hospital, there was a divine visitation with words and visions. All the words, all the visions have now manifested. But the door did not close, and the next steps in life are evident. Last Thursday in this house and Monday night at the San Francisco home, Sam gave his farewell addresses to privacy and tranquility. There is no time now when interviews are not sought, when office work is not done, and when there are other aspects of both spiritual and material business. For the next five days in a row at least, there will be cameras and sound equipment recording the spiritual dances, the sacred lessons, and the daily life of a man who was marked for spiritual leadership by so many holy men and egotistically rejected in previous years with a single exception—these all being a priori rejections.

Murshid's diary letter to Anandashram today reflects a shift in his expression of how he's going to manifest in Geneva. Only two days ago, Murshid told Shamcher in a letter, "But now, after a life's effort with constant doors shutting in my face, at least I shall be heard, which is something."

Could it be that Murshid's many sermons on "big ears" (the importance of listening) have been taken to heart? What Murshid writes to Anandashram sounds like it. I read these remarks years later as preludes to Murshid's silence in Geneva.

Sam's theme which may be presented to a conference of great spiritual teachers and ecclesiast[ic]s is not going to be "Love ye one another." (Sam is amused by the number of people in audiences who interrupt saying, "Why don't you preach and teach more love?", not aware that rude interruptions are self-evident demonstrations of the lack of love and the dominance of a dualistic outlook.) So Sam will present instead "Respect ye one another."

This is very difficult, for Sam has as his *koan*, so to speak, the first words of Handel's *Messiah*, "Every valley shall be exalted and every hill laid low; the crooked places made straight." But how is a little valley going to express itself amid a throng of mountains who because of their very nature are unable to bow before each other. Nevertheless, this will be the theme.

This is the night cameras film the Wednesday night meeting at the seminary in San Anselmo. My failure to remember much of Murshid's talk is redeemed by tapes the film crew make tonight. My thanks to Fred Cohn for permitting me to reproduce here a big chunk of Murshid's talk. As is typical of Murshid's lectures, the delivery is stream of consciousness, rapid fire, and full of gusto. Murshid darts from one subject to another according to the rhythm of his mind, making points, editorializing, and embellishing the story with examples from his own life.

This is Murshid in real time. Sometimes his words stop and start, switch to a different subject, and go on a new vector without finishing what he started. I have added bracketed inserts to help the reader follow. Murshid in real time may be tedious, but it's Murshid live, speaking without notes to several hundred people. Murshid used to say, "You know what the sutras are? Words that came out of the mouths of enlightened men." The talk tonight begins like a sutra in the making.

All right, a chair up here please for the guru, roshi, murshid, all in one. I'm the first guru, roshi, murshid, I think, in existence in the history of the world. I always feel like Nasr-ed-din Hoja (Murshid says it so it sounds like "Coga," which means *imam*—a Muslim scholar—in Turkish), getting up and sitting down. Do you know what I'm going to say?

He asks this sitting up straight in his chair, like a Zen master. Regulars at Murshid's are familiar with this Nasr-ed-din story. The *mullah* (religious leader) asks if the audience knows what he's going to say. The audience says, "Yes, we know what you are going to say," Nasr-ed-din says, "You give the talk, then." The next night Nasr-ed-din asks, "Do you know what I'm going to say?" And the audience, one day wiser, says, "No." The *mullah* then tells them they are a bunch of dummies. After giving the audience a good look around, Murshid continues,

And if you do [know what I'm going to say], well, you're a bunch of idiots, because I'm not going to say that, because sometimes I take just the opposite tack from Nasr-ed-din Hoja and just keep on jawing. Now, the other night some of you were at my house and our good friend Dr. Warwick came in with the group, and he spoke something I don't understand. He spoke *for* love, and he spoke *against* ecstasy. Now this is a very difficult thing for me to understand, because I find that love should produce a certain type of ecstasy, and ecstasy, if it's real, will produce a certain kind of love.

So when he was gone, I asked who would give me the riddle that would solve the problem that he brought up, and some of them got it. This is perhaps very unfair, but the answer was, of course, *sour grapes*.

Now I don't think that's true of him at all, but I think the implication's there. And a lot of people go and speak against ecstasy, and they don't know what it is, and a lot of people speak for it, and they don't know what it is.

Tonight, too, I shall have to pass through such a stage in certain dances, [the Krishna dance, when he dances like Lord Krishna playing his flute] wherein the sense of ego self just entirely disappears, and you feel like you're an actor on a cosmic stage, performing a role because you can't help performing it. But the role is real and you're unreal. When you get into this lofty state, you don't necessarily have a sense of self.

The other night I went to hear a man some of you know—I'm not necessarily going to mention his name—who spoke for cosmic consciousness and then attacked almost everybody he ever heard who had cosmic consciousness.

Why? The unspoken question lingers. Murshid answers,

Because he has never had it or anything like it. He just read something in a book that somebody had it. And the man who had it, that he quotes, is Dr. Bucke [Richard M. Bucke, author of *Cosmic Consciousness*], who had it maybe once, or maybe a few times. And so Dr. Bucke wanted to collect a number of instances of other people [who had cosmic consciousness], and like all good Americans—God only looks upon the Aryans, except on very rare occasions, which is a bunch of nonsense, because cosmic consciousness can come in any form, almost.

For example, when people of the African races have cosmic consciousness, it always comes with ecstasy. But when people of the Mongolian races have it, it very often comes with sobriety. Now what are you going to say about it? That's the way it comes. Now if anybody has any question about it, I will ask them just one simple question: Give me the list of Negro comedians and give me the list of Chinese comedians. It's very obvious because that's the way they have their divine experience: one through sobriety, and the other through intoxication. That's the way they're made. And what is better than the other? That's a bunch of nonsense. Even to bring the subject up, this shows the person doesn't have it. Besides, in that state you don't feel differences from others. You don't feel that, and it's so easy to start a bunch of condemnations. Anybody's adept at that; gosh. For example—I'm not going to ask you to raise your hands—do you know anybody that hasn't attacked some group or other down at Santa Barbara?

Well, I don't. This is California politics, and I recently arrived here from the Upper Peninsula of Michigan. Moineddin comes from Iowa City. We don't know or much care about spiritual politics connected with Santa Barbara. And Murshid got it right away.

Everybody's up with all kinds of criticisms. Well, all right, I'm not going to say anything about it. But you see, it's so easy. Now I'm not going to say that there isn't right or wrong implied. I'm not going to say that at all. But there is a certain sense, and in my sense, right is not in a sober state, it's always in a transcendent state, where you rise above individuality. You rise above group divisions, and you come into a world of understanding. Walt Whitman said, "In all men I see myself." But how many of you ever found any Whitmanians that believe that? They'd quit. They'd have to quit, if they were honest, because they don't choose to see themselves in everybody else.

This is exactly the kind of rigorous thinking that Murshid is teaching us. The Whitmanians would have to quit because they don't live the outlook of their mentor. How many hippies present have been in academic settings where followers of the Great One are referred to like this? Not many.

They just don't choose it. They form a Whitmanian Society, and this is quite typical of our age. I am blackballed by practically every cosmic or world organization, and one reason that I am blackballed is that I admit the existence of a rival group. That's far worse to them than the criticizing. They can stand the criticizing. You know, one time there was a conference of all the world's religions. They came to London, and at that time they were trying to prove [*sic*] each other. And one group came and said, "All religions are true. But now there is a new age coming, and the new religion takes the place of all the old religions without rejecting the old religions." Everybody thought that group was the finest. On the last day a delegation of another group came in: "All religions are true. But now is the time to have a universal religion without displacing the old religion, but the universal religion." And all the people looked around. This was an impasse. So the leader of the second group said, "I'd like to ask the leader of the other group a question. What was your year of revelation? "1844," the first man answered. "Thank you, ours was 1834!" Well, you know...

There is a break in the tape at this point. Murshid picks up again with:

But one thing about these people, they won't even recognize the existence of the other persons. The other persons aren't evil, because they never lived. And I am going to a peace conference. Nearly all the persons that say they are there for a peace conference refuse to admit the existence of certain persons. So they refuse to admit their existence. Isn't that interesting? You show me a universal organization in San Francisco, or even this country, and I can name historical characters of whom they refuse to admit their existence. Now, how in God's name are we going to have any peace in the world then, [when people] just refuse to admit their existence?! So I am going to Geneva soon, for a world peace conference, and I know what is going to take place.

There is no break in the tape here, just a change of subject.

You know, I could have been famous long ago. And all I had to do was sign on the dotted line, but I didn't. That's all. Everybody decided there would be world peace. That's it. Maybe it was a petition.

This is another one of those starts that stops, and then Murshid goes in a different direction.

I read a little article today. Art Hoppe wrote something about the misguided voters. So I wrote him about how there is a character all ready to lead the misguided voters. His name is Sam Yorty [the mayor of Los Angeles at the time]. A number of years ago, Los Angeles had a mayor, and they had gangsters. And the chief of the gangsters—the two of them, the mayor's brother and the chief of police—they saw to it that nobody from Chicago could settle into Los Angeles, because they were saving the city from gangsterism. So people from Chicago weren't welcome, and if anybody came from Chicago, they were immediately chased away. And in Los Angeles, there were several crimes of which you could be guilty of. For example, if you saw a crime committed, you were immediately a criminal. If you were a friend of somebody who saw a crime committed, you were suspect. So they removed the criminals and they removed the suspects.

But we kind of got tired of it, and we had a recall election—the other two Sams [Yorty and I don't know who the other Sam is] and myself, who were busy in that recall election. You know it was a very honest election, absolutely honest. The police counted the ballots. Well, you see, every now and then they slipped somebody in who wasn't a policeman. Maybe an honest person put on a policeman's uniform. The mayor got recalled. The police got disestablished. Maybe some of you wish they would [recall the mayor] here now, but that actually happened there, and this pushed Sam Yorty up, and he's been running around like this ever since, and to me, he's so much like a comic opera character, I can't have any ill will toward him.

What does this comic opera view of southern California politics give me? It reminds me that Murshid used to sing songs from Gilbert and Sullivan on the way home from these Wednesday night meetings where this talk is delivered.

So I said he [Sam Yorty] is going to be the leader of the misguided voters. But at least he lived! You can't con him out of existence. We want a world peace program. You got to omit all reference to any historical character who ever did anything contrary to your idea. Your idea is supreme. What happened is unsupreme. So a number of years ago, I was the advisor, like I am now, to a great world peace conference. Now the difference between that peace conference and this one: This world conference is made up of holy men and prelates and clerics and recognized religious leaders, and the other one was made up of holy men and prelates and recognized religious leaders and heads of governments and heads of Mafia and heads of Tammany [the political machine in New York City] and so on, and they were talking.

And I said, "As soon as these men get together, we're starting a new world war." So I wasn't allowed to attend the conference, and the life I saved would be my own, because all they did was tear into each other beautifully; and the next thing, the world war started almost immediately after that.

Now who do you think we're fooling? If you have read Edward Carpenter [Walt Whitman's teacher], or Edna St. Vincent Millay ["The world stands out on either side/ no wider than the heart is wide"], or occasionally some great mystic, they will say, like Jesus, "Whatever ye do to the least of these my creatures, ye do it unto me."

And you don't have peace by stamping out anybody whatsoever. You don't have it that way, and this is a tough thing to get. I joined a peace organization up in Washington. Nearly everybody recommended it. They had fourteen plans for Vietnam. One came from U Thant [secretary general of the United Nations]; one came from a Vietnamese; and all the rest from Americans! What do you think of that?

No other people counted. Not even the Vietnamese themselves, outside this one person. Now how are we going to have world peace under such circumstances? How are you going to have it? You can have all the ideas you want, but as long as we have ideas, we are going to have wars. Ideas and wars go together. This is a hard one to get: Ideas and wars go together. When you get into ecstasy, you don't have any ideas any more: You stand above them. There is a phrase about "peace beyond understanding." But we don't want to get "beyond understanding"; we want to be "*under* understanding." We want not "understanding," but "under understanding." And we're going to stay there.

I read some phrases in the Prajnaparamita Sutra Sunday, and it lays down particularly what you can't have salvation with. ["If a son or daughter wishes to study the profound *Prajna-Paramita*, he must first get rid of all ideas of egoselfness."] It lays down absolutely, specifically, and particularly what you can't have salvation with. ["Let him think thus: Personality? What is personality? Is it an enduring entity? Or is it made up of elements that pass away?"]. And it gives us exactly what's presented to us by the philosophers, and the churches, and the cliques, and the cults. They'll read the thing, and they'll do exactly contrary to what's there.

So this is a pretty hard thing to do. If you want peace you'll have to experience it. I've been jawing a lot, so let's try to experience just a little bit of peace. And I think this is also a good time, while doing this, to have first a group *darshan*, and some of you who didn't have *darshan* last time will be allowed to come up.

This is the night I receive Murshid's *darshan* (see the photo at the head of the chapter) when I get in line holding the movie camera.

March 12, 1970, Thursday

Vocha Fiske arrived Tuesday and witnessed the whole spectacle last night. Today, Murshid makes breakfast for her. He later remarks in a letter to Russ Joyner,

The public exhibition last night under camera klieg lights and sound equipment did not touch my ego so much as the breakfast I made for Mother Divine Vocha Fiske this morning. Of course Vocha had a full view of rather successful efforts and also she having been connected with stage and screen and speech arts was better able to judge the worthiness or unworthiness of these efforts than most people.

Of course, Vocha loved everything. The above passage from Murshid's only letter today, dictated to me at the *khankah*, is part of four pages that rehearse in Murshid's expansive style all the old sins of General Semantics against a man they knew as "Sam." Here, in just one sentence, Murshid alludes to three such "sins."

I am concentrating on attending a world peace conference, a conference where the floor is open, and where referents are required from the worthy and unworthy, and the passing of great names coupled with emotional chairmen will not avail.

March 13, 1970, Friday

During at least one (to Saadia) of Murshid's five letters today, the film crew is present with camera rolling while Murshid dictates. Murshid mentions this distraction to Saadia on two occasions.

Why do I enjoy Murshid's letters to Saadia so much? I can see him instructing someone else, and I don't have to take the heat. When Saadia apparently uses the Islamic equivalent of our "Oh, well," and says she'll "leave it to Allah," Murshid explodes.

> One is not assured if one defaults, if one follows the pious platitude of "Leaving it to Allah." Action on one's own part has in the past brought both financial betterment and respect, and lack of action has brought both financial loss and disrespect.

God helps those who help themselves. Buddha says, "Work out your salvation with diligence." Lack of *rajas*, action, could be construed as a shortcoming of India—all these thoughts are behind Murshid's words to Saadia. In an Islamic version of Murshid's anti-*tamas* crusade that Nancy (February 15, 1970) and Indian Vice-President Giri (March 1, 1970) heard about recently, Murshid comes out strongly for taking action. "In the past one has always won by action and always lost by default. No exceptions." Murshid tells Saadia, "Pious verbalisms may cause people to be pleased with their egos, but this does not always avail in outer matters. On previous occasions, actual action has always brought success."

To the American Friends of the Middle East (AFME), Murshid speaks in the vernacular for the third time (see February 11, 1970, for the first two examples).

> And before a conference of the leading ecclesiast[ic]s and holy men of the world, I am going to present a case which will be heard, *inshallah*, for real recognition of human beings by human beings, and no more crap, and I call it crap, from men in high places with very un-pious sentiments, increasing confusion.

A copy is sent to the Department of Near Eastern Languages at Berkeley, with a repeat of information included in the AFME letter concerning Murshid's wish to endow the department with a bequest from his will. His considerations are his anticipated inheritance of considerable size, and the department's reflection of his values.

An epistle from Gandalf's Garden in London "pleases us no end," Murshid writes to people whose identities I don't know, and whom Murshid addresses as "Beloved Ones of God." Gandalf's Garden has responded, asking: *Why two robes?* This is a response to Murshid's comment (February 28, 1970) about wearing both a Sufi and a Korean Buddhist robe.

Murshid answers, "The robes are being worn for ritualistic and credential purposes. Yes, I shall also wear them of course in visiting any Pakistani restaurant, etc."

Another question comes, and Murshid recognizes their reticence to promote the dances. He lets them off the hook while hooking them, the way teachers do, with contradictory language. "It is not necessary to promote dancing, and it is also wise to introduce it, but the same applies to chanting, which does not require such a large space, to lectures and teachings, etc."

Don't promote dancing, Murshid says, but it would be wise to introduce it, along with lectures, chanting and teachings. Without explaining that he leads dances outside or that friendly relations with a local Sufi group could provide space, Murshid adds, "Much will depend upon the weather, and also your relations with the Sufi group."

March 14, 1970, Saturday

Word comes from Shamcher that he's in good spirits and good health and this causes Murshid to remark that he's "terribly relieved." It is touching indeed when Murshid turns at the end of his letter to comment at length about Shamcher personally—something he rarely does, being mainly concerned with either his own experiences or issues.

From what you tell me and what you feel, I believe your life's work will be accomplished. I hope your health will be in good enough condition that you may be able to see some of the results yourself. One does feel awkward when one's closest colleagues are withdrawing from manifestation. But this has to be.

Shamcher, who became my mentor when we lobbied for OTEC (ocean thermal energy conversion), reflectively tells me on his deathbed that he isn't going to see the realization of OTEC—the "life's work" Murshid refers to—and can't predict that I will, either.

Concurrent, again, with the writing of this letter is the presence of the film crew in Murshid's home. While Murshid is being filmed dictating to Wali Ali, my job is loading and unloading four hundred-foot magazines of 16 mm color film for award winning cameraman Robert Frank.

Fred Cohn brought Frank from New York to produce footage about Murshid to show to investors for *Sunseed*. Frank is a former beatnik. The beatnik's love for dark coffee houses shows in his cinematography. Frank, who doesn't use a light meter, concerns me with his love for shadowy realism. It diminishes the message if the colored clothes our women wear look drab. We are a spiritual group promoting light. Beauty is part of the message. Filming at the *khankah*, Frank and I have a run-in over how much to light the inside, him preferring the natural shadows.

On the day we are filming Dr. Warwick's group climbing Mt. Tamalpais, I am alarmed when I take a reading with my light meter and discover the f-stop setting on Frank's camera is ridiculously low. I react by opening the aperture of his camera while he is shooting. Frank doesn't appreciate it, even though that's what camera assistants are supposed to do. We have words, with me arguing again for light. But he's the boss.

In the end, I am vindicated, but it is a Pyrrhic victory. Fred has to discard all the footage Frank shot on Mt. Tamalpais. The film looks like it was shot after sundown. "Day for night," they call it in the movie business. Even though it was a bright sunny day with blue skies and puffy white clouds, the film is garbage. The sunlit colors of the rocks, the greens of the trees and shrubs aren't there. The exposure is too dark even for the lab to lighten up.

March 15, 1970, Sunday

Murshid has me read Wali Ali's postcard to Paul Reps. Murshid and Reps don't write any more. The card tells Reps that Inayat Khan's wish for Murshid to be an exoteric leader is happening. Then Murshid tells me that I will go with him geographically, spiritually, and socially. He says Jemila and I will be good friends—not like brother and sister, but with understanding about the cosmic significance of our relationship. Murshid mentions my *remarriage*. He says he wants me to get to this decision for myself—or not—from within, by meditation and vision, rather than from something he tells me outwardly. I can rely on him for strength, Murshid says, but have to find my own wisdom. Murshid mentions again that it will "benefit him personally" if I marry Saadia. Only God knows what Sufi Barkat Ali said to Murshid about a marriage for Saadia back in Chapter 23. As far as her new last name "Chisti," Sufis often adopt the last name of the namesake of their order; in this case, Moineddin Chisti. And I know without him saying it that "there is no compulsion in Sufism" (al-Ghazzali). After all this guidance, I am heavy in thought all day, contemplating the involuntary loss of my wife and the support of my Murshid. I cry in the bathtub when I read in a Sufi book called *The Purpose of Life*, by Hazrat Inayat Khan about the need for hope when you are disappointed; faith in your own pure motives; and perfection as an achievable reality.

There is a continual desire working in every soul to see things perfect according to one's own conception of perfection; and as one goes on with this desire, observing, analyzing and examining things and beings, one becomes disappointed and disheartened, and besides one becomes impressed with the lack one sees in conditions, in persons, in beings. No doubt there is one thing that keeps one alive, and that is hope...

Hopelessness can be overcome by faith... It is very interesting to study the lives of the great in the world. We find that some great people have almost arrived at the fulfillment of their undertakings and just before they had reached the goal they have lost it; and there have been some great people who have attained the ultimate success in whatever they have undertaken. You will always find that the souls of the former kind are the ones who were gifted with great power and yet lacked faith, while the others were gifted with the same power, and that power was supported by faith...

For life is an opportunity, and desire has the greatest power, and perfection is the promise of the soul. We seek perfection, because perfection is the ultimate aim and the goal of creation. The source of all things is perfect; our source is perfect, our goal is perfect; and therefore every atom of the universe is working towards perfection, and sooner or later it must arrive at perfection consciously. If it were not so, you would not have read in the Bible, "Be ye perfect as your Father in heaven is perfect." (*The Sufi Message of Hazrat Inayat Khan*, vol. 1, pp.225, 226, 228)

March 16, 1970, Monday

Out of the blue, Murshid addresses Rabbi Alvin Fine of San Francisco. After remarking that "not a single Rabbi or Imam has ever answered any letter proposing any kind of meeting between one and another," Murshid challenges the Rabbi to break this trend. "I am not asking anything from anybody, but I should like to see on rare occasions some cleric step forward and do something to end both the useful and useless wars of the moment."

Murshid begins to share his whimsical style, formerly reserved for columnist Art Hoppe, with sympathetic politicians such as Congressman Paul W. McCloskey, Jr. I particularly like Murshid's epithet for news gathering organizations the Associated Press (AP) and the United Press (UP), calling them "the diabolical God UP-AP." Similarly entertaining is Murshid's use of the phrase "semi-divine" to describe the U.S. State Department's policies that divide mankind. Murshid puts the blame squarely on the government—and, it must be said, the disconnect between the people and various unaccountable government agencies is worse in the twenty-first century. Murshid says,

I blame the State Department and foreign service for the easy manner in which they accept presumable news from these sources ["the diabolical God UP-AP"], and are not so open to anything that comes from the mass of citizenry. There is a vast difference between accepting ideas from the masses, and accepting valid reports therefrom. The result is a tremendous barrier between ourselves and nationals of other lands who would like to be friendly, but are barred because policies are considered semi-divine, and news reports from other than official groups are entirely disregarded.

March 17, 1970, Tuesday

It was the *Playboy* article that equated Murshid's *darshan* gaze with that of the Buddha at Gumps. Murshid knows Martin S. Rosenblatt, the vice president of Gumps Department Store. He is a man Murshid acknowledges today in a letter as "having been the person who most instilled me with the realities and cultures of the peoples of that part of the world," meaning "the Thais, the Burmese, the Mons and Khmers, the Chams, the Indo-Chinese of all sorts." Murshid dangles before Mr. Rosenblatt the possibility that he can obtain Gandharva Buddhas "for the Rudolph Schaeffer School of Design, or for some other museum, or even for you," informing him that "the great art museum at Lahore is under obligation to me personally both for missions I have accomplished and for my knowledge of Buddhist art." In the second paragraph, Murshid touches on his family background.

My late father Jacob E. Lewis of Levi-Strauss and Company taught me neither trade nor gave me an education, apologized on his death bed, and his estate has been so handled by the executors Wells Fargo and Company that I am in no material need.

There is talk about two details in Murshid's will: his shunned attempt to make the Asian Studies Department at Berkeley a "grand beneficiary," and the chair of Robert Clifton, which will go either "to Dr. Kozicki or to Dean Carroll Parrish of UCLA." The former may have been an attempt to make a bequest. The latter speaks simply of the gift of a chair, not an endowment. Murshid stresses at the beginning and end of this letter that "this is a sort of bon voyage letter and is hardly a request." The whole exercise seems to be, like so many of Murshid's expressions, a divine inspiration, the outcome of which, if any, will be left to God.

And for the next four days, there is no correspondence, as Murshid lives his everyday life and concentrates on Saturday's Spring Festival.

March 22, 1970, Sunday

I worked yesterday assisting the film crew, which filmed the Spring Festival at Lake Nicasio in the middle of Marin County, less than fifty miles north of San Francisco. The cameraman was not Robert Frank, and all the beauty of the costumes, the people, and nature was captured on color film. Murshid shares his retrospective on the event to Anandashram.

Yesterday Sam presented a Spring Festival for the young. It was also the birthday of Gavin Arthur, who was always a warm admirer of Papa. It was very different: There were 200 to 250 people there, practically all young. They joined in the dances and chants. They love to recite *Ramnam* and Hare Krishna and Sufi sacred phrases. It is a totally different world; it is a totally new world.

Some of the young women surprised Sam with a Sita dance. When they completed, Sam put on a Ram ceremonial; then they all joined together in a Ram-Sita performance. This was not India. This is the America of today, a very different America. This will also go down on record, because there were television cameras and sound equipment and all technical paraphernalia.

The height of the moment came when Sam performed *Ras-Lila* [the Krishna dance]. One cannot describe this because in it there is no sense of being. There is [a] sense of mergence. One becomes the instrument of God, so to speak. This is what the young people want. This is what they expect. This is what they respect. My friends, it is a New Age. It is an age of warm delight in the Divine Presence.

After a long day at the lake, Murshid retired to San Francisco and conducted the Saturday night class and, as he told Anandashram, "Everybody came."

March 23, 1970, Monday

The beginning of today's letter to Swami Swahananda and the end of Murshid's letter to Saadia capture the mood of the day. To the Swami, Murshid says, "This is a sort of letter of farewell for the time being." He tells Saadia, "When one told the Arab neighbors that one would not accept any praise or thanks, but that we are all demanding, *Alhamdu Lillah!* they smiled in joy, and in time, *Inshallah,* the world also will smile in joy."

March 24, 1970 Tuesday

Today Murshid offers Shamcher the following summary of the Spring Festival on March 21th.

Anyhow on Saturday we celebrated a joint Spring Festival and Gavin's birthday and some 200 people participated—I mean participated. There were others present, including quite a few technicians. We performed a lot of the elements of "Dances of Universal Peace" and also the astrological dances for Gavin, as suggested by Pir Vilayat, and lots more. One group put on a special woman's dance; another, a "psychic drama," and there was choral singing based on principles coming out of Helmholz and Dane Rudhyar. Gavin raved—he has never permitted me to express myself, nor have a lot of others, including all the European professors of Oriental philosophy of which the passing generation was so proud.

On Monday, two days after the Spring Festival, the film crew that still includes me followed Murshid to the New Age health food store. Murshid tells Shamcher,

Yesterday a joint interview with my friend Fred Rohe at the New Age health food store was recorded. It was under very difficult circumstances. There was a constant barrage of customers, even during the hours when trade is supposed to be lax.

Today Murshid confronts Surendra Mohan Ghose, one of the eminent Indians cited earlier (see March 1, 1970), which surprises me in view of the fact that Ghose recommended Murshid to R.L. Adamson. Murshid agrees with Ghose's statement that India has a spiritual message for all the world, but counters,

I do not see it necessarily coming to the world through the agency of your countrymen. It is with considerable sorrow that I face an awkward fact that many of your countrymen and their friends simply do not accept Indian history.

For Murshid to lecture two eminent Indians this month—the president and a congressional leader—shows that for a dervish the trappings of power are not intimidating. The inner freedom of dervishes allows them to speak the truth, when and how they choose.

March 25, 1970, Wednesday

"My dear Haridas," Murshid begins, as he continues his personal vendetta against Haridas Chaudhuri of the Cultural Integration Fellowship,

I was practically the first man you met in reaching this land. I had enough faith in Indian philosophies and in you as a representative of them. One of the most memorable incidents of my life—and it certainly stands out like a sore thumb— came when your esteemed teacher Dr. Chatterji of Calcutta University attacked me before he was even introduced or I was introduced, as one of those Americans who was sitting at the feet of the, to him, detestable Germans and Europeans whom we have paraded as experts in Oriental philosophy. This is going into my autobiography, of course, or into my biography...

Besides preventing Murshid from presenting anything, Chaudhuri made the mistake of using the word "integration" in his business name. Murshid's experience of Chaudhuri's not living up to his business name cuts deep.

I am not so much opposed to your methods as to your absolute uncalled for barriers against other methods, and this in the name of integration. It is too bad... The desire for leadership is not necessarily evil, but it seldom accomplishes what is sought. Fare you well.

The *San Francisco Chronicle* religion correspondent, Lester Kinsolving, answered Murshid's letter dated January 24th. Today Murshid writes to him,

I have a most delightful letter from you. I don't know whether you are criticizing me or Jesus Christ, to put me in his company is indeed an honor. Where I differ from many traditional religionists, no doubt, is that I lean over to accept any words and teachings which presumably emanate from Jesus Christ. Some of these are in the Gospel of Thomas. I certainly do not request that others take this as a scripture. I do not know how well acquainted you are with my favorite American author, Mark Twain, nor do I request that other people also admire him, but in his *Extract from Captain Stormfield's Visit to Heaven*, consciously or unconsciously he gives a key [continuing to study and learn] to maintaining any age, and I mean just that, any age...

Kinsolving's curiosity, piqued by Murshid's first letter, inspires him to ask Murshid how old he is.

As to my age, I am a veteran not only of the Santa Barbara earthquake, but the San Francisco earthquake! I am living at the bottom of Bernal Heights where even before the earthquake and fire, they said to me, "Go fly a kite," and I did. Also I have been writing: "My efforts to become a Pied Piper have failed miserably; only the young show up."

I cannot tell anything new to anybody that doesn't want to learn. I am about ready to leave this city to attend a conference of the religions of the world, great and not so great religions. In one sense I carry credentials of different outlooks which the scribes and pharisees say are in conflict with each other. But I am American enough to accept Walt Whitman's, "In all men I see myself."

I am not trying, or rather, I have not tried to reach the press about this conference of the world's religions. No doubt it is not *exciting* enough to be news. There are plenty of passages in the New Testament where emphasis is made on loud ears and soft tongues. But Tibetan Buddhism goes even further, where the Saint Milarepa is pictured having his hands up to his ears. Yet it may be wrong also to try and impose this or anything on anybody, when one is working for the cause of peace.

I am in utter revolt against our present culture, and every sort of dialectic, whether it comes from Karl Marx, or Hegel, or the Hegelians, or all those who establish premises based on their own speculations and not on the experiences of themselves or others. I am a dotard enough to have accepted the words of the great Clemenceau: "War and peace are two things too serious to entrust to diplomats and generals." But whether we are communists or anti-communists, or anti-anti, we seem to be more bound by dialectics than by either Clemenceau or wisdom. So I am going with those [in Geneva] who are giving a try to having some sort of peace, not dominated by diplomats and generals.

Richard Harvey of the East-West Foundation in Boston has been picking Murshid's brain on numerous subjects in their recent correspondence. Richard, whom we will encounter in Boston, asks about the Hopis. Murshid answers,

I do not know much about the Hopi rites or cosmic teachings, but I do believe that all the Southwestern part of this country was once a sort of holy land, where masters have appeared. There are enough remnants of engineering and agriculture to support this belief along with more evident information known to others.

Richard asks Murshid if he knows anything about Tibetan Buddhism. Murshid replies in the negative, with so many qualifications that one may doubt the negative.

I do not know very much about Tibetan Buddhism. Yes, I have been initiated into it. Yes, I have read all of Talbot Mundy. I have a colleague here [Dr. Warwick] who is a Rimpoche—he is half European, half Asian, and his father was in the same initiatory group as the marvelous Alexandria David-Neel. While I have not much knowledge of Tantra, I have performed *mahamudra* [which he presents at Lama in June], and at times feel like an incarnation of Saint Marpa. I was also connected with the belated Roerich Museum of New York.

In order to help Richard recognize us when he picks us up at the airport in Boston, Murshid offers this guidance: "I am a very small man with a Santa Claus-like beard and should be accompanied by my esoteric secretary Mansur Johnson, who is young, tall, handsome, and of a blond, Vandyke-ish appearance."

I am driving Murshid and Vocha Fiske to San Francisco from Novato today when Lloyd Morain stops by the *khankah*. Lloyd Morain at the *khankah* is a first, and I'm sorry I missed witnessing this meeting with Murshid. Murshid's intent is to hook up Vocha, who has a collection of Japanese art to sell, with a former president of the Japan Society, Mr. Shibata, who owns the Daibutsu, an oriental art store on Fillmore Street.

In the evening we go to a lecture on Japanese art at the Rudolph Schaeffer School of Design, where Murshid has taken classes and another roommate, Zeinob, is currently studying.

March 27, 1970, Friday

According to Murshid's letter today to Shamcher,

A surprise letter of apology came from Paul Reps [perhaps Wali Ali's card to Reps mentioned earlier stimulated this]. This is most wonderful. Another apology of sorts came from Lloyd Morain. [This is how Murshid interprets his visit to the *khankah* Wednesday.] We have now dedicated our kiln which was part of the methodology of attempting to spread the message. Everything looks beautiful and wonderful on this eve of departure, Praise to God!

I have been upgrading the electrical system at the *khankah*, and there is one more circuit breaker to be installed to complete my work before we go.

Responding to Lloyd Morain's visit to the *khankah* Wednesday, Murshid writes Morain that he's sorry he missed him. After cleverly weaving at least six examples of outrages Murshid had endured at the hands of Morain and others into his letter, Murshid tells a story at the end, in which the character involved could be considered Christ-like. *Whatsoever ye do unto the least of these my brethren, ye do it unto me,* Christ says in the Bible verse implicit behind this story. By telling it, Murshid suggests to me, if not Morain, *The guy you persecuted is like Christ.*

Last week I was sent for, to visit a mental hospital. I have never visited mental hospitals. I have seen your presentations of Fritz Perls and Carl Rogers and others. I have considered this outside my fields. But to my amazement there was considerable success in bringing the girl down to normalcy during the period of my visit. A lot of things are like that, and a lot of things may be like that.

To philosopher Oliver Reiser, Murshid reveals his true feeling about Morain's gesture: "One of the best greetings possible at this time has been the fact that Lloyd Morain called at my home in Novato, California, which is a commune."

Murshid tells UC Berkeley Oriental Languages Professor Lewis Lancaster, who was a disciple of Nyogen Senzaki, about Vocha Fiske's information: There is a disciple of Nyogen Senzaki's who wants to "establish a chair in Zen at the University of Chicago." Murshid lobbies for California as the site for a Senzaki Zen Center and dangles the possibility of Senzaki's tea ceremony equipment before Lancaster, telling him, "Certainly if a Zen center continuing and commemorating the works of Shaku Soyen and Nyogen Senzaki would be established here in California the ceremonial equipment would 'naturally' go to it."

March 28, 1970, Saturday

The rush of activity on the last day of correspondence before leaving late tonight for Switzerland is apparent in the conclusion of a letter to R.L. Adamson in Australia.

On account of the necessity of my departure almost immediately to attend a conference of the world's religions at Geneva, Switzerland, this letter itself may on account of the shortness of my time, exhibit weaknesses therefore.

Murshid and I are taking the redeye to New York City. We experience a half hour delay leaving San Francisco International Airport due to an air traffic controllers' slowdown. We leave around 11 P.M. To Fred and Corinne Reinhold, Murshid writes before leaving,

Last week after a program dedicated to the dangers from alcoholism, the [TV] station owner immediately editorialized on the dangers of drugs. I am not defending drugs. I am concerned with the terrible harm done by subjectivisms of all sorts parading as knowledge, and parading as science. The next day after a program showing how London had cleaned up its smog, the head of the station gave another scare editorial on the dangers of pollution. I have felt, and many scientists, indeed most scientists, agreed that there is one danger greater than that of the use of chemical poisons on plants, and that is the widespread interjection of comparatively ignorant people into what should be dispassionate discussion.

Murshid and Mansur arrive Sunday morning in New York at 7:30 A.M. Eastern Time. Our body time is three hours earlier. It is raining when we arrive. It snows when we walk to Easter services at the Community Church of New York at 40 East Thirty-Fifth Street. To W.D. Begg of Ajmer, India, Murshid wrote before leaving,

Your letter of 17th March arrived just as secretary Mansur and I prepare to leave this part of the world for a conference of the great religions meeting at Geneva, Switzerland. We are presumed to discuss what religion can do to promote world peace. This is a field in which I personally have been engaged most of my life but which has been aborted because the religious leaders of the world, whatever else they may say, are too often concerned with the prowess of human personality than with Divine Experience...

It is raining after church, when the husband of Marion Martini, Murshid's cousin, picks us up and takes us to their home for a dinner being prepared by Marion. We eat carrots, beans, ham and cauliflower, cake, and root beer. Afterwards, Mr. Martini takes us to J. F. Kennedy International Airport.

Murshid wrote yesterday to Joyce Best in Middlesex, England—the daughter of an old Sufi who shifted his devotion from Hazrat Inayat Khan to Meher Baba—and identified himself as "one of the last living direct disciples of Hazrat Inayat Khan."

I do not recall whether a letter was written to you in 1967 when I was preparing to visit Great Britain [and work on pollution issues], but Allah ruled it otherwise, for one had an attack of ptomaine compelling one to be in the hospital for some time, and afterwards something like a miracle occurred in that one's efforts to spread the Message of God, which had previously always failed, now suddenly began a career of success.

We board the Swissair plane in New York at 6:20 P.M. after a two to three hour delay. In the air, we eat chicken breast with morel sauce, rice pilaf, green peas in butter, salad, chocolate coated pineapple bits, cheese and crackers, and coffee. To an old friend named Irene, Murshid said in a letter yesterday,

Somewhere along the line our correspondence has been interrupted. I hope nothing is wrong... [Elliott is in the hospital] but there is now agreement that it should not interfere with my career, which seems to be getting along very well indeed.

Secretary Mansur Johnson and I will be leaving in a few hours to fly to Geneva, Switzerland. We are going to attend a grand conference of the religions of the world who hope to do something to promote peace and understanding. After that we go to London to meet young people [Gandalf's Gardens] and study plant life [Kew

464

Gardens] and related subjects [the Royal Asiatic Society, the Buddhist Society, F. Clive-Ross, Marco Pallis, Martin Lings, the U.S. Consulate]. No doubt we shall also be visiting museums [the British Museum] and theaters. I understand springtime is very beautiful there, and this is something I wished to see all my life.

When the plane starts to land, the pilot says, "Ground time in Geneva is 9:14 A.M." It is Monday, March 30, 1970.

Epilogue

Perfection includes both aspects

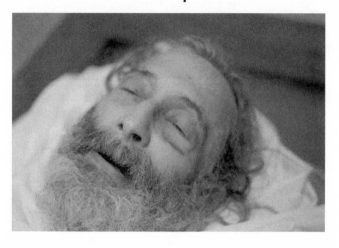

I am not sending anybody any copy of this. I am leaving this to you. I feel that your present stand uniting the superior spiritual outlook with the inferior materialistic outlooks lead[s] one to perfection. Perfection includes both aspects, and so this blending of the "up" and the "down" brings about a balancing in life which is fully in accord with the teachings of mysticism. The studies in AWARIFU-L-MA'ARIF [written in the thirteenth century by Shaikh Shahabudin Umar bin Mohammad-i-Suhrawardi] are giving me so much which, when blended with the teachings of Hazrat Inayat Khan and with my own outer and inner investigations, that I feel we can have a full continuation of Sufism. Murshid does not agree with some of the trends of the day, let us say toward combining religions; promoting studies in comparative religions; looking toward false universalities which are selective; etcetera, and play little part in the awakening of the soul of man. Perhaps Murshid seems almost fanatical in his stress on esotericism. Inayat Khan did not come into this world to promote studies in comparative religion; to found a new faith rivaling others; or to promote any form of universal brotherhood which was or is discriminatory, personality leaderships, or prowesses of any kind. These may come, of course, but they should never be dominant. (Murshid's letter to Mansur, November 6, 1970)

Some people have complained about the abrupt ending of this book. It is true: the ending is abrupt. I could have shared more details about the Temple of Understanding conference in Geneva. I could have published details from thirty of Murshid's last letters to me, which included either personal communications or copies of letters to others that he shared with me from September to December, 1970. The final one was dated December 14th, two weeks before he slipped and fell on December 28th, 1970, and a little over a month before he died, January 15, 1971. But the truth is—as I wrote in Chapter One—shortly after the meeting in Geneva, I became Murshid's "former secretary," which is how he characterized me in a letter November 4, 1970, to a man we met in Geneva, Mr. Asha Merchandani from Bombay, India. This book wants to be true to the Sufi dictum that one should teach only what one knows. It would not be a memoir if I researched and wrote about six months in the life of Murshid that I didn't witness. That's why the ending is abrupt.

Still, I know it is the lack of closure at the end of the book that bothers people. Please listen carefully. It is as it is because abrupt was how Murshid's passing seemed to so many of us. We didn't want to believe that a man so alive and vibrant could be taken from us as fast as the swipe of a scimitar guillotining a head from a body.

And then there is art. And the circularity of life and death. Another reason I end the book like this is for art's sake. You will remember that I provide details in Chapter One that chronologically belong at the end of the book. The intention is to invoke a circle and suggest to the reader: reread, and get stuck repeatedly, as I do, on a single sentence that embodies some noble aspect of the man known as Murshid. You may go high and dissolve in tears or soar dry-eyed in ecstasy. If so, please join me in saying, *Thank you, Murshid.*

Dramatis Personae

Principal Characters (422) in Alphabetical Order

A

Adams, Ansel: (1902-1984) a legendary, fine-art photographer of wild America.
Adamson, R.L.: associated with Aquarian Arcane College in Liverpool, Australia.
Affifi, Abul Ela: wrote *The Mystical Philosophy of Muhyid Din-Ibnul Arabi.*
Ahmed, Shamseddin (aka S. Ahmed): a disciple in Lahore, Pakistan.
Akbar, Emperor: (aka Akbar the Great) (1542-1605) a wise and enlightened ruler.
Alawi, Shaikh Ahmad al-: (aka Sidi El-Alawi) subject of Martin Lings' *A Sufi Saint of the 20th Century*; recognized Murshid's *makam* when he came to San Francisco.
Albanese, Margaret: a poet friend of Murshid.
Ali, Sufi Barkat: Murshid's Murshid in Pakistan.
Alpert, Richard: see Ram Dass.
Amertat: see Fred Cohn.
Amin: (aka Stan Quance) a disciple, b. 1943.
Amina: (aka Katherine Erikson) a disciple, b. 1941.
Anandashram: in Kanhangad, South India; the ashram founded by Papa Ramdas.
Arasteh, Reza: wrote *Rumi the Persian.*
Arberry, A.J.: (1905-1969) English translator of Rumi and others.
Aristophanes: (c. 448-380 BC) Greek playwright.
Arlock, William: associated with Great Books of the Western World.
Arthur, Gavin: (1901-1972) astrologer; grandson of U.S. president Chester Arthur; friend of Murshid.
Ashby, Thad and Rita: Mansur's LSD connection in Mexico.
Ashvaghosa: (or Avaghosa) (AD 80-150) considered India's greatest poet until Kalidasa in the fifth century.
Atiya: (aka Charlotte Brautlacht) hosted Murshid, Saul, and Mansur in Seattle.
Atkinson, Dr. Henry: secretary of the World Church Peace Union.
Auliya, Nizamuddin: (1238-1325) a saint of the Chishti Order; disciple of Fariduddin Ganjshakar; teacher of Amir Khusro.
Austin, Jack: a friend of Murshid in England; edited *The Western Buddhist.*
Austin, Leonard: a personal friend of Murshid.
Avalokitesvara: the Bodhisattva of compassion in Buddhism.
Azam: an Israeli Arab.

B

Baba, Meher: (1894-1969) an Indian avatar; attracted Rabia Martin, whose successor, Ivy Duce, Baba supported to start Sufism Reoriented.
Baer, Steve: designed the architectural dome at Lama Foundation.

Bahm, Archie J.: (1907-1996) philosophy professor at the University of New Mexico.

Bailey, Alice A.: (1880-1949) a popular psychic.

Baipal, K.S.: Consul General at the Indian Consulate in San Francisco.

Baptiste, Walt and Magana: yoga teacher friends of Murshid.

Barbara: (aka Ayesha Moffat) a disciple, b. 1944; mother of Summer.

Basira: (aka Gypsy Updike) a disciple, b. 1946.

Beck, L. Adams: wrote *Garden of Vision*.

Begg, W.D.: (aka Mirza Wahiduddin) from Ajmer, India; newsletter editor; wrote *The Holy Biography of Hazrat Khwaja Muinuddin Hasa Chishti* and *The Big Five of Sufism in India*.

Bell, Gertrude: (1868-1926) traveled in the Middle East; friend of Lawrence of Arabia.

Besant, Annie: (1847-1933) a leader of the Theosophical movement.

Best, Joyce: from Middlesex, England; the daughter of a longtime Sufi.

Bethmann, Erich W.: director of research at American Friends of the Middle East in Washington, D.C.

Bhajan, Yogi: (1929-2004) *kundalini* yoga master from India.

Bhakti (Engle): mother of Jelila Fraley; wife of Fatha Engle, who was one of Hazrat Inayat Khan's secretaries.

Bibijan: the aunt of Saadia Khawar Khan; (not to be confused with Suzanne D'Mitrieff aka Bibijan).

Blighton, Father: (aka Rev. Earl) founded The Holy Order of MANS in San Francisco.

Bloom, Alfred: professor at the University of Oregon in Eugene.

Bois, J. Samuel: author of *The Art of Awareness*: a text on General Semantics.

Brand, Stewart: editor of the *Whole Earth Catalog*.

Brautlacht, Charlotte: see Atiya.

Brinner, Dr. William M.: chairman of the Department of Near East Languages at UC Berkeley.

Bruner, Helen D.: director of public relations for American Friends of the Middle East.

Brunton, Paul: (1898-1981) wrote *A Search in Secret India*.

Bucke, Richard M.: author of *Cosmic Consciousness*.

Buddha: (c. 560-480 BC) the fountainhead of Buddhism, born in India.

Bulwer-Lytton, George Edward: (1803-1873) wrote *The Coming Race*.

Burbank, Luther: a horticulturalist; knew Inayat Khan; lived in Santa Rosa, California.

Burckhardt, Titus: wrote *Introduction to Sufi Doctrine*, b. 1908.

Burdick, Eugene and William Lederer: wrote the novels *The Ugly American* and *Sarkhan*.

Burton, Phillip: (1926-1983) U.S. Representative from California.

Byron, Lord: (aka George Gordon) (1788-1824) English Romantic poet.

C

Caen, Herb: columnist with the San Francisco Chronicle.

Cage, John: (1912-1992) experimental musician and composer.

Cameron, George: (aka Yusuf) a secretary of Pir Vilayat's.

Carl: see Moineddin.

Carlebach, Schlomo: (1925-1994) the singing rabbi; founded the House of Love and Prayer in San Francisco and Moshav Or Modiin, near Tel Aviv, Israel.

Carpenter, Edward: Walt Whitman's teacher.

Carson, Rachel: (1907-1964) wrote *Silent Spring*.

Carter, Boake: radio commentator, b. 1899; said, "In time of war the first casualty is truth."

Carus, Paul: (1852-1919) American philosopher, born and educated in Germany; wrote *The Gospel of Buddha*.

Cassim, Dr. K.M.P. Mohammed: a correspondent of Murshid's from Ceylon.

Cayce, Edgar: (aka the sleeping prophet) (1877-1945) a popular psychic and medical clairvoyant; established Association for Research and Enlightenment (ARE) in Virginia Beach, Virginia.

Cayce, Hugh Lynn: son of Edgar Cayce, associated with ARE.

Cerminara, Gina: wrote *Many Mansions*.

Chandrasekar, Dr.: India's best demographer, according to Murshid.

Channon, Ram Lal: Murshid's Indian guru for secular affairs.

Chatterji, Dr. S.C.: professor at Calcutta University in India; teacher of Haridas Chaudhuri.

Chaudhuri, Haridas: (1913-1975) sent to the United States by Sri Aurobindo; founded the Cultural Integration Fellowship in San Francisco in 1951.

Chishti, Khawaja Moinuddin: (1141-1236) founded the Chishti Order of Sufis in Ajmer, India.

Clark (Brown): a pre-1967 disciple of Murshid.

Clary, William: art dealer in San Francisco.

Clemenceau, Georges: (1841-1929) appointed Prime Minister of France in 1917.

Clifton, Robert: (aka Phra Sumangalo) a Buddhist who witnessed the effects of U.S. foreign policy in S.E. Asia.

Cogswell, Sibley: a disciple, b. 1947.

Cohen, Alan, PhD: a representative of Meher Baba.

Cohn, Fred: (aka Amertat) a disciple, b. 1943, director of the film *Sunseed*.

Cohn, Julie: a disciple, Fred Cohn's wife.

Cook, Ruth: an employee of Field's Book Store in San Francisco.

Cooper, John Sherman: (1901-1991) a Republican U.S. Senator from Kentucky.

Corda, Sheikha Vera: (aka Vera Van Voris) a contemporary of Murshid's whom he made a Sheikha.

Cowell, Henry: (1897-1965) American composer and author; teacher of John Cage.

Crumb, R.: an underground, San Francisco cartoonist.

D

Dalton, John: (1766-1844) English chemist and physicist.

Daniel (Lomax): (aka Abdul-rahman) a disciple, b. 1944; one of Murshid's secretaries.

Dara: (aka Buzz Rowell) accompanied Sheila to India.

Davenport, Clara: (aka Selima) a disciple, b. 1944; wife of Phillip Davenport, mother of Kevin and Shirin; Mansur's Greek dance partner.

Davenport, Phillip: (aka Vasheest) (1943-2001) a disciple; husband of Selima, father of Kevin and Shirin; editor of the revived *San Francisco Oracle*; lead sheet writer for the Grateful Dead; singer in the Sufi Choir.

David-Neel, Alexandria: author of books about Tibet, e.g. *Magic and Mystery in Tibet*.

Deed, D.M.: wrote an article on Jonah.

Devi: (aka Debbie Churney) a disciple, b. 1952.

Dignaga: (AD 480-540) Indian Buddhist philosopher and logician.
Diskul, Princess Poon Pismai: Thailand's president of the World Fellowship of Buddhists from 1963-1984; attended the Temple of Understanding conference in Geneva.
Dixon, Jeane: (1918-1997) a popular psychic.
D'Mitrieff, Suzanne: (aka Bibijan) Pir Vilayat's secretary in Los Angeles.
D'Olivet, Fabre: (1767-1825) French philologist, mystic, and Hebrew scholar.
Donkin, William: wrote *Wayfarers*: Maher Baba with the God-intoxicated.
Douglas-Klotz, Neil: (aka Saadi) scholar and Sufi Murshid; student of Moineddin Jablonski; edited *Sufi Vision and Initiation*.
Doyle (Wegner): a disciple.
Drew (Langsner): a disciple.
Duce, Ivy: (1895-1981) successor of Rabia Martin; follower of Meher Baba; founder of Sufism Reoriented.
Durkee, Barbara: (aka Asha) co-founder of Lama Foundation in New Mexico.
Duncan, Isadora: (1878-1927) dancer; revolutionist.
Dunne, Peter Finley: associated with the Temple of Understanding.
Durrani, Professor: Pakistani yogi; Sufi; renowned physicist.

E
Emerson, Ralph Waldo: (1803-1882) American author, poet, and philosopher.
Erickson, Richard: director of the Alumni Association at UC Berkeley.
Ets-Hokim, Jeremy: San Francisco businessman.
Evenson, Admiral: associated with American Friends of the Middle East.

F
Fakir, Asoke: a Bengali, embraced by Murshid at a meeting.
Fatha (Engle): see Bhakti.
Fatima: (aka Pat Lassar Jablonski) a disciple, b. 1946; Moineddin's wife.
Ferlinghetti, Lawrence: beat poet, b. 1919; contemporary of Jack Kerouac; opened City Lights bookstore on Columbus Avenue in San Francisco.
Fernandez, Zoso (Paul): chief disciple of Nyogen Senzaki.
Ferry, Diane: a disciple.
Fine, Rabbi Alvin: resident of San Francisco.
Fish, Nancy: an actress; one of Murshid's goddaughters.
Fiske, Vocha: Murshid's friend, often referred to as "divine mother."
Fiyazaddin Sahib: (aka Fayazuddin of Hyderabad) the exoteric head of the Nizam-un-din Chishtis in India.
Fleming, Dean: lived at Libre in Colorado.
Fraley, Jelila: wife of Bob Fraley (aka Muni) and daughter of Bhakti Engle.
Frances (von Briesen): a co-founder of Lama Foundation; Hans's sister.
Frank, Robert: b. 1924 in Zurich, Switzerland; documentary film-maker.
Frank (Welch): (aka Halim) a disciple, b. 1944.
Franklin, H. Bruce: English Professor, b. 1934; author at Stanford and Rutgers Universities.
Fung, Dr.: minister of the Buddhist Universalist Church in San Francisco.
G
Galbraith, John Kenneth: b. 1908 in Canada; Berkeley-educated economist; U.S. ambassador to India in the early 1960s.
Gandalf's Garden: a group of hippies in London.

Gandhi, Mohandas K.: (aka Mahatma Gandhi) (1869-1948) leader of the struggle for India's independence.

Garrett, Eileen: a popular psychic.

Geeting, Baxter M.: professor of Speech in Sacramento, California.

George (Matthews): a disciple.

Ghazzali, Abu Hamid al-: (1058-1111) Sufi mystic born near Mashad, Iran; wrote *Niche of Light*.

Ghose, Sri Aurobindo: (1872-1950) established Sri Aurobindo ashram in Pondicherry, India.

Ghose, Sri Surendra Mohan: Indian congressional leader; recommended Murshid to the Australian, R.L. Adamson.

Gibbings, Rev. Cecil: served Longthrope Vicarage in Peterborough, England.

Gilbert, W.S., and Arthur Sullivan: (1836-1911 and 1842-1900, respectively) creators of comic operas loved by Murshid.

Ginger: see Jehanara.

Ginsberg, Allen: (1926-1997) Beat poet; wrote *Howl*.

Giri, V.V.: (1894-1980) Vice President of India from 1967-1969; President of India 1969-1974.

Goddard, Dwight: compiled *The Buddhist Bible*.

Gold, Marc: a disciple.

Gottlieb, Lou: (1924-1996) commune leader at Morning Star Ranch in Sonoma County; former bass player for the Limeliters.

Govinda, Lama Anagarika: (1898-1985) a Tibetan Buddhist born in Germany; author of *The Way of the White Clouds*.

Gupta, P.K.: an Indian friend of W.D. Begg.

Gurdjieff, George Ivanovitch: (1872-1949) Armenian spiritualist and author.

H

Haeckel, Ernst: (1834-1919) German comparative anatomist, best known for saying, "ontogeny recapitulates phylogeny."

Hafiz: (1317-1390) Sufi poet buried in Shiraz, Iran.

Hammarskjold, Dag: (1905-1961) Swedish statesman; Secretary-General of the United Nations from 1957 until his death.

Hans (von Briesen): a Lama resident; Frances's brother.

Harvey, Richard: associated with East-West Foundation in Boston.

Hathaway, Bill: local friend of Murshid.

Hawkins, Dr. Alma: professor at the UCLA Dance Department.

Hassan (aka Sigmund Herz): a disciple, b. 1946; husband of Jehanara.

Hayakawa, S.I.(Don): President of San Francisco State and a U.S. Senator from California.

Hawthorn, Nathaniel: (1804-1864) American novelist; wrote *The Scarlet Letter* and *The Great Stone Face*.

Hedgepeth, William and Dennis Stock: visited Lama Foundation researching *The Alternative*: Communal life in new America.

Hegel, Georg Wilhelm Friedrich: (1770-1831) a German philosopher.

Helen and Ray: Saul's friends living in Klamath Falls, Oregon.

Helmholz, A. Carl: a nuclear physicist at UC Berkeley.

Hoffmaster, David: a disciple, b. 1947; Murshid's housemate.

Holmes, Steward W.: English professor at Castleton State College in Vermont.

Holzhauer, Betty: Mansur's mother.

Hoodbhoy, Samir A.: Executive Secretary of the Pakistan Students Association of America.

Hoppe, Art: columnist with the San Francisco Chronicle.

Howard (Mussell): a pre-1967 disciple of Murshid.

Hubbard, Earl: edited *The Center Letter* from Lakeville, Connecticut.

Hujwiri, Ali ibn Uthman al-: (aka Data Gang Baksh) (AD 988-1073) wrote an ancient Sufi treatise *Kashf al-Madjub*.

Hunt, Ed: Murshid's elderly housemate in the late 1960s, briefly.

Hussain: (aka Dennis H. McGinley) a disciple.

Hussein, Dr. Zakir: (1897-1969) third President of India 1967-1969.

Huxley, Aldous: (1894-1963) English author, wrote *Brave New World*.

I

Iamblichus: (c. 250-325 BC) Neoplatonic philosopher; wrote the *Life of Pythagoras*.

Ibn Arabi, Muhyi al-din: (1164-1240) mystic born in Spain; died in Damascus.

Iqbal, Mohammed: (1877-1939) Urdu poet-philosopher; instrumental in the creation of Pakistan.

J

Jaffe, Raymond: official at the Experimental Collegiate Program at UC Berkeley.

James (Pickard): a disciple, b. 1943.

James, William: (1842-1910) worked in and between physiology, psychology, and philosophy; wrote *The Varieties of Religious Experience*.

Jasmine: (aka Jill Cogswell) a disciple, b. 1948.

Jefferson, Thomas: third President of United States (1801-1809).

Jehanara: (aka Ginger May) a disciple, b. 1946, wife of Hassan Herz.

Jelaleddin: (aka Jeremy Cave) a disciple, b. 1934.

Jemila: (aka Carolyn Buckmaster Johnson) a disciple, b. 1943; Mansur's wife.

Jennings, C. Robert: author of Playboy magazine's article about Murshid.

Jeremy: see Jelaleddin.

Jesus: gave teachings that Murshid took seriously, e.g. "Whatsoever ye do unto the least of these, my brethren, ye do it unto Me."

Jilani, Abdul Qadir: (1077-1166) Sufi saint buried in Baghdad.

Johnson, Otis and Mabel: Mansur's grandparents.

Joyner, Russell: office manager of the International Society of General Semantics.

K

Kaplan, Dr. Abraham: pupil of Daisetz Suzuki.

Kapleau, Philip: Zen master; author of *The Three Pillars of Zen*.

Kelly, Frank: associated with Center for the Study of Democratic Institutions in Santa Barbara, California.

Kennedy, Susan: staff person in Congressman Phillip Burton's office.

Kennett, Roshi: (1924-1996) founded Shasta Abbey, Mt. Shasta, California.

Keyser, Cassius: (aka C.J. (Jackson) Keyser) (1862-1947) wrote *Humanism and Science*.

Khalif Akbar: (aka Jim Simmons) a disciple, b. 1946.

Khan, General Ayub: (1907-1974) President of Pakistan (1962-1969).

Khan, Fazal Inayat: grandson of Hazrat Inayat Khan, son of Hidayat Inayat Khan.

Khan, Hazrat Inayat: (1882-1927) brought the Sufi Message to the United States in

1910; established the Sufi Movement; one of Murshid's teachers.

Khan, Hidayat Inayat: son of Hazrat Inayat Khan; Vilayat's brother, b. 1917.

Khan, Maheboob: (1887-1948) Hazrat Inayat Khan's brother.

Khan, Pir Vilayat Inayat: (1916-2004) son of Hazrat Inayat Khan; Hidayat's brother; established the Sufi Order.

Khan, Saadia Khawar: born in Pakistan; a disciple and goddaughter of Murshid; studied at Cornell University in Ithaca, New York.

Khusrau, Amir: (1253-1325) poet, favorite companion of twelfth-century saint Nizamuddin Auliya with whom he is buried near Delhi.

Kingsolving, Lester: a religion correspondent for the San Francisco Chronicle.

Kirby, M.T.: (aka Sogaku Shaku) a student of Shaku Soyen, Murshid's teacher in 1920; introduced Murshid to Nyogen Sensaki.

Korty, John: film director.

Korzybski, Alfred: (1879-1950) wrote *Science and Sanity*: an introduction to non-Aristotelian systems and general semantics.

Kosygin, Alexei Nikolayevich: (1904-1980) in 1964 succeeded Krushchev as Premier of the Soviet Union.

Kozicki, Dr. Richard J.: taught a class on Southeast Asia at UC Berkeley; lived in Burma and Malaysia.

Krishna: (c. 3228-3102 BC) appeared in India for 125 years; gave the *Bhagavad-Gita* (Song of God); danced with the gopis, including Radha; considered an avatar.

Krishnabai, Mother: the spiritual consort of Papa Ramdas at Anandashram, Kanhangad, Travancore-Cochin, South India.

Krishnadas: (aka Duncan Pierce) a disciple.

Krishnamurti, Jiddu: (1895-1986) adopted in India by Annie Besant; subject of a documentary by Amertat Fred Cohn at KQED in San Francisco.

Kuchel, Thomas: (1910-1994) Republican U.S. Senator from California 1953-1969.

L

Lachelt, Theodore: Murshid's lawyer.

Lal, Dr.: associated with Indian Consulate in San Francisco.

Lama Foundation: a mountain community in New Mexico.

Lame Deer, Archie Fire: wrote *Gift of Power*.

Lancaster, Lewis: UC Berkeley professor.

Lansdale, General Edward Geary: (1908-1987) author of *In the Midst of Wars*: an American's mission to Southeast Asia; a CIA legend; a hero of Murshid.

Laura (Mathison): a disciple.

Leach, Margaret: Pir Vilayat's summer camp coordinator.

Leadbeater, C.W.: leader in the Theosophical movement.

Leary, Timothy: (1920-1996) popularized the use of LSD.

Lee, Chingwah: art dealer in San Francisco.

Less, Lonnie: (aka Shahabudin) hosted Murshid in New York City.

Lewis, Elliott: Murshid's brother.

Lewis, Jacob E.: father of Murshid Samuel L. Lewis.

Lewis, Murshid Samuel L.: (aka Reverend He Kwang and Sufi Ahmad Murad Chisti) (1896-1971) initiated a revival of the Sufi outlook in the West.

Lindstrum, Charles and Miriam: old friends of Murshid.

Lingo, T.D.: associated with the Adventure Trails Survival School in Black Hawk, Colorado.

Lings, Martin: author who wrote *A Sufi Saint of the 20ᵗʰ Century*: Shaik Ahmad al-

Alawi: His spiritual heritage and legacy.

Lytton, Bulwer: (1803-1873) wrote *The Coming Race.*

M

Maharshi, Ramana: (1879-1950) among the most renowned Indian sages of the twentieth-century; lived at the holy hill of Arunchala in South India.

Malalasekera, Dr. G.: the United Nations representative from Ceylon.

Mansur: (aka Otis Johnson) a disciple, b. 1941; one of Murshid's secretaries.

Marcia (Pavolic): a disciple, b. 1943.

Marpa: (1012-1096) known as the Translator; translated scriptures he brought from India into Tibetan; teacher of Milarepa.

Martin, Murshida (Ada) Rabia: (1871-1947) Inayat Khan's first *mureed* (disciple) in America; extended invitation in 1923 for Khan's second visit to the states; appointed Murshid her *Khalif* (representative).

Martini, Marion: Murshid's cousin.

Marty (Peller): a disciple.

Mary Sue (Sitton): a disciple, b. 1939.

Marx, Karl: (1818-1883) a socialist philosopher.

Mathieu, Bill: (aka Allaudin) musician; composer; a disciple; director of the Sufi Choir.

Matthews, George: a disciple.

McCandless, Mrs.: a literary collaborator with Nyogen Sensaki.

McCloskey, Jr., Paul N.: U.S. representative from California, b. 1927.

McCoy, Don: established Olompali Ranch.

McGee, Norman: Murshid's godson.

McLellan, Nusi: an old friend of Murshid.

Medlock, Julie: a North American living at Sri Aurobindo's ashram, Auroville, near Pondicherry in India.

Melvin: (aka Wali Ali Meyer) a disciple, b. 1942; one of Murshid's secretaries.

Merchant, Deepak: son of K.T. Merchant.

Merchant, K.T.: Indian professor.

Milarepa: (1052-1135) Tibetan saint; student of Marpa the Translator.

Millay, Edna St. Vincent: a poet Murshid adored; wrote, "The world stands out on either side, no wider than the heart is wide."

Mir, Mian: (d. 1635) a Sufi saint from around the time of Akbar.

Miura Roshi, Issho: wrote *Zen Dust* with Ruth Fuller Sasaki.

Mohammed: (570-632) the last of the prophets; received the Qur'an; founded Islam.

Moineddin: (aka Carl Jablonski) (1942-2001) a disciple; Murshid's chosen successor; Fatima's husband.

Moore, Marianne: (1887-1972) an American poet.

Morain, Lloyd: secretary of the International Society of General Semantics.

Morris, Craig, and Donald E. Thompson: wrote *Huanuco Pampa.*

Morse, Samuel: (1791-1872) invented the telegraph and Morse code.

Moscone, George: (1929-1978) senator in California's legislature; murdered while mayor of San Francisco, along with gay activist Harvey Milk, by City Supervisor Dan White.

Mosley, Rufus: described as a saint; one with whom Murshid had a love attunement.

Mossman, Ruth: from Modesto, California; friend of Murshid.

Mary, Mother: (aka Mary Mae Hoffman Maier) (1894-1970) spiritual seeker; proprietor of The Inn at Mt. Shasta, California.
Mundy, Talbot: (1879-1940) wrote *Om, the Secret of Ahbor Valley.*
Murphy, George: (1902-1992) U.S. senator from California from 1965-1971.

N
Nakagawa Roshi, Soen: (1907-1984) abbot of Ryutaku-ji in Japan; friend of Nyogen Sensaki; teacher of Philip Kapleau.
Narita, Hiro: a cinematographer; worked with John Korty.
Nasr, Dr. Seyyed Hossein: a professor from Iran who taught at Harvard.
Nasr-ed-din, Mulla Kwaja: a comic character in Sufi stories.
Nathan (Benjamin Johnson): son of Mansur and Jemila, b. 1966.
Needleman, Jacob: philosophy professor; offered classes at UC Berkeley Extension in San Francisco.
Nicholson, Reynold Alleyne: (1868-1945) wrote *Idea of Personality in Sufism.*
Nietzsche, Friedrich: (1844-1900) a German philosopher.
Nizami, Pir-O-Murshid Hassan Sani: grand master of the Chishti order in Delhi.
Nottingham, Professor: offered classes on Asian religions.
Nur-un-nisa: daughter of Moineddin and Fatima.

O
OTEC: acronym for ocean thermal energy conversion; a technology for producing electricity from ocean water; promoted by Shamcher.
Ouspensky, Petyr Demianovich: (1878-1947) Russian-born mathematician and mystic; played St. Paul to Gurdjieff's Christ.

P
Pallis, Marco: (1895-1990) wrote about Buddhism.
Parisa: (aka Ruth Wintheil) a disciple, b. 1939.
Parrish, Dean Carroll: of UCLA, visited in Los Angeles by Murshid; formerly, a secretary of Murshid.
Pat: see Fatima.
Patel, A.B.: a leader of the Sri Aurobindo Movement.
Patel, Villabhai: gave Murshid an interview in India.
Patterson, Elizabeth: a resident at the Meher Baba Center in Myrtle Beach, South Carolina.
Paul (Rognlie): a disciple, b. 1947.
Perls, Fritz: a psychologist connected with the Esalen Institute.
Plato: (c. 427-347 BC) Greek philosopher; student of Socrates; teacher of Aristotle.
Power, Richard: author of *The Life and teachings of Joe Miller.*
Premanand, Trikanand: grandson of Papa Ramdas.
Price, Iru: Lama Govinda's host in San Francisco.
Priebe, Reverend Harold: resident of Ojai, California.
Pythagoras: (c. 569-475 BC) Greek philosopher and mathematician famous for his theorem, $a^2+b^2=c^2$.

Q
Qadiri, Hazrat Faqir Nur Muhammad Sarwari: (1888?-1960) born in Northwest Frontier Province of Pakistan; wrote *Irfan.*

R

Rabbit, Peter: lived at Libre, an artist's community, in Colorado.

Radhakrishnan, Dr. Sarvepalli: (1888-1975) second President of India (1962-67).

Rahman, Tengku Abdul: (1903-1990) the first Prime Minister of Malaysia.

Ram Dass: (aka Richard Alpert) joined with Timothy Leary to popularize LSD, b. 1941; author of *Be Here Now.*

Rama, Swami: (1925-1996) wrote *Living with the Himalayan Masters.*

Ramakrishna, Sri: (1836-1866) his message was his God-consciousness; teacher of Swami Vivekananda.

Ramdas, Swami: (1884-1963) founded Anandashram near Kanhangad in South India; wrote *God Experience.*

Ranganathananda Maharaj, Swami: a Vedanta student of Swami Shivananda in the Ramakrishna school of Swami Vivekananda, b. 1908; considered by Murshid "the greatest man in the world."

Rapp, Dorothy: secretary of the Temple of Understanding.

Reinhold, Fred and Corinne: personal friends of Murshid.

Reiser, Oliver: professor in the Philosophy Department at the University of Pittsburg.

Renee (Sager): a disciple, b. 1920.

Reps, Paul: (1895-1990) (aka Saladin) a disciple of Hazrat Inayat Khan; friend of Murshid; author who compiled *Zen Flesh, Zen Bones.*

Rhys-David, Thomas William: (1843-1922) and his wife, both English scholars of the Pali language.

Robinson, Lois: a psychic.

Roerich Museum: 319 W. 107th Street in New York; founded by Russian painter Nicholas Roerich (1874-1947).

Rohe, Fred: proprietor of New Age health food store in San Francisco.

Rosenblatt, Martin S.: vice president of Gumps department store in San Francisco.

Rosenthal, Harry: Murshid's uncle.

Ross, F. Clive: English Editor of the journal *Studies in Comparative Religion.*

Rudhyar, Dane: (1895-1985) astrologer and author.

Rumi: (aka Maulana Roum, or Jelaluddin Rumi) (1207-1273) poet inspired by Shams-i-Tabriz.

Russell, Bertrand Arthur William: (1872-1970) Nobel Prize winning British philosopher; anti-nuclear activist.

Ruth: see Parisa.

S

Sadiq, Major Mohammad: Murshid's friend in Pakistan who healed cancer and blindness.

Sahib, F. Mawlawi: head of the bureau of Arab information in San Francisco.

Sai Baba, Bhagavan Sri Sathya: Indian guru, b. 1926, has 10 million followers.

Sa'id, Abu: (AD 967-1049) Sufi sheikh born in Turkmenistan, disciple of Abu al-Fadl and Abu 'Abbass.

St. Denis, Ruth: (1879-1968) a spiritual dancer.

Sakran, Frank C.: executive secretary of the American Council on the Middle East.

Saladin: (1138-1193) a Kurd born in Tikrit, Iraq; recaptured Jerusalem from the Crusaders.

San, Master Seo: (aka Hyoo Jung or Chung Hur) wrote *Text for Zen Buddhism*, b. 1520.

Sapp, David: accompanied Mansur and Phillip to the Ram Dass interview.
Sasaki, Sokei-An: (1882-1945) transmitted the dharma; one of Murshid's Japanese Zen teachers; married Ruth Fuller (whose daughter from a previous marriage was Alan Watt's first wife); met Murshid in 1930; died the day before Murshid arrived for another visit.
Sasaki, Ruth Fuller: wife of Sokei-An Sasaki; wrote *Zen Dust* with Issho Miura Roshi.
Satchitananda, Swami: (1914-2002) revered yoga master from India.
Saul (Barodofsky): a disciple, b. 1939; Murshid's *Hakim* (physician).
Savio, Mario: (1942-1996) leader of the Free Speech movement at Berkeley.
Schaeffer, Rudolph: founded the Rudolph Schaeffer School of Design in San Francisco; friend of Murshid.
Scherbatsky, F.I.: (also Shcherbatskoi, or Stcherbatsky, Th.) (1866-1942) wrote *Buddhist Logic.*
Schuon, Frithjof: (1907-1998) author of *Understanding Islam* and *Gnosis.*
Scipio Africanus Major, Publius Cornelius: (c. 236-183 BC) Roman general who defeated Hannibal in the Punic Wars.
Secrist, Elsie: associated with Edgar Cayce's Association for Research and Enlightenment (ARE).
Sekhar, Dr. Chandra: Indian demographer.
Senzaki, Nyogen: (1876-1958) Soyen Shaku's student; a Zen Buddhist teacher of Murshid.
Seo, Master Kyung Bo: Murshid's Korean Zen Master; a disciple of Chinese Zen Master Tai Hsu.
Shaku, Soyen: (1859-1919) attended Parliament of Religions in Chicago in 1893; teacher of M.T. Kirby and Nyogen Senzaki.
Shamcher: (aka Bryn Beorse) Norwegian engineer; a disciple of Hazrat Inayat Khan; friend of Murshid; built OTEC plants in three sizes at UC Berkeley's Sea Water Conversion Laboratory; lobbied the federal government for OTEC from 1976-1979.
Shankaracharya: Vedantic scholar, b. AD 788.
Shams-i-Tabriz: Jelaleddin Rumi's spiritual consort.
Sharab and Paul: a couple; friends of Murshid.
Shawn, Ted: Ruth St. Denis' dance partner.
Sheila (McKendrick): (aka Sheyla) a disciple; resident of Olompali ranch; went to India with Dara.
Shereef, Pir Dewwal: spiritual advisor to Ayub Khan; in 1962 appointed Murshid representative of the University of Islamabad in Pakistan.
Shibata, Mr.: owner of the Daibutsu, an Asian art store on Fillmore in San Francisco.
Shikoh, Prince Dara: (1615-1659) eldest son of Shah Jahan; defeated and beheaded by his younger brother Aurangzeb in a struggle for the Moghul throne.
Shirin (aka Marion Doyle): a disciple, b. 1944.
Sibley (Cogswell): a disciple, b. 1947.
Silver, Ralph: Nancy Fish's husband.
Singer, Milton: wrote *Krishna: Myths, Rites, and Attitudes.*
Sitara: hosted Murshid, Saul and Mansur in Everett, Washington.
Slosberg, Mr.: a banker at Wells Fargo in San Francisco.
Smith, Huston: MIT, Syracuse, and UC Berkeley Professor of Philosophy and Religion; author of *The Religions of Man*, re-released as *The World's Religions.*

Smith, Russell: Murshid's former boss; associated with the Asia Foundation.
Smuts, Jan Christiaan: (1870-1950) South African statesman and soldier.
Snow, C.P.: (1905-1980) wrote *Two Cultures and the Scientific Revolution.*
Snyder, Gary: Zen, Beat poet, b. 1930; won Pulitzer prize for *Turtle Island.*
Snyfeld, Louise: numerologist for Hollywood notables.
Sorenson, Ted: advisor to President John F. Kennedy.
Stockwell, John: associated with the World Union in San Francisco.
Subhuti: the foremost disciple of Buddha in The Diamond Sutra.
Suleiman the Magnificent: (1494-1566) Turkish Sultan for 40 years; rule marked the apex of the Ottoman Empire.
Summer (Moffat): daughter of Barbara, b. 1965.
Suzuki, Daisetz: (1870-1966) Japanese Buddhist scholar; student of Soyen Shaku.
Swahananda, Swami: a pupil of Swami Ranganathananda Maharaj based in San Francisco.

T
Tai-Hsu: a Chinese Zen Master; author of *Lectures in Buddhism.*
Tamalpais: a 2,571 foot mountain in Marin County, just north of San Francisco.
Tansen: a great musician at the court of sixteenth-century, Moghul Emperor Akbar.
Tart, Charles: a psychologist.
Taylor, Dan: a disciple.
Tedesco, Frank: a disciple.
Terry, Walter: author of *Miss Ruth.*
Thant, U: Secretary-General of the United Nations, serving from 1961-1971; from Burma; succeeded Dag Hammarskjold.
Thien-An, Thich: (1926-1980) a Vietnamese Zen master; wrote *Zen Philosophy, Zen Practice.*
Townes, Charles H.: Nobel Prize winner in Physics.
Trebitsch-Lincoln: (aka Dr. Ruh) a Buddhist psychic who saw clearly.
Trikanand, Sheela: wife of Premanand Trikanand.
Tussman, Joseph: employee of UC Berkeley Experimental College.
Twain, Mark: (1835-1910) humorist, novelist, wit.
Tyberg, Judith: (1902-1980) a disciple of Sri Aurobindo; founded the East-West Cultural Center in Los Angeles.

V
Van (Beasley): a disciple, b. 1946.
Vashti (Morgan): a disciple.
Vilayat: see Pir Vilayat Inayat Khan.
Vivekananda, Swami: (1863-1902) a student of Sri Ramakrishna; attended the Parliament of Religions in Chicago in 1893 to present Indian philosophy.
von Stahl, Lottie: a clairvoyant.
Voris, Vera Van: (aka Murshida Vera Corda) (1913-2002) met Murshid in 1937.

W
Wachob, Bill: Mansur's cousin.
Wadia, A.P.: economics guru to K.T. Merchant.
Wagner, Eugene: a Buddhist; spiritual advisor to the Maharani of Sikkim.
Wali Ali: see Melvin.

Wallace, Schatsie (Charlotte): knew about Sri Aurobindo's ashram.
Wallace, Craig: resident of Ross, California.
Warwick, Dr. & Rev. Neville: Tibetan Buddhist friend of Murshid.
Watts, Alan: (1915-1973) popularizer of Zen.
Wayne (Jaekel): a disciple.
Weismuller, Johnny: an Olympic swimmer, played Tarzan in the movies.
Welch, Holmes: a Harvard professor; wrote *The Buddhist Revival in China.*
Welch, Lew: (1926-1971) Beat poet; poetry instructor of Murshid at UC Berkeley
    Extension; disappeared in the Sierra Neveda foothills at Gary Snyder's in 1971.
Whiteman, Luther: co-author with Murshid of *Glory Roads.*
Whitman, Walt: (1819-1892) ecstatic American poet who said, "In all men I see
    myself."
Wilde, Oscar: (1854-1900) wrote *The Picture of Dorian Gray.*
Wills, Lynn: Vilayat's youth secretary in Los Angeles.
Wood, Seth: old friend of Murshid from Marin County, California.

Y

Yasutani Roshi, Hakuun: (1885-1973) Zen Master; teacher of Philip Kapleau.
Yeager, Elizabeth: counseled by Murshid.
Yorty, Sam: (1910-1998) Mayor of Los Angeles 1961-1973.

Z

Zaehner, R.C.: taught at All Souls College in Oxford, England; wrote *Hindu and
    Muslim Mysticism.*
Zeinob: (aka Clair (Gwen) Bernham) a disciple, b. 1947.
Zenji, Hakuin: (1686-1769) Zen master in the Rinzai school; first asked, "What is
    the sound of one hand clapping?"; wrote *The Embossed Tea Kettle.*
Zitko, Dr. H. John: founder and president of the World University.

Glossary of Terms Mentioned

Abdal: people who fulfill a function far transcendent to ordinary or even extraordinary human roles. Murshid was an Abdal, and the sense he gave of this function was "chameleon."

Abdul: slave of.

Advaita: the doctrine of nondualism.

Ahankara: self-consciousness.

Ahmadiyya movement: established in 1889 by Hadhrat Mirza Ghulam Ahmad (1835-1908). Hadhrat Ahmad claimed to be the expected reformer of the latter days, the Awaited One, the Mahdi, the Messiah; has over 200 million adherents in 178 countries.

Ajna: the third eye or sixth chakra.

Akasha: ether.

Akhlak Allah: the manner of God.

Alaya: a place.

Alaya-vijnana: a storehouse of consciousness.

Alhamdu Lillah: all praise is due to God.

Allah Mansur: God is victorious.

Allaho Akbar: God is great.

Amal: one of eight parts of the Sufi method of realization; means the same as Samadhi; see also Kalama, Nimaz, Wazifa, Ziker, Fikar, Kasab, Shagal.

Ananda: bliss.

Anandavada: a state of bliss.

Anatta: no self.

Artha Sastra: an ancient Indian treatise on economics and politics written by Chanakya (350-275 B.C.). The term is made up of *artha*, material prosperity and *sastra* (or, *shastra*), knowledge.

As-salaam aleikhum: peace be upon you.

Asura: a demon.

Auliya: the plural of Wali, friend.

Azan: the Muslim call to prayer.

Baraka: blessing.

Bayat: an initiation.

Bhumis: stages on the way, in Buddhism.

Bismillah: in the name of God.

Bodhi: awakening.

Bodhisattva: someone who vows to work for the awakening of all humanity.

Buraq: the winged animal that was Mohammed's means of conveyance during the Miraj; esoterically, it symbolizes the breath.

Buzurg: a grade in the spiritual hierarchy described by Hazrat Inayat Khan. "The work of the *Buzurg*...is to help by the power of his soul those who wish to

advance spiritually." (*The Sufi Message of Hazrat Inayat Khan,* vol.9, p.129); see
also Pir, Wali, Ghauth, Qutb, Nabi, Rasul.

Cherag: (lit. light) the title of one appointed to lead the Universal Worship Service
of Hazrat Inayat Khan.

Dargah: a shrine or tomb.

Daroods: affirmations.

Darshan: a blessing through the eyes; see Tawajjeh.

Deva: an angel-man.

Dharana: concentration.

Dharma: (lit. that which supports or holds together) the teachings of Buddha.

Dharma Dhrishthi: right views.

Dhikr: see Ziker.

Dhyana: meditation or concentrated awareness.

Dorian Gray: the protagonist who does not age, in Oscar Wilde's eponymous
novel.

Ekayana: the clear, bright, shining light from which all manifestation comes.

Elhami: a dream in which a divine message is given either in letters or a divine
voice.

Enceinte: pregnant.

Er-rahim: the merciful.

Er-rahman: the compassionate.

Fakir: one who practices fikar.

Fana: assimilation or effacement; annihilation, as it is defined by R. A. Nicholson
translating al-Hujwiri.

Fana-fi-lillah: assimilation in God.

Fana-fi-rassul: assimilation in the world teacher.

Fana-fi-Sheikh: assimilation in the teacher.

Farishtakhaslat: angel-man.

Feringhi: a foreigner.

Fikar: (a transliteration of the Arabic *fikr*) to repeat a sacred phrase mentally.

Fudo: (lit. immoveable one) a guardian of the Buddhist faith.

Futa: a waist-cloth.

Gatha(s): in Sufi studies, teachings for the first three grades.

Ghauth: the fourth degree in the spiritual hierarchy of seven degrees. "The
influence of the Ghauth is wider than Wali. He gives up his personality wholly
to the divine guidance... [and creates] an atmosphere of protection from natural
disasters." (*The Sufi Message of Hazrat Inayat Khan,* v. 9, p. 130); see also Pir,
Buzurg, Wali, Qutb, Nabi, Rassul.

Githa(s) in Sufi studies, teachings for grades four, five and six.

Githeka: advanced teachings for the generality.

Hadiths: recorded teaching tales derived from the life example of Prophet
Mohammed.

Hajj: the required pilgrimage to Mecca for Muslims.

Hakim: physician.

Hal: a state of consciousness; see also Makam.

Halim Taba': poorness of spirit.

Hara: the solar plexis.

Hejira: (lit. flight or migration) for Western Sufis Hejirat Day is the anniversary
of Hazrat Inayat Khan's departure from Bombay for the west on September
13, 1910. Hejira for Muslims signifies the flight of Mohammed from Mecca to

Medina in 622 A.D. and marks the beginning of the Islamic calendar.

Hridaya: heart.

Ilham: divine inspiration.

Ilm: knowledge.

Imam: a prayer leader in Islam.

Inshallah: God willing.

Ishk: love.

Ishk Allah: God is love.

Ishk Allah mahbud Lillah: God is love, lover and beloved.

Jabrut: in Sufi terms, the world of the angels, love; "power" in the Lord's prayer.

Jagat: the body.

Jelal: strength.

Jemal: beauty.

Jhanas: meditations.

Jinn: (lit.genius) for Murshid, a type of soul, rather than an invisible order of powerful beings.

Kaaba Allah: a building fifteen meters square in Mecca; the point toward which Muslims worldwide direct their prayers.

Kalama: the declaration of faith, "There is no God but God"; see also La illa ha el il Allah.

Kasab: a breath practice.

Kashf: insight.

Kemal: perfection.

Khalif: representative.

Khankah: a place of Sufi prayers.

Khatimal-Mursaleen: the seal of the divine messengers.

Khatum: closing.

Khayali: a dream in which the actions and thoughts of the day are reproduced; see also Naqshi.

Khilvat: seclusion.

Kundalini: energy.

Kurukshetra: the battleground in the Bhagavad-Gita.

La illa ha el il Allah: the Sufi Ziker as given by Sufi Murshid Samuel L. Lewis ("There is no God but God").

Lahut: in Sufi terms, the source, luminosity; "glory" in the Lord's prayer.

Madzub: a God-intoxicated being.

Mahabbat: divine love.

Makam: station; a lasting state of consciousness; see also Hal, Wujud.

Malakut: in Sufi terms, the world of the jinn, inspiration; "kingdom" in the Lord's prayer.

Manas: mind.

Manusha: man or rational being.

Mast: a God-intoxicated being.

Ma'sum: to be without sin.

Miraj: (lit. ascent) Mohammed's night journey to heaven; see also Buraq.

Mudra: a gesture.

Mujahada: self-mastery.

Mujahadat: to live a purgative life.

Mullah: a religious cleric in Islam.

Mureed: a transliteration of the Arabic word *murid*; means disciple.

Murshid: spiritual guide.
Mushahadat: the contemplative life.
Mushahida: contemplation.
Nabi: a prophet of God. "His work is mainly the giving of the message in the form of warning, awakening, preaching, teaching, and inspiring those to whom he may be sent." (*The Sufi Message of Hazrat Inayat Khan*, v.9, p. 130); see also Pir, Buzurg, Wali, Ghauth, Qutb, Rasul.
Nada Brahma: the sound of God.
Nafs: ego; also, breath.
Nafs-i-selima: a refined ego.
Nafs-kushi: crushing the ego.
Nakib: a spokesman for the esoteric community.
Nakshibandi: symbology.
Naqshi: a dream in which the real meaning is disguised by a symbolic representation; see also Khayali.
Nimaz: prayer.
Nirtya: a type of yoga involving dance.
Pancha sila: refers to the five precepts, in Buddhism.
Paramitas: perfections, in Buddhism.
Pir: the leader of a religious group or sect; also, a grade in the spiritual hierarchy of Hazrat Inayat Khan. "The work of the *Pir* is helping individuals toward the unfoldment of their soul." (*The Sufi Message of Hazrat Inayat Khan*, vol.9, p.129); see also Buzurg, Wali, Ghauth, Qutb, Nabi, Rasul.
Pir Dahan: the voice of the prophet.
Prajna: insight.
Prajnaparamita Hridaya Sutra: (the Heart Sutra) regarded as the summation of the wisdom of Buddha, i.e. non-attachment and the doctrine of emptiness; ends like this: *Gate, Gate, Paragate, Parasamgate, Bodhi Swaha* (Going, coming, having gone completely beyond, gone altogether to the totality, O what an awakening, all hail)!
Pranayama: from *prana* (breath) and *ayama* (stopping) a breath practice.
Prasad: blessed food.
Prema: divine love.
Puja: a devotional ritual.
Qalbi: a dream showing the opposite of the real happening; see also Ruhi.
Qutb: In the spiritual hierarchy above Ghauth, "[a Qutb] has, to a lesser or greater extent, power over all elements as well as influence upon life. Under him there is a dominion in which he is responsible for the order and peace of souls. He governs a country or nation spiritually." (*The Sufi Message of Hazrat Inayat Khan*, v.9, p.130); see also Pir, Buzurg, Wali, Ghauth, Nabi, Rasul.
Rahmat: divine compassion.
Rajas: activity.
Rasul: (or Rassul) a world messenger. "[a Rasul] comes for all people at the time of the world's need, and brings with him that inspiration, influence, and power which will harmonize humanity." (*The Sufi Message of Hazrat Inayat Khan*, v.9, p.130); see also Pir, Buzurg, Wali, Ghauth, Qutb, Nabi.
Ruhi: a dream showing the real happening; see also Qalbi.
Ryazat: esotericism.
Sadhu: a renunciate.
Sahasrara: the crown center or seventh chakra.

484

Salat: prayer.

Saluk: a sober person, or Apollonian in the Greek sense where Apollo and Dionysius represent the mental and the emotional. In Islam, Abu Bakr is a *saluk* (who has *sahw*, sobriety) and Ali has *sukr* (intoxication).

Samadhi: a state of oneness.

Samma Dhrishti: right sight.

Samsara: the cycle of life and death.

Samskara: subtle impression created by one's thought or action.

Sangatha(s): in Sufi studies, teachings for grades seven, eight, and nine.

Sangha: community.

Sangitha(s): in Sufi studies, teachings for grades ten, eleven, and twelve.

Satori: a Zen Buddhist term for enlightenment, sudden awakening.

Sattvic: refined.

Satyagraha: (lit. holding to truth) reliance on God.

Shagal: the practice of being one with the inner sound.

Shahud: bearing witness that God alone exists.

Sheikh: (or Shaikh) elder or teacher; it is the tenth grade initiation for the Western Sufis.

Shifayat: a conductor of healing ceremonies.

Shirk: polytheism.

Silsila: (lit. a chain) a spiritual lineage or chain of transmission.

Skandhas: in Buddhism, the five principle components of personality—form, feeling, thought, intention (*samskara*), and consciousness (*vijnana*).

Soma: an hallucinogenic creeper from the succulent family; mentioned in the *Vedas*.

The Sorcerer's Apprentice: a fable that begins with an old sorcerer giving his apprentice chores to perform while he is away from their workshop. The apprentice soon grows tired of filling a tub with water so he enchants a broomstick to do it for him, but uses a form of magic in which he is not fully trained. The workshop floor is quickly awash in water and the novice does not know the magic word that will stop the broom. In despair, he splits the broom in two with an axe, but each piece then takes up a pail and continues fetching water at an even faster rate. Just when a disasterous flood seems most immanent, the old sorcerer returns to break the spell and save the day.

Spiritual hierarchy: "According to the Sufi conception, there are seven degrees in the spiritual hierarchy, which can be distinguished as different stages of responsiveness; in other words, of higher initiation." (*The Sufi Message of Hazrat Inayat Khan*, v.9, p.128); see also Pir, Buzurg, Wali, Ghauth, Qutb, Nabi, Rasul.

Sushumna: the center of the spinal column.

Talib: a disciple.

Tamas: sloth.

Tamasic: slothful.

Tapas: heat.

Tashbih: a string of prayer beads.

Tassawuf: Sufism.

Tassawuri: an expression of outward attunement and effacement.

Tat Twam Asi: thou art that.

Tattvas: elements.

Tauba: repentance.

Tawajjeh: a blessing through the eyes; see Darshan.

Tawbat al-inabat: to repent for fear of God's greatness.

Tawbat al-istihya: to repent for shame of God's beauty.

Thummim: perfections.

Tumo: heat, in Tibetan.

Urim: lights.

Urs: a commemoration observing the anniversary of the death of a holy one; promotes the belief, "Verily death is the bridge which unites friend to friend." (*Sayings of Mohammed*)

Vairagi: a renunciate.

Vairagya: indifference.

Vedas: the most ancient Indian expression of divine wisdom.

Vijnana consciousness.

Vajrayana: (lit. "indestructible vehicle") esoteric, as in Vajrayana Buddhism.

Vijnanavada: a state of consciousness.

Wali: (lit. one who is very near) a friend; also, a grade in the spiritual hierarchy of Hazrat Inayat Khan. "[T]he initiate whose will has come close to the divine will and he shows it in the harmony which reigns in his own life...with his friends...with an adversary...with the changing weather...with all that he eats and drinks...the place he lives...with all atmospheres. And so his will becomes the will of God; the will of God becomes his will." (*The Sufi Message of Hazrat Inayat Khan*, v.9, pp.129-30); see also Pir, Buzurg, Ghauth, Qutb, Nabi, Rasul.

Waswas: suggestions of the devil.

Wazifa: a sacred phrase.

Wujud: a state of consciousness; interchangeable with Hal.

Ya Azim: the highest.

Ya Haqq: O Truth.

Ya Hayy: O Life.

Ya Kafee: God is the remedy.

Ya Shafee: God is the healer.

Ya Wahabo: O Inspiration.

Yantra: in art, an interlocking matrix of geometric figures, circles, triangles and floral patterns.

Zavaliat: relates to the downward cycle; expiration as opposed to inspiration.

Zen-shi: a Zen master.

Ziker: (a transliteration of the Arabic *zikr* or *dikr*) remembrance; for Sufis, to remember God by repeating his name, Allah, in some form.

Bibliography of Books Mentioned

Affifi, Abul Ela. *The Mystical Philosophy of Muhyid Din-Ibnul Arabi.* Lahore: Sh. Muhammad Ashraf, 1964.

Aflaki, Shams al-Din Ahmad (d. 1360). *Legends of the Sufis: selected anecdotes from the work entitled The Acts of the Adepts (Menaqibu l'arifin),* Edited by James W. Redhouse. 3rd ed. London; Wheaton, Ill.: Theosophical Pub. House, 1976.

Aristophanes.; Aeschylus.; Sophocles., and others. *Fifteen Greek Plays.* New York: Oxford University Press, 1943.

Baba, Meher. *Listen Humanity.* Edited by Don E. Stevens. 5th ed. New York: Crossroad Pub., 1998.

Baer, Steve (b. 1938). *Sunspots: collected facts and solar fiction.* Albuquerque, N.M.: Zomeworks, 1977.

Bahm, Archie J. *The World's Living Religions.* New York: Dell Pub. Co.,1964.

The Bamboo Basket (serial publication). San Francisco: American Buddhist Order, 1967-?.

Beck, L. Adams (d. 1931). *Dreams and Delights.* New York: Dodd, 1926.

Beck, L. Adams. *The Garden of Vision: a story of growth.* New York: Farrar & Rinehart, 1929.

Begg, W.D. *The Holy Biography of Hazrat Khwaja Muinuddin Chishti.* Tucson: The Chishti Sufi Mission of America, 1977.

Beorse, Bryn. *Every Willing Hand.* New York: Hu Press, 1979.

Biography of Pir-O-Murshid Inayat Khan. London and The Hague: East-West Publications, 1979.

Blum, William. *Killing Hope.* Monroe, Maine: Common Courage Press, 1995.

Brand, Stewart. *The Next Whole Earth Catalog: access to tools.* Sausalito, Calif.: Point; New York: Random House, 1980.

Brunton, Paul. *The Secret Path: a technique of spiritual self-discovery for the modern world.* London: Rider, 1969.

Bucke, Richard M. *Cosmic Consciousness: a study in the evolution of the human mind.* New Hyde Park, N.Y.: University Books, 1961.

The Buddhist Bible: favorite scriptures of the Zen sect; history of early Zen Buddhism, self-realisation of noble wisdom, the diamond sutra, the prajna paramita sutra, the sutra of the sixth patriarch. Edited by Dwight Goddard and Introduction by Huston Smith. Boston: Beacon Press, 1970.

Burckhardt, Titus. An *Introduction to Sufi Doctrine.* Lahore: Sh. M. Ashraf, 1959.

Burton, Richard F. *The Arabian nights' entertainments, or, The Book of a Thousand Nights and One Night.* Chosen and arranged by Bennett A. Cerf. New York: Modern Library, 1996.

Carson, Rachel. *Silent Spring.* Boston: Houghton Mifflin, 1962.

Cerminara, Gina. *Many Mansions.* New York: Sloane, 1950.

Coghlan, Ronan. *The Illustrated Encyclopaedia of Arthurian Legends*. London: Claremont Books, 1996.

Corelli, Marie (1855-1924). *A Romance of Two Worlds*. Los Angeles: Borden Pub. Co., 1947.

Darshana International: an international quarterly of philosophy, psychology, psychical research, religion, mysticism & sociology. Edited by J.P. Atreya. Morabadad: Darshana International, 1963-?.

The Diamond Sutra and the Sutra of Hui-neng (the 6th Patriarch). Translated by A.F. Price and Mou-Lam Wong. Berkeley: Shambhala, 1969.

Donkin, William. *Wayfarers: Maher Baba with the God-intoxicated*. Myrtle Beach, S.C.: Sufism Reoriented, 1988.

Douglas-Klotz, Neil. *Desert Wisdom: sacred Middle Eastern writings from the Goddess through the Sufis*. San Francisco: Harper San Francisco, 1995.

Dowland, Jessie E. (Khalifa Nargis). *Between the Desert and the Sown: the way of the disciple*. Southhampton, [U.K.]: Sufi Movement, 1923.

Ellis, Havelock. *The Dance of Life*. New York: Modern Library, 1929.

Emerson, Ralph Waldo. *Essays*. Introduction by Irwin Edman. New York: Crowell, 1951, 1926.

ETC: a review of general semantics (serial publication). Fort Worth, Texas: Institute of General Semantics, 1943-present (2006).

Ghose, Aurobindo. *The Life Divine*. New York: E.P. Dutton, 1953. 1951.

Giri, Varahagiri Venkata. *Civilization at the Crossroads of Destiny*. Bangalore: Indian Institute of World Culture, 1969.

Goethe, Johann Wolfgang von (1792-1842). *Faust: Part 1*. Translated by Bayard Taylor and Bayard Quincy Morgan. New York: Crofts Classics, 1946.

Govinda, Lama Anagarika. *The Way of the White Clouds: a Buddhist pilgrim in Tibet*. Berkeley: Shambala, 1970.

Hawthorne, Nathaniel. *The Great Stone Face*. Kila, Mont.: Kessinger Pub. Co., 1991.

Hedgepeth, William and Dennis Stock. *The Alternative: communal life in new America* (New York, 1970). Toronto, Ontario: Collier Books, 1970.

Huineng (638-713). *The Sutra of the Sixth Patriarch*. Edited by Paul F. Fung. San Francisco: Buddha's Universal Church, 1964.

al-Hujwiri, 'Ali B. 'Uthman Al-Jullabi. *Kashf Al-Mahjub*. London: Messrs. Luzac and Company Ltd., 1970.

The Hundred Thousand Songs of Milarepa. Translated and annotated by Garma C.C. Chang. Secaucus, New Jersey: Carol Publishing Group, 1962.

Huxley, Aldous. *Brave New World*. New York: Perennial Classics, 1998, 1932.

Huxley, Aldous. *The Perennial Philosophy*. New York: Harper & Row, 1945, 1944.

Iamblichus's Life of Pythagoras. Edited by Thomas Taylor. London: J.M. Watkins, 1965, 1818.

The Iron Flute: 100 Zen Koans, with commentary by Genro, Fugai, and Nyogen. Translated and edited by Nyogen Senzaki and Ruth Strout McCandless with an Introduction by Steve Hagen. Boston, Tokyo: Tuttle Publishing, 2000, 1964.

Joyce, James. *Ulysses*. New York: Random House, 1946.

Kapleau, Philip. *The Three Pillars of Zen: teaching, practice, and enlightenment*. New York: Harper & Row, 1966.

Khan, Hazrat Inayat. *The Complete Sayings of Hazrat Inayat Khan*. New Lebanon, N.Y.: Sufi Order Publications, 1978. (Includes *The Bowl of Saki, Gayan, Vadan, Nirtan*.)

488

Khan, Hazrat Inayat. *The Sufi Message of Hazrat Inayat Khan*. 12 vols. London:
Barrie and Rockliff, 1960-67. Books and chapters cited from these volumes,
which contain thirty-seven books, include: *The Metaphysics of Sound;* "The
Intoxication of Life" in *The Alchemy of Happiness; Rasa Shastra; A Sufi
Message of Spiritual Liberty; Mysticism; Sufi Mysticism;* "Reincarnation" in *The
Phenomenon of the Soul; Una (a play); The Inner Life; Confessions; Moral Culture;
The Way of Illumination; The Purpose of Life; Cosmic Language; The Path of
Initiation and Discipleship*.
Khan, Hazrat Inayat. *Tales: told by Hazrat Inayat Khan*. Compiled by Mansur
Johnson. New Lebanon, N.Y.: Omega Press, 1991, 1980; Warsaw: tCHu
(Translated by Magdalena Tarnowska), 2005.
Khan, Pir Vilayat. *Toward the One*. New York: Crown Press, 1974.
Khan, Pir Vilayat, "*The Introduction and Instructions in Meditation*", "*The Training of
Breath*", and "*Introduction to Vision*." Sufi Order, Photocopy received by author,
1968.
The Koran. Translated with notes by N.J. Dawood. London: Penguin Books, 1956.
Korzybski, Alfred and Cassius Jackson Keyser. *Manhood of Humanity*. Lakeville,
Conn.: International Non-Aristotelian Library Pub. Co., 1950.
Korzybski, Alfred. *Science and Sanity: an introduction to non-Aristotelian systems
and general semantics*. Lakeville, Conn.: International Non-Aristotelian Library
Pub. Co., 1958.
Krishna: Myths, Rites and Attitudes. Edited by Milton Singer. Honolulu: East-West
Center Press, 1966.
Krishnabai, Mother. *Devotee's Diary*. Kanhangad, S. India: Anandashram, 196?.
Lame Deer, Archie Fire (b. 1935) and Richard Erdoes. *Gift of Power: the life and
teachings of a Lakota medicine man*. Introduction by Alvin M. Josephy, Jr.,
Santa Fe, N.M.: Bear & Co., 1992.
Lansdale, Edward Geary. *In the Midst of Wars: an American's mission to Southeast
Asia*. New York: Harper & Row, 1972.
Lederer, William J., and Eugene Burdick. *The Ugly American*. New York: Norton,
1958.
Lewis, Samuel L. *Introduction to Spiritual Brotherhood: science, mysticism & the new
age. (*aka *Toward Spiritual Brotherhood)* San Francisco, Novato: Sufi Islamia/
Prophecy Publications, 1981, 1972.
Lewis, Samuel L. *Spiritual Dance and Walk*: an introduction from the work of
Murshid Samuel L. Lewis (Sufi Ahmed Murad Chisti). San Francisco: Sufi
Islamia Ruhaniat Society, 1978.
Lewis, Samuel L. *Sufi Vision and Initiation*. Edited by Neil Douglas-Klotz. San
Francisco & Novato: Sufi Islamia/Prophesy Publications, 1986.
Lien, Carsten. *Olympic Battleground: the power politics of timber preservation*. San
Francisco: Sierra Club Books, 1991.
Lings, Martin. *A Moslem Saint of the Twentieth Century: Shaikh Ahmad al-'Alawi, his
spiritual heritage and legacy*. London: Allen & Unwin, 1961.
Lytton, Edward Bulwer. *The Coming Race*. New York: George Routledge & Sons,
1880-1889; Mokelumme Hill, Calif.: Health Research, 1967.
Melville, Herman. *The Confidence Man*. New York: Norton, 1971.
Migot, Andre. *Tibetan Marches*. New York: Dutton, 1955.
Miller, Joe. *Great Song: the life and teachings of Joe Miller*. Edited by Richard Power.
Athens, Ga.: Maypop, 1993.
Miura, Isshu and Ruth Fuller Sasaki. *Zen Dust: the history of the koan and koan*

study in Rinzai (Lin-chi) Zen. New York: Harcourt, Brace & World, 1967.

Morris, Craig & Donald E. Thompson. *Huanuco Pampa: an Inca city and its hinterland.* New York: Thames & Hudson, 1985.

Murshid Sam Archive, unpublished teachings cited include: Murshid's *Commentary on The Inner Life,* by Hazrat Inayat Khan, *Commentary on Everyday Life,* by Hazrat Inayat Khan, *Commentary on Insight,* by Hazrat Inayat Khan, *Commentary on Superstitions, Customs and Beliefs,* by Hazrat Inayat Khan, *Commentary on Nakshibandi (Symbology) Gatha,* by Hazrat Inayat Khan, *Commentary on Moral Culture,* by Hazrat Inayat Khan. Also included are citations to or selections from Murshid's *Six Interviews with Inayat Khan, Candidate's Gathekas, Walk Papers 1-10, Breath Papers 1-8 by Murshid, Breath* (39 paragraphs), *Spiritual Architecture,* and *The Lotus and the Universe.*

Nicholson, Reynold Alleyne. *The Idea of Personality in Sufism: three lectures delivered in the University of London.* Lahore: Sh. Muhammad Ashraf, 1964.

Nicholson, Reynold Alleyne. *Studies in Islamic Mysticism.* Cambridge, [Eng.]: The University Press, 1967.

Pistis Sophia: a Gnostic miscellany, being for the most part extracts from the books of the Savior to which are added excerpts from a cognate literature. Edited by G.R.S. Mead (1863-1933). Secaucus, N.J.: University Books, 1974.

Plato. *The Republic.* Edited by Allan David Bloom. New York: Basic Books, 1968.

The Psychedelic Review (periodical journal). Edited by Timothy Leary and Richard Alpert, 1963-71.

Qadri, Faqir Nur Muhammad Sarwari. *Irfan: a true and unique book of divine knowledge.* Kulachi: Abdul Rashid, 1978.

Rama, Swami. *Living with the Himalayan Masters.* Honesdale, Pennsylvania: Himalayan Institute Press, 1978, 1999. 16th printing, 2001.

Ramdas, Swami. *God-Experience.* Bombay: Anandashram, 1963.

Ramdas, Swami. *In the Vision of God.* Bombay: Bharatiya Vidya Bhavan, 1962.

Ramdas, Swami. *World is God.* Kanhangad, S. India, 1955.

Ram Dass. *Be Here Now, Remember.* New York: Crown Pub., 1978, 1971.

Reps, Paul. *Ask a Potato.* New York: Doric Pub. Co., 1967.

Ronan, Coghlan. *Encyclopedia of Arthurian Legends.* London: Claremont Books, 1996.

Rumi. Jalal al-Din. *Discourses of Rumi* (Fihi ma Fih). Edited by A.J. Arberry. Richard, Surrey: Curzon Press, 1993, 1961.

Rumi, Jalal al-Din. *Tales from the Masnavi.* Edited by A.J. Arberry. London: Allen and Unwin, 1961.

Sasaki, Sokei-An. *Holding the Lotus to the Rock*: the autobiography of Sokei-An, America's first Zen master. Edited by Michael Hotz. New York: Four Walls Eight Windows, 2001.

Sayings of Mohammed. Illustrated with wood engravings by Boyd Hanna. Mount Vernon, N.Y.: Peter Pauper Press, 1958.

Senzaki, Nyogen and Eido Shimano. *Like a Dream, Like a Fantasy.* Tokyo: Japan Publications, 1978.

Seo, Master Kyung Bo. *Text for Zen Buddhism.* (typescript held by author).

Shaku, Soyen. *Sermons of a Buddhist Abbot.* Chicago: Open Court, 1906.

Shcherbatskoi, F.I. *Buddhist Logic.* Gravenhage: Mouton, 1958.

Smith, Huston. *The Religions of Man.* New York: Harper, 1958.

Studies in Comparative Religion (periodical journal). Edited by F. Clive Ross. London: 1969-?.

Tai-Hsu. *Lectures in Buddhist.* (typescript held by author). Paris, 1928.

Tennyson, Alfred (1809-1892). *Poems. Selections.* New York; London: Knopf, 2004.

Terry, Walter. *Miss Ruth: the "more living life" of Ruth St. Denis.* New York: Dodd, Mead, 1969.

Thoreau, Henry David. *A week on the Concord and Merrimack rivers; Walden, or life in the woods; the Maine woods; Cape Cod.* New York: Literary Classics of the U.S., 1985.

Townes, Charles H. *Making Waves.* Woodbury, N.Y.: American Institute of Physics, 1995.

Twain, Mark. *Captain Stormfield's Visit to Heaven.* New York: Harper, 1952.

Vivekananda, Swami. *Raja-Yoga.* New York: Ramakrishna-Vivekananda Center, 1955.

Watt, W. Montgomery. *The Faith and Practice of Al-Ghazali.* Lahore: Sh. Muhammad Ashraf, 1963.

Welch, Holmes. *The Buddhist Revival in China.* Cambridge [Mass.]: Harvard University Press, 1968.

The Western Buddhist. (serial publication). Edited by Jack Austin. London: Garrett & Campbell, 1953-1989.

Whiteman, Luther and Samuel L. Lewis. *Glory Roads: the psychological state of California.* New York: Thomas Y. Crowell Co., 1936.

Wilde, Oscar. *The Picture of Dorian Gray.* New York: Modern Library, 1992.

Wright, Harold Bell. *The Eyes of the World: a novel.* Chicago: The Book Supply Company, 1914.

Yogananda, Paramahansa, *Autobiography of a Yogi.* Los Angeles: Self-Realization Fellowship, 1972.

Zaehner, R.C. *Hindu and Muslim Mysticism.* New York: Schocken Books, 1969.

Zen Flesh, Zen Bones: a collection of Zen & pre-Zen writings. Compiled by Paul Reps. Rutland, Vt.; Tokyo: Charles E. Tuttle Co., 8th printing, 1965.

Zenji, Hakuin. *The Embossed Tea Kettle.* London: G. Allen & Unwin, 1963.

Index

A

A Sufi Saint of the 20th Century (Lings), al-Alawi's use of ziker, 64
abdal, 206, 383
abdul, 252
Abdul-rahman. *See* Daniel (Lomax)
"Abstinence," 32
Adams, Ansel, 220–21, 467
Adamson, R.L., 426–27, 442, 458, 462, 467
advaita, 165
Affifi, Abul Ela, 57, 467
ahankara, 300
Ahmadiyya movement, 240
Ahmed, Shamseddin, with the following entries: 216, 284, 301, 334, 352, 396,
    about, 477
Ajna, 301
Akasha, 36, 67, 153
akashic records, 401
Akbar, Emperor (Akbar the Great): contribution of, 419, 423, 467; criticisms of,
    193–94; descendant of, 55; Emperor of India, 364, 367, 377, 392; engraving of,
    100; Fathepur Sikri, 89; significance of, 377
aklak Allah, 117-8, 345
Alawi, Shaikh Ahmad al- (Sidi El-Alawi): about, 467; *baraka*, Murshid's, 75;
    confirmation, meaning of, 47; Hollywood, visit to, 341; mystical experiences,
    213; *A Sufi Saint of the 20th Century*, 64, 322; wife, lost his, 55, 337
Alaya Vijnana, 131, 384, 385
alaya, 131, 170, 270, 384-5
alaya-vijnana, hyphenate existing entry, so it reads: 384-85
Albanese, Margaret, 44, 145, 467
alhamdu Lillah, 53, 218, 431, 458
Ali, Sufi Barkat: about, 467; engagement cancellation, 206; Saadia, marriage of
    Murshid to, 455; Sufi teacher, chief, 368; teacher, Murshid's, 218; wire, sends
    important, 365
Allah (musical rendition), 387
Allah mansur, 321
Allaudin. *See* Mathieu, Bill
Alpert, Richard. *See* Ram Dass
amal, 390-91
American Friends of the Middle East, 453
American Humanist Association, 222

Gold, Marc, 270, 292, 471
Gordon, George. *See* Byron, Lord
Gospel of St. Thomas, 245, 260–61, 266, 409
Gottlieb, Lou, 134, 471
Govinda, Lama Anagarika: about, 471; *Buddhism and Modern Thought*, 286; health
 food store, 321; as host, 92, 113; "Infinite Compassion," 165, 169; meeting, 169,
 171–73, 177–79; as speaker, 113, 162–63, 165, 169; spiritual political fireworks,
 125–26
The Grateful Dead, 87
Gupta, P.K., 435, 471
Gurdjieff, George Ivanovitch, 80–81, 112, 235, 268, 417, 471
Gypsy Updike. *See* Basira

H
hadiths, 252, 367, 431
Haeckel, Ernst, 446, 471
Hafiz (poet), 85–86, 471
hajj, 216, 283
hakim (physician), 429-30
hal, 53, 194, 301, 386
halim taba', 108
Halim. *See* Frank (Welch)
Hammarskjold, Dag, 393, 471
Hans (von Briesen), 425, 471
hara, 31, 121
Harvey, Richard, 417, 423, 435, 446, 460, 471
Hassan (Sigmund Herz), 471; commando raid, 286; interview with Murshid, 227;
 khankah, 62, 71, 278; picture, 2; poem, Murshid's, 141; Prophesy Pressworks,
 155, 164, 230, 259, 321; social gathering, 132; *tassawuri*, 128; torpor, correction
 for, 99
Hathaway, Bill, 28, 176–78, 471
Hawkins, Dr. Alma, 401, 438, 471
Hawthorn, Nathaniel, 321, 471
Hayakawa, S.I. (Don): about, 471; approval, seeking from, 135; derision of, 171–72,
 212, 222; as enemy, 75–76, 224, 368; General Semantics, 225, 229, 231, 233;
 "intolerance" of, 71; law and order stance, 224; letter, Murshid's, 76, 225;
 papers, rejected by, 117; San Francisco State College, 192; as senator, 369; Zen
 challenge, 96–97
Hedgepeth, William, 298, 471
Hegel, Georg Wilhelm Friedrich, 256, 460, 471
hejira, 345, 356-57
Helen (Saul's friend), 324, 354–55, 361, 471
Helmholz, A. Carl, 458, 471
Herz, Sigmund. *See* Hassan
Hoffmaster, David, 45, 335, 418, 426, 471
Hollywood, 287, 290, 295, 323, 341, 423
Holmes, Steward W., 173, 471
Holy Order of MANS, 123, 196, 233, 244, 245, 263, 266, 278
Holzhauer, Betty, 20, 322, 471
Hoodbhoy, Samir A., 245, 472

Jemila (Carolyn Buckmaster Johnson): about, 472; angel's, surrounded by, 88, at home, 110; as chief dancing disciple, 170; Bolinas dinner, 27; Carolyn's spiritual name, 23; consequences of leaving Khankah, 349, 373, 376; hosting Huston Smith in Marquette, 78; Mansur's dreams of, 23, 24, 334, 338, 345, 359, 371, 385; Mansur's love for, 37, 39, 289; marriage relationship with Mansur, 37, 55-57, 289, 303-304, 305, 306, 320, 327, 328, 329, 333-34, 335, 337-338, 341, 342, 348, 359, 362, 363, 365, 370, 375, 378, 383, 385, 403, 455; movie role, 41; Murshid's practices for, 68, 197, 230; pottery class, 208, 278; psychedelics, 247; Vilayat and, 87, 320-321, 322, 323, 324, 325, 338-339, 383, 403-4; visit with Schwartzes', 52-53;

Jennings, C. Robert, 204–205, 472

Jeremy (Cave). *See* Jelaleddin

Jesus Christ: about, 472; appearance of, 59; beliefs, Murshid's, 413; contacting, Murshid's challenge, 137; *darshan* process, 117, 121; *Gospel of St. Thomas,* 245; Impressions of, Murshid's, 15; manifestation in sound, 103; mergence experience of, 51, 93; mystic undertanding of, 431–32; practicing, Murshid, 146, 155; reincarnation of, 76; Sermon on the Mount, 108; as Sun in human form, 392; teachings of, 108–109, 220, 240, 409, 451; vision of, 12; "walk," 243; Words of, Murshid speaking the, 424; world mission, 397

Jews, 130, 324, 338, 389, 395

jhanas, 113-14, 162, 366, 441

Jilani, Abdul Qadir, 67, 472

jinn, 55, 99

Johnson, Benjamin. *See* Nathan

Johnson, Mabel, 322, 472

Johnson, Otis. *See* Mansur (Otis Johnson)

Joyce, James, 99

Joyner, Russell: about, 472; *Civilization at the Cross-Roads of Destiny,* 442; International Society of General Semantics, 71, 76, 117, 166, 221; letter, Murshid's, 232, 233, 243, 255–56, 440, 452; warefare, end of, 242, 246

Jung, Hyoo. *See* San, Master Seo

K

kaaba Allah, 10-12, 26, 86, 171, 226, 380, 429-30

kalama, 390-91, 396

Kanhangad (Travancore-Cochin, India), 23, 473

Kaplan, Dr. Abraham, 104, 472

Kapleau, Philip: about, 472; *The Three Pillars of Zen,* 33, 113, 116, 155, 167–68; Zen Master, 328

karma: of Aurobindo movement, 399; bypass, 254; cosmic, 404; enemies and, 365; good, 92, 163, 167, 169; intentions and, 369–70; Olompali ranch fire, 195; wealth and fame, 284; yoga, 159, 346, 416

kasab, 154, 390-91

Kashf al-Mahjub, 99, 143-44, 209, 317, 472

kashf, 90, 95, 102, 366, 444

Kelly, Frank, 222–23, 472

kemal, 152, 207

Kennedy, Susan, 200, 369, 472

Kennett, Roshi, 386, 406, 472

Keyser, Cassius (C.J. (Jackson) Keyser): about, 472; General Semantics,

146, 204, 233, 253, 260, 261, 266, 272, 328, 333, 338, 344, 345, 354, 359, 361, 362, 371, 385, 397, 408, 444, 446; early family life, 19; experiences *samadhi*, 232; interviews: Huston Smith 112, 119, Timothy Leary, 246-48, Baba Ram Dass, 305; initiations of: second grade, 44, fourth grade, 115; meeting with Gavin, 220; on a fast, 59; receives *nakib*, 317; receives transmitted robe, 118; resemblance to Christ, 359; Shamcher, interrogation of, 186; spiritual name given, 48; successor to Whiteman-Lewis, 243, 246; "Toward the One" practice, 55, 196; translation of Allah Mansur, 321; travels alone, Lama, 288-99; travels with Murshid: Lama, 16-17, northwest, 354-62, Los Angeles, 435-39, Geneva, 462-464; 472, 474

manusha, 427
Many Mansions (Cerminara), 67
maqbara (grave), 15
Marcia (Pavolic), 32, 44, 119, 148, 163, 170, 259, 260, 282, 319, 328, 349, 411
Marpa (translator), 54, 376, 461, 474
Martin, Murshida (Ada) Rabia: accusations by, 197; as hypocrite, 143, 148, 191; money, organization's, 84; special diet, 51; spiritual papers, handling, 74, 474; as successor, 379–80, 391
Martini, Marion, 446, 463, 474
Marty (Peller), 411, 474
Marx, Karl, 256, 460, 474
Mary Sue (Sitton), 355, 411, 434, 474
Mary, Mother (Mary Mae Hoffman Maier), 355, 475
Mathieu, Bill (Allaudin), 387, 474
Mathison, Laura. *See* Laura (Mathison)
Matthews, George, 411, 433, 474
May, Ginger. *See* Jehanara
Maypoles, 291, 320
McCandless, Mrs., 294, 332, 474
McCloskey, Jr., Paul N., 423, 456, 474
McCoy, Don: about, 474; in India, 209; Olompali ranch, 68, 74, 109, 151–52, 168, 195, 249, 334
McGee, Norman, 67, 69, 173, 367, 474
McGinley, Dennis H. *See* Hussain
McKendrick, Sheila. *See* Sheila (McKendrick)
McLellan, Nusi, 437, 474
Medlock, Julie: about, 474; India, living in, 92; letter, Murshid's, 33, 102, 168, 169, 176, 177, 185, 302, 303, 341, 402, 417, 446; letter to Murshid, 144, 151, 162; permits, refusing to obtain, 127; Pondicherry, 107; recital, Christmas, 66; Sri Aurobindo Ashram, 346
Melvin (Wali Ali Meyer): about, 474; interview with Murshida Duce, 379-80; Islamic studies class, 230; journal, daily, 229; meeting with, 95, 164; name, spiritual, 353, 372; poetry writing, 153, 164; religions of Asia, traditional, 220–21; secretary, 184, 185, 282, 285, 306; student, first, 178
Merchant, Deepak, 474
Merchant, Prof. K.T., 138, 444, 474
mergence: in divine spirit, 95; with God, 457; with Jesus Christ, 51, 93; mystical, 10
messiahism, 376
Meyer, Wali Ali. *See* Melvin
Milarepa (saint), 27, 54, 129–130, 376, 460, 474

Muslim, 151, 193–94, 245, 264, 283, 295, 324
Mussell, Howard. *See* Howard (Mussell)
mystical experiences: Alawi, Shaikh Ahmad al- (Sidi El-Alawi), 213; Baba, 415;
    disciples, Murshid's, 330; in Japan, 212–13; Murshid, 397, 403–404, 415–16,
    432; Oriental philosophies, 344–45
Mysticism (Khan), definition of, 90
The Mysticism of Sound (Khan), 43, 79, 401

N

nabi, 129, 145
nada Brahma, 73
nafs, 108-9, 283,
nafs-i-kushi, 109
nafs-i-selima, 432
Nakagawa Roshi, Soen, 92, 96, 127, 332, 475
nakib, 317, 321, 357
nakshibandi, 52, 150-51, 346, 424
naqshi, 93
Narita, Hiro, 144, 277, 475
Nasr, Dr. Seyyed Hossein: *about*, 475; Clive-Ross, supporting, 235; fashion display
    by, 313; intellectualization, world leader in, 48–49; letter, Murshid's, 334,
    338; Mohammed experience, Murshid's, 333; muslims, Murshid lecturing,
    394; mystical experience, Murshid's, 264; Saadia's friend, 150; San Francisco
    visit, 313, 324; *tawajjeh* of Hazrat Inayat Khan, 94; Temple of Understanding
    conference, 366
Nasr-ed-din Hoja, Mulla Kwaja, 448, 475
Nathan (Benjamin Johnson): about, 475; babysitting, 131; birth of, 20; child
    rearing, 166, 234, 265, 305, 307, 311; dreams about, 24, 42; Jemila's travels and,
    337, 341, 383; Mansur's separation from, 55, 289; with Summer, 110, 138; wine
    store with Murshid, 317; traveling with Mansur, 17.
Needleman, Jacob, 475; cult methodologies, exposing the, 374; dervish dancing,
    366; humility, need for, 402; letter, Murshid's, 331–32, 380, 393–94; on
    "messiahism," 376; mysticism for intellectuals, 375–76; Psalm, reading 137th,
    262; spiritual movements, contemporary, 373; teacher, Mystical Experience, 267
New Age: communes, 303, 334; community, 152, 425; dances, 298; Gandalf's
    Garden, London, 177; Ghose, Sri Aurobindo, 271; health food store, 240,
    321, 323, 404, 409, 458; Lama Foundation, 271; leaders, 406; life styles, 297;
    press interpretation, 156–57; principles, 231, 271; proof of, Indian films as,
    281; spirituality, 7, 53, 203, 414, 450, 457; typology, Murshid, 405; *Whole Earth
    Catalog*, 347; women, oracular function of, 201
Niche of Light (al-Ghazzali), 61
Nicholson, Reynold Alleyne, 57, 61, 475
Nietzsche, Friedrich, 256, 475
nimaz, 390
nirtya, 162
Nizami, Pir-O-Murshid Hassan Sani: about, 475; inspiration, ways to, 147; letter,
    Murshid's, 154; meeting, 10; spiritual brotherhood, lacking, 288; teachings of,
    11, 23, 50, 84, 85, 117, 137; tomb visit, New Delhi, 41, 281, 283
Nottingham, Professor, 192, 212, 291, 475
Nur-un-nisa (daughter of Moineddin), 425, 434, 475

O

Ocean Thermal Energy Conversion. *See* OTEC
Olivet, Fabre d', 90
Olompali ranch: as commune, 249, 252, 282; dancing, 166; disciples, Murshid's, 81; fire at, 192, 195; founder, Don McCoy, 68, 74, 151, 195; invitation declined, 288; meditation papers, recorded at, 98; meditation weekend, 87; *pranayama* (breath work)., 154; spiritual dedication, 92
Organicism: The Philosophy of Interdependence (Bahm), 244, 338
OTEC (Ocean Thermal Energy Conversion), 384, 416, 454, 475
Ouspensky, Petyr Demianovich, 268, 475

P

Pallis, Marco, 212, 236, 464, 475
pancha sila, 264
paramitas, 386
Parisa (Ruth Wintheil), 233, 243, 259, 265, 267, 268, 475
Parrish, Dean Carroll, 281, 438, 457, 475
Pat (Lassar Jablonski). *See* Fatima
The Path of Initiation and Discipleship (Khan), initiation tests, 122-23
Patel, A.B.: about, 475; humility, lacking, 402; as Indian, eminent, 442; letter, Murshid's, 219, 222–23, 254, 299, 301–302, 344, 395, 396, 397, 399; letter from, 399; Sri Aurobindo movement, 300; World Union International Centre, 22, 291, 344, 375, 377
Patel, Villabhai, 280, 442, 475
Patterson, Elizabeth, 341, 345, 353, 380, 396–97, 475
Paul (Rognlie), 411, 475
Paul. *See* Fernandez, Zoso
Pavolic. *See* Marcia
Pearls from the Ocean Unseen (Khan, H.I.), 43, poor in spirit, 109
Peller, Marty. *See* Marty
Perls, Fritz, 97, 128, 462, 475
Perversion (Khan), neglect a cause of, 37
The Phenomenon of the Soul (Khan, H.I.), 43
Phrasumangalo. *See* Clifton, Robert
Pickard, James. *See* James (Pickard)
Pierce, Duncan. *See* Krishnadas
Pir Dehan, 26, 86
pir, 129
Plato, 96, 228, 271, 475
Playboy magazine, about, 191–210; Anandashram, 198; article, 456–57; Fiske, Vocha, 198, 209, 212; Lachelt, Theodore C., 198, 199; lawsuit insight, 203
Power, Richard, 475
The Power of the Word (Khan, H.I.), 43
prajna, 102, 209, 344, 354, 367, 382, 417, 422, 442
Prajnaparamita Hridaya sutra, 408, 452
pranayama (breath work), 154, 164
prasad, 170
prema, 203
Premanand, Trikanand, 323, 434, 436–38, 475
Price, Iru, 104, 113, 125, 126, 131, 171, 475

128, 131–32, 145–47, 160, 170, 253, 327, 329; picture, 140, 263, 267; as spiritual advisor, 55; subscription, 236; Tai Hsu's manuscript, 104
Wahiduddin, Mirza. *See* Begg, W.D.
Wali Ali. *See* Melvin (Wali Ali Meyer)
wali, 61, 129, 206
Walk Papers 1-10, 77
walking meditation, Abraham walk, 308; *Allaho Akbar* practice, 109; Astrological-Occult walk, 133; Avalokiteswara walk, 243; Buddhist Master walk, 163; centers of concentration, 94; chanting *wazifas* with *mudras*, 88–89; class on, 42, 43, 61; Easter services walk, 463; etheric breath walk, 285; fire walk, 152; general, 24–25, 49, 50, 66, 82–83, 121, 129, 135, 148, 159, 166, 175, 220; Hindu walk, 26; holy walks, 411; Jesus walk, 121, 135, 243; manifesting walk, 103; Mercury walk, 408; Mother Krishnabai walk, 99; Murshid walk, 93, 237; Mystical walk, 133; Neptune walk, 264; Pakastani walk, 26; Prophet Mohammed walk, 133, 134; Ramdas walk, 99; saint Mian Mir walk, 63, 98, 100; saints' walk, 446; shopping teachings, 112; Saturn, Mercury and Jupiter walk, 419; Saturn and Jupiter walk, 419; solar plexus, 121–22; Sun, Moon, Mars, Venus, and Mercury walks, 134; "Toward the One" walk, 30–31, 100; *Walk Papers 1-10*, 77, 266
Wallace, Craig, 169, 479
Wallace, Schatsie (Charlotte), 222, 479
Warwick, Dr. & Rev. Neville, 47, 479
waswas, 99
Watts, Alan, 68, 76, 98, 126, 169, 171, 479
"Way of Breath, the Way of Heart," 68, 182, 220, 236, 238–39, 239, 300, 468
The Way of Illumination (Khan), what happens to the prophet's son, 323
Wayfarers: Meher Baba with the God-Intoxicated (Donkin), 238
Wayne (Jaekel), 411, 479
wazifa, 33, 53, 64, 82-3, 87-88, 157, 185, 195-96, 200, 390
Wegner. *See* Doyle
Weismuller, Johnny, 437, 479
Welch, Frank (Halim). *See* Frank (Welch)
Welch, Holmes, 253, 254–55, 370, 479
Welch, Lew, 372, 378, 392, 432, 479
The Western Buddhist magazine, 126, 321, 367
Whiteman, Luther, 12, 86, 243, 246, 372, 384, 479
Whitman, Walt, 185, 224, 330, 425, 450–51, 460, 479
The Whole Earth Catalog, 288, 347, 468
Wilde, Oscar, 479
Wills, Lynn, 289, 479
Wintheil, Ruth. *See* Parisa
Wood, Seth, 182, 479
World Is God (Ramdas), 139
"World Union," 222–23, 254, 291, 299, 344, 375, 377
The World's Living Religions (Bahm), 234, 335
wufud, 194, 273

Y
ya azim, 200
ya haqq, 30, 196
ya hayy, 30, 196

List of Illustrations

(All photos by Mansur Johnson, except Chapter 17's photos of the author by Dennis Stock from his book with William Hedgepeth *The Alternative*, with thanks to Collier Books, the group photo including the author on page 335 and the back cover photo of the author—both by unknown photographers—and the shot of Murshid on page 459 by Sylvaine Vaucher of Geneva, Switzerland.)

518

Acknowledgements

When I approached Shabda Khan, the head of the Sufi Ruhaniat International, about this book and paraphrased Murshid's statement that a few people working together can change the world, it had been 37 years since my first journal entry in September, 1967. As the reader knows, I began reviewing my esoteric journal and wrote the first draft of this book in 1981. I took up the project again in 1995 with the help of Elaine Surya. She was living at Lama Foundation at the time. I rented a computer and drove to Lama where I worked for four weeks on a second draft. I am eternally grateful to her for providing companionship and a place to work during this time.

After three additional drafts the book failed to interest a major publisher and I imagined it would only be published posthumously. At this time of few allies, there were two intrepid souls who were willing to read the entire 700 page manuscript. I am grateful for the support of Jami at the Southwest Sufi Community in Silver City, New Mexico, and Haqiqa Bear in Charlottesville, Virginia. I also want to thank Saul Barodofsky for reviewing a portion of the manuscript at this time.

Murshid languished until 2004 when Shabda took my floppy disk to Kinko's and produced a copy of *Murshid* that he could more easily proofread. He provided a welcomed list of improvements, which only made the book better. About this time Wali Ali Meyer also read the book and his enthusiastic support furthered the project. But there would be no project without Neil Douglas-Klotz. He generously took over the unpaid position of project manager and helped advance the book at every stage. He hired an editor in South Africa, Jennifer Woodhull, and he engaged his Sufi brother in Berlin, Jelaluddin Hauke Sturm, to design the book. But beyond his contributions to this book, he accomplished what I knew needed to be done and he accomplished; namely, to spread the message of God throughout the world with the Dances of Universal Peace.

I would never have met the publication deadline without assistance from my son Nathan who helped with the bibliography, glossary, dramatis and index. And I am especially grateful to Deborah Perry who worked tirelessly by my side for two years editing and proofreading the final drafts of the book. Her work was a love-offering given as the author's girl friend. Without Nathan and Deborah, Hauke and Jennifer, Shabda and Neil, this book does not happen. Thank you all. Thank you very much. To those whom I may have omitted unintentionally through the failure of my memory, I am sorry. And for any errors and omissions in the book, I take full responsibility.

May the message of God reach far and wide!

Mansur Johnson
Fairfax, California
May, 2006